CONCORDIA UNIVERS
GV14.5.S53
PRINCIPLES AND PRACTICES OF
Y0-DLW-997
3 4211 000035620

WITHDRAWN

PRINCIPLES AND PRACTICES OF
RECREATIONAL SERVICE

PRINCIPLES AND PRACTICES OF RECREATIONAL SERVICE

JAY S. SHIVERS
The University of Connecticut

THE MACMILLAN COMPANY, New York
COLLIER-MACMILLAN LIMITED, London

© Copyright, Jay S. Shivers, 1967

All rights reserved. No part of this book may be reproduced or transmitted in any form or by any means, electronic or mechanical, including photocopying, recording or by any information storage and retrieval system, without permission in writing from the Publisher.

First Printing

Library of Congress catalog card number: 67–14193

THE MACMILLAN COMPANY, NEW YORK
COLLIER-MACMILLAN CANADA, LTD., TORONTO, ONTARIO
PRINTED IN THE UNITED STATES OF AMERICA

To My Mother
La dame aux cheveux de lin . . .

PREFACE

Three major concerns prompted the writing of this book. For some time, there has been the need for a single volume that would present in easily understood and sharply defined language the fundamental concepts governing the field of recreational service. Of primary importance to the student is the need to understand what principles really are, as opposed to expedient policy, or current practices. A text was needed that would identify the chief components and concerns of the field, and provide supporting data to illustrate how closely standards of practice and common techniques come in achieving the ideal as signified by the principle. Finally, there is the need to research what history has to provide for a contemporary comprehension of how ideas, philosophy, terminology, and practices developed.

Although the book is divided into two distinct parts, fundamental and applied principles, it is an indivisible entity. Each principle, definable and separate by itself, is nevertheless closely related to all other principles which together form the basis for the field of recreational service. These clearly individual concepts combine to compose all the features, facets, functions, and responsibilities of which the field of recreational service is composed. In this book the basic ideas of the field of recreational service have been gathered, and an attempt has been made to study their meanings, logical relationships, and classification.

A survey of the literature on leisure, recreation, and recreational service shows an uneven development in the ideology of the field. Some ideas have been developed to their most profound degree by early thinkers. Some early ideas have had to wait until the writers of a later time could complete them. Some ideas have been organized according to a logical system or rationale; some have been taken piecemeal and adapted to systems in which justification for such placement has no rational basis. Some ideas have degenerated through misapplication or poor conceptualization from their earlier levels of excellence.

Any attempt at taxonomy discloses several groupings of fundamental ideas. The first of these relates to certain qualities of the experience itself. The second set of ideas concerns the relationship of recreation to other phenomena. The third deals with the values of recreation. This presentation is not merely a summary or accounting of the many play and recreation definitions and theories. Rather, it has been designed to promote a clearer concept of the word *recreation,* and to integrate a positive selection of ideas in this particular area of thought that may be systematized into a logical philosophy. It is concerned with what recreation *is* as well as how recreational service is accomplished.

A textbook author has an obligation to readers beyond listing current practices, pro and con; he should also indicate personal preferences and beliefs. It is not enough, moreover, to offer two sides of a given question and let the student choose the view which apparently meets his needs or fits into his frame of reference. When an idea is appealing, or believed in strongly, to be silent about that concept is less than scholarly. There are certain parts of specific chapters that appear to fly in the face of reality, currently accepted practices, definitions, and terms. These have been included because they establish the author's proclivity to these concepts. Such views reflect ideal situations that are not current practices. Sooner or later, however, people will begin to demand these services.

This text, although primarily concerned with the public or governmental sector of the field of recreational service, is equally involved with the private and quasi-public sector. Although specific, legal impingements and financial factors have bearing only upon the public sector because of legal requirements, almost every chapter, and certainly every principle, has direct meaning and value for the provisions of recreational service in this society regardless of where they originate.

The book was written to enable students to gain greater knowledge of the field. Of considerable significance, as well, is its utility as a handbook of preferred practices for professional practitioners in the field. It is useful in that it illustrates and exemplifies techniques for successful accomplishment of operational phases of recreational service in all of its ramifications. It employs, in detail, the most worthwhile ideas dealing with administrative aspects of the agency, and all of the pertinent management and supervisory methods designed to achieve success when working with laymen and professionals alike. There are guidelines for policy statements, standards for personnel management, administrative methods for executing policy, and techniques for effecting the most competent and comprehensive service possible.

The book has attempted, moreover, to cover the important historical developments of the field, and the transitional and derivative phases which led to the establishment of recreational service as an indispensable, applied social science in contemporary society. It is not, however, the last word. In a field of continuous change and dynamic proportion there will be a constant need for literary materials prescribing newer, better, or more effective methods for offering recreational opportunities to people. The principles, in all probability, will remain relatively unchanged, although future outlooks and different emphases may require their modification. As values undergo change, and as more people are exposed to more purposeful and intensive education, the orientation of public recreational service will also adjust to situational needs. At this time, and with the value system of this culture operating in context, this book appears to meet the demand for the kinds and levels of information presented herein.

J. S. S.

Storrs, Connecticut

ACKNOWLEDGMENTS

It is with a deep sense of personal satisfaction and gratitude that I indicate my appreciation to those who have provided needed information, concepts, and support in the development and completion of this manuscript.

I am indebted to Jack Woody, Superintendent of the Miami Beach Department of Recreational Service, and Howard Crowell, formerly General Superintendent of the Detroit Department of Recreational Service, for contributing ideas on the organization and administration of public departments. Mr. Crowell and his excellent staff did much to assist me in obtaining administrative charts that are utilized in the text. Permission from the City of Detroit to publish the departmental charts of the recreational agency is hereby acknowledged.

I wish to thank Dr. Hollis F. Fait, Professor and Supervisor of Graduate Studies and Research, The School of Physical Education, The University of Connecticut, for his comments and assistance concerning the chapter on research. I also express my appreciation to several individuals who have given needed assistance in the development of sections of the text: Joseph Trepasso, Director of Recreational Service, Town of Branford, Connecticut, Mrs. Glee Tate, Program Director of the Waco YWCA, and Mrs. Rhoda Booth, Director, Camp Kearsarge, Elkins, New Hampshire, for programming suggestions and applications. Appreciation for their helpful comments, practices, and valuable suggestions is expressed to the members of the Connecticut Recreation Society.

Finally, I express my deepest affection and esteem for my wife, Rhoda Shivers, for her constant support and contribution to my professional growth and writings. I thank my son, Jed, who in many ways served as a stimulus in helping me to complete this work.

CONTENTS

PART I Principles of Recreational Service

1. **INTRODUCTION**   3
   Development of Principles—Standards—Techniques—Summary

2. **LEISURE**   12
   Leisure and Human Development—Civilization and Leisure—Near-Eastern Contributions to Western Culture and Leisure—Ancient Western Civilizations and Leisure—An Overview of Post-Roman Leisure—Leisure in America—Class, Culture, and Leisure—The New Leisure and Recreational Service—The Economics of Leisure—Urban and Suburban Development Fosters Recreational Service—The Acceptance of Leisure and Recreational Activity—Summary

3. **RECREATION**   46
   Instinct as Motivation—Instinct Theories of Play or Recreation—Hedonism as Motivation—Homeostasis as Motivation—Recreation: Definitions and Concepts—Summary

4. **LEGALITY**   92
   Supremacy, Sovereignty, and Police Power—Recreational Service Establishment and Legislation—The Way Ahead—Summary

5. **SOCIAL MOVEMENT**   111
   The Recreational Movement—Summary

6. **PUBLIC RECREATIONAL SERVICE**   118
   Functions and Responsibilities of Recreational Service—Values of Recreational Experience—Equality of Opportunity—Social Limitations on Equality—Summary

7. **CONSERVATION**   149
   The Public Domain—The Threat of Megalopolis—The Threat of Exploitation—The Threat of Encroachment—Typical Outdoor Recreational Areas Furnished by Conservation—The Incompatibility of Recreational Use and Conservation—The Compatibility of Recreational Use and Conservation—Summary

8. **LEADERSHIP**   177
Human Needs and Motivation—Leadership and Learning—Leadership and Individual Differences—Leadership as Instruction—Counseling—Leadership and the Individual—Social Behavior—The General Characteristics of Leadership—Summary

9. **PROFESSIONALISM**   192
Recreational Service as a Profession—Education—Humanitarianism—Nonpredictability—Variability—Technique—Professional Association—Professionalization of Recreational Service—The Recreationist-Professional Practitioner—Summary

PART II   Practices of Recreational Service

10. **RESEARCH**   219
An Introduction to Research—Forms of Scientific Research Which Can Be Employed in the Field of Recreational Service—The Outcomes of Research in Recreational Service and Their Use—Significant Problems in Recreational Service—Summary

11. **ADMINISTRATION**   240
Organizational Concepts—Financial Support—Summary

12. **COORDINATION**   304
Human Nature and Social Organization—The Guarantees of Government—Community Organization and Coordination—Coordinating Councils—Coordination Through Other Efforts—Summary

13. **SUPERVISION**   327
Foundations for Supervision—Supervision Is Leadership—Supervisory Functions—Supervisory Techniques—In-Service Education and Development—The Effects of Supervision—Summary

14. **PROGRAMMING**   354
The Identification and Classification of Recreational Activities—Planning Factors in Programming—Summary

15. **PLANNING**   385
Planning Procedures—Public Land Use for Recreational Services—Social Examination—Factors Influencing the Program—The Agency Structure—Departmental Jurisdiction—Community Viewpoint—Summary

16. **EDUCATION**   420
Public Education as Necessity—Staff Requirements—Standards of Practice—Producing the Educational Program—The Organization of the Department—Summary

17. **EVALUATION**   450
Measurement, Evaluation, and Appraisal—Evaluation and Appraisal for Recreational Service—Why Evaluation Is Necessary—Methods of Evaluation—Determining Attitudes and Related Concepts—Summary

APPENDIX 491
    Sample Ordinance for the Creation of a Board, Commission, or Council of Recreational Service

INDEX 497

PART I

Principles of Recreational Service

# Chapter 1

INTRODUCTION

Any discussion of principles usually connotes a logical study of the primary problems of recreational service in its distinctive phases, which sets forth the most valuable, reliable, and useful consequences of investigations and judgments from practice. The object is mainly to provide guidance for students and practitioners of recreational service. The treatment of principles, therefore, is eminently of a practical nature. Generally, any study of principles is concerned with results of practice; however, this interpretation is vitally concerned with the exploration of primary causes and foundations for the practice of recreational service. Thus, this volume is divided into two nearly distinct parts: the first section dealing with basic assumptions fundamental to the organization and establishment of the social institution known as recreational service; and the latter relating to the best available results of recreational service theory and practice.

A principle is recognized as a universally accepted concept based upon evidence or prior experience which governs behavior. Although basic beliefs may constitute a principle, founded upon the most valid data currently available, it is rarely immutable fact and is subject to modification as new scientific information provides evidence that requires revision. However, some principles have come to be of such long-standing duration that they are taken as axiomatic and may be looked upon as laws of nature. Whether or not a principle is a natural law can be decided by the application of all the contemporary knowledge available relating to the subject matter. Even though scientific information is undergoing constant change as a result of new insights gained by better methods of procedure and better instruments of evaluation, concepts accepted as principles should vary little if they are, in reality, principles.

Any statement of belief is not a principle. This is particularly true if the statement is flavored with prejudiced information, distorted by bias and ignorance, or falsely predicated on illogical reasoning. The validity of a statement is determined by distinguishing between factual evidence and unsupported assertion. Unfounded generalizations may be the basis for prejudicial belief, but are usually unverifiable and are backed by a relative lack of scientific fact and objective reason. If concepts are of a factual nature, they will stand the test of confirmation or denial. It may also be stated that there are no principles which cannot be supported by scientific facts and that few concepts will prove valid as principles if they are not based on scientific fact. An avowed principle may be true insofar as the facts are known. These facts have to be scrupulously analyzed. The stability, reliability, and validity of the data used must be established before any demonstration of the truth or falsity of the concept may be attested. The details of securing data concerning a subject to be recognized as a principle, the skill of those who study and interpret the collected data, the relevancy of the data, the date of the data, and other interrelated factors have to be weighed before a principle can be established. Perhaps the chief recognition is one of limitation in that environmental and social pressures have a tendency to impinge upon objectivity so that the consequences may be biased. Any inference made from collected material must bear the burden of some subjectivity as an additional factor.

> It is conceivable that any individual, given all the contemporary knowledge available that has a bearing on a particular subject (broad sampling of expert opinion, all available scientific evidence, and a knowledge of the experience of past and present in terms of practice), could from this data derive the principles and standards which would be valid. With the provisions that all of the relevant data must be assembled, and that average to superior intelligence must be applied to interpretation of the relationships inherent in the material, an individual could work out the important principles which are the self-evident truths involved.[1]

Every profession relies upon scientific facts from which its basic principles may be established. The fields that are more readily recognized as professional and that progress most rapidly are those which have the greatest amount of time, money, and educated personnel engaged in areas of pure and applied research. The most distinct field of investigation that has remained almost completely untapped has been that of research in recreational service. Because recreational service is completely dependent upon the scientific methods of dealing with human behavior and the utilization of statistics to support its endeavors, more thought should be given to these fields of research. Statistical inquiry which is readily available to researchers in the field of recreational service must be utilized with greater scientific control so that findings will be more precise, comprehensive of the areas in which this work must be carried on, and more responsive to the needs of the field. Principles of recreational service based upon scientific facts will be affected by the current findings of scientific research.

The field of recreational service is still beset with rules of thumb. Stan-

---

[1] Natalie Marie Shepard, *Foundations and Principles of Physical Education* (New York: The Ronald Press Company, 1960), p. 201.

dards and policy are enacted as the result of accepting statements without discriminating between fact and fancy. Simply because an idea has been announced and followed for a given length of time does not make it a principle. Many practitioners follow some pattern that has been devised by an "authority," although there has been no scientific analysis of the facts upon which to substantiate the concept. Typical of these behaviors is one concerning the amount of recreational space which every community should attempt to set aside for the people. It has been stated that each community requires not less than one acre for every hundred persons in residence within the community. How was that figure developed? By what scientific process did the need for one acre per hundred people become acceptable? The need may very well exist and the concept may be, in fact, a principle; but if it is, then there should be some basis for a comparative investigation as to the validity or improbability of the idea. A whole series of studies need to be performed wherein commonly held principles and the standards which are derived from these principles are subjected to careful analysis and verification.

A composite list of the important principles concerning recreational service given detailed treatment in the chapters to follow must include

1. Leisure—human society, the development of culture, and the status of leisure in the behavioral patterns which produced social advancement.
2. Recreation—foundations, definitions, conceptualizations, and new understandings of the use of the word *recreation* and the behavioral manifestations which it describes.
3. Legality—legislative enactments and public policy which have given rise to the social philosophy of recreational service as a governmental function on every level. The provision of service as itemized in the Constitution of the United States and the several states which legitimize recreational service as an instrument for health, education, and social welfare.
4. Social Movement—the historical growth of the recreational service movement in the United States and supporting ideologies for such a development.
5. Recreational Service—the concept of a field of endeavor in its many ramifications as a continuing need of people.
6. Conservation—the need for natural resources, the destruction of natural resources, and the ambivalence of modern society toward its great natural phenomena.
7. Leadership—the professional practitioner (recreationist), practices necessary to implement and maintain recreational service operations, and the responsibilities incidental to conduct soundly established programs.
8. Professionalism—the concepts, practices, and requirements for professional practice, education, and a body of ethical procedures.

6   Principles of Recreational Service

9. Research—the need for continued inquiry, methods of investigation, applied research, and identification of field problems.
10. Administration—the presentation of an administrative manual for use by practitioners as well as a graphic description of the recreational service agency. This principle exemplifies the need for a detailed statement of procedures, rules, regulations, and policies concerning all facets of agency operation.
11. Coordination—the requirement of continuous cooperation and coordination of public recreational service agencies with all other community agencies for the effective, efficient, and economical utilization of facilities, manpower, materials, and program ideas. Close cooperation and consideration are necessary in order to maximize recreational services at the community level.
12. Supervision—basic leadership practices, in-service education, and staff development techniques for the production of more highly competent recreationists.
13. Programming—the essential activity necessary to meet the obligation of the recreational service agency to its constituency and the methods by which programming is accomplished.
14. Planning—the comprehensive analysis of the community, its character, necessities, and the techniques for organization and operation.
15. Education—the need and methodology for the organization and conduct of interdepartmental communications and external public relations procedures and practices.
16. Evaluation—the processes by which the recreational service agency may more effectively serve the leisure needs of people.

The scientific establishment of principle has tremendous value for the professional practitioner and for the professional occupation. The function of principles is one of identification of purpose, the technique of achieving goals, and the instruction of individuals in choosing alternative possibilities predicated on the consequences of discriminate selection. Critical thinking in the search for the reasons why is essential to the study of principles. The principles of the recreationist indicate the value and breadth of his experience and education. They become the hallmark of his professional status. They are the foundations for his capacity to confront and resolve specific problems that occur in his situation. Principles are guiding rules to action. They shape the behavior and conduct of the practitioner as he attempts to meet the circumstances in which his position places him.

DEVELOPMENT OF PRINCIPLES

Historically, a variety of factors has focused attention on man's recreational experiences and the services which have occurred in his leisure. The application of comprehensive activities operating for the social, physical, and cultural benefit of people has been sponsored by a varied group of agencies and individuals in many societies. Recreational activities are so manifold and extensive in expression that they represent nearly every form of approved human behavior. The scope and medium of experiences emphasize their necessity and value in whatever culture they have appeared. The diverse manifestations of leisure acts and the services incidental to them clearly indicate that salient or covert principles are in effect. Primary hypotheses and assumptions do exist and account for the widely separate means developed by different agencies and for the stressing of certain program instruction and experiences in these varied groups and places.

Principles are truths whose bases stem from scientifically corroborated facts and logical concepts. The source of principles is primarily from logic, biology, philosophy, anthropology, sociology, and education. Facts derived from these studies become the fundamental premises upon which are built systematic concepts for behavioral guidance. However, it should be noted that individuals may state beliefs that rest upon nonsense, prejudice, emotional bias, or on reasons that cannot be corroborated. Under these conditions, discriminating and valid action is unlikely, but nonetheless undertaken. Generalizations, for example, are quite often based upon knowledge which is predicated upon thinking that cannot be verified. The person who justifies his actions on the stated belief that ". . . nice guys finish last" bases his view on a falsely interpreted fact. Attitudes which are held and supported by misrepresentations have just as much power to influence subsequent actions as do valid principles. The significant fact is that principles denote statements which can be validated, whereas attitudes—even those which rest upon long use—without adequate factual confirmation, cannot be termed principles even though they influence behavior.

As a consequence of research efforts, specific facts are established and give rise to a parallel need. This comparable need develops in terms of the explication and application of the findings of verified research. Many people are in the position of knowing what to do, but are uncertain about putting their knowledge to practical use. They are acquainted with theory, but are strangers to methods of practice. Scientific data need interpretation for action. Agencies of recreational service functioning within the private as well as the public sphere will progress more rapidly when they rely upon the two-fold system comprising principles, e.g., scientific foundations of research plus logical implementation through careful and accurate interpretation and application.

Principles are the last best compilation of ideas which standardize behavior so that the most effective performance can be accomplished. The principles herein presented are organized in such a way that there is a logical progression from a broad base of social-historical data to a narrowly specific rationale of applied principles which practitioners can, and currently are utilizing, as best practice.

STANDARDS

Standards are an immediate and direct outgrowth of principles. A standard is a commonly held practical procedure for the implementation of the principle. Standards are developed as precise means for effecting the execution of generalized rules of action. Because they are more numerous than principles, they are influenced by distinct situations and conditions. They are relatively flexible and subject to modification and do not have the same total commitment to invariability as do principles. The principle serves as the ideal goal toward which all activity is aimed. The standard is the action taken in attempting to reach the ideal. The need for standards is discovered in the requirement for organization, consistency, reliability, identification, and the sense of security and endurance in the conduct of social institutions.

Standards may be correctly or incorrectly oriented, they may be purposeful or ambivalent, stable or of short duration; but whatever they are and however they are placed in effect, they include the operational techniques and are supposedly guided by principles. It seems inconceivable that standards can be set up which are disoriented to the clear purpose identified by principles. Nevertheless value judgments are made by human beings and are subject to the same biases and miscalculations that influence their creators. There are other reasons for a less than perfect standard implementing any given principle. More numerous than principles, standards attempt to meet the ideal from polar positions. The end result may be the same, but the actions taken to gain the end in view may be quite divisive. Standards are only as strong, reliable, and permanent as the human mind that formulates them can make them. Again, the factor of the human ego, personality, behavioral dynamics, and the pressures of environment upon the standard-maker at any given time may result in measures which fail to fulfill the functions for which they were designed. Allowance for the role of human nature and personal motives cannot be omitted from the concept of standard making.

Standards are particularly significant to the purposes, range, and stability of recreational service. Principles of recreational service cannot operate without effective standards for their implementation. However valuable a principle may be, it will be of small benefit if the standards that are supposed to effect its idealization are static and without the necessary means to innovate, initiate, or boldly question current practices. If, on the other hand, standards are developed which forthrightly provide the *modus operandi* for producing services that comply in every respect with the principle, then the field of recreational service and the people who constitute its clientele will be well served.

TECHNIQUES

Even more numerous than standards, techniques are the very practical day-to-day means for performing the work of the agency in the field of recreational service. Just as standards serve as the implementation of principles, so too do techniques become the specific devices for the implementation of standards. Techniques are even more subject to variation and impermanence than the aforementioned factors. Techniques are often expedients and are pragmatically used. If a practice is successful it will be utilized regardless of whether it meets the requirement set forth by the principle and standards of which it is a consequence. Thus for example, a basic principle is concerned with the provision of recreational service for all people. This principle demands a wide range of activities which will appeal to the greatest number of people within the community to be served. However, the technique used may be to offer opportunity to a limited number of people through the inclusion of sports and games without adequate arrangement for other experiences. The basis for such thinking is that the routine provision of sports and games invariably succeeds in attracting a definite number of participants. The stability of numbers of participants in such activity will help to justify the department's request for funds or facilities. The inclusion of other activities within the program may be considered too unsure in terms of the number of individuals who might participate and therefore leaves the department open to harassment or censure for using public funds without justifiable results. Farfetched as the example may read, it is nonetheless used time and again by some administrators to vindicate their program and policies which are extremely limited. In fact, there is no defense for the omission of a well-rounded and extensive program of various activities. The pragmatic view prevails among those who have not been professionally prepared to assume recreationist positions or among those who do not recognize or understand the nature of the function of recreational service agencies.

This is not to be taken as an attack upon techniques. A good technique is practical and sure. It does the necessary work according to the policies, standards, and principles to which it is oriented. It is a way of performance or rapid execution of some appointed task. It may be simple or complex, but in any case, the technique must conform to and be absolutely guided by principles. Briggs and Justman assert:

> The surest way of finding a solution for a new problem is not to draw solely on a composite of old experiences, but to possess sound fundamental principles and to know how to apply them.[2]

[2] Thomas H. Briggs and Joseph L. Justman, *Improving Instruction Through Supervision* (New York: The Macmillan Company, 1952), p. 406.

There is little question that a series of techniques are requisite for competency in carrying out the principles of recreational service, but, as will be obvious, complete reliance upon the technique of expediency without guidance or understanding of principles can result in experiences and values which are less than standard at best and unfortunate or negative at worst. The main difficulty in attempting to resolve problems that occur in recreational service by the use of common techniques is that two program situations are rarely if ever identical. Intrinsic and conditional factors vary from individual to individual, time to time, activity to activity, group to group, and environment to environment. A technique that proves successful in one of these situations may not be successful in the next. More is needed than an array of techniques on which to fall back when a situation demands improvisation and creativity on the part of the recreationist. Principles are necessary to guide the selection and steps of action for appropriate techniques as well as to originate new methods when conditions require them. The field of recreational service must be controlled and guided by a definite set of principles by which optimum values can be gained for and by people. Otherwise, recreational service continues in a haphazard, trial-and-error, and inept manner. Such operation is not only wasteful of time, money, and effort, but it tends to deteriorate the image of a field which needs all of the public support it can gain.

SUMMARY

The above statements should not be understood as a condemnation of techniques nor as a suggestion that techniques are not absolutely essential for carrying out the practices of recreational service. Techniques are basic to the provision of recreational service. Skillfulness and technical information are necessities. When the objectives are defined and standards have been set, then the achievement of the entire operation hinges upon the technical competence and adroitness of the recreationist. Recreational service is a technical field which calls for specialized and prolonged education and sound experiences before one is adequately prepared in its various techniques. Principles are essential if techniques are to be correctly channeled, but principles can never abrogate the basic role which techniques play in executing the procedures and practices of daily recreational service.

SELECTED REFERENCES

BRIGHTBILL, CHARLES K. and HAROLD D. MEYER, *Recreation: Text and Readings.* (Englewood Cliffs, N.J.: Prentice-Hall, Inc.), 1953.
BUTLER, GEORGE D., *Introduction to Community Recreation,* 3rd ed. (New York: McGraw-Hill), 1959.
CARLSON, REYNOLD E., THEODORE R. DEPPE, and JANET R. MACLEAN, *Recreation in American Life.* (Belmont, Calif.: Wadsworth Publishing Company), 1963.

DANFORD, HOWARD G., *Recreation in the American Community.* (New York: Harper and Brothers), 1953.
DAVIDSON, ROBERT F., *Philosophies Men Live By.* (New York: Holt, Rinehart & Winston), 1952.
GEIGER, GEORGE R., *Philosophy and the Social Order.* (New York: Houghton Mifflin Company), 1947.
HALL, EVERETT W., *Philosophical Systems.* (Chicago: University of Chicago Press), 1960.
MEYER, HAROLD D. and CHARLES K. BRIGHTBILL, *Community Recreation: A Guide to its Organization,* 3rd ed. (Englewood Cliffs, N.J.: Prentice-Hall, Inc.), 1964.
MOORE, GEORGE E., *Principia Ethica.* (New York: Cambridge University Press), 1959.
NASH, JAY B., *Recreation: Pertinent Readings, Guide Posts to the Future.* (Dubuque, Iowa: Wm. C. Brown Company), 1965.
Recreation for Community Living, Guiding Principles. (Chicago: The Athletic Institute), 1952.
ROBINSON, DANIEL SOMMER, *Principles of Reasoning,* 3rd ed. (New York: Appleton-Century-Crofts), 1965.
SCIACCA, M. F., *Philosophical Trends in the Contemporary World.* 2 vols. (South Bend, Ind.: University of Notre Dame Press), 1964.
WOOD, ROBERT BROTHER, *Principles and Problems of Ethics.* (B. Herder Book Company), 1962.
YUKIC, THOMAS S., *Fundamentals of Recreation.* (New York: Harper & Row), 1963.

Chapter 2

LEISURE

PRINCIPLE: In each age when man has had and utilized leisure in positive ways, then cultural advancements have been largely made. The arts and sciences, but particularly the humanities, have been developed extensively out of the creative use of leisure. Free time, constructively used, advances society, enriches individual life, and produces massive cultural development.

LEISURE AND HUMAN DEVELOPMENT

One of the most illuminating methods for an understanding of present concepts is to view them from an historical perspective in order to appreciate their progression from distant origin to contemporary meaning. Leisure was a part of culture before civilization came into being. It has been a part of human society from a time prior to when man learned how to communicate within his species.

In the beginning there was only survival. Until man learned how to make fire at his own discretion, preserve whatever food he could find or kill, have an adequate water supply, build or locate an easily defensible habitation against marauding foreign groups and savage animals of the infra-human species, his every thought was focused on just staying alive.

It is during the initial period of the Third Interglacial period that *Homo neanderthalensis* makes his appearance. Approximately 120,000 years ago these first men wandered over what is today the central plains of Europe. They had learned to use fire, began to seek protection from inclement weather in crevasses and caves, and because they were of a more intelligent form than were the subhuman creatures of the Paleolithic era, they were able to withstand the rigors of their harsh environment and survive.

When man took to the caves he had to dispossess bears, lions, and other animal cave dwellers. He did not penetrate very far into the cave recesses because he had no means to light his habitation. He was not capable of utilizing a torch or fabricating a taper, although he had fire. He still depended upon rock barricades, fire, and finally stone or wooden implements to ward off attack. He was a hunter who was hunted. When he went in search of food, he killed the smaller fauna simply because he could not tackle the massive size and ferocity of the larger mammals. If he was fortunate enough to come upon a large animal, sick, wounded, or carrion, or was able to exploit the large mammals' difficulties as they became mired in boggy places or at treacherous water crossings, he was then able to kill them. The Neanderthal men partially ate their kill where it fell; but they brought the big marrow bones back to their retreats to crack and eat at leisure. Eating, then, became the first pleasurable activity to be engaged in when survival aspects were taken care of and the hazard of attack or counterattack was not imminent.

Man and Leisure

During the Fourth Glacial period the first true man appeared and swept all before him. He either used the Neanderthalers as slaves or exterminated them, for in the later Paleolithic period the Neanderthalers are an extinct species. Forty thousand years ago, *Homo sapiens* appeared. The difference between the two species is marked. It is likely that *Homo neanderthalensis* neither spoke nor communicated in any symbolic way. The remains found in the grotto of Cro-Magnon in Dordogne, France, indicate that these truly human Paleolithic people brought the human race a matchless step forward. They were certainly more intelligent than any living creature before them. These earliest true men were artists. They drew and painted on any smooth surface which could take their implements. Their drawings on cave walls and cliff faces attest to this. They not only drew and painted, but carved as well.

In all likelihood, they did not fear attack by other men or animals, at least not as much as their predecessors had. They hunted the hairy mammoth as well as bison, reindeer, horses, and aurochs. With their greater intelligence, and their moderate environment, they were able to live a more secure life. Thus, when the urgencies of the hunt were over, they had leisure. What they did with their leisure has been recorded for posterity. The cave dwellings and assembly places of the Cro-Magnards are alive with pictorial representations of the animals they hunted, tamed, or ate. Ivory, bone, and clay carvings and statuary also attest to their artistry. Although the drawings never showed depth perception, but were generally done as side views, they nevertheless indicated a high degree of skill and vividness still preserved in the caves of Spain and France to this day. That they used a variety of pigments to make various hues in painting is seen from cave paintings as well as from opened graves. Color was a primary medium which they used in life as well as death. Body decorations were painted on and evidence suggests that females of this species were well coiffured. If there was time to paint, draw, and establish some system of burial, and for the women to be provided with elaborate hair styles, there must have been much leisure. Inasmuch as the paintings have been found in the inner recesses of the caves, these people must have known how to fashion some form of candle or lamp. They were far advanced over their earlier Paleolithic forebears.

However, as thousands of generations passed, the environment grew harsh and finally destroyed this race. The hunters were no longer capable of hunting as the herds thinned out and vanished. What finally caused the Later Paleolithic men to disappear can only be surmised. Drought, disease, famine, or flood may have decimated and effected extinction of the race. Whatever it was, the hunters waned, and, some 10,000 years ago, a new race of men prevailed—Neolithic.

The Neolithic age is characterized by five distinct features: (1) the polished stone implement; (2) agriculture, i.e., some form of plant cultivation; (3) the utilization of pottery and weaving; (4) domesticated animals; and (5) cookery. The chief tool was the handax, which also made an excellent weapon. Neolithic man used bow and arrow in hunting and fighting. Because he had the bow, he probably also had some form of stringed instrument. There is little doubt that if he carved whistles from bone then he also used hollow reeds as pipes upon which to play. He knew how to stretch skins over hollow tree trunks and over drum bases made of pottery. There is no evidence of when men began to sing, but inasmuch as he had musical accompaniment, and some verbal communication, songs were sung.

That man has always had some leisure is something that cannot be challenged. In this culture, stone, initially, and then metal became part of life. First copper, discovered by accident, then in like manner the alloys of bronze and brass were smelted. Presumably men began to smelt iron as early as 3,000 years ago. Trade in preservatives such as salt, bronze weapons, and tanned skins, and a variety of ornamental minerals, e.g., jade and gold, were transmitted over great distances.

That he had the time to think and invent is self-evident for it is only when the individual can stop his intensive occupation of survival that culture flourishes. Neolithic man possessed some leisure. With it he developed speech, primitive writing, some art, metal tools, agriculture, primitive religious rituals, symbolisms, and tribal taboos. Much the same settled way of life was being led by Neolithic man 10,000 years ago, as was being led by peasants in some rural areas of Europe in the early eighteenth century. The age of the caucasian in Europe, of which the Neolithic Period was the first phase, was still going on until the modern era of power-driven machinery.

When man first discovered fire and could tell somebody else how to build a blaze from pyrites and tinder materials, when the older generation was able to pass on instructions concerning the handling of sharpened stones, wooden implements, and eventually metals, when food could be cultivated instead of chased, then man had leisure and human culture began to progress.

We have seen that throughout the development of human culture some leisure has been present. Anthropologists, among others of the scientists devoted to the study of the development of man, have indicated that recreational experiences, in some form, were a direct outgrowth of the possession of leisure.[1] There are indications that preliterate societies utilized leisure and recreational activity as both an instructional vehicle as well as a monument to man's aesthetic and creative tendencies.[2] When man began to gain some control over his environment and, by chance, learned to use providentially provided materials as utensils, he fashioned vessels made of clay for containing his food and water. In order to enhance these purely utilitarian products he decorated them with ocher or other coloring substances; thus he played with his articles, which we now see as artifacts in many museums of natural history. As more sophistication came to man's personality over succeeding thousands of years, he expressed his feelings upon the walls of caves as well as on his pottery, thus, symbolizing and transmitting his ideas concerning the creatures he met and the life he lived.

The method by which primitive man exerted control over his environment could not be by mechanical contrivances. Nevertheless, he had manpower at his disposal. Gatherings of families or clans into tribal groups, and tribes into communal living produced the first step in social organization which ultimately led to the development of law. Tribal customs based upon certain taboos, superstitions, and the like served to guide and formulate what was later to be known as political, martial, economic, religious, educational, and family institutions of the social order. Although it is true that there was no differentiation between these varying activities during the emergence of man from his preliterate stage to the civilized complexity of more highly developed systems, these practices made way for the social structures that have evolved. The ethos of civilization and culture finds its earliest seeds in the Paleolithic and Neolithic ages.

CIVILIZATION AND LEISURE

Where man's civilization, of the higher order, first existed is not well known; but evidence suggests that the societies which arose as men settled the fertile river valleys of the Nile in Egypt and the Tigris and Euphrates, called Mesopotamia, are perhaps the two oldest and demonstrably the most sophisticated and cultured. By 4000 B.C., settled communities had existed in these areas for some time. These civilizations contained continuously inhabited structures and some code of law by which the dwellers abided for not less than two thousand years prior to the uniting of the states of Upper and Lower Egypt by Menes in 3800 B.C.

The most ancient communities of these civilizations were formed from the city-states of Sumer—Ur, Eridu, Kish, Susa, Larsa, and Uruk. That within these communities recreational activity was part of religious festival

---

[1] Julius Lippert, *The Evolution of Culture,* translated and edited by George P. Murdock (New York: The Macmillan Company, 1931), p. 415.
[2] George R. Stewart, *Man: an autobiography* (New York: Random House, 1946), p. 118.

and rite has been well represented.[3, 4] The growing complexity of life along these river banks required some form of governmental organization and far-sighted leadership to forestall chaotic uprisings and disorder when natural calamities, i.e., floods, famine, and plague, despoiled the land; or to direct and command the population to their appointed tasks in maintaining the food supply, diking the rivers, and operating an army either to subjugate their neighbors or to prevent their conquest by others. There emerged a king-priest class who commanded the respect of their followers, grew to dominate and reign over the great masses. Such individuals had a great deal of leisure and utilized it to plan social development. These figures were endowed with divine stature and represented as having been descended from the gods.

From this beginning there developed a separate social classification which in turn initiated definite institutions characterized by an orientation toward the maintenance of life. The formulation of social stratification and the rise of these institutions became a powerful force in organizing all of the people so that the job of daily living was facilitated. Agricultural, political, religious, martial, and other tasks were performed cooperatively with the full knowledge that division meant dissolution and probable destruction by invaders. The well-defined social institutions provided for the creation of king-priest and the establishment of the first aristocracy and leisure class. As the community grew, the two functions were separated. Class and caste division also were nourished by tradition which looked upon this status as completely normal. With the stratification of class, the kings utilized priests as their councilors and much that the priestly class ordained had the sanction of the king's authority. The priests were probably more intelligent than the average man and passed much of their time in contemplation. Spending time in this manner they had a chance to develop rituals dealing with metaphysical concepts, originate many taboos based upon seasonal cycles or other natural occurrences, and instigate mystical signs and symbols to give them an apparent command of the occult and supernatural world.

It is an interesting fact that it was the priestly order of ancient Sumeria (ca. 4000 B.C.) who utilized games, dance, and other recreational acts to dignify ritual and sacrifice to their gods.[5] In this instance the games held a deadly significance as illustrated by the human sacrifices made to propitiate the gods; all done in a play-acting form.[6] Artifacts from this culture indicate that children had dolls with which to play. Art was used to express creativeness as well as historically significant happenings on scrolls, tables, walls, and

---

[3] Sabatino Moscati, *Ancient Semitic Civilizations* (New York: C. T. Putnam's Sons, 1957), pp. 55–66.
[4] Edward Burnett Tylor, *Religion in Primitive Culture* (New York: Harper and Brothers, 1958), 539 pp.
[5] Johan Huizinga, *Homo Ludens* (Boston: The Beacon Press, 1955), p. 15.
[6] R. R. Marett, *The Threshold of Religion* (London: Methuen & Co., Ltd., 1914), pp. 42–68.

utensils. Dancing, in the ritual of temple ceremonies, was also used to express emotion, depict events, and explain traditional activities carried on as part of the daily lives of the inhabitants of these civilizations.[7]

Dancing, as a matter of course, has become one of the recreational activities in which all people participate and through which many cultures have contributed certain symbolic steps, movements, or physical attitudes.[8] Nowhere is this seen more clearly than in the "dance of life" creations of specific African tribes. The hunter could no more engage in the pursuit of hunting and killing the lion than he could fly, without first performing the dancing rite of this entire experience. The dance graphically tells the story of the hunt, the chase, the cornering of the quarry, the manifestations of courage under threat of claw and fang, the final assault of the hunter, the kill, and then the trophy gathering. Unless the adult who participates in the hunt actually goes through this symbolic dance, he feels himself in mortal danger and cannot perform adequately. The whole idea of dramatizing what is to happen, this play-acting of real life, is part and parcel of reality. One cannot take place without the other. In this situation the play on life becomes as meaningful as the reality of the hunting episode; more so if possible, because the former is the open-sesame to the latter act. Rhythmical movement, becoming dance, probably developed out of the boredom which the individual experienced during whatever free time he had. Although the dance presumably became established as a result of individual leisure, such dancing as accompanied religious ritual was obligatory rather than of a recreational nature. The ceremony required the dance and could not proceed without its performance. Nevertheless, dance has almost universally become associated with leisure activity.

NEAR-EASTERN CONTRIBUTIONS TO WESTERN CULTURE AND LEISURE

With the growth and complexity of social institutions, there also emerged a trend toward governmental organization with one powerful ruler retaining the headship to which all others of the community must pay respect and devotion. From 3600 B.C. in the Mesopotamian and Egyptian societies, this social complexity evolved into a distinct separation of classes; so that the political and military function was given into the hands of a central figure, the king. The mystical rites were handed to priests, and these rites included most, if not all, of the arts and sciences of the day including religion. The rest of the populace were left with the burden of cultivating the crops, engaging in commercial and trade enterprises, and generally increasing the material wealth of the state.

[7] W. D. Hambly, *Tribal Dancing and Social Development* (London: Witherby, 1926), pp. 133–135.
[8] Robert H. Lowie, *An Introduction to Cultural Anthropology* (New York: Rinehart and Co., Inc., 1947), pp. 171–174.

Briefly, there arose a series of societies ruled by an individual given divine-right powers. Among these were the Babylonian, Hittite, Assyrian, and Persian empires. Several books could be written about each of these kingdoms on every aspect of cultural importance, but it is only to the leisure and recreational element that we turn.

Sumer and Akkad

During the age of the Sumerian unification, in which the city-state of Sumer rose to power over the southern fertile crescent communities, the area between the Tigris and Euphrates rivers constituted a most prized possession. For the thousand years between 3600 B.C. and 2600 B.C., there were countless struggles and periodic wars between the mountain and plains dwelling peoples. This strife lasted through several kingdoms and did not abate in intensity until after 1900 B.C. In the northern section of the Plain of Shiner, the state of Akkad held sway over this region which then became known as Akkadia.

These two hostile states were decidedly different. The Sumerians were a well-disciplined agrarian civilization, whereas the Akkadians were desert nomads without the military training or organization to confront the heavy infantry of the southerners. During the centuries when these two states engaged in border wars against one another there was comparative peace within the internal areas. However, sometime around 2370 B.C. the Semitic chieftain, Sargon, known to history as "The Great," led his lean archers against the Sumerian host and defeated them in a conclusive battle. He swiftly consolidated his conquest by invading the entire land, and pushed his claims from Elam in the east to the Mediterranean Sea in the west and the two rivers in the north.

Although the Akkadians had conquered in battle, they were gradually engulfed in a wave of fraternization as they adopted Sumerian ways, including the technique of measurement, arts and crafts, commercial organization, metal smithing, a calendar and numbering system. Sargon's forced union of Akkadia with Sumeria changed the Akkadian standards of living and it was the latter civilization which prevailed over the simpler Semitic culture. The Semites left their desert life for town living. With town life there was intermarriage and adoption of the vernacular tongue of the Sumerians as well as their style of writing, which was cuneiform.

With the civilizing influence of the towns imposed upon the Akkadians, they settled in the land and it became the Sumerian-Akkadian empire. When these formerly vigorous and warlike Semitics began to acquire the cultural attributes that had developed over a period of two thousand years in the then independent Sumeria, they ceased to be have-nots and became the leisured aristocracy. They hunted and participated in many outdoor sports and game activities including chariot racing, but they regarded manual labor, especially that of agriculture as the province of inferiors. After several generations, the former conquerors became an integral part of the civilization which they originally overthrew in war. There was an exchange of religious, political, and social ideas, and in the process of refinement, the conquerors lost some of the pioneering hardy spirit that had impelled them to fight. Thus, the Semites turned aristocrat, relied more and more on others to enforce their rule, and depended upon mercenaries and lesser hirelings, thus laying themselves open to invasion by other up-coming lean and hungry men.

The Sargonid dynasty lasted less than two centuries, but it is an era filled with creative artistic works among which are the Sargonid seals, cut from stone and depicting men and animals in violent action.[9] The art of sculpturing was raised to its highest form in terms of human development at that stage. As the militaristic thrust and hardihood of the Akkadians were lost as a result of civilizing influences together with the new found leisure, which as aristocrats, they enjoyed, fresh incursions of warlike people took place and the Sumerian-Akkadian empire was overthrown in 2300 B.C. under the direction of the city-state of Ur.

Babylon

From the west came the Semitic people who settled in a rural village, called Babylon, located on the Euphrates upstream from Ur. After three generations of intermittent warfare these Amorites succeeded in bringing much of what was then western Asia under their political and military control, surpassing Ur as the central seat of government, and having Babylon as its capital city. Under their great king Hammurabi (ca. 2100 B.C.), the first Babylonian empire was founded.

During the period of Hammurabi's dynasty, Babylonia flourished as the greatest commercial and political expression of that time. The arts, particularly literature and graphics, were generally developed to an extremely high form not to be repeated in that ancient time.[10] Many recreational activities were indulged in by members of the upper classes, specifically hunting, fishing, riding, wrestling, swimming, and the exercise of a variety of weapons both for war and leisure. Typical of the philosophy of Babylon is this illustration told about the hero Gilgamesh.

> O Gilgamesh, why dost thou run in all directions?
> The life that thou seekest thou wilt not find.
> When the gods created mankind,
> They determined death for mankind;
> Life they kept in their hands.
> Thou, O Gilgamesh, fill thy belly,
> Day and night be thou merry,

---

[9] C. Leonard Woolley, *The Development of Sumerian Art* (New York: Charles Scribner's Sons, 1935), pp. 126–130.
[10] C. H. W. Johns, *Hastings' Dictionary of the Bible*, Extra Vol. (New York: 1906), p. 584.

Daily arrange a merry-making,
Day and night be joyous and content! [11]

The orientation of "live for today" and enjoyment of life is self-evident. This rationale predates the earliest of the hedonistic philosophers of ancient Greece. It connotes the pleasurable existence which the upper classes could afford as a result of the pyramidal society on which Babylonian culture rested. Documentation of the history of the rise of the Babylonian empire, the enterprises of peace and war which were carried on throughout the 400-year dynastic period, the myths, fine arts, dress, habitation, religion, and literature can be found in many texts as well as archaeological sources.[12] Gradually, Babylon grew decadent. Its militaristic capacity was greatly reduced as it became more highly civilized. Its art was prolific as was trade and commerce. But the fruits of a leisured society came under the covetous eyes of warriors from the East and by 1750 B.C., the empire that had been Babylon gave way to the Kassites who ruled, and in turn were absorbed into the Babylonian culture as a whole, until the twelfth century B.C.

Assyria

To the north of Babylon, Assyrian power had consolidated. The Assyrians raised warfare to a fine art and under Tiglath Pileser I, they conquered all of Mesopotamia, and forced Babylon to submit to them in 1150 B.C. However, their conquest was not absolute and for four hundred years a power struggle ensued between Assyrian military might and Babylonian force. It was not until the middle of the sixth century B.C. that a third Tiglath Pileser arose to found the New Assyrian empire with the final conquest of Babylon. The Assyrian empire lasted only until a new crop of lean and hungry men came from the Southeast to overthrow the 150-year old Assyrian kingdom. The Semitic nomads came from Chaldea and in alliance with the Medes and Persians from the north, they captured Nineveh in 606 B.C. The Chaldean kingdom, with Babylon as its capital, lasted until Cyrus the Persian successfully attacked and defeated it in 539 B.C.

Thus the story of civilization is repeated in successive centuries as conquest follows conquest in an almost rhythmic pattern, with intermittent warfare occurring as fresh invasions from border races inevitably bring about the collapse of the more settled former invaders. The Sumerians give way to the Akkadians who in turn interbreed with the Sumerians and lose their identity as a distinct people. The Sumerian-Akkadian empire languishes and is set upon by other peoples. The Babylonians defer to the

---

[11] James B. Pritchard, ed., *The Ancient Near East* (Princeton, N.J.: Princeton University Press, 1958), p. 64.
[12] A. H. Sayce, *Babylonians and Assyrians, Life and Customs* (New York: Charles Scribner's and Sons, 1900).

Assyrians, who in turn give way to the Chaldeans and Syrians, the northern Hittites swallow the Syrians and they become Aryanized, the Medes and the Persians then dominate until they are finally subjugated by the Greeks.

The Tigris and Euphrates civilizations existed for some 4,000 years. As Winckler states in his 1907 text, *The History of Babylonia and Assyria:* "Eridu, Lagash, Ur, Uruk, Larsa, have already an immemorial past when first they appear in history." Those civilizations created out of man's need for social organization and his cultural appreciation for and use of leisure have left an indelible stamp upon human history. Leisure, not necessity, is the mother of invention. Only when the individual has the time to survey his needs, beyond mere survival, and appreciate the significance of creating something aesthetic out of a utilitarian item or something utilitarian out of natural materials does the veneer of culture thicken to become civilization.

The Hebrews

Although the Israelites were never politically as significant as the kingdoms of Chaldea, Babylon, Assyria, or Egypt, their place is recorded in history because Judea or Canaan was the most direct route for both trade and warfare between Egypt to the south and the Hittites, Assyrians, Syrians, and Babylonians to the north. The land occupying this position was, therefore, almost constantly undergoing attack and conquest, or, as a tributary state, paying indemnification to some foreign power. Small and militarily insignificant as this country was, it nevertheless had a long and troubled history. However, inclusion is made of this nation and its culture because the writings of this people have made significant ethical and religious contributions to western civilization as well as documentation of leisure concepts and recreational pursuits.

The Patriarchs of the Old Testament came upon the scene of history sometime in 1800 B.C. The Pentateuch, or first five books, provide the reader with a basic idea of the history of man and the record of his daily life. It recounts the flood, which appears widely in ancient Near-Eastern histories. This may have been an account of some great submersion which occurred in the Mediterranean valley during the Neolithic era.

In *Genesis* a history of the founding fathers is given, along with the migration of Abraham from Ur of the Chaldees, in which a covenant is made with the deity identified as Yahweh, later anglicized to Jehovah. The next six books of the Bible recount the consolidation of Israelite fortunes in Canaan, the migration of Jacob's tribe to Egypt, the story of Moses, the giving of the laws, the exodus and wanderings of the Jews in the desert before reaching Canaan.

The Hebrews never really held Canaan, for in reading the Bible one learns that the Philistines consistently held the fertile seacoast region of the south and the Canaanites and Phoenicians remained steadfastly in possession of the northern border areas. The initial victories of Joshua were never repeated and the *Book of Judges* becomes a recital of the trouble, defeat, and failure which the Israelites experience. The people soon lost their faith and deserted to pagan gods. They became a people of many races. Under the leadership of several prophets and heroes they continued to wage intermittent warfare, never completely successfully and usually with a disunited front, against a series of enemies. They were conquered by the Moabites, the Canaanites, the Midianites, and the Philistines.

Then the first king arose.[13] Saul was no more successful against countering invasions than were the judges and priests before him. He and his army were overwhelmed at the battle of Mount Gilboa by the Philistines. His successors were David c. 990 B.C.) and Solomon (c. 960 B.C.). The end of the reign of King Solomon was also the end of Hebrew plans for expansion and glory. A schism developed between the northern and southern sections of the country as two separate kingdoms, Israel and Judah, were established. The rest of the history consists of regicide, fratricide, religious conflicts, political maneuverings, mistaken alliances, and intrigues, which go on for three centuries.

Israel was finally swept into captivity in 721 B.C. by Shalmaneser of Assyria. Judah remained partially sovereign until 604 B.C. when Nebuchadnezzar II annexed it and several decades later transported the majority of the people to Babylon. There the Jews remained for more than two generations. Upon their return, under the protection of Cyrus the Persian, in 539 B.C. a great change is noted in the character of this people.

> They went a confused and divided multitude, with no national self-consciousness; they came back with an intense and exclusive national spirit. They went with no common literature generally known to them . . . and they returned with most of their material for the Old Testament. It is manifest that . . . the Jewish mind made a great step forward during the Captivity.[14]

Out of this travail an intellectual awakening began and flourished to the extent that a moral force of intense power was created. Ethical concepts to guide the entire community were established. The capability of human grace and perfectibility runs throughout this prophetic religion, and is seen in the subsequent establishment of Christianity and Islam as a direct outgrowth of Judaism.

But beyond the creativity and monotheistic aspect of the Jewish religion, there is a dominant meaning for leisure and recreational experiences. The entire concept of the Sabbath or day of rest is applicable here. The statement "Have leisure and know that I am God," [15] exemplifies the idea that some time had to be set aside from the ongoing functions of daily life when

---

[13] I Samuel, viii.
[14] H. G. Wells, *The Outline of History* (New York: Garden City Publishing Co., Inc., 1921), pp. 230–231.
[15] *Psalm* lxv, 11.

man was free to worship his creator. Man was supposed to work from sunup to sundown in whatever vocational capacity he showed talent, but at some point in his life, and periodically thereafter, he must give thanks to the God in which he had faith. Every seventh day was devoted to this offering of thanks and sanctification. Thus the Sabbath was a day of leisure, free from the obligations of toil, and concerned with the revitalization of the individual through prayer, feasting, and appreciation of a god-given world.

Other recreational experiences noted in Hebrew life were the usual hunting and fishing activities as well as the utilization of more warlike and defensive instruments such as the sling, the bow, javelin, and short sword. Many biblical passages refer to a variety of physical activities and one of the outstanding examples of this is Jacob's wrestling with "the Angel of the Lord." [16] Dancing, singing, and the playing of musical instruments are also recorded in Hebrew literature. Repeatedly, religious rites are celebrated with song, instrumentation, and dance; [17] but through it all the underlying cultural expression of Jewish life revolves around the Sabbath and the leisure which it brings.

ANCIENT WESTERN CIVILIZATIONS AND LEISURE

Parallel with the ancient Near-Eastern civilizations another culture arose on the island of Crete, the remains of which at the capital of Knossos indicate an advanced civilization much of which is now submerged beneath the Mediterranean. This island civilization is at least as old as that of Sumer, but it was only about 2500 B.C. that political unification occurred. For the next thousand years, the Cretans lived in peace, prosperity, and safety. They developed commerce with every civilized nation in the known world. Secure in their island citadel and immune from invasion for more than 3,000 years, the Cretans were free to perfect their leisure habits. Their artisans utilized skills to produce a high form of textile manufacture, sculpture, painting, lapidary work, and amenity conveniences which closely approximate those of our modern life.

Excavations show that the people of Crete were able to devote much time to the leisure arts and that they participated in a variety of recreational activities such as shows, festivals, bull-fights, gymnastic exhibitions, dance, swimming, wrestling, and other sports. Crete presents a picture of a vibrant, unrestrained, exuberant life, expressive of good-living as illustrated by the luxurious conditions surrounding the aristocrats at the expense of the enslaved masses.[18] It is apparent that security, when survival needs are satisfied, allows for leisure. Wherever humans have been safe for

[16] *Genesis,* 11, 24–25.
[17] *II Samuel,* **vi,** 5, 12–14, 16, 20.
[18] Helen Gardner, *Art Through the Ages* (New York: Harcourt, Brace and Company, 1936), pp. 101–120.

any length of time, they have been able to develop their arts and standards of living and other benefits to culture to an amazing degree. It is not surprising, therefore, that the Cretans were able to accomplish just such a record in light of their immunity to invasion and comparative freedom from want.[19]

The Hellenic Age

As a sea power Crete probably sent out colonies to the nearest shores, one of which was the Peloponnesus. From 1600 B.C., specific communities actually rivaled Knossos as centers of Cretan culture, and after the sacking of Knossos in 1400 B.C., Mycenae became the chief city of this branch of old Minoan, or Aegean, culture, known as the Mycenaean civilization.[20] This culture, about which much art forms have been gathered, lasted until the twelfth century B.C., when a final and engulfing invasion from the north by the Dorians completely overwhelmed it and dissolved its manifestations into a dark age of three centuries.

It is abundantly clear that a continuous series of minor invasions from the north harried an indigenous people who inhabited Arcadia and Attica from 1800 B.C. to about 1400 B.C. The incoming Hellenic people gradually imposed their language and in turn were culturally absorbed by the non-Hellenes. It is not until the Dorian invasion of 1200 B.C. that a cultural break is noted. The chaotic period of death and destruction, upheaval and internecine warfare terminates, perhaps from sheer exhaustion, in the eighth century B.C., after which in a renaissance of culture classical Greece begins to emerge.

The Greeks and Leisure. If one is to discuss with any correctness the influence that Greek thought has had on western leisure theory and philosophy, we must first survey the structure of the Greek mind which conceived and directed such intellectual pursuits of knowledge as ethics, morality, and education. To do this one must be made aware of *aretê* and the consequences this ideal had on all Greek achievements, including play, and subsequently on what we call recreation.

Aretê combined the idea of what is best in all things and is worthy of emulation and adoration—complete mastery. The Greeks saw *aretê* in terms of animate and inanimate objects. A thing had *aretê* if it was able to perform more than merely efficiently; it had to perform excellently in the manner for which it was created. This view applied to men as well.

The formation of the Greek national character takes its mold from a history of its culture, beginning in the aristocratic arena of early Greece, where human perfection was a coveted ideal towards which the superior class of the society was steadily trained and educated.

[19] M. I. Finley, "The Rediscovery of Crete," *Horizon,* **VII,** No. 3 (Summer 1965), 65–75.
[20] H. R. Hall, *The Ancient History of the Near East* (New York: The Macmillan Company, 1935), pp. 56–67.

We can find a more natural clue to the history of Greek culture in the history of the ideal of *aretê,* which goes back to the earliest times. There is no complete equivalent for the word *aretê* in modern English: its oldest meaning is a combination of proud and courtly morality with warlike valour. But the idea of *aretê* is the quintessence of early Greek aristocratic education.[21]

The ancient tradition of heroic power was not enough to satisfy the chroniclers of a younger era. Their concept of *aretê* hinged upon a combination of noble actions and noble thoughts. Human perfection was the ideal that joined exalted deeds with nobility of mind. It is this concept of unity forcing its way into the very foundation of the Greek code of life which has been handed down to us in the modern meaning of recreation.

Unity and wholeness seem to be the salient features of the Greek psyche. Unity and wholeness are best described by Kitto when he states:

> The sharp distinction which the Christian and the oriental world has normally drawn between the body and the soul, the physical and the spiritual, was foreign to the Greek—at least until the time of Socrates and Plato. To him there was simply the whole man. The Greek made physical training an important part of education . . . because it could never occur to him to train anything but the whole man.[22]

The above discussion has been presented because it is intimately bound up with the subject of recreation. It has been introduced to show the direct lineal descent, as it were, of modern recreation philosophy with its concepts of the rebirth of harmony within the individual from the idealistically contrived values of excellence and oneness of the ancient Greeks. Such a tracing is necessary to support the thesis that recreation is really the alleviation of the awareness of tension and the reunification or rebirth of the individual in mind and body.

In the Greek cultural pattern there emerged a two-fold reason for the existence of leisure which gave rise to the great intellectual, artistic, creative, and other achievements. One was the owning of domestic, factory, and mine-working slaves upon whose shoulders the leisure of the well-to-do rested. The other aspect is the simplicity in which the Greek lived. The standard of living and the basic necessities of life were quite far removed from what we would consider to be the bare needs of today. Then too, it must be remembered that the Greek citizen saved time by not having to travel to work and back home, that there were no conventional hours of work. Kitto has put it quite well:

> Again, the daily round was ordered not by the clock but by the sun, since there was no effective artificial light. Activity began at dawn. We envy,

---

[21] Werner Jaeger, *Paideia: The Ideals of Greek Culture* (New York: Oxford University Press, 1943), **1,** p. 5.
[22] H. D. F. Kitto, *The Greeks* (London: Penguin Books, Ltd., 1951), p. 174.

perhaps, ordinary Athenians who seem able to spend a couple of hours in the afternoon at the baths or a gymnasium (a spacious athletic and cultural centre provided by the public for itself). The Greek got up as soon as it was light, shook out the blanket in which he had slept, draped it elegantly around himself as a suit, had a beard and no breakfast, and was ready to face the world in five minutes. The afternoon, in fact, was not the middle of his day, but very near the end of it.[23]

It is significant to note that such leisure as the Athenian had was directed to contemplative study of philosophy, rhetoric, civic service, and artistic creativity. Leisure to the Greeks, especially to the Athenians, was not conceived as many of us see it today. Leisure was a period to be put to practical use in learning (education), or in public participation of government. It was free time which was utilized to benefit the society in which the Greek citizen, that is, the nonslave lived.

How different is our conception of leisure. Many think of it as anything but in terms of practical or educational usage. Many consider it, in its usual connotation, as the antithesis of work, labor, or study; as a time for loafing rather than living. The Greeks took their leisure seriously and spent it wisely in the pursuit of knowledge for living. People of our modern civilization take their leisure and use it to no purpose. We spend our time by letting it pass, killing it so to speak, with no thought as to what we can make with it. The Greek concept of leisure was one of participation, stimulation, learning, and living. Our concept of leisure is a time for doing nothing or, at best watching someone else do what we either will not or are not skillful enough to do. This might be considered as too sweeping a condemnation of our leisure practices, but it is indicative of what our culture does with its free time.

The purpose of this book is not to indict or condemn leisure pursuits of people. In fact, it is believed that leisure activities may be one phase of possible recreational acts, but it is the purpose of this section of the study to show the relationship of Greek educational philosophy as the taproot for modern recreation thought.

Because leisure was a basic ingredient which produced one of the world's greatest cultures, it was natural for its use in the education of the young. The word *schola* is Greek for leisure, and we derive the English word *school* from it.

> Of course reasoned the Greek, given leisure a man will employ it in thinking and finding out about things. Leisure and the pursuit of knowledge, the connection was inevitable—to a Greek.[24]

The love of play and the desire for freeing men for the most important aspects of their lives, namely participation in government, artistic works,

---

[23] Kitto, *op. cit.*, pp. 134–135.
[24] Edith Hamilton, *The Greek Way* (New York: W. W. Norton & Company, Inc., 1942), pp. 31–32.

and the never-ending search for knowledge impelled the Greeks to use leisure as a time for creative activity. Edith Hamilton put it in a slightly different way:

> The Greeks were the first people in the world to play, and they played on a great scale. If we had no other knowledge of what the Greeks were like, if nothing were left of Greek art and literature, the fact that they were in love with play and played magnificently would be proof enough of how they lived and how they looked at life. They had physical vigor and high spirits and time, too, for fun.[25]

The Greek concept of education is joined with freedom; and their concept of freedom is tied up with leisure. It is the combination of these two factors, freedom and education, in conjunction with *aretê* or excellence on which a philosophy of leisure can be based. These separate facets of a single whole form what to the Greeks was completeness and what can be thought of as the unification of man's mind and body to produce the complete man—at peace with himself and his environment. All his faculties are in harmony and there is no awareness of tension, strain, or discord in any part of him. He is truly re-created.

The Romans

Traditionally Rome is supposed to have been founded by Aeneas of the Trojan house of Priam somewhere about 1200 B.C. Many myths describe in minute detail the construction and development of Rome by Romulus. However, these stories, for such they are, do not stand the test of critical evaluation and are merely part of the elaborate heritage of folk lore to which the uneducated masses subscribed in the days of ancient Rome.

The Neolithic Italian culture existed before 3000 B.C. For five hundred years thereafter there was little change in that stagnant society. It was not until foreign migration starting in 2500 B.C. that progress in social culture was made. During the Chalcolithic age metalworkers from beyond the Alps began to move into the region of the Po Valley, and it is basically from these emigrants that Italy was to gain its first knowledge of civilized life.

While the people of the Italian boot were adopting themselves to Chalcolithic culture (about 1700 B.C.), a new wave of invasions began in central Europe. The Achaeans moved into the Greek peninsula, and ripples of migrant pressure were felt throughout the northern Mediterranean region. One of these groups left a deep impression upon the peninsula Italians —the "Terramara people." It was through profound contact with the Terramara people that great advances in both material and cultural institutions were made.

Some six centuries after the initiation of the Chalcolithic culture into Italy, a new flood of migrations brought violent repercussions to the lands lying along the Mediterranean sea. One result was the Dorian invasion of

---

[25] *Ibid.*, pp. 21–22.

Greece and another was the drive southward by the then inhabitants of the Po Valley to new locations in the central region of the peninsula.

About 800 B.C., Italian culture underwent another remarkable change for the better when invaders from Asia Minor, the Etruscans, overran much of western Italy. They rapidly transformed the land which they conquered. They taught the Italic natives how to drain the swamps, log the forests, and introduced grape and olive agriculture into the country. The local iron, tin, and copper mines were successfully worked, and the practical trades of smithing, stone masonry, carpentry, and weaving soon made their appearance. Timber was transformed into ships, which were soon plying the trade routes between Italy, Sicily, Sardinia, and Corsica.

Once their initial landings and position had been consolidated, the Etruscan aristocrats began to enlarge their sphere of influence. They went south and invaded Latium and Campania, thus, probably founding Rome. The Greeks, too, had colonized parts of the Italian peninsula, and when the Etruscans headed south, it was only a matter of time before the two would clash. From the sixth century on, the two peoples were almost continuously occupied by war. It was not until 535 B.C., that an alliance between Carthage and Etruria combined to expel the Greek colonists from Corsica. By 500 B.C., however, the tide in Campania and Latium had turned against the Etruscans, and after repeated revolutions on the part of the native populations, the Etruscan empire toppled. The growing power of Rome was an important factor in this decline of the Etruscans. Between 500 B.C. and 265 B.C., Rome first became the dominant power and then engulfed and united all of Italy into one state.

Life and Culture in Early Rome. Life was simple and somewhat crude during the third century B.C. The weakening of class distinctions and the lack of a very wealthy or very poor class mitigated against a heterogeneous culture. The economy was based on agriculture. Traditions were what men lived by and family unity was very strong. There was little of the aesthetic quality about these Romans and they cared little for the niceties of civilization.

Under such conditions work, rather than leisure, was the central theme. Thus everyone in the family worked hard and lived simply. Yet even in these times of simplicity and frugality there was leisure and the diversions that free time usually spawns. Religious holidays were numerous. Citizens were still obliged to attend public hearings and pass on laws in Rome. Markets or fairs were held every ninth day in and about the capital as well as in the rural areas.

Slaves in early Rome were usually captives of war. In this simple society they were usually utilized as agricultural laborers. There were so few slaves during this period that they contributed little to the leisure of their respective owners. It was not until much later that the introduction of large numbers of captives from Asia, Greece, and central Europe, and their cruel exploitation by their owners for purposes of luxury and vice, made slavery the abomination which it became. As might be expected, the early Romans, having to cope with harsh environmental conditions, both human and natural, did little in terms of cultural achievement, i.e., the fine arts and literature. However, in the eminently practical arts of architecture, road and aqueduct building, they were unsurpassed.

Life and Culture After the Roman Conquest. From 265 B.C. Rome began to dominate the western Mediterranean world. During their consolidation of the Italian peninsula, their wars seemed largely defensive. However, as they continued to win so also were there new frontiers to protect. This led to increased expansion. Inevitably, their sphere of influence clashed with that of Carthage, who, up to that time, controlled much of the western Mediterranean area. The resultant conflicts were the Punic wars. Rome emerged victorious and by 200 B.C. was well on the way to imperial overlordship of the Mediterranean world.

With Carthage defeated, Rome became the strongest military power in the civilized world. Again, new frontiers led to new antagonisms with attendant wars, both of defense and of aggression. The stage was set for Rome's assumption of power over the eastern Mediterranean. Up to about 200 B.C., Rome's foreign policies had been based on opportunism and had had little contact with the Hellenistic states. Now she came into direct contact with them and was involved in an endless series of wars. As a result of these wars, Rome emerged, in 167 B.C., as the dominant power in the eastern Mediterranean as well as the western. From that time until the decline of the Roman Republic in 79 B.C., Rome engaged in a series of major and minor wars which brought into subjugation all of the former kingdoms and empires of the ancient Near East as well as Asia Minor, Greece, Spain, and the Danubian region.

One of the unfortunate results of this imperial expansion was the decadence of the society. A salient effect of the increased wealth and might of the Roman people was a marked inequality in economic status between the rich and poor. Slave labor replaced free labor and depressed wages were the consequence. The well-to-do no longer performed the manual labor nor lived the simple life to which their ancestors had adhered. A new leisure class arose—the aristocratic rich.

Public festivals and amusements became more numerous and varied both for rich and poor. From Campania came the gladiatorial combats, initially held in Rome in 264 B.C. This custom did not gain popular support until after 200 B.C. Theatrical performances, horse racing, and acrobatics were some of the events held to entertain the public. By 50 B.C. the aristocracy, by virtue of its reliance upon slave-worked agriculture and other commercial enterprises lived a leisure existence on a scale hitherto unknown. As Van Sickle states:

> Indeed, many of the richer members and the spendthrifts who strove to imitate them at times adopted gaudy splendor and coarse luxury which

was the scandal of their own and later times. Eating, drinking, flashy clothes, expensive furniture, handsome slaves, and gambling cost these worthies enormous sums, and they went to the most absurd and revolting lengths to procure the objects of their desire.[26]

Yet, for all this apparent depravity and shocking activity, there is abundant proof of a rich cultural development during this period. The Romans were very creative and found means of self-expression in both the fine arts and literature. Architecture, sculpture, and painting flourished. History, poetry, oratory, and the didactic essay were integral parts of Roman literature. Roman architecture formed a style of its own. An age that had leisure produced Virgil, Horace, Livy, and fine arts which cannot be denied acclamation.

The years of gradual decline and abandonment of the Republic because of the corruption and degradation of senatorial power and the illegal office-holding of some men during emergencies cannot be laid on any single person. When the first Tribune of the people was murdered, the basic sanctions were lifted and one consequence was the rise of a variety of warlords who hastened the decline of the Republic. After the Triumvirate and subsequent rise of Gaius Julius Caesar as a general and statesman, the fate of the Roman Republic was sealed. Civil war between Caesar and Pompey, proscription of enemies, dictatorship, assassination, and the war of succession heralded the Augustan Principate.

Early Imperial Society. The aristocracy stood at the top of Roman society. These were the wealthy few who, through ownership of estates and shares in commercial ventures, or by corrupt methods in politics had gathered the economic means to pursue a life of luxury. Their estates were cultivated by tenants and slaves. With abundant leisure and, therefore, opportunities for education, this group followed cultural pursuits that were denied to the great masses of the people. The urban middle class, or curials, also enjoyed excellent educational opportunities. Through wise investments, a strong sense of civic duty, and other reasonable factors, they served Rome diligently until they were financially ruined by sustaining the cost of imperial government in the third century A.D. In the fourth and fifth centuries, its surviving members were no more than slaves of the state.

The urban proletariat was a composite of hard-working, frugal freemen, hired laborers, and slaves. Because of slave competition, wages were very low and most workers lived a life of squalor and bare existence. In Rome, the emperors had to take over the task of feeding and amusing the populace and these people shared in the free entertainment, public baths, food distribution, and other doles which the local ruling class saw fit to present. Much more numerous than the city masses were the peasants who culti-

---

[26] C. E. Van Sickle, *A Political and Cultural History of the Ancient World From Prehistoric Times to the Dissolution of the Roman Empire in the West* (New York: Houghton Mifflin Company, 1948), pp. 341–342.

vated the soil. Although slavery never was the principal ingredient used for agricultural production, some slaves were utilized along with free peasants. Agricultural implements were primitive at best and the peasants worked very hard for a small return and little leisure.

Generally, the peasant's life was a hard and bitter one. He had to pay his rent and taxes and face forced labor drafts and other imperial levies. He had little or no part in the brilliant, if wasteful, urban life which produced the appearance of great prosperity for the Empire in the second century A.D., and educational prospects were nonexistent. Culturally, the peasant was backward and his freedom, such as it was, became a farce at the end of the third century.

For the 250 years after Augustus' death, the Greco-Roman culture of the Empire was sustained by the intellectual and aesthetic traditions of its past, but the decay of classical culture had already begun. During the first century of this era much was produced that was valuable. Then routine and stagnation set in, and for the next century a rapid decline in taste and artistic form is noted. Van Sickle states:

> Literature succumbed to a taste for showy rhetoric and to blind worship of the past, and of the arts only architecture was producing anything which was destined to win the approval of later ages. Science and philosophy lingered a little longer, but before the accession of Diocletian they, too, had succumbed to the forces which were bringing the classical world to an end. The decline of economic prosperity, the breakdown of political order, the weakening of urban life, the growth of political absolutism, and a caste-ridden social order—all contributed to create an environment in which none of the distinctive products of earlier ages could flourish. Hence, they withered away . . .[27]

Late Imperial Society. The decadent fourth and fifth centuries witnessed the fall of the classical tradition in the Roman empire as well as the destruction of orderly government, sophisticated urban life, the economy, art, literature, science, and philosophy. This was closely followed by an almost complete lack of artistic activity. In the harassed and regulated cities of the fourth and fifth centuries, survival, rather than leisure and the wealth to indulge in free time experiences, was the controlling interest. There was no longer sufficient economic support for building programs and artistic creativity was displaced in communities continuously under attack by invading barbarians as well as supposedly protecting soldiers and rapacious bureaucrats.

The general view of society at this time is one of conformity, complicity, and stagnation. The urban middle class had been crushed and no longer existed. The wealth, leisure, and consequently the culture of the late Empire was to be found only in the possession of the great senatorial landlords,

---

[27] *Ibid.,* p. 523.

who lived in seclusion on their vast estates. Their wealth was drawn from the land, and was created as a result of slavery.

The Empire was doomed to destruction. Many factors influenced the inevitable decline of the Empire and it is not known just what specific conditions contributed to the final dissolution of Imperial Rome. The splendors of the classic era were routinized and strangled by an effete aristocracy or ignorant peasantry. The indulgences of the senatorial aristocracy amid the ruination of the other classes were scandalous. In every period of ancient and the later Roman Empire, there are traces of degeneracy. For sheer waste and brutality, the gladiatorial contests and orgiastic or sybaritic ways of living cast a pall which the ensuing Dark Ages could not dispel. There is little wonder at the condemnation of leisure by members of the various Christian sects during the following 1400 years. A final commentary on the social conditions of Imperial Rome is offered by Johan Huizinga:

> Rome grew to a World Empire and a World Emporium. To it there fell the legacy of the Old World that had gone before, the inheritance of Egypt and Hellenism and half the Orient. Its culture was fed on the overflow of a dozen other cultures. Government and law, road-building and the art of war reached a state of perfection such as the world had never seen; . . . The Roman Empire . . . was spongy and sterile in its social and economic structure . . .
>
> Rome in its later days . . . was slowly degenerating and being suffocated under a system of State slavery, extortion, graft and nepotism, circuses and amphitheaters for bloody and barbarous games, a dissolute stage, baths for a cult of the body more enervating than invigorating—none of this makes for a solid and lasting civilization. Most of it served merely for show, amusement and futile glory.[28]

AN OVERVIEW OF POST-ROMAN LEISURE

The grandeur that was Rome was copied to a large extent from the Hellenistic culture. The Romans adopted the leisure style of the Greeks but added certain refinements and debasements. Thus the gladiatorial schools for slaughter were developed as well as daredevil competitive events. In the period of the Empire, leisure excesses were so prevalent and leisure so demeaned that a negative reaction was formulated against all things recreational. This reaction is disapproval of most leisure activity, seemingly purposeless experiences, and has remained in one form or another with all Western cultures since the early Christian Church denounced frivolous conduct, particularly after Saint Augustine wrote against sensuousness in human affairs. We may see this inference to this very day in terms of the 1961 U.S. Supreme Court ruling upholding the legal propriety of the blue laws.

[28] Johan Huizinga, *Homo Ludens* (Boston: The Beacon Press, 1950), pp. 174–176.

Ideas concerning leisure have been found in the literature of many historical periods. The reason for not including all the ages in which man had leisure is that many are repetitive and are not necessary in order to illustrate the basic principle of leisure. No mention is made of the Medieval or Renaissance periods, in any but the most superficial manner, because writers of those eras utilized the classical Greek thinkers as models for educational principles and philosophic ideals. In these instances the cultural development would merely be a restatement.

After the decline of the Roman Empire and the rise of other national states in Europe, leisured classes still persisted in the performance of activities that met with great resistance from the organized church. However, with the arrival of the age of chivalry, the knightly contests and tournaments became the leading recreational and leisure activities of the day. The centuries between A.D. 800 and A.D. 1000, commonly known as the Middle Ages, produced manifold activities of a recreational nature. Hunting, warfare, falconry, and courtly romance were the favored activities of the leisured while the great mass of the public practiced archery, vigorous dancing, and the common sports of running, wrestling, throwing, and jumping. Villagers participated in the passion plays, market days, festivals, pageants, parades, fairs, and other numerous recreational experiences. Animal baiting was also a common practice and gambling was the rule rather than a rarity.

The clergy took a dim view of the excesses which occurred during leisure, such as it was, and deprecated most leisure activity. The Roman Church was particularly disinclined to view with favor certain forms of dance, gambling, gaming, musicales, and masques. This religious censure resulted in a general ban against most hedonistic activity, specifically that which was associated with leisure. But the aristocracy, while paying lip service to the church, still participated in many of the illicit activities against which there was a clerical taboo. Pleasure seeking continued to flourish and the promotion of amusements, sports, games, and other leisure experiences proliferated.

The Renaissance, or re-birth of learning, witnessed a resurgence of secular thinkers over theological sanctions. The day of the courtier, as exemplified by Bayard, Cellini, or Castiglioni, arrived with the religious reformers. The temporal court was the center of romantic, political, and cultural activities exemplified by the lavishness of the Medici and the Borgias. However, the excesses of political intrigue and secular living which reached into the hierarchy of the Vatican also produced a countering force known to history as the Reformation. During the rapid spread of Protestantism one of the leading figures, whose influence had a profound effect upon Western civilization, was John Calvin of Geneva. Among his precepts are those teaching that man's salvation is only for the elect. He also taught that original sin is passed on to all mankind and that no man could rise out of the state of disgrace without God's help. There was much stress upon God's anger and vengeance. Calvin's view of leisure can be seen from an inordinate emphasis upon leisure being idleness and idleness equated with the devil. This concept was to dominate clerical understanding of leisure for the next five hundred years. In fact, the completely orthodox Calvinistic condemnation of leisure has been part of the Protestant ethic which has tended to govern the lives of most people of the Western World to this day.

The Enlightenment, on the other hand, further freed men's minds from dependence upon supernatural fears and ignorance, and set out to perfect human society. This was a time for learning and creativity. Leisure activity was commented upon in a more favorable light. The humanist orientation played a great part in the recovery of leisure as an important aspect of human life. From this liberation of thought there also developed more reasonableness toward activities performed in leisure. The great educators began to stress the child's needs for recreational experience. Locke, Comenius, Montaigne, and Froebel contributed much to the trend that revitalized the use of recreational activity in the formal school setting. It was the men of this group who influenced subsequent recreational and leisure activity development through their writings and practice.

LEISURE IN AMERICA

Colonial America was the seat of religious dogmatism as well as a hodgepodge of political and social colorings. The colonies of the seventeenth and eighteenth centuries were under the theological domination of Calvinistic thought. Particularly were the New England colonies under the pressure of Puritanism. Under the leadership of Joseph Cotton and Cotton Mather, the Protestant ethic indicated specific taboos and restricted social movement. Their teachings of predestination, frugality, and an intolerance for leisure and recreational activity profoundly influenced later modern social life. In New England, although not elsewhere, most forms of recreational experience were prohibited by law.

During the years immediately after the colonies were settled on the American continent, and especially in the New England communities, the attitude toward play was decidedly unfavorable. This was an era of frontier settlement and terrible hardship. Survival was uppermost in men's minds. Consequently, productivity in the way of material goods and services became the measure by which men lived. The early colonists bringing with them as they did the orthodox preachings of the Reformation, specifically Calvin's concepts of unconditional predestination, limited atonement, and irresistibility of grace, sought to stamp out the human desires for pleasure and amusement by limitations and prohibitions on what man might do in the daily process of living.

The unproductivity of the land and the stunning experience of frontier living combined with the stark pessimism of puritan life in forming a philosophy that valued only frugality, hard work, self-discipline, and strict observance of civil and religious codes. Such an approach to life considered play to be "the devil's work" and any time not given over to productive work or worship was wasteful and therefore condemned. In such a society where survival was a daily pressure, legislation surpressing activities called play was readily accepted by the people. The magistrate was the law, the law was the literal interpretation of the Bible, the Bible was handed to men from God, and God was to be obeyed.

Time passed, and the struggle for existence ceased to pervade all the waking hours of a man's life. The problem of meeting each day eased. Land was fenced off for common pasturage, protection, and tillage. A man now had time to talk of social issues with his neighbor. Meeting grounds, later to become parks, were established as the stress of emergency living seemed to be over. When the agricultural economy was firmly built, trade and commerce, first between colonies, and then with foreign contacts, allowed a leisure class to develop. Men still performed their daily work, but those with more financial security, those with land holdings, mineral rights, or other valuable assets, found others to carry on the more onerous, detailed, and time-consuming tasks which, in turn, provided certain blocks of unoccupied time for these privileged few. This wealthy minority constituted the ablest, best learned, and highest positioned people and sometimes the most astute, ruthless, and unprincipled people whose background and education made them long for the modes of living which had been left behind in England and on the European continent. Men of such breeding reverted to their accustomed pleasurable pursuits, and soon bowling on the green, cricket, horse racing, fox hunting, card playing, dancing, musical concerts, theatrical entertainments, and the common sports became the recreational activities of the day.

As the vigor and aggressive leadership receded from Calvinistic idealism, people tended to find replacement in other concepts whose outlooks were more pleasing to their new-found security. By 1700, the Dutch settlers of the eastern seaboard pursued many pleasures within the environs of public houses. In addition to drinking, games similar to modern golf, handball, skating, tennis, and sleighing in season, and the more indiscreet activities such as gambling and prostitution were carried on. These leisure activities spread throughout the colonies, despite denunciations from the pulpit, and by the time of the American Revolution (1775–1783), masques or theatre parties, balls, entertainments, extravagant dances, drinking, gambling, animal baiting, and other equally censured, but nonetheless pleasurable activities were flourishing during leisure.

Again, as it had during the colonial settlement period, recreational ideas underwent a change after the War of Independence. Once despised and condemned, recreational activity assumed a place in all parts of the American social scene. The eastern seaboard cities and towns had their social gatherings, but the back country farmers and frontiersmen, living on the edge of the wilderness, remained relatively untouched by the quest for diversion initiated by their urbanized cousins. Utilitarian recreational activities were most popular in rural areas. Cooperative group experiences and efforts such as barn raisings, sheep shearing, corn husking, crafts, church suppers, quilting bees, town meetings, turkey shoots, and community dances tended to draw the interest of rural people who realized that many useful benefits accrued from cooperation in getting a particular job done.

The migration of people seeking a new and better life on the western side of the Appalachian Plateau helped to spread the doctrine of equalitarianism, the natural rights of man, and humanitarian faith rather than aristocratic privilege. This westward movement brought with it the isolation of the frontier and freedom from conventional restraint associated with east coast living. The recreational activities centered in the home, and the family was the social world by which the individual was surrounded until that time of year when road or river travel permitted all the families of one district to meet for common feasting, dancing, marketing, or other such enterprise. Life was severe and short for the unwary settler and the pleasurable pursuits of social intercourse and other recreational activity were few and far between.

In effect, then, recreational activities of the rural and frontier regions mixed play and work. The natural elements as well as survival techniques were utilized. In the well-developed and settled areas of the East and later on in the West, as civilization inexorably pushed back the frontier, a leisure class grew and its typical recreational experiences were games of chance, extravaganzas, the more aesthetic entertainments, and other forms of individual and social activity.

The years between the Civil War and 1900, saw advancing forms of a mechanistic technology, the explosive effect of Darwin's biological theory of evolution, and a humanitarian appeal; all exerting pressure for a new approach to the latest discoveries of the day. The advances made in the physical and biological sciences produced such profound changes in the world view of man, his relationship to his environment, and the possibilities for his education that not only was reappraisal necessary to reconcile these diverse concepts, but a radical change was patently required if any practical use was to be made of these facts and new knowledge.

Education began to take rapid professional strides as labor, a newly awakened force in the economy of the United States, insistently demanded a place. There was a call for more education better fitted to the demands of those who worked at the manual trades, and for their children upon whose shoulders their hopes for better living rode. As education progressed, it carried with it, albeit more slowly, the field of recreational service. Industrialization and mass production called for new techniques. The demand for more efficient methods in turning out goods and services throughout the manufacturing and heavy industrial world stressed advances in communications, transportation, metallurgy, scientific analysis, and chemical research necessary to produce more and cheaper goods.

With the new technology, advanced techniques in science and industry after 1865, turned the attention of educators and those connected with the economics of the country toward utilitarian and materialistic philosophies of life. Businessmen wanted an education that would orient their workers to a useful type of practical knowledge. They were eager to underwrite institutions of learning that would produce an employee who could fit into their particular form of economic enterprise. Coupled with this outcry for a utilitarian education was the swift growth of the natural sciences. Science became the byword for industrial growth and development.

The consequences of this rapid acceleration in an area of learning that had formerly reposed behind ivy-covered walls was to open new vistas to the intellectually minded. Where the natural sciences had languished under the eyes of the academicians of the classical idealism school, there now appeared a movement away from faculty psychology doctrines.

The conflicting forces unleashed by Darwin's evolutionary views in 1859, struck with smashing impact upon the classical humanities. Deeply penetrating investigations in the biological and physical sciences produced empirical evidence which when opposed to customary theological views of the time caused widespread anguish and dismay among traditionalists. Still, the faculty psychologists remained. The philosophical absolutists refused to give ground to this evidence. Crusty, hide-bound conservatives were disinclined to accept the evidence of natural science. The struggle for intellectual and academic supremacy between idealistic humanists and revolutionary scientists intensified in the decade after the publication of *Origin of Species*.

But the great weight of scientific matter and knowledge could not be denied. Encouraged by the demand for better ways of doing things through industrial crafts, which needed the sciences for operational inventions, the natural and physical sciences gained ascendancy over the humanities in the institutions of higher learning, and a new round of philosophical thinking was inaugurated.

CLASS, CULTURE, AND LEISURE

Thorstein Veblen wrote extensively on the leisure concept as a product of social stratification. His outstanding work, *Theory of the Leisure Class*, is an example of a reversal of the trend toward considering leisure as the only time for creativity. The book, which was published in 1899, had almost instantaneous critical reaction. To many who read it, Veblen appeared to have written a satire against aristocracy everywhere. He was taken to task for having dared to question time-honored activities and customs of what he called "the leisure class." Veblen's polemic was conditioned by what he observed in the America of the late 1800's. He wrote a satire, or at least satire was utilized in his work, but it was not directed against an aristocratic class. It was pointed toward exposing the envy in which the aristocratic class was held by all other social levels.

Veblen produced some thought-provoking ideas concerning what he described as unrestrained or conspicuous spending in order for one class to live up to its conception of possession at the expense of all others. He described the leisure class as having evolved from a predatory stage to a quasi-predatory stage where, instead of outright naked force to reduce all competitors to subservience, there is a reliance upon constituted authority to enforce customs of ownership. Veblen looked upon the ownership class as diametrically opposed to productive labor. The occupations of this class were institutionalized as religious order, government administration, warfare, education, and sports. In these occupations the leisured class could carry on their interest in pecuniary gain without crossing the line of producing gain through labor. This could be seen in the activities of those engaged in war or government, where gain is received by the honorable processes of annexation and naturalization. He also described the early differentiation out of which the distinction between a leisure and a laboring class developed as a dichotomy maintained by male and female work in the earliest stages of savagery; an invidious distinction out of which came industrial and nonindustrial occupations at the next highest level of culture.[29]

The term *leisure* as utilized by Veblen is taken to mean nonproductive use of time.

> Time is consumed non-productively (1) from a sense of unworthyness of productive work, and (2) as an evidence of the pecuniary ability to afford a life of idleness.[30]

This show of pecuniary ability gives rise to vicarious leisure, that is, an exhibition by the possessor of goods, services, and other decorative but nonessential devices. This is manifested by the utilization of servants, and the vicarious leisure of the wife as a symbol of the master's wealth and power. Conspicuous leisure from productive activities is by far the more classical and inclusive principle of the leisure class plan.

A striking concept which Veblen invested in his thesis is diametrically opposed to conspicuous waste and considers man as having an impulse or instinct of workmanship. This instinct, the court of last resort in the human organism, rationally lauds what is economically effective or productive in life and condemns economic waste or inutility.[31] This scale of economic worth is closely associated with the moral scale of behavior and the aesthetic scale of refinement. It is not an inclination towards effort, but a desire for accomplishment. Thus, an intelligent person wants to believe

---

[29] Thorstein Veblen, *The Theory of the Leisure Class: An Economic Study of Institutions* (New York: The Macmillan Company, 1899), p. 4.
[30] *Ibid.*, p. 93.
[31] *Ibid.*, p. 92.

that he is useful, and he generally wants to see others performing at some productive task or plan. This trait of workmanship leads to productive creativity and leisure, therefore, becomes just another area of time set aside for certain activities having hedonistic qualities.

According to Veblen, recreation held a mediating position between the instinct of workmanship and the instinct of sportsmanship. The latter is an expression of an aversion to labor and is thus a part of the code of the leisure class.

> The leisure class canon demands strict and comprehensive futility; the instinct of workmanship demands purposeful action. The leisure class canon of decorum acts slowly and pervasively, by selective elimination of all substantially useful or purposeful modes of action from the accredited scheme of life; the instinct of workmanship acts impulsively and may be satisfied, provisionally, with a proximate purpose.[32]

Sports give the individual an excuse to exercise skill and predatory actions. As long as the individual reacts to life with naive impulses, sports will compensate his instinct for workmanship. By satisfying the two prerequisites of conspicuous waste and proximate purposefulness, any given activity can maintain its position as an historic and accustomed form of proper recreational activity.[33]

> In the sense that other forms of recreation and exercise are morally impossible to persons of good breeding and delicate sensibilities, then, sports, are the best available means of recreation under existing circumstances.[34]

The leisure class of Veblen's book contemplates a life devoted to pleasure based on a nonessential expending of wealth derived by manipulation of industrial products or workers through ownership and/or exploitation. The meaning such a thesis has for the field of recreational service is recognizable by its implication of a new concept concerning social service which might more nearly equalize leisure expenditure for all groups of people to satisfy the desire of social classes in the American culture. Another pointed implication is an awareness of creativity performed in other than leisure pursuits. This unique concept challenges customary ideas on the worthiness or usefulness of acts performed in leisure as opposed to those performed in nonfree time.

THE NEW LEISURE AND RECREATIONAL SERVICE

The increasingly important role played by recreational activity is due to a variety of causes beginning with those which gave rise to the industrial

---

[32] *Ibid.*, p. 258.
[33] *Ibid.*, p. 260.
[34] *Loc. cit.*

revolution. The age of discovery brought the age of invention; the age of invention brought the age of power; the age of power brought the age of leisure. As in the past, new technical processes have improved production methods to the extent that it has become practicable to reduce the hours of work with corresponding increasing returns to the workers. Accordingly, within the past sixty years, the hours of factory labor have been reduced in some industries from sixty per week to thirty-five. State and federal legislation has imposed restrictions upon the number of hours which minors and women might be employed. Along with the curtailment of hours of manual labor have gone equal limitations upon white collar work and employment in the professions.

A shift in interest by the public health agencies from curing gross environmental producing ailments to procedures that will extend life and physical effectiveness, so that the average person may contemplate from twelve to twenty years of life expectancy after retirement, should have considerable effect upon the activities of leisure. The science of medicine has done much to reduce poor health among the aging. As science pushes back the frontiers of the unknown, it will surely find remedies for the diseases that now account for most morbidity at advanced ages.[35] Consequent increase of leisure of older adults and proportionate growth of their interest in community recreational service programs must be anticipated.

That the American people have been extremely ingenious in devising ways to employ their leisure is apparent to everyone. The amusements, entertainments, and diversions designed to provide vicarious experience and the activities organized to induce direct participation are literally inexhaustible. The variety of activities is as great as the range of human capabilities. They partake of nearly all of the innate capacities for feeling and action and are multiplied by the development which these capacities undergo in the experience of living. Their complexity is increased by inventive genius and they are not limited by the requirements of utilitarianism but are conditioned only by their ability to give human satisfaction and enjoyment. Innumerable hobbies practiced by individuals and group activities in literature, science, craftsmanship, games, sports, music, art, and clubs abound. There are reported to be 150 million aquatic enthusiasts, 25 million bowlers, 8 million tennis players, 4 million golfers, 30 million softball players, 30 million fishermen, and unnumbered archers, riders, hunters, walkers, boaters, collectors, birdwatchers, ad infinitum.

Creativity and Leisure

Coincident with the decrease in hours of work has been the increased dependence of people upon activities of leisure for full expression of human faculties. In the preindustrial era, a worker found an outlet for a wide range of his faculties in his vocation. Work was not highly competitive,

---

[35] Jay S. Shivers, "Recreational Service for the Aging," *Journal of the Association for Physical and Mental Rehabilitation,* **XIV** (November–December, 1960), p. 170.

but was performed leisurely. It was varied in the skills which it employed. It not only gave opportunity for creative experience and invention and for the individual to place the stamp of his own genius upon the character of the product, but also provided opportunity for social intercourse in the productive processes. Work was life in the full.

Today work in the trades and professions alike is restrictive in its employment of the worker's full potential. His success is almost in direct proportion to the degree of his specialization. In the factory he often uses the accessory and not the large skeletal muscles. This does violence to his physiological and emotional balance, and so he must find relief in big muscle activity during leisure. In his recreational pursuit he discovers opportunities to live creatively and to give expression to the wide assortment of human capabilities with which he is endowed, but which atrophy through disuse if not released and cultivated in leisure.

> Because the satisfaction of basic human needs was inherent in the work of our predecessors, they did not need as much time for recreational activity as we do today. Few of us, at the present, can see the completed result of our labors, and even if we do we cannot readily identify ourselves with a particular product since we may have performed only one of the thousands of operations required for its completion.[36]

The need for individuality and self-expression is necessary in an environment that restricts conduct and demands conformity. Creativity allows the individual to realize his known skills and latent talents. It is during leisure that the individual engages in experiences that are uniquely his own. Because freedom is the essence of recreational pursuit, the individual is free to select his leisure activity and participate to the limit of his being, affording him a chance to shake off the confines of routinized daily living and slip into the realm of highly personalized self-determination. In no other activity is the individual free to be as uninhibited as he desires. However, recreational activity is *not* escape from life. What the individual does in his leisure inevitably affects the kind of person he is or will become. Because man is known to do what he wants to do when he wants to do it during leisure, there is the chance that he will seek creative activity in his free time in order to satisfy his basic needs for achievement.

THE ECONOMICS OF LEISURE

Fortunately the processes which changed the nature of work and reduced its hours created a greater national wealth. This made possible many improvements and commodities which were needed if leisure was to bring compensatory satisfactions and values. Much of this wealth has been

---

[36] James A. Baley and Jay S. Shivers, "Recreational Activity and Family Health," *The American Recreation Society Bulletin,* **XII** (February 1960), pp. 8–9.

reinvested and consumed in the processes of further production; much has been wasted in wars and other enterprises which produced no social values; and much of it has been expended upon social betterment, education, and recreational activity.

Realization of the potential values of our leisure has been enhanced by the increased national wealth. Many leisure activities require materials and services which cannot be had without expenditure of money. Whereas it is true that some of the activities which rank at the top of the recreational scale, in terms of value, are free gifts of nature, others are unquestionably denied the individual if he cannot purchase the requisite commodities or services incidental to their enjoyment. The benefits of leisure before World War II had never been as universal as they are today. This was due, in part, to the unequal distribution of wealth. Yet, an expression of monetary expenditures of America's free time would show that with very few exceptions almost every family spent some money for recreational services, materials, or activities this past year. Even when individuals did not have the necessary economic means for providing themselves with certain recreational commodities, they were assisted by the public and other community facilities which are open to all. These include not only those available through agencies specifically established for recreational services such as parks, playgrounds, and beaches, but those which are offered by public schools, youth serving agencies, churches, libraries, and other community enterprises. These facilities are still not uniformly distributed nor are they by any means adequate for existing needs, but they are increasing in number as demand is created for them.

URBAN AND SUBURBAN DEVELOPMENT FOSTERS RECREATIONAL SERVICE

Urbanization of the population has provided a fertile soil for the growth of leisure activities. The reasons for the phenomenal increase of public recreational service agencies in cities rather than in rural communities may be explained by the traditional conservatism of rural populations to accept new governmental functions. The disinclination of rural people to facilitate the establishment of leisure-oriented agencies probably stems from the distrust that most ruralities have for governmental enterprise of any kind. Further than this is the historical concept, which rural living has espoused, of work being opposed to leisure activities. Urban dwellers, on the other hand, have tended to be liberal and progressive in their outlook, willing to accept many new governmental services. There appears to be an almost socialistic willingness to allow government the responsibility for establishing agencies which will serve the needs of people. With a rapid development of urban centers there is a corresponding growth of municipal recreational service departments.

The noticeable migration of farm families to cities each year is part of the urban movement developing in the United States. Approximately one million farm families moved into cities between 1940 to 1945. Today, more than 72 million people live in a relatively few urban centers. The great significance of internally migrating populations for leisure and the subsequent growth of public recreational agencies is that the sharp line of distinction which once probably marked the difference between rural and urban living no longer exists. There is less distinction and more similarity between urban and rural life than there has ever been. With the rise of the suburbs the accent has been a movement away from the central city, but close enough to utilize the commercial and recreational facilities. Suburban living and rural dwelling have literally become the same thing because of the advent of television and the great mobility which improved methods of transportation, including the private automobile, provide. With technological improvements a decided interest in the provision of public recreational service has just recently become apparent in rural and suburban areas. An increasing number of rural communities, i.e., from 800 to 2,000 people in 1961, have been very much concerned with providing recreational facilities and activities, particularly for their children, and also for adults. This is evident throughout the South as well as in many other rural regions of the country. The development of full-time public recreational service departments is somewhat slow in the most highly countrified areas due to the small numbers of people who can afford to be taxed for the professional leadership and facilities which are necessary and the lessened need for creative satisfactions due to the self-sufficiency attained in agricultural processes.

THE ACCEPTANCE OF LEISURE AND RECREATIONAL ACTIVITY

The growth of the field of Recreational Service has also been accelerated by the breakdown of traditional cultural prejudices and religious taboos. A philosophy more tolerant of leisure and recreational activities and one which recognizes their importance from the standpoint of human and social value has gained general acceptance. It is a function of sectarian systems to prescribe the moral code by which it intends its membership to abide. This is particularly true of the universal axioms as the specific branch or ideology defines the truth. Its power is tradition and ritual. As time has passed, however, the clergy have seen their members increasingly affected and influenced by the consequences of a highly technological society. Time, in terms of value, utilization, and understanding, has been strongly affected by economic reorientations. As work has receded from the pre-eminent place it occupied in previous societies of Western culture, ecclesiastical revision has come about concerning the place of leisure in the life of man.

The church, by the very decrease of working time, has been forced to consider leisure as an incorporated element in systematic philosophy and theology.[37] Thus, the Calvinistic tradition which views work as the antithesis of leisure has been dispelled for the most part. The church has in many instances entered into the support of leisure and recreational activities, particularly and significantly adopting the techniques which have been developed by practitioners in the field of recreational service. In the pluralistic culture of America it would be difficult for any one clerical system to suppress much recreational experience which is performed in the new leisure. Even the most fundamentalist sects are developing recreational aspects for use in their own churches. The modified attitude against recreational activity and leisure pursuits has assisted the great development of recreational service by public agencies and the new awareness of leisure by private groups and persons. Although there are still laws prohibiting certain recreational activities on Sundays, and a minor academic prejudice against the applied arts, the tendency to ascribe an insignificant role to leisure activity is breaking down rapidly.[38]

SUMMARY

The nuclear age is also an age of massive human leisure. In no epoch of the past has there ever been a hope, if not full realization, of free time available to nearly everyone, free from unremitting toil. In all cultures, past and present, some leisure has always been available, but in earlier times only a privileged few were able to enjoy it. Historically, only the aristocratic class could ever afford leisure. Whenever there were slaves in any society, leisure was a commodity, i.e., something to be purchased. The rise of leisure can be traced to the recapture of time from that devoted to the imperative needs to obtain food, clothing, and shelter. In a social order built upon slavery, free time was available to those who owned slaves. Development of civilization with organization, division of labor, mechanization, mass production, and automation brought leisure within the grasp of all. Whenever time could be gained through the institution of labor-saving devices, e.g., the wheel, better agricultural implements, irrigation methods, sailing vessels, steam, internal combustion engines, and atomic power, then, and only then, did leisure accrue and tend to become a universal possession.

Reaffirmation of the principle of leisure will serve to assist the reader in assimilating the entire discussion. From an historical view of human development and cultural achievement throughout the thousands of centuries since the first true man had the time to think, leisure has been an element of life. Significant advancements in culture have been largely due to man's creative use of whatever leisure he has had. Free time, used to increase

---

[37] Josef Pieper, *Leisure, The Basis of Culture,* translated by A. Dru (New York: Pantheon Books, Inc., 1952), p. 26.
[38] Agnes Durant Pylant, *Church Recreation* (Nashville, Tenn.: Convention Press, 1959), pp. 9–17.

one's knowledge, ability, or for providing benefits to a community and by extension to society as a whole, affords a matchless step forward in the progress of civilization.

SELECTED REFERENCES

CHARLESWORTH, JAMES C., *Leisure in America: Blessing or Curse?* (Philadelphia: The American Academy of Political and Social Science), 1964.

COWELL, F. R., *Culture in Private and Public Life.* (New York: Frederick A. Praeger), 1959.

DE GRAZIA, SEBASTIAN, *Of Time, Work, and Leisure.* (New York: Doubleday and Company), 1964.

DEMCZYNSKI, S., *Automation and the Future of Man.* (New York: Hillary House Publishers, Ltd.), 1965.

DOUGLASS, PAUL F., et al., eds., *Recreation in the Age of Automation.* (Philadelphia: The American Academy of Political and Social Science), 1957. The Annals of the Academy, Vol. 313.

FISK, GEORGE, *Leisure Spending-Behavior.* (Philadelphia: University of Pennsylvania Press), 1963.

GREEN, ARNOLD W., *Recreation, Leisure, and Politics.* (New York: McGraw-Hill), 1964.

JAMES, E. O., *Primitive Ritual and Belief.* (London: Methuen and Company, Ltd.), 1917.

KAPLAN, MAX, *Leisure in America: A Social Inquiry.* (New York: John Wiley & Sons), 1960.

KEPHART, CALVIN, *Races of Mankind Their Origin and Migration.* (New York: Philosophical Library, Inc.), 1960.

KRAMER, SAMUEL N., *History Begins At Sumer.* (New York: Doubleday & Company, Inc.), 1959.

LARRABEE, ERIC and ROLF MEYERSOHN, eds., *Mass Leisure.* (New York: The Free Press), 1958.

LOWIE, ROBERT H., *An Introduction to Cultural Anthropology.* (New York: Rinehart & Company, Inc.), 1947.

PIEPER, JOSEF, *Leisure, The Basis of Culture,* rev. ed. (New York: Pantheon Books, Inc.), 1964.

SAMUEL, HERBERT L., *Leisure in a Democracy.* (New York: Cambridge University Press), 1949.

TYLOR, EDWARD BURNETT, *The Origins of Culture.* (New York: Harper & Brothers), 1958.

WISSLER, CLARK, *Man and Culture.* (New York: Thomas Y. Crowell Company), 1923.

Chapter 3

RECREATION

> PRINCIPLE: It is necessary that total conscious intellectual absorption occurs if the individual is to achieve recreation. This state of being, an integral part of human behavior, is not qualified nor affected by time, place, activity, or will. It is completely subjective, beneficial to the individual, and can never be construed as debilitating in nature.

In order for the reader to more fully grasp the concept which this principle embodies, a complete discussion of the philosophical development of the term *recreation* is included. Basically, this chapter is an analysis of a variety of theories of play and recreation in order to arrive at a meaningful and understandable definition that can be applied to human behavior.

Why do people play? Do people have to be motivated for recreation? If recreation is a human need, what is its essence? It is presumed that the answers will depend upon the definition of motivation and its components. For purposes of this discussion, recreation and play will be treated synonymously. Recreation is defined as a nondebilitating, consummatory experience.

Recreation, like any other word, is an abstract symbol, having many meanings, depending upon the context in which it is used. Although the word *recreation* suggests leisure activities or other experiences of relaxation, pleasure, or satisfaction, it does not reveal precisely what is meant by the single term. Recreation in and of itself means nothing; it has no form, nature, or function until the human mental process develops a rationale and places the word within a given situation. When this is done, recreation is traditionally seen as a conscious act performed. It is that, but it contains a more inclusive meaning as well.

INSTINCT AS MOTIVATION

For many recreationists and writers of today, the term *instinct* is the rallying point around and on which they base motivation for activity. Throughout the literature of this field, there are many theories dealing with instinct as motivation for human behavior of all kinds. Generally, instinct definitions have taken the form of mind mastery or stimuli, i.e., the controlling of external pressure through reactions of response to these stimuli. Environmental processes are a continuous source of these stimuli and they incite the mental apparatus. Internal stimuli, those of the somatic field, the neuro-chemico-muscular variations in the body organs that impel response have been called instincts. The basic difference between internal or somatic stimuli and environmental or external stimuli is that the individual cannot withdraw from the somatic as he can from environmental stimuli.

Instinct is conceived as the mental messenger of a perpetually active force initiated within the organism and traveling to the mind from the physical body. Instinct is thought of in terms of mental causation of an evolutionary nature. It is a mental movement which arises from bodily origins. It is a borderline symbol, relating to mind and body. It acts as a constitutional spur in the mind, as a continually changing item. In the psychoanalytic sense, the word *instinct* was used in an attempt to build psychology on a biological foundation and thus negate the artificial separation of psyche and soma, or mind and body.

Instinct has been represented in several ways. An eclectic overview would show that four factors are to be found in different theories: the drive, the aim, the object, and the source. Drive is defined as dynamic energy causing action or reaction. The aim of an instinct is to remove tension. The object is environmental, i.e., outside of the somatic field by or through which instinct is satisfied. The source of an instinct is that projection in a body organ the incitement of which is reflected in the mind by the instinct.

In some instances instinct has been thought of as acts that are accompanied by consciousness, which marks them off from such reflex acts as are unconsciously performed. Instinctive acts are those similarly performed by all members of the same, more or less, restricted group of animals but which are subject to variation and to subsequent modification under the guidance of individual experience. Only on occasion of their initial performance are acts purely instinctive, all subsequent performances being in some degree modified by the experience afforded by previous behavior of like nature and the results it achieves.

> The characteristic feature of the instinctive act is itself instinctive because at the presentation to sight or hearing it calls forth a mode of behavior of like nature to, or producing like results to, that which affords the stimulus.[1]

What is spoken of in terms of instinct tendency is, in any species, the expression of a considerable number of particular responses each of which is congenitally linked with a specific presentation of stimulus. The traditional instincts included one which was termed *play*. Whether instinct was

---

[1] "Instincts," *Encyclopedia Britannica*, Vol. **XIV** (Cambridge, Eng.: The University Press, 1910), p. 650.

a reflex action or unlearned purposive behavior, play was a part of it. In separating the two concepts of instinct, that of reflex movement from unlearned purposive reaction, a leading reference of the day printed this statement:

> On biological grounds a distinction can be made . . . from this point of view, the instinctive movement unlike the reflex, is that which involves the whole organism. The animal crouches in fear, advances in anger, disports itself in play.[2]

Thus, the instincts in man, though developed to a lesser degree than those found in insects, are quite numerous but probably less powerful because of the molding capability of man's nervous system. Instincts are supposed to include actions that are similar to reflexes, i.e., sneezing, smiling, coughing, crying. However, there are reactions which are called *large general tendencies*.

> The tendency which makes us take the world of perception as a world of real things; the empathetic tendency, which makes us humanize our surroundings; the tendencies to imitate, to believe, to dichotomize. Certain movement complexes expressive of the emotions must also be considered instinctive.[3]

This then has been the expressed reasoning contained in instinct motivation for play or recreation. The instinctivists say that recreation is instinctive in human beings just as play is instinctive in the lower animals. The instinctivist argument follows the line of reasoning that although the instinct to play or recreate has been suppressed to a great extent in children, and even more so in adults, it is never completely abolished. Whereas there is no empirical method by which to determine whether play is an instinct in man, there is nothing to prove that it is not. There are, on the other hand, more logical explanations of the play phenomenon in man than instinct affords.

Play is recognized in animals, below the human level, as instinctive. This assumes that animals do not reason logically but survive through instinct patterns of behavior. When the same activity is observed in human infants or young children it is called something else, i.e., random movements or imitation. How can it be known that such activity is not play? The older child, if left completely alone, will not sit still; he will move about, talk to himself, construct make-believe images, or indulge in day dreams, all quite unlearned and not imitative. This line of thought supposedly shows instinctive action. Perhaps, however, the mental pictures which the child summons during this period are strictly those with which he has had prior

---

[2] "Instinct," *New International Encyclopedia,* Vol. **XII** (2nd ed.); (New York: Dodd Mead and Company, 1928), p. 228.
[3] *Loc. cit.*

experience. The physical activities have presumably been learned during the developmental or large muscle stage of his physiological growth.

Recreation or play is considered to be a response to stimuli and situations that have not been learned through prior experience; thus it is considered instinctive. Going one step further, the carrying point for this doctrine emphasizes that man instinctively turns to recreation or play in order to satisfy a felt need. He does not experience or receive the unifying force of recreation in other activities so it is through leisure diversions that this instinctive craving is met. The instinctivists believe that recreation is a universal need, not because of its possible values to the individual such as refreshment or mental stimulation, but because it is instinctive to the human animal and experiencing certain stimuli compels this need to be filled.

INSTINCT THEORIES OF PLAY OR RECREATION

The two earliest play theories based on instinct as motivation were the Kamesian relaxation theory and a similar theory by the German educator Johan Gutsmuths. In essence, both of these theories stressed the recuperative powers in play and the instinctive seeking-after of such activity as a method of relaxation from the labors of the day by the human or lower animal. Gutsmuths was under the impression that instinct for activity creates the impulse or stimulus to play and that boring or prolonged sieges of dull activity afford another permissive situation in which men were stimulated to play.[4] In this theory the hedonistic doctrine expressed the main play objectives. Gutsmuths also presented, as incidental, the view of play as a preparation for later life, a concept that was seized upon and expanded to its greatest extent by Karl Groos. Thus the earliest play theories accepted as instinctive those motivations for activity which are now termed play or recreation.

Other play theorists accepted and added to this type of thinking. G. T. W. Patrick published *The Psychology of Relaxation,* in which he upheld the relaxation theories and stated that children must play because of inherited patterns or tendencies which impel them to act. He based this motivation on what he called, "the great multitude of old racial habits" and "deep seated human instincts."[5] A much more detailed description of Patrick's theory is presented in Mitchell and Mason's *Theory of Play* as well as in Lehman and Witty's *The Psychology of Play,* and is therefore not elaborated upon here.

Of all the instinct theories of play or recreation motivation, the views of Herbert Spencer have affected theoretical considerations more than any

---

[4] J. C. F. Gutsmuths, *Spiel zur Uebung und Erholung des Korpers und Geistes fur die Jugend* (Erzier zu Schnepfenthal, 1796), pp. 38–44.

[5] G. T. W. Patrick, *The Psychology of Relaxation* (New York: Houghton Mifflin Company, 1916), pp. 34, 65.

other. Perhaps this has occurred because it was one of the earlier works attempting to define the nature, meaning, and function of play. Spencer's theory of "surplus energy," sometimes miscalled the Schiller-Spencer theory of play, has been cited as a major contribution to the knowledge of play by more eminent writers than almost any other work. Surplus energy is expressed in sensory motor activity above that energy needed to satisfy basic biophysical needs. This theory served as a basis for the writings of Karl Groos and his successors, and can be found in almost every book dealing with play theory.

Spencer viewed play as a gratification of an instinct, usually of a survival type of action.[6] He felt that play was a result of impulses received from continuously active stimuli originating within the physical organism and streaming into the mind from the somatic field.[7] Thus, in his chapter on the development of the human nervous system, he laid the foundation for the theory of surplus energy. He realized that play was broad enough in scope so that it could not be explained by one manifestation alone. He therefore adopted Schiller's views on art and play, not to the same extent, nor even with all of the implications to be found in Schiller's concept, but with enough of the original aesthetic principle to avoid the pitfall of using one absolute base as a definition.

Karl Groos, the German philosopher, published two important works concerning play theory. One, on the play of animals, became the groundwork for his subsequent treatment involving the play motive in man. His basic understanding of play is ". . . that it is, in short, preparatory for the tasks of life."[8] Groos concurred with Spencer's surplus-energy theory of play, but he felt that it was not complete. In accordance with that belief he expanded Spencer's line of reasoning to include practice for adult life.

Although Spencer himself felt that such a practice theory would not answer the motivation question in play, Groos turned this idea around because he did not feel that the surplus-energy concept alone was the correct motivational representation. Groos further presented the recreation or relaxation theory of play and the surplus-energy theory of play as being diametrically opposed.[9] Groos' attempt to utilize the surplus energy theory of Spencer materialized in his concept of play as a cathartic agent. Play, in his view, represented a built-in control activated by an instinctive urge for expression. Although he stated that the cathartic value of play was of minor importance in comparison to the self-development aspect, he nevertheless thought it important enough to devote several articles to it.[10] He expressed his attitudes about play as catharsis in terms of emotional reactions to

---

[6] Herbert Spencer, *The Principles of Psychology* (New York: D. Appleton and Company, 1873), **II**, p. 631.
[7] *Ibid.*, pp. 647–648.
[8] Karl Groos, *The Play of Man* (New York: D. Appleton & Co., 1908), p. 361.
[9] *Ibid.*, pp. 365–366.
[10] Karl Groos, *Der Lebenswert Des Spiels* (Jena: Gustav Fischer, 1910), pp. 20–21.

painful stimuli; in other words, he assumed that in play harmful impulses as a reaction to instinctive tendencies would be avoided.[11]

Throughout his entire treatment of play, Groos maintained an unvarying approach and attitude toward play. He consistently reiterated, whether discussing what he called the psychological, biological, physiological, aesthetic, sociological, or pedagogical views of play, that it was nothing more or less than ". . . the agency employed to develop crude powers and prepare them for life's uses, . . ." [12]

The criticisms of Groos' theory seem to have been well founded, but he had his adherents as well. One of these writers, taking the Groos theory as his basis and continuing on to discuss, interpret, and point out the value of ". . . our best of Germans and chief teacher in this matter . . ." was Joseph Lee. A contemporary of Luther H. Gulick and a student of child development, Lee did much to enhance the prestige of the recreational service movement during its formative years early in the twentieth century. His enthusiastic interest in play as an educative device for the child was fully brought out in his book, *Play In Education*.[13] In this work he extolled the virtues of Groos and detailed his own idea of play in human life. Although Lee was not an innovator nor a particularly profound scholar, he nevertheless performed a distinct service to the entire recreational service movement as a speaker, writer, and demonstrator of the value of play and recreational activity.

Lee predicated his whole philosophy on play as growth and on its readying the individual for future activities as an adult. Throughout his writings, his educational views were colored by a faculty psychology approach. For Lee, there was no explanation of play motivation other than instinct.

> Man's cardinal qualities, the activities through which he is to make and hold a place in the world's competition, are given in his leading instincts; and these instincts take charge of him in plastic infancy and mould him to their ends.[14]

Lee defined *play* as "All pursuits that justify themselves." How this coincides with his idea that the play instinct leans towards an ideal seems difficult to understand, unless one interprets his statement to mean that play is an end in itself and that all motivation for play is play.

Lee seems to deal in contradictions. He conceives of play as growth, i.e., having value because it prepares the individual for life. At another time he makes a complete turnabout and states that play ". . . represents the

---

[11] Karl Groos, "Das Spiel als Katharsis," *Zeitschrift fur Padagogishe Psychologie*, **XII,** (1911), 353–366.
[12] Groos, *The Play of Man*, p. 375.
[13] Joseph Lee, *Play in Education* (New York: The Macmillan Company, 1916), pp. 3, 6–7.
[14] *Ibid.*, p. 10.

nonutilitarian motive" by which he implies that play serves no other end but itself.[15] He is as positive on one side as the other. Yet for all his seeming nonuniformity of thought, Lee has expressed a position worthy of more profound masters. Aside from his dependence upon the practice-instinct theory of play and his acceptance, partial though it may have been, of the surplus-energy theory, he formulated an idea, the implications of which should assure him of a permanent place in recreation philosophy; he rejected the hedonistic doctrine as a play motive.[16]

He was aware of an even more important facet of play, its consummatory quality, although he never elaborated it to a satisfactory conclusion. It is reasonable to assume that the psychology and educational theories of his day would not logically have led him to such a radical interpretation of the consummatory qualities of play. He did recognize that play captivated the player to the extent that:

> In successful play a child does not know that he is having a good time; he does not know that he is having a time at all; time, in fact, has ceased to exist along with self-consciousness.[17]

However, he tenaciously clung to instinctual motivation and there is no indication that he ever fully realized the content and the opportunity that was offered to him. In the last chapter of his book he described play for adults as recuperative, thus identifying himself with others who have made the same claim. Whether recreation or play is recuperative or relaxing is not a consideration here, inasmuch as such attributes, if anything, do not explain the meaning or nature of play or recreation.

The play instinct, covering as it does groups of instincts, stimulates several interests or brings about an interest in a different set of objects or focus of attention. This is clearly shown before the onset of puberty. It would appear necessary therefore that recreationists be made aware of the psychological and biological factors during their professional learning experiences. Such education, along with technical preparation, would enable the recreationist to choose the most favorable moment when the individual is instinctively interested in a group of objects to encourage proper modes of reacting to these objects.[18,19]

In opposition to the practice theory of play was G. Stanley Hall, whose monumental work on child development and education culminated in his recapitulation theory. In essence, this theory maintains that the key to present behavior lies in the past. Hall thought of play as motor habits whose best index ". . . is found in the instinctive, untaught, and non-

[15] *Ibid.*, p. 55.
[16] *Ibid.*, p. 255.
[17] Lee, *loc. cit.*
[18] *Ibid.*, pp. 38, 62–67.
[19] Joseph Lee, "Leadership," *The Normal Course in Play* (New York: Playground and Recreation Association of America, 1925), p. 111.

imitative plays of children which are most spontaneous and exact expressions of their motor needs." [20] He always stated that play motivation was instinctive and that these instincts were of an epochal nature. In play the human organism relives each stage in the development of man throughout his time on earth. Such explanations of the nature of play have largely been found to be invalid. Although heredity may have a part in the formation of attitudes towards objects and actions, how much a part, if any at all, it plays is unknown.

Among the followers of Hall's theory was George E. Johnson, one of the first recreationists in the United States. Johnson felt that although Groos' practice theory was acceptable and whereas surplus energy contributed to a favorable climate for play, it was nonetheless a basic reliving of cultural stages in the development of man that really defined play as an instinctive motivating force.[21]

Notwithstanding the fact that many writers have credited something which they call the play instinct (perhaps for want of something better) as being the motivating force of human play, other experts who are also instinctivists discount play as one of the instincts. Probably, the most comprehensive and lucid treatment of this view is L. L. Bernard's work on instincts in which he has categorically denied the existence of a play instinct. He stated in part:

> . . . we shall be compelled to repeat our former statement that play represents no concrete describable and definable unitary or structural fact, unless it connotes a concrete method of playing. Play is a word, an abstraction, . . . It is a synthetic concept, a word image, symbolizing all or more than one of the concrete ways of playing. The word play, when signifying an instinct either represents structurally all the ways of playing or it represents less than all. If it represents less than all, it should be described in terms of those activities and structures which it does represent and not in terms of the general word play.[22]

A scholar in the field of anthropology, Leo Frobenius, in his book *The Cultural History of Africa,* was adamant in his protestations against the instinctive theory of play. He conceived of play as something other than instinct and devoted much consideration to a consummatory view of play. He contended that:

> Instincts are an invention of helplessness when compared with the sense of reality. Science discovers the play drive as an appearance which is

---

[20] G. Stanley Hall, *Adolescence* (New York: D. Appleton and Company, 1906), p. 74.
[21] George E. Johnson, *Education By Play and Games* (Boston: Ginn and Company, 1907), p. 13.
[22] L. L. Bernard, *Instinct: A Study in Social Psychology* (New York: Henry Holt and Company, 1924), pp. 343–344.

noteworthy because it already appears in the child naturally so without having anything to do with education.[23]

To some, this appearance, unlearned in form, meant instinct. To Frobenius, it decidedly meant a mental process of permutation and creative imagination.

HEDONISM AS MOTIVATION

Many recreation and play definitions have been based upon pleasure seeking as the source of motivation and the factor that operates as the stimulus for continuing such activity. The doctrine of eudaemonism, and subsequently epicureanism, is contrasted to hedonism because the former concepts were based upon value judgments, i.e., the good life and the attainment of happiness were considered to be an aim rather than the cause or motivation. The *summum bonum* of Aristotle involved the moral values of ethics and principle. It was said that man should seek happiness, that he ought to try for the highest good. Such a doctrine did not concern itself with happiness as motivation nor did it state that man acts for pleasure. The latter view presents a much different philosophy. Hedonism is predicated on the principle that man acts in search of pleasure; pleasure is the motivational force that drives him to perform certain acts or to behave in a particular way.

Sigmund Freud's earlier writings abound in the expressions of the hedonistic doctrine, better known as the pleasure principle. The infant, according to this principle, begins life with an intense desire for pleasure; all his activities are carried on with the intent of deriving pleasure from them. If some prior activity has given him pleasure then he seeks to re-create that pleasurable circumstance.

Another psychologist committed to the hedonic concept was L. T. Troland, who devoted several chapters of his book on human motivation to this belief. He felt that past experiences, whether favorable or unfavorable, pleasant or unpleasant, modify neural patterns. Through such change behavior becomes regulated by emotion.[24] Hedonism teaches that individuals tend to continue activity that elicits pleasure and avoid situations or behavior that evokes unpleasantness. This has been widely accepted as a theory of human motivation. E. L. Thorndike contributed to this idea when he wrote that the strengthening of neural bonds is achieved by repetition in accordance with the laws of effect, frequency, and recency. The law of effect is based on the premise that an appropriate successful act that leads to satisfaction survives, or is "stamped in," and thereby takes prece-

---

[23] Leo Frobenius, *Kulturgeschichte Afrikas Prolegomena zu einer historischen Gestaltlehre Schicksalskunde im Sinne des Kulturwerdens* (Zurich: Phaidon Verlag, Inc., 1954), p. 24.

[24] L. T. Troland, *The Fundamentals of Human Motivation* (New York: D. Van Nostrand, 1926), pp. 278–279, 290–306.

dence over unsuccessful or frustrating ones which are "stamped out." [25] Under this law, the satisfying situation is sought or maintained, whereas annoying situations are avoided as much as possible. Thus the organism seeks the pleasurable and learns to avoid what is not pleasurable.

The pros and cons of the law of effect fill many pages of psychological literature, and many errors have been committed in the name of Thorndike's theory. He very clearly differentiated between satisfaction and pleasure, but several writers have tended to ignore this distinction. Although no empirical study has yet been made on human beings which clearly defines the experience under study, the delimitations of the conditions, the facet of behavior to be considered, or the neural pattern of the individual under investigation, many readers assume, wrongly, that pleasure and satisfaction are synonymous, contrary to Thorndike's implications.

The hedonistic principle is consistently referred to as an explanation for recreational activities. Nearly every person will answer in the same way when questioned as to the reason for engaging or participating in what they term play or recreational experience. The response will usually be: "Because I like it" or "Because it's fun and I receive pleasure from it" or "Because it pleases me." Thus, it is taken for granted that pleasure is the prime motive that influences the individual toward performing or engaging in so-called recreational activities.

The following definitions of play and recreation clearly reflect this hedonistic concept:

> Recreation, in contrast with work, has its own drive and is enjoyable. The chief drive in recreation is the pleasure it affords.[26]

> The chief aim in play is satisfaction or pleasure, but in much the same way is this true of life as well.[27]

> The primary objective of recreation is to give pleasure, enjoyment, and happiness to individuals and groups . . . every other objective is secondary to this one . . . in all matters relating to evaluation, measurements are in terms of the abundance of joy, happiness, and pleasure that accrue to individual and group.[28]

> Play may be defined as activity undertaken for pleasure, or as an expenditure of energy for the pleasure inherent in the process of expending it . . . one cannot imagine or even conceive of play without pleasure, for pleasure is its very root.[29]

[25] E. L. Thorndike, *The Fundamentals of Learning* (New York: Columbia University Press, 1932), p. 183.
[26] Martin H. Neumeyer and Esther S. Neumeyer, *Leisure and Recreation* (New York: A. S. Barnes and Company, Inc., 1936), p. 147.
[27] Elmer D. Mitchell and Bernard S. Mason, *The Theory of Play* (New York: A. S. Barnes and Company, 1935), p. 90.
[28] Harold D. Meyer and Charles K. Brightbill, *Community Recreation* (Boston: D. C. Heath and Company, 1948), p. 24.
[29] Austin Fox Riggs, *Play: Recreation in a Balanced Life* (New York: Doubleday, Doran & Company, 1935), pp. 16–17.

The same adherence to hedonism can be found in much of the literature on play and recreation. Many of the writers and theorists have held to surface manifestations of action or behavior rather than seeking out the underlying or basic patterns of stimuli influencing behavioral action.

Freud, in his earliest writings, stressed the pleasure principle as motivating individual behavior. However, with the publication of *Beyond the Pleasure Principle,* Freud modified his basic concepts to refute the pleasure principle as the sole force for motivation. The observation that prompted this change was centered around masochism. In his later work he abandoned hedonism as motivational and developed an environmental concept of behavioral stimulation. According to Freud, the situation in which the individual finds himself restricts or prohibits certain actions while requiring others. The individual is compelled to accept reality and face daily living. Under such circumstances no individual could be considered to act merely for pleasure.[30]

Perhaps a more important aspect of Freudian psychology, for an understanding of the meaning of recreation, deals with the psychoanalytic theory of play. Again, catharsis is a part of the phenomenon. The Aristotelian idea of dynamic emotional release in play roles reached its most profound conceptualization in the sublimation theories of Freud. In *Beyond the Pleasure Principle,* Freud observed the play of an infant whose activity involved throwing small toy objects away. Seeing this pattern of behavior, Freud investigated and discovered that the child's mother usually left him alone for long periods of time. The child, in an attempt to master this renunciation situation, acted out this frustrating experience by playing a game, i.e., throwing his toys away and out of sight. Psychoanalytic study has shown that the need to master an unpleasant or traumatic experience scores a central part in child play.[31] As Freud says:

> It is easy to observe how, in every field of psychical experience and not merely in that of sexuality, an impression passively received evokes in children a tendency to an active response. They try to do themselves what has been done to them. This is a part of their task of mastering the outside world, and may even lead to their endeavoring to repeat impressions which they would have good reason to avoid because of their disagreeable content. Children's play, too, is made to serve this purpose of completing and thus, as it were, annulling a passive experience by active behavior.[32]

Although the doctrine of hedonism, as a psychological theory of behavioral motivation, appears to be waning, there have been some important recent developments from experiments by animal psychologists under laboratory conditions which give rise to some pertinent questions. No ex-

---

[30] Sigmund Freud, *Beyond the Pleasure Principle* (London and Vienna: The International Psycho-Analytic Press, 1922), pp. 15–16.
[31] R. Walder, "The Psychoanalytic Theory of Play," *Psychoanalytic Quarterly,* Vol. II (1933), 208–224.
[32] Sigmund Freud, *Collected Papers,* James Strachey, ed. (London: The Hogarth Press and the Institute of Psycho-Analysis, 1950), p. 264.

planation of motivation as pleasure seeking would be complete or valid without a reference to the Nebraska Symposium, which involves studies by Harlow, Brown, and Butler on aspects of motivation.[33] Among the experiments reported is the investigation of discrimination learning through visual exploration by rhesus monkeys, by Butler at the University of Wisconsin Laboratories. In the light of these experiments it appears as though a strong case can be made for the hedonistic or appetitive concept. However, such conclusions as were drawn from these experiments can also be explained in terms of psychological homeostasis.

As explained in Harlow's paper,[34] it is conceivable that a complex organism, when conditioned by certain environmental stimuli, will adjust toward those conditions as either its mental and/or physiological adaptability apparatus undergoes transformation. One of the important factors differentiating higher orders from lower orders of animals is the ability to adjust. Inasmuch as homeostasis is a condition of adjustment and balance in the chemicophysical sense, it is presumably possible to extend such an adjustment mechanism to the mind.

The satisfaction received by the monkeys when they were able to look out a window after having solved a particular problem might be explained as an adjustment process to which the animal's mental and physical receptors were conditioned. When deprived of the privilege of looking out the peep-hole, a psychological imbalance may have occurred which resulted in the behavior observed. The deprivation may have produced anxiety factors or tension, or it may have been the animal's attempt to reduce this condition of stress in order to regain balance. Yet, this is only conjecture because it is not known whether pleasure seeking as a motive really exists, and if it does, how much or how little a part of the principle may have played in this situation.

Another feature of Harlow's paper is the continual reference to the elimination of homeostatic drives, as opposed to externally aroused drives, which, he states, are of such intenseness as to be inimical to learning.[35] However, Brown has challenged this point of view on the grounds that the homeostatic drives are rarely of such concentration as to be of importance to human learning.[36] In any case, whether hedonistic drives or biological drives are responsible for behavior manifestations in complex organisms has not yet been clearly indicated. There appears to be fairly good support for the theory that biological drives are the basis for human behavioral acts, whereas, any suggestion that hedonism can safely be validated by experiments which have already been conducted is open to serious question.

Rejection of hedonism as the basis for motivating human behavior, and

---

[33] Harry F. Harlow, "Motivation as a Factor in the Acquisition of New Responses," *Current Theory and Research in Motivation* (Lincoln, Neb.: University of Nebraska Press, 1953), pp. 24–27.
[34] Harlow, *loc. cit.*
[35] Harlow, *loc. cit.*
[36] J. S. Brown, "Problems Presented by the Concept of Acquired Drives," *Symposium on Motivation* (Lincoln, Neb.: University of Nebraska Press, 1953), p. 1.

thus play or recreation, is supported on three distinct judgments. First, the theory that the organism is motivated by the prospect of a pleasurable response, is, in fact, paradoxical. Seeking behavior has most nearly come to be associated with unpleasant manifestations. What is sought is generally what is needed and lacking: one seeks rest because of weariness; companionship because of loneliness; food and drink because of hunger and thirst. In these cases the factor that influences action is unpleasant. In many cases the pursuit of pleasure, *per se,* is doomed to failure. Pleasure may be typically generated as a by-product or effect of specific actions.

In questioning Troland's theory of prior hedonism, an example of the act of a parent frantically diving into a body of water to rescue a child could hardly be thought of as the pursuit of pleasure, yet prior experience has modified the neural patterns of the parent and has effectively determined the course of action, which, under the stimulus of the situation, forces the parent into the water regardless of swimming capability. Thoughts concerning pleasant or unpleasant feelings hardly ever arise at the moment of stimulation.

Secondly, a question of semantics becomes part of any discussion of the hedonistic doctrine. In this instance the difficulty lies with the terms *seeking* and *avoiding*. Usually, no difficulty is experienced in differentiating seeking from avoiding, but occasionally both terms can be used with identical meaning in a peculiar circumstance: the steelworker seeks safety by avoiding the furnace; the trapped miner seeks air to avoid suffocation. In these cases the individual may not be aware of his objective, but when observed from a disinterested point of view, one is never sure of the goal.

Thirdly, hedonism restricts the behavioral effects of pleasant and unpleasant to acts of seeking and avoiding; such a restriction is far too limiting. Pleasantness or unpleasantness is probably encountered as often by passive noncommitment as by active pursuit. Pleasantness or unpleasantness are probably effects rather than causes. These are surface manifestations of many factors which serve as motivational stimuli in human behavior.

HOMEOSTASIS AS MOTIVATION

According to one theory, human behavior is stimulated by a drive to reduce or relieve organic or tissue needs. In the struggle for survival, the organism that does not fulfill the insistent demands of physiological needs soon deteriorates and then ceases to exist. Through conscious desire in some cases, or by general ill-feelings, the body makes known its needs so that the organism can mobilize its functional apparatus for response. The process by which the body continues to produce the chemical balance necessary to maintain life has been called *homeostasis*.[37] This concept holds that the

---

[37] W. B. Cannon, *The Wisdom of the Body* (New York: W. W. Norton & Company, Inc., 1932; rev. ed., 1939), p. 24.

body is an intricate chemical manufacturing plant, limited by organ structure, and dependent upon autonomic stimuli for effective maintenance of proper chemical relationships so that organic balance (equilibrium) is preserved. The process by which such equilibrium is maintained is homeostasis, a condition of adjustment designed to satisfy physiological needs.

Rignano has clearly enunciated the principle of homeostasis with this statement:

> Every organism is a physiological system in a stationary condition and tends to preserve this condition or to restore it as soon as it is disturbed by any variation occurring within or outside the organism. This property constitutes the foundation and essence of all 'need,' of all 'desires,' of all the most important appetites. All movements of approach or withdrawal, of attack or flight, of seizing or rejecting which animals make are only so many direct or indirect consequences of this very general tendency of every stationary physiological condition to remain constant . . .[38]

This same principle has been stated by Raup as what he calls *complacency,* an adjustment ratio wherein a consummatory or fulfilling act completes a relationship that has been disturbed. Raup stresses the idea that maintaining homeostasis is the fundamental factor, not only of behavior, but of all life processes. His principle of complacency suggests that behavioral adjustments are related to the organism and its environment. The healthy organism maintains homeostasis through the process of adjustment. Raup further wrote that the condition of equilibrium is continuously interacting, i.e., always dynamic.[39] Thus, this theory considers that human behavior moves away from equilibrium when physiochemical balances are disturbed, toward it when meeting the need, and through it to continue human activity.

In his chapter on complacency and the autonomic nervous system, Raup comes to grips with what might be termed psychological homeostasis. He refers to the psychological state of the organism as the thing that gives rise to behavior. Continuing this line of thought, he introduces the concept of the nervous system as a mechanism which serves the whole organism and eases the condition of stress as that organism seeks to adjust. The whole question of metabolic reaction to environmental stimulation is opened. The nervous system is thought of as the means whereby favorable relationships are maintained.

Relating concepts of equilibria to behavior patterns, Raup asserts that any disturbance of these little known equilibria reveal themselves in the psychological factor of complacency and its imbalances. When equilibrium is fully restored, complacency develops. Maladjustment, therefore, is a

---

[38] E. Rignano, *The Psychology of Reasoning* (New York: Harcourt, Brace and Company, 1923), p. 6.
[39] R. Bruce Raup, *Complacency: The Foundation of Human Behavior* (New York: The Macmillan Company, 1925), p. 42.

60 Principles of Recreational Service

disturbance of balance, i.e., lack of equilibrium between the organism and its surroundings. All behavior, then, is the effect of movement toward complacency or restored equilibrium. Because the maintenance of homeostasis affects psychological activities as well as tissue needs, mental adjustments reflected in behavior activities are affected.

Perhaps the most important implication of Raup's view of the dynamism of homeostasis is the progressive nature of this idea. Homeostasis is not stable. As the organism reaches equilibrium it is concurrently creating new tensions, proceeding to throw itself off equilibrium. This would appear to fit present knowledge of both physiological and psychological functions. Thus the physical laws of energetics, principally the second law, would be involved in a system concerning free and bound energy.[40]

> . . . whenever there is activity of any kind in the part of the organism considered there is also a using up of energy. The cells are worn down, but there is also a corresponding heightened process of building up the cell. This metabolic process goes on just because there is activity in the part, throwing the energy condition off of equilibrium, and thus compelling a drive back toward that state.[41]

Psychological homeostasis is merely the term given to mental complacency or equilibrium and is not separated from physiochemical effects, because whatever disturbs even the most obscure tissue appears to influence the whole organism. Any type of activity might be an example of psychological homeostasis. The painter may be engrossed for any number of hours in his painting and never once be concerned with the function of his brush. The whole self is at ease as far as brush utilization is concerned. Yet, in the course of the effort something might occur to the brush-relationship, and complacency disappears. The hairs of the brush may become loosened or tend to hold too much paint. Attention is turned toward the removal of the difficulty so as to return to the condition that was interrupted. The brush-relationship now enters into those processes that define changes in activity directions; furthermore, it will perpetuate itself until such time as some action so resolves it that the former condition of unconcern is restored. In this example, mental focus was directed toward the disturbing element which served as motivation for behavioral actions. This may be true for all behavior patterns.

If homeostasis is the condition that motivates behavior in human beings, it must also serve as the motivational stimulus for recreation. Just as there are physiochemical needs for equilibrium in the organism, there is also a psychological need for equilibrium which reveals itself as the environment changes during the daily experience of living. When the individual consciously or unconsciously realizes imbalance in his life he tends

[40] Raup, *op. cit.*, p. 16.
[41] *Ibid.*, p. 65.

to move toward a rebalance in which harmony and accord between the self and environment are found. This balance may be restored through recreation.

The distinguishing feature of recreation is the consummatory quality which sets up or regains for the individual the equilibrium lost during impact with environmental forces. The consummatory act is characterized by complete absorption. During such intense concentration consummation displaces any maladjustment so that harmony is restored or re-created in the individual. The whole concept of the consummatory act depends upon and helps to explain the principle of homeostasis. In recreation, a need is met and satisfied. The satisfaction continues until some other disturbance enters the psychosomatic field, at which time equilibrium is lost and the process repeats itself. Thus the process is dynamic and perpetual.

The principle of homeostasis has been further refined and classified for inclusion in psychological systems attempting to interpret human behavior. The psychologists, Snygg and Combs, claim that the preservation of the individual's self, the "I," makes logical and consistent all human behavior.[42] Whether or not action is directed toward life preservation, suicide, or any other activity affecting the physical being, the concept of the phenomenal self can explain human behavior.

> The phenomenal self includes all those parts of the phenomenal field which the individual experiences as part or characteristic of himself.[43]

Thus, all behavior may be explained and even predicted in the light of the individual's desire to maintain a concept of himself, i.e., what he believes to be his actual self. The one basic human need is determined to be predicated on the desire for self-esteem. All other so-called needs or drives are in reality subservient to this one.

> From birth to death the defense of the phenomenal self is the most pressing, most crucial, if not the only task of existence. Moreover, since human beings are conscious of the future, their needs extend into the future as well, and they strive to preserve not only the self as it exists but to build it up and strengthen it against the future of which they are aware. We might combine these two aspects in a formal definition of the basic human need as: the preservation and enhancement of the phenomenal self.[44]

Seen from the phenomenological view, such seemingly diametrically opposed propensities as a life or death wish can be placed in context and may appear quite logical as a manifestation of the enhancement of the individual's phenomenal self. By this is meant a desire on the part of the

---

[42] Donald Snygg and Arthur W. Combs, *Individual Behavior* (New York: Harper and Row, 1949), p. 54.
[43] *Ibid.*, p. 58.
[44] Snygg and Combs, *loc. cit.*

individual to gratify some aspect of his self-esteem. He may do this by appearing in one situation with a concern for "What will people think (of me)?" and in another by his reaction to physical privation or to a surfeit of physical goods. The phenomenal point of view is a psychological system based on the impact of culture upon the individual. It is a ready device for the explanation of behavior in terms of environmental pressures on the physical and mental existence of the organism as it attempts to adjust to the culture of which it is a part.

Snygg and Combs also suggest a conceptualization of goals differentiation. As the organism matures and seeks to gain an idea of self in its surroundings, goals arise to which the basic need, preservation and enhancement of the phenomenal self, is directed. Techniques, or the methods by which goal attainments are carried out, develop in the same way and are also differentiated as experience dictates. Three classifications of techniques are suggested

1. Mastery of people and/or things.
2. Identification with powerful forces, i.e., pressure groups, individuals in control, or dominant ideas.
3. Physical change in the somatic organization.

The first two classes of techniques are self-explanatory, but the third needs some clarification. In order to regain self-esteem, peer status, or other restoration of the phenomenal self, the individual may seek excitement usually associated with activities ranging from minor sports and games to drug addiction. The inherent stimulus derived from excitement results in an increased feeling of power and effectiveness which uplifts the lagging or humiliated self-esteem and gives heightened vigor to the individual.[45] This exhilaration is commonly sought in competitive activities, in exhibition of artistic or creative accomplishment, or in antagonistic and compulsive behaviors that may overstep social taboos in certain circumstances. The explanation offered for human behavior and the motivation stimulating such behavior is an all-inclusive doctrine of the phenomenal self based on homeostasis. Behavior is produced by the organism's need to maintain a constant.

RECREATION: DEFINITIONS AND CONCEPTS

Few definitions of recreation or play have been presented in any but stereotyped terms. Most definitions have assumed the inocuous exterior of smoothed-over clay in which any individuality or peculiarity is hidden. Each may be worded differently, but the net effect has been to produce conformity and total identification with what have been considered absolutes.

[45] *Ibid.,* p. 76.

Problems of Inadequate Conceptualization

Although there have been few, indeed too few, recreationists and educational philosophers who hinted at more broadly defined terminology, none has really stated what recreation is. The practice has been to explain recreation in limited terms of function or use; thus the field has accumulated definitions which are singularly restrictive. By misapplication or through faulty concept building, common definitions present only the one way, the ultimate way, in which anyone can recreate. It is said that these definitions allow for freedom of choice (if one discounts human conditioning factors as abrogating free choice). Although presumably based on selectivity, they are offering only one choice. One can argue that these offer freedom, to act or not to act, but in reality there is no choice.

Traditional definitions of recreation have been founded upon five concepts. These include when recreation occurs (in leisure), why recreation occurs (prime motive), how recreation occurs (freedom of choice), what occurs (activity), and in what context it occurs (virtue). On these bases restrictive meanings have been applied to prevent many human activities from being termed recreational either in quality or connotation. The real difficulty in talking about the where and the what of recreation has been that people have not coined a sharp enough terminology that could be used to guide future thinking and to suggest new possibilities. The problem, then, is not that these questions of when, why, what, and how have been asked, but that they have been answered in such a manner that their definitions become useless as a guide to future activities.

In the past as well as in the present, recreation has been viewed as the antithesis of work or labor. It has been thought of as value derived, contributing to mental health, physical well-being, creativity, personality development, satisfaction, self-assertion, pleasure, and so on *ad infinitum*. Further than this, recreation has been subdivided into activity classes that range from antisocial on the lowest level to creativity on the highest level. Thus, it has been explained as everything from the universal panacea to merely sports and games or physical exercise and art.

The Leisure Concept. The leisure concept has always had an inordinate following among writers in this field beyond any justification in proportion to its relationship with the recreative experience. Basing recreation on leisure pursuits, or defining recreation as the use of leisure, distorts the entire picture. Such a narrow view effectively omits the vast possibilities of recreative behavior during other than leisure.

Recreation has been described as a way for man to supplement and complement his hours of stress and labor with activities that bring relaxation and rejuvenation. It has suffered from being made synonymous with time not required for satisfying the incessant need for food, clothing, or shelter. Historically, therefore, recreation has come to mean those activities performed during leisure; time that is not spent in vocational pursuits, education, or in attending to natural physiological acts. Thus, even the word *leisure* has been spoiled by making it synonymous with time in which nothing significant occurs. It would appear that what has been described is not recreation but leisure activity. There is a great difference between the two. What has developed is a gross misrepresentation in which a part becomes greater than the whole.

The foundation for a leisure concept of recreation was laid in fifth century B.C. Greece and reached its fullest ideational flowering during the lives of Plato and Aristotle. However, the leisure of those Greeks had a different meaning than the leisure of today. For the early Greeks, leisure was education. It was a time set aside for creativity and learning. Sometime in the centuries that followed the decline of Greek civilization, leisure, as the Greeks knew it, also declined. From an exhalted level, which would befit a symbol for cultural achievement, educational betterment, and democratic ideology, leisure plummeted to depths of depravity during the days of the early Roman emperors and may only now be recovering from two thousand years of social misinterpretation.

On all sides one hears about the moral decay of American society because of its lack of wholesome use of leisure. Various acts of delinquency are cited as occurring during the leisure of individuals; and such acts are held up for critical concern and inspection as further evidence of the downhill path our culture is taking. Whether or not such criticism is valid does not lift the awesome burden which leisure carries. In the minds of many it is to be spent, without thought of usefulness either to the individual or to his community. Leisure must go a long way in order to be anything like the prototype conceived by the Greeks.

It would be admirable to equate the Greek concept of leisure with recreation because that idea covered, almost completely, every phase of human activity in which the Greek participated; everything, that is, except his narrow trade activities. One might almost say that the Greek concept of leisure included vocation, at least the vocation of governing and managing the affairs of the state. One used his leisure in the duties of citizenship, which of course, demanded freedom from the necessity to produce goods and services.

The Greeks looked upon ordinary work as drudgery fit only for slaves. To be sure there were free artisans and craftsmen to create the sculpture and ornamental buildings which decorated his cities, but by and large, the common labor of soil tillage, commercial carriers, sailors, anything that smacked of nonaristocratic demeanor was viewed as wearisome toil to be engaged in only by captives of war and other servants. It came to mean that everything in which the Greeks gloried, enjoyed, or respected as aristocratic privilege was performed during leisure; everything else was relegated to the backs of slaves. There is small wonder that this concept seemed so attractive to later writers. The attraction stimulated these people to look upon leisure as recreation. Because leisure was antipodal to work, so was recreation. Each succeeding generation of writers read a little more of the leisure concept into the definition of recreation until the two became so merged as to be identical.

The writers whose views support the concept of equating leisure with recreation have generally followed the same line of reasoning regardless of the terminology. Probably the outstanding champion of the leisure-recreation equation is G. Ott Romney. His popular book, *Off The Job Living,* by its very title suggests the path to follow in order to achieve recreation. The whole line of thought in Romney's book precludes any possibility of recreation performed in other than leisure. He rests his case on defining recreation as ". . . all those things the individual chooses to do on his own time off the job for the gratification of the doing." [46] Recreation is off the job living, off the job living is leisure, *ergo* recreation is leisure.

In two of his books, L. P. Jacks has described the art of living. He calls it an indivisibility, something that cannot be divided into compartments. All facets of life which include "work and play, labor and leisure, mind and body, education and recreation, are governed by a single vision of excellence and a continuous passion for achieving it . . ." [47] Jacks feels that all of these pairs of terms are synonymous. He states that there is no sharp distinction between labor and leisure, "because the labor occupation of one man is often the leisure occupation of another." [48] Whether this statement is true, and it undoubtedly is, is not the question in point. Jacks tries to equate a behavioral act (labor) with something (leisure) that is not an act, but merely a segment of time. Labor is an activity performed by the individual as a result of some motivation; leisure is not an action, nothing compels it; it is outside the realm of human behavior. One simply cannot equate symbols of human behavior and terms representing concepts that are beyond the scope of human behavior.

H. Allen Overstreet's *A Guide to Civilized Leisure* is perhaps the most inclusive representation of the synonymity of recreation and leisure. Almost every page is devoted to activities which are called leisure but which are commonly known as recreational. The *Guide* tells what there is to do with leisure, how such time can be utilized, where participation may be enjoyed, why participation should be engaged in, and sums up with the statement that "Leisure that is worth the living must issue out of a work-life that is equally worth the living." [49] If leisure grows out of work then it must be a part of work. Although this would seem to be inconsistent with dictionary meanings of leisure, the idea is advanced. The following definitions are also examples of this type of thinking:

[46] G. Ott Romney, *Off The Job Living* (A. S. Barnes and Company, 1946), p. 16.
[47] L. P. Jacks, *Education Through Recreation* (New York and London: Harper and Brothers, 1932), p. 1.
[48] *Ibid.*, p. 98.
[49] H. A. Overstreet, *A Guide to Civilized Leisure* (New York: W. W. Norton & Company, 1934), p. 19.

> For the individual, recreation may be any wholesome leisure experience engaged in solely for the satisfaction derived therefrom.[50]
>
> Functionally, recreation is the natural expression of human interests and needs seeking satisfaction during leisure.[51]

Arthur N. Pack is another writer who has substituted leisure, as a period of free time, for a manifestation of human behavior. In his book *The Challenge of Leisure,* Pack asserts:

> . . . that the only essential difference between work and play is the presence or absence of the element of necessity, we must logically admit that practically any human occupation may become an absorbing leisure time activity provided it is not pursued primarily for commercial reasons. In leisure the motive is the important thing.[52]

By stating that leisure can have a motive he classifies it with behavior. Not only is the basic assumption incorrect, but it is carried to an absurdity. If Pack had been speaking of play or recreation, the above paragraph would more nearly mean what it intends to say.

The Neumeyers, in *Leisure and Recreation,* explain recreation in sociological terms as:

> . . . including many types of activities which are undertaken for their own sake and not for any reward or goal beyond themselves, and which are relatively free, spontaneous, and enjoyable. Such activities are motivated primarily by interest and give more or less immediate satisfaction.[53]

Once again the reader is made aware of an underlying pleasure principle in the motivation of recreation. However, there is another significant feature of this definition which has meaning for the act itself: no mention is made of when such activities may be performed. Implied in this description is the cognition that recreation can be performed under any circumstances, i.e., any place in time and not limited to leisure. Although the definition tends to limit recreative acts to those pursuits entered into for their own sake, it nevertheless paves the way for an extremely broad interpretation of recreation as a manifestation of behavior. According to the Neumeyers' definition, even vocational, educational, and various physiological activities could be defined as recreation if, during their performance,

---

[50] Harold D. Meyer and Charles K. Brightbill, *Community Recreation, op. cit.,* p. 28.

[51] Gerald Fitzgerald, *Leadership in Recreation* (New York: Ronald Press, 1951), p. 3.

[52] Arthur N. Pack, *The Challenge of Leisure* (New York: The Macmillan Company, 1934), p. 59.

[53] Martin H. Neumeyer and Esther S. Neumeyer, *Leisure and Recreation, op. cit.,* p. 7.

they elicited pleasure, satisfaction, and enjoyment on the part of the participant. One would have to stretch both the imagination and the precise meaning of this definition, but such an implication is present.

In the Neumeyers' view, leisure is time, free from obligatory activities; it is not to be confused with idleness nor with recreation. Recreation is recognized as a type of leisure activity. Further than this, an attempt is made to show the integration possible between recreation and work:

> Work can be playful and be recreation motivated. All agreeable and enjoyable work has a large element of recreation in it. The same can be said of education, which may be drudgery or a pleasant experience.[54]

Thus, recreation is conceived as a behavioral act that can be performed at any time the individual is so inclined. It is not measured nor defined as a specific time but as an act taking place in time.

Defenders of this position include George B. Cutten, late President of Colgate University, Weaver W. Pangburn, and Eugene T. Lies. President Cutten, in his book *The Threat of Leisure,* says, "Leisure comes as the antithesis to compulsory work . . ."[55] Leisure has come to the American culture through the technological advances made possible by modern industrial methods. In an automated society, leisure, i.e., time free from occupational demands, provides extended periods which may be given over to indiscriminate application of energy. Thus, Cutten states:

> To enjoy leisure is only one way to use it, and it is likely to lead one to its misuse. I am still old fashioned enough to think that leisure may yet give an opportunity for work. The laborer today has more leisure than his father had, yet I do not believe that he is happier. Work is still the divine opportunity rather than the cruel tyrant. I cannot think of happiness as the sole product of leisure, and misery as the complement of work. Success, not in industry or business or in professional life but in lifemaking, depends upon work and upon more than eight hours of it; and true happiness depends upon successful lifebuilding.[56]

Leisure, then, is considered as time free from the occupational hazards of monotony and boredom. It is a time for education, a time for learning the uses to which leisure may be put. Recreation, a manifestation of human behavior, can be performed during leisure. It combines the aesthetics and the trades through a spirit of self-expression thereby uniting two of the more important features of man's life: his need for activity and his desire for achievement.

W. W. Pangburn in his book, *Adventures in Recreation,* states:

[54] *Ibid.,* p. 159.
[55] George B. Cutten, *The Threat of Leisure* (New Haven: Yale University Press, 1926), p. 15.
[56] *Ibid.,* pp. 122–123.

Leisure and recreation are not the same. Leisure is free time after work. It spells opportunity for the activities of life not necessary for making a living.[57]

Pangburn also suggests that recreation is an activity that has its own drive and is carried out without any need of reward. It is its own end and has no ulterior purpose. It means refreshment and, most important, self-expression for the individual.

Eugene T. Lies has taken a dictionary definition of leisure as "freedom from necessary occupation or business."[58] He sees a vast amount of free time, produced by the machine age, being utilized for both creative and recreative ends. His setting is the school where education for the recreational use of time can be taught.

Although it may be true that leisure activity can potentially be recreational, this is not always the case. To make synonymous two such distinct terms as *leisure* and *recreation* immediately casts a pall over the validity of this definition. Leisure is time. Time may be viewed subjectively or objectively. If subjectively, then it exists only so long as the individual realizes that it is passing. In other words, there is no time outside of individual consciousness. If viewed either as a continuum or as a series of intervals, passing and spending regardless of individual awareness, then it is objective.

Recreation, however, has nothing to do with time, aside from being a particular behavior that takes place in time. An apt simile would be the camper in the forest. The camper, as a human being, cannot be defined in terms of the forest, yet his action takes place within the forest. Recreation is to be considered as individual behavior. If recreation is behavior, it may or may not be a visible phenomenon, depending upon the individual receiving its impetus from physical and psychological stimuli in an attempt to retain or achieve equilibrium within the organism.

Viewed from this perspective, one can discern with remarkable clarity how palpably incorrect it is to equate these two utterly dissimilar terms. It is like trying to compare an apple and an orange and calling them the same because they are both round, both fruit, and both tree grown. It is obvious that they are different, so different that to explain them as identical is inconceivable. Yet, this very thing has been allowed to happen in the case of recreation and leisure. Even by qualifying leisure and investing it with *use* and *activity,* it still comes no closer to being identical with recreation. Add both of these words to leisure and one has free time that is used. Wholesomely utilized or not makes little difference. The phrase still does not explain what recreation is, far less what it entails. Worst of all it completely eliminates and ignores the largest body of human activities—those that take place outside of leisure.

[57] Weaver W. Pangburn, *Adventures in Recreation* (New York: A. S. Barnes and Company, 1936), p. 10.
[58] Eugene T. Lies, *The New Leisure Challenges the Schools* (Washington, D.C.: National Education Association, 1933), p. 18.

The Prime Motive Concept. By prime motive is meant the causal factor which determines individual behavior towards a particular activity. Traditionally, recreation has been conceived as a self-motivating activity, i.e., it differs from all other activities not only in the sense of the values derived when it is performed, but also *why* it is performed. Basic motivation, which includes the individual's attitude toward any given thing, is the criterion which effectively excludes education, various physiological acts, vocation, and religious experience from being recreation. In the view of many, the basic tenet of recreation is that it is primarily engaged in for its own sake and for the fun of it.[59] The activity is executed for the pleasurable feelings aroused. Therefore, primary motive—in this instance, fun—excludes all activities from being considered as recreation if they are not engaged in primarily for fun.

There is always the question of the distinction between work and recreation. Both represent activities which may give self-expression, satisfaction, and fun to the individual. Both may contribute to the well-being and be totally absorbing for the individual. The main difference, as it has been described, is that vocation is motivated by the promise of economic advantage together with certain psychological values, whereas recreation is motivated presumably for its own sake or for the fun of it. The difference between work and recreation is the reason for which the activity is undertaken.

Recreation supposedly carries with it its own drives, whereas vocation seems to need a reward, prize, or other extrinsic motive to stir the individual to action. If we are to believe this, then many of the activities being carried on by professional leaders under the aegis of recreation are not really recreational. They are vocational because the participant is urged on, not by the inherent interest of the activity, but for the promised reward at the conclusion of the activity. An example would be the common assertion that one ought to exercise or engage in sports for the sake of building a healthy or stronger body. In the sense of this discussion, this is pure vocationalism.

There are two possible reasons for this problem: (1) the activities are presented without any thought of planning that includes potential participants; and (2) activities have been presented in such a manner as to conflict with standards of acceptance.

Participation becomes reward-centered; the prize becomes all important. Our leadership has glorified the winner, the hero, the champion to such an extent that anything less than winning is considered failure. Huge bonanzas are paid; the individual is surrounded by commercialized amusements which offer get-rich-quick schemes. Recreational departments which continue to offer league-type tournaments flourishing on the promises of bigger and better trophies, cross-country travel, and audience adulation have helped to create this one-sided value system.

[59] James E. Rogers, *The Child and Play* (New York and London: The Century Company, 1932), p. 25.

As Bucher has written:

> There are other evils which make the practice of stressing the 'winner' educationally unsound. This is true especially in the area of sports. Undue pressure is placed on the participants, parents become overenthusiastic, immature children become over-stimulated, the health of the individual is overlooked, excessive publicity often times is bad for the 'star' contestant or the 'star' team, unsportsmanlike play is resorted to, and a sound standard of values is disregarded.[60]

Few will quarrel with competitive activities or even of recognition for being the best in a class, game, event, or other participatory act; the quarrel is rather with the amount of emphasis that is placed on the incentive so that a completely biased view is brought about. In another aspect of this reasoning too much stress has been placed on the mass or crowd activities and not enough time or importance has been placed on individual encouragement and stimulation. The thinking behind this emphasis of mass versus the individual has been centered in the public recreational agencies and schools. All too often budget-minded boards or other authorizing agencies have to be "sold" by the number of participants engaged in the activities of the department or system. This has led to thinking in terms of numbers. If a department can receive so much money for X number of participants, then it follows that more participants mean greater budgets.

The result of this all too common situation is that spectator sports and other mass activity enterprises are programmed while individual opportunities and services, or even small groups of people and their needs are generally overlooked in the rush for the large crowd. Thus, the differentiation between extrinsic and intrinsic values is somewhat overlooked, probably unintentionally, by "promoters" or "businessmen" operating in the guise of recreationists. This unintentional identification of work and recreation is of considerable significance in the dogma of the field.

There are several volumes concerning play and recreation which do not differentiate between work and recreation, i.e., which assume that work and recreation have overlapping content. This bone of contention between the traditionalists and the more progressive writers takes the form of defining both work and recreation in terms of time performed, motivation of the individual, and the opportunity for choice.

The traditionalist defines work in terms of its being performed in nonleisure, being of an obligatory or compulsory nature, and having an economic motive. The progressive may be aware of relative distinctions between work and recreation, but he minimizes that distinction; in general, he focuses attention on the fact that any work requires periods of rest even though such work allows the individual to maintain a high level of intel-

---

[60] Charles A. Bucher, "Must There Always Be a Winner," *Recreation Magazine,* **XLIX** (October 1956), p. 364.

lectual activity. Although creative work is not something to be avoided, there should be periods that may be termed relaxation. Even though creative work may produce complete satisfaction and pleasure in the participant and thus be similar to play, time must be taken to refresh and restimulate the individual.

In analyzing this concept of the relationship between work and recreation one must recognize that the majority of practitioners in the field of recreation regard their organized, or even privately conducted, activities, performed in leisure, to be recreational. It is only on the theoretical or educational level, and then in too few instances, that thought is given to the shading between these two types of behavior. A typical pronouncement which shows the position of those who view work and recreation as having overlapping areas is taken from *Principles of Education* by Chapman and Counts.

> The line between recreational and other activities, however, cannot be rigidly drawn, because by imperceptible gradations the one type of activity shades off into the other . . . Even in the field of vocations there are many cases where, because the individual expresses himself fully in his calling, work becomes identified with play.[61]

A typical statement which shows the position of those who view recreation and work as completely distinct is taken from Riggs:

> Work might be defined as the purposive expenditure of energy toward objectives to which the worker holds himself responsible, whereas play is the expenditure of energy just for the joy of expending it in that particular way . . . In short, play must not only give pleasure in itself, but must also be utterly carefree . . . To complete the definition by contrast, work is activity bound by purpose and responsibility and may or may not be pleasurable.[62]

Regardless of how the work-recreation concept is viewed, both schools of thought are agreed that recreation must produce satisfaction for the participant whereas such is not necessary for work, however desirable it might be. Both are convinced that work demands conscious effort over a sustained period of time whereas recreation is an immediate experience demanding only the moment.

This same thinking is also met in another important area of human activity, that of religion. Generally religion is not considered a form of recreation even though there are many aspects of similarity between the two. Again primary motive or individual attitude is taken as the criterion

---

[61] J. Crosby Chapman and George S. Counts, *Principles of Education* (New York: Houghton Mifflin Company, 1924), p. 296.

[62] Austen Fox Riggs, *Play: Recreation In a Balanced Life* (New York: Doubleday, Doran & Company, Inc., 1935), p. 18.

for stating whether or not this activity is recreational. There can be no question that early human experience in religion with its rites and ceremonies had significant recreational overtones just as there are ceremonies in various religions of today which contain predominantly recreational themes. However, for all intents and purposes, all of the recognized religious sects, groups, or denominations have as their primary purpose the glorification and adoration of their god-symbol, whatever it might be. Under these conditions and with primary motive explained in this way, religion could not be conceived as recreation.

Problematically, the question of recreational value must arise when prime motive is considered. This question is: what value is derived from recreation if it is entered into only for fun? Is not fun to be construed as value? If fun is the value, then doesn't it rule out the aspect of prime motive?

A thing has value for us, as individuals, because we know from experience what it is worth. We evaluate both material objects and intangibles, i.e., feelings, attitudes, pleasure, or pain on the basis of prior experience, seldom, if ever, at the moment of experience. We are prone to say that a thing is good or bad depending on our previous experience or learning and relative to the particular situation in which we are placed. We appear to seek activities that afford us pleasure and satisfaction rather than the opposite. This is also true of the values derived from recreation. However, the value received from a recreational activity as opposed to a nonleisure activity, it is said, is that in the former the activity is engaged in for its own sake, it is valuable for itself for what it does to or for the individual. Nonleisure activities, on the other hand, are engaged in primarily for the latent value to be received, be it economic reward or some other asset. Notwithstanding the fact that nonleisure activity may be just as enjoyable, satisfying, or self-expressive to the individual concerned, it is not recreation.[63]

By its very tone, the common usage of recreation would have the world believe that the elemental reason and main purpose for its being is fun regardless of the seriousness involved in the activity. It is unequivocally stated that recreation is desired for the pleasurable feeling created in the individual. Happiness is its characteristic.[64] Thus, when all the derived values are removed, when the camouflage and pseudopurposes are stripped away—then, we are told, only fun remains, there being no other urge to act.[65]

Other problems arise with the concept of primary motive, for there are antisocial acts as well as low order escapist activities which then come under the heading of recreation. This enigma is neatly side-stepped by some

---

[63] George D. Butler, *Introduction To Community Recreation* (New York and London: McGraw-Hill Book Company, Inc., 1948), p. 3.
[64] Meyer and Brightbill, *op. cit.*, p. 24.
[65] Riggs, *op. cit.*, p. 25.

writers who include such activities in a scale, stating that they are recreational if they carry within themselves their own drives to action, i.e., if they are ends in themselves regardless of how vulgar such acts are and how low on the scale they are placed.[66] However, it is only the most broadminded of professionals who would dare thus to classify as recreation acts that are antisocial in nature. In the majority of cases the entire area of immorality is disposed of by placing the word *wholesome* or *worthy* before the rest of the definition. In this way the profession maintains an aura of ethics and morale pride.

Yet, a true definition of the word *recreation* must spell out explicitly just what recreation is. It must include negative aspects, if such there are, as well as the positive. If the prime motive concept is valid, then there must be excluded education, work, physiological acts, and other activities not performed in leisure. Most of the above-mentioned activities are performed either to keep the individual alive, to propagate the species, or to gain profits other than fun. Even though these acts may have pleasure or satisfaction as a secondary aim, perhaps even as a primary aim, they are not to be considered as recreation. Eating and sleeping, which under certain circumstances are extremely pleasurable, or the eliminatory process which under varying psychological conditions becomes pleasurable, are considered only in terms of their supposed primary purpose, whether consciously desired or not, and are therefore nonrecreational.[67]

One considers physiological activities to be those that are necessary to keep the individual alive. In this way the implication of societal taboo is averted by classifying the procreative act with physiological functions. Nevertheless, there still remains the stumbling block of explaining sexual relations when social taboos are not present. In this instance the sex act presents every indication of being a recreational activity inasmuch as it meets all the requisites of definitions now in current use.

The Virtue Concept. The history of the virtue concept of recreation draws upon its heritage of early Greek society where leisure was used so that a man could perform worthy acts, enhance his culture, and live an ethical life. From that period and having that concept to live up to, all professional definitions have adhered to the virtue concept by insisting that its activities be worthy or wholesome. This is most clearly seen in the numerous volumes and pamphlets written on character building through recreational experience and in the adoption by a National Education Association committee of the wording, "worthy use of leisure." This standard has been so ingrained that its inclusion as part of the *Recreation Platform* issued by the combined committees of the American Recreation Society, American Association for Health, Physical Education and Recre-

[66] J. B. Nash, *Philosophy of Recreation and Leisure* (St. Louis: C. V. Mosby Company, 1953), pp. 93–95.
[67] J. F. Brown, *The Psychodynamics of Abnormal Behavior* (New York: McGraw-Hill Book Company, 1940), p. 190.

ation, and the American Association of Group Workers, was almost mandatory.[68]

The virtue concept inevitably grows out of the prime motive concept. It has been stated that most crime is eliminated from the recreation definition even though there are many antisocial acts which have fun or pleasure as their basic motivation. Various acts of juvenile delinquency, such as vandalism or fighting, may have fun as their primary motive, at least outwardly. The inner psychological problems manifested in these acts may be quite different, but the individual who engages in immoral or criminal acts may actually believe that such activity is fun or that it evokes pleasurable sensations for him. By the clever insertion of "worthy" or the phrase "not antisocial in nature," the whole issue of unethical practices, immorality, and crime is completely disposed of; as if the field could, by definition, eliminate the fact that many antisocial acts may be recreation for the individual pursuing that line of conduct.

Among the values which have been ascribed to recreation has been the bolstering of ego and self-esteem in individuals, especially children who have experienced failure in school or in other social contexts.[69] Recreation is valued because it develops character in the individual, strengthens his personality, and helps him to achieve satisfaction in making a social adjustment to his environment. Although this may be true, it is not recreation itself that deserves such tribute, but activities performed by individuals in the hope of attaining recreation.

This may appear to be a radical thought but on closer inspection it may prove to be quite logical. It would be inconsistent with current recreation definitions to explain recreation in any way except as activities performed during leisure, along with other qualifications. If, however, recreation is defined in terms of human behavior, i.e., as a nondebilitating consummatory experience, motivated by equilibrium-seeking within the organism, then the entire picture changes. Asserted in this manner all human activities become potentially recreational and the activities engaged in regardless of their moral qualities become steps in the attainment of recreation. They have inherent values in themselves, whatever they might be, but these values are incidental to achieving recreation. Hence a criminal bent on lawbreaking would be attempting to find his phenomenological self in criminal pursuit in order to regain his organismic balance. If during the committing of a criminal act he did achieve recreation, that act would have value for him in relation to his need provided there is no following sense of guilt. If, on the other hand, a policeman played at his hobby of collecting stamps in order to assert his phenomenological self and did not achieve recreation, the act would have no value for him in relation to his

---

[68] Office of Education, *Cardinal Principles of Secondary Education* (1918, Bulletin No. 35).

[69] S. R. Slavson, *Recreation and the Total Personality* (New York: Association Press, 1946), p. 23.

need. Thus human actions whether socially acceptable or not may have recreational value for an individual depending upon his psychological need and in relation to his personal ethics in satisfying that need. In other words the virtue concept is null and void when speaking of recreation as a product of human behavior.[70]

This does not mean that recreationists advocate unethical conduct, nor does it mean to say that immoral, criminal, selfish, or other negative behavior is necessary in order to achieve recreation. It infers that recreation as behavior may include all human activities and must be so considered in order for a true definition to be given.

The Freedom Concept. The typical axiom recited by the professional and layman alike is that recreation is indulged in on a purely voluntary basis. It is free, not in the economic sense, but on the foundation of independence of thought, movement, and action. It carries with it the idea of liberty, personal and social. Within acceptable bounds the individual does what he wants to do when he wants to do it. Various members of the recreational service field have stated that recreation cannot be prescribed, ordered or forced, for to do so would prejudice its meaning and deny its attractiveness.

> Although there are countless activities that may be considered recreation, it is generally agreed that all recreation activity has certain basic characteristics. One is that the person engages in it because he desires and chooses to do so, without compulsion of any type other than an urge from within.[71]

In this way, recreation is strictly defined and limited to those acts which are elected. If recreation, however, is defined in terms of consummatory experience, it does not matter whether the individual is forced into an activity or enters into it for any other reason. Any activity has potential recreation value if it demands some clear-cut action as well as thought.

One of the more difficult problem areas concerning recreation and the freedom concept has been in the field of therapeutic recreational service, i.e., recreational activities conducted in mental, general medical and surgical, long-term custodial, chronic, rehabilitation, and penal institutions. There has generally been a lack of acceptance of recreational service on the part of other professions in the institutional field. Only in recent years have there been any breakthrough and the granting of peer status to recreationists. The problem can be stated in terms of effects. Has recreational activity been used as simply diversion or is it therapeutic?

Another question in this area involves the use of prescription. Those who feel that recreational activity can be prescribed see no conflict between

---

[70] Clarence E. Rainwater, *The Play Movement in the United States* (Chicago: The University of Chicago Press, 1922), p. 8.
[71] Butler, *op. cit.,* p. 4.

prescription and voluntary participation because of the way in which prescription is defined. Others who oppose prescription do so on the basis that prescribed recreational activity immediately ruins any value that voluntary participation has on the participant. If therapy is defined as anything that helps or aids recovery, then assuredly recreational activity is therapy. If, on the other hand, therapy is defined as the scientific treatment by the application of specific remedies for diseases, then it is unlikely that recreational activity, as presently practiced, is therapy.

In any case, with recreation defined as behavior, in contradistinction to particular activities, it no longer matters whether recreational activity is prescribed. It may very well be taken as therapeutic, and the obtaining of individual prescriptions for patients will not destroy the value that it has for them. Prescribed recreational activity, provided it is recreational, may prove just as effective and therapeutic as activities voluntarily entered into. In many observable cases, recreational experiences which have been prescribed for various patients have proved very stimulating and absorptive for them, although at first there was resistance. When this occurs, it is generally due to unfamiliarity with the activity or subject rather than to any inherent dislike because of prior experience. Strangeness or unfamiliarity breeds fear of failure or anxiety; thus, the unwillingness and apparent hostility toward new outlets. Any human activity may potentially be recreation or have recreational value for an individual whether he consciously seeks it or not.

Objections to this concept might well take form as farfetched questions to test the validity of this statement. Samples of these tests could consist of questions concerning war, crime, forced labor, or other occupations that usually carry distasteful connotations. Does war have potential recreational value? Yes! But the consequences of combat or the strain undergone in the manifold emergencies one finds in a battle atmosphere would appeal only to a certain type of individual. Yet, because recreation is so highly personalized, there are some people who could conceivably find in a war activity a consummatory experience (not death) and achieve recreation. Huizinga realized that there was play in war:

> Ever since words existed for fighting and playing, men have been wont to call war a game . . . The two ideas often seem to blend absolutely in the archaic mind. Indeed, all fighting that is bound by rules bears the formal characteristics of play by that very limitation.[72]

Huizinga always refers to war as a cultural function that presupposes certain rules recognized by all. Once war becomes total war, as we know it today, it loses its limiting rules and becomes simply criminal violence. Notwithstanding the fact that war today is total war there are still some individuals who regard it as a game. One is reminded of that unnamed

---

[72] Johan Huizinga, *Homo Ludens* (Boston: The Beacon Press, 1950), p. 89.

British officer who, during the Suez Canal dispute in 1956, stated that the fight was "jolly good sport," taking the view that war is a sport with rules to observe. This might lead to a consummatory experience but only where the activity involved complete absorption.

This possibility can also hold true for other activities which are in the main distasteful. The very fact that a human being is engaged in the action clears the way for recreation to take place. The dullest, most repetitious job imaginable might require an automatic control for hand manipulation but it still leaves the mind free to wander. In such circumstances the dull mechanical job performance can pave the way for free flights of the imagination which at later times may be transformed into action. Thus, thought leading to action or action leading to thought may characterize the consummatory experience.

The criminal act may also be recreation under certain qualifying circumstances. If a burglar is intent upon looting a safe, the opening of that safe may completely absorb him. His concentration upon the clicking tumblers might require such intense effort that he could be completely absorbed in this pursuit. The thought of financial gain may enhance the act, but it is the act itself which provides the thought access to recreation. It does not matter in which activity the individual is engaged as long as he attains a state in which he is beyond tension or stress. Although it may be possible to reach consummation through total absorption in any activity, external stress or internal body chemistry reactions can cause dissolution within the individual and prevent total absorption. The unity and harmony achieved during moments of consummation may be withheld because of tension factors.

Whether or not the individual has guilt feelings because of participation in an activity of dubious ethical value depends upon his own value system and the type of conduct acceptable in his community. Thus, a habitual thief, liar, cheat, prostitute, or other immoral individual can feel perfectly free of tension or other stresses while engaging in antisocial activities as long as the culture of which he is a product accepts such conduct. Even if the culture does not accept immoral behavior, the individual may still regard his behavior as normal and acceptable due to a complete absence of moral standards or pathological factors. If such is the case, immoral action might well lead to recreation. On the other hand, where actions, regardless of social acceptability, cause feelings of guilt or tension, unity or harmony is not possible and complacency will not be attained. When an individual steals time from one activity to participate in another, there may be guilt feelings. When this happens the unity derived from recreation and the value that this has for the individual cannot be attained, regardless of surface feelings of pleasure. An individual may fool himself into thinking that he is having fun or even that he has received something of value for his misbegotten efforts, but in reality he has only succeeded in repressing his true feelings of guilt or other tension producing factors. He may, therefore, feel that he is attaining recreation, but he does not emerge from the activity with a re-born or "new-man" feeling, which one receives from recreation, because the unity feature is lacking.

This "new-man" sensation is better described as the "ahhh" feeling. It has been experienced by countless millions engaged in various and sundry activities which humans have performed since time immemorial. It is the feeling that the dedicated golfing "duffer" receives when, for the first or hundredth time, he hears the sweet click of clubhead meeting golf ball and watches as the sphere rises straight and true to hum down the fairway and alight some two hundred plus yards away. It is the feeling doctors, lawyers, teachers, researchers, businessmen, and all other professionals and laymen alike have achieved in their respective callings. It is "the job well done." Yet this feeling is produced only when complete absorption occurs. Stated more simply, it means that the degree of concentration leading to total absorption is not as great when some guilt thought or other tension producing strain is present. More often than not recreation will not be obtained by the individual who is engaged in an activity in which he has no right or should not be. Any part of the mental process that prohibits complete unity of mind and body also prohibits recreation. It is only when there is a consummatory activity leading to unity that recreation exists.

This concept does not eliminate the fact that many antisocial acts have recreational value for the individual who pursues this line of behavior. Antisocial acts seldom contribute to the unity of man's nature. Unethical practices and degrading activities seldom produce a sound mind in a sound body, nor are they conducive to peace of mind for the individual concerned. Criminal and immoral practices probably cause more worry and tension than acts which are in line with moral behavior and conduct, but such feelings of guilt or lack of guilt depend upon the value system of the individual and his social environment. To a lesser extent other delinquent acts or minor breaches of a given society's code are also included in this class.

A unique characteristic of the re-created feeling is that it can be repeated. This duplication or reproducing quality can elicit the same satisfying response or feeling of well-being regardless of the number of times the action is performed. The same responses to certain acts may be eternally evoked in the same person, and more wonderful still, the act is never dulled or boring, nor is the consequence tarnished or jaded in any way. Once the recreational act has been discovered it never loses its ability to fully consume or absorb the participant, especially, although not necessarily, if it is highly competitive.

This does not say that interests never change. One is aware that the changes in the interests of an individual are somewhat determined by emotional, environmental, and physiological growth factors. These factors push forward several interests or bring about an interest in a different set of objects as illustrated very clearly at the onset of puberty or menopause.

Nevertheless, it can be just as clearly indicated that adults, whatever the changing interest pattern is, at times do revert to activities and interests that once held their attention as children. Witness some of the social gatherings which adults attend or the convention tactics and antics that adult males go through. The solemn rites in various orders and organizations are throwbacks to the love of secrecy that children have.

Having defined recreation in terms of values which are derived, time of performance (leisure), and free choice, the term is carried to extreme proportions. It is described as basic to the democratic process of individualism, as a cure-all for the ills of mankind, as the sociological answer to mental illness, juvenile delinquency, high blood pressure, and personality difficulties.[73] Nowhere has this type of thinking been more clearly spelled out than by G. Ott Romney in *Off The Job Living*. He states:

> Release from strain, translation from self-concern to absorbing interests and the concurrent discovery of the friend you can be to yourself, by *rest, play* or *doing* something you really want to do—such is the insurance recreation writes against the mill-run miseries and ills of too much self.[74]

The definition most used in this context, or the one that typifies the current trend of thinking in the recreational service field is:

> . . . a voluntary participation in any wholesome activity for the personal enjoyment and satisfaction derived from the doing, producing a refreshment of strength and spirit in the individual.[75]

This definition is a composite of all those that have been described in the preceding pages and which are in use up to this time. It neatly side-steps all activities having any moral taint, delimits the scope of activity to include only leisure activities, and states that the democratic ideal of free choice or electivity must be present.

The Activity Concept of Recreation. One of the least innocuous concepts of recreation in current use is that which sets up the criterion of action as the measuring rod by which experiences will be known as recreation. In this instance recreation is set up as a going, doing, active type of behavior. Pre-eminent in this outcry against passivity has been Jay B. Nash, an outstanding educator in the fields of recreational service and physical education. In his book *Spectatoritis,* published in 1932, he laid down several explicit points concerning the recreative act as an active process.

> Recuperation may be defined as the rejuvenation of the body after work. It is, however, not wholly relegated to inertia—doing nothing. Recupera-

---

[73] John E. Davis, *Play and Mental Health* (New York: Barnes and Company, 1938), pp. 60–61, 64, 135, 139.
[74] Romney, *op. cit.,* p. 16.
[75] American Recreation Society, Hospital Recreation Section, *Basic Concepts of Hospital Recreation* (Washington, D.C.: The Society, September 1953), p. 4.

tion is obtained in action—action with a 'glide-stroke relationship.' The body recuperates, regains its equilibrium, much more quickly in an atmosphere of happiness, joy—the play attitude.[76]

He further stated that "The thesis of this discussion is that the central motive of our behavior is struggle—doing." [77]

Nash's concept rests upon the Greek formula inscribed on the facade of the olympic stadium—"strip or retire." This meant either prepare for active participation or withdraw from the arena, as there was no place for spectators. He questions the majority who sit in the stands, admire skills they do not possess, and secure whatever exaltation lies in the vicarious thrill of escape and in shouting:

> The looker-on, the victim of spectatoritis, brings neither joy to himself nor heritage to his people. Living is struggle, competition—a hope-fear relationship. Remove that and you remove satisfaction. Competition exists not only in sport, but in every zestful act.[78]

In another book, Nash depicted leisure activities in terms of level or status drawn in a pyramid or triangular form. This drawing represents, not only levels of behavior, but also the amount of activity or passivity which the individual exhibits in participating. Thus, at the base are antisocial acts and inertia, whereas at the apex are socially acceptable acts, creative acts, and participating acts.[79]

Although it seems logical to assume that active participation would bring about a deeper absorption and lead to a consummatory experience, such is not always the case. Passive appreciation, intellectual browsing, so to speak, may be as deeply absorbing and recreational as any active participation can be. It might be stated that contemplation is really active because it requires some effort and may be equally exhausting as hard labor or other strenuous activity. However, in the way that Nash utilized the term it appears that what he means by active is actual physical participation. This concept also restricts the definition of recreation but not so completely as other concepts mentioned in preceding pages. Although it is true that Nash conceived of recreation as activity performed in leisure, he nevertheless is willing to include activities which would ordinarily be classified as nonrecreation. His thesis is mainly concerned with leisure activities and although he attempts to solve the problem of deciding which activities are better suited for individual choice, he recognizes the semantic problem of delineating work from play and recreation from education.

The activity concept is not a negative restriction. It has been formulated

---

[76] Jay B. Nash, *Spectatoritis* (New York: Sears Publishing Company, Inc., 1932), p. 65.
[77] *Ibid.*, p. 195.
[78] *Ibid.*, p. 190.
[79] Jay B. Nash, *Philosophy of Recreation and Leisure,* pp. 93–96.

to associate participation with the recreative act in opposition to activities which promote loafing or other completely passive amusements.

Harold Rugg and William Withers have this to say about the action concept as it relates to recreational activity:

> We are an active and creative people, yet we have increasingly tended toward conformity and group behavior in recreation . . . Perhaps Americans find the trend toward passivity and 'spectatoritis' wholly satisfying. But recreation has a greater social significance than mere escapism and relaxation. Recreation is one of the realms in which creative powers are developed and broader perspectives discovered.[80]

Rugg and Withers and Nash have hit upon one of the more complicated features of recreational life. In the action concept this feature becomes more and more assertive. The problem of the spectator is one that needs a fully detailed explanation. Out of the action concept grows the problem of the spectator: empathy or escape. At certain times and in specific places the problem of empathy asserts itself. Does the spectator escape his surroundings or does he empathize? Is it catharsis through participation or vicarious pleasure through escape?

The difference between these two terms is characterized by the psychological implications for the individual. Escape is a behavior pattern that acts as a mechanism for adjustment. Like other forms of behavior, it is part of the homeostatic process. The individual initiates this type of behavior in order to ease the tension of inner stresses or environmental pressures. In this attempt at adjustment the individual may call upon the mechanism of escape. Escapism may be the method by which a desired end can be attained and it is usually carried on outside the world of reality. It is sealed off, as it were, from the hectic struggle for existence in that it is compensatory, through the imagination, for physical or mental inability.

For some people escape may be a way of "getting out of themselves." They drop the cares and burdens of daily living and either play at or become somebody else. This type of activity is generally pleasurable. It may be observed in many of the spectator-type events where skilled individuals are in competition, although it may occur whenever or wherever admired qualities are found. The spectator may have had the skill at one time and no longer possesses it or never had it and would have liked it.

Such behavior reflects satisfaction through imaginary representations that are not attained in true experience. Thus, the imagination is utilized to compensate for certain personal lacks and to achieve success quite easily. The spectator may slip from the confines of strain and frustration to the fancy and make-believe of leisure activities. Regardless of the activity, whether it is highly developed sports and games or daydreaming, individuals

---

[80] Harold Rugg and William Withers, *Social Foundations of Education* (New York: Prentice-Hall, Inc., 1955), pp. 600–601.

tend to forget themselves and identify with being someone or something else. In this way they satisfy their longings or desires to be what they are not and thus achieve vicarious pleasure.

Empathy, in opposition to this, is an identification from actual experience. Empathy is a process by which the individual completely identifies himself with the object of his immediate experience because a past experience under similar or identical circumstances has occurred. Thus, a person can say to another who is undergoing some trial or tribulation or an extremely happy event, "I know exactly how you feel." This is not to be confused with sympathy. Sympathy is a feeling for, i.e., the one who sympathizes wishes that the misfortune never occurred; whereas the empathizer feels with the individual because he has actually experienced the sensation. This may be pleasurable or unpleasurable. In the context of which this is written the spectator may empathize with the performer, competitor, or artist and gain a certain freedom of expression through cathartic reaction.[81] This can be illustrated by college football. The graduate or former player may receive immense satisfaction by the process of shouting and armwaving as he cheers his team on. In some instances such an individual may empathize with an on-field player; feeling the tension, reliving the force and drive of straining bodies and pounding pulses. He may re-create in his mind's eye the movements and pace that he once knew. Outwardly this pent up emotion may give way to shouts and hysterical body contortions in order to release the tensions that have been built up during the identification process. Empathetic cartharsis, in the spectator sporting events, is most usually of the pleasurable variety. It consists of physical effort and exertion as an outcome of psychophysical stress. The physical reaction of outburst stimulates the entire organism and results in a feeling of well-being.

The empathetic reaction may also occur during exhibitions of an aesthetic nature. Thus, the same physical reactions may occur from the stimulating effects of an opera, art exhibit, dramatic production, or other spectator performances. Whereas the cathartic expulsion may be of a more quiet nature, i.e., no shouting or violent body contortions, there may still be the physiological expression of quickened breathing, perspiration, faster pulse rate, and other physical manifestations that show some physical exertion taking place. This reaction may occur during the performance or make its appearance immediately upon its conclusion. Thus, the wild outburst of applause and hysterical acclaim that accompanies a spectacular performance by some artist may be not only an appreciation of the artistic accomplishment, but a cathartic release of pent up emotion.

The concept of action poses the problem of empathy or escape in citing what would appear on the surface as a manifestation of passivity or at best active appreciation. No definite conclusion can be drawn concerning

[81] Wilhelm Worringer, *Abstraction and Empathy* (New York: International Universities Press, Inc., 1953), p. 6.

this phase of leisure activities because only the participating individual can make known the type of response or behavior mechanism he utilizes at a particular point in time. The action concept is then incomplete because it considers only physical activity as a criterion for making a judgment. Action may be of the intellectual variety as well as the physical. True recreation, however, combines both of these elements. Clear-cut action developed out of purposive thought as a consequence of past action allows the individual to re-create himself.

This is the consequence meted out to all the activities which confront the human being in his effort to adjust to the constantly changing scene of daily living. The professional definition is strict in its interpretation because it cannot afford to be associated with any other meaning. Although there are a few professionals on the fringe of the practicing field who discern conflicts or grey areas between what is called recreation and other activities, the great majority see only black and white. Yet this black and white pattern reflects a distorted image of what recreation really is.

Play and Recreation

Recreation is so highly personalized that any effort to assign its usage and limit its area to a small segment of human action is fruitless. Yet, this restraint continues to be applied. When the term *recreation* is mentioned, the word immediately suggests pictures of relaxation, entertainment, spectator sports, and any nonserious activity. Used in this way it connotes a strictly nonutilitarian type of activity.

Play and recreation are symbols expressing the same idea. Much confusion has resulted from differentiation of these words which are in fact interchangeable. Play has been used by many to show contempt for an individual's action, i.e., one disparages another by saying, "All he does is play." One speaks of acts that do not seem appropriate by saying, "Don't play around! Be serious!" People continually place the words *play* and *seriousness* in opposite categories. One generally speaks of play as something a child does. One says to a child, "Stop playing like a baby and act like a man." What is really meant is: "Your actions are bothering me, and I have no time to understand them." To the child his actions may be perfectly intelligible; he is playing. He plays in all seriousness, i.e., with fixed attention. The rude voice of the adult shatters this play-existence because, not understanding the profoundness of what is occurring, the adult assumes it to be meaningless.

The child plays with all the devotion and energy of which he is capable. Whether the play is concerned with listening to a story, chasing another, manipulation of objects, or just dreaming, the child is intently and completely absorbed in what he considers real and therefore serious. The child is probably aware that he is only playing at being something or somebody, that such play is not real life; but nevertheless, during the course of the play he may empathize with whatever he imagines and, for that short instant,

84 Principles of Recreational Service

may be what he plays at being. The child exalts his play in the same manner as the adult who pays homage to the tee and golf ball. Such play is deadly serious to the player. The same feelings are evoked in child play as in what adults call their play, the only difference being that adults have dignified their play by calling it recreation. There is no difference between the two symbols. Whatever results from this intense preoccupation, the feelings, sensations, or effects are the same. This is not to say that play is nonserious. There are many times when child and adult play are light and frivolous, but behind the facade of the tensionless and comic is the probability of serious purpose.

Another confusing aspect concerns attitudes toward work and play as each shows infringement upon the other. Some people putter or work around in their garden, tool shed, or kitchen at the end of a working day. Some people work at perfecting their skill at any number of sports, games, or musical pursuit. Others work at play. These people try hard to have fun, to divert themselves, to find relief from boredom. They invest their leisure, money, and effort in order to achieve a modicum of satisfaction; and they work hard to attain that feeling. Is this work or play? Conversely, there are those who do all of these things and consider that they are merely playing around, i.e., getting their recreation. What is the standard by which one can say that one thing is work and another is play?

The same attitude prevails with regard to work and recreation. Many people express the view that recreation is the antithesis of work, that its main function is to divert, relax, and rebuild the individual's strength for another round at the strenuous task of living and working. Statements have been made to the effect that recreation is the wholesome use of leisure, time free from work. Some definitions concerning play, recreation, and work show how ambiguously they are used.

> But the word 'recreation' is broad enough to include play in its every expression and also many activities not thought of as play—music, the drama, the crafts, every free activity and especially creative activity for the enrichment of life.[82]

> Summing up the formal characteristics of play we might call it a free activity standing quite consciously outside 'ordinary' life as being 'not serious' but at the same time absorbing the player intensely and utterly.[83]

> There is a very common misunderstanding of the play of children among adults which arises from their confusing it with recreation. Recreation is relief from toil. It is intended for the rest and rebuilding of wearied muscles and nerves and spirit. It may take any form, but it is always lacking in seriousness and usually has value only in re-creating the mind and the body for the more serious work of life. The play of the child does

---

[82] John H. Finley, "What Will We Do With Our Time?" *Recreation* (November 1933), p. 367.
[83] Huizinga, *op. cit.*, p. 13.

not correspond to the recreation of the adult, but to the work of the adult. Play is the most serious activity in which the child engages.[84]

As one reads over the preceding statements from authorities in the field a certain confusion must develop as a result of there being no clear distinction between play and recreation. The experts do not agree. They tend rather to disagree on what constitutes the proper definition for the terms involved. Witness the following: attitude, time, activity, or value difficulties that accrue when discussing the separate structure of play and recreation. Each is supposed to take place during leisure. Each is composed of a peculiar attitude which expresses itself in pleasure. Each is set in a free-choice atmosphere. Each is self-activated, i.e., motivated or carried along by its own drive. Each completely absorbs the individual. Each takes many forms. Each has been interpreted as being broader or larger in scope than the other and therefore includes the other. Each is serious. Each is not serious. Each is different but the same. In other words, no one knows precisely wherein the difference lies, or for that matter what makes the difference; yet a few claim that there is a decided difference. That difference would appear to be man-made. Every characteristic that has been listed in the name of play has also been attributed to recreation.

Not only has there been a great confusion in the semantics of play and recreation, but much of the literature of the field has intensified the confusion rather than alleviated it. Prior to the early 1930's, there was a preponderance of literature on the meaning, nature, psychology, and value of play; today the literature of the field has come to focus on recreation and its exploration. Before 1900 few writers even mentioned the term *recreation* as a subject for discussion; after that time the two terms were treated with recreation in the subordinate position. Today, in many of the books on education and recreation major import is given recreation, its structure, meaning, and value; whereas play is included only as a secondary consideration.

Probably, the most valuable suggestion would be to accept or to assume that recreation and play are synonymous. For all practical purposes, when an individual speaks of his play he refers to recreation and when he recreates he does so in the spirit of play. The individual does not give any thought as to whether he plays or recreates; he just exhibits a pattern of behavior. The main consideration is that these symbols are interchangeable and have the same meaning, structure, and value.

The Unity Concept of Recreation. It is not surprising that the professional definition and interpretation of recreation, as an act, should be what it is inasmuch as the entire field has been conditioned by and is a logical outgrowth of Aristotelian precepts and philosophy. Any definition or philosophy based on the teachings of the absolute, unchanging, immutable

---

[84] Henry Curtis, *Education Through Play* (New York: The Macmillan Company, 1916), p. 12.

truth placed within man's reach, such as the Aristotelian world view, can under no circumstances be anything but biased toward what it considers to be that truth or absolute good. In the contemporary views of many, the truth regarding recreation is that it consists of voluntary participation performed in leisure for pleasure or satisfaction as a means of gaining recreation or in order to gain refreshment. Everything else is ignored regardless of the values to be derived from participation or lack of participation by the individual.

In defining recreation, it must be realized that there are no absolutes! Secondly, it must be kept in mind that any definition is a concept of the subject concerned, initiated in the mind and projected or developed as a consequence of acts, or ideas of acts, which may prove fruitful if adapted to human experience. Finally, it must be remembered that any concept of recreation is developmental in content; factors involved in its substance are subject to change and are continually changing. Recreation, then, may be said to be dynamic.

In most subject matter whatever is depicted to be its essence is the thing that gives it meaning. If the essence of a subject or substance is meant to be its primordial element which, if removed, so changes the structure or form of the subject that its original character becomes so completely altered as to defy description, then essence is a final end. In terms of this explanation and under these circumstances recreation could have no essence. It must be defined in terms of a *concept of essence*. Concept, by its inclusion, changes the interpretation from finality to an on-going or changing product. The obvious intent for explaining the essence of recreation in terms of conceptualization is to show it as evolutionary rather than as an absolute. Recreation is any consummatory experience, nondebilitating in character.

The conceptual essence of recreation is theorized as being oneness or unity. This unity or physical and mental harmony which man captures by a consummatory experience appears to be a constant or finality because it does not seem to change within the life span of any human being. Nevertheless, it is always changing. It is continually translated in the mind of man from an idea to a reality, but it is still different in each individual's view. Such an idea may be likened to a flowing stream. The water maintains a basic appearance; the channel, except for deepening, holds true; but the stream continues to flow. It never is the same at any two times. Its chemical properties vary by the second; yet for all practical intents and purposes, the stream looks and is the same.

In analyzing what recreation is, it is found that only one condition is necessary by which unity or harmony is brought about. An intense absorption must seize the individual's attention so that everything outside of whatever he is participating in loses its significance for the period of time in which his whole attention is engaged. This can never be a piece-meal affair; it is either all or nothing. In losing himself, the individual finds himself.

The anthropologist, Leo Frobenius, knew well the intense absorption that play had for the individual. In his book *The Cultural History of Africa,* he devoted a section to the subject, calling it "To Be and To Play." He stated that human beings behave according to the dictates of their own nature, that they attain complacency which is a product of an absorbing interest, and that their complacency gives way to disharmony under the influence of internal and external interferences. The characteristic feature of human animals is that they have the ability for absorption and dissolution which influences the development of ethos. In relating the completeness of absorption as it affects children at play Frobenius says:

> I have shown . . . what devilish power lies in the game that children play. Whoever has naturally active children knows what it means to tear the child away from the game and tell him he has to go home. In fact, when we are dealing with the intensive play of children we work with the basic source out of the holiest ground waters of all culture and with one of its greatest powers for creation.[85]

In this manner Frobenius explains his concept of the consummatory act. Consummation for him is the grace of play, where men are engrossed by the nature of things, and where the highest grace is the capacity for devotion. Thus, the consummatory act is intimately connected with aesthetic creation and it is through this medium that culture develops. He conceived of the development of culture as a process of living experience in which the individual was completely absorbed in the natural ebb and flow of creativity and extinction. The consciousness was enmeshed in this rhythmic pattern, compressed through reflex action to an outward expression of emotion in aesthetic form. In this way play served to bring about the consummatory act. This consummatory process is possible because the mind is free to concentrate on the pursuit at hand without mental reservation that time taken up in the immediate act should be spent or devoted to other more useful, necessary, or mandatory activities.

Finally, recreation is absorption leading to unity, balance, or harmony. One follows the other as surely as day follows night. Without absorption or consummation there can be no unity nor equilibrium; if unity is not the outcome of the consummatory experience it is not recreation. In this respect, total absorption may be brought about by almost any activity or pursuit engaged in by human beings and when achieved, will result in varying degrees of complete and intense concentration. In any case, unity or equilibrium, i.e., the uniting of the physical with the spiritual or mental processes, is complete at the time of consummation. It is from this vital sensation or dynamism of feeling that the receiver truly becomes reborn, reawakened, or re-created. However, it must be remembered that equilibrium is not nirvana, quiescence, or lack of action, but a dynamic balance

---

[85] Leo Frobenius, *Kulturgeschichte Afrikas, Prolegomena zu einer Gestaltlehre* (Zurich: Phaidon Verlag, Inc., 1954), p. 24.

between the individual and all stimuli. It is an adjustment which is satisfying to the organism.

Thus, the only value to be truly recreative is that of absorption or consummation. In other words, recreational value arises from the consummatory experience the individual may undergo in any activity. Recreation, however, is the unification of mind and body brought about by consummation. Such a distinction is not only logical but necessary. If consummation was the end product, this concept would be just as biased as the leisure-time proposition. With unity as the base and post behavior as an outcome, this is a dynamic concept.

The basic difference between recreational value and recreation is in time rather than degree. Recreational value will be noted after the consummatory experience has occurred whereas recreation occurs at the time of the consummatory experience. With this type of definition to go by, primary motive is no longer a consideration or criterion by which an act may be classified as recreation. As it has been implied antisocial acts as well as socially acceptable activities, including religion, education (schooling), vocations, various physiological acts—in fact most human activities which have for so long been classified as nonrecreational—have potential recreation value and are indeed potentially recreation.

In defining recreation as a progression or pragmatic concept, the logical consequences that such a definition has for human activities and conduct must be explained. The unity of mind and body (psyche and soma) brought about at the time of consummation is recreation. This unity or wholeness is predicated upon the organism's continual attempts to attain equilibrium. Because all behavior is a product of the organism maintaining organization and manifesting itself in acts seen by the individual as phases of phenomenological self, then any act may become recreation. Recreation as a product of behavior is also a part of behavior. This is explained by understanding recreation as the aim of organismic action, i.e., as equilibrium and as a functional process of thought and action.

SUMMARY

Theorists who have favored instinct as motivation for human behavior do not include play as one of the human instincts. However, several psychologists have felt that if instinct is thought of in terms of responses to stimuli and environmental conditions that have not been learned through past experiences, then recreation or play might well be instinctive. Suggestions have been made that man instinctively turns to play in order to satisfy racial habits, to practice for later life skills, to fulfill the need for relaxation, or to expend surplus energy.

That human beings are organisms possessing certain characteristics prior to birth which influence the kinds of traits that each will display during life is almost universally accepted. Much of the controversy over instinct boils down to the question of whether that concept really explains anything and whether so-called instincts are, in fact, instincts at all. Man, being a complex product of psychosomatic energy in dynamic form cannot be anything but active. It would be an unwarranted assumption that man's innate nature should be one of inactivity.

Psychologists differ among themselves regarding their views on the problem of instincts. Freud's theory of the death instinct seems to have been influenced by the biological theories current at that time. These theories were largely based on the second law of thermodynamics which applies only to closed systems. Because the phenomenon of life can only occur in open systems, the principle of entropy is not applicable in these circumstances.

There is to be found in the various psychiatric views the unitary theory of instinct. According to this theory, there is a single primary instinct, the life instinct, the aim of which is to keep the life processes of living systems in continuous operation. This is accomplished by driving negative entropy from the environment. Death results from environmental interference with the life instinct. The same idea was expressed by Ferenczi as early as 1913, and Freud's earlier writings were dominated by similar views. Following *Beyond the Pleasure Principle,* Freud's observation of a behavioral manifestation, which he called *masochism,* caused him to modify his basic concepts.

Instead of using the term *instinct* to explain behavioral activity, other psychologists refer to stimuli, the structure of the nervous system, the internal chemistry of the body, past behavior, and similar determinants. This occurs because instinct has accumulated such a wide variety of meanings that no scientific exactness can be applied to it. Historically, the concept of instinct has become so encrusted with customary meaning and ambiguity that its utility as a scientific term has been lost. Consequently many behavioral scientists have dismissed explanations of behavior as instinctive and have substituted other terms with more explicit and descriptive meanings.

The whole question of the hedonistic doctrine as the motivational stimulant appears to have been proved either obsolescent or not quite valid. The paradox contained within the doctrine prevents its continued acceptance. Because seeking activities are generally conceded to accompany unpleasant conditions or situations, the basis for the doctrine of pleasure seeking presents difficulties of logical explanation. It has been found that conscious and active seeking after pleasure usually makes realization of such a goal impossible to achieve. Pleasure more often accompanies an activity as an effect or a by-product and is not considered as causal.

The principle of homeostasis has come to receive wide acceptance, especially among scientists who deal with biochemical, physiochemical, or electrochemical phenomena. It has been accorded wide popularity among psychologists who see in homeostasis the fundamental basis for human behavior. It has been noted that body chemistry continually seeks to maintain equilibrium among its products, and therefore, within the organism as a whole. Directly related to this aspect is the metabolic condition of the organism upon which behavioral activities are built. Just as the physio-chemical balance is concerned with equilibrium in the somatic field, psychological homeostasis is concerned with maintaining equilibrium in the psyche or mental field. Psychological homeostasis, also called complacency, attempts to direct the mental state into a condition where there is unawareness of tension or stress. This is achieved during moments of complete concentration or absorption of the individual in any activity which does not subject the organism to mental or physical debilitation, guilt, or degradation. During this period of consummation the individual is restored to a state of harmony within himself as well as toward his environment, a mind-body-situation relationship.

Recreation is characterized by its consummatory nature. It has the power to seize and hold the attention of the individual to such an extent that the very meaning of subjective time and environment disappears from view. In this respect it fulfills the need for psychological homeostasis. Recreation receives its motivation from the organismic movement toward equilibrium, based upon metabolic and environmental conditions. As such it is part of human behavior.

There are many aspects of psychology that can be explained in terms of biology and physiology. It is also true that in the more complex organisms there are blank spaces or unsupported assertions and analogies in the relationship between psychology and physiology. There is, however, an increasing acceptance of homeostasis and the implications that this concept has for behavioral motivation. If psychological homeostasis is an acceptable explanation for recreational motivation, then it abrogates the pleasure principle as its main aim and instinct as the drive that causes spontaneous action. Under these circumstances a new definition must be offered in order for recreation to be meaningful.

The concept of essence provides the basis for a definition of recreation. It is the realization of totality, i.e., complete integration by the individual within himself. This is the recreational focus. Unity is its conceptual essence —the re-creation of man's sensitivities, sensibilities, and rationale. What the individual loses during moments of frustrating experience, his equilibrium and sense of proportion, may be regained through the unifying power of recreation. By broad identification, the consummatory concept defines recreation as the product and process of eqilibrium seeking within the human organism. It provides the basis for a theory of recreation and a concomitant philosophy utilizing the social psychology of pragmatism. A complete and radically new idea of the meaning, value, and process of recreation has been postulated: it is any nondebilitating, consummatory experience.

SELECTED REFERENCES

Cannon, Walter B., *The Wisdom of the Body*. (New York: W. W. Norton and Company, Inc.), 1932.

Carlson, R. E., T. R. Deppe, and J. R. Maclean, *Recreation In American Life*. (Belmont, Calif.: Wadsworth Publishing Company), 1963.

Danford, Howard G., *Creative Leadership in Recreation*. (Boston: Allyn and Bacon), 1964.

Dewey, John, *Art as Experience*. (New York: Minton, Balch and Company), 1935.

Huizinga, Johan, *Homo Ludens: A Study of the Play Element in Culture*. (Boston: The Beacon Press), 1955.

Louenfeld, Viktor, *Creative and Mental Growth*. (New York: The Macmillan Company), 1949.

Nash, Jay B., *Recreation: Pertinent Readings*. (Dubuque, Iowa: Wm. C. Brown Company), 1965.

Neumeyer, M. H. and E. S. Neumeyer, *Leisure and Recreation*, 3rd ed. (New York: The Ronald Press), 1958.

Read, Herbert, *Education Through Art*. (London: Faber and Faber, Ltd.), 1943.

Sapora, A. V. and E. D. Mitchell, *The Theory of Play and Recreation*, 3rd ed. (New York: The Ronald Press), 1961.

Shivers, Jay S., *An Analysis of Various Theories of Recreation*. Unpublished Doctor's thesis, University of Wisconsin, 1958.

Worringer, William, *Abstraction and Empathy*. (New York: International University Press, Inc.), 1953.

Chapter 4

LEGALITY

PRINCIPLE: The establishment of agencies providing benefits to the public which are considered essential to the general health and welfare are sanctioned by the state through constitutional measures. The administration of certain functions for effecting promotional services cannot be left to happenstance or private exploitation and therefore become the foundation for legislation to advance such governmental responsibilities.

Constitutional provision for governmental undertakings to enhance, protect, or secure a better life for the constituency has been a part of the American system since the inception of the republic. While constitutional enactment has been the living frame of reference for the restriction of governmental power over the life and liberty of individuals, it has also been the document by which justifiable governmental arrogation of power to enable it to carry out its functions is based. This interesting and apparent dichotomy developed because of the time in which the framers of the constitution lived as well as their own ideology. It must be remembered that the men who formulated the constitution were products of enlightened humanism. They were steeped in the German romantic tradition and were passionately devoted to the doctrine of individual liberty and the natural rights of free men. Therefore, it is not surprising that that constitution is a document of limitation on government with more emphasis on the restriction of governmental power than on its utilization. However, the men who designed it never foresaw the growth and development of the United States to the degree that it has attained; yet they provided for an elasticity which enabled the Constitution to develop with the changing times. The Constitution is not a document of specificity, but one of generality. Thus, the original source of power by government has been able to keep pace with the exigencies that time brings. Still, if the framers wanted less government control how is it that such a powerful force as *Police Power* came into being?

SUPREMACY, SOVEREIGNTY, AND POLICE POWER

In effect, the aftermath of the revolution and the drawing up of a constitution enumerating a tripartite Central Government also established two levels of government existing side by side. Nevertheless, the constitutionalists did not want to repeat the same mistakes and weaknesses that attended the original Articles of Confederation. To offset the possibility of a central government without the necessary power to perform its functions and to prohibit the assumption of sovereignty by the states, with all of the prerogatives which the term *sovereignty* implies, the framers created a document that draws its strength, centrality, and power from "We the people . . ." rather than the states. The Constitution is itself irrevocably opposed to the concept of state sovereignty. Although the United States is composed of fifty autonomous political entities, by design and fact the law of the land was not created from them as sovereign states. The preamble essentially explicates the entire question that the Constitution was the act of the nation, not the states. All of the states form, but they did not create, the United States.

Supremacy

The supreme law in this country is the Constitution. The supremacy clause has been challenged several times, but there has never been any question as to what level of government is sovereign or what foundation provides it with that supremacy. If there had been any question it was effectively settled after the Civil War rebellion and reaffirmed in Supreme Court decisions from that time on. The acts of the National Government are defined as the operational supreme law in this country. This status is conferred upon them as a result of their independence from other sources for enforcement. Thus, federal mandate is enforceable in every court because there is no dependency on state origin. The states do not have the authority to hinder in any way or supervise the performance of federal law. The Constitution is "the written instrument agreed upon by the people . . . as the absolute rule of action and decision for all departments and officers of the government . . . and in opposition to which any act or rule of any department or officer of the government, or even of the people themselves, will be altogether void." [1]

Sovereignty

The absolute, incontestable, and arbitrary right to govern is unknown in the United States. Sovereignty, then, is antithetical to the concept of government under which the United States was founded. The Federal Government itself is one of limited powers, expressly enumerated, delegated, or implied by the Constitution. In such an instance the Constitution is itself sovereign, with the supreme power to govern not residing with any legal or executive body. Only in the sense that the United States of America does not owe allegiance to a superior form of government and that it may,

---

[1] Thomas McIntyre Cooley, *A Treatise on the Constitutional Limitations Which Rest Upon the Legislative Power of the States of the American Union* (Boston: Little, Brown and Company, 1868).

if it so desires, carry out its functions on a unilateral basis (which acts it may have to enforce with arms) can it be called sovereign. In reality, however, there is only the sovereignty of law. The reasons for this are plain. In a free society disputes must be weighed in the courts and, regardless of the judgment handed down, accepted.

In this country, the establishment of fundamental precepts in an organic law which is enforced by a judiciary branch as the supreme law is necessary because of the extreme diversity of population. There can be no arbitrary enactment of government due to the separation of powers within the Federal Government as well as between the nation and the states. Finally, each state is submissive and answerable to the supreme law. As Schwartz has maintained:

> One can go further and assert that the rule of law is utterly dependent upon the existence of a free society whose political institutions are endowed with authority to promote such freedom . . . The rule of law is thus both the effect and the cause of the American system of government. Representative democracy without the rule of law is a contradiction in terms. At the same time, the supremacy of the law, enforced by the courts, can only be effective in a democratic society; it is that kind of society alone that is really willing to submit conflicts to adjudication and to subordinate power to reason.[2]

The several states have never had total authority, nor have they ever been sovereign. Never in American history was any state ever recognized as a sovereign. Regardless of common misconception of "states' rights" or the statement that each state is supreme within its own border, no state has any unbridled right to act without subordination to the Constitution. Inasmuch as all states are restrained and limited in their actions they cannot be sovereign. Furthermore, they owe allegiance to the United States and may not attempt to perform acts that are expressly set aside for the Federal Government to enact. But the Constitution, generalized as it is, leaves to administrative discretion the formulation and substantive activities by which daily government becomes operational. It is this facet of law to which attention is turned.

Police Power

Because the Constitution does not specify the precise functions of government nor make any mention of state regulations for internal security, other than to indicate the limitations of the Federal Government, no ready device for protection and service remains to each state except police power. Until recent years, police power has simply meant regulation of conduct, prohibition of certain actions, and the maintenance of public order and safety. Government, particularly in the states, was of a restrictive nature.

---

[2] Bernard Schwartz, *The Powers of Government,* Vol. I (New York: The Macmillan Company, 1963), p. 29.

It seemed to exist to inhibit life rather than to promote it. This concept of governmental function was largely exercised as a result of the depression years, 1930–1940, although there had been inroads into the purely regulatory aspect of government prior to 1835. Those functions of government which we take for granted, i.e., police and fire protection, were originally in the hands of private citizens, as was the postal service and education. When it was determined that these responsibilities of public safety and welfare could most effectively be carried out by publicly controlled agencies, then the government undertook to carry them out.

The power to provide protective and preventive services by governmental bodies within the state is the police power. This power literally controls all citizen behavior within the state's boundaries. Essentially, it was originated ". . . to establish laws and ordinances of reasonable and wholesome content, with or without penalties, and not in conflict with the constitution, for the security of the general health, safety, morals, welfare, and prosperity . . ."[3] It is this power that provides the state with the right and responsibility for the provision of services of a recreational nature. Initially, this may have been used as a restrictive device, namely for the control of prostitution, gambling, and licensing of certain activities to prevent the depletion of natural and game resources, but with the passage of time its effects have taken much more of a promotional form than formerly. Today, the state is largely concerned with the provision of social, educational, cultural, and developmental opportunities which are actively encouraged in recreational experiences. Other legislative forms, rather than the police power, have been passed to provide recreational service to all people at every level of government.

RECREATIONAL SERVICE ESTABLISHMENT AND LEGISLATION

Recognition by government that recreational service, and the concomitant experiences thereby produced, is a vital and necessary part of society and a proper function of public agencies has done much to establish the movement as an important social force. Indication of governmental effect upon the impetus of the movement may be seen in its most salient form at the community or municipal level. Nevertheless, federal and state governments have had profound influence upon the provision of recreational services by acquiring regional and extensive areas whose recreational capacity and potential have been invaluable in supplementing local services. State legislation has paved the way for local implementation of recreational services. The Federal Government has done much to promote state action by undertaking surveys, offering consultation, and in many ways provoking state legislatures into expanding their respective views for the provision of recreational services.

[3] George Hjelte and Jay S. Shivers, *Public Administration of Park and Recreational Services* (New York: The Macmillan Company, 1963), pp. 10–11.

Federal Interest

An example of governmental influence on the recreational service movement may be illustrated by the Congressional enactment of 1832, whereby the Arkansas Hot Springs area was set aside for public ownership and utilization, instead of private exploitation, because of the supposed therapeutic value of the springs. This act was the forerunner of additional area acquisitions which subsequently culminated in the establishment of the National Park Service. The National Parks are essentially recreational areas administered by the National Park Service, a bureau of the U.S. Department of Interior. These parks are maintained, to a great extent, in their natural condition for the benefit and enjoyment of all the people. Preserved in national parks are spectacular canyons, caves, mountains, wilderness regions, forests, waterfalls, rivers, geysers, volcanoes, glaciers, lakes, hot springs, giant trees, and paleontological remains. The National Park Service has constructed roads and trails to enable visitors to reach various points of interest. Hotels, lodges, cabins, and camp grounds have also been made available. Park naturalists and rangers are on hand in several of the parks to conduct those interested on hikes, nature study walks, and to explain the phenomena encountered along the trails. In the evening, campfire programs, illustrated lectures, and other recreational activities are conducted. Some parks have museum and library collections. New parks are being acquired as the population growth demands additional space. Delaware Water Gap National Recreation Area, Indiana Dunes National Lakeshore, Assateague Island National Seashore off the Virginia coast, and the world's only underwater park at Key Largo Coral Reef off the Florida Keys are some of the newest acquisitions.

Although Yellowstone National Park was created in 1872, followed by Yosemite and Sequoia in 1890, the National Park Service was not established until 1916. This Service has as its major function the administration of all the national parks, 84 national monuments, 54 military and historic parks and sites, 3 national parkways, and the system of National Capital Parks in the District of Columbia and its environs. This includes administration of the National Recreational Demonstration Areas and Reservations, the best known of which are located at Lake Mead, Nevada, Shadow Mountain, Colorado, and Grand Coulee Dam in Washington.

Many federal agencies have recognized the essential aspect of recreational experience in the lives of people and have acted to provide opportunities that might otherwise be lost. More than forty federal agencies in seven departments have responsibilities for offering direct or indirect recreational services. Among these are the Department of the Interior with the National Park Service, mentioned earlier, the Fish and Wildlife Service, the Bureau of Roads, Bureau of Indian Affairs, Bureau of Reclamation, and the Bureau of Outdoor Recreation; the Department of Health, Education and Welfare with the Children's Bureau, Office of Vocational Rehabilitation Administration, Office of Education, and the Public Health Service; the Department of Agriculture with the National Forest Service, the Soil Conservation Service, and the Extension Service which offers advisory recreational service to state departments of agriculture as well as to the 4-H Club activities; the Department of Commerce with the Area Redevelopment Administration; and the Department of Defense with the Corps of Engineers, who have done much to augment recreational spaces and specialized sites through dam building, flood control, and rivers and harbor construction. The Tennessee Valley Authority, The Veterans Administration, the Urban Renewal Administration (formerly the Federal Security Agency), the depression-inspired Works Progress Administration, the Civilian Conservation Corps—all discharged notable achievements in direct and incidental provision of recreational service and did much to inspire a great deal of state and local legislation for the organization and operation of recreational service departments.

It is not the intent of this chapter to supply the names, duties, and offerings of a recreational nature of all the federal agencies involved, but merely to suggest that such legislation as was enacted by the National Government to initiate these services did more to develop the legal establishment of recreational service as a governmental function than almost anything else. Surely private groups and individuals such as Jane Addams, Jacob Riis, Joseph Lee, Luther Gulick, and others did an enormous amount of work in pioneering the American recreational service movement. Nevertheless, it was still necessary for government to pass suitable legislation for the movement to gain legal status and establishment.

State Intent

Early state interest and recognition of recreational service as an important facet of social living were manifest in the beginning of state park development and systems. Such acquisitions for this type of area probably resulted from a desire on the part of the states to emulate the Federal Government's reservation of natural sites as potential recreational spaces. However, it is in the enactment of legislation that the state has recognized the general need of the total population for recreational services. Perhaps the first instances of state awareness came through the passage of legislation allowing the utilization of school properties for recreational and other civic purposes. In addition, the subsequent development of recreational services by some state agencies, including consultative and direct leadership from universities and colleges, extended such activities. Today, many state recreational services are rendered by the following agencies: conservation, agriculture, natural resources, parks, planning, youth, library, education, higher education, highway, fish and game, forests, and when created, recreational service commissions, departments, boards or other state-designated authority.

The first state to enact legislation allowing schools to be used for community recreational purposes was Indiana in 1859, although no school funds were permitted to support this project. However, when New York State authorized the City of Rochester to provide community use of schools for recreational purposes in 1907, it also allowed school funds to be made available. This was the first time that such a step had ever been taken by a state legislature and the experiment attracted much favorable attention and emulation. A logical question which arises is, Why was such a long period of time necessary between the Indiana enactment, the Rochester experiment, and the major state developments for recreational service in 1945? The following factors may be cited for this retarded pace and may lead to some answers:

1. Inadequate knowledge of the need for and significance of recreational experiences in human life.
2. Failure to understand the need for planned provision of recreational opportunities.
3. Inadequate education of state legislators by recreationists to explain the need for state action and concern for recreational services.
4. A disinclination to organize and coordinate the recreational functions charged to various state agencies, such as they were.
5. Lack of understanding concerning the need for a state authority to undertake primary responsibility for the provision of leisure opportunities and recreational services at the state level.
6. A disinclination to expend or appropriate funds for promotional projects.
7. The prevailing political philosophy that the state was a restrictive rather than a promotional body.

With all of these detrimental aspects, it is remarkable that such permissive legislation was ever enacted in the latter half of the nineteenth century. It took two world wars, a panic, a depression, and a vast communications network before state governments awoke to common needs. Even after 1920, only twenty states had passed sufficient enabling legislation effecting public recreational service. The first true state authority was established as recently as 1945 when North Carolina passed a law creating its Recreation Commission. In 1947, California passed a bill creating a state recreational service commission, which, in 1959, was consolidated into the Department of Natural Resources. Vermont established a state board in 1947 after the governor appointed a state director of recreational service in 1944. Other states have legislated the creation of recreational bureaus, divisions, or other appropriate office designations in a variety of state departments whose primary function may or may not be recreational. In many instances it is incidental to the major concern of the agency; in some instances it is the primary function of the agency. New Hampshire has a recreational service division in its forestry department; Kentucky has a similar division in its conservation department; Florida and Missouri have recreational divisions in their respective developmental and resources agencies. Louisiana has a little-used recreational division in its Department of Parks. The states of Wisconsin, New York, Pennsylvania, Indiana, Connecticut, Illinois, and Washington employ recreationists in a variety of departments including their respective Youth Boards or Commissions, Mental Health Departments, or Health Departments to provide consultive and demonstration projects throughout the state. Michigan has a State Interagency Council for Recreational Service within its Department of Commerce. Indiana has recently appointed a state director of recreational service as has Washington.

State Enabling Legislation. The chief legislative enactment by which the state recognizes its responsibilities for the provision of recreational services to its constituents has been broad enabling acts. For the most comprehensive, intensive opportunities and tangible means of offering state support for these functions, permissive legislation signifying local prerogative for the operation and administration of departments supplying recreational programs have been most effective. During the initial phase of the recreational service movement, when children's playgrounds were being established in cities, state enabling laws for local recreational service were not significant because after the historic Missouri Act of 1875, which gave rise to the "Home Rule" law, large municipalities depended upon their charters for the required power.

There is no state without some legislation on its books applicable to or affecting some aspect of state and local provision for recreational services. In many cases, state law stipulates the local bodies in which the operation of public recreational service will reside. Generally, but not always, such authorization includes the power to appropriate funds, acquire land, develop areas, construct facilities, and employ suitable personnel. In a few states, laws directing the operation of recreational services designate specific cities by class, counties, townships, special districts, regional government, and school districts as the recreational authority. Several states have passed a single organic law of such an inclusive nature that the local legal subdivision has complete autonomy in selecting the agency to provide recreational services.

The characteristic feature employed by broad general recreational service enabling legislation is the empowering of any division of local government to organize, operate, and administer a public tax-supported recreational program for all of the people. The general law also permits legal cooperation between two or more corporate entities, e.g., city-county relations; municipality-school district relations; or special district-city relations. It must be remembered that enabling acts are permissive and not mandatory in binding local governments to perform recreational functions. Special purpose and regulatory acts, aimed at the conduct or operation of a specific phase of recreational service are authorizations and requirements to act. Typical of the language usually written into broad enabling legislation is the following statement:

> Any local legal subdivision of the state may select an existing agency of government or create and establish a new agency to have direct responsibility for the organization and operation of recreational services for the citizens of the community. The agency shall be directed to do all of those things necessary and incidental to the provision of such services and shall be supported by tax funds. Said agency shall join or cooperate with one or more extra-corporate or other legal subdivisions of the state in executing the functions for which it was established.

In some instances, however, state enabling legislation is quite narrow and restrictive. Such legislation not only designates the agency to be authorized which will administer recreational services, but is usually explicit in dealing with how the agency will be financed, how much of the tax dollar can be expended on facilities, the types of facilities and their number, the titles of personnel to be employed, the classification of local government to which this act may be applied, and other regulations which are tacked onto the bill. Enabling legislation, other than to focus local government attention on the need for recreational service, in recent years has not been as important as formerly because of the wider use of home rule legislation. Even in states where home rule has not been universally adopted, recreational enabling legislation is getting away from the narrow form and moving toward broad acts which can encompass most local customs and probabilities.

State enabling acts for recreational service should be of the broadest type to provide the widest latitude to local governments in determining the procedures best suited for them in their organization, maintenance, and operation of public recreational services. Any restrictive provisions that tend to hinder or prohibit the logical development of recreational services should be shunned.

Progress is being made, but it is neither constant nor is it uniform. Variability is justified and desirable, depending upon the traditions and financial resources available for funding specialized agencies. However, the states are and have been notoriously slow to approve recreational service as a primary responsibility and direct function of the state. This unfortunate situation is being improved as the request for recreational services continues to grow unabated and increases current pressures upon legislatures. With a highly literate and vastly informed public, the states are finding it difficult to turn a deaf ear to the incessant demand for more and competent services of a recreational nature in order to take advantage of leisure opportunities available to nearly all citizens.

Local Action

American cities are no longer dominated by absolute state control. State constitutions have been amended or completely rewritten, in some instances, to grant municipalities a large measure of self-control, whereas in other cases measures have been taken to limit the worst abuses of the legislature's power. The state is no longer free to handle purely local matters nor regulate local jurisdictions. States must adhere to constitutional law. One of the greatest acts of emancipation of cities from state legislative abuse and regulation was municipal home rule. The exact meaning of home rule does not suggest complete freedom from state influence. Rather it means that state control will be exercised where such matters of state-wide concern are involved, and that in problems arising from local situations, authority will reside with the community so involved. Essentially, municipal home rule may be defined as the power of the city to control, regulate, and dominate its own affairs. Chiefly, the whole home rule concept has to do with local autonomy and the way in which public services are carried out. Today, municipalities, particularly the urban giants, are attempting to provide comprehensive recreational services conducted by professional personnel. But it was not always so.

Prior to 1850, private influence was the dominant force in the progress of the recreational service movement. The establishment of sandpiles on the schoolgrounds of Boston in 1885 was sponsored by a private body. It was not until 1899, that tax funds were utilized to support recreational functions in the Boston school system. New York City had the foresight to develop Central Park in 1853, but only after the turn of the century could any real public recreational service movement be discerned in the city. Yet, there is a basic principle working which implies that recreational service is a fit subject and responsibility for municipal concern. School administrators seemed to be the first professionals to apply this principle, for the school systems of several cities pioneered the provision of recreational services years before municipal government finally accepted recreational service as a public function.

Citizen petitions to the school committee of Boston forced approval of the use of school property for recreational purposes in 1901. Following suit, New York City's school board established recreational centers in several schools. This plan was the forerunner of the school-community center plan now extant in New York City. In 1902, the City of Chicago erected two large field houses in the South Park system which were financed by a $3,000,000 bond issue. In 1903, New York City organized the Public School Athletic League. Los Angeles was the first city to operate recreational services on a community-wide basis under a special playground commission and by 1907, St. Louis, Oakland, and Minneapolis had organized recreational service authorities. Rochester was the first city to make full use of its school buildings as recreational centers in 1907, and Newark, Milwaukee, and Boston soon followed the pattern.

The first two decades of the twentieth century actually brought recreational service, as a public function, to the attention of municipal authorities. The progress that was made during that time was tremendous by virtue of the innovational idea of promoting these services. It must be reiterated that the concept of operating public agencies for the purpose of making recreational opportunities available through tax support was considered radical. Indeed, there are communities today which still have that notion. Nevertheless, there was a determined movement by progressive jurisdictions to enact statute, code, and legislative implementation whereby recreational services could be offered as widely as possible by public agencies.

Tremendous impetus was given to municipal legislative enactment for recreational services by the consequent rise of free time and the reduction of working hours during the period between 1920–1950. As Fitzgerald stated, "The forty-hour week was the signal for educators, recreationists and public officials to give increased thought to and provision for extended recreation facilities and programs." [4] The ten years of depression following the boom years of the twenties served as a great stimulus to the recreational service movement. Municipalities, acting with federal funds, put men to work in constructing facilities and developing property which, upon completion, were utilized for recreational activities. Local communities reacted to the deepening calamity by making new efforts to provide for citizen betterment. Laws were passed whereby public and private agencies might work out cooperative actions. Federal recreational projects greatly multiplied local jurisdictional activities. The municipalities responded with emergency measures to gear federal aid and developmental programs to supplement and complement existing programs. The means for setting up a municipal establishment to assume complete authority for the operation of recreational services after the withdrawal of federal assistance was nothing short of phenomenal. Cities, which never before had considered such responsibility, reacted to the emergency with plans, personnel, and action supported by new legal enactments. On the whole, then, the principle of recreational service as the direct responsibility of city government was really espoused and accepted during this time. Significantly, state enabling legislation for recreational services also received much stimulation with the result of providing a stable base for local improvement and consideration of recreational service as an important segment of municipal function.

World War II emphasized the need for increased funds and leadership within municipal programs. With ten million men and women in the armed services and millions more employed in defense-related industries, towns were forced to plan for a mobile and newly rich population. Small communities that never before had experienced transient populations were

[4] Gerald B. Fitzgerald, *Community Organization for Recreation* (New York: A. S. Barnes and Company, 1948), p. 30.

swelled by nearby armed forces centers. Cities had to organize to compensate for the needs developed by war conditions. Many citizens took the opportunity to become active in community affairs on a scale hitherto unknown, and recreational councils, committees, and boards were established. Public and private agencies and organizations were forced to coordinate their activities and this association led to increased confidence and cooperation in the planning and direction of recreational services to meet community needs. In the aftermath of war some letdown in the feverish activity was to be expected. It came, and with it the apathy that has so often been the traditional hallmark of conservative government. Everyone expected some depression to come after the war years and so a wave of economic moves and retrenchments were instituted. Departments were consolidated for "economy" reasons, recreationist positions were left vacant or abolished. When the economy continued to expand, then state and local governments began to leave their conservative ideas behind.

The Korean police action, followed by a resumption of the cold war caused considerable apprehension and once again placed the United States on a limited war footing. The young men who went to war and returned had been exposed to a better recreational service provision than had been their relatives of the two preceding wars. Inasmuch as the Selective Service Act, originally passed in 1939, had never been repealed, many young males were exposed to a variety of well-organized and operated recreational services administered by Special Services in the military branches. When the soldiers returned to civilian life it seemed natural to expect such services to be provided by local government. A new round of committee and council hearings within the municipality, and communities of all sizes, became commonplace as this younger generation sought to convince local authorities of the need for expanding existing departments or establishing new services of a recreational nature. In the ten-year period after the cessation of hostilities in Korea, the gross national product had soared to more than one-half trillion dollars. The Federal Government has created a space agency and is busily absorbed in placing a man on the moon. The fantasies of "Buck Rogers in the 25th Century" seem to be closer than many think. New York City electrical workers have won a twenty-five hour week and other unions are demanding a greater share of the nation's economic boom. There is a new leisure, greater economic means, a higher incidence of mobility, faster methods of transportation, a mass means of communication that offers tremendous news coverage and instantaneous appreciation of the facts while they are becoming history. Americans in 1967, have the wherewithal to do what they want to do when they want to do it. This places increased responsibility for the planning, development, and conservation of recreational facilities and spaces on all levels of government.

How are the various levels of government meeting this challenge? There

104 Principles of Recreational Service

is a vast appreciation of the need for recreational services by all people. This has manifested itself in terms of the coordination and joint planning by all levels of government and the pumping of tax dollars by the Federal Government directly into local as well as state coffers to be spent for acquiring recreational areas and open space.[5] The assumption of state responsibility for recreational services, the passage of new legislation for the establishment of state authority in which this primary function will reside, and the increased incidence of state stimulation to local government as well as tax support for planning and developing recreational service systems have had a considerable influence in several sections of the United States. Since the beginning of the organized recreational service movement in America, considerable pressure has been exerted upon local jurisdictional phases of organized recreational opportunities. The actual accomplishment of all communities, within the last forty years, concerning provision of recreational services to all represents a great step forward in social achievement.

Additional progress is being observed daily as this movement succeeds in gaining the interest and effort of state and national levels. To this must be added the remonstrance that this effort is a long way from reaching its goal although municipal and other local governments are attempting to satisfy public requirements. The widespread importance of recreational opportunity and experience in the American way of life makes mandatory additional legislative enactment to fulfill the early promise of comprehensive service and equal opportunity for all people.

THE WAY AHEAD

Still, there is much to be done and much is being done, stimulated by a major population increase, a decrease in suitable space for recreational purposes, the high density of population in urban centers, the growth of strip cities or megalopolis, automation and its by-product massive leisure, great population mobility, and cheap money. Spurred on by these pressures and obvious deficits, new legislation is being enacted to afford necessary recreational opportunities for people everywhere.

Federal Legislation

Some ten years ago, a senator from Utah introduced in Congress a bill authorizing a federal recreational service within the now-abolished Federal Security Agency. The bill was never brought to a vote and subsequent bills of this type have met the same fate. Since that time, the Federal Government has created the National Recreation Resources Review Commission, which performed invaluable service to the growth and spread of the national recreational movement through its surveys of present and potential

[5] *The Urban Renewal Program Fact Sheet* (Washington, D.C.: Housing and Home Finance Agency, Urban Renewal Administration, 1961), p. 4.

recreational needs, and led directly to the establishment of the Bureau of Outdoor Recreation in the Department of the Interior. Although this is a step in the right direction, it hardly meets the clear and present needs of urban centers and the more than seventy per cent of the total population who comprise their respective constituencies. What is really required is a Federal Bureau of Recreational Services, situated in the Department of Health, Education and Welfare or in the newly created Department of Urban Affairs and Housing. Such a bureau would be the action agency of the National Government in all matters concerning recreational projects. This agency would provide broadened recreational service directly to states and local governments as requested. It would serve as the coordinating body at the federal level for agencies involved in direct or indirect provision of recreational services so that optimum utilization of national recreational spaces and programs could be made without duplication. Such a bill would authorize technical assistance to any governmental agency relating to the most economical use of potential space for recreational purposes, design and functional use of a variety of buildings, personnel standards, and recreational activities. The coordination function called for in the establishment of such a federal bureau now rests with the Bureau of Outdoor Recreation. However, this Bureau is oriented to open space and natural resources, and although it is supposed to provide planning consideration for urban centers, its official designation and primary efforts are hardly likely to be focused in that direction. The population increment will largely be contained in present metropolitan areas. High density cities are projecting an even larger population forecast during the next twenty to thirty years. This country will need an agency whose chief orientation is to the plight and possible solutions of urban centers. The problem of providing recreational planning and coordination, and effecting more competent services to the metropolitan areas will be resolved by a federally constituted agency whose primary function it will be to work with, by, and for the modern city.

A Federal Bureau of Recreational Service would compile, publish, and disseminate specialized data including statistics relating to recreational expenditures, facilities, and pertinent research being carried on in the field. Provision would be made to list all agencies having any responsibility, and the nature of the responsibility, for recreational service as well as the agencies which can offer financial assistance for the rendition of recreational service. The bureau should be empowered to fund researches relating to educational, professional, or practical demonstration projects. Included, then, would be pilot community programs which might lead to the full-time establishment of local recreational service departments, educational studies made by institutions of higher education for a variety of investigations leading to the promotion of more competent services, and assistance to state and local agencies for the development of areas and facilities having primary recreational use. Finally, it would call for the abolition of the

Bureau of Outdoor Recreation and its placement as a division within the new Bureau of Recreational Service, thus insuring coverage of rural and sparsely populated regions as well as urban areas without needless waste of funds or futile duplication. Any legislation authorizing such an agency would not impair or disrupt the authority or responsibility of any other department or office within the Federal Government, except as that noted herein.

That such an act is needed cannot be doubted. When it will receive congressional attention is questionable. However, the Congress will be forced to act as the full force of urban congestion and population expansion create the demand for increased federal aid. The significance of recreational experience to American culture and society is self-evident, and action by the Federal Government is needed in a field so vital to national life. To prevent widespread exploitation of natural resources for a few rather than all can only be performed when such areas receive federal protection. Present recreational services of the Federal Government are inconsistent, directed to regions which are already rich in natural resources, and not effective in sections that are highly populated and where open spaces are at a premium or are almost depleted. A distinct need for guidance on the part of state and local governments, if the development of recreational services is desirable, as well as their movement for express action may be hastened by federal stimulation. Legislation of the type described will be forthcoming within the next decade; it cannot be otherwise. The need is undiminished now and will continue to increase as population increases. Population forecasts indicate that by 1970, more than 200,000,000 people, at a minimum, will live in the United States. It is not farfetched to predict that the Federal Government will have to act where other levels of government cannot.

State Legislation

Coordinated planning and action on a state-wide level seems to be the chief means of ensuring adequate provision of recreational opportunity for all of the people. Current action of states in the development of recreational services is one consequence of the deficits which the states have allowed to build up over the years. Now, there is realization of the importance, to many groups, of a service of a recreational nature, and states are attempting, even if belatedly, to secure legislation that can facilitate ways to satisfy needs. The structure of state government, together with the collection of agencies having some responsibility for recreational service, requires a plan that can meet the diverse needs of people as well as the special needs of the particular state. The whole concept of state-wide planning must be made with the same scrupulous care for the degree of difference to be encountered in individual states as is made for variability at the local level. The characteristic aspect of recreational experience is its wide latitude and impact upon human life; this factor does not change regardless of the governmental level which endeavors to promote it. For this reason, the several states have undertaken particular recreational responsibility and interest, motivated, no doubt, by the same stimuli which have prompted local actions along the same lines.

Any legislation that is proposed will have to consider the following:

1. The collection, arrangement, and analysis of all legislation pertaining to recreational service within the given state as well as the nature of legislation enacted in other states relating to the same issue.
2. The thorough investigation of recreational service responsibilities and functions currently assumed by state agencies and the means whereby improved cooperation between such departments may be facilitated.
3. The determination of various means by which public awareness and recognition for recreational services in community life can be fostered, organized, and maintained.
4. The assembly, collation, and classification of current investigations on recreational service within the state produced by both state and local agencies.
5. The implementation, insofar as is feasible, of legislation authorizing one central state body to be responsible for the major functions of providing recreational services to the state-at-large.
6. Based upon these studies, the development of a state-wide plan for the design, construction, and maintenance of recreational facilities; systematic acquisition of land and water areas, to be held in perpetuity, for recreational purposes; the development of space and facility standards to which all local governments may apply for matching grants-in-aid; and personnel standards, set in cooperation with institutions of higher education offering preparatory curricula in recreational service education as well as professional organizational personnel policy statements, to ensure competent practice.

State governments must be encouraged to pass legislation for the establishment of a recreational service authority independent of other state departments and directly responsible to the governor.

Only with the proper legislation establishing a central state authority can it be hoped that the essential services will be effected. Total recognition of individual as well as group and corporate needs will serve as the motivational factors for providing those functions which are an integral part of any state level agency. Legal enactment of bills for the authorization of recreational service as the sole responsibility of *one* state agency will be reflected throughout the state by increased assistance to local communities in the organization and administration of recreational provisions. Devices such as a consulting program available to all communities upon request can be attainable only when it becomes a prime duty of the state authority. Although other state agencies may rightly have primary, secondary, or incidental recreational responsibility, their respective functions should be facilitated through a high degree of coordination so that they can be aided in offering such services. The state authority, in its coordinative capacity, can also act as the medium by which the collection, analysis, and dissemination of recreational service information of all kinds may be exchanged between agencies. Furthermore, the state is the only level at which responsibility is at once the basic focus of attention in urban and rural regions. Thus, both corporate and unincorporated areas and their populations are assured of continuing recreational services. Finally, the state agency is in the best position to promote, as well as determine, professional personnel standards for potential certification procedures and to assist in the recruitment and placement of recreationists.

Local Legislation

The entire concept of recreational service being a proper function of local government has received widespread recognition. As government is a social institution created by people for the provision of necessary and elemental services, which by individual means could not be so economically or effectively performed, the processes by which recreational opportunities are made available to citizens is especially adapted to the province of local administration. Every person in the community supports local governmental functions by a system of taxes and other money raising measures and obtains in return a level of service consistent with the ability of the community to provide these services. The history of the recreational movement indicates the past recognition of the local jurisdiction to concern itself with recreational services. Current awareness by local governments of the necessity to serve all of the people all of the time presents communities with the precept that total opportunity means financial responsibility and operation of a public department whose prime purpose it is to place at everyone's disposal the program, leadership, and facilities for wholesome enjoyment of leisure.

There is no intent here to discuss the administration of public recreational service, but to treat the procedure by which local authority can be empowered to perform. Essentially, the local civil subdivision must either take advantage of a charter or home rule grant, or, if these enactments are not established, any existing state enabling legislation for the declaration of legal assumption of recreational service functions. As is well known, there are many legislative forms for the establishment of local community recreational service. Whatever type of ordinance or statute it takes to create a department according to local tradition, and influenced by state grants of powers to perform, should be taken.

The organizational patterns and legal recourses for the establishment of operating authorities for local recreational service administration are as varied as individual communities make them. One outstanding factor which remains, however, is the need to accept, as an integral part of government, the function of recreational service. Once this is recognized, the creation of a separate authority becomes almost mandatory. There is increasing evidence, based upon historic precedence, current social mores, and potential technological progress, that leisure and opportunity for recreational experience are primary factors of the American way of life. Where required, in the absence of established governmental forms to perform, special recreational service districts of a regional character should be organized. Such agencies would have legal authority to function within or without corporate areas, and not be limited by geopolitical boundaries if the agencies' functions could be carried on successfully. This kind of recreational authority is provided ". . . with grants of power formerly retained by both city and county and assigning to it explicit functions for designated activities . . ."[6] concerning recreational service.

SUMMARY

When some aspect of social existence has been found to be of importance to the general welfare, then legal sanction is applied to bring that experience into public domain by empowering some agency with the necessary authority, financial support, and personnel commensurate with its significance in individual, local, state, and national life. Such has been the case of recreational service and the myriad opportunities which it offers to all people. Acting for the common good and without dependence upon other governmental agencies, the recreational service authority must possess the same status and receive the same treatment as other local or state departments enjoy. Sound and broad legislative enactments are the most reliable measures to ensure adequate, effective, and official recognition of this logical public service. The people are best served when enlightened legislators enact laws which provide for wide latitude and great discretionary powers in the provision of recreational services.

SELECTED REFERENCES

CORBETT, P. E., *Law and Society in the Relation of States.* (New York: Harcourt Brace and Co.), 1965.

CORWIN, E. S., *Constitution and What It Means Today,* rev. ed. (Princeton: Princeton University Press), 1958.

CORWIN, E. S., *National Supremacy: Treaty Power vs. State Power.* (New York: Peter Smith), 1965.

EDMUNDS, PALMER D., *Law and Civilization.* (Washington, D.C.: Public Affairs Press), 1959.

FISHER, MARGUERITE J. and DONALD G. BISHOP, *Municipal and Other Local Governments.* (Englewood Cliffs, N.J.: Prentice-Hall), 1950.

---

[6] Hjelte and Shivers, *op. cit.,* p. 16.

GARBER, L. O. and N. EDWARDS, *Law Governing School Property and School Building Construction.* (Danville, Ill.: Interstate Printers and Publishers, Inc.), 1964.

———, *Law Governing the Financing of Public Education.* (Danville, Ill.: Interstate Printers and Publishers, Inc.), 1964.

GRAY, HAMISH R., *Law of Civil Injuries.* (New York: Hillary House Publishers, Ltd.), 1965.

JENKS, C. W., *Law, Freedom and Welfare.* (Dobbs Ferry, N.Y.: Oceana Publications, Inc.), 1964.

JENNINGS, I., *Law and the Constitution,* 5th ed. (Mystic, Conn.: Lawrence Verry, Inc.), 1963.

MOBERLY, Walter, *Legal Responsibility and Moral Responsibility.* (Philadelphia, Pa.: Fortress Press, 1956.

PHILLIPS, JEWELL C., *Municipal Government and Administration in America.* (New York: The Macmillan Company), 1960.

ROSENBLUM, VICTOR G., *Law as a Political Instrument.* (New York: Random House), 1955.

SHEPPARD, PAUL, *Sovereignty and State-Owned Entities.* (New York: Twayne Publishers), 1965.

SOWLE, CLAUDE R., ed., *Police Power and Individual Freedom.* (Chicago, Ill.: Aldine Publishing Co.), 1962.

Chapter 5

SOCIAL MOVEMENT

> PRINCIPLE: Imbalances in society inevitably generate a counter force or action designed to alleviate such conditions. Generally, dissatisfaction with mores, disintegration of traditions, disparity of economic power, bigotry, political negligence, or necessity of not having essential needs met has caused social upheavals, both of a positive and negative type, which may be termed movements.

THE RECREATIONAL MOVEMENT

The recreational movement grew out of social situations which were products of population migrations, urbanization, industrialization, mass education, mobility, mechanization, and leisure. According to Dr. Clarence Rainwater, the recreational tradition was part of the culture brought to these shores by men of an enlightened age. The cavaliers of the Tidewater region in the Virginias and Carolinas lived a rich recreational existence. Even Puritan New England, which at first suppressed recreational opportunities, was forced to concede recreational activity a place in the life of the people. Colonial America had a rich heritage of the recreational life. Nevertheless, the recreational tradition in the American culture suffered a decline during the formative years of national growth and development as a result of an expanding urban structure with its congestion, an overwhelming devotion to materialism and commercialism, and the basic isolation of rural districts. However, with the passage of time a movement of great impetus and inherent value spread throughout the country. Its inception may have been from a parallel development in the field of education in the middle 1800's or with the establishment of sand gardens for children in Boston in 1885. Regardless of the initial stage, this social movement has revitalized American life. The Neumeyers have this to say:

> Pioneer leaders sensed the situation and called attention to the necessity of providing recreation for the masses, especially for the underprivileged groups. Various organizations and agencies began to do something about it and pioneered in establishing new ways of meeting a felt need. One event followed another, resulting in a more concerted effort and a spread of attempts to provide new forms of recreation for people who otherwise lacked opportunities for them. As the movement progressed, objectives

and standards emerged, leaders were trained for the supervision of recreation, transitions took place in the program of activities, and the movement progressed through various stages of development.[1]

Recreational Service and Divisions of Culture

The recreational service movement is in part a response to the changing functions of the family. Urbanization, mass mobility, and communication have removed the family from its former position of centrality and placed the recreational pattern surrounding the home environment into the school, the church, the neighborhood, the recreational center, and the community at large. Because there is more leisure, more money with which to do things during leisure, and wider horizons as a result of mass communications and education to identify a variety of leisure pursuits, the home is the scene of less recreational activity. But with this apparent family-recreational disintegration there has been an upsurge in individual interest in community patterns of recreational service and public affairs.

Among the trends to be observed in connection with the current pattern of recreational services are the provision of spaces and facilities in which mass as well as individual recreational opportunities may be fulfilled and the increasing diversity of comprehensive programs which include aesthetic, educational, cultural, social, as well as physical experiences. More and more communities throughout the nation are organizing and operating full or part-time recreational service departments financed from public funds. Educational devices to inform the public of the massive opportunities available are in keeping with identification of governmental functions for the promotion of public welfare.

The broadening of recreational horizons by stimulating interest and effort on the part of would-be participants to the possibilities that await them may have to begin artificially. However, once the experiment has started, the activity generates enough interest to perpetuate itself and to ignite the individual's ideas of further experiences. This objective is often accomplished through the organizational efforts of the recreational service movement. The agencies which make up the movement and the personnel involved form the resources for stimulation. In the final analysis, it is to the schools that the entire movement must turn for the educational emphasis of skills for leisure. A main responsibility of the educational system must be for the beneficial uses of leisure and the enrichment of recreational living.

One of the great social movements to appear in the era of technological change is that of recreational service and its objective of providing a great opportunity for the cultural enhancement of life. Although there is no one national recreational program, there are many community patterns which would appear to make the movement one of national significance. Increas-

---

[1] Martin H. Neumeyer and Esther S. Neumeyer, *Leisure and Recreation: A Study of Leisure and Recreation in Their Sociological Aspects,* 3rd ed. (New York: The Ronald Press Company, 1958), p. 64.

ingly, state and federal governments are providing agencies, finances, and leadership in securing perpetually dedicated areas and facilities for the development of recreational pursuits. That the movement will continue to grow in the second half of this century is a certainty. Its past and contemporary trends are therefore offered to illustrate what has been and what might be.

The Recreational Service Movement in the United States

In the late nineteenth century the establishment of the public recreational service field was initiated. In 1885, the first public tax-supported recreational facility was created in Boston when a sand pile was placed in a mission yard to provide a safe area where children could play. The idea, brought back from Germany by Dr. Maria Zakrewska, was so popular that school grounds soon had sand piles on them. In 1889, the City of Boston budgeted tax money to meet part of the expense which the provision of a directed program made necessary. Boston also established the Charlesbank Outdoor Gymnasium in 1889, and created the forty-acre Franklin Field in 1894. The Boston School Committee appropriated $3,000 for public recreational purposes in 1898.

New York City converted a tenement area into what is now known as Seward Park, under the promptings of Jacob Riis and his antislum newspaper campaigns. This park, developed at a cost of $1,800,000, was phenomenal for the year 1897. In 1899, the New York City School Board allowed school property to be utilized for recreational purposes, specifically playground activities. Newark, New Jersey, also consented to the use of school property for recreational functions. In Chicago, the Neighborhood Guild, inaugurated to relieve the plight of the poor in 1887, was followed by Hull House in 1889. The first private summer camps were established in 1880. The Young Men's Christian Association, established in 1851, and the Young Women's Christian Association, established in 1866, originally for other than recreational purposes, became extremely interested in the possibilities that recreational activities might have for and on their respective programs.

These few examples indicate the importance that was attached to organized recreational service. In the brief period of 15 years, between 1885 and 1900, tax-supported recreational service agencies began to attain official sanction from legally established municipal departments.

The growth of recreational service as a function of government which parallels in time the acquirement of almost universal leisure represents one of the interesting public developments of the present century. Previously regarded as purely the prerogative of the individual citizen in his private capacity, recreational service is now considered a field of human activity in which government must manifest some concern and render some aid. Under the police power authorized by the supremacy of organized government, leisure activities, which were early stigmatized as being harmful and destructive, were regulated or prohibited. The laws restricting certain activities on the Sabbath, laws regulating hunting, fishing, prize fighting, gambling, traveling circuses, and dispensing of alcoholic beverages, are examples in point. Only in the present century, and then only within the last forty years, has government in the United States gone generally beyond the province of regulation and control to assume a more positive function of "promoting the general welfare" through recreational service.

Urbanization brought crowded living conditions and many new ideas for commercialistic enterprise. The beer gardens of Philadelphia, amusement parks, extravagant settings such as the Barnum and Baily circuses, an upsurge in theatre attendance, the advent of baseball in 1859, all served to spearhead what was to become a vast movement serving the recreational needs of people. As early as 1830, colleges had allowed their students to participate in outdoor games and had begun to build gymnasia. During the late 1860's athletic clubs of all kinds appeared in colleges.

Although the focus of municipal politicians was on an expanding economy, the lack of citizen enlightenment and absence of an aroused public opinion resulted in recreationally blighted communities. The consequences of this political ineptitude allowed forests to be cut down indiscriminately and replaced by brick and steel, and cement structures; streams were damned and rerouted to accommodate thoroughfares; rivers were allowed to become polluted by industrial and domestic waste; warehouses and wharfs obliterated the waterfronts. We reap the harvest of this imprudent action. Traffic, both pedestrian and vehicular, filled the streets as homes with open spaces disappeared from the American scene. Railroad apartments and multi-storied dwellings replaced private homes in the urban center. In rare instances some municipalities actually planned for park and other recreational spaces, but in nearly all cases urban development meant urban blight.

The Park Movement. Parks in the American culture had their beginnings as far back as 1565, when the first known municipal plaza, or central open space, was built in St. Augustine, Florida. Many of these regions were first settled by the Spanish, which had a decisive influence on the architectural style of the facilities that were constructed. Spanish architecture always employed open porticos and plazas to enhance a structure, and this custom was repeated in the New World. Moreover, it is quite logical that cities in the southern and southwestern sections of the country would construct open spaces within the city, for in this way the inhabitants could take advantage of the relatively mild climates which prevailed in those regions.

The park movement in America was, until the beginning of the present century, primarily a movement for the improvement of the aesthetic appearance of certain areas. Apart from the rapid increase in the number of parks, the most significant development in the movement has been the change in concept of the function of the park. Parks are now considered as places of pleasing and attractive appearance which are set aside for varied forms of recreational activity. Another interesting development has been the establishment of large parks away from the center of cities and regional parks accessible only by automotive means of transportation. The local areas formerly considered as neighborhood parks are now thought of as playgrounds and recreational centers. The trend is toward providing an attractive open space where vigorous physical recreational experiences may be provided—the signs prohibiting such activity are no longer so prevalent as previously.

The Mid-century Years. By 1950, a well-established need for recreational service on every level of government had developed in the United States. In this year, the National Recreation Association received reports from more than 2,000 communities operating public recreational service agencies.[2] These reports showed that the number of playgrounds had increased twelve times since 1910, and indoor recreational centers had increased thirty-three times during the same period. The first national conference on aging occurred in 1950, during the Truman administration, and was repeated in 1961. One of the ten topics devoted to gerontological problems was that of free time activities.

Perhaps the most visible program to take place was "Mission 66," a ten-year master plan for the development of modern recreational facilities and sites in the National Parks. Started in 1956, the program has already been responsible for the construction of a new lodge at the Mt. Rushmore Memorial, camp grounds of excellent quality at Theodore Roosevelt National Memorial Park in North Dakota, recreational facilities at Lake Meade National Recreational Area in Nevada, and many other observable and highly necessary constructions. This has been one of the most outstanding contributions made to the recreational life of the American people. "Operation Outdoors" is the Department of Agriculture's Forest Service corresponding program and effort to keep up with the expanding use of the national forests.

In 1958, the Outdoor Recreation Resources Review Commission was activated and the survey performed by this group led to the creation, in 1962, of the Bureau of Outdoor Recreation administered in the Department of the Interior. This Bureau, as an action agency, serves in a consultant capacity to state and local subdivisions concerning the planning and development of parks, historical areas, wildlife and waterfowl areas, and other outdoor recreational spaces. The Soil Conservation Service of the U.S. Department of Agriculture under Public Law 566, as amended by the Food and Agriculture Act of 1962, may provide up to fifty per cent of the cost of the land, easements, and rights-of-way for reservoir and other facilities required for recreational activity. These are only a few examples of the continual assistance given by federal agencies to the recreational service movement.

[2] *Recreation and Park Yearbook: Midcentury Edition* (New York: National Recreation Association, 1950).

The states, too, have been partially effective in promoting services of a recreational nature to their constituents during the sixties. Many states have begun to implement a shared cost system for the acquisition of open spaces for recreational purposes and not a few have long-term plans for regionalizing within their borders to make more efficient recreational service developments. Most states have planning boards or departments that have primary responsibility for the planning and construction of regional recreational facilities which tend to equalize recreational opportunities for people. Some states even provide consulting services to local communities.

SUMMARY

By 1900, only a few cities had made provision for public playgrounds, but rapid advancement has been made, and now nearly all cities have recreational areas available, some with highly organized programs supervised by professional practitioners. Writing in 1921, Clarence E. Rainwater traced nine transitions in the play movement:

> (1) From provision for little children to that for all ages of people; (2) from facilities operated during the summer only, to those maintained throughout the year; (3) from outdoor equipment and activities only, to both outdoor and indoor facilities and events; (4) from congested urban districts to both urban and rural communities; (5) from philanthropic to community support and control; (6) from 'free' play and miscellaneous events to 'directed' play with organized activities and correlated schedules; (7) from a simple to a complex field of activities including manual, physical, aesthetic, social, and civic projects; (8) from the provision of facilities to the definition of standards for the use of leisure time; (9) from 'individual' interests to 'group' and community activities.[3]

Twenty years later, George Hjelte was able to formulate five additional modifications:

> (1) From a 'play' movement to a 'recreational' movement; (2) from a local municipal only, to a state and national movement; (3) from programs detached from public education, to programs integrated with the educational curriculum and system; (4) from organization limited to urban communities to that inclusive of sub-urban and rural areas as well; (5) from an organization largely under quasi-public control with subsidies from public funds to full acceptance of recreational service as a public function.[4]

---

[3] Clarence E. Rainwater, *The Play Movement in the United States* (Chicago: The University of Chicago Press, 1922), p. 192.
[4] George Hjelte, *The Administration of Public Recreation* (New York: The Macmillan Company, 1940), p. 16.

To these transitions may now be added the following: (1) From programs operated by laymen to those operated by professionally prepared, and, in most instances highly qualified practitioners; (2) from an amenity service to one which is considered essential to the health, welfare, and cultural development of all people; and (3) from a voluntary field of service to a professionalized occupational field of applied social science.

Recreational experience is universally recognized as one of the basic needs in human life. When a need has been identified and deemed significant to society, then governmental authority, as well as private and philanthropic enterprise, enter to help administer such needs for the mutual benefit and welfare of all concerned. It is well known that recreational activity is an aspect of life of such importance that modern society would be barren and suffer an inestimable loss without such a mode of expression.

SELECTED REFERENCES

BREDEMEIER, HARRY C. and JACKSON TOBY, *Social Problems in America*. (New York: John Wiley & Sons, Inc.), 1960.

CUBER, JOHN F. and WILLIAM F. KENKEL, *Social Stratification in the United States*. (New York: Appleton-Century-Crofts), 1954.

FURFEY, PAUL H. and MARY E. WALSH, *Social Problems and Social Action*. (Englewood Cliffs, N. J.: Prentice-Hall, Inc.), 1958.

HEBERLE, RUDOLF, *Social Movements: An Introduction to Political Sociology*. (New York: Appleton-Century-Crofts), 1951.

HIMMELSTRAND, U., *Social Pressures, Attitudes and Democratic Processes*. (New York: Humanities Press, Inc.), 1965.

HOFFSOMMER, HAROLD, *Sociology of American Life*. (Englewood Cliffs, N. J.: Prentice-Hall, Inc.), 1958.

JENNINGS, H., *Societies in the Making*. (New York: Humanities Press, Inc.), 1965.

KING, C. WENDELL, *Social Movements in the United States*. (New York: Random House), 1956.

LIPSET, SEYMOUR M. and REINHARD BENDIX, *Social Mobility and Industrial Society*. (Berkeley, Calif.: University of California Press), 1959.

MARTINDALE, DON A., *Social Life and Cultural Change*. (New York: D. Van Nostrand Company), 1962.

MURDOCK, G. P., *Social Structure*. (New York: The Macmillan Company), 1965.

WARNER, W. L. and P. S. LUNT, *Social Life of a Modern Community*. (New Haven: Yale University Press), 1941.

WEINBERG, SAMUEL K., *Social Problems in Our Time*. (Englewood Cliffs, N.J.: Prentice-Hall, Inc.), 1960.

ZNANEICKI, F. W., *Social Relations and Social Roles*. (San Francisco, Calif.: Chandler Publishing Company), 1965.

Chapter 6

PUBLIC RECREATIONAL SERVICE

> PRINCIPLE: To the end of providing equal opportunities to engage in recreational activities for all people, as a function of government, the field of public recreational service has no other reason for existence.

All of the efforts by public agencies designed to help people lead more satisfying lives through the enhancement of their physical, mental, social, and cultural capacities by active or passive participation within recreational experiences may be deemed services. Services may be performed for monetary return, for altruistic purposes without extrinsic motives, for a combination of these reasons, or out of necessity created by cultural forces requiring such endeavors if the organization of a specific society is to survive.

Commercial enterprises perform services for profit. Humanitarians provide services because of their belief in, and the need to promote, human dignity. Certain individuals and organizations are motivated by a blending of humanitarian dedication and economic gain. Only public service, growing out of governmental establishment, performs functions which are thought to be essential for the preservation, stabilization, and advancement of the ideological order through the promotion of the public wellbeing. Services are usually intangible products, the effects of which enable recipients to perform their individual functions better. The improved performance, in turn, either modifies the environment (social or natural), so that particular activities may be engaged in, or mitigates conditions to the extent that the individual is able to achieve some satisfaction or enjoyment as a result of a given experience.

FUNCTIONS AND RESPONSIBILITIES OF RECREATIONAL SERVICE

All of the functions and responsibilities undertaken by the recreational service agency are necessary, but incidental to the chief reason for establishment of such agencies. Everything that the agency does is performed with one objective—the direct or indirect sponsorship, operation, management, and administration of activities of a recreational nature within a comprehensive program. All other acts are important only to the extent that they contribute to a more effective end product, i.e., the creation of an environment whereby participants may engage in a variety of recreational endeavors.

The recreational service triad consists of leadership, finance, and facilities. Each of these aspects is necessary if a well-planned, comprehensive program containing a variety of activities is to be offered. No one questions the fact that people are capable of assuming individual responsibility for achieving recreational experiences by themselves. However, in an ever-expanding society of specialists, many people simply do not have the monetary means to construct suitable areas or facilities for participation in motor skill, dramatic, art, craft, and other experiences requiring special spaces, places, direction, or financial outlay. The public recreational service agency makes all of these things available to the greatest number of people at the least possible cost to them and further provides the competent personnel to guide, instruct, or lead activities of this type.

Among the coincidental services which the public recreational service agency performs in carrying out its prime responsibility are organization, administration, education, coordination, conservation, planning, evaluation, supervision, and programming. The net outcome of the sum of these functions is the offering of the broadest schedule of recreational activities from which the individual may choose for his satisfaction.

Organization

In order to carry out the objective of bringing participants into contact with a recreational activity, a certain amount of organizational arrangement must be made. Basically, organization concerns the establishment of the agency, the specification of its functions and responsibilities, the structure of its internal system—i.e., employment of line and staff personnel to operate the agency and produce those services which result in recreational activities—and the performance of those necessary adjustments within the community so that the most effective, efficient, and economical utilization of available professional leadership, volunteers, spaces, areas, physical plants, facilities, equipment, and financial support can be made. The objective of organization is attained when the most complete provision of recreational experiences is formulated so that the public has the opportunity to satisfy individual needs.

Administration

To carry out the policies assumed as a result of the institution of the public recreational service agency and guided by those principles adopted during the organizational establishment, the process of direction, management, and control that is termed *administration* is initiated to operate the agency. Administration is the medium by which all segments of the agency are coordinated in the production of activities for the recreational benefit of agency constituents. Operationally, administration is divided into at least eight subdivisions for the most efficacious outcomes relating to activity offerings: personnel management, fiscal management, recording, planning, maintenance, public relations, research, and programming. Administration within public recreational agencies is wholly concerned with techniques for the conduct of effective services that can be supplied to the citizens of any community at minimum cost, maximum efficiency, and without repetition of other agency functions.

Education

Every recreational service agency has an obligation to keep the public informed about the agency, but beyond that it has an instructional obligation to perform. It should attempt to educate citizens to the variety of activities in which they can engage, not only for public relations purposes, but also in terms of equipping the individual for enjoyable and valuable pursuits during leisure. The enrichment of life, enhancement of personality, enlargement of personal viewpoints, teaching of skills, and the guidance of people in selecting leisure activities that will be reflected in creative achievement are all part of this procedure. The significant development of appreciation for and participation in worthwhile leisure activities is an instructional goal. An ofttimes neglected, but nevertheless important. contribution that recreational service agencies may make to the steady utilization of common means of enjoyment is the effort to make available opportunities in an environment wherein people find it conducive to learn. This does not have to be formal education. The entire process can be informal and concomitant with the provision of a well-balanced program. Something for everybody, rather than stereotyped and routine acts may be the most effective method by which individuals will be educated to appreciate personal capacity and potential for achievement and the satisfaction that achievement brings.

Coordination

No one single agency can provide all of the services necessary to meet the needs of each individual within the community. Even when there is established a public recreational service agency, the time of operation, personnel, and experiences offered simply cannot keep pace with the diverse needs of people. The limitations upon any one agency are not insurmountable. Some coordinating effort within the community must be arranged so that all of the people are reached. Public recreational agencies must cooperate and coordinate their services with all other agencies so that the most comprehensive program of recreational experiences can be offered.

Each agency in the community, whether public, private, or quasi-public, has something in its program, structure, or orientation to offer to people.

These agencies exist to serve people. They have the specialized personnel, financial resources, physical plants, material, or pieces of equipment necessary to supplement and complement the natural and physical resources of other agencies. By judicious counsel, joint planning, and cooperative attitudes, all agencies within any community may more effectively meet social recreational needs of people. These efforts may very well provide recreational services to almost all of the people all of the time without jurisdictional dispute, duplication of functions, or expensive and needless monetary expenditures. Coordination may be the purposive process by which strangulating competition for the same group of participants, at the same time, is decisively eliminated and where each person may be the recipient of a more highly competent and extensive series of services.

Conservation

Public recreational agencies must acquire, develop, and otherwise maintain areas for the recreational values which are derived from the utilization of such spaces by the public. Insofar as is possible these agencies must protect any natural resources within their jurisdiction. Such preservation is extended to fish and wildlife as well as flora and whatever wilderness exists within the area under control. The entire concept of conservation deals not only with the continuing use of natural resources in such a manner as to avoid depletion, pollution, or destruction, but also with the controlled maintenance through scientific management and the sustained development of replenishable resources.

Because the public is poorly informed on the current status of the nation's natural resources it behooves those agencies involved in the conservation process to establish lines of communication with every means applicable and at their disposal. Unfortunately, the day of unlimited natural recreational resources is largely over because of the exploitation and spoilage by private interests and shortsighted governmental officials. Unquestionably the time has arrived when properties must be operated with a minimum of waste and destruction. It has become necessary for governmental agencies to regulate natural resources and areas for the benefit of the country as a whole. Local agencies have the responsibility to provide the same control in their jurisdictions. Land and water areas are necessary for comprehensive recreational activities. Unless space is preserved against encroachment for any reason, it is used up and cannot be replaced.

In order that the public may enjoy whatever there remains of primitive or wilderness areas, recreational service agencies must acquire and set aside these spaces, in perpetuity, so that present and future generations have the opportunity to see and appreciate the wonderful scenery and wildlife, and those who wish to follow wilderness experiences may be accommodated. It is unlikely that any municipality will have an area that can be remotely termed primitive or wilderness, but to the extent that open and natural places are still available, these should be preserved. This need is most particularly apparent in large urban centers where the density of population far outstrips any of the reserved natural areas.

Planning

The systematic acquisition and logical development of property and physical plants based upon a long-term priority schedule is one aspect of planning. Public recreational agencies must provide adequate facilities in order to safeguard the health and welfare of the participants, provide for the conservation of accessible natural areas and resources for the perpetual use and value of the people, and control expenditures on a need basis in coordination with local, district, and regional plans.

Planning is the method by which current status of the locality under investigation is determined. It is concerned with the collection, analysis, and evaluation of the physical and natural areas and resources of the community in order to assess whether adequate provision of recreational spaces and structures for all of the people is present; it compares population movement, trends, and density with property and facility needs; and it provides a method by which the agency may incorporate community preparedness for future growth, cooperative endeavor in realizing the significance of recreational service to the community, and a device whereby undesirable conditions may be alleviated.

Planning is an exploratory technique that attempts to develop sound procedures for the orderly selection, acquisition, construction, and maintenance of land and water spaces which can serve the immediate and future needs of residents and transients of the local community. It is the principal means of gathering information upon which a master plan can be based so that a more highly skilled and effective service can be rendered. The main purpose of planning is the collation of evidence, both existing and forecastable, that affects the jurisdiction's competency to initiate and administer an ever more valuable and effective recreational service to its people. Planning for recreational service is an integral part of total community planning. The interrelationship of all community factors, of which recreational service is but one, is a necessary objective in the analysis of local needs.

Evaluation

The comparison of present recreational services to proposed services, and the contrast between one community's recreational service operation with another of the same type, is the process utilized to determine the adequacy, ability, and comprehensiveness of departmental offerings. Evaluation is concerned with every aspect and function of the department. It is a technique designed to measure current output against specified goals.

Every recreational service agency must undergo evaluation continually in order to establish and maintain an optimum recreational service for the people it serves. Significantly, objectives of evaluation are not the same as the process of evaluation because the end product is improvement, whereas the procedure is simply one of contrast and qualitative or quantitative measurement. Thus, there are typical ends which evaluation seeks to determine:

1. The actual level of performance or adequacy of the subject under consideration.
2. Any shortcomings that currently exist.
3. Unsatisfactory fulfillment of service needs.
4. Personal and physical or natural resources that may be utilized.
5. Suggestions for favorable reform.
6. Policy relating to priority for action.

There is no function of the agency that may not profit from evaluative action. Just as the operational procedures and standard duties of the department may be studied for improvement, so too, can all personnel and their responsibilities be subjected to the same evaluation. The objectives will remain, but they will tend to fall in the qualitative rather than the quantitative category. Objective and subjective examination of personnel efficiency is within the purview of evaluation. Unless all factors relating to the provision of recreational service within the community are adequately considered, the inquiry will be deficient and indecisive and will not offer any substantial, accurate, or valid means for effecting improvements and abolishing the insufficiencies involving the subject under investigation.

Supervision

The leadership process of supervision has two distinct functions: (1) guidance and direction of participants within the program of recreational activities sponsored by the department; and (2) the maintenance of personnel standards of competency and effectiveness of departmental employees. Supervision may be effected by reliance upon authority and headship or it may be the outcome of communication and understanding between people. If the latter technique of human relationship is used, as it should be, then more satisfactory behaviors can be expected, feelings of reliability and loyalty may be engendered, and the personality needs of people will be better met. Being able to understand individual behavior patterns is one of the important areas of specialized knowledge acquired by the professional and this skill is especially required within the supervisory process.

The highly successful supervisor is an individual whose participating followers are not acutely aware of being led, whose supervision is indirect, and who works with and through others rather than with dependence upon a superior position. Naturally, this type of leadership depends upon the previous experiences, level of competence, motivation, intelligence, and status of those who are participating in the activity. Supervisory factors of participants' activity depend, to a great extent, upon the mental contact, desire, enthusiasm, age, skill, and environment in which the recreationist works.

Supervision is important in terms of encouraging worker resourcefulness on the job. There is also responsibility for the guidance and in-service education of line employees, direction of certain phases of the over-all program of activities, and interpretation of administrative policies to lower echelons as well as the elimination of grievances which tend to undermine staff effectiveness. The success of supervision can be measured in relation to increased worker competence and participant attendance and enjoyment of program offerings. In general, the supervisor will perform a variety of functions, such as:

1. Understanding the recreational needs and interests of those whom the program will serve.
2. Providing direct leadership, when required, with individuals within the program.
3. Guiding volunteers toward providing better service in their performance.
4. Directing, controlling, and maintaining facilities and their usage in order to produce a maximum amount of service at the lowest possible cost.
5. Coordinating, through scheduling and conference, the use of recreational structures, facilities, and spaces.
6. Keeping abreast of current techniques and practices in the field of recreational service in order to assist and guide program worker improvement as well as to make supervisory personnel more competent.
7. Offering direct counseling, in-service education, and participating in field observation to enhance worker competence, morale, and be in a position to offer valid advice and reliable appraisal of worker performance.

Programming

In essence the *sine qua non* for any recreational service agency is based upon provision of opportunities for the public to engage in recreational experiences. Programming is the chief means of carrying out the prime responsibility for which the agency is created. Adequate programming is derived when the agency can offer a varied, stimulating, and well-balanced selection of activities that meet both individual and group needs. The program itself must appeal to different age groups of both sexes and take into consideration such aspects of social life as economic means, educational background, vocational experience, religious beliefs, ethnic, racial, and environmental status, and physical and mental capacity to perform. Some activities will be routine by virtue of the fact that they appeal to all. However, some activities will be programmed on the basis of individual differences and special needs or interests.

Programming is the process by which the agency brings together the participant, the activity, and any specialized facility or space, and whatever instructional or leadership direction is necessary for successful engagement in and enjoyment of the experience. It involves the establishment of a master calendar of events on a community-wide basis which is subdivided into hourly, daily, weekly, and monthly activities. These activities may be programmed to direct attention to some common theme so that there is, or appears to be, a progression of experiences culminating in a central event. There may be routine activities whose universal appeal makes mandatory their inclusion on a daily basis. There may be intermittent or irregular routine activities which have application, but whose more frequent use may lead to undue fatigue, harassment, or boredom. There are special events or unique spectacular events performed once or less than three times throughout the year; and there are special interest experiences which may coincide with holidays, memorials, anniversaries, ceremonial occasions, or ethnic and religious patterns as needs are demonstrated.

The main purpose of programming is to create opportunities whereby people are assisted in achieving the maximum benefit from direct or indirect participation within any given activity. Programming has extreme ramifications, the details of which cannot be fully explained here. However, the program of any recreational agency should contain as many activities as there are professional staff and volunteer workers to give guidance and instruction on a continual, regular, and adequate basis. Programming may account for some of the following activities offered free of charge and with any necessary instruction in order for participants to achieve satisfaction: athletics, games, art, crafts, dancing, dramatics, outdoor and nature experience, music, social, educational, civic, and special projects. Such activities should be scheduled either where there is a high degree of interest and potential participation, or for exposure of people to activities which may stimulate participation by their very unfamiliarity. Programming is clearly one of the most vital segments of the agency's work. Through this function the justification of agency establishment is readily explained.

VALUES OF RECREATONAL EXPERIENCE

Many values have been ascribed to recreational activity and these are essentially why recreational service has been promoted for the well-being of participants. The movement has promulgated a wide variety of experiences which include these basic values thought to be of extreme importance in enhancing life itself.

Physical Fitness

Although physical fitness is a specific state of physiological conditioning which is subject to change in terms of muscle tone and endurance, certain recreational activities of a gross motor nature in amounts suited to the needs of the individual, will, with regular participation, contribute to the development of functional power and stamina, and also have a significant effect on the physiological structure of the musculature, the skeletal system, and the vital organs of the body. Vigorous muscular activity induces development that will enhance the ability of the individual to work up to capacity with less fatigue and more effectiveness.

The improvement of physical vigor and the release of hostility, caused by the sublimation of certain feelings, through competitive experiences or individual acts in a social setting provide satisfaction for the need to participate in motor activities. Because a great number of people take part in physical activities for the sense of achievement they attain, the experience is one where significant behavior toward others is highly developed.

Health

Among the many factors which contribute positively to the development of health is joyous activity. Certain activities have an important hygienic effect. Of equal significance from the standpoint of health is the emotional release which nearly all recreational activity affords and the effect of joyousness in activity upon the organism through the functioning of the endocrine glands.

Public recreational service seeks to provide activities, largely in the out-of-doors, because of the appreciation of its health-building and health-conserving values. The programs of public recreational service are designed in part to counteract the effects of sedentary occupation and the strains of daily life, which would promote degenerative diseases as a result of insufficient motor activity.[1] During leisure, public recreational programs afford opportunities for continuation of health habits, moral conduct, and increased individual development. Activities for all ages are thus employed to supply that form of exercise and mental or emotional involvement which may be missing from other aspects of living. It therefore contributes to the maintenance of the whole man.

Satisfaction

The limitations placed upon most individuals by the scope of satisfaction in his gainful occupation enhance the importance of recreational activity and provide an objective toward which recreational service may move. More and more, people must depend upon their recreational outlets for the continuation of the developmental processes begun during childhood. When a vocation is entered, a limited range of skills will tend to be employed—the rest should continue to find expression and further development in recreational offerings. Public recreational service, through such activities as it may provide, creates an opportunity for balanced development and for a continuation of education in lines pursued, not for utilitarian purposes, but for pure satisfaction.

The impulses that are the bases for creative art, music, literature, and

---

[1] Warren R. Johnson, ed., *Science and Medicine of Exercise and Sports* (New York: Harper & Brothers, 1960), pp. 403–437.

drama are to be found in almost everyone to a variable degree. Potentially, everyone is an artist, musician, interpreter, and dramatist. There is no more thrilling experience for the individual than to discover some modicum of creative capacity in one of these fields. People may be literally born anew by such discoveries in their recreational experiences. Through well-planned leisure programs, opportunities for discovery of latent talent may be created and a new type of art patron developed, namely, one who has had personal experience in the arts and whose appreciation for the creative efforts of others is, therefore, more real. For too long the development of art has been left to the professionals. Through planned leisure, art may be restored to the amateurs and a real folk art may emerge. This will make for a happier people.

It is not necessary to justify recreational service as a means of accomplishing preconceived objectives. It is true, however, that benefits to people will accrue from participation in recreational activity. But the recreator is not always conscious of them. Accomplishment of objectives is somewhat impeded by too serious contemplation of them by the subject. He is primarily interested in the *affect* and only incidentally in the *effect* of the experience. The affective state of satisfaction is, therefore, the primary objective of recreational participation.

This truth must be recognized in planning public recreational service. At the same time it is necessary to discriminate between levels of satisfaction. There must be an effort to improve the quality of appreciation and response. This raises the inevitable question as to whether a public recreational agency should provide a program in accord with "what people want" or "what the people should have." This question is usually answered in the enabling legislation that gave original authorization for creation of the agency or inauguration of the program. State enabling acts authorizing the establishment of systems of public recreational service frequently set forth the purposes of the legislature in enacting the legislation, and are almost always stated in terms of public welfare. The view may be justified, therefore, that it is a mandatory obligation of a public recreational agency to offer facilities and a program of activities which will tend to accomplish the desired social objectives. At the same time the facilities and program must meet with public approval, or participation in the activities will not eventuate. The problem is one of providing facilities and programs which induce participation in activities that contribute to desired objectives, in a manner immediately and primarily satisfying to the individual. This, of course, calls for the greatest skill in planning and the highest degree of leadership.

Safety

Another aim of public recreational service is safety education and prevention of accidents. The earliest playgrounds were advocated as necessary in order to get small children off the streets which were becoming unsafe as play places. This continues to be an important objective because, in most congested urban areas, the only alternative to outdoor play on a playground is the public street. The recreational center goes further than this, however, for it eliminates the most dangerous practices in play, provides safe equipment, and through competent leadership instructs safe practices. By developing skill in play activities, much of the hazard inherent in body contact sports and games, or in activities which require individual strength, coordination, and flexibility, is avoided. Awkwardness is replaced with skilled practice when professionals are employed to guide the program. Modern recreational systems also make continual studies of causes of accidents and unsafe conditions on the public areas and devise means for their removal.

Social Intercourse

Social needs have to be satisfied throughout life. There are always situations where people have to meet, mix, get along, or adjust. Social activities of a wide scope have a place in any program where socially approved actions are desired and where good mental health is an objective. The relationships developed as a result of such social intercourse contribute to the development of empathy, sympathy, catharsis, personal value, and self-expression.

Through recreational activity a person may find for himself a satisfying place among his fellows. He may cultivate the basic human virtues of courage, justice, patience, and fairness. He may learn to live happily among his peers, to make his contribution to the good of all and to feel that he is wanted, needed, and appreciated. These are the basic needs of the social animal. In playing together people learn to live together and to adjust to the ramified and complex relationships which society imposes upon them.

Cultural Achievement

At the present time the tremendous drop in working hours which today's machines make possible allows for vast opportunities for everyone, in a recreational context, to select and move toward those ends that seem good to him. The selection and method may be wise or foolish, worthwhile or stupid, but it will only be by education that the habits of decision are influenced toward the wise and worthwhile or the foolish and trivial. Individual satisfaction and self-realization will be a consequence of how well the educational process has taught him to enjoy and employ his time in recreational experiences.

All decisions concerning human behavior patterns are important. Every alternative relating to the activities in which people engage is an educational selection because it gives guidance and direction to the path of human development. For this reason recreational opportunities have a marked influence on the maturation and development of personality and character.

Being the selection of individual choice, recreational activity is an accurate indicator of personal interests and goals.

If this is true, then recreational activity is a concern of education and the agencies by which education is transmitted. Individual growth through recreational experiences must not, cannot, be left to chance situations or accident. Recreational living must receive the careful and deliberate planning of those whose professional duty it is to provide service to the public in an educational capacity. Provision for recreational experience must be as skillfully guided as is preparation for the job. In many instances educational opportunity for cultural development through recreational experiences is even more pronounced than are opportunities on the job.

Heretofore, the total amount of leisure not only has been small in quantity but it also has been in the possession of few. Now it is an almost universal possession. There are those who still question whether the American people will prove themselves equal to the opportunities which this heritage bestows upon them by using this leisure for the improvement of the national culture, or whether through its misuse the culture will be profaned. Civilization, according to H. G. Wells, is a race between the forces of education and disaster. Public recreational service, as a part of education in the broadest sense, is playing an important part in this race.

Ethical Practices

A distinctive ethical code is the characteristic of a professional field. It is a primary objective of the field to provide service to all people within the province of its auspices and to perform in a way that can cast no shadow of doubt upon the ethical practice of the recreationist. The professional's unique knowledge and skill carry with them certain moral responsibilities. The ethical code of professional practice is a special instrumentation of ideal precepts, formed from an awareness of the particular functions attributed to the unique field for which it was established.

The ethics of practice require the recreationist to provide the best possible service which his professional preparation and experience make available. It is his duty to afford varied opportunities of a recreational nature where people may satisfactorily achieve such experience. By his very practice the recreationist must adhere to the principle of equalitarian service regardless of the social, economic, racial, religious, educational, or political affiliations of his prospective clients. It is an item of his professional ethic that he offer equal opportunity for recreational satisfaction in the most attractive manner possible.

By definition, recreational experience is inherently moral. Nothing about the term reveals any intent for physical, social, or psychological disintegration. On the contrary, recreational activity is conceived to be of benefit to the participant. Leisure may be utilized immorally or recreationally, and it is the function of the professional practitioner to guide people into activities that have been proved beneficial. The recreationist is concerned ethically with human behavior. He must provide services that will induce people to participate recreationally rather than wastefully.

Democratic Ideals

Recreational service recognizes the essential dignity and worth of the individual. He is accorded a place commensurate with his capacity and willingness to serve. His success is determined by his ability to produce and to cooperate with others. Democratic ideals are concerned in the individual's acceptance of the rights of others and in his employment of processes which preclude infringement upon the equitable acts of others. He must recognize the rules of the game even as he recognizes the regulations of society. As an individual, he may select specific recreational experiences, the time devoted to them, and those who will be his companions in such a venture. Yet, full enjoyment of his recreational activity requires submission to the collective choices and to the self-imposed laws. This is the essence of democracy. If it becomes the rule of life in recreational pursuit, it will be difficult to follow another principle in other areas of living. Recreational opportunity in America is in conformity with the democratic ideal and fosters its general acceptance and application.

As the economic, civic, and social organization has become more complex, requiring increasing regimentation of people even in a democracy, the freedom which people may still enjoy in leisure stands out in bold relief. The democratic principle of freedom strongly persists in leisure. The same necessity for regimentation in productive industry does not exist in leisure, although there is an ever-present danger that the people might unwittingly yield this freedom to self-appointed or elected dictators. Dictators in totalitarian nations have demonstrated how leisure may be organized to serve the will of the dictator and the purpose of the state. The Declaration of Independence of the thirteen original colonies of the United States declared that "life, liberty and the pursuit of happiness" are among "certain inalienable rights" with which "all men are endowed by their Creator." The right to pursue happiness in leisure must be considered a basic precept in American democracy. In protecting this principle in leisure, the democratic ideal is sustained.

It is this concept of freedom in leisure that imposes upon society the necessity of educating people for leisure. Democracy has been said to contain the seed of its own destruction. This is certainly true in relation to leisure. Individuals may interpret liberty as license, rather than as freedom with concomitant responsibility. The individual, therefore, may freely neglect to take advantage of leisure for purposes of growth and development; he may even waste it in vulgarity, mediocrity, and debauchery. He may destroy his body, his mind, and his finer sensibilities by excesses in leisure; or he may develop his powers and enhance his knowledge, talent, and satisfactions by creative utilization of leisure through recreational endeavors.

EQUALITY OF OPPORTUNITY

Every person has the innate right to pursue his dreams and must be given the opportunity to fulfill his needs (within societal approval) as he has the capacity to achieve without artificial hindrance or restriction. The only limitation upon individual achievement should be biological potential and social acceptability. Age, sex, race, ethnic origin, religion, economic worth, political affiliation, and social status are all considered as being artificially contrived restrictions if, because of them, any man is prevented from participating in an activity which would otherwise be socially acceptable. Social acceptability in this instance has nothing to do with regional traditions or biases. Social acceptability simply means that the activity is not immoral, injurious to life, detrimental to the health, welfare, or safety of the individual so engaged or to anyone directly or indirectly associated with the experience.

The only criterion that is utilized is whether or not each individual has had an opportunity to take advantage of activities offered, not whether he has actually participated. There is no stipulation as to the amount of service received. In fact, equality of service is neither possible nor feasible because of the great disparity in individual differences. To the extent that some people need a good deal more of attention than others in terms of instructional assistance, personal guidance, activity direction, or other supervision, there will always be a disproportionate amount of services administered. This will occur by the very nature of recreational services. There are too many people in comparison to the number of professional personnel employed within the field and in no way can every person be reached. This is a physical impossibility. The usual way of reaching the recreational needs of people is by attracting a small group so that specific individual service can be performed or by programming for mass activities. Only in special situations will the recreationist be able to work on a one-to-one basis, and these will be cases where the physical or mental capacity of the participant is so limited as to make any other possible work method untenable.

Thus, the field of recreational service is concerned with equality of opportunity. Every man must be given his share, his opportunity to perform. Whether he utilizes this opportunity or not is incidental. That he be given the chance to take part is the only fact. Insofar as this opportunity is one of recreational experience, it is limited to those satisfactions which may be gained through activities in a recreational context. But beyond the opportunity to participate or not to participate, recreationists have the professional obligation of providing stimulating activities covering all phases of human living. There must be something for everybody. Activities should range as wide as the human mind is capable of expanding, with emphasis upon those events which tend to inculcate achievements in social, cultural, and educational experiences.

It is meet that recreationists have an educational function as well as their program function because only when attractive and positively suggestive activity ideas are offered will individuals want to take part. Although it is important to make the experience available, it is of equal importance that the activity is of such a nature as to excite and entice participation; particularly is this true when there has been no previous experience. Professionalism demands that each person's personal horizon be widened so that there is a better chance for life enrichment. If the recreationist can open a new door to satisfaction and achievement through ingenuity and attractive activity presentation, then he is performing his duty in a competent manner. After all, this is the purpose for which he is employed.

SOCIAL LIMITATIONS ON EQUALITY

All men are not created equal, nor does the Constitution of the United States attempt to make such a statement. The true meaning of the constitutional statement is an idealistic concept of all men being equal under a justly administered legal system, under God (if such a belief is part of the individual's rationale), and, because all men are endowed with the unalienable rights to life, liberty, and the pursuit of happiness, equality of opportunity. All men are different by virtue of genetic inheritance, environment, and other factors. Even identical twins have some basic personality, physical, and social distinctions because, according to Newton's law, two bodies cannot occupy the same space at the same time. Each individual, therefore, sees objects just a little differently than does anyone else. This is not only a physical phenomenon, but an emotional or psychological one as well. Environmental stimuli and pressures cause different reactions to the same set of facts or conditions in different individuals and give rise to differing opinions, attitudes, biases, and extremes of behavior.

Because we cannot all have the same points of view and because we are characterized by specific physical, mental, and other differences, the idea of equality, except as an abstract form, is meaningless. Yet, there is, or should be equality. Even in a great working democracy, where the law is supposed to be administered impartially and where justice is tempered with mercy, equality is a sometimes thing. Economic means has often played an important role in securing one verdict from either judge or jury when, in fact, another judgment should have been handed down.[2] However, court room discrepancies are rapidly dying as great new legal gains are made in jurisprudence. The now famous Gideon, Escobedo, McLaughlin, Mapp, Jones, Dorado, and Riser cases tried in various state supreme courts and the United States Supreme Court have done much to eradicate

---

[2] "Criminal Law," *Time* (Feb. 21, 1964), p. 78.

inequalities due to economic status while giving greater protection to individuals in criminal cases.[3]

But this is an imperfection of human nature rather than a revocation of the principle of equity. Until the last few years it could also be said that a wealthy individual by reason of his wealth might secure more highly competent and effective counsel before the law. The poor man was either denied access to highly polished advocates or his limited means made him incapable of understanding his inferior status and his lack of adequate defense. Affluence is itself an unequalizing force in society. Nowhere has this been more apparent than in the law courts. Seldom, if ever, have wealthy persons been condemned to death for capital crimes. Almost inevitably poor persons have been so condemned. Even where there is blatant misuse of office, or where felonies occur, the wealthy do not ever suffer the degree of punishment, in terms of penal servitude, high fines, or both, as do the poor. Nevertheless, all men should be equal before the law.

Cynicism aside, and with knowledge of the inability of the human factor to achieve perfection in many or all aspects of social intercourse, the ideal of equality must be made a constant effort on the part of all who seek to serve other people. Wherever professionals view human dignity and the pursuit of excellence above materialism, there equality for all has a chance for development as a common part of life instead of the rarity in which it is usually found.

Age

During no other period of American life has there been such a concern for the problems of old age as has been produced in the last fifteen years. More than 18 million people are classified as aged because they have reached 65 years or more. This means that about ten per cent of the population fall into this category. Public concern continues to grow as an increasing number of people reach the age where they are considered to be economically useless, victims of advancing health hazards, dependent or partially dependent upon others for basic necessities. All too frequently, society arbitrarily assumes that old age makes a sudden appearance at 65. This may be seen from the commercial propensity of forcing retirement at 65. It is fallacious to assume that there is any specific age at which a person becomes old. This physiological process may occur at any time. Individual differences in personality reflect the same degree of difference in aging. Physiologically, the internal organs age at varying rates and with different intensities. Externally, eyes and ears are not necessarily impaired in their functions at the same rate, nor to the same degree. In fact, some individuals never lose these sensory functions.

Not only are there great individual differences as to the onset of specific physical decline, there is also the psychological aspect of aging which is

---

[3] "Courts," *Time* (Jan. 21, 1966), pp. 48–49.

probably more apparent and important. Psychological deterioration is the more likely manifestation, although its measurement is more difficult to determine. Intense forms of senescence are readily observed in terms of loss of memory, inability to concentrate, inability to learn new skills, insecurity, suspiciousness, living in the past, and other features. It must be understood, however, that these indications of aging do not occur in all individuals at the same time nor are they symptomatic of the aging adult at the same rate.

Adjustment to the changes of aging is, essentially, a subjective matter. It can be achieved when there is opportunity rather than rejection. Because society as a whole creates roles, biases, social values, status, agencies, organizations, and services, the personal problems of old age have their mirror image in the social environment. Society and the individual communities have provided a favorable environment for the development and self-fulfillment of other age groups and they must create the same climate for the older adult. American society recognizes and rewards self-sufficient and contributing citizens. It ignores or allows disproportionate existence to those who have outlived their usefulness—at least as far as some people are concerned. Medical science has discovered ways by which life can be prolonged for from ten to twenty-five years after the individual reaches 65.

> In recent years there has been effort on the part of society to provide for the recreational and social needs of older people. Some have labeled the programs 'superficial' and the activities 'busy work' but, at any rate, there has been a real growth of organizations for and by the aged. In a few localities, civic and other organizations have provided club rooms or game centers where the older person can spend his time at shuffleboard or cards, or, as one such 'club' boasts, where checkers, 'both regular and Chinese,' are available. It is undoubtedly true that some of the aged are able to spend their days more pleasantly and with less concern over 'what to do' as a result of the existence of such centers. But life for the aged is still far from being purposeful and useful, and some oldsters complain that it more resembles 'playing at living' than living itself.[4]

Isn't this a sad commentary on one of the most enlightened societies in the world? The denial of a worthwhile role for the aged, in any of the areas comprising social existence, excludes them from equal opportunities to achieve in economic enterprises (unless they are financially independent), in civic responsibility, and even within the family. There are no easy solutions to this problem, for the issues are bound up with basic needs, understanding, attitudes, and education.

---

[4] John F. Cuber, Robert A. Harper, and William F. Kenkel, *Problems of American Society: Values in Conflict* (New York: Henry Holt and Company, 1956), p. 294.

Youth

The limitation on youth in a society which dotes upon youth seems to have built-in contradictions. Nevertheless, this society attempts to give with one hand while taking with the other. It is expected of the adolescent that he act in a manner that conforms with adult societal standards, although he is, in fact, treated as a child. Confusion as to moral attitudes and standards confronts the adolescent on all sides. He is at once admonished to go to school, stay in school, and then select a vocation in which he will be able to earn his livelihood. This has been the time-tested formula since societies were first organized. Unfortunately, in this era of modern technology and varied occupations, there is an attempt to force the individual, from early childhood through young adulthood, into a preconceived mold that may not actually meet his particular needs and differences. All too often, great emphasis is placed upon peer competition. "Why can't you be like Johnny? He always gets high marks," is an anguished cry from some parents who refuse to believe that their child cannot perform as well as someone else's child.

"You're going to college whether you want to or not," is another common parental statement. For whom is this college education? In many instances it is not for the recipient, but for the parent or for the parent's unconscious desire to have his child accepted into a society where a college education has become a partial open-sesame to economic and social status. The plethora of blatant sexual stimulation at the most provocative age is completely inconsistent with moral preachments concerning the conduct of sexual relationships. Adolescent behavior, imitative of adult behavior, is consistently rejected by the adult community even though adult morality and conduct under certain conditions is either absolutely reprehensible or questionable at best.

Adolescents, as do adults, have leisure. What they do with that free time concerns the entire community and by ramification, society as a whole. They may have no inclination to use whatever leisure they have in anti-social ways, but in not a few instances, this is the only way possible to them, because no other avenues are open. Recreational activity based upon what the traffic will bear proves too costly and usually does not meet adolescent needs. The growing youth wants an interesting, exciting, absorbing, and long-term experience. He wants to be with his own kind and not dominated by adults, although he is generally willing to concede that social standards must be maintained for the benefit of all. Public recreational service may be able to meet the needs of youth through the variety of activities available within the departmental program. Recreational service that provides equal opportunities for all youths to participate in experiences which can be valuable and creative is a most constructive proposal. Communities should provide extensive year-round public recreational services for adolescents. Even where the total cost of such a program appears out of proportion, the per-capita cost of such a system, to the taxpayer, is extremely low.

But the provision of such activities by the public recreational service department is not the entire answer to the problem of adolescence. Most, if not all, of the problems of youth are mirrored in society at large. Economic deprivation, poor mental health, sexual frustration, delinquency, and other failures are not to be found only in adolescence. They are integral parts of the social order. The cause may be adult ineptitude and an ineffective society. The recreational inequality engendered by this inefficiency may be observed through the following:

1. Lack of cooperative effort on the part of the entire community. Disunity and bickering among those community agencies who should be interested in and manifest concern about youth. Misunderstanding about youth needs and leadership.
2. Inability of community agencies to reach all youth. Ineffectiveness of program and understaffing of agencies makes this effort a failure.
3. Adult domination of youth activities. The adult planners leave youth out of program planning and operations. As a result adolescents react by nonparticipation or hostility. Too often activities that are derived from adult opinion are based upon recall rather than inventiveness and have no connection with the youth needs of today. What was "good enough for my grandfather" is no longer good or even necessary.

Sex

All cultures have traditionally held the female as an inferior creature. The manifestation of this fact can be validated by scanning recent history and recalling the suffragette movement. That this has been a world-wide disservice to the distaff side does not make it any more logical or right. Although this country has grown beyond its rural "American way of life" and has now entered upon a growth rate with urbanized foundations, it is still bound to old mores. Only in very recent years has there been any noticeable modification in programming for females. Most public and private recreational service agencies are content to program for the male. Enter any agency on any given day and the activities of a physical nature will provide the accuracy of that statement. Whether this is true because of incompetence upon the part of the programmers or because of ignorance, or both, is a moot point.

Recreational agencies have historically been devoted to youth rather than any other age group, to males, and to those who utilize the center or facility. There has never been a concerted effort to go out and recruit female participants into the program. Even when concerned individuals protest against this inequitous arrangement, little is done to change the pattern. Frequently, the program is developed around gross motor skill activities which appeal to the young males. Thus, football, basketball, baseball, and other team sports are initiated. These grow into major or minor leagues and tournaments, as the case may be, and have as their devotees youth and young adult males.

There is an intrinsic feminine disdain for gross motor activities because of the so-called "perspiration concomitant" which happens to be part of the game. It is considered unfeminine to participate in strenuous sports and girls simply do not wish to appear to be unfeminine. Presumably this attitude has something to do with their marriage potential. Nevertheless, this bias against sports participation by females is being successfully countered as a result of the popularization of gymnastics for women and girls, swimming, and bowling. There has been a noticeable upsurge in women's track and field events as a consequence of the past few Olympic Games, and more and more women are participating in golf, snow skiing, and riding as well as aquatics, i.e., water skiing, scuba diving, and surfing. However, the majority of women still prefer to engage in less strenuous activities. Recreational agencies continue to neglect the program experiences which are more likely to draw a feminine crowd. Perhaps this is in part the result of the inability of those in charge to lead or direct such activities. Many times the department has a former athlete as its executive. Such an individual cannot or does not appreciate nonathletic and noncompetitive experiences. It may very well be easier to organize and operate many leagues and tournaments than it is to direct and produce a stage drama, lead a chorus, supervise an orchestra, conduct a dance festival, organize an art or sculpture class, book group, and literary program, or find the skilled people who are employable or who will voluntarily undertake these functions. For these several reasons the female sex has been neglected and is still being omitted from receiving an equal share of recreational service by the public agency charged with this responsibility. Some private agencies, with direct interest in females, e.g., YWCA, Girl Scouts, Future Home-Makers of America, Girls' Clubs, Junior League, and so on, do have activities specifically geared to appeal to females. But this does not make for equal opportunity within public agencies.

A noticeable gap exists on the playgrounds where even the youngest children, both male and female, should find equal opportunity. If there are organized activities available, they are generally of the "Little League," "Little Guys," "Midget" or some other appellation signifying that the game is for little *boys,* not girls. If any attempt is made to include coeducational activities it is a skimpy affair at best and a farce at worst. The tendency to relegate females to the role of spectators, passive participants, and "off-to-the-siders" is still very real and very much a part of current recreational practice. Obviously such practice makes the word *equality* something that is found only in textbooks.

Economic-Social Status

Part of the initial social movement which later came to be known as the recreational service movement was instigated as a welfare or relief program. It was born as a result of the waves of immigrants being tossed into the melting pot of this country, and as the result of the new urbanization with its slums, ghettos, and demoralizing human values. The concept of service to the poor, slum-ridden, foreign-born, illiterate, and low social status person has never been completely erased from the practice of recreational service. As Hutchinson states:

> . . . no such entity as a special recreation neighborhood should exist in a city officially supporting recreation activities by taxes. Residential neighborhoods, slum districts and those in between deserve consideration only because of need. Neither superficial standards nor pressure group activities should influence recreation efforts so that one section of the community gains at the expense of the other.[5]

That such neighborhoods do exist in our largest cities cannot be disputed. Why they exist at all is the prime question. The special neighborhood is a throwback to the social welfare aspect of the movement. It has been thought that certain classes of people, particularly low-end socioeconomic groups should receive the greatest share of public facilities, leadership, and organized program activities. On the other hand, there are those who feel that recreational facilities, leadership, and activities should be parceled out to the better neighborhoods because the people who count live there. Little thought is given to any concept of equality when either of these conditions prevails.

On occasion, political, social, or economic pressure groups will demand the construction or development of certain recreational facilities within the immediate environs of the neighborhood which they represent. The "ward heeler" does this as a part of the campaign pledge made to voters in his district or as a sop to his supporters. The well-to-do ask for parks and other beautifying facilities because such areas tend to cause property values to rise when they are adjacent to or within a reasonable distance from a given place. All of these factors make demands upon the type and quality of service which the public department can render to all of the people of the community. The function of the public department is to provide equal opportunities for all of the people without distinction as to economic or social status. Recreational service, as a public tax-supported function, exists for all of the people regardless of their economic or social characteristics. The public agency can no more provide one type of facility, program, and leadership to a specific class or group, and do a creditable job for the entire community, than it can afford to plan for only one neighborhood and leave the rest of the community to fend for itself. Such inequity would surely meet with honest cries of outrage from the citizens who are being discriminated against—at least one is led to believe that would happen. But it does not; for many departments do function in precisely

---

[5] John L. Hutchinson, *Principles of Recreation* (New York: A. S. Barnes and Company, 1951), p. 178.

that discriminatory way, either for one segment of the total population with token activities for the rest or with inequitable expenditures of budget for one group and nothing for anybody else. As Butler has said:

> Every community recreation program should 1. Provide equality of opportunity for all. This democratic principle applies particularly in the field of recreation. For example, as far as possible all neighborhoods should have adequate playgrounds, not just a favored few. Facilities and programs should be sufficiently broad and well distributed to enable all the people to be served.[6]

Some progress is being made to offset the pressures that tend to favor the few at the expense of the many, but the condition is a current problem. Practices which attempt to operate facilities and administer activities for one group militate against the common principle of equal opportunity for all. To overlook the whole so that one part may benefit is not merely shocking, but may eventually prove disastrous to the public agency. As improved communications are developed, better understanding and recognition of the function of recreational service will also grow. The public will disavow its support of any agency that cannot or will not provide the service for which it was created.

Education

To the extent that individuals have not had prior experience with or instruction in leisure skills other than a few motor activities, they are hindered from participating in the remarkable variety of recreational activities available within public programs. This lack of exposure to enjoyable experiences does much to mitigate potential performance. If the individual has not previously attempted specific activities, it is likely that he will be less inclined to do so because people do not like to be placed in uncomfortable or unfamiliar situations or positions. When the individual must function on a lower level of competence, under conditions that either make him defensive or frustrate him, or without any appreciation for activities that have not been a part of his educational preparation, he is hindered from considering these activities and is therefore offered an unequal share of recreational items from which to choose. Such a condition may be largely brought about by the individual himself, but in many communities throughout the country, inequitable educational programs prevent people from achieving through leisure arts because they are nonexistent in the curriculum.

Channeling the development of people is not sufficient if the outcome of such direction does not consider off the job living as well as vocational experiences. Occupational provision through formal schooling facilitates

---

[6] George D. Butler, *Introduction to Community Recreation* (New York: McGraw-Hill Book Company, 1949), p. 229.

the essential functions by which society carries on. However, life is more than existence, and the process of education influences living (in the fullest meaning of the word) and is, in turn, affected by it. Living is not only occupational; it has recreational connotations as well.

Education must prepare the individual so that an appreciation and a taste for worthwhile leisure activities will be accomplished. Individual proclivity for one kind of activity instead of another is generally learned. Activity which is fulfilling to one person may be dissatisfying to someone else without the same experience and education. Biological factors may have some bearing upon a given predisposition toward a specific form of activity, but the individual's attitude toward and taste for one form of leisure activity as opposed to another is largely acquired. Therefore, learning is of primary significance in defining what activities a person will engage in with a maximum of satisfaction. No individual is born with a taste for reading good books, skillfully participating in a variety of motor activities, or performing great music. These proficiencies are acquired slowly and usually only with painstaking care. During the learning phase much support must be rendered to the potential performer, by way of praise, stimulation, and prediction of potential ability to compensate for the often painful presentiments when something new or unfamiliar is attempted. With diligence, the practice of new functions becomes pleasurable as increasing skill makes the performance smooth and easy thus providing satisfaction. Nevertheless, in the procedure of educating towards desirable kinds of activity, supplemental rewards having some extrinsic value will do much to reinforce individual perseverance and productivity.

As Phenix has stated:

> A considerable segment of most people's time is spent in recreation. Furthermore, unlike work, there is an almost universal presumption in its favor. It is neither punishment nor an evil or unpleasant necessity. It is usually regarded as a reward and an undeniable good. Being freely chosen, it is also a reliable reflection of personal interests and goals. For these reasons recreation is certain to exert a marked influence on the development of character. It is therefore not appropriate that recreation should be considered a subsidiary educational concern. Personal growth through recreation cannot safely be left to haphazard arrangement, accidental circumstance, and the vagaries of momentary inclination. Provision for recreation needs as careful deliberate consideration as preparation for the job. In some respects the educational opportunities in the former are even greater than in the latter.[7]

The education of people for their intelligent discrimination between valuable and worthless activities is a function of the learning process. Whenever the educational process is blighted by poorly prepared and equipped

---

[7] Philip H. Phenix, *Philosophy of Education* (New York: Holt, Rinehart and Winston, 1958), pp. 243–244.

instructors, for reasons of bias, or because authorities have no conception of the need for such acquisition, then the individual will be slighted and the criteria by which people judge the relative value of activities will be impaired. To the extent that this impairment of judgment exists the individual cannot fairly distinguish between the more and the less desirable and worthy forms of leisure experience. If the individual does not have a basis from which to select recreational experiences which may prove to be of greater satisfaction, enjoyment, and value to him, then he has been the victim of inequity within the educational system and is ill-prepared to find living outside of existence.

Ill and Handicapped

Perhaps the greatest inequity relating to recreational service has been contained within the basic principle of equal opportunity to all of the people all of the time. Certainly, this principle has had little application toward the ill and handicapped persons in a variety of settings whether they be in treatment centers or in the community itself. This principle has been warped to the point where it must be translated to mean equal opportunity to all, except the ill and handicapped. What has been behind this apparent indifference by community recreationists? Even more startling has been the disinclination of competent medical authorities to utilize recreational services within the hospital environment. Recreational service has largely been confined to long-term, custodial, or chronic treatment hospitals, the Veterans Administration hospitals, and mental health institutions of various types. Few general hospitals, either public or private, have instituted recreational services as a part of patient rehabilitation or adjunctive therapeutic aid.

Recreational service as an integral part of the medical team is a recent arrival and addition to commonly accepted medically oriented treatments. It is not surprising, therefore, to discover that little is known of the outcomes which such therapeutically involved functions should have. It is not a therapy in the true sense of the term, because no positive results can be shown regarding the application of recreational experiences to patients under diffuse circumstances and involving the full range of physical and mental disabilities to which the patient is subjected. No conclusive evidence has yet been brought to medical attention which would unhesitatingly assure physicians that the involvement of patients within recreational activities would materially benefit the patient. Some experimentation has been carried out in various places, but to date, these have proved inconclusive. There is a great deal of personal observation which tends to support the inclusion of recreational services within treatment centers as a means of assisting, in some way, the rehabilitation of patients who have been afflicted by some mental disorder, but beyond these subjective *medical* opinions there is little or no empirical proof. Nevertheless, recreational programming is carried on in hospitals, nursing homes, or homes for the aged. The only reasonable explanation for including such a function as a part of the medical program is that it seems to help.

There is almost universal agreement on the futility of providing a recreational service program in a general hospital which deals only with acute medical incidents. However, even the smallest general hospital will have not less than half of its bed space occupied by patients who either have progressed beyond the acute stage in their recovery or who were never on the acute list at all—for example, those in the hospital for tests, examinations, observation, or prolonged treatment, i.e., anything lasting more than three days. The acute patient's stay in the hospital generally lasts between three and eight days, depending upon the specific reason for his admission. For minor surgery, the patient will be in pain, traumatized, and in no condition to know or care what is happening around him during the first twenty-four hours after his initial operation. Within three days he may be sufficiently recovered to be released from the hospital. The duration of pain and other postoperative shock and weakness depends upon the severity of the incident, whether major or minor repair was made, the physical condition of the patient prior to the operation, and his ability to recuperate. The more drastic the surgery or treatment, the longer will be the required recovery period and the hospital stay. What do these patients do after they have recovered sufficiently to begin to take notice of their surroundings? Aside from the normal routine of injections, tests, periodic visitation by medical personnel, feeding, and eliminatory acts, what do these recuperating patients do for the next one to eight days and nights? In many instances nothing, with concomitant boredom, impatience, and other frustrating manifestations making their appearance. "Well, we are not running a resort hotel," "My patients cannot do anything," are comments made frequently by hospital administrators. "Funds are limited, costs are high and getting higher, only those vital medical services which are proved essential to the competent treatment of patients can be provided." These answers are obviously supposed to relieve the needs of patients.

As if to complement the absence of recreational service within the hospital the external community has offered little or nothing by way of recreational services to the ill and handicapped.[8] Shut-ins, permanently disabled, mentally retarded, blind, deaf, mute (not those who have communicable diseases), out-patients of mental hospitals, all require the same recreational services as do normal people because as human beings they all have the same physical, social, and psychological needs. As in some hospitals, community authorities are either unwilling, unable, incompetent, or ignorant of the need to provide such services. As in the hospital environ-

---

[8] Jay S. Shivers, "Equality: A Challenge to Community Recreational Service Leaders," *Recreation In Treatment Centers,* Vol. **3**, pp. 5–8 (September, 1963), Washington, D.C.: The American Recreation Society, Inc.
Connecticut Department of Health, *Miles To Go,* Report of the Connecticut Mental Retardation Planning Project (Hartford: State Health Department, Office of Mental Retardation, 1966), pp. 63–73.

ment there is the question of the value of recreational service, as an unknown quantity, in terms of its effect on disabled citizens. Surely there are other more essential functions that need to be performed, i.e., fire, police, sanitation, public works, and so on. That recreational activity falls within private purview anyway seems to be the general opinion.

Some reactionary community and economy-minded hospital authorities will continue to deprive the ill and handicapped of a fair share of services which they should receive, just as in the past medical advances were looked upon with suspicion if not with hatred, because they broke with tradition or required a little bit more intelligence than current practitioners then had. As Cuber and others have said:

> Advocates of dissection, Harvey's theory of the circulation of the blood, the theory of percussion, asepsis, antisepsis, vaccination, etc., met with violent opposition from the practicing physicians and the public of their day. Yet today these theories and practices are part of the very heart of medicine. The chief reason for such opposition was that preconceived values were encroached upon by the new theories and techniques. Resistance to technical and theoretical medical progress was as strong a century or so ago as resistance to social medical progress (change in the methods of distributing medical services) is today. Harvey, Pasteur, Lister, Ehrlich, and other proponents of new technical theories and methods were even more denounced by defenders of what was then the *status quo* . . ."[9]

In the same way can we now say that advocates of recreational services to the ill and handicapped in whatever environment they inhabit are, if not reviled, ignored, suspect, and condemned, opposed in many ways. The descendants of the people who drove Semmelweis insane and almost forced Waterhouse out of medicine are inflicting their *status quo* arrangements on the ill and handicapped in relation to their receiving opportunity for recreational experiences.[10]

Explicit evidence as to the therapeutic value of recreational activity for the ill and handicapped person has not yet been confirmed. But to the extent that recreational experience has proved to be of value to people in general, there is no reason to believe that atypical persons would not also benefit from such participation. Confronted with the same problems, in many cases much more complex as a consequence of the disability, the ill or handicapped person requires at least the same chance as his more fortunate brother to associate himself with and in various groups which offer the possibility of enjoyment through recreational activities.

---

[9] J. F. Cuber, R. A. Harper, and W. F. Kenkel, *Problems of American Society: Values in Conflict, op. cit.,* p. 89.
[10] Jay S. Shivers, "Equality: A Challenge to Community Recreational Service Leaders," *Recreation in Treatment Centers,* II (Sept. 1963), 5–8.

Regional Deficiencies

The vagaries of nature being what they are, certain regions within the territorial limits of the United States have been fortunate to have an abundance of scenic vistas, mountains, caverns, deserts, glaciers, gorges, inland waters, coastal areas lapped by ocean, sea, sound, or gulf, temperate climates, and other natural phenomena which, by their very existence, make the region more susceptible to leisure experiences. Conversely, the absence of natural wonders has created areas of flat uninteresting land, cold in winter, hot and humid in summer, wet in the spring, but perhaps magnificent in autumn. These areas, too, have capitalized on whatever nature has presented. However, there are areas that have nothing whatever to recommend them in terms of supplying recreational settings to people. These may be the island communities dotting the great plains region of the country or the numerous industrial towns which once participated in newly emerging industries, but are now left to dry up in an economy that no longer needs the labor or raw material.

About the imbalance of nature, little can be done. Man may create artificial waterways and lakes by damming and constructing canals, but he can do less when it comes to repairing desolate, stark, nonfeatured terrain. These factors may come under human domination and control eventually, but such deficiencies of geographical location, topography, and weather are not validly included in regional dislocation. They may be partially contained by the development of man-made facilities and structures which can compensate in some way.

The real regional disparity comes in terms of political understanding or the lack of it, economic means or the lack of it, local mores, urban congestion, rural sparsity of population, population movements, and the establishment of recreational service agencies to provide the leadership and direction for equalizing opportunity.

Political shortsightedness accrues from elected officials who view the recreational service department as a waste of tax money and an agency that can be lopped off the municipal budget during times of retrenchment. Coupled with this lack of appreciation of the functions of the recreational authority is the politician's constant compromise toward a variety of pressure groups which force him into expedient, rather than logical, actions, the consequences of which are recreationally blighted areas within the city. Particularly is this true in the great urban centers of this country where the costs of acquisition of built-up property, demolition of condemned buildings, and the construction of modern public structures and facilities are extreme. The covetous politician casts his eye upon park lands as a means of reducing some of the cost of appropriation. The sad fact is that such encroachment is not only for parking lots, streets, and other mundane reasons, but for vitally required schools, hospitals, police stations, and so on. In spite of the apparent justification for taking park and other recreational spaces for public building, the end result is to create a city without breathing space. Once the land is taken over by asphalt or concrete, it can never be utilized as a park. The expedient of saving the tax-payers' money generally ends with a future appropriation of many times the original "saving" when the community has to buy new property for its recreational areas; presuming that such property is acquirable. The fallacious idea is that it costs the city less if park land is taken. In reality the city is denuded of its necessary green places which are never replaced. The danger then is that the politician and appointed officials have not planned for construction needs and often transfer open space to another department because it is easier to do this than to buy on the market. Without adequate facilities, e.g., parks and reservations, there is a reduction in the kinds of recreational experience which can be programmed. Lacking open spaces, people are denied equal opportunity to participate in activities requiring places of this type.

Economic resources that are limited prevent the community from establishing a department geared to the provision of recreational service. Communities without the financial means cannot afford to develop facilities, much less employ qualified leadership for the direction and operation of a department. Whenever funds are in short supply, the program suffers or those who would ordinarily benefit from participation within the program suffer because they have to do without.

Urban congestion, which presses more people into less space and limits the amount of service, and the number of opportunities available to each individual because of the absolute disproportion between professional workers and recipients of the service lead to inequality. Inadequate facilities and recreational spaces to serve the needs of the inhabitants tend to make their appearance in highly congested neighborhoods of cities. In too many instances slum areas and the central section or core of the city has been allowed to deteriorate as the rim has expanded and become increasingly more residential. Consequences of allowing recreationally blighted areas to exist lead to a movement away from the heart of the city, an absence of open space, and by default, commercial, light manufacturing, loft, and warehouse establishments take over.

The scarcity of rural population often negates governmental provision for recreational services. When the population of any given area is very small as in the case of many rural regions, there are economic limitations upon the agencies that can provide services. Usually, rural areas can only count upon the school district because county government is not adequate to the task of supplying adequate leadership. Often, rural dwellers have been unwilling, or uncaring enough, to tax themselves so that some central authority is enabled to undertake the responsibility for performing those functions designed to establish recreational services. Rural populations, generally made up of agricultural workers, have been disposed to view government organization, of any form, in a dismal light. With millions of rural people leaving their districts to migrate to cities, the disparity between land area and people living in the rural region has become extreme. To those families who remain, the lack of an established agency to which the individual may turn when seeking services of a recreational nature, the poor or limited financial resources, and inadequate facilities, program, or direction all indicate a basic inequality due to sparse population. The state seems to be the final source of redress and many state governments, finding themselves heavily taxed to offer aid to great urban centers with their millions of people, consider rural districts with few people to be somewhat less important.

Leadership Inadequacies

Incompetence like illiteracy steals opportunity from people. Those who cannot read find that much of life's enjoyments, as well as necessities, are beyond them. Incompetency or the inability to perform adequately is perhaps the most damaging factor to the provision of equal recreational opportunity and service to people. Almost every other inequity can be overcome if the recreationist has the intelligence, drive, ingenuity, and dedication it takes to function under adverse circumstances. When the worker is incompetent, every advantage working to benefit the program is negated because the success of organized recreational service is chiefly dependent upon the quality and effectiveness of the leadership available to it. The inept are either poorly prepared to negotiate the sometimes delicate public relations so necessary to the maintenance of a sound public image or they are incapable of offering attractive activities which make up a well-balanced program appealing to all potential participants.

Incompetency in the worker cannot be hidden because it is always and immediately reflected in terms of the program. A worker who does not have the skill or knowledge required of the recreationist cannot offer the variety of recreational experiences which must be afforded if people are to be well served. Usually, there is a tendency to present activities that limit participation to those who are highly skilled or that call for overloading of the program with athletics, thus eliminating a majority of the public without offering compensating efforts. Activities may be proposed without prior plan or consideration of people's needs. This action often develops because chance rather than purposeful choice is depended upon for success. In many cases the incompetent relies upon a specific group of activities, whether they fit the situation or not, and these are continually offered. Under such conditions the program becomes stagnant and denies ample opportunities to citizens to perform in patterns which may be more meaningful to them.

Incompetency results from any of the following factors: (1) a lack of intelligence which precludes any satisfactory performance; (2) a lack of knowledge necessary for the provision of comprehensive recreational services in a given environment; (3) a lack of skill and/or experience for functioning in terms of a particular assignment; or (4) a lack of initiative, desire, or enthusiasm for the accepted responsibility. Any of these, by itself or in a combination, when applicable to a worker, results in inefficient operation, ineffective rapport with the public, disorganization or deterioration of the program, and an intense form of inequality.

SUMMARY

It is the function of all governmentally constituted recreational service agencies to provide opportunities of a comprehensive and varied recreational natural for all of the people within the community served. To this objective, all of the duties, responsibilities, and standard operating procedures performed by the agency are supportive, but incidental to its chief goal. Everything which the agency does, it does in order to carry out the purpose for which it was established, namely furnishing competent leadership, providing adequate and safe places, and financially supporting the most balanced and varied recreational program possible. Anything less than this standard is unfortunate and inadequate. When the public places its trust in some agency and the agency fails to deliver satisfactory service, the consequences are often disenchantment with the program and ultimate replacement or abolishment of the agency. Sometimes, nonfeasance by a public recreational service agency may be caused by political intrigue, a nonsupportive city administration, or incompetence within the department. Whenever any of these factors is operational, the taxpaying citizens will bear a heavier burden.

In order to perform its vital function, the public recreational service agency must also maintain adjunctive services for greatest efficiency, economy, and effectiveness. These staff or technical services include organization, administration, education, coordination, conservation, planning, evaluation, supervision, and programming. The outcome of such supportive functions is the offering of the most comprehensive schedule of recreational opportunities from which each person in the community may choose for individual satisfaction and enjoyment.

Essentially, recreational experiences provide specific values to individuals who participate, thus promoting intellectual, physical, and emotional development. Recreational activities engender a sense of well-being and may best bring about self-expression, involvement, enjoyment, satisfaction, self-control, and an enhancement of life not offered by other experiences. Among these values are thought to be physical fitness, health, aesthetic appreciation, socialization, equality, sound value judgments, and freedom of choice.

The provision of recreational service demands a high degree of skill, knowledge, sound judgment, reliability, and intelligence. The burden of programming falls upon the recreationist who must bring all of his natural and learned forces to bear on the problem of comprehensive and varied experiences which can satisfy diverse public demands. There must be constant evaluation and appraisal of the program. The recreationist cannot allow the program of activities to become static. Basic activities, such as motor skills, arts, crafts, music, dramatics, camping, interest groups, and so on, should always be available. However, the recreationist must be certain to build continually on these experiences as demand is created for them and as competent leadership becomes available to promote them. Departments of recreational service must consistently offer opportunities for people to grow recreationally. They must provide the means and the leadership to allow participants and potential participants ample opportunity to select experiences which can widen their horizons and achieve satisfaction for them. Recreationists must indeed be leaders of leisure and serve as resources for the public. Public departments of recreational service must continually experiment with new ideas to create additional opportunities for the people which they serve.

SELECTED REFERENCES

CALIFORNIA, *Publications of Division of Recreation,* Department of Parks and Recreation, Resources Agency of California, Documents Section, Sacramento, Calif., various dates and publications.

DOELL, CHARLES F. and GERALD B. FITZGERALD, *A Brief History of Parks and Recreation in the United States.* (Chicago: The Athletic Institute), 1954.

GEORGIA, *Municipal Recreation in Georgia,* Georgia Recreation Commission and Georgia Municipal Association, Atlanta, 1962.

KRAUS, RICHARD G., *Recreation and the Schools.* (New York: The Macmillan Co.), 1964.

LaGASSE, ALFRED B. and WALTER L. COOK, *History of Parks and Recreation.* (Wheeling, W. Va.: American Institute of Park Executive, Incorporated), 1965.

MAINE, *A Recreation Plan for Maine.* (Augusta: The Main State Park Commission), 1956.

MEYER, HAROLD D. and CHARLES K. BRIGHTBILL, *State Recreation: Organization and Administration.* (New York: A. S. Barnes and Company), 1950.

NEW JERSEY, *New Jersey Statutes Relating to Public Recreation.* New Jersey Department of Conservation and Economic Development, Division of Resource Development, State Bureau of Parks and Recreation, Trenton, N. J., 1965.

NORTH CAROLINA, *Publications of the North Carolina Recreation Commission.* Raleigh, N. C., various dates and publications.

Recreation and Park Yearbook. (New York: National Recreation Association), 1961.

Recreation for Your Community. (New York: National Recreation Association), 1954.

VERMONT, *Recreation In Vermont.* State Recreation Board, Montpelier, Vt., 1958.

WASHINGTON, *Report of the Washington State Parks and Recreation Commission.* Olympia, Wash., 1964.

Chapter 7

CONSERVATION

> PRINCIPLE: It is part of the professional obligation of recreationists and the agencies in which they serve to protect, preserve, and maintain the natural resources of the public domain against all forms and methods of waste, pollution, destruction, and encroachment in order that the provision of recreational experiences in outdoor places for present and future population's utilization, enjoyment, and value may be accomplished.

Space, the places in and on which recreational activity can occur, is an essential and critical commodity to the field of recreational service. There must be designated areas set aside so that people can participate in experiences of a recreational nature, either as spectators or as active participants. Yet, on every side, land is being gobbled up, taken away, broken, cut, excavated, constructed upon, developed, leveled, tunneled into, or hidden under layers of concrete and asphalt. The trees and grass are fast disappearing from the scene of human habitation. The fish and wildlife that once abounded in many regions are being killed off by the number one predator—man, and his civilization. But more important, restrictions are being imposed upon systems of recreational service because they are unable to accommodate the growing population, the megalopolitan spread of strip cities, the widespread pollution of water, and the encroachment by private, commercial interests as well as by governmental agencies which take park and varied recreational resources and spaces and utilize them for purposes other than for which they were originally intended. The waste of forests as a result of fire, soil erosion, the wholesale destruction of landscapes as a consequence of wanton strip-mining operations, each leaves a needless blight upon the face of the land. All of these factors, some related, some correlated, by the sheer immensity of useless exploitation or foolish spoilage of property and natural areas cause the attrition of available space for use by the public as a recreational resource.

A great deal of conflicting opinion exists between those who see in land a great storehouse of natural history, scientific, aesthetic, and cultural values which must be preserved and those who are mainly interested in the profit that can be garnered from economic utilization of these same resources. A similar dichotomy exists between those who wish to preserve open spaces for recreational purposes in their primitive state, i.e., as wilderness, and other equally dedicated individuals who seek to open up these wild regions by constructing access roads, utilities and other amenities. The idea of multipurpose utilization of land has tended to divide those who want to preserve the land as opposed to those who want to conserve the depletable resources. Questions and problems must be faced concerning whether wilderness regions shall be preserved without undue civilizing influences, for the use of only those hardy spirits who have the necessary interest, dedication, and rugged individualism to "pack-in" to the back country; or whether road systems shall be expanded so that thousands, instead of tens, will have access, and thereby reap the benefit of, the natural environment. The purist states that wherever man goes he destroys the balance of nature in some way, and brings with him a civilizing pattern that tends to ruin the essential harmony. Protagonists of this view point to the fact that with great mobility, leisure, and economic means many more people have the inclination to visit the great natural wonders and get back to the soil—but only if roads, accommodations, and other conveniences precede them. The wilderness is there for those who want to see and use it. If agencies begin to develop access roads and scar the vista with resorts, and in the process cut the timber and eliminate the wildlife, then, obviously the wilderness disappears. There is no happy medium.

Still, the chief emergency exists in terms of available space for the conduct of recreational activities. When all is said and done, space is the prime necessity. Space must be acquired for a variety of structures in which recreational activities occur; space is necessary for sports and game purposes, for every aspect of the comprehensive program. No recreational program is complete unless it provides both indoor and outdoor experiences throughout the year in order to meet the diverse needs of people. Available, accessible, and economically acquired land is the key to these problems. Yet the public agency is losing land on every side. Infringement by other public agencies, by purchase which takes the land out of the market, by development of private investors, and by other legitimate and even illegitimate means has created a crisis in terms of needed land for a growing and mobile population.

This nation was endowed by nature with an abundance of riches and varied resources. The productive capacity of this country has been enhanced by having minerals to mine, land to cultivate, scenery to enjoy, waters to control, develop, and fish, and timber resources to carefully manage and utilize. The flora and fauna have provided both food, clothing, and recreational activity. But what was once considered limitless and inexhaustible has, after study, come to be recognized as a steadily diminishing resource. Nevertheless, some planning and management has developed which has led to the perpetuation and provident utilization of natural resources for, among other things, recreational purposes.

THE PUBLIC DOMAIN

Almost the entire area of continental United States was acquired by either purchase, treaty, or conquest. Lands thus owned by the Federal Government constituted the public domain. Chief acquisitions were gained from the Louisiana Purchase of 1803, and treaties with Spain for Spanish Florida in 1819, with Great Britain in 1846, with Mexico and the cessions made to the United States including California, Utah, Nevada, and what are now Arizona and New Mexico in 1848, the annexation of Texas and the Texas Purchase of 1850, the Gadsden Purchase of 1853, and the Alaska Purchase from Russia in 1867. Nearly all of the land west of the Mississippi River was acquired by either purchase or treaty arrangement. At one point the public domain included about seventy per cent of the land area of the United States. Early ideas concerning the public lands were oriented to private sale, which, it was believed, would raise enough revenue to support the Federal Government. Other policies were concerned with encouraging western settlement and initiating routes of transportation to help assure the economic development of the country.

Through an ordinance of 1784, land grants were made to the veterans of the American Revolutionary War and later to those of the War of 1812. The Homestead Law of 1862, the Timber Culture Act of 1873, the Timber and Stone Act of 1878, and the Desert Lands Act of 1877 and 1890 disposed of vast areas of the public domain. Huge land grants were made to the railroads, which did much to exploit this subsidy. Approximately 64 million acres of swamp lands were granted to states with the intent that these would ultimately prove valuable if properly drained. The Morrill Act of 1862 took additional public land and granted it to states for the establishment of institutions of higher education, usually specializing in mechanical trades, mining, agriculture, and technical fields.

This program of disposing of the public domain permitted the development of the naturally rich agricultural lands as well as timber, mineral, grazing, and related resources. The public domain, however, was administered so poorly that the consequences of outright theft, trespass, and piracy by private and corporate interests left a residue of whatever could not be immediately turned to cash profit. This remainder was available for later reservation and much of this land constitutes the great land resource out of which our national parks and forests and other recreational areas have been carved.

In the latter part of the nineteenth century, Congress passed a number of laws leading to the conservation of natural resources at the federal level. In 1872, the Yellowstone National Park, containing more than two million acres, was created from the public domain. In 1897, an act for the useful administration of national forests was passed. The various acts cited above, and that of 1891, stopped the exploitation of the rich timberland in the

Rocky Mountain and Pacific Coast states. However, the best timber and grazing lands had already passed from the public domain into the hands of corporate and private interests. Fortuitously, the residual lands were left in the public domain and now amount to more than 180,000,000 acres which have been reserved for the general welfare of the people as national parks, forests, Indian lands, reclaimed areas, national recreational areas, monuments, wildlife and game refuges, and defense needs. The present public domain is restricted chiefly to the far western states, Nevada, Arizona, Utah, New Mexico, Wyoming, Oregon, Washington, California, and Idaho. Much of it is at high elevations and in remote locations. Nevertheless, it is there for those who wish to follow wilderness travel.

The Federal Government now owns about 455,000,000 acres, of which 89 per cent was once part of the original public domain. The Government either purchased the additional 42,000,000 acres or was the recipient of gifts from private or corporate donors. The Reclamation Act of 1902 withdrew almost 20,000,000 acres from the public domain, while the Antiquities Act of 1906 resulted in the reservation of more than 9,000,000 additional acres to make up the eighty-five national monuments which have since been established by presidential proclamation. The Weeks Law of 1911 made possible the purchase of lands at the headwaters of navigable streams for inclusion in the national forest system. This law permitted acquisition of lands in the eastern part of the United States as well as other sections of the country. The Wildlife Restoration Act of 1937 provides for federal aid to states for the purchase and development of land under state aegis for the primary objective of wildlife conservation. The Soil Conservation Act of 1935, along with the establishment of the Tennessee Valley Authority in 1933, did much to prevent soil erosion and utilized the natural resources of water and land for the public good.

The twisted history of the attenuation of the public domain is blotched by error, immorality, and crass exploitation of magnificent land and the soil, forests, water, and other mineral resources. Although the settlement of the great plains and regions west of the Mississippi River to the Pacific Ocean contributed incalculably to the development and economic enrichment of the country, this aspect of American history is generally identified as one of waste and irresponsible mismanagement of the country's unsurpassed natural resources. Between 1900 and 1940, millions of acres of these capital assets around the Great Lakes and the South that had been formerly given away for nothing, or at such a minimal cost as to be negligible, began to revert to public ownership. The chief reason for this reversion was the leaching out of anything of value which these lands possessed by their private owners who allowed the soil to erode, the forests to be cut and burned, and the mineral resources to be wasted or so depleted that it became uneconomical to work them.

World War II caused the conservation of natural resources to lose much impetus.[1] However, the Materials Disposing Act of 1947, which stopped much of the circumvention of mining laws and the reenactment of the Water Pollution Control Law in 1953, went a long way in assisting the reenforcement of conservation practices. With the change of administrations in 1960, several important conservation measures were enacted by the Congress which have and will continue to have far-reaching effects upon the entire outdoor recreational movement. Public Law 87-383, Wetlands Acquisition Program, was passed in 1961 and authorizes loans for the acquisition of wetlands for waterfowl habitats. Public Law 87-703, Food and Agriculture Act, was signed into being in 1962 and authorizes a ten-year pilot land use reconversion program that establishes a cost-sharing procedure for farmers who will take idle farmland and convert it for recreational usage. Public Law 87-874, Omnibus Bill for Rivers, Harbors, and Flood Control, was passed in 1962, and authorizes the U.S. Army Corps of Engineers to construct, maintain, and operate recreational facilities at water resource development projects which are under the control of the Department of Army. Public Law 88-29 established in 1962 the Bureau of Outdoor Recreation within the Department of the Interior. This Bureau acts as a coordinating agency for the more than 29 other federal agencies involved in the provision of recreational services and will further provide technical assistance to counties that are establishing outdoor recreational areas and programs. The Bureau will also be the administering agency for the Land and Water Conservation Fund under Public Law 88-577, passed in 1964 and implemented on January 1, 1965. Money in the Land and Water Conservation Fund is available for outdoor recreational needs of public agencies and may be received through state designated funding agencies on a matching fifty-fifty basis with the Federal Government. Such funds as are received may be utilized for the following objectives: (1) for the preparation of a statewide master plan for outdoor recreational needs; (2) for the acquisition of land and water areas for recreational purposes; and (3) for the development of public recreational areas and facilities.

Perhaps the most far-reaching enactment of the 88th Congress was to pass Public Law 88-577, which went into effect September 3, 1964. This statement is made in reference to the creation of the National Wilderness Preservation System, established to protect the nation's wilderness. The act is a compromise, as much legislation is, which takes from the national forests and other federally owned lands specific areas and sets them apart in order to, as the enactment states, "secure for the American people of present and future generations the benefits of an enduring resource of wilderness." The compromise was between those who want to preserve and

---

[1] Metal ore and timber resources were required for the war effort and conservation practices dealing with the materials were restricted, if not completely abolished, during the war years. New roads were cut through wilderness areas because concern was manifested for expediency and not toward any idea of what natural resources those roads would destroy.

conserve the wilderness areas for the recreational, educational, and cultural uses to which it may be put and those who would place forest resources to commercial and other-than-wilderness uses.

The wilderness has been carved out of federally owned acreage covering a total of 9.1 million acres under the provisions of the new act. These areas had previously been classified as *wilderness, wild,* and *canoe.* Now, however, they will all be designated as *wilderness.* This law does absolutely nothing to the forest lands. Insofar as the U.S. Forest Service is concerned, it will continue to administer these lands. General public utilization of these areas has been increasing in recent years and the Forest Service will, no doubt, cut a few more trails, maintain its policing operations and planned management. However, instead of the wilderness being merely a part of a national forest or public land, subject to some controlled commercial operations, acreage specifically classified as wilderness will be perpetually reserved and preserved.

The new 9.1 million acres of wilderness within the 186 million-acre national forests is located in 54 areas in 13 states and ranges in size from 5,400 acres to 1.2 million. All of the land is in western states except 5,400 acres in New Hampshire, 21,155 acres in North Carolina, and 886,673 acres in Minnesota. The New Hampshire wilderness lies along the slope of Mount Washington in the White Mountains National Forest. The North Carolina wilderness areas are Linville Gorge, a rugged chasm in the Pisgah National Forest, and Shining Rock located in the same forest. The Minnesota wilderness is the largest area east of the Rockies. It is the Boundary Waters and Canoe Area in the Superior National Forest, a region known for its beautiful lakes and superb fishing. Areas in Arizona, Colorado, California, Idaho, Montana, Nevada, New Mexico, Oregon, Washington, and Wyoming are those which have been designated as wilderness preserves. Montana and Wyoming have the largest wilderness acreages already set aside, but Idaho has the greatest wilderness potential of all.

But even with the Federal Government doing more to protect great areas from desecration and spoilage, and to preserve the forest and wilderness areas from exploitation, commercial infringement, and other land-use encroachments, there still remains a hostility to these actions and an uphill struggle against vested interests bent upon destroying these scenic wonders and scientific phenomena.

THE THREAT OF MEGALOPOLIS

Perhaps there is no greater danger to open space than the phenomenon of ever increasing urbanization. Where once this country existed as a rural and agrarian nation, it now resides in metropolitan complexes that continually expand and is broadly based on a vast interdependent empire of mass communications, transportation, industry, and scientific technology. All of this has irrevocably led to the growth of strip cities and urban sprawl.

This country is surrounded by and engulfed in megalopolis—the current meaning of which is the continual expansion of huge center cities, suburbs, and fringe communities developing in a lineal manner to cover many regions and states along both seaboards, the Great Lakes area, Gulf Coast, and the island empires in the heartland of the Midwestern states.

With the surge of the megalopolis several factors are at once noted. There is the necessity of increasing highways between and through satellite communities as traffic load increases and existing highways become obsolete. There is a concomitant loss of fish and wildlife as the spread of cities continues to make land uninhabitable for wildlife. Water pollution, as a result of industrial and human waste being poured into rivers and streams, has adversely affected fish life and the recreational use of fresh water. Woodlands and forests are being depleted by man-made fires as well as poor management. Open spaces for recreational purposes still exist, but they are at an increasing distance from where people work and reside.

The rapid development of the suburbs was an attempt to compromise with the disparity of easy accessibility to recreational areas and employment areas. However, the growth of suburbia tends to eat up just that much more open space as developers buy up former farm lands or woods, and vacant fields and construct gerry built citified suburbs. The growth of suburbs in concentric circles around the rim of central cities has necessitated the need for improved methods of transportation. Hence, as people seek relief from the core of central cities and move to outlying areas that become the suburbs and satellites of the core region, then new demands are made for more rapid means of transportation and the vicious cycle of additional highway development, with its encroachment upon open space, begins anew. As urban complexes grow they create escalation effects upon areas just outside of the city. People move out of the core and into these outer regions, which puts pressure on all of the natural resources within that region. The consequence of the megalopolis is a deterioration of open space, natural resource conservation, and all of the attendant ills of encroachment.

Urban encroachment on the land can be observed as part of the machinations of investors who speculate in land. As cities grow, they follow major traffic routes. Population seeking housing outside of the city's core also follows the traffic route. The ensuing housing development appears from the air as spokes radiating from a hub, but without any rim. Consolidation of the spaces between the spokes follows and when these areas are filled, additional migrations take place and the city expands in ever widening circles. Investors, noting population trends, quickly buy up whatever land is available between the densely populated zones of the city and the rural areas. Without intelligent planning and zoning, these outer areas are allowed to deteriorate while the land speculator reaps a profit from his investment as the value of property increases far beyond what it costs in taxes and capital gains to maintain such property. As Von Eckardt states:

Such unused land may profit the speculator but it is most expensive to the community—and not only in aesthetic terms. Such land can no longer be considered for the orderly planning of floodwater impoundments, roads, sewers, schools and other vital facilities. New housing that is actually built is pushed farther and farther away from the city. This means longer and more expensive sewers, more utilities and roads, and greater transportation problems.[2]

One result, of course, is urban blight.

THE THREAT OF EXPLOITATION

Man's greed has probably done more harm to his natural wealth than any other single destructive force. Not content to take what he needs for survival and profit, man has wantonly destroyed naturally endowed areas simply for pleasure and because he ignored the fact that natural resources do not exist in inexhaustible supply. But there are those who see in a variety of natural resources the glitter of monetary return far in excess of what has to be invested. These individuals and corporate agencies would deface and spoil natural areas and mineral resources to reap a greater profit. In some instances, corporate investments can be coincidental with the preservation of natural resources, but too often, profit blinds the corporation and the conservational methods that should be taken are not or are done in half measure with a resultant pollution or complete demolition of the resource.

Typical of the acts of exploitation is one in the state of Connecticut, where the Yankee Atomic Power Plant has requested and received permission to construct its buildings at Haddam Neck on the Connecticut River. The operation of the plant will necessitate the utilization of the river waters to cool the reactor. Superheated water will then be discharged back into the river in such volume that the temperature of the water will rise not less than 20 degrees above its normal temperature. There is some controversy concerning the precise results of this operation. Conservationists claim that the superheated water will create a thermal barrier in the river and effectively kill the game fish. Power plant personnel say that even if a thermal barrier develops, there is little likelihood that the fish will not be able to swim through it. It is a well-known fact that raising the temperature of the water effectively reduces the chance of survival of cold water fish, such as shad. However, no testing has been performed at this time and the outcome of the power plant operation will not be determined for some years to come. In the meantime, on the off-chance that the fish might not be adversely affected by the discharge of hot water into the river, the plant will continue with its operations. The cost to recreational

---

[2] Wolf Von Eckardt, *The Challenge of Megalopolis* (New York: The Macmillan Company, 1964), p. 53.

fishermen will be tremendous if the results are negative. However, there is a solution. If the power plant would consent to refrigerate the water prior to discharging it into the river there would probably be no adverse effect on the fish. The corporation which owns the plant is reluctant to do this initially because of the cost—probably two million dollars—but is perfectly willing to ruin fishing in the river if their estimates are proved incorrect. Instead of requiring experimentation before granting approval of the plant, the state commission charged with responsibility for supervising such operations has simply allowed the corporation to construct its buildings, with the "wrist-slap" restriction of requiring the construction of a refrigeration procedure within a five-year period if the shad are killed by the thermal barrier produced by the plant. Of course it might eat into the profits of the company if they were to be on the safe side and not discharge heated water into the river, but the company is willing to take that chance—for the public—despite a concerted outcry against this by interest groups.

The radiation produced by the plant and discharged into the river is not in any appreciable amount to destroy plants and other life in the river—so an expert has testified. Whether or not the latter is true, the fact remains that a private company is so concerned about reaping a bigger profit that it has refused to establish safeguards which would absolutely prevent the spoliation of the river. The reasons why a state agency, whose responsibility it is to protect the public's interest in such cases, would allow the plant to operate before scientific tests can be made to determine the true facts is quite another question.[3] The only impression to be gained is that the state is more concerned with the taxes it might collect from the plant than with the conservation of its natural resources.

Another act of exploitation is taking place in the state of New York, where a utility company is attempting to situate a power plant at one of the loveliest scenic views along the Hudson River in the highlands. The question under consideration is whether aesthetic values are worth anything when they come in conflict with corporate needs. The Consolidated Edison Company of New York has requested the Federal Power Commission to grant a license that would allow the firm to build a $160-million hydroelectric power installation at Cornwall, New York. The company states that under the law the FPC has no right to take aesthetic values into account in rendering a decision. The Scenic Hudson Preservation Conference, which has been leading the conservation fight against the installation, strongly asserts that the FPC not only has the right but is obliged to consider these values as the basis for making a decision.

Consolidated Edison plans to demolish the north front of Storm King Mountain by blasting and gouging out of the rock wall enough room for a

---

[3] Daniel L. Leedy, *Water as a Recreation and Wildlife Resource.* Report to the Agricultural Board, National Academy of Sciences, National Research Council, Washington, D.C., Oct. 20, 1965.

giant power plant supplied by water from a huge storage reservoir located high above the plant in the Hudson Highlands. Water would be pumped from the river into the reservoir during the night and be discharged through tunnels during the day to generate power as required for capacity periods of New York City's never-ending electrical demands. The current would be transmitted across the Hudson by submarine cables, then mainly by overhead high-tension lines to New York City. These high-tension lines would require a pathway not less than 150 feet wide for the distance between the plant to the city and would thus take additional woodland and recreational space out of accessibility. Aside from the acquisition of public domain for corporate uses, the entire concept of spoiling a scenic wonder for millions of people is casually shunted out of the way by a company whose only thought is a favorable profit statement. Commenting upon this entire procedure on the editorial page, the *New York Times* had this to say:

> An examiner for the F.P.C. has found in favor of Con Edison and against the conservationists, mainly on economic grounds. He has upheld the company's contention that its plans would not seriously impair the scenic beauty of the area, but has not ruled specifically on its claim that the Federal Power Act does not permit the F.P.C. even to consider esthetic values. Now Scenic Hudson has filed a brief asking the full commission to rule on this highly important point. Under its broad powers to protect the public interest, the F.P.C. certainly should accept its responsibility to preserve a great national heritage—a region of unspoiled natural beauty and historic national traditions dating back to the beginnings of the Republic. Unless it does so, Con Edison's plea can become the entering wedge for despoiling the entire area.[4]

Certainly, this is blatant exploitation of the public domain for economic gain at the expense of natural beauty and those who are yet unborn.[5] Destroying this natural wonder will positively earn money for the corporation, but it will also cost the people an expense in terms of values which no amount of money can buy.

Apparently the State of New York has been unwilling to grant the necessary protection to the Hudson Highlands region, but would rather be the recipient of future revenues engendered by taxing the company. One result has been the stimulation of federal interest in this situation. The following letters, relative to the Hudson Highland problem, were received from New York's two senators.

> This beautiful river area is one of the most scenic and historically important regions of our state. You can be assured of my determination to preserve it, not only for the use of New Yorkers but for future generations

---

[4] Editorial, "Protecting the Highlands," *The New York Times,* September 8, 1964, Sec. C, p. 28.
[5] "The Hudson," *The New Yorker,* Vol. **XLI**, No. 30 (Sept. 11, 1965), 41–43.

whose need for wilderness area and outdoor recreation space will increase. As you know, I have sponsored legislation in the Senate to establish a Hudson Highland National Scenic Riverway and am working to secure its passage.[6]

As you may know, I introduced in the Senate on March 4, 1965, legislation to create a Hudson Highlands National Scenic Riverway. This legislation, similar to that introduced by Congressman Ottinger in the House, will help conserve the natural beauty of the Hudson River Valley. I hope it will be passed in the near future. The Federal Power Commission's recent decision on granting Consolidated Edison's license application makes it all the more important that we pass the Riverway Bill, because preservation of the lower Hudson's breathtaking beauty depends on preventing further scenic encroachments.[7]

Significant developments have occurred since the Consolidated Edison project for the development of a hydroelectric plant on Storm King Mountain near Cornwall, New York was first approved by the Federal Power Commission in March, 1964. The United States Appellate Court acting on a petition by the Scenic Hudson Preservation Conference against the plant's construction, sent the proposal back to the Federal Power Commission for a complete review. Apparently, there were both procedural irregularities as well as factual discrepancies which prompted the court's action in December, 1965. Early in 1966, the United States Supreme Court refused to review the Appellate Court's decision. This action may open the way to other petitions by interested parties when the aesthetic interests of people come into conflict with purely economic ramifications. Thus enjoined, the Federal Power Commission may well have to consider other than economic development in its certificating processes.

California is another state which has commercial interests gnawing at its priceless heritage from the mesozoic period of evolution. For many years commercial timber companies have acquired vast stretches of the public domain where the giant redwoods grow. These companies have systematically logged the trees until, at present, there are some areas where one can travel for miles and not see a single tree—only stumps, a visual reminder of the graveyard of vanishing forests. After a lapse of 56 years, the Federal Government is again showing interest in preserving a dwindling breed of tree dating back to the mesozoic age.

In 1908, Theodore Roosevelt established Muir Woods National Monument, thus putting the Federal Government on record as obliged to preserve California's mammoth coastal redwood trees. Since that presidential proclamation, and despite state and private acquisition of redwood stands for parks, the number of acres of redwoods has been reduced from two

[6] Letter from Jacob K. Javits, United States Senator, Washington, D.C., Feb. 11, 1965.
[7] Letter from Robert F. Kennedy, United States Senator, Washington, D.C., March 11, 1965.

million to 750,000. Of 300,000 acres of virgin redwoods still in existence, only 50,000 remain safe from being cut over by lumber companies.

Because further delay in acquiring these virgin stands might forever end the once vast resource of redwood forests, the Federal Government is considering appropriate action to safeguard these trees for the benefit of the public. In a report released on October 8, 1964, the National Park Service recommended the federal purchase of up to 53,000 acres of additional redwood forest for national parks. The report advances two points: (1) The redwoods represent a priceless national asset; and (2) preservation of these trees would provide an economic boom for northern California. In the first instance, public interest in these trees has been evidenced over a period of many years, particularly by visits from people from all over the world and the United States. These interested persons have been willing to contribute substantial amounts of money for the purchase, dedication, and preservation of groves of redwoods. Since 1902, private citizens have poured more than $10 million into efforts to preserve the redwoods. Much of this money has been directed through the "Save-the-Redwoods League," a group founded in 1918 that carried on a nation-wide fund raising campaign and information program. Californians have spent another $9 million in taxes to create the state's 28 existing redwood parks. Another good reason for saving these trees is the fact that they grow nowhere else on earth.

The strongest opposition to expansion of redwood parks has come from the logging concerns and their employees, who view conversion of privately owned forests into parks as a threat to northern California's economy. Within days after the National Park Service report, the Redwood Empire Association, representing the major lumber companies and other northern California *commercial interests,* criticized the plan as economically disastrous. The Park Service disagrees because its report estimates that within five years after the establishment of the new redwood parks, some one million visitors annually could be expected to visit the three counties containing these trees. Within 15 years, the number of tourists would increase to two million annually. Within five years, tourists would spend approximately $3.6 million annually on food, lodging, gasoline, and souvenirs. The expanded parks would generate $11.2 million worth of business within 15 years.

The lumbering concerns are not so worried about the economy of the area as they are about making additional profit by cutting the extremely valuable trees. In spite of vital public interest in the redwoods and the undoubted fact that these giants are priceless, the exploiters want to disregard public need in order to capitalize on a rapidly dwindling part of America's natural resource.

Even state agencies, whose normal responsibility is to protect the general interests of the public, succumb to the easy money to be gained by exploiting natural resources at the expense of the very people it is charged with by law, to protect. More specifically, the National Wilderness Preservation System provides that the wilderness areas shall remain open for prospecting for at least twenty years, ending December 31, 1983. Conservationists and recreationists who battled for the passage of this act wanted more restrictive legislation on wilderness areas so that such loopholes in the law would not be used for the advantage of a few to the discomfort of all the people. Yet, this has been allowed to occur. The wilderness act was a compromise between dedicated conservationists and some influential members of the Congress who would not support the bill if it had contained restrictions on new mining claims upon passage. The congressmen represent mining and other vested interests. Nevertheless, the law was enacted with the compromise feature built into the bill as an open invitation for individuals to exploit these regions. While a few Forest Service employees believe that the mining provision is not an open invitation for would-be prospectors, Forest Service officials actually believe the opposite to be true. Apprehensions are apparent in the obvious attempts being made, under the appearance of mining claims, to circumvent the letter of the law in order to obtain individual preserves, literally estates, in the wilderness areas, much like private domains with all the rights of hunting and fishing.

Some Forest Service officials in Washington point out as examples of state exploitation the advertisements published in western states which proclaim good fishing and hunting on small mining claims at prices of from $2,000 to $5,000 each. Officials believe that some people may receive the impression that they will not have to do any mining and will be safe in using the land as a vacation resort. How unfortunate to observe state governments more interested in obtaining revenue from such doubtful sources than in protecting the rights of the public by adhering to the spirit as well as the letter of the law.

THE THREAT OF ENCROACHMENT

Lands which have already been dedicated and set aside for recreational purposes, such as parks, playgrounds, preserves, wilderness areas, beaches, nature trails, and other outdoor areas are under constant threat of encroachment by other public agencies seeking land upon which to construct vitally needed facilities. There is no question that communities need schools, streets, police and fire stations, hospitals, and low rent housing, among other of the more essential buildings, but communities also need parks and recreational areas easily accessible and available for people. When recreational places are taken for buildings of various types they are seldom, if ever replaced. The land, once it has been torn up, cemented over, and built upon, is lost forever to people as a recreational site. Public agencies are under the mistaken impression that land so taken is economical for the city. Such recreational lands, like parks, do not have buildings or other structures already developed on them. The land is already owned by the city, and it is easier to build a road through a park or to build a hospital or school on park property than it is to acquire comparable property on the open market and demolish any buildings that are situated on the site.

Misunderstanding of the economics of this form of encroachment is predominant among shortsighted politicians who view the immediate savings to the city, by acquiring park property for building purposes, without realizing that it will eventually cost the city many times the amount that was "saved" to purchase new property in replacement. For example, the construction of a hospital upon park property will simply cost the community the total sum of actual construction. Inasmuch as the city owns the land, the property is merely transferred to the proper department. However, as demand for more recreational spaces grows—because of an increased population, and particularly because such a population is more aware of the need for recreational areas as a result of better education and communication—the city will have to acquire new sites to satisfy its residents. The acquisition of new property within the modern city is unusually expensive. The additional expense develops because land values rise along with the growth of the city and because urbanization generally means that the land has been used for buildings or other structures that will have to be demolished before the site can be utilized as a recreational facility. All of this adds to the expenditure caused by short-term thinking.

Property which is required for the location of vital community needs other than recreational experiences should be purchased regardless of immediate cost. Neighborhoods slated for urban renewal projects and old buildings and other undesirable structures are the sites which should be used for police stations, access roads, garbage disposal plants, water works, sanitation garages, and hospitals. If these structures are not situated where they will do the community the most good, then other buildings should be condemned and razed. Recreational facilities specifically parks, which are allowed to be destroyed to make way for streets and other public utilities can never be replaced in their natural state. If the community has to wait to acquire such areas, the cost of this acquisition will be many times the original price of the property that was encroached upon, and probably will cost much more than the entire development which replaced the original park. Parks, situated within the crowded neighborhoods of cities and in their core, are almost impossible to replace once they have been taken for other than recreational uses. The city and its population are much the poorer when there are no park areas in the central section of the community.

Typical of the narrow views prevalent are the incidents which occurred in several cities throughout the United States in 1964. In New York City three separate proposals to divert parks for other than park purposes were made. During February, the Board of Estimate of the city overrode the objections of its own Planning Commission and approved the conversion of a 1.35 acre section of Morningside Park from park use to a site for a new public school. Although this is one of the most congested neighborhoods in the City of New York, the Board of Estimate nonetheless transferred the land to the Board of Education for construction and stated that New York had more park land than any other city in the United States, and besides, the area in question was rocky. The fact that there are more people living in the City of New York than in any other city of the United States apparently did not impress the Board of Estimate sufficiently for them to leave the park intact. In July, the Commissioner of the Department of Real Estate for the city proposed that public housing be constructed in the northern section of Central Park as well as in other New York Parks. The Commissioner of Parks had this to say:

> This is a continuation of a short-sighted tendency to attempt to use park properties to resolve problems in sites for schools and other public buildings. This proposal to use park lands for the construction of apartment houses is nothing new. Similar proposals have been defeated in the past because they would deprive the public of park facilities for an interminable length of time while other land was cleared and new facilities constructed and would violate the inalienability of park land. . . . If this proposal is in any way encouraged, it will mean that park lands are no longer inalienable, and that the rights of the majority of citizens and their children through the enjoyment of the irreplaceable natural features of park landscapes can be sacrificed at temporary expediency.[8]

In September, a proposal of the Sanitation Department to build a garage on an undeveloped portion of Alley Park in Queens was attacked by the chairman of the City Planning Commission who is reputed to have stated that, "Park lands should not be diverted to other uses, however worthy." This stand foreshadowed a sharp conflict between the Planning Commission and the City's Site Selection Board. The Planning Commission opposed the proposal because the use of the park for a garage would eliminate nearly four acres of park land, would result in a steady flow of sanitation trucks through the park, and would make it impossible to provide for a suitably planned development of surrounding park areas.

Historic Bushnell Park in Hartford, Connecticut, has been all but dealt a death blow by the State Highway Commission when that body approved plans for extending a new interstate access road through part of the park. Much park land is already taken up by the State House of the Legislature and this latest move will effectively destroy any further park use of this once beautiful and truly historic city park, situated in the center of the community. By running an overpass through one section of the park, its utilization as an open space for recreational purposes will be drastically curtailed. The Hartford metropolitan area is rapidly increasing in size of

[8] Letter from Newbold Morris, Commissioner, Department of Parks, NYC, December 2, 1964.

population and will soon have a rather congested area at its core, yet the only open space will be replaced by a highway.

During the summer of 1964, the stand of trees along the Charles River Drive in Boston was threatened by the Boston Public Works Department which wanted to raze the trees in order to widen the parkway. A determined group of citizens opposed the move, took their case to court, and obtained an injunction against any action being taken to destroy the trees.

Even when laws are passed to preserve specific lands, e.g., the Wilderness Bill, there are examples of public pressure against the wilderness found within the act and elsewhere. Illustrations of this are ascertained by examining provisions in the bill. The Gore Range-Eagle Nest Primitive Area of Colorado is made up of rugged rock-climbing peaks and spectacular ridges. Forest Service officials had tentatively decided that an undetermined amount of land at the southern tip of this area, but not exceeding 7,000 acres, should be made available for Interstate Highway 70. Now, the Secretary of the Department of Agriculture is authorized by the law to remove the acres, if he determines that the action is in the best public interest. This would be done when the Secretary reviews whether the primitive area should be included in the wilderness system. He also may recommend the addition of other lands, not now within the area, to replace the 7,000 acres that may be cut.

These incidents are typical of what is happening with greater frequency throughout the country. With increasing demands being made upon land for many purposes, recreational service agencies are in direct competition to acquire new lands and even to retain what they now hold.[9] A sharp look needs to be taken at the present and future needs of the population if confusion and conflict are not to make chaotic the proper designation of land use patterns. But even more vital is the necessity to prevent continued encroachment upon park and other recreational areas.

TYPICAL OUTDOOR RECREATIONAL AREAS FURNISHED BY CONSERVATION

Either as a necessity or a frill, society believes that outdoor recreational pursuits are important to the health, welfare, and happiness of people. For this reason the establishment of governmental parks, forests, and other facilities within municipalities, counties, and states, and federally has been brought about at great tax expenditure. These range in scope and kind from the neighborhood playground to the great preserves of wilderness to be found in national forests as well as the scenic beauty of the magnificent national parks. One of the most significant uses of our outdoor areas is for recreational purposes. With the increasing leisure, money, and information, and the nearly universal use of private cars and other methods of transportation, as well as the construction of highway facilities into the

---

[9] Peter Farb, "Disaster Threatens The Everglades," *Audubon Magazine,* Vol. **67,** No. 5 (Sept.–Oct., 1965), 302–309.

most attractive regions of the country, tens of millions are now utilizing natural areas in place of the hundreds of thousands of a few years ago.

Among the facilities which can only be provided if proper conservation procedures are taken are:

Roadside Rests. A large proportion of those who travel by automobile to reach the outlying recreational facilities must spend not less than six hours driving. They do not generally plan to utilize facilities that are closer to their homes, but seek a distant site for their final destination. They are chiefly interested in picnicking and resting in attractive locations along the main highways, of which there are now over 5 million miles in the United States. All public areas should be situated in suitable locations and not the typical uninteresting, nonscenic, gouged-out spot at the side of the road that one usually finds. Even where commercial forestry is practiced, roadside stops, particularly along streams, glens near waterfalls, overlooks, and other attractive sites should be retained for recreational development.

Campgrounds. Many vacationers, especially those traveling by automobile, with or without trailers, plan to spend their leisure in camp-site areas. This requires recreational planning and landscaping of high quality. The camping areas must be located away from roadsides and main trails so that complete freedom from noise and the dust stirred by automobiles may be enjoyed. The segregation of particular areas for camping purposes offers an effective method for the control and guidance of people in their utilization of the outdoors. Facilitating participant use without a great many restrictions provides access to attractive settings while maintaining these sites. Conservation methods have to be observed if camping areas are not to be misused. When campgrounds are insufficient to accommodate the number of users, certain destructive tendencies are observed. Soil becomes impacted as a result of overuse, vegetation is destroyed, and the fertility of the area is seriously affected. In some instances careless or ignorant users vandalize trees and bushes in their search for fuel. At times, the novice camper may hammer nails into living trees on which to hang clotheslines, bedding, and other paraphernalia. Trees may be scraped, scarred, and even knocked over by automobiles. As Brockman so well states:

> Proper planning and development of campgrounds are vital to the best use of recreational areas. Good planning not only preserves recreational interests for use by future generations but also ensures everyone of an equal opportunity for enjoyment, provides the maximum number of camp spaces consistent with the character of a given area, and fosters maximum efficiency and economy of operation as well as public safety.[10]

Parkways. Many individuals enjoy viewing an attractive scene rather than being a part of it. For this reason, and because they may also like con-

---

[10] C. Frank Brockman, *Recreational Use of Wild Lands* (New York: The McGraw-Hill Book Company, 1959), pp. 234–235.

tinual change, travel along routes that have deliberately been selected for unusual geologic formations, relatively primitive areas, heavily forested regions, or unique scenic or historic sites affords a recreational experience. The parkway is easily accessible to metropolitan areas. Through the acquisition of sufficient land to allow the development of the property as a continuing belt of heavily wooded land, a reasonable degree of rough terrain often supplies an impression of solitude and remoteness. Space, water, ground cover, and whatever animal life may be found along the parkway play an important role in the preservation of such a resource. Unless conservation of plant and animal life is performed, the constant stream of traffic will soon obliterate the natural environment.

Picnic Areas. Picnic areas may be set aside in almost any park where adequate planning has been arranged for those facilities. Typically, the picnic site can consist of a table, a low stone, brick, or cast-steel fireplace with a secured grate, a nearby fresh water outlet, and toilet facilities. Certain sanitary precautions must be observed in order that the site does not quickly deteriorate as a result of indiscriminate refuse disposal. Toilet and drinking facilities should conform to modern health standards and practices. Conservation practices which will ensure the preservation of the area must provide protection of trees and shrubs from damage, trampling of soil, and the resultant destruction of grassed areas. Control can be gained by rotation of the sites as well as by the emplacement of equipment which cannot be moved to other locations. Specific parking places will also lessen the damage that can accrue as a consequence of unrestricted parking.

Reserved Timbered Areas. Within recent years special areas having unusual scenic values have been set aside for use and enjoyment. These are categorized as exceptional lands that are of such interest and uniqueness that they must be preserved. Examples of such areas may be found in the redwood groves of California as well as the white pine areas of New York, Pennsylvania, and New Hampshire. These sections have been set aside for their scenic, scientific, or historic interest and also as wilderness areas intended to preserve large tracts of remote virgin timberland without encouraging permanent dwellings or the extension or construction of highways.

Wilderness Lands. Considerable popular sentiment has been developing for the preservation of primitive or remote lands that contain few if any permanent inhabitants, provide no essential means of transportation, and are of sufficient size so that one may travel for several days or even a week and not retrace or cross his line of travel. Visitors to these outlying areas are expected to provide their own means of travel by either walking or horseback, and the primitive features of the region are to be protected and preserved. Accessibility, even by helicopter, is limited and only those willing to carry their own gear and sturdy enough to explore these vast spaces are afforded an unsurpassed opportunity to see lands of superlative views and awe-inspiring majesty. All roads, settlements, commercial operations, and most power and reclamation projects are or should be prohibited. Some trails and temporary shelters may be provided.

Wilderness areas are generally situated in regions of high altitude, in remote places where commercial values are low, and scenic and aesthetic values are high. These areas do not lend themselves readily for timber production because of their slow rates of growth, their inaccessibility, and their low-quality forests. About 200,000 acres, or 300 square miles, of this type of forest is considered adequate minimum size for a wilderness area. It is expected that those attracted to these wilderness areas must travel on foot or use pack and saddle horses, boats, or canoes as a means of traversing these areas. Those primarily interested in camping, mountain climbing, and hiking in remote and solitary regions will enjoy such recreational experiences at minimum expense.

State Parks. Nearly every state has some land set aside as part of a state park system. These areas are situated at some distance from metropolitan regions although they may be reached by excellent state highways. They contain some wilderness areas, camping and aquatic facilities, and sometimes sports and game areas. They may be heavily or lightly utilized depending upon their approximation to large urban centers. Even when they are densely populated and heavily used by people who reside in nearby cities, the character of the parks is maintained because these people do not penetrate very far into the interior of the parks. The visitors are content to utilize the fringe picnic and other amenity facilities which are located along the edges of the area. Thus, one of the conservation problems in state parks is that of distributing use so that certain areas are not permanently damaged or destroyed.

The National Parks. The most impressive of the outdoor resources dedicated primarily to recreational experience may be said to be the national parks.

> At best the national parks present the scenic masterpieces of this country, with a spatial setting appropriate to such presentation, and indeed a part of it. Considered in this way, such intangibles as beauty, majesty, and grandeur of the scene become natural resources subject, unless conserved, to marring and in some instances, if pressures for commercial use are not constantly resisted, to utter destruction.[11]

The National Monuments. The national monuments are areas set aside, less for unique scenic interest, than for historic, scientific, or cultural value. Most of the monuments have been established by presidential proclamation. A few have been established by acts of the Congress. Although the more scenic monuments may be found in the western part of the United States and the historic sites located in the East, there is a fair distribution of

---

[11] Shirley W. Allen, *Conserving Natural Resources Principles and Practices in a Democracy,* 2nd ed. (New York: McGraw-Hill Book Company, 1959), p. 196.

national monuments throughout the country and they provide a series of highly enjoyable recreational experiences. In a few instances monuments may become national parks, as has been the case of Grand Canyon, Zion, and Olympic national parks which were first reserved as monuments. The national monuments range in size from one acre to 2½ million acres.

> The most significant difference between a national park and a national monument is found in the comparative value and quality of the natural resources to be preserved, each park being supreme in its special scenic or scientific field. Fortunately no conflict exists; a national monument that is found to possess the outstanding qualities required can, with the approval of Congress, be transferred to the status of a national park.[12]

National Forests. National forests are located largely in the Rocky Mountains and Pacific Coast States where almost three quarters of the total acreage of forests of this type are found. This was the original development, as most of them were established from the public domain. The gross acreage of national forests approximates 190,000,000 acres. The lands are largely of second-growth and cut-over timber in the East and virgin timber in the West. However, a good portion of the forests is situated in high altitude regions which make them less valuable for commercial exploitation because of poor quality timber or inaccessibility. The forests themselves are extremely valuable for watershed, forage, and recreational purposes as well as for timber production. These areas are extremely attractive, an indication of which may be observed from the 9.1 million acres recently withdrawn from the national forests for the wilderness preserves. They are now more generously distributed throughout the country as a result of recent purchases of forest lands by the Federal Government. Fishing, camping, hiking, hunting, trapping, and the construction of temporary summer homes by permit are some activities which are enjoyed in national forests.

Protection and preservation of the natural resources offer inherent recreational values which would otherwise be marred or completely demolished. Unless competent plans are put forward, the damage to recreational lands will be of such proportion that their continued use will be negligible. Basically, conservation of the outdoor properties for availability by the public will stand as the best method of preserving such facilities over the longest period of time.

THE INCOMPATIBILITY OF RECREATIONAL USE AND CONSERVATION

There is an inconsistency between conservation and the utilization of natural resources for recreational purposes. The two ends appear to be

---

[12] A. F. Gustafson, C. H. Guise, W. J. Hamilton, Jr., and H. Ries, *Conservation in the United States* (Ithaca, N.Y.: Comstock Publishing Associates, 1949), p. 307.

inimical. On one side there is an almost fanatic concern on the part of conservationists to *preserve* the natural places without any alteration and to stop whatever imbalances in the ecological processes man-made inroads have made. To this objective the avowed intent of certain conservationists seems to be to keep all of the outdoors just as though population pressures and economic incentives did not exist, i.e., leave primitive areas as if contemporary civilization had never come to the United States. This means that the great outdoors cannot be used.

The paradox of use versus nonuse is best exemplified in the various reports and statements sent out by federal and state governments which list an increasing number of conveniences and amenity services, thus almost removing the reasons for going away from the normal routines of modern living. New roads providing greater access to the wilderness are constructed, electric outlets, flush toilets, modern restaurants, lodges, swimming pools, and all of the devices which can so readily be found in urban living are being included as part of the governmental development of outdoor recreational places. At the same time, these agencies are also decrying the tremendous influx of people clamoring to get to wilderness, as well as park lands, in order to find whatever they conceive to be their personal recreational satisfactions. The simultaneous objectives of use and preservation are mutually exclusive.

Examples of the statements issued by governmental agencies showing their concern for both conservation and use include

> . . . to acquire typical portions of the original domain of the state which will be accessible to all of the people . . . conserve these natural values for all time; administer the development, use and maintenance of these lands and render such public service in so doing, in such manner as to enable the people of Florida and visitors to enjoy these values without depleting them . . .[13]

> To preserve large forested areas and marginal lands along rivers, small water courses, and lakes for recreational use different from that given by the typical city park, and so that these tracts may remain unchanged by civilization, so far as possible, and be kept for future generations.[14]

> The chief function of this Division is to conserve for all time for the use and enjoyment of the people of Indiana certain areas of typical Hoosier scenery in its original state. . . . it should protect and preserve such areas and in so doing provide access to them, provide means for their fullest and most complete enjoyment by the people, . . .[15]

> First, that the national parks must be maintained in absolutely unimpaired form for the use of future generations as well as those of our own

---

[13] Florida State Senate: "The Collins Bill," Senate Bill 441, 1949.
[14] G. W. Williams, "Wise Laws Gave Impetus to Illinois Park System," *Illinois Revised Statutes (1963)*, Vol. 2, Chap. 105, Sec. 466(3).
[15] Indiana Department of Conservation, Division of State Parks, Lands and Waters: "Description of Properties and Facilities," n.d. (Mimeographed).

time; second that they are set apart for the use, . . . and pleasure of the people; . . .[16]

The twin purposes of the establishment of such an area as a national park are its enjoyment and use by the present generation, with its preservation unspoiled for the future; to conserve the scenery, . . . by such means as will insure that their present use leaves them unimpaired. . . .[17]

Every one of these laudable statements is, in fact, a contradiction in terms of meaning. There are statements which indicate that the original or primitive aspects of acquired lands will be preserved in perpetuity. On the other hand, there are statements that these very same lands are to be made highly accessible to the public for its use and enjoyment. There cannot be preservation and utilization at one and the same time. If people are continually encouraged and educated to enjoy the natural setting, there will, if for no other reason, be less of the natural environment for the present population, and much less for future populations to enjoy.

With an increasing population and competition for land by an expanding urbanization, the wilderness will eventually disappear. Man is by nature an extractor and exploiter and for this reason his presence in areas that were once primitive has destroyed much of the natural regions. Land acquisition for recreational and primitive areas will never be able to be maintained with a continuously expanding population. The modern American has committed himself to an urban existence that does not look with favor upon life in the primitive outdoors. As Green has written:

Except for use and consumption, the outdoors actually receives little attention. In part to serve his own comfort and convenience, the hypothetical average American prefers a 'human scale' in his natural setting. He is not 'a lover of nature in all her moods,' whether that man-made personification be romantic or classic. What the nature poet may describe as sublime and awesome, or static and calm, fails to stir his imagination. . . .[18]

Contemporary existence dictates that man's leisure will be spent in an urbanized environment. For this reason there is little knowledge engendered about the outdoors. Understanding of and familiarity with the natural environment produce an attitude toward the preservation of scenic settings and unspoiled areas; lack of knowledge and the skill to participate in activities that require competence in the outdoors promotes difficulties and makes enjoyment almost impossible. Unfamiliarity and ignorance encourage

---

[16] Jenks Cameron, "The National Park Service: Its History, Activities, and Organization," *Service Monographs of the U.S. Government*, No. 11, Institute for Government Research (New York: Appleton-Century-Crofts, Inc., 1922).

[17] U.S. Department of the Interior, National Park Service: "Annual Report of the Director of the National Park Service to the Secretary of the Interior for the Fiscal Year Ended June 30, 1932," Washington, D.C., 1932.

[18] A. W. Green, *Recreation, Leisure, and Politics* (New York: The McGraw-Hill Book Company, 1964), p. 13.

behavior that lessens the value of an area. Acts of vandalism, littering, deposits of refuse in formerly beautiful locations are yet another indication of the human presence in and damage to natural lands. The recreational worth of wilderness is adversely affected by and in conflict with most of civilization's influence.

A tremendous increase in tourist travel has occurred since the National Park Service was established in 1916. During that year more than 300,000 visitors took advantage of opportunities to visit the parks. In 1965, the number of users of the national parks amounted to well over 90 million, while the federally owned forests attracted in excess of 120 million visitors. With the systematic exhortation, on the part of governmental agencies, to the public to enjoy themselves at these various facilities a continually greater number of campers, hikers, viewers, tourists, and other vacationers will descend upon the parks and forests. There is little doubt, then, that these recreational consumers must eventually overrun the wilderness and obliterate it. In order that the public may enjoy the phenomena provided by a bountiful nature, observe wildlife in its natural environment, and live, however briefly, for a period in primitive areas, governmental agencies have highly developed the recreational features of these wild regions.

> Accommodations for visitors at hotels, lodges, and camps are provided to meet the needs or desires of every class of tourist. Facilities are available for those who wish to pitch their own tents. . . .
> Excellent road systems give access to the more important centers. Trails for walking and horseback travel are generally available for those who wish to penetrate even the most remote sections. By using these trails the visitor really gets to know the parks.[19]

However, a great deal of conflict has been stirred up by the methods in which parks are being opened. Many believe that the wilderness cannot be maintained under such conditions and that the very features which make it wilderness must be impaired by these developments. Serious questions can be raised in relation to the terms *use* and *preservation*. Additional queries may be made about what constitutes need and what is the greatest good to be obtained for the largest number of people; or even if the greatest good for the majority is ethically consistent if it denies or infringes upon the rights of minorities. These questions are not simply theoretical semantics, but have practical application to problems confronting recreationists at this time.

One more example of the paradoxical position of the government concerning the preservation (conservation) and utilization of natural resources is the proposal to nearly obliterate the most awesome of America's natural wonders —Grand Canyon of the Colorado. The Grand Canyon is regarded by many as the world's most magnificent spectacle. Nowhere else can be seen such

---

[19] A. F. Gustafson, *et al.*, *Conservation in the United States, op. cit.*, p. 304.

a combination of geologic history, the erosive power of water, and brilliant coloring. This formidable gorge, 217 miles long, from four to eighteen miles wide, and approximately one mile deep, was cut by the Colorado River over a two million-year period. As the vast plateau upon which it is situated was elevated and the rushing river water was able to cut into the sedimentary rock, the canyon was formed. Many layers of varied colored rocks reacted differently to the weathering process, which accounts for the fantastically eroded cliffs, buttes, pinnacles, and ledges, brilliantly colored in blues, reds, purples, grays, and other hues. One can also learn about the nature of plant and animal life which coexisted during the epochs when the Grand Canyon was being formed. The many trails that descend from the rim to the canyon floor pass shale abounding in the fossilized remains of plants, animals, and their traces. Now, for all of its loudly proclaimed desire to preserve and conserve natural resources for the recreational enjoyment and scientific wonderment of this and future generations, the Federal Government, through its Bureau of Reclamation, has designs upon Grand Canyon which would destroy its scenic grandeur and ruin its recreational, natural historic, and geologic impact. In an editorial, *The New York Times* states:

GRAND CANYON NOT FOR SALE!

The Grand Canyon of the Colorado is one of the world's great scenic marvels, a masterpiece of nature's creative sculpturing of the earth over vast periods of time by wind, rain, frost, and most of all by a free-flowing river. It is a mile-deep open book of the geologic ages, with layer upon colorful layer of sandstone, limestone and shale down to the dramatic inner gorge where the river is exposing the oldest known rock on earth.

Under the proposed Pacific Southwest Water Plan, nearly half of this inner gorge of 279-mile-long Grand Canyon would be flooded behind two hydroelectric power dams. Bridge Canyon dam would back water almost one hundred miles upstream—all the way through Grand Canyon National Monument and thirteen miles of Grand Canyon National Park. Marble Gorge dam, just upstream from the park boundary, would inundate the first in the series of Grand Canyon gorges and would further shrink and artificially control the normal flow (already affected by Glen Canyon dam) of the remaining unflooded miles of river in the national park.

The basic function of these dams is simply to provide dollars from the sale of generated power with which to help finance the water development program of the Southwest. The Bureau of Reclamation contends the dams are essential. Yet there is mounting evidence that reasonable, even far less costly and more efficient, financing alternatives do exist.

In a beautiful and authoritative book on the canyon, "Time and the River Flowing: Grand Canyon," just published by the Sierra Club, less costly thermal power plants using abundant fossil fuels are suggested as one possible solution to the financing problem. In addition to savings in cost, thermal plants would save much-needed Colorado River water, which reservoirs behind the dams would lose through evaporation and percolation.

Much has been said by the dam proponents of how small an area of the total canyon would be affected by these dams and reservoirs. Yet it is the very heart, the most significant creative force that gives meaning to the canyon scenery, which would be destroyed. That is the living river.[20]

So many appeals to members of the House and Senate were made by an aroused public and professional practitioners in the fields of conservation and recreational service that the Department of the Interior has now abandoned its attempt to completely destroy the Grand Canyon. Only the upper reaches of the Colorado River will be dammed. Bridge Canyon Dam, which would have backed water through the spectacular gorge itself, has been stopped for the present. In a letter received from the Interior Department, the following information may be of interest:

> In recognition of the deep concern expressed by many people for preservation of our scenic resources, a request for authorization of Bridge Canyon Dam is being deferred, as recommended by the Bureau of the Budget, to permit further evaluation of the scenic, recreation, and power values and power revenues involved in this development. Authorization for construction of Marble Canyon Dam, however, is being recommended.[21]

An alert citizenry must keep ever vigilant and be ready to oppose crass waste and improper use of the national heritage of natural resources whenever it occurs.[22,23] Constant scrutiny of governmental functions and responsibilities is required if timeless benefits to all of the people are to accrue. Such instances where public demand restricts governmental interference, waste, or destruction of the public domain prove that the people's voice can be heard and that an aware citizenry can make their demands felt and satisfied. However, eternal preparedness to cry out against infringement of any person's right to the great natural preserves of this country is the price that must be paid.[24,25]

[20] Editorial, "Grand Canyon Not for Sale!" *New York Times,* Dec. 20, 1964, Sec. E, p. 8.
[21] Letter from L. W. Daniours, Acting Assistant Commissioner, Bureau of Reclamation, United States Department of the Interior, Washington, D.C., June 1, 1965.
[22] Hugh Nash and Carl Hayden, "Storm Over the Grand Canyon," *Parks and Recreation, I,* No. 6 (June, 1966), pp. 496–501, 524–525.
[23] Editorial, "Shadow Over Grand Canyon," *New York Times,* July 31, 1966, Sec. E., p. 9.
[24] Jay S. Shivers, Beware: The Spoilers Are On The March," *Recreation,* **LVIII**, No. 9 (Nov., 1965), 448–450.
[25] Editorial, "New Tragedy in the Everglades," *New York Times,* Aug. 7, 1966, Sec. E., p. 8.

THE COMPATIBILITY OF RECREATIONAL USE AND CONSERVATION

If conservation is seen as the regulated use and management of depletable natural resources so that their durability is prolonged for the longest period of utilization, if it means the careful management of replenishable resources to afford continual utilization without obliteration, permanent damage, or destruction, then there is no polarity between recreational use and conservation. These aspects of conservation can and should be carried out by recreationists and those who have direct interest in the development and maintenance of natural phenomena.

The meaning, importance, and goals of conservation have greatly expanded within recent years. Conservation is chiefly a local problem, although its results have regional and sometimes national implications. It must fit the local social and economic requirements. Although the immediate objectives differ from region to region and state to state, the ultimate aims are fairly consistent. For example, in some areas conservation attempts have the utilitarian objective of conserving water for irrigation, power, or drinking purposes. In some states an adequate supply of cover is necessary for the forage of animals. The development of the most attractive scenic and aesthetic effects can be accomplished only if growing forests are maintained. Soil conservation to prevent erosion or the washing of soils into streams, lakes, and rivers is of tremendous significance in certain regions. Conservation of natural resources is of importance in every part of the country. Conserved forests are the habitats of fish and game. Outdoor recreational areas would be less valuable if there were no trees, grass, or flora. Thus, multipurpose conservation has been given wide status.

One of the most important uses of natural resources is for recreational purposes. It would, for example, be almost impossible for most people to use their leisure for any sport or game, for receiving a sense of awe and a feeling of adventure, if they did not have access to the outdoor environment. Rolling land, rugged terrain, hills, mountains, panoramic vistas, forests, waterways, wildlife, and a variety of flora—all make a significant contribution to the recreational experiences of people everywhere. The satisfaction to be obtained from participating in high-quality recreational activity in the outdoors requires space, unique terrain, cover, and in specific situations, recreational experience must be the chief use to which these natural resources are employed.

In terms of this discussion the recreational facilities usually found in municipalities that permit outdoor activities are mentioned because land, which is the essence of designated recreational space, is part of the natural resources. However, dominating attention will be given to those areas that generally constitute the reservoir of natural resources in the outdoors, e.g., wilderness, water, fish, game, and forests. These natural phenomena may be used for many purposes, alternately, simultaneously, or exclusively for and dedicated to recreational use. The varied recreational resources such as favorable climate at different times of the year, diversified terrain, and topographical features that are scenically, scientifically, or historically interesting are unequally distributed throughout the country, and probably account for the spasmodic utilization of land and the differences in the kind and extent of outdoor recreational experiences.

The scattering and uneven arrangement of physical resources stress the need for well-conceived plans in relation to immediate and potential utilization of natural areas. There is not merely the requirement of additional space to be set aside, withdrawn from the public domain, particularly for a variety of recreational activities, but it seems obvious that many types of outdoor recreational experiences are in harmony with other forms of land utilization. When such compatibility is feasible, methods must be worked out so that the most effective diversified land use can be developed. Ultimately, only intelligent coordination and scientific management of the land will encourage the most beneficial recreational use by the greatest number of people, in accordance with the continuity of all essential land values. In any event, natural resources can be diminished or obliterated. The perpetuation of recreational values obtained from the outdoors will occur only if conservation practices are performed.

To the degree that natural resources, specifically land, are diversely affected by nearly all of man's activities, the whole concept of conservation is consistent with recreational use. If not for conservation, i.e., the deliberate and directed maintenance of natural resources, then soil depletion in the face of accelerated erosion would continue unabated. Waters, cleaned in defiance of pollution caused by industrial development and the expansion of metropolitan areas, would be useless. Scenic, historic, or archaeological areas preserved in opposition to the flooding of these resources, as a result of the erection of dams and the formation of artificial lakes, would be lost forever. Prevention of the destruction of forested regions, grazing lands, promiscuous drainage of swamps and marshes, all of which affect the natural cover, habitat, and ecological balance of fish, game, and wildfowl, makes their preservation possible. The perpetuation of wilderness areas provides experiences to be gained in no other setting. But without conservation, the values to be preceived from passive or active participation in outdoor recreational environments would be impossible, or at best so reduced that only those lands in private ownership, which adhered to conservation practices—if such lands had the features described—would provide valuable recreational experiences, and then only for the select few.

SUMMARY

The protection of important recreational lands is of infinite significance, because they are particularly subject to damage as a consequence of overexposure to an irresponsible public. Specifically, careful attention must be given to the extent and method of the development of such land as well as to the type of activities conducted there. Although the public may not fully realize the notable recreational features unless sufficient means for their inspection and investigation are provided, it must be recognized that construction of any sort interposes components that are contrived and affected and thus destroy the natural values for which interest was originally aroused. For this reason continued physical development of outstanding outdoor recreational places should be held to a strict plan. Amenity facilities may be included in plans for the utilization of outdoor areas, but they should be minimized and never viewed as being more valuable than the natural resources themselves. Perhaps it is better to sacrifice *some* consumer comfort and convenience than to forever destroy natural areas with artificial elements.

SELECTED REFERENCES

HARRISON, C. WILLIAM, *Conservation: The Challenge of Reclaiming Our Plundered Land.* (New York: Messner), 1963.

HARRISON, C. WILLIAM, *Conservationists and What They Do.* (New York: Franklin Watta, Inc.), 1963.

HIGHSMITH, RICHARD M., et al., *Conservation in the United States.* (Chicago: Rand McNally), 1965.

HOGNER, DOROTHY CHILDS, *Conservation in America.* (New York: Lippincott), 1958.

HUBERTY, MARTIN R. and WARNER L. FLOCK, *Natural Resources.* (New York: McGraw-Hill), 1959.

LIVELY, C. E. and J. J. PREISS, *Conservation Education in American Colleges.* (New York: The Ronald Press), 1957.

KRUTCH, JOSEPH WOOD, *Grand Canyon: Today and All Its Yesterdays.* (New York: William Morrow and Co., Inc.), 1958.

LEYDET, F., *Time and the River Flowing.* (San Francisco, Calif.: The Sierra Club), 1965.

RAY, J. R. JR. and R. H. FUSON, *Resource Conservation in the United States.* (Dubuque, Iowa: Wm. C. Brown Co.), 1965.

SCHULZ, W. W., JR., *Conservation Law and Administration.* (New York: The Ronald Press, 1953).

SHANNON, WILLIAM V., "The Battle of the Canyon Is Joined" *The New York Times* (July 31, 1966), Sec. E, p. 4.

SMITH, ANTHONY WAYNE, "The North Cascades" *National Parks Magazine,* Vol. 40, No. 223 (April, 1966), p. 2.

SMITH, GUY H., *Conservation of Natural Resources,* 2nd ed. John H. Wiley, 1958.

UDALL, STEWART, *Quiet Crisis.* (New York: Holt, Rinehart and Winston), 1963.

U.S. DEPARTMENT OF THE INTERIOR, *Quest for Quality.* U.S. Department of the Interior Conservation Yearbook. (Washington, D.C.: U.S. Government Printing Office), 1965.

———, *The Population Challenge . . . What it Means to America.* U.S. Department of the Interior Conservation Yearbook No. 2. (Washington, D.C.: U.S. Government Printing Office), 1965.

Chapter 8

LEADERSHIP

> PRINCIPLE: One of the primary functions of the recreationist is the leadership of people by teaching them about their almost unlimited potential for participation in wholesome leisure experiences. Leaders in the field of recreational service must offer instruction of leisure arts and skills through every feasible method which promotes individual awareness of personal capacity for enjoying a variety of rewarding recreational opportunities.

Of necessity, leadership has been thought to be the influence of a single person with other people in such a manner that specified goals are achieved. Although the above statement is probably valid, it raises certain questions. Whose goals are achieved? In what manner are individuals so involved with a designated leader that they follow him? How does leadership offer a climate for instruction? Will individuals accept instruction in activities or about a subject of which they have had neither previous experience nor familiarity? All of these questions are directly related to the social phenomenon of leadership and the processes by which it is effected.

Leadership is authentic when democratic processes are followed. It is in this procedure that all members of any given group participate in decisions which will ultimately affect the group and its aims. Decision making has been thought to be the essential facet by which leadership is known. In any situation, it is the leader who makes the decision which the group then follows. However, the decision-making process allows each person to project his ideas in such a manner that the result can cause consensus and become the plan which the group will follow. Before any decision can be made, several important objectives must be made known. First, all of the alternative concepts which are pertinent to any decision must be recognized; second, the relevancy of these alternate modes of behavior and their probable outcomes must be analyzed; finally, one course must be selected as having the most value and greatest degree of probability of successful achievement for and by the group.

The single aspect of group participation within the decision-making process is validation of the democratic orientation of leadership. Each member of the group has the right to offer ideas and preferences and to have equal opportunity for his proposals to be heard and utilized. Thus, the individual is more closely bound to whatever project upon which the group decides because he has had a chance to assist in planning the activities. Total commitment to the activities of the group and participation by all members of the group are essential to democratic leadership. However, group members must be prepared to contribute their suggestions, attitudes, and performance in the selection and the accomplishment of aims.

Unfortunately, not all group members are sufficiently experienced or ready to take part in the decision-making process. Some may have been conditioned by previous situations to accept plans, policies, and decisions ready-made for execution. They may be simply unaccustomed to self-expression, problem-solving procedures, and projecting the probable consequences to be derived from making a choice of several possible courses of action. Such involvement may be quite unfamiliar to them and may cause insecurity and a lack of confidence. Group living requires a different orientation and basic instruction in decision making. These are attitudes and skills that can be learned in a democratic atmosphere. Above all, the communications network within the group must be freely available and clear. The surest way toward learning democratic procedures and practices is through the widest dissemination of information to the participants.

In the most practical sense, leadership is not only displayed by a single individual, acting and exerting influence with others as a consequence of his projected self-image. Leadership depends upon an interaction between the leader, the group, and the situation in which the group finds itself at any given time. The leader may symbolize group ideas and/or ideals. He may be best able to express group concepts and desires. The leader has much to do with channeling group action toward a specific set of goals and he thus works indirectly or through others to achieve this purpose. The leader may therefore be characterized as one who manipulates the environment so that group members actually perform the direct tasks that lead to whatever objective they seek. Leadership is largely catalytic. It is through the leader that events are started, arranged, and oriented. It is the leader's continuing stimulation of the group that usually makes them persevere so that ultimate success is assured.

HUMAN NEEDS AND MOTIVATION

Satisfaction of human needs may be achieved when social, physiological, and psychological needs are met. The probability exists that these are not separate factors, but that they act interchangeably and that each facet exerts some influence upon the behavior of the individual. Typical of human needs are those which involve status, personal worth, recognition, and security. Status concerns the place of the individual within a specific social environment. It is usually associated with membership in a particular group or some acclamation either tangible or intangible. Each person has a sense of self-esteem which may be said to reflect his concept of his worth as a human being. An individual may be able to perform satisfactorily and contribute more successfully when he feels that his dignity is accepted even though his status is limited or low.

> Man is an individual but at the same time he is a social being. He wishes to develop his own personality and self-respect; he desires opportunity to achieve and to create, and he delights in the self-assurance that derives from possessing real ability and the chance to use it. . . . Indeed, self-esteem is founded only in part upon an inner conviction of worth. To a large extent it is a by-product of recognition given by other.[1]

Recognition is bestowed upon the individual by others. Recognition imparts a real feeling of belonging and participation for it constitutes an explicit method of understanding and communication between people. Basically, recognition means that the ideas and actions of an individual are accepted and utilized by others who accord the recipient a place in the community, whatever it may be.

Security is the result of having status, being recognized, and realizing personal dignity. When an individual is secure he is able to function in a more intensive and competent manner, and does not fear to explore or to innovate nor to participate and contribute more fully to group life. The secure person has a heightened sense of belonging and is, therefore, freer to offer suggestions and comments for and upon group life without apprehension or worry that he will be rejected or that the group will omit him from its plans. Security enables better communication to exist between group members and encourages a greater degree of rapport and empathy. With security, apparent dangers or conflicts can be confronted and usually overcome successfully, for there is a concomitant build-up of morale and cohesiveness as group members unite to attack common problems or plan to reach certain objectives in concert.

Motivation

Stress or tension is produced in the individual when needs are unmet. Man's behavior is oriented toward the satisfaction of his needs. The urge to reduce tension and thus satisfy social needs is motivation. An understanding of man's needs will present knowledge of human motivation and this, in turn, will lead directly to the comprehension of why people behave the way they do in given situations. All people are motivated to act in ways that will tend to alleviate tension, satisfy specific desires, and achieve a sense of social fulfillment. Motivation has to do with feelings of anxiety that arise when the attainment of social goals is thwarted, or when

---

[1] American Business Leaders, *Human Relations in Modern Business* (Englewood Cliffs, N.J.: Prentice-Hall, Inc., 1949), p. 21.

an individual pictures himself at a higher level than he is able to realistically attain. Motivation also serves as a stimulus for behavior when the individual aspires to some level of achievement that may be within his capacity or potential.

People work in a variety of ways to fulfill their social needs. When needs are being met in a routine manner there is no stress upon the person to strive or make demands of himself. He is satisfied with the *status quo*. However, when certain needs become urgent and there are blocks that deny the satisfaction of those needs, then the individual utilizes his intellect and energy to bypass the hindrance and is therefore in a state of tension. In this dynamic condition between the individual and his environment, the unsatisfied need acts to motivate him toward the achievement of his aims. He is thus compelled to behave in ways that will lead to eventual or immediate satisfaction or ultimate failure. The distinguishing feature of the *status quo* and dynamic interchange is significant. In one instance there is no reason for movement. All conditions within the environment remain fixed and apparently there are no goal-strivings. People are satisfied with what they have and are simply not interested in pursuit of objectives which may lift them out of their placid orientation. On the other hand, leadership flourishes and is, in fact, dependent upon states of stress, flux, and dynamic interchange. One of the requirements for leadership to exist is conflict and the lack of resolution of factors which block the attainment of objectives so that particular needs, generally social, may be satisfied. The leader is usually looked upon as the instrument by which social needs can be satisfied and the leader's success is directly related to his ability to use whatever intellectual or special knowledge he has to satisfy or seem to fulfill the needs of his followers. His influence with his followers stems from his power to mitigate problems which thwart them.

When an individual is in a state of unfulfilled need, there arises a condition of tension within the organism. When such need is not satisfied, because of some internal or external hindrance, a behavioral pattern emerges that is organized around the object thwarting fulfillment. Depending upon the intellectual capability of the person involved, the rigidity of the barrier to satisfaction, and the leadership available, i.e., the agent having the power to reduce the problem into component parts and resolve it, either tension will remain with frustration and disintegration as the outcome or the need will be satisfied and goal attainment secured. In any case, the consequences will depend upon the need, the readiness of individuals or the group to function, the leadership potential, and the difficulty of the problem to be overcome.

LEADERSHIP AND LEARNING

The leader has an all-consuming concern, that of achieving some object, presumably the position of leadership within a group. He has a need to attain social status through leadership exertion. Concomitant with his need to lead is a very definite concern for those who make up his following. In this respect, therefore, the leader has influence with his group and it accords him the position of leader. The choice is reciprocal. The leader, as far as the group members are concerned, has the necessary qualification, perhaps personal magnetism, intelligence, or technical skill, to enhance their status or make easier their attainment of some goal which they all hold in common. It might be the ability to solve some problem or conflicting situation which directly affects the group's stability or establishment. In the same manner, the leader requires followers, for without them there is no leadership. He provides the direction and ideology that will assist them in the attainment of a specific aim and they provide the necessary environment for the leader to satisfy his need.

The leader aids the group in its goal attainment, by providing an outline of behavior for them to follow. Perhaps the group must conform to rules and regulation of conduct by which it may sooner reach its desired prize. Whatever conditions prevail for the group to achieve its goal is of basic business to the leader. It can be stated that the leader facilitates the climate in which success is reached by teaching group members to adapt themselves to their present environment. In point of fact he is teaching them and is directing their behavior. If improved behavior can be generated, the likelihood of need satisfaction is more probable. Leadership may therefore be partially defined as the manipulation of the situation so that learning can occur. Learning may be defined as an improved pattern of behavior whereby problems or conflicts are analyzed and solved.

LEADERSHIP AND INDIVIDUAL DIFFERENCES

Learning, or the development of improved behavioral patterns, is constantly made difficult by the diversity, intensity, and distribution of individual differences. The leader must take into account the range of individualization in his attempts to assist in the development and improvement of his followers. To the recreationist, the professional obligation of teaching others to appreciate and ultimately participate in recreational activities with which they may have no previous experience requires a high degree of leadership ability. The methods and hypotheses upon which such action is based is the subject of this section.

To some, individual differences means that only by working with each person separately can any account be taken of the numerous differences that characterize people. However, the recreationist rarely, if ever, obtains the chance to work with one person, for the ratio between recreationists and laymen in nearly all communities is extreme—usually one to 1,000 plus. Small towns may employ one or two recreationists in a population of 20,000 or less, whereas large urban centers may employ one hundred or more recreationists. The ratio of professional to layman is still extreme in the latter instance because the urban center has a population in excess of 100,000. Nevertheless an understanding of individual differences does not preclude working with people in groups. The two concepts are not mutually exclusive. There is no innate contradiction between working as a group member and simultaneously participating in activities that have a direct appeal for, and are adapted to the physical or psychological capabilities of the individual. The leader who appreciates the need to adjust the learning activity according to differences among individuals organizes the experiences of the members so that each of them can proffer a specific contribution to a common group interest.

As an integral part in the leadership process, each participant is allowed and encouraged to take part in the choice and planning of the experiences in which he will engage. This method is more likely to develop individual capacities and skills than a method whereby no contributions are solicited from group members—i.e., they merely watched others participate, simply competed, or performed. Effective guidance of the recreational activity necessitates a knowledge of the traits and background of each client by the recreationist. To the extent that the recreationist will get to know all group members, but will rarely meet all of the potential participants who seek recreational activity through the department at mass and/or spectator events, he must be well versed in the techniques of diagnosing whatever weaknesses the individual has and then show that person how to overcome them and improve his likelihood for successful achievement.

Individual Characteristics and Learning

Any recreational program in which instruction is significant must consider the facts about individual differences. There is, for example, in any of the activities included within the program propensities for a wide range of characteristics with which individuals are equipped. The arrangement of talent most nearly approaches the normal frequency curve. This is reliable for motor skills, educational experiences, general intelligence, art, craft, dramatic, and musical faculties, as well as most, if not all other innate and learned talents. There is valid evidence to support the contention that the intensity to which the individual possesses varied characteristics also differs. In many instances the skills that have been attained are not developed to the same degree. We observe some people who have a high degree of skill in motor movement and no talent for art or music. Other people have a many-faceted talent, seemingly good at whatever they put their head or hand to; while others appear to be unskilled and without a modicum of talent for anything.

People do not all gain to the same degree from the same activity because of their varied levels of intelligence, their previous exposure to and experiences in activities, their readiness to learn, their proclivity for the task, and their willingness to make the effort. They do not react in the same manner to a given stimulus. People are also unlike in terms of their respective speed of maturation, e.g., physiologically, psychologically, intellectually. They differ in terms of ability to master certain skills. These variations are determined by both nature and nurture.

The individual should be appraised according to his present capacity, environmental background, maturation rate, and potential. The recreationist is in the best position to assist the individual to take the greatest advantage of his experiences, and the recreationist must do so on the basis of needs, interests, attitudes, and potentialities of each group member. The need is for a flexible recreational program operated by a professional staff competent to adapt activities to fit the mental and physical capacities of people. Simultaneously, earnest consideration must be given to the problem of developing the necessary skills, attitudes, and interests that can be engendered only by instruction when there has been no prior acquaintance or experience on the part of the agency's clientele.

LEADERSHIP AS INSTRUCTION

Instruction is seen as being both developmental and remedial. Based upon an analysis of the individual's record in group living, his stated interests, capabilities, and experiences, the recreationist attempts to lead the individual to achieve objectives that are important to him and the agency. The agency prepares a variety of recreational experiences that, if undertaken, will eventuate in a well-rounded personality and the development of wholesome attitudes and skills for leisure. The essential factor is the provision of a comprehensive program that will ensure coverage of individual differences among participants. Leadership also has a guidance function. It is a technique that requires the establishment of an atmosphere most conducive to wholesome growth and development of individual potential and the creation of conditions that encourage and support the growth of all group members in the social recreational setting.

Leadership may be regarded as an empathizing ability which is focused on some end in view by both leader and follower. Instruction may be regarded as the most effective sympathetic means available for the educational development of the participant. The fundamental purpose of the recreational agency is to provide the environment so that people can live more effective daily recreational lives. As such practice is instituted in a democratic context, instruction—one form of leadership—acknowledges the value of creative human individuality and attempts to inculcate in each group member the attitude, skill, and capacity to estimate and scrutinize any conflicts that confront him and the social group to which he belongs. The recreational program must offer an attractive, socially acceptable, stimulating environment, which consistently provides the participant with new, as well as familiar, possibilities that keep him active and directed toward desirable goals.

The recreationist, acting in a leader role, has an instructional obligation to all those who utilize services of a recreational nature for which the agency is responsible. He must perform a teaching function beyond that of developing skills in experiences to which the individual may have had prior exposure. The recreationist's instructional function is performed by broadening the horizons of would-be participants by informing them, and if needs be, luring them by all ethical means to try activities that might prove beneficial to them. Perhaps this may well be the most difficult task of the leader, but the value for the follower can be of immeasurable importance. The recreationist must find ways for the continued expression and expansion of the individuality of his agency's constituents. In order for the recreationist to function effectively, he must have a sympathetic understanding of individuals and be able to empathize with them. He must understand the needs, talents, and capabilities of his group members at any time and guide them into experiences that will be worthwhile and enhance their lives. He is prepared to give guidance and direction by virtue of his knowledge of people and those experiences which have constantly proved effective. His knowledge of recreational activities should be such that he is able to influence group members in their selection of experiences that will correlate with what they seek in terms of group and individual satisfaction.

Those experiences which add to social integration and organization, an arrangement through which all members have the opportunity to participate, should be high on the list for inclusion within the program. The recreationist must utilize his leadership powers to permit the free expression of individuality, but must, nevertheless, be prepared to assume direction when the membership requires. This does not mean authoritarian control, but merely a channeling of interest so that the basic objectives for which the group was formed is not lost. He must know the needs and abilities of the individuals with whom he is dealing and must simultaneously organize the environment which will most effectively offer satisfaction of these needs and develop these abilities. In order to gain maximum influence with the group and thereby greater support, he must counsel participants so that their goals are not beyond their capacity. Guidance of the selection of activities that fall within the scope of existing experience is necessary so that a bridge between the familiar and the unknown can be made. Working from the known and moving on to activities which are new requires a natural and normal progression evolving without sudden gaps. The lead-up sequences must be of a type that promise smooth continuity from old (familiar) to new. Stimulating new ideas and the development of power to perform with confidence so that exploration of additional experiences may be furthered without undue stress is part of this technique. The implementation of such a plan can come from the recreationist's original suggestions, but support for it can only be gained when group members adopt the idea as their own and contribute their concepts and efforts. The recreationist has the added responsibility for the dynamic interaction that epitomizes group life and the conduct of information which is most important to the perpetuation of the group. Unless all members have a direct link with intercommunications their support and personal contributions weaken until the group dissolves. Without the group, there can be no leadership.

COUNSELING

That leadership is best which is least apparent or restrictive. For this reason, counseling is innate in leadership as an instrument to help the follower more fully understand his role within the group and play a greater part in group living through self-understanding. Opportunities for counseling are present in many recreational group situations. Most groups are small and provide a maximum direct contact in which the technique of indirect leadership or nondirective counseling can be most effective. Indirect leadership, where the recreationist expresses his influence through other members of the group, is most nearly like nondirective counseling. Where group members have the capacity, education, background, and skill to maintain their own affairs and move in satisfying and appropriate directions, the situation is best suited to nondirective counseling.

The counseling technique is utilized to establish modifications of opinion and conduct. Thus, it can institute a climate where conflict from within can be overcome in order for the group's common objective to be reached. Basically, it is concerned with individual attitudes and adjustments. It does not attempt to arrogate to the counselor the direction of an individual or group. Instead, it constructs a situation where the counselee is confronted by his immediate situation and the counselor reflects the counselee's problems and conflicts in such a way that the latter gains psychological insight into his frustration. With understanding of the reasons why he acts the way he does, problem-solving may result instead of thwarting. The leader uses this technique if he really believes in a permissive, participative, democratic process.

LEADERSHIP AND THE INDIVIDUAL

Interpersonal behavior is the basis for leadership. There is good reason to believe that individuals who have the ability to empathize with others are in a better position to gain influence and thereby hold leadership status. This particular social sensitivity to others is a significant factor of overall skill in working with people. Leaders apparently have this attribute to a rather high degree.[2] For this reason the leader is better able to recognize, and thereby counsel more effectively, concerning the problems which the follower faces. The true leader, one who exists in a democratic rather than an authoritarian environment, understands others because he does not impose his own attitudes and knowledge. He establishes rapport or mutual feelings of confidence, between himself and those who are his potential followers. Such social perception enables the leader to determine the

---

[2] K. Chowdhry and T. M. Newcomb, "The Relative Abilities of Leaders and Non-Leaders to Estimate Opinion of Their Own Groups," *Journal of Abnormal and Social Psychology*, **XLVII** (1952), 51–57.

needs and desires of the members of the group in which he works and to develop shared goals toward which each member works.

Dynamic interaction is a direct consequence of empathy. Interpersonal behavior has augmented potential when there are clear lines of communication between the leader and his followers. The likelihood of attainment of leader status is tremendously enhanced when understanding is conducted freely and easily. If recipients and communicants can find the means of expressing themselves, and, in so doing make themselves understood as well, the probability that leadership attempts will be made successfully is encouraged. Leadership requires a high degree of communication. The individual who has developed his skill in social perception is in the best position to exploit that skill in effecting communication with others. For this reason, the whole process of interaction has a direct and determinate impact upon successful leadership attainment.

The ability to empathize gives the potential leader enough insight into the responses of the members of the group with which he would exercise influence that he is able to predict their respective behaviors. The ability to correctly estimate group members' feelings and attitudes involving any idea also provides the leader with a greater degree of control and initiative in planning ahead. If he is able to foresee how his followers will react to certain situations or conditions, he is better able to avoid conflict and unnecessary hindrances to his proposals. Of course the ability to predict the behavior of any given individual within a group varies directly with the degree of intimacy that one person has with the other, the intensity of interest and familiarity, and the intelligibility or direct line of communication established.

With interaction the strength of influence on behavior is magnified.[3] Because leadership is defined as influence with others, it is apparent that predictability of behavior leads to increased interaction. This means improved rapport and efficacy in dealing with people. The results of heightened security, more frequent contact, and the responsiveness of individuals to ideological stimuli form the basis for the assumption of the leadership role. Thus, leaders are agents of modification, people whose behavior, ideas, or ideals affect others to such an extent that these others change and focus their attention or energies on some object or in some direction which the leader espouses.[4] In fact, the *status quo* is abhorrent to the leader. He cannot exist in a static situation. He achieves through group action born of personal interaction.

---

[3] J. W. Bennett and M. M. Tumin, *Social Life* (New York: Alfred Knopf, 1948).
[4] R. T. LaPiere and P. R. Farnsworth, *Social Psychology* (New York: McGraw-Hill Book Company, 1936), pp. 308, 371–377.

SOCIAL BEHAVIOR

Social behavior is not inborn. It must be developed over a long period of time, and is often a painful and frustrating process to the individual. Perhaps the most significant aspect of socialization is in learning to get along with other people. Because most recreational experiences occur in a social context, the desirability for instructing the individual in the processes of social development is of utmost importance both to him and to those who make up his extrapersonal environment. During infancy, the child must learn to get along with members of his immediate world, his family. As he matures and goes to school he must learn to adapt himself to others who may represent authority as well as social beings who have certain needs and desires of their own. Slowly there is the realization that adjustment to the social milieu in which there are various colors, creeds, classes, and ethnic patterns presents some difficulty, but not of insurmountable odds. As the individual advances to puberty and beyond, there is heterosexual attraction and other stimuli. With adulthood the individual is confronted with essential social, political, economic, marital, and legal tasks that demand his full time and attention. In order to compete within the community of his choice, he must learn to behave in accordance with the customs and codes dictated by the socioeconomic activities of society. As life draws to a close, the individual is faced with difficult adjustments due to declining physical facility, economic constriction, health problems, and lessened social responsibility. Again he must learn to live and get along with diminished functions, narrowing social movement, and increased leisure.

In order for the leader to effect the ideas and goals which he wants to accomplish, he must understand the concepts of individual differences, human development, learning, and social psychology. The various stages of social responsiveness which people undergo, the adjustments which they must make to their external environment and whatever internal stimuli motivate them, are all part of the complex which the leader must grasp if he is to lead. As a leader, the recreationist also has the task of instructing those who fall within his purview so that his professional obligations to people can be transacted. Direct knowledge of social behavior is vital to the recreationist, for his efforts in meeting personal needs through recreational experiences hinge upon his comprehension of what those needs are throughout the life span.[5]

---

[5] Elizabeth B. Hurlock, *Developmental Psychology*, 2nd ed. (New York: McGraw-Hill Book Company, 1953), p. 444.

THE GENERAL CHARACTERISTICS OF LEADERSHIP

The preceding pages have clarified many of the instructional aspects of the leadership phenomenon. Principles and explanations have been expounded. The general characteristics of the instructional embodiment of leadership may be described without a great deal of ramification at this point.

The instructional factor of leadership with which recreationists must contend is directly concerned with the encouragement and guidance of people in ways that will teach them of their own ability to find recreational experiences. This admits both the extemporaneous learning procedures that are part of the natural environment of the individual and the directed learning processes that are derived from the constructive manipulation of the environment, recreationist leadership, or other positive motivation. Leadership requires broad knowledge, rare insights, intricate skills, and a dynamic personality. The demands for leadership appear overwhelming, but they are valid. Perhaps the foregoing is the reason why there are few leaders and many followers. Leadership is not a trifling affair; it cannot be performed successfully by ignorant incompetents devoid of personality who hold narrow views or have limited experiences. The intelligent, broadly prepared, positive personality with talent and skill is absolutely necessary to the recreationist-leader.

Origin of Necessary Information

1. The way human beings grow and develop.
   Knowledge of biology, anatomy, physiology, psychology, and kinesiology.
2. The way the social order develops.
   Knowledge of sociology, anthropology, political science, and social institutions.
3. The way in which political theory is developed.
   Knowledge of social institutions, political doctrine, and history.
4. The way in which democracy emerges.
   Knowledge of the democratic process, social justice, and the laws of equity.
5. The way in which social criticisms develop.
   Knowledge of philosophy, ethics, customs, codes, mores, religious teachings, and the theories of critical thinking.
6. The way individuals, groups, and environments reciprocate and affect one another.
   Knowledge of the psychological process, group dynamics, societal organizations, personality development, pressure groups, and the effects of the physical environment upon human personality.
7. The way instruction affects the individual in contemporary society.

Knowledge of the processes of human learning, human behavior, social environment, and an understanding of human needs.
8. The way research may be applied to affect leadership.
Knowledge of the technique of research, the application of the scientific method, the processes of critical analysis, diagnostic techniques, and the effect of value judgments upon leadership problems.

Particular fundamental understandings are important. Recreationists must recognize and implicitly believe that:

1. The needs, wants, and desires of individuals are the most sensible points of departure for learning activity and continuous motivation.
2. The recreationist can assist learning only when he understands the concept of individual differences and the mental and emotional make-up of the individual.
3. Unacceptable behavior or conduct that is pointless can be redirected and made beneficial through leadership, not headship.
4. Only the individual is capable of learning. Learning is accomplished if there is a desire to learn, not limited by mental deficiencies.

Taken altogether, leadership is neither a routine procedure nor a series of logical steps from which will come some pat answer or solution every time. It is prototypal, resourceful, imaginative. Leadership is not a standard operating procedure; it is a truly intellectual pursuit. The routine use of maxims and regulations, a robot obedience to and dependence upon time-honored techniques will not result in leadership. Leadership requires rather the adroitness to question, to innovate, to originate procedures to satisfy the dynamic demands of human beings in any given situation. Leadership insists upon ingenuity in forecasting the responses of others, the ability to think clearly and rapidly, and to use language in such a way as to activate thinking, as well as the talent to keep complex and remote behaviors channeled and moving toward a desirable goal without simultaneously coercing or assuming an authoritarian role. Leadership necessitates technical knowledge and an experiential background of considerable depth and breadth in working with people.

SUMMARY

Leadership is a combination of three factors, all of which must be present and interacting if a leader is to emerge and valid leadership is to develop. The three aspects concern the need of a group for leadership, the need of an individual to be a leader, and a specific situation or environmental condition of stress or crisis which requires resolution. All of these ingredients must be present or leadership does not occur. The recreationist functions in a leader capacity as he resolves environmental problems of a recreational nature. In his work with individuals, aggregates, classes, and groups, he must guide, direct, and otherwise lead people to where they can achieve satisfaction within recreational contexts.

The recreationist must understand and have insight into human motivation. He must be aware of the clear and present manifestations of behavior as well as of the remote and hidden causes for them. As a leader, the recreationist aids people in fulfilling personal desires centered around social needs. As he instructs, gives guidance, or assists individuals to take their rightful place within group situations so that they may become part of the decision-making process, he instills an improved pattern of behavior. Through activity participation in some respects, and group living in others, the recreationist-leader attempts to provide the means whereby individuals may offer suggestions or influence outcomes within the group. Democratic practice wherein each person is accorded the right to be heard and respectfully evaluated is part of the instructional function of the recreationist.

Leadership is not performed on an intuitive basis, on the application of common sense to a given condition, or upon experience alone. Successful leadership depends upon the ability to make modifications, cut new paths, create methods, adapt familiar measures to unexpected situations, and seek variety in meeting the ever-changing demands of people in contemporary life. Normally, experience and critical evaluation of the experience will play a vital part in gaining and enhancing skill, but all experience and analysis are clarified by the preparatory education in basic information.

Leadership skills may be gained through determined discriminating inquiry of one's personal experience or indirectly through knowledge gained theoretically. In the final analysis all skills of leadership require practical application for validation. Leadership in the field of recreational service, as with all occupations that deal with human behavior and personality, is absolutely insistent upon the use of sound judgment, ingenuity, creativity, enthusiasm, and intelligence. Specifically it requires the utilization of a vital, facile, and original intelligence.

SELECTED REFERENCES

ANDERSON, LYNN R. and FRED FIEDLER, "The Effect of Participatory and Supervisory Leadership on Group Creativity." *Journal of Applied Psychology*, 48:227–36, 1964.

BEAL, GEORGE M., J. M. BOHLEN, and J. N. RAUDABAUGH, *Leadership and Dynamic Group Action*. (Ames, Iowa: Iowa State University Press), 1962.

BROWNE, C. G. and T. S. COHN, eds., *The Study of Leadership*. (Danville, Ill.: The Interstate Printers and Publishers), 1958.

CAMPBELL, DONALD T., *Leadership and Its Effects Upon the Group*. (Columbus, Ohio: Bureau of Business Research, Ohio State University Press), 1956.

DUBIN, R., *et al., Leadership and Productivity*. (San Francisco, Calif.: Chandler Publishing Company), 1965.

FIEDLER, FRED E., *Leader Attitudes and Group Effectiveness.* (Urbana, Ill.: University of Illinois Press), 1958.
HALL, DAVID M., *Dynamics of Group Action.* (Danville, Ill.: The Interstate Printers and Publishers), 1960.
HOLLANDER, E. P., *Leaders, Groups, and Influence.* (New York: Oxford University Press, Inc.), 1964.
LIPPITT, GEORGE L. and EDITH SEASHORE. *Leader and Group Effectiveness.* (New York: The Association Press), 1962.
PETRULLO, LUIGI and BERNARD M. BASS, eds., *Leadership and Interpersonal Behavior.* (New York: Holt, Rinehart and Winston), 1961.
SHIVERS, JAY S., *Leadership in Recreational Service.* (New York: The Macmillan Co.), 1963.
STOGDILL, RALPH M., et al., *Leadership and Role Expectations.* (Columbus, Ohio: Bureau of Business Research, Ohio State University Press), 1956.
STOGDILL, RALPH M., *Leadership and Structure of Personal Interaction.* (Columbus, Ohio: Bureau of Business Research, Ohio State University Press), 1957.
WHITE, WILLIAM R., *Leadership.* 2 vols. (Boston, Mass.: Forum Publishing Company), 1951.

Chapter 9

PROFESSIONALISM

> PRINCIPLE: The rendition of the most competent, objectively performed skills at the command of the recreationist, with the concept of enhanced individual worth uppermost, is the primary function of the professional practitioner.

All of those ethical acts, which devolve upon the recreationist, relating to best practice, applied knowledge, educational pursuit, and humanitarian ideal are the result of the attainment of professionalism. Professionalism is the manner in which certain practices are carried out and the steps taken to ensure that specific standards are being met. It stems from practice within a field which is considered a profession or one which is attaining professional status.

The field of recreational service in the modern world is a significant social force with potential influence upon all people. Public institutions that render services of a recreational nature, no less than private organizations with historic traditions of service, are outstanding among the long-lived agencies of culture. Nearly every person is touched in some way by the enterprise of the practitioners and students engaged in recreational service. In an endeavor as potentially vast and important to the well-being of people, it is necessary that considerable attention and purposeful thought be given to the occupation and status of those who are recreationists. The effectiveness of service to all people primarily rests upon these professional practitioners. The examination of professionalism in its ramifications and the criteria upon which a profession may be established constitute the main problem to be settled in support of the principle stated at the beginning of this chapter.

RECREATIONAL SERVICE AS A PROFESSION

Any category of practitioners who become concerned about their role and position in society has recourse to seek recognition as a professional group. The more intensive their realization of their social function and obligation, the greater is the aspiration to become a profession. Frequently, leaders in the field of recreational service demand higher standards of personnel and increased professionalization, for they are conscious of the fact that this avenue is the most direct means of securing improvement in the status of recreationists, in their conditions of work, and also in the kinds of services effected by the variety of agencies which employ them.

Perhaps the most frustrating question asked is whether or not recreationists are professional. In order to clarify the position of the practitioner and answer the question, the definition of what a profession is must be offered. If the practice of the recreationist fits the standard by which profession is defined, then the answer is obvious. If, for one or more reasons, the work of the recreationist does not meet the qualitative criteria, then modification of practice and education would normally be required.

The term *profession* clearly symbolizes a complex of indicators. The recognized professions evidence all or almost all of these factors; they are acknowledged in their pre-eminence, and are surrounded by other vocations displaying one, some, or few of these features. The vocations which occupy the position of centrality and are thus termed *professions* have certain marks that distinguish them from all other types of occupation. The essence of professionalism is intellectual insight applied to the ordinary course of human events, obtained as the consequence of prolonged and particularized education in the acquirement of a specialized technique.

As Carr-Saunders and Wilson have so explicitly stated:

> The practitioners, by virtue of prolonged and specialized intellectual training, have acquired a technique which enables them to render a specialized service to the community. . . . They develop a sense of responsibility for the technique which they manifest in their concern for the competence and honour of the practitioners as a whole—a concern which is sometimes shared by the state. They build up associations, upon which they erect, . . . machinery for imposing tests of competence and enforcing the observance of certain standards of conduct.[1]

The characteristic that most singularly distinguishes the profession from other occupational fields is the concept of responsibility. Responsibility here is defined as the rendition of services in such a manner as to combine good judgment with humanitarian effort and ethical conduct. All professions work with people. The closer an occupation comes to providing services to people directly and the further it remains from working with things, the more it may be likened to the centrality of profession. Thus, humanitarianism becomes the key trait by which the profession is characterized. On one hand, vocations such as engineering or architecture may appear as professions because of the theoretical knowledge and prolonged study necessary to gain technical proficiency. However, on closer inspection, these fields, although scientifically based and aesthetically formulated, tend to work with the applications of the science to things rather than with people. They are more concerned with material constructs than with human needs.

---

[1] A. M. Carr-Saunders and P. A. Wilson, *The Professions* (Oxford: The Clarendon Press, 1933), p. 284.

Law, which is founded upon the study of human institutions and is not scientific, *per se,* is basically involved with the problems of people and the variety of individual needs which social pressures produce.

Another characteristic of the acknowledged professions is the formation of associations, the main objective of which is to evaluate and test for the specialized competence necessary in the technique of the field. In the development of the technique that is unique to the field and the responsibility that accompanies the possession of an intellectual competence, there also exists a concomitant need for the maintenance of an ethical code. The association initiated by the professional group has, among its chief aims, the obligation to safeguard the general public and the practitioners through the institution of a register of qualified persons. The register is a minimum set of standards set up and administered by professional personnel of the field. It is the least qualitative measurement of whether or not an individual is competent to function as a member of the profession. More usually than not, it is a quantitative device relating to the educational preparation and experiential background of the individual who wishes to practice.

The professional code of ethics, always developed from an association of professional personnel, provides specific behaviors by which the professional is guided in his practice and enforces the observance of particular standards of conduct. Such a code may delimit acts that are detrimental to the profession, to society, and to practitioners. It may govern a range of actions from the acceptance of fees for service to the concept of privileged communication between client and professional. In whatever way it is observed and administered, the code of ethics is part of the humanitarian principle that segregates the profession from other occupations.

If a definition of the term *profession* is necessary, then it may be conceived as a vocation in which an affirmed knowledge of some specialized field of learning or science is utilized in its appliance to the ordinary course of human events or in the practice of an art based upon it.

EDUCATION

To prepare a person for effective practice the acquirement and deliberate utilization of special knowledge not readily accessible to laymen is a necessary part of professionalization. Only by way of a particular series of educational experiences does the recreationist begin to understand the fundamental premises that make up his responsibility. In these basic assumptions and hypotheses are contained the insights of method and technique. But beyond the surface promise of *how* an effective performance is derived are the reasons *why* specific functions are instituted and maintained. There are many instances where nonprofessional people, skilled and competent volunteers, can effectively perform for the benefit of those participating within the program. They may have skill or talent in any of the activities on which the total program is constructed. These same individuals can make up a cast for a play, paint or draw a picture, repair a faulty gadget, or serve in many utilitarian ways. They may perform effectively without recognizing the sequences of actions taken nor having any grasp of why they do the things that they do. The recreationist, on the other hand, needs to know certain skills that will be used within the program and also the related needs of human beings upon whose satisfaction these procedures are based. The professional practitioner must be more than routinely competent. He must understand the underlying principles and the foundations of the necessary standards and skills of performance.

Thus it follows that a practitioner who knows only methods or techniques of application without understanding the rationale for his practices merely follows a trade and is not engaged in a profession. The practitioner who has little to recommend him but experience without education may know many techniques that allow him to attain peculiar ends with tremendous results, and still have no concept of what he has done to achieve the desired consequences. The recreationist not only has the ability to perform successfully, but also has a profound knowledge of subject matter pertaining to the nature of individual differences and human personality, social values, personal growth and development, mass communication and the learning process, human ecology, and an unqualified comprehension of the foundational concepts and theoretical insights that are used to formulate organization and administration of agency services.

The recreationist is not professional merely by reason of knowing specific methods of programming, leading activities, or organizing group experiences. The professional practitioner must have conceptual insight concerning the essential facts and philosophy on which the accomplished techniques and standards for action are based. Conceptual understanding is not simply an abstraction without practicality. It is vital to the practitioner on eminently utilitarian grounds. Theory provides the foundation for improved practice and for handling situations which are extraordinary. Standard operating procedure may suffice for routine assignments, but in extreme conditions or at times where exceptional instances demand resolution, only the insight gained by intellectual command of fundamental assumptions allows enough impetus and facility to change outdated or unreliable techniques and innovate. Thus conceptual insight makes possible the type of practice where unusual and exceptional circumstances are met by creativity and experimentation. The practitioner who only memorizes rules instead of learning to understand the guiding theoretical concepts on which the rules are founded runs the risk of becoming rigid and static. Routine skills and standard techniques do not always offer the correct methods or answers, particularly when new conditions require new methods and answers. As Phenix has so aptly stated:

> Dynamic and flexible practice is possible only when the guiding theoretical framework is comprehensive enough to include unusual and novel

circumstances and to suggest promising avenues for experimentation. The educator who has merely learned to follow the rules is lost in cases where there are no rules or where they give the wrong results. Only the professional who has sufficient theoretical understanding to modify old procedures and create new ones is in a position to turn such emergencies into opportunities rather than failures.[2]

If such an assumption is correct, and there is no reason to disbelieve it, then it must also be valid that the professional education of recreationists cannot be considered satisfactory when the preparation deals only with program techniques and management practices. To be fully effective a mandatory inclusion of studies that offer basic instruction in the behavioral sciences, learning process, and social milieu must be provided. Of particular significance is knowledge of the primary historical, social, and cultural facts pertaining to recreational service, of psychology, philosophy, and those interdisciplinary studies which can offer theoretical fundamentals in the applied sciences. To these prerequisites the critical aspects of professional education for recreationists must contain the following essentials: (1) a high degree of knowledge and demonstrable skill in three or more program activities; (2) a thorough understanding of recreational service, its philosophical rationale, ability to analyze the component concepts upon which it is based, and ability to interpret intelligently and relate recreational concepts to other spheres of human endeavor; (3) the development of the ability to communicate, to transmit as well as receive ideas for the furtherance of human effectiveness through recreational achievement; and (4) the mastery of the theoretical foundations and validated facts upon which standards of practice are built and through which the advancement of improved recreational service may be effected.

HUMANITARIANISM

As America has, in the modern era, progressed within the democratic political frame of reference, it has also continued to move toward an interdependence which is intrinsic in the urbanized culture. The goal of society has, therefore, been increasingly focused on the provision of individual development and utilization of personal capacities which can contribute to the entire community and society-as-a-whole. Today's professions are chiefly concerned with a concurrent development of the individual rather than with functions that merely promise survival. It is rapidly becoming recognized that the development of the individual and all humanity grows out of knowledge of man. In order to serve society, the profession must serve each person. Logically, recreational service, which is directly committed to the well-being of people, has begun to focus attention upon highly skilled services as well as show a concern for the individual being

---

[2] Philip H. Phenix, *Philosophy of Education* (New York: Holt, Rinehart and Winston, 1958), p. 159.

served. Ethical obligation, applied intelligence, and professional assistance are oriented to the individual within a given environment in terms of what the person needs and what he wants.

The professions are those fields that are established primarily to serve humanity through the organization and administration of services to advance individual welfare. They all deal with people, serving them as individuals, in relation to human well-being. The professional practitioner is required by laymen because he has a specialized competence essential to the needs of the recipients. Thus, in providing services to people, the practitioner does things with and for them. In receiving these services the layman reacts relative to what he is and how he feels about them. Historically, the professional practitioner has been vitally interested in offering his services in ways which are valuable, thus enabling the recipient to profit from the elements received—physically, mentally, socially, intellectually, and culturally.

In addition, the practitioner is sought after because the individual has specific problems which he is unable to resolve. The professional, with his technical skill and competence, is able to offer a solution to the person who may not have the knowledge required or the personal adequacy to mitigate his difficulty. The professions normally specialize in working with people under these circumstances. The rendition of professional functions is predicated on the basis of support for the recipient. No service can ever be made which tends to subvert the individual's ability to make his own decisions. If, through the provision of professional acts, the individual's capacity for self-management is diminished, then those acts lose their effectiveness and assume a threatening guise.

As Towle has written:

> Furthermore, respect for the total person in every profession implies that concern for one area of his welfare must not ignore his general welfare. Respect for the integrity of the individual implies that, in administering to his physical health, we take into account his mental and emotional needs and responses and that, in administering to his intellectual needs, we do not ignore the physical or social self. Respect for the integrity of the person implies also that his rights to self-determination within social limits be regarded, that individual differences be appreciated—in short, that the professional relationship be oriented at all times to his identity as a person with rights as well as obligations.[3]

NONPREDICTABILITY

Another criterion which marks the profession is the factor of nonpredictability. To the extent that the practitioner cannot predict, with any accuracy, the outcome of the problem he confronts as he works with

---

[3] Charlotte Towle, *The Learner in Education for the Professions As Seen in Education for Social Work* (Chicago: The University of Chicago Press, 1954), p. 4.

people, the closer he approximates the professional occupation. The more confused and dimly perceived is the consequence of the service offered by the practitioner the surer it is that he belongs to a profession. Why is this true? Fundamentally, this proposition stems from the humanitarian concept that is the single most important segregational standard between the profession and any other vocation. Other fields of endeavor may approach the centrality of profession through educational prolongation, codes of ethics, or organization, but the real professions, from the ancient fields of law and medicine to the youngest—education, social work, and recreational service—have these in common, plus the responsibility of working with people.

It may be seen that occupations which work with things, e.g., any of the trades, sales personnel, advertising personnel, engineers, etc., may provide a service to people by offering them food, clothing, shelter, transportation facilities and amenities. However, to render these, things rather than people become significant and uppermost in the view of these vendors. Tradesmen, i.e., carpenters, masons, plumbers, electricians, repairmen, work with things; sales and advertising personnel sell things or promote things; amenities personnel offer services which are tangible and therefore may be listed as things. Even such scientific fields as architecture or engineering work with things. The same is true for chemists, pharmacists, and the military establishment. All of these occupations work with material, equipment, facilities, or formulae whose consequences can be predicted with certainty. They do not work with unknown factors, they deal with something, the results of which can be predicted with mathematical precision. Unquestionably, some of these fields are going to be involved with problems that baffle the mind, but only for a brief moment, and then merely because additional knowledge has not been added to the archives of the field. When knowledge is acquired, complete predictability results. There is no confusion, there is less concern with unknown factors. Every act is seen with clarity and understanding. The technique is faultless. Step by step the work goes forward until a finished object or performance has been accomplished. Such is not the case with those fields primarily working with human beings. Each individual brings with him a separate problem or set of problems. Each person, because he is an individual and is unique in the universe has an infinite capability to react in ways that cannot be predicted with any degree of accuracy. No one can ever say with certainty what any human being will do under any given set of circumstances in any given environment. Thus it may be stated that the nearer to absolute predictability one gets in his vocation, the further he is from employment in a profession.

This idea may engender some protest from fields that wish to be considered as professions, but if one assumes that humanitarianism is the chief characteristic of the profession, then nonpredictability follows. It may also be said that the typical profession exhibits certain distinct factors, and that other occupations approximate this condition of complex characteristics more or less intensely, because they have some of the same factors in common with the acknowledged professions. Nevertheless, the denominator of humanitarianism indicates how closely each field approaches, owing to the possession of these traits in complete or fragmented development.

VARIABILITY

In much the same manner as the factor of nonpredictability testifies to the remoteness or approximation of a vocation to the central tendency of profession, so too does the feature of variability. In this sense, variability has to do with the variety of problems which confront the practitioner during his service. Those occupations dealing with finite objects or material goods have comparatively less variables to contend with in solving problems whereas those occupations confronted by a great range of variable factors come closer to the infinite variety faced by the professions in dealing with the human factor.

Machinists, for example, have few variables in their work. They are basically concerned with the variables of stress, tolerance, malleability, rigidity, fissility, tensile strength, and other structural facets. These are readily accounted for and whatever compensation is necessary can be adequately measured for a completed product to take form. Recreationists, on the other hand, have an infinite array of endless problems which they must face as they deal with people. The needs, desires, wants, and problems of people coupled with the unknown of human behavior evoke an unlimited set of variables. There are no sequential steps that can be taken which will solve a similar problem found in one or more persons each time. What may work well for one individual may fail with the next under identical conditions. The technique utilized may be faultless, but there can never be a guarantee that it will succeed even though it has been successful at a prior time. No formulae have yet been created which can determine exactly the reactions of human beings.

In all probability, those occupations which tend to few variables have a lesser proximity to professions which have an infinite complex of variables with which to operate. The more scientifically oriented and less personalized is the field the further it is from true professional status. Fields which are dehumanized to the extent that inanimate objects are their sole concern or where only the application of a science is employed have less of the profession in their calling. Vocations based upon scientific knowledge which is specifically applied to the everyday lives of people, or where knowledge is founded upon human institutions and then made responsible to the service of humanity are, in all likelihood, professions.

TECHNIQUE

It has developed that technique or special competence, obtained as the result of intellectual preparation, is one of the chief distinguishing factors of professions. The possession of a technique gives the practitioner a knowledge denied to most other people, or endows him with skills which the average individual does not own. Does the recreationist possess some special competence? Does he have a particular technique and knowledge which the average person does not have? Opinions diverge quite sharply on this point. From one point of view, the recreationist, not only does not need special competence, he does not have any. Any person can perform the functions of recreationists, it is said. Volunteers have many skills that are used in a great variety of activities within the recreational service program and they are not specifically prepared in professional curricula. Therefore, the recreationist cannot pretend to possess any exceptional skills, competencies, or knowledge which the average intelligent individual does not have.

The supposition on which this nonprofessional concept of recreational service rests is that recreational service is made up of activities which are so natural that it requires nothing more than ordinary good sense to organize and administer them. The commonly held fallacy that it is not necessary to teach a child to play because it is instinctive is part of this antiprofessional tendency. Those who oppose professional preparation and deny a specialized technique do so on grounds that anyone, who is of at least average intelligence, by daily association with the problems and responsibilities of the recreationist position will automatically learn all of the functions and solutions by observation and trial and error practice.

In contrast the assumption upon which the professional view of recreational service is based declares that specific knowledge and special skill are vital for the recreationist to be competent. Simple association and intelligence are not sufficient for the organization and administration of recreational services. The orientation and philosophy to which the student is exposed in professional education programs develop feelings and attitudes that will make it possible for him to think and function appropriately and effectively. Disciplined thinking, increased capacity to perform competently, objective service to people, understanding those with and for whom one works, a high degree of skills, an ability to transmit instructions concerning skills, and the knowledge to organize and operate a comprehensive program of recreational services do not take place in any way but by deliberate design. The best environment for obtaining technique is not a matter of common knowledge, and the average individual neither has the time nor the guidance to master the knowledge or functions of the recreationist.

The affirmation of recreationists to special knowledge and technique can be validated through the generally accepted, reliable, and thoroughly tested department of learning of applied social science which makes up professional preparation. The consequences of utilizing professional leadership as opposed to nonprofessionals in practice should amply substantiate superior achievement. Special competence through professional education invariably produces a categorically superior practice to that accomplished by persons without this particular technique and knowledge.

PROFESSIONAL ASSOCIATION

Up to this point attention has been focused upon the factors on which professions are founded. But a special competence may be an actuality and men may practice it, and nevertheless there is no profession. A profession can exist only when a technique is practiced in common and a relationship is developed between the practitioners. These ties of commonality can be structured in one way only—that of a definitive association.

The professional society has a four-fold function. The first is the testing of professional competence. This is not to be construed as professional education. Far from educating the future practitioner, the profession, through its various committees within the society, has inaugurated an examination mechanism to evaluate what the higher institutions of education have taken responsibility for, i.e., technique as a consequence of prolonged intellectual preparation. Usually, the professional group studies, evaluates, and then institutes certain minimum standards for competence which would-be practitioners must attain. Tests of competence have generally been of the written, oral, and in some instances, the practical type, presided over by practitioners. Where institutions of higher education are willing to examine, the associations are amenable to recognizing a university degree as admitting entry to the profession.

Examinations are the accepted method of testing for special competence and theoretical insight. True professions rarely admit unexamined individuals to membership. However, on occasion, special dispensation is granted to a particularly outstanding practitioner who has not had the advantage of technical study. This rear door approach to membership in the professional association is one that can be used infrequently at best, and then only with the highest discretion.

The second function of association is one of discrimination. Any exclusiveness attached to the field is practiced with the sole idea of shutting out the incompetent. For no other reason can exclusiveness be justified, other than to expose those individuals who cannot measure up to minimum standards for qualification as practitioners. When an individual is incompetent, it is primarily up to the professional society either to bring pressure to bear upon that person so that he may not inflict his incompetency upon a trusting public, or to cause whatever legal action is required to disallow that individual from continuing in the field. The field of recreational service has never proceeded to this action, probably because it has no power to prohibit local jurisdictions and private agencies from employing incompetents. Beyond this, there is an added factor of lack of licensing by state bodies which would force would-be practitioners to meet minimum standards for practice in the field.

Professions regulate membership conduct and practice through a procedure called registration. The register, then, becomes a statutory governing body for the profession, empowered by the membership and the executive to draw up certain standards of practice, education, ethics, and personal behavior to which all practitioners must adhere. Initially, registration makes no distinction between those who came on it because of their achievements, both educational and experiential, and those who are accepted by virtue of being practicing workers. However, once a specific period of time has elapsed after the register is in effect, only those individuals who can demonstrate reasonable attainment through educational preparation and practice are accepted and registered.

The field of recreational service has attempted to promote registration of qualified persons as an initial action prior to more stringent regulations being effected. At first, registration is an association's private means of indicating acceptable and qualified practitioners. However, registration is a forerunner of state licensing procedures. Registration implies certification or the authentication of the recipient's assertion of special competence. With special competence to perform, there is also the suggestion of a grant of privilege to those who are registered. Privilege carries with it certain immunities and responsibilities. Except in cases of negligence (and incompetence invariably produces negligence), recreationists should be immune to litigations filed against them when they act *in loco parentis* and damage in some form accrues as a result of an individual's participation. They should be allowed the same type of privileged communication as is given to lawyers or physicians. By granting these privileges, the state should rightly expect the recreationist to assume full responsibility for his activities as a professional person. In order to protect its constituents from misfeasance or malpractice by persons operating in the field of recreational service without competence to practice, the state can institute licensing procedures. Thus, a licensing system developed by state government would necessarily have to turn to the professional association for criteria on which to base the minimum standards applicable for the competent performance of the recreationist.

But who shall say whether or not an individual is competent to practice in the field? What are the minimum standards which any potential recreationist should obtain prior to presenting himself for induction into the field? Actually, the professional association is in the best possible position to ascertain the adequacy or readiness of a practitioner to meet any licensing requirements which a state body would administer. It can establish criteria of performance by which the potential practitioner can be measured. However, this is, at best, only a partial answer for creating acceptable standards to which the potential recreationist must conform. The key to competency lies with professional preparation in recognized institutions of higher education. To the extent that the professional preparation offered by universities and colleges is the same in terms of studies and content, the licensing agency as well as the registering body may find that education can be made to perform an initial screening function in determining practitioner competency.

Whatever examinations may be utilized to evaluate competency, the association's registration board may require certain educational qualifications before allowing the would-be practitioner to advance to any other practical demonstration of competence. The registration board could, of course, exempt the recipient of a baccalaureate degree with a major in recreational service education from some of the examinations. Nevertheless, the association would have to delegate some of its authority to the pertinent faculties of those universities where professional curricula exist. A council whose representatives are selected from accredited institutions would then be able to formulate national criteria by which professional programs could be standardized. In this way, the registry board would be assured that insofar as intellectual insight and theoretical knowledge were concerned each would-be practitioner, who held an appropriate degree from a recognized college, must have the same minimum educational background and could then be fairly tested with all other applicants for induction into the field.

It stands to reason, therefore, that weak programs of recreational service education undermine the reputations of all colleges and universities. A profession of recreational service with poor admission and scholastic standards critically reduces the effectiveness and quality of professional preparation at all levels. Lack of explicit accreditation standards for recreational service education permits any institution to engage in the preparation of potential practitioners. Local loyalties and political considerations being what they are, it is almost impossible to control the quality of educational preparation for the field of recreational service except through a nation-wide system of voluntary accreditation which gives support to high quality institutions and calls attention to those which have either paper curricula or fail to come up to standard. Only in this way can evaluating bodies be assured of some common learning technique to be equitably distributed among those who seek employment in the field of recreational service. Without the basis of professional education as a fundamental premise for further testing the entire concept of professionalism must be abandoned.

To offset the possibility of poor preparation, the council for accreditation would surely sanction only those institutions offering professional courses conducted by qualified faculty as well as offering research, library, affiliational, and other necessary resources for the complete education of future recreationists.

The primary function of a registration authority is to control access into the profession, on the presumption of course, that employing bodies want to hire individuals who are certified as competent to perform the duties for which they are paid. To administer this function the board of registry must have the authority to maintain the register and the right to enroll, or to refuse to enroll, a name upon it. Given this authority, its supervision over entry would be final. It must be understood, however, that the board of registry would ultimately be responsible to the executive body of the professional association. In establishing criteria for entry, the recognition of diplomas from accredited universities as admission to the register, after an initial period of practical experience has been achieved, would form the chief means of induction.

The essential responsibility of the registration authority is to ensure the effectiveness of licensing procedures. The wherewithal to encourage institutions of higher education to broaden the preparatory program so that the disadvantages of early specialization could be overcome would also be made the province of this authority. This might be elicited by testing for a high standard of general education in any examination process to be given. Beyond this, it could stimulate the extension of both theoretical and practical education within the university itself and promote practical field work as part of the professional curriculum.

When the state finally recognizes the value of contributions made by certain fields and occupations as being necessary to the general health, education, or welfare of its constituents, then it moves to safeguard the public by requiring that specific standards be maintained. In some instances, the state requires licensing procedures as a simple means for taxing purposes or in order to be better able to police the dispensation of goods and/or services which might be harmful to the public good. However, when the state becomes aware of a field's service to people it may require that certification be established to ensure a minimum standard of competence among those who practice. If this step is taken, and licensing procedures are initiated, the state automatically confers prestige upon the field and provides special privileges to it, e.g., exclusive use of occupational name and practitioner title. The process of licensing is the best method by which the status of an occupation and its practitioners can be raised. Because the grant of privilege and prestige attaches to the field so endowed, the state also acts to supervise professional preparation to ensure competent functioning. Licensing to ensure professional competence means common recognition by the state, the general population, and other professional peer groups. Through this procedure, the field which has its practitioners licensed, obtains many rights among which are: sole utilization of a professional title or designation, privileged communication, and so on.

But certification itself, rather than licensing, is the prerogative of the professional association. Not only the public is hurt when incompetents attempt to function in a profession; the recreationist and the entire field of recreational service are penalized in terms of loss of public confidence and a downgrading of status. Thus, it is vital that admission to professional prestige and recognition be policed by the professional society itself as it is concerned with the potential practitioner's capability. In fact, only professionals are really competent to determine whether or not an individual is qualified to practice in their field. A system of accreditation for institutions offering professional preparation in recreational service education, an internship program for those who successfully pass within the curricula, and some form of rigid induction examination prior to registration and employment should be the standardized procedure in order that certified recreationists shall be produced.

The third important responsibility of the professional body is the establishment of a distinctive code of ethics, meaning thereby a salient ideal of conduct, expressed in several different rules, and prescribed, no doubt, by varied authorizations, but founded upon two broad principles which pervade the professional realm. The first is the protection and probity of the profession itself. The second principle is the ideal of objectivity in service.

When an individual becomes a member of a profession, he undertakes a responsibility to perform honorably and faithfully. He has an obligation to serve the interests of the public. The obligation of the professional to perform his services to the best of his ability, without prejudice against the recipient, is generally conceded in all professions. The only question here is what is in the best interest of the recipient? All other factors are subordinate to this paramount issue. Thus, the recreationist must employ all of his skills and knowledge to provide the best possible service to those who would partake of them. The field of recreational service will gain the confidence of the public which it serves when its members abide by the faithful performance of their special skills and collectively administer whatever censuring and regulatory machinery may be required to insure compliance. Incompetents must not be allowed to practice nor can the profession allow its membership to become lax in the attainment of high standards of skilled performance. This concept is basically one of self-preservation. Without it, the public would soon consider the recreationists with contempt. In order to gain public esteem and achieve status, the principle of internal security should be operable in the association. It is largely a professional society's task to maintain an assured standard of ethical practice. Sanctioning conduct of recreationists is necessary if only for the advantage which accrues to the field as a whole.

Professional objectivity is the other foundational factor upon which rests the determination of ethical practice. The professional person has an essential obligation to his agency's clientele or to his employer. It is an attitude of dedication to the field heralded by an overwhelming sense of responsibility; it is characterized by the self-respect engendered through service given rather than of attention to or interest in self-aggrandizement. The professional person who gave a lower standard of service to people who, in his opinion, "did not count," where his status might not be enhanced in the eyes of governmental authorities, would be regarded as a dishonorable individual by his professional peers. Some practitioners might restrict their service to political figures, the very wealthy, or to the famous personality in an attempt to surround their practice with an aura of status not granted when providing service to "ordinary" people. The prestige thus acquired might endow the practitioner with higher status within the organization for which he works, but would lower him in the eyes of fellow practitioners. The very fact that the phrase *professional quality* is in common usage assuredly suggests that an ethical code demands behavior which primarily considers the needs of the individual to be served and the quality of the work performed. As Phenix has written:

> The second foundation is the ideal of disinterested service. According to this ideal, the true professional does not engage in practice solely for personal satisfactions or financial rewards, nor does he do his work faithfully merely for the honor of the profession, but he is also motivated by the pure ideal of rendering service. He finds intrinsic value and a sense of fulfillment in making available his special ability for the welfare of others. The vocation of the professional at its highest is one of service rather than of gain for individual or group. The professional is a trustee to whom has been given the stewardship of gifts which are for the good of all. It is this spirit of disinterestedness which gives to a profession such nobility, elevation, and honor as it may deserve.[4]

The professional person has one mandatory role to observe in all of his dealings with people after he has accepted as his vocation a field which is devoted to humanitarian service—he is obliged to serve the interests of the public. The professional must provide all of those techniques and services, which are his to command, and place them at the behest of whosoever requires them. He cannot ever allow personal bias or whimsical discrimination to influence his best judgment or skill in his practice. For him, every man must receive whatever technique, or resource is required for that person to attain equality of opportunity.

Finally, professional associations must necessarily have some judicial machinery for implementing whatever code of ethics is established for the field. Every profession has the power to exclude from its association those who do not observe specific rules of conduct and conform to certain standards of behavior. Exclusion and other disciplinary measures have generally been deemed necessary to offset the poorly qualified worker whose incursions upon the public are often ill-advised and harmful.

The existence of disciplinary powers within the professional association is required for two chief reasons, i.e., the maintenance of a high standard of technical competence and the fulfillment of a moral standard. The concept of technical proficiency may be construed to mean all of those practices in effect throughout the field which are generally considered to be of such type that their inclusion will lead to the most beneficial contribution for the public which the agency serves. Moral standards are considered to be related to the prohibition by professional peers of high reputation and competency of any disreputable, infamous, or reasonably disgraceful conduct. Exclusion from membership should rest primarily on moral grounds rather than technical competence because technique necessitates the utiliza-

---

[4] Philip H. Phenix, *Philosophy of Education* (New York: Holt, Rinehart and Winston, 1958), p. 169.

tion of judgment rather than mere routine and each practitioner must have some leeway in exercising his intelligence in the service of the public. If, however, the recreationist is confronted with litigation as a result of negligence (which, it would seem, can arise only from ignorance and incompetence, and is found guilty of the charge, then the association should also undertake to remove that person from the register of the association and any certification concomitant with it. If such action could bring about the prohibition of that person from ever practicing within the field of recreational service, so much the better for the field and the public. Publication of the name of any person against whom such action is taken might have a most salutary effect on potential misfeasants inasmuch as no employing authority of any consequence would want to take the chance of hiring a person whose morals or technical competence was questionable. Such drastic action would follow only if, in the eyes of professional peers, the transgression was quite outrageous or of such turpitude as to warrant it. The distinctive feature of a valid profession, as that appellation is generally construed, is not simply the possession of disciplinary powers, but the ultimate purpose for which they are used.

In a professional association, some sort of executive council provides for the examination of practitioners for actions that are detrimental to the reputation and interests of the field. This adjudicating body or tribunal is specifically convened for hearing any charges or pleas. The membership of the tribunal must always be composed of professional practitioners. It cannot be too strongly stated that professional conduct has been, in the main, created by professional thinking; and the maintenance of such standards should be left to the enforcement of professional practitioners.

Fundamentals of equity demand that any hearing, which could imperil a practitioner's status on a professional register or demean his reputation in a professional association, must be held before a properly constituted adjudicating board or tribunal, specifically authorized to hear such preferments. Every member of the tribunal must receive prior notice of the proceeding at which a charge is to be reviewed, although the hearing is not nullified or impaired in any way if every member does not attend. However, not less than two thirds of the tribunal so appointed should appear at any hearing in which a charge is to be heard. The accused must receive all specifications of charges alleged, and shall be heard in any defense of same if he so desires. The functions of adjudicator and prosecutor cannot be performed by the same person. For that reason, any member of the tribunal who may have been active in bringing charges against the accused must disqualify himself from sitting in judgment. These are only minimum requirements in order to ensure equal justice for the accused. It is not the intent of this section to prescribe the legal niceties or hearing procedures to be observed. Suffice to say that in circumstances where the professional society initiates judicial machinery to maintain its ethical code, the tribunal may, and usually does imitate the proceedings of law courts.

208 Principles of Recreational Service

One warning is necessary. Frivolous charges may sometimes be made against a practitioner on grounds of technical incompetence because that person does not follow the usual line of reasoning or the accepted philosophy which a majority of his fellows profess. The hazard in subjecting an individual to a tribunal of his peers without the possibility of appeal is horrendous. In this instance, the danger would perhaps be grounded not in too great an affirmation upon the maintenance of a standard operating procedure, but in the ease it would provide for witch-hunting. The divergencies of theory and concept of recreational service, and even of the terminology used, among educators and practitioners in recreational service are wide-spread. Equally infamous is the enmity shown by the protagonists of one philosophy or orthodoxy towards the advocates of another, and the *empressement* of each faction to enjoin a pet theory upon the rest of the profession. Human nature being what it is, the fear of allegations either true or false, against upholders of an heretical point of view is always present. The temptation to use the authority which a professional society provides to its judicial tribunal as a means of punishing those who adopt or do not adopt the practice of any given philosophy or theory is a clear and present danger. It cannot be reiterated too often that offenses having to do with morality rather than technical competence should fall to the province of the association's tribunal, although where negligence has been or can be shown, in fact, the society should act to rid itself of an incompetent.

PROFESSIONALIZATION OF RECREATIONAL SERVICE

To the extent that the field of recreational service exhibits the central characteristics which validate any profession, it is approaching the social status usually reserved only for the traditional vocations of law, medicine, and theology. However, on the basis of the central tendencies which distinguish the professions from quasi-professions and other occupations, then recreational service falls somewhat short.

To best illustrate this concept, **Figure 9-1** is offered on page 209: Let the outer ring of **Figure 9-1** represent all of the unskilled occupations. Let each successive inner ring represent the vocations that require a higher degree of skill or technique. Let the innermost rings represent all of those fields that require prolonged education for proficiency as well as technique. Let only those rings falling within the G orbit stand for vocations that are dedicated to humanitarian service and have prolonged education for specialized technique, associations established for the transmission of knowledge within the field, and the institution of an ethical code for practice. Let absolute center or P stand for the validated professions that possess all of the traits that act as criteria, e.g., prolonged education, specialized technique, humanitarian dedication, a master association that possesses complete authority, qualifying examinations for induction into the field, a code

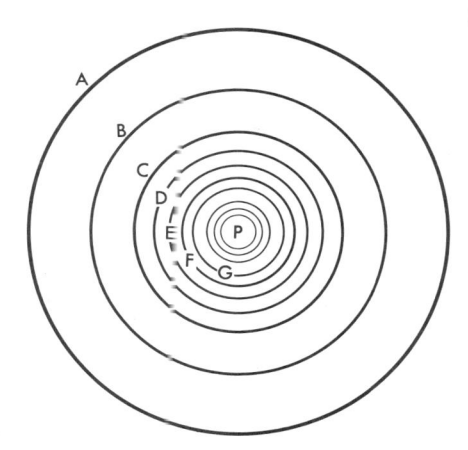

Figure 9-1

of ethics, judicial machinery for the enforcement of moral behavior and ethical practice, and the registry of practitioners or other certification procedures.

The closer a field approximates the conditions of centrality, the more acceptable it becomes as a profession. Some fields may appear to have all of the qualifications necessary, but upon close examination they are found to be deficient in one or more criteria. The further from center a field moves, the more evidently it is a trade or occupation. Because humanitarian service and prolonged education are the distinguishing features of the profession, the neglect of either one of these hallmarks precludes recognition as a profession. Even where these traits are present, unless they are *required* of the practitioner, and not voluntary, they do not meet the qualifying standards. Professional association is required, but again, all of the items which set the real professions apart from other fields of endeavor must be operating. Thus, a field may have a professional society, but the society may not have judicial machinery for enforcement of ethical practices, required registration for practice, peer examination for induction, nor the certification procedure which guarantees technical competence.

As to whether or not the field of recreational service is a profession, one has only to examine the criteria laid down and compare the characteristics of this field with true professions. There is no question about recreational service being dedicated to humanitarianism. This is the basis of its establishment and function. It has no other reason for being. The field is absolutely oriented to the development of human welfare through recreational experiences. Insofar as prolonged education is concerned, there is a trend now operable for requiring would-be practitioners to have certain minimum education. However, this is not a universal requirement nor does the education even have to be professional. There is such a wide gap between vacancies in the field and professionally prepared people to fill those vacancies that desperate communities and agencies of every kind will employ almost anyone—whether he has been well educated or not. It will take some time before a prolonged professional educational sequence is absolutely required of individuals who wish to practice in the field of recreational service. Today, this is still a voluntary process, left up to the individual and not a part of the obligation required for induction. Nevertheless, as more communities face the leisure challenge and as more information is disseminated concerning the field, today's apathetic public may become aroused and concerned enough to demand well qualified and professionally prepared practitioners. When that time arrives, the field of recreational service will move inexorably closer to professional status.

Finally, there is a question relating to professional association. There is not one, but several, professional societies and associations claiming a hold on the recreationist. Each may represent a distinct specialization or orientation, but there is no one master organization to which all of these diverse groups belong, nor is there any one governing body to which these societies may belong which speaks for the field as a whole and represents all practitioners to the public. At this time, successful efforts have finally been made to consolidate five formerly separate and distinct associations into the National Recreation and Park Association. A great forward step has been taken in the process of professionalization of the field as a result of this merger. However, there are still splinter and other professional speciality organizations which may remain outside of the greater body. Under these conditions, the idea of peer examination, registration, certification, ethical codes, and other association practices are less meaningful and in most instances nonexistent. Although the aspiration toward professional status is very apparent and much effort is being made to promote professionalism among practitioners in the field, recreational service has neither reached a point where this can be brought about immediately, nor will it achieve its goal until all of the mandatory requirements are met. At best, it may be said that the field of recreational service is a quasi-profession attempting to approximate the centrality of the true profession.

A Professionalizing Program

In order that recreational service as a vocational experience can acquire the features which professions have, a seven-point program is here defined. By adhering to the conditions described, the achievement of professional status may result.

1. A broad educational program directed at the general public must be initiated at the earliest moment. By improving the image of the recreationist, the entire field can be strengthened. Opportunities must be found for the dissemination of information through a variety of media which tend to raise the status and promote the image of the recreationist. The establishment of television and radio programs depicting the recreationist in practice must be suggested to major networks.

2. The provision of increased understanding and support of the field of recreational service must be engendered. Individual practitioners and state societies should prepare an information service to individuals and groups. Such a service would provide speakers before lay groups, make better use of mass media, and distribute a selected list of films, books, feature stories, and other audio-visual materials to lay groups through the offices of the professional society. A direct line of communication must be maintained with community leaders, local, state, and federal legislators particularly in relationship to current developments in recreational service. The field must obtain cooperation from other interested groups for the adequate support of recreational services, and sponsor a continual series of lay and professional conferences on recreational service problems of wide significance on the local and state level.
3. Promotion and dissemination of research applied to recreational service should be an integral part of association practice. The attention of all practitioners and educators should be called to the outstanding publications and studies being made in the field. Worthy new texts, master's theses and doctoral dissertations, applicable journals, and current experimentation must be widely known.
4. The development of more highly competent practitioners through required professional education programs should be made obligatory. The entire process of recruitment focusing attention upon capable and willing young people in preparing for leadership roles in recreational service should be undertaken. Encouragement of scholarships and other financial benefits to students should be made. The establishment of administrative internships should become part of the joint responsibility of educators and practitioners. The sponsorship of workshops, conferences, studies, and projects devoted to the development of leadership skills can be augmented.
5. Establishment of one master professional society organized to meet the diverse needs of the various specializations within the field of recreational service should be implemented at once. Such an association of practitioners can do much to promote the needed legislation for the stringent licensing of practitioners. The procedure of registration, exclusion, ethical codification, examination, and accreditation will all be fulfilled when there is general agreement on a single official society capable of representing all recreationists. The supreme importance of such an association cannot be underestimated in the movement toward professionalism. Such an organization could be made up of autonomous groups, each represented on the governing board of the society. In spite of the fact that each speciality would be represented and be able to conduct its affairs independently of the parent body, the main characteristics of a professional society would be placed into effect through the master organization. Thus, a national registry board, practitioner certification, the ethical code, judicial enforcement, examination for induction, and

cooperation with institutions of higher education for their accreditation by the association would be provided.
6. The involvement of state legislative bodies for the licensing of recreationists as well as for the establishment of state offices, commissions, or departments of public recreational service can be implemented through individual state associations. The writing and enactment of laws implementing licensing procedures which would require minimum obligatory professional education and a specified standard of practice would do much to extend the influence of professionalization. Through such licensing, many communities and agencies not now aware of the field and its practitioners might be made so aware. Beyond that, improved status, salary policies and practices, and enhanced positions within agencies might be effected. From such legislation might also come the employment of only registered and certified recreationists commanding a level of recognition consummate with the high degree of competence earned through prolonged education and intellectual insight.
7. The extension of professional practice throughout the field and the observance of and conformity to a published ethical practices code must be maintained. Practitioners should attempt to identify problems of legislation, recreationist supply, and community awareness and recognition affecting the field. The development of proper programs to resolve or alleviate these problems must be achieved. There must also be developed agency policies which recognize and reward the special contribution made by career recreationists as distinguished from part-time volunteers or workers.

THE RECREATIONIST-PROFESSIONAL PRACTITIONER

The term *recreationist* is defined as professional practitioner in the field of recreational service. But what does professional really denote. The true professional is unique among people because he can demonstrate a special technique, has attained an intellectual insight and a logical theoretical basis for his vocation, and has developed high standards by which he maintains ethical practices in a life's vocation. At the same time, the professional is representative of all people for by his very dedication to the service of humanity he is a part of every man. The recreationist, to be professional, must adhere to the regimen of prolonged education, objective and ethical conduct in his practice, and a continual search for that which is true. When the practitioner reaches the status of recreationist he should not become affected in his manner nor should he become snobbish and condescending. This advanced prestige should neither make him feel superior to or exclusive of others. It should rather integrate him more completely with those whom he would serve, for by the ideal of humanitarian service he is inseparably associated with people.

Howard G. Danford has succinctly characterized the recreationist in the following terms:

> The professional leader is motivated primarily by ideals of service rather than money. . . . He believes that people, not activities or facilities, are the most important thing in the world and that the basic purpose of recreation is to enrich the lives of people. . . . Since people are the most important thing in the world, the professional man respects all human beings and is interested in their welfare.[5]

There are many ways in which the specific professional characteristics can be observed and expressed. However, the three chief premises upon which all recreationists should base their practice and conduct are presented as being fundamental for professional responsibility.

Occupation with the Public Welfare

The primary concern of the recreationist is always to act for the best interest and welfare of the participant. Because recreational service is a field that seeks the total development of the individual through experiences which are recreational in nature, no practitioner can correctly name himself a professional unless he is unquestionably dedicated to that objective. For a practitioner to comport himself in such a way so as to reap self-benefit, either of status, economic means, or psychological preferment, is to disobey the principles of professionalism. The individual participant places his faith in receiving qualified and ethical service from the recreationist. It is, therefore, obligatory for the recreationist to abide by that belief through provision of experiences which will enhance the participant's skill, mental acuity, and personal satisfactions. The practitioner who violates this concept has no right to the claim of being a professional.

Continual Search for the Truth

A second fundamental factor determining the professionalism of the practitioner is his concern for and pronouncement of the truth. The recreationist must never close his mind to alternative points of view. He should challenge misrepresentation and demagoguery wherever he finds them with whatever the true facts indicate. The two common opposites of truth are ignorance and misconception. Ignorance is a complete lack of knowledge about any given subject which precludes an understanding or recognition of the truth. Misconception, on the other hand, is undeniable error having its basis in faulty reasoning, biased opinion, or deviation from true facts. The practitioner can never allow himself the error of expediency of conforming with majority pressure which is prejudiced in favor of any individual or

---

[5] Howard G. Danford, *Creative Leadership in Recreation* (Boston: Allyn and Bacon, 1964), pp. 100–101.

group. He must have professional objectivity and the courage of his convictions to withstand faulty reasoning even if such is the attitude of many. The recreationist needs to develop moral intelligence.

> Moral intelligence may be defined as the ability to discern what is right or true, regardless of social pressure or mass opinion to the contrary. It is, perhaps, the one quality of intelligence which can be taught and learned by diligent search. Moral intelligence is, in fact, 'good character.' It consists of behavior which excludes immorality, both from thought and action. Lip service, sanctimonious platitudes and hypocrisy are foreign to this quality.[6]

The recreationist must stand prepared to convincingly justify his actions on the basis of true facts. To mislead or deliberately falsify information, because it might lead to the request for more than mediocre performance, is an act that is unworthy of a professional person and one that is unethical. The recreationist must bend his full intellect to the collection and analysis of all pertinent facts regarding the provision of recreational services. His sincerity and devotion to the cause of truth dismisses pretentiousness. Through the intelligent apprehension of knowledge concerning the field, particularly in his performance, the professional recognizes his own limitations as well as competencies. He weighs various ideas carefully, closes his mind to no consideration unless it has neither merit or application, and is conspicuous by his reasonable attitude.

> The leader constantly searches for additional knowledge which can be useful. He is always intent upon discovering faster, better, stronger, more adequate, more productive, and less expensive and time consuming processes. . . . The restless mind is one which is not satisfied with just getting an answer. It wants to know the reasons why. The inquiring mind is never content to wear blinders or follow the well-rutted path without determining if there are other paths to follow or if there is a wide world beyond the blinders.[7]

Dedication to Ethical Practice

The differentiation between a mediocrity and a professional person comes, essentially, in terms of expressed attitude toward one's vocation, peers, field, and self. Dedication is one form of loyalty. It is perseverance, constancy, and integrity of purpose against all odds. The principal condition is complete selflessness. The dedicated person creates high standards of practice and then lives up to them. As Brubacher has written:

---

[6] Jay S. Shivers, *Leadership in Recreational Service* (New York: The Macmillan Company, 1963), p. 257.
[7] *Ibid.*, p. 466.

The professional person knows so vastly more than the layman that the latter is almost completely at a disadvantage in determining whether the professional service he is receiving is to his best interest or not. Consequently the professional person must take extra precaution to assure his public that he is not confusing his own personal interests with theirs. The only way he can unmistakably do this is to put their interests unequivocally ahead of his.[8]

The chief method by which the recreationist can assure the public of his dedication to ethical practice occurs in the high regard in which he holds professional competence and technical skill, and in the way in which he carries out his own responsibilities and obligations. If he is sensitive and totally devoted to those professional activities which ethical considerations make mandatory, he must naturally offer his expert knowledge and technique chiefly for the public's service. Monetary reward, although necessary and significant in any man's life, is definitely of lesser importance to the concept of public service and social welfare.

SUMMARY

If the field of recreational service and the practitioners who compose its personnel wish to achieve professional status in this society, a completely different approach from the methods currently in use is necessary. In this day, when technological advancement and an increasingly enlightened public demand highly competent, proficient, and effective recreational workers, we no longer can tolerate unprofessionalism. Of necessity, practitioners must set their house in order. They must accept the criteria that govern the longer established professions and adopt the methods, principles, and standards that differentiate professional fields from other occupations. The closer the field of recreational service comes to approximate the conditions which the older professions have already achieved, the sooner will it be recognized by these same professions and society in general.

Among the criteria commonly assumed to endow an occupation with professional characteristics are humanitarianism, objectiveness, research, prolonged esoteric education, common technique, association of peers, and an ethical code of practices. Subordinate standards supportive of these essential factors are concerned with induction into the field, peer examination, reciprocal accreditation, standardized nomenclature, state sanction through certification, professional licensure, registration, judicial procedures to remove incompetent or unethical practitioners, and a national education program designed to inform the public about the field of recreational service and its practitioners, thereby insuring future material for recruitment into the field.

[8] John S. Brubacher, *Modern Philosophies of Education,* 3rd ed. (New York: McGraw-Hill Book Company, Inc., 1950), p. 115.

In an age of cybernetics, automation, and thermonuclear power, it is no small supposition to foresee a time when all decision-making functions will belong to those who have become professionals, or who are at least under professional persuasion. With the rise of specialized technique to keep pace with increased knowledge and technology, there will be a concomitant increase in personnel engaged in intellectual occupations. This will be most valid for the field of recreational service and its incumbent practitioners. Opportunities for specialized and prolonged education are gradually being extended and required. It is not unthinkable that the future will belong to those who have the education and talent to seek careers as recreationists. To the extent that more highly competent individuals are being professionally prepared for careers in recreational service a more efficient provision of services should be engendered. Even more significant is the consequence of such education upon the field in general where the aspiration to see professional techniques completely and capably used would furnish a selfless motive. Professional education, particularly those courses dealing with ethics and objective practice, will imbue the would-be practitioner with the idea, ideal, and desire of humanitarian service rather than self-aggrandizement. The education of the professional person is as much an indoctrination program as it is a preparation for future practice. Professional pride and quality in the effective offering of recreational services, would become a compelling force.

SELECTED REFERENCES

BRUBACHER, ABRAHAM R., *Teaching: Profession and Practice*. (New York: Appleton-Century-Crofts), 1927.

CARR-SAUNDERS, ALEXANDER M. and P. A. WILSON, *The Professions*. (Oxford: The Clarendon Press), 1933.

DURKHEIM, EMILE, *Professional Ethics and Civic Morals*. (New York: The Free Press), 1958.

LANDIS, BENSON Y., *Professional Codes*. (New York: Bureau of Publications, Teachers College, Columbia University), 1927.

LEWIS, ROY and ANGUS MAUDE, *Professional People*. (London: Phoenix), 1952.

LYNN, K. S., ed., *Professions in America*. (Boston, Mass.: Houghton Mifflin Company), 1965.

MASSEY, HAROLD W. and EDWIN E. VINEGARD, *Profession of Teaching*. (New York: Odyssey Press, Inc.), 1961.

TAEUSCH, CARL F., *Professional and Business Ethics*. (New York: Henry Holt and Company), 1926.

ZNANIECKI, FLORIAN, *The Social Role of the Man of Knowledge*. (New York: Columbia University Press), 1940.

PART II

Practices of Recreational Service

Chapter 10

RESEARCH

PRINCIPLE: In order to make every facet of recreational service efficient and effective so that each person may benefit more completely, a continuing inquiry by scientific methods to determine the most reliable means of solving recreational problems is mandatory.

The purpose and principles of recreational service, as indicated in this book, are to offer specific opportunities for people to achieve optimum development and satisfaction through their participation in activities of a recreational nature. The developmental process is extremely complex, conditioned as it is by various factors. Some of these factors are inherent in the individual, some in the recreationists who attempt to assist people, some in the program of activities, some in the groups to which the individual belongs, some to the social milieu in which the individual finds himself, and some in the extrapersonal environment which subjects the person to certain pressures, modes of behavior, or conditioning features.

The entire process of providing recreational service, and the incidental influences which these services have upon the individual recipient, must be scrupulously studied. The intricacies of human behavior and the social institutions which have been formulated by men are rather complex systems requiring thorough analysis. It is probably correct to state that much of what is taken for granted today will inevitably be found to be erroneous in the future simply because additional knowledge and insight into human nature and better comprehension of social complexities will be available to tomorrow's social scientists.[1] Rapid progress has been made in the physical sciences during the last twenty-five years. The same great progress can be expected in the applied social sciences during the next twenty-five years. Many illustrations of faulty, inaccurate, or incomplete knowledge have been cited in previous pages. It is also valid to say that present knowledge of this field makes it imperative for recreationists to accept with caution many of the so-called standards, facts and techniques so widely held as true.

[1] "Bobby Joins His World," *Look*, Vol. **30**, No. 23 (Nov. 15, 1966), pp. 84–93.

AN INTRODUCTION TO RESEARCH

Research may be broadly defined as any logical inquiry for truth, which is restricted to a specific subject that has, for purposes of investigation, been planned in problem form and regularly defined. Its chief objective is to discover facts not previously known. It may be comprised of historical research as the only means of information or as orientation for an original and direct experience; it may involve appraisal or evaluation as well as fact determination; and it may include the collation of data in concert with the rules of science. Recreational service being what it is should not be limited to any single form of research. In the search for knowledge one may study a variety of concepts, occurrences, items, individuals, and organizations; emotions and estimates; and conduct and procedures; as well as their composition, common components, and affiliations; their source, development, and immediate social orientations; and their meanings, values, and utility.[2]

A superior and much too frequently overlooked method of recreational service research is that of systematic evaluation. Program, supervision, leadership, administrative processes, techniques, and operations as well as persons, subjects, judgments, and organizations may all be examined by systematic evaluation, both from the orientation of standards initiated through an analysis of literature and by experimentation in controlled situations. Such evaluations can be informal, such as are performed by almost all field practitioners, or of the more systematic type performed by research specialists. Research also includes the quest for confirmable claims. One may be thoroughly persuaded of some fact, but the search is not finished until whatever evidence is available can be classified in a way so as to be believable by others. Many persons who attempt to carry out research fail to understand the necessity for such presentation which is both a responsibility and an obligation. To satisfy this obligation, problems to be investigated must be meticulously stated and scrupulously defined. The information upon which conclusions are to be reached must be assembled and tabulated in a way that omits any question as to their authenticity, sufficiency, and thoroughness. There must be emphasis on the factors of accuracy and adequacy of data-collecting measures of all kinds, and the method of documenting data. The meaning of the data must be intelligible to all interested parties. The data must be examined and arranged from a number of distinct and pertinent ways evidencing the diverse ways by which people view them. The description of findings must be correct, adequate, and restricted to the data collected. Where personal opinions are injected, attitudes expressed, or judgments interposed, they must be clearly identified. The reader should never be uncertain as to where factual statements finish and subjective judgments begin.

[2] Allen L. Edwards, "Experiments: Their Planning and Execution," *Handbook of Social Psychology,* ed. Gardner Lindzey, Vol. I (Reading, Mass.: Addison-Wesley Publishing Company, Inc., 1959). pp. 259–287.

Methods of Research

The layman assumes that mechanical and scientific progress will continue to press back the areas of the unknown and that research will always be an on-going process. A steady increase in the knowledge of any field, particularly that of recreational service, is unlikely unless there is a constant supply of professionally educated personnel specifically prepared for this significant work. The accretion of knowledge does not come about in a vacuum nor is it the consequence of circumstance; quite the opposite, it requires consistent effort by intelligent and highly specialized people who devote their lives to advancing human knowledge by pushing back the limits of ignorance.

It is not a misrepresentation to state that almost all of the valuable discoveries and improvements in contemporary civilization were derived through systematic research. The reasons for this become quite clear when it is realized that the principles and techniques of research which are so effectively employed have not been available only to the modern researcher. The knowledge that man has in his possession is the painfully gained result of an extremely slow process extending from man's primitive origins. As his knowledge has increased, so has his comprehension of the methods by which truth may be known. Everyone learns new concepts and specific facts either by trial and error, personal experience, accident, authority, history, tradition, logic, philosophy, and scientific inquiry.

1. *Trial and Error.* One of the most common sources of knowledge consists of deliberately attempting certain acts, e.g., analyzing chemicals or experimenting with schedules, roles, items, in the hope that one will prove to be correct for the purpose for which it is intended. Once a correct response has been found, it is learned and probably transmitted to others and thus the precious store of knowledge about a given thing is accumulated. Of course, this is an extremely arduous, painstaking, and wasteful process. Nevertheless, in the beginning, it was probably one of the only means by which new facts and ideas could be learned.

2. *Personal Experience.* One of the ordinary ways by which the truth is learned is through one's own personal experience and observation. Nearly all of primitive man's early concepts of himself and his environment must have been shaped by this method. The gathering of whatever knowledge there was must have included the drawing of generalizations from particular incidents which occurred and were observed. The restrictions upon this means as applied to the problems of recreational service stem from the complexities of the situational factors of the field; the conditions limiting recreational events are not always readily performed, and the information collected can be very unreliable arising from biased judgments, fancy, and guesswork rather than upon factual measurement. This is not to say that some, or even a good deal of truth might not be learned from personal observation and experience; on the contrary, even with such limitations it

is obvious that keen minds, educated to the techniques of incidental observation and the rules of logic, can produce valuable generalizations from this source. Personal experience can be a worthwhile root of evidence. However, it is probably best fitted for the part of initial concepts rather than as the final word.

3. *Accident.* Just as man probably discovered how to smelt copper, i.e., by the chance putting of lumps of copper ore among ordinary stones in the construction of fire pits for cooking purposes, so too have other facts come to him through accident, provident blunders, or blind luck. One need only recall some of the great scientific discoveries which would appear to have been observed by happenstance. Several examples come to mind: the discovery of radiation as the result of the inadvertent exposure of a photographic plate to an ore sample containing radioactive materials; the discovery of penicillin because a test dish containing the mold had been left unwashed; and the discovery of the first vaccine for syphilis, as a consequence of accidentally placing the six hundredth and sixth experimental material on a hot stove. There were many other combinations of fortuitous circumstances, all of which advanced man's knowledge and allowed him to progress and build up a permanent body of useful information about the world.

4. *Authority.* The measure of authority as a wellspring of truth is reliable only to the extent of the knowledge contained by the authority. As knowledge of involved processes becomes more conclusive, dependence upon authority reaches greater proportions. Contemporary society, with all of its complexities, breeds a host of authorities whose specialized skill and knowledge enable them to provide expert guidance and information in solving problems. However expert an individual is in any given field of endeavor, he still does not know all about every aspect of that field. The recreationist may be reasonably expert in the practice of recreational service, but he cannot be an authority in every single phase of the field. In those areas where his knowledge is limited or incomplete, he must attempt to determine solutions to his problems by various methods, one of which is to consult with experts. Even though the recreationist may not be adequate to meet every exigency that confronts him, he is technically competent in a great many areas and is prepared for areas where he has incomplete command by his knowledge of resources. The recreationist knows where to find expert assistance, either of a written nature or by personal advice from a consultant. The value of such assistance will depend upon the technical proficiency of the authority and the factual information at his disposal.

It cannot be reiterated too often that even the most outstanding authority available can be mistaken. However, there are occasions when a problem will lend itself more readily to the expert advice than it does to other research methods. In the field of recreational service there are experts whose long and intimate experience dealing with specific problems of leisure leadership, administration, planning, evaluation, or other specialization makes them undeniable sources of information that is probably as significant and profitable as may be gained elsewhere. Nevertheless, all authorities are fallible and the use to which their findings are put must be carefully evaluated.

5. *History*. The historical method offers an instrument by which immediate experiences may be enlarged upon by recalling similar episodes or possible solutions from remote times. Through the careful study of records, reports and previous conclusions, activities, ideas, and facts may be secured. If the worker is to be made more competent in his functions he must rely, to some extent, upon the documents and other historical data which serve as vicarious experience. The agency has a history which each worker should know. Even the newest employee must be appraised of the policies and practices of the department and the reasons for their development, use, or disuse. The relation of the superintendent to the board of recreational service, the history of the community which the agency serves, and the modifications of population, economy, age group, or any number of changes which may affect the recreational program and services offered by the agency should be made known to the agency's staff.

Analysis of historical documents must often take the form of critical comparisons between contemporary language and the original meaning of the language used in the documents. Differences in shadings, tone, and literal interpretation can destroy the author's true meaning, and thereby make inaccurate and misleading the current interpretation given the document. Problems which arise as a result of modification in language, dialectical variations, the author's personal biases, the fallibility of the author as an observer, or the author's interpretation of a fact or event which he learned from hearsay, are the bases for critical suspicion of historical sources.

History has a significant contribution to make to all personnel associated with the provision of recreational service in the community. However, historical evidence must be analyzed very carefully lest erroneous conclusions be drawn as a result of uninformed observation or biased attitude. The documents with which the historian must work are usually less accurate and reliable than other evidence derived from scientific sources.

6. *Traditions*. Some individuals rely upon a traditional way of doing things, "because it's always been done this way." This unfortunate frame of reference may occasionally serve as one source of information. It is probably least reliable as a source of information, although there are some traditions in various communities that need to be observed if the worker is to be effective in his leadership. There is a practical value of knowing a community's traditions, but it should also be remembered that tradition is not necessarily correct, ethical, or valuable. What may have served a useful purpose at a lower level of development may now be absolutely worthless. Just such traditional methods for carrying out the objectives of recreational service may be offered to the new worker as a consequence of inertia and

a lack of desire to change. It is easier to remain static than to constantly seek new ways or to question old ways. Lack of adequate knowledge may cause the individual to fall back on traditional means.

7. *Logic.* The logical method represents a progressive step as a way by which man can accumulate knowledge. Syllogistic or deductive reasoning is the method by which the validity of a given concept may be tested. In this procedure, two initial statements which are adduced to be true will inevitably lead to a conclusive third statement. Thus, it is stated that a conclusion logically deduced from reliable premises is itself always reliable. Naturally, the suppositions are that each facet of the preliminary statements is true, that all pertinent material has been carefully examined, and that all extraneous matter has been discarded. In this manner the preliminary premises are supposed to be perfect. Unhappily the deductive method of reasoning is sometimes faulty. Unless there is scrupulous attention to all details the probability of error in the preliminary premises may result in a wrong or unrelated conclusion. This form of reasoning, from the general to the specific, is sometimes too much concerned with semantics and speculation. However, when used in connection with inductive reasoning, i.e., the utilization of specific facts which produce a general inference, the sequence produced is closely akin to what is conceded to be modern scientific research.

8. *Philosophy.* Another more systematic source of truth is philosophy. Through the utilization of historical research, personal observation, and logical reasoning, the study of epistemology, ontology, metaphysics, ideology, and orthology, the philosopher attempts to supply answers to the questions of life. The study of the fundamental principles of knowledge, the values, goals, and logical derivations of truth is within the province of philosophy. The philosophers of recreational service, leisure, and recreation have been extremely helpful in providing theories of human motivation in terms of recreation, in raising questions about recreational practices in view of the objectives of recreational service and recreation, and in their critical estimation of the values produced and provided by the field. It is truly stated that no practitioner is well prepared for his work in any community if he has not had an opportunity to study the philosophical foundation of the field. Such information offers an historical view of the field and provides a larger view than what the individual can know from either practical or contemporary experiences. Philosophy should be used specifically to formulate values, aims, and guiding rules to action for the field.

9. *Scientific Inquiry.* The scientific method of research differs from all other sources of truth or knowledge. It is based upon the concept that every observable phenomenon has a natural explanation. It assumes that new data may be collected at any time and that whatever conclusions are drawn must rest upon clearly substantiated evidence. Through the use of a variety of measuring devices, a more systematic and refined scrutiny of facts, and,

if necessary, through contrived and controlled experimentations the scientific method of inquiry can be carried out. The application of this method to all facets of recreational service problems is one which may prove to be the most effective tool for the solution of many of the complex situations and unanswered questions which now confront the field.

Within the field of scientific inquiry, several types of research may be ascertained (1) the production of evidence through determined fact which involves a search for facts without any attempt to generalize; (2) internal criticism which largely utilizes the technique of inductive and deductive reasoning to derive solutions to problems. This method is applied when dealing with value judgments, ideologies, principles, and foundations of knowledge where ideas rather than facts are being dealt with; and (3) comprehensive research. The process consists of specific steps comprised of identification of the problem to be studied, collection of all pertinent facts, choice of alternative possibilities, analysis of the alternative proposals, refinement of data concerning the possible solution, and the selection of the alternative which meets all of the facts as the best solution.

The Scientific Method

The typical characteristics of the scientific method which make it so advantageous over other forms of investigatory procedures is that it appeals to the natural order of things in the most logical sequence. First, any problem is approached in terms of the observable facts, i.e., to look and see—the determination of whether a thing is present or absent. Second, the technique of detailed and ramified analysis breaks intricate phenomena into more simplified categories in order to make them amenable to solution. With understanding gained by unraveling complex natural processes into comprehensible units, man is able to work out controls and exert his dominion over his environment. Third, science employs a more natural and logical explanation for observable phenomena. Thus, man is able to make hypotheses based upon very careful observations of known facts. The hypothesis is generally looked upon as a tentative or working assumption. The suppositions thereby formed are regarded as a point of departure from which the investigation starts. Such provisional theories consist of possible explanations of any data which may be valid or false, or of all the varied answers which the researcher may find for the study. Once the hypothesis has been tested to determine if there is any substantiating evidence for its support, a temporary theory can be formulated which will tend to direct the study toward more fruitful and clearer sources of knowledge.

The hypothesis may be viewed from two different points. It may be looked upon as a generalization which has been formulated as a consequence of a thorough investigation into any given problem. In this instance the hypothesis is substantiated by undeniable evidence. It may also be regarded as a working proposition, during the initial phases of some study, which acts to guide the researcher in collecting additional data and, perhaps, reaching a final and correct solution.

Another characteristic of science is its objectivity or freedom from pre-study prejudices and emotional convictions. Science is, or should be, disassociated from violations of the truth as a result of personal bias for or against some idea, proposal, person, or thing. It can never be indulgent of popular sentiments regardless of what the facts show. Scientific inquiry stands above all personal commitments to cause or personalities. In its true sense, science frees the mind from the ordinary course of human events in order that the investigator can view new concepts with candor, without artificial restraint, and without ignoring evidence that disproves an initially held point of view.

The progress of scientific knowledge is made as a result of the most careful analysis and appraisal of all facts objectively measured and tested. The work of the scientist is correlated with his ability to employ sophisticated instruments to evaluate collected data. The more highly accurate the instruments are made, the more refined and quantitatively adequate are the data produced. Instead of reliance upon estimates, the researcher is enabled to measure precisely whatever is under analysis. With relevant items of assessment the values may be statistically compared. By employing the most logical and systematic of all quantitative media, the science of mathematics, the most accurate rendition of phenomena being studied may be gained. Starting with scrupulous attention to each unit of the issue in question, the investigator compiles related information into the most expressive classifications and awards every fact with a specific numerical designation or value. These in turn become items on a normal frequency distribution curve. By summarizing the measures in such terms as means, medians, modes, standard deviations from the mean, and coefficients of correlation, quantitative treatment of data can provide greater accuracy and significance.

FORMS OF SCIENTIFIC RESEARCH WHICH CAN BE EMPLOYED IN THE FIELD OF RECREATIONAL SERVICE

In the foregoing pages there has been a concern with the essential principle of research and an orientation to the general attitude and approach that is required in order to utilize research. The application of scientific methods to the study of leadership in recreational service, administrative procedures, supervision, demography, program standards, personnel management, participant behavior, planning, and evaluation has taken many forms. Usually, the problems confronting the recreationist are quite clearly defined. Sometimes they apparently defy description. In any event, once the problem has occurred to the researcher and has been weighed and accurately detailed, the initial method for solution must be an investigation of all the available relevant ideas, facts, and opinions concerning the problem. This investigation invariably leads to the formation of some explanatory suppositions. Such tentative generalizations offer valuable assistance to the search for knowledge by channeling the attention of the worker to salient aspects of the problem under study.

The Hypothesis

The hypothesis must admit the use of deductive reasoning and the implication of results able to be compared with the derivatives of observation. It cannot conflict with natural laws which are held to be valid. It must agree with the facts of observation. Sufficient evidence must exist to support the hypothesis. The hypothesis must be tested to determine whether it is correct. This testing process is performed by collecting and examining data. Research methods are ways by which the hypothesis is tested. In order to validate the hypothesis data is required to serve as the foundation for any solution to a given problem. The analysis and categorization of the collected information in a way which tests the working supposition for validity are also necessary.

One of the techniques developed to test hypotheses has been the application of the null hypothesis to recreational service problems. In using the null hypothesis the investigator assumes that chance rather than a clearly defined cause has produced the consequences which have been observed. Two or more items under investigation having been taken from the same homogeneous population can be differentiated only by chance as a causative factor. This supposition is tested by mathematical examination of the data in question to determine the sampling distribution, i.e., the pattern into which they fall, and the probability that an item declinating as much as that found in the observed sample would arise merely from chance. This procedure is standardized by the development of tables from which the required values are taken. There is little question that this method of stating hypotheses will come to be of increasing value and use when research workers in the field become accustomed in its application.

Although there be many ways of discovering evidence and of examining and classifying it for purposes of research, they can all be defined under the following forms: (1) historical, (2) descriptive, (3) experimental, and (4) clinical. In any given investigation, it is frequently necessary and desirable to use several of these research forms in combination. The decision to utilize one or more of these methods will depend upon the type of problem requiring solution and the availability of data.

The Historical Method

The study of records and other documents in order to learn new facts constitutes historical research. Current concepts, attitudes, and modes of behavior can be better understood in light of information gathered by the historical method. Data gathering of an historical nature is invaluable in establishing a long-term study of any given community or region. In order to determine contemporary mores and to apprehend traditions in a selected subculture of society, the origins and growth sequences of these mores and traditions may be gathered from written records and other visual material. Among the documents from which historical data may be collected are

1. Legal records. Legislation, statutes, ordinances, court records, minutes of meetings, annual and/or daily reports of agency operations, public records of various agencies, contracts, wills, deeds, charters, licenses, certificates, and other instruments which, by their very nature, require accuracy and completeness as well as careful preservation.
2. Mass media accounts. Newspaper reports, radio transcriptions, magazine articles, television pictures, and cinema may be used to amass documentary information.
3. Personal accounts. Autobiographies, biographies, memoirs, diaries, and letters constitute confidential information which may or may not have been written with the knowledge of future publication. The more intimate the material, the less likely it would have been set down with premeditation for future disclosure and the more likely it contains considerable detail of actual opinions.
4. Published literary works. Historical summaries, scholarly reports, literature of the times, essays, poems, novels, and dramatic productions often indicate a close approximation of the life and activity of a period.
5. Artifacts. Plastic and visual art, music, ruins, monuments, sculpture, architecture, and certain types of engineering may provide invaluable data about a prior period.

Historical research is a method of testing a hypothesis by discovering and examining information from written or visual records. Although this method is widely used in all areas of investigation, it specifically applies to the literary fields. Once discovered, historical data must be analyzed for accuracy, validity, applicability, and genuineness. To ensure that an historical study offers undisputed evidence, the investigator must believe without doubt that his data are absolutely pertinent, factual, and adequate.

The Descriptive Method

The data secured by the descriptive method is typically quantitative. It involves a way of obtaining precise facts about the status of some phenomenon and draws valid conclusions from those facts. In normative-survey research, an attempt is made to describe a condition of something in terms of norms. It is a method whereby prevailing conditions may be determined. For example, a recreational service department which makes a population study will thereafter have a sound basis for planning future facilities and employing additional staff. Such a study may seek answers to the following questions: What is the average daily attendance of participants at different recreational facilities, at different age levels, at various times of the day or evening? To what extent does a specific socioeconomic group participate in a given series of recreational opportunities? What is the per participant cost of leadership instruction in different activities and for different age groups? What recreational activities appear to best meet the needs of people at different age levels and from a variety of socioeconomic backgrounds? What are the kinds, amounts, and quality of materials, supplies, and equipment found in each of the several recreational facilities throughout the community? These are the numerous fact questions that the normative-survey tries to answer.

In the comparative-causal survey the researcher's objective is to authenticate some supposed cause-and-effect relationship in the phenomenon under study through application of the logical principle of congruity. These studies are usually made through the orderly review of items within their natural environment without artificial interposition of any factors. This method provides a significant means of investigating the complex problems of recreational service, where the introduction of controlled environments will not furnish accurate or valid conclusions. Among phenomena studied might be the specific differences in the leadership performance of professionally prepared as opposed to nonprofessionally educated recreational service workers, the intellectual characteristics of good and poor administrators, the developmental aspects of successful and unsuccessful recreational programs, and the like.

Among other surveys or descriptive forms is the public opinion poll with its attendant sampling technique. In such surveys, it is usually impossible or uneconomical to personally contact the entire group to be measured, and therefore it is necessary to select a representative sample of the total population from which the required information is to be obtained. The sample may constitute only a small part of the population, but must be large enough quantitatively to be reliable. The most important consideration here is that both size and representativeness of the sampling have a great bearing on the data obtained. The ideal sample is an exact duplicate of the population of which it is a part. There are statistical tables which are of invaluable assistance in deciding upon the proper size of the sampling which should be utilized in any given survey.[3] The reader is here referred to any one of the current textbooks available on methods of research and evaluation which deal in statistics.

The Experimental Method

In the experimental investigation the researcher's objective is to validate some assumed fact or relationship in which controlled conditions are established for examining the supposition. The artificial development and control of something under study has become a widespread method for

[3] Allen L. Edwards, *Statistical Methods for the Behavioral Sciences* (New York: Holt, Rinehart and Winston, 1964), pp. 472–476.

testing cause-and-effect relationship. This has specifically been true in laboratory situations where the phenomenon to be tested can be manipulated and where all conditions can be so controlled that chance is entirely eliminated. The technique is the logical development of basic principles formulated as the method of agreement and the method of difference. The method of agreement avers that, if the conditions leading up to a given circumstance have in each instance only one common factor, said factor is the cause. The method of difference, on the other hand, proposes that, when two or more phenomena are the same with the exception of only one factor and if a specific occurrence is the consequence of that factor, then the appearance of differences may be traced to the single factor.

There are other patterns of experimental research and these take three distinct forms: the concurrent method, the residual method, and the coexistent variable method. The concurrent method is considered to be most generally reliable. In this type of research both the methods of agreement and difference are used jointly. Thus, the conditions of agreement and difference must be met so that the cause of the phenomenon can be identified. One common factor has to be determined as present in all of the instances in which a specific phenomenon occurs. The application of the method of difference is used to determine that the phenomenon never occurs when the unique factor is absent. When both methods point inescapably to one conclusion, the researcher may be reasonably certain as to the cause.

The residual method determines cause through the process of elimination. When the particular factors causing certain parts of a given phenomenon are recognized, then the remaining aspects of the phenomenon must be caused by the remaining or residual fact or factors. Although the experimental method has recently been widely utilized in field research, the conditions for field research are normally less well controlled than those of laboratory research. In instances where the concurrent and residual methods cannot be applied, the technique of coexistent variables or concomitant variations may be attempted. This method illustrates variance probability. When two things consistently vary together, then either the changes in one are caused by the changes in the other, or both are effected by some common cause. In covariational investigations, interest is turned toward the concomitant variation of things. The results are described as regression equations or as coefficients of correlation. This method will probably come into wide use among research oriented recreationists for the study of the more complex problems of recreational service. The statistical techniques utilized in this method are briefly expressed below.

Statistical methods assist the researcher mainly to evaluate and more accurately define the information as well as to determine the degree of correctness of the calculations used. The fundamental premise upon which statistical formulae are based is that of probability. The theory of probability suggests that when a large enough sample of most factors is collected, the items will tend to group themselves around a central point. Thus, it is probable that a theoretical curve exists which, if a large enough sample of items is collected and analyzed, will be found to be symmetrically curved because the items will be distributed over a bell-shaped pattern. Quantitative facts will be grouped around a central point and also rather evenly in both directions from the average. Typically, the measures of central tendency are useful to explain in abbreviated form the average value of a whole order of data. For example, what is the number of participants who utilize a given playground or center at any time of the day or evening? What is the age distribution of individuals who participate within the recreational program? What is the salary of administrators in the field of public recreational service in a given state? The arithmetic mean or average of these facts can express all of these facts in terms of central tendency. Also useful in calculating central tendency are medians and modes. The median is a measure which indicates the exact middle of the range of data. The mode simply indicates the measurement which occurs most often within the sample.

The standard deviation is a measure of dispersion or the spread of scores. In the normal frequency distribution, one standard deviation from the mean would indicate those items of the sample which fall in the range immediately to the right or left of the mean and includes 34.13 per cent of the area on each side of the center. Two standard deviations from the mean would include 47.72 per cent of the range on either side of the mean, while three standard deviations would comprise nearly the entire range of items sampled, or 99.74 per cent. Inasmuch as the normal probability curve is open-ended the last percentages may be infinitely hard to define.

In any statistical investigation the calculation of the standard deviation would be beneficial. In analyzing a survey of population interests, the researcher could compile data from several different samples of the total population with which he is working. After determining the mean score for each group, the scores are tabulated in order to examine whatever differences occur. By comparing the curve of distribution with a normal curve a more accurate mean score for all of the samples can be obtained. When utilized in this way, the standard deviation becomes the standard error.

Calculations of the standard deviation may aid in determining the relative significance of specific kinds of data. Significance has to do with the degree of confidence the investigator can attach to the data under study. Any conclusion reached as a result of sampling some part of the population must be at a level of confidence that clearly shows a definable pattern without the probability of chance involved as a causative factor. There are several factors which affect lack of certainty about samples. Perhaps the most obvious is the size of the sample, e.g., is it adequate for what it is supposed to do. Even with a large sample of items within a given population there is the factor of variability which will inspire uncertainty. Uncertainty may be expressed by a simple formula: degree of uncertainty concerning the average equals observation fluctuation divided by the number of observations. The standard error, being a meaningful measure of variance, can be obtained for as many averages as there are within a given sample. When the standard error is defined for each of two averages, the standard error for the difference between these two averages may also be calculated. The standard error of the difference is normally larger than the standard error of either of the averages. Once the size of the difference and the standard error of the difference are known, significance of the difference will also be known. The ratio derived from dividing the difference by its standard error is usually called the critical ratio. A critical ratio of not less than 2.5 is necessary before any degree of confidence can be assumed about differences in the sample drawn from the larger groups.

Critical ratio is utilized in many studies, but there are refinements of methods. The t test is one. When samples are grouped in twenty-five cases or more, t is almost always identical with the critical ratio. The F test is another method most often used. The F test allows the investigator to examine the significance of an entire group of differences. In some studies, the researcher may use Chi square to test the significance of results. This technique is utilized when the subjects under investigation are categorized rather than actually measured.

Some research involves correlation. Correlation is concerned with the relationship between two sets of data in a given study. It is most frequently used for determining the answer to such questions as the following: What is the precise relationship between occupation and recreational pursuit? What is the result of public relations in stimulating participation within a recreational program? What effect do age, sex, social status, educational background, experience, climate, traditions, and so on have on the potential and/or actual participation within the recreational program by a given population?

The degree of relationship is usually expressed as a coefficient of correlation and it may take any value from -1.00 to $+1.00$. If no correlation exists between items being compared, the coefficient is zero. Where the degree of relationship is positive, but imperfect, a ratio of .30 is commonly considered significant. Negative correlations exist when the ratio between the two variables is inverse. Certain hazards arise in dealing with statistical calculations of this type. Care must be taken to validate whether two or more items compared have a valid relationship to each other. Statistics at best are estimates and cannot be equated with precise measurements.

There is now coming into more general use a variety of group methods of experimentation which offer a method of dealing experimentally with human beings outside of the laboratory. The group methods provide the means for investigating human subjects more directly. The experimental method of the single variable form is typically characterized by one of three forms: (1) the unit group method; (2) the identical group method; or (3) the rotated group method. In the unit group method a single known factor is added to or subtracted from a group and the consequent modification, if any, is determined. In the identical group method two groups of individuals are studied simultaneously. These two groups must be as nearly identical as possible. Having secured the two separate but equivalent groups, the researcher adds or subtracts the experimental factor to one of the groups. After the experimental item has been applied, the two groups are examined to learn whether significant modifications have occurred. In the rotated group method two or more equivalent groups of subjects are used. The experimental factor is applied to each group on a rotated basis. In this latter method, identical aspects need not be as severe as in the identical group method, and the researcher may conduct his experiment with several rather than with only two groups.

The Clinical Method

In the clinical study the investigator's purpose is to learn the cause or causes pertaining to some condition or phenomenon. It amounts to the scrupulous examination of every facet of the life and behavior of one person. This same technique may also be utilized when studying groups, communities, specific regions, or a particular mode of social behavior. In recreational service research, which has a tendency to reflect sociological research in general, the survey and the clinical study are often used to supplement and complement one another, for there is a close relationship between the two forms.

The information collected in the clinical study may be ascertained from diverse sources. Important among these are the personal statements of the subject, letters, diaries, or logs, medical and social evaluations, the accumulated records of a variety of social institutions, public and private agencies, and the public record of mass media. Such material must be examined and authenticated in much the same way as is done for historical research. Research of this type usually strives to obtain a thorough description of the individual or group under study and also to identify the chief cause or causes leading to the current status or situation of the individual or group.

THE OUTCOMES OF RESEARCH IN RECREATIONAL SERVICE AND THEIR USE

What are the results of research carried on in a variety of settings by recreationists and specialists? The products of such research are numerous; and although it is not the author's purpose to detail these results here, some reference to them appears to be needed as an orientation or point of departure for those who intend to investigate and participate in the systematic study of the field of recreational service and its improvement. A brief synopsis would include the following:

1. Facts, standards, and concepts that contain the immediate results of research investigations:

a. Programs differ in their capacity to attract and retain participants.
b. The cost of recreational leadership varies and is standardized nowhere.
c. Good leadership promotes greater participant activity.
d. No cost studies have been made to determine salary levels on a standardized basis in any part of the country.
e. Each individual is unique and differs in capacity.
f. Females mature more rapidly than do males.
g. Programs must account for individual differences.
h. The education of practitioners in the field of recreational service to their professional responsibilities and in professionalism is necessary.
i. Environmental factors affect the program.
j. Planned recreational programs do not affect juvenile delinquency.
k. The recreational agency cannot provide or substitute for the home environment.
l. There are physiological limitations to the acquisition of motor skills.
m. The mentally retarded have recreational needs.
n. The mentally retarded can participate in a variety of recreational activities within the public setting.
o. Success should be a part of group activities.
p. There is a form of collective recreational behavior which affects selection and participation in activities.
q. Almost 60 billion dollars of discretionary income was spent for some form of recreational activity in 1966. This spending is increasing.
r. There is an inverse ratio between consumer (participant) use and maintenance at present. Recreational usage versus maintenance of natural resources.
2. The explanation of suppositions indicating that:
a. Research methods which can be applied to physical phenomena may also be utilized in determining human behavior and social institutional phenomena.
b. The provision of recreational service to all of the people all of the time is mandatory.
c. The concept of charging for the use of public recreational facilities is undesirable.
d. The assumption that recreational service agencies, of all public agencies, should charge for services even though the department is tax-supported is untenable.
e. Recreational service should be part of every local government.
f. Statistical evidence is valuable in dealing with human questions.
g. Recreational service must concern itself with all of the attendant needs of a professional vocation.
h. Support of public recreational service can be equalized.
3. Definitions were rendered:
a. Of terms, such as *recreation, recreational, leisure, play, recreationist,*

recreator, administrator, program, professional, professionalization, profession.
   b. Of goals, such as the achievement of which promote the greatest satisfaction, enjoyment, social acceptability, physical fitness, mental health, social capability, ethics, and skill.
4. Development of intellect for the critical analysis of issues affecting the field.
5. The improvement of observation and the perpetuation of the scientific method in determining problems and seeking their solution.
6. Techniques that are the foundation of concepts concerning research procedures.
4,5,6. These aspects of research are needed. The outcomes are in doubt at this time. These problems are still considered to be in the developmental stage and are not at all in widespread practice now.

Of course, this is not intended as a complete listing of research outcomes. The products of research are too numerous to be presented here in any but a sketchy outline. Nevertheless, the magnitude of information generated by research in the field of recreational service is noteworthy and should act as a stimulus for the production of better programs by more highly proficient and professionally oriented personnel. Much has still to be done to overcome the conditioned inertia that infects many practitioners. There is currently available a good deal of information which has been documented and authenticated. The knowledge, principles, and facts already catalogued simply have not been put into practice. There is a noticeable gap between theory and operation; only a minor part of what is known has been utilized in the promotion of more useful methods. The problem of acquainting recreational service practitioners with, and bringing them to a point where they recognize the significance of, research so that they will make use of the derivatives is an intricate one.

How to Locate Research

The problem of finding research literature is not a simple matter of routine. On occasion, even those who really are interested in examining the facts pass over important guides as not being relevant. Knowing what is pertinent and applicable is a skill that should be developed in all recreationists. Although the typical practitioner may not have easy access to much of the research that is produced at institutions of higher education, such material is available with very little effort. There are also publications that specialize in the rendition of research reports. These should be perused faithfully, even though the implications for recreational service practice may not be immediately recognized. Most of the best writings will be found in a variety of journals, i.e., *Phi Delta Kappan; Recreation In Treatment Centers; Lancet; Review of Educational Research; Child Development; Journal of Gerontology; Journal of Educational Psychology; Educational Leadership; Jour-*

nal of Educational Sociology; American Sociological Review. Authors of these articles have contributed their efforts because they feel that the information has application to the field.

Conversion of Research Products to Practice. The objective which professionals seek is improved recreational service. This outcome will be discovered in part in the documentation of historical, logical, philosophical, and scientific research. Rarely will the practitioner find all of the facts organized to such an extent that he will be able to apply them operationally. More usually, the facts and principles derived from research are synthesized. The recreationist must learn how to apply the summarized findings in ways that will make more effective the service that he can offer. Typically, suitable methods for application of the facts and principles involved will be indicated in the original research; otherwise it will be necessary for the recreationist to use his ingenuity, creativeness, and technical ability in devising new methods. By invention or combinantion of old and new techniques, the findings of research may be instrumental in improving recreational programs and the results obtained from such improvement should be wholly beneficial.

A broad investigation must be made of the problems affecting the translation of research findings into field utilization. A study of the resources available to such a procedure is required. From such a program the following techniques may be discerned as having significant influence for application of basic research to field improvement.

1. The organization of research producing and resource classifying centers by state agencies, preferably a state recreational service commission as well as institutions of higher education. Cooperatively with these agencies, institutes, conferences, workshops, symposia, and other educational meetings should be initiated to explore needs, translate current research findings to practical applications, and make readily available pertinent facts and principles by which local problems may be resolved.
2. Transmit educational information concerning research currently underway or proposed within a distinct region, district, or locality. Assistance may be given by preparing a monthly publication on research that has been completed.
3. Arrange for technical assistance, e.g., specialists, to perform needed research on current problems. If a central research facility is established, coordinated efforts of researchers and practitioners could result in better application of scientific procedures to operational efforts.
4. Assist in the publication, dissemination, and utilization of resource materials produced through recreational research. Coordination could be developed with state commissions, regional agencies, commercial publishers, institutions of higher learning, and in-service education programs through cooperation with state professional societies and local departments of recreational service.

5. Attempt to stimulate and otherwise encourage positive efforts to coordinate the work of existing professional groups, regional and district agencies, associations, or committees as their output relates to the translation and effective use of research.

SIGNIFICANT PROBLEMS IN RECREATIONAL SERVICE

Invariably, textbook authors have included, in any explanation of research methods and findings, some statement on problems that trouble them or that require further research. To the extent that the field of recreational service has problems of major import that have never been examined, much less scientifically researched, a separate volume might be produced on this subject alone. It has been the objective of this chapter to offer a more encompassing treatment of research needs for the field of recreational service, rather than to supply a list of problems. The content has therefore been extended to include the significant items influencing the product of the scientific method and its integral techniques, as applied to the field of recreational service. Nevertheless, an itemization of some outstanding problems is offered as an indication to researchers of an even more extensive list relating to the multiform factors which should dominate field productivity and practice.

1. How can effective and appropriate standards of professionalization be established and made acceptable to operating agencies?
2. What is the most effective ratio between recreationists and population?
3. How can professional personnel ratios between functional workers and participating individuals be standardized?
4. Should recreationists be licensed by state agencies as are other service field personnel?
5. Is it feasible to have some sort of national board examination and reciprocity agreement if certification and/or licensing procedures are adopted?
6. How can the field of recreational service achieve recognition among other socially acceptable and recognized professional fields and agencies to the degree that special educational preparation is required for its personnel?
7. What should be the place of the Federal Government in the conduct of public recreational service?
8. How can municipal (local) governments be made to recognize their primary responsibility for the provision of recreational service to their constituents?
9. How can operating agencies performing a recreational service function be made to employ only professionally educated and qualified personnel?

10. Should regulatory legislation be enacted, much as it is for medical practitioners, in terms of whom may professionally practice in the provision of public recreational service?

SUMMARY

An emphasis has been made in this chapter relating to the method of scientific inquiry and research methods applicable to the field of recreational service. Stress has been placed upon the extreme care that must be observed and maintained in determining the facts and principles of this field. What appears to be fact may well be opinion, based upon ignorance or long outmoded tradition, and not fact at all. A number of methods for ascertaining facts has been indicated in man's intensive search for the truth about his environment and himself. Man's initial method for deriving some idea about the world in which he lives is from personal observation. As man has developed from a survival existence to what he is now pleased to call civilization, his ideas produced traditional ways of doing things and a reliance upon authority, history, chance, and philosophy. During the last century, the scientific revolution has enabled man to discard many of his biases, superstitions, and reliance upon unfounded opinion gained through ignorance. Instead there has slowly developed the means for examining natural phenomena in such a way as to bring more systematic and logical refinements to the observation. Perhaps the most important device to be created for the identification and authentication of what the truth is has been the scientific method. Its many ramifications may be found in nearly every aspect of the literature of this and other scientifically based endeavors.

The idea of logical inquiry and research based upon the scientific method along with the more important forms of scientific methods have been discussed. The emphasis upon the scientific method is readily observed and its advantages are manifest for various reasons, chief among which are (1) facts to be derived are objectively rather than subjectively obtained, and when the method is strictly enforced, prejudice is removed; (2) any generalizations made rest upon evidence that can be observed; (3) the employment of reasoned inquiry can result in the simplification of apparently unfathomable enigmas; (4) the formulation of tentative hypotheses as a point of departure for directed research is of great assistance in obtaining knowledge; (5) the utilization of experimentally contrived situations can produce an understanding of otherwise unintelligible phenomena; and (6) specialized techniques utilizing arithmetic means to measure the collection and treatment of information are superior to methods basing results on less valid and reliable means. In order to solve present problems confronting the field of recreational service, a wide variety of techniques must be used coordinately if the most meaningful data are to be produced with accuracy. The purpose of research is to solve problems. The objectives of research in recreational service are characterized by verified evidence, scrupulous attention to source and collection of facts, and the need for complete objectivity in handling whatever information is derived from the investigation.

SELECTED REFERENCES

Cohen, Lillian, *Statistical Methods for Social Scientists, An Introduction.* (New York: Prentice-Hall), 1954.

Edwards, Allen L., *Statistical Methods for the Behavioral Sciences.* (New York: Holt, Rinehart and Winston), 1964.

Fisher, R. A., *The Design of Experiments,* 3d ed. (Edinburgh: Oliver and Boyd), 1942.

Good, Carter V., *Introduction to Educational Research,* 2d ed. (New York: Appleton-Century-Crofts), 1962.

———, *Essentials of Educational Research.* (New York: Appleton-Century-Crofts), 1966.

Griffen, John I., *Statistics: Methods and Applications.* (New York: Holt, Rinehart and Winston), 1962.

Larson, Leonard A. and Rachael D. Yocum, *Measurement and Evaluation in Physical, Health, and Recreation Education.* (St. Louis, Mo.: The C. V. Mosby Company), 1951.

Ostle, Bernard, *Statistics in Research: Basic Concepts and Techniques for Research Workers.* (Ames, Iowa: Iowa State University Press), 1963.

Richmond, Samuel B., *Statistical Analysis,* 2d ed. (New York: The Ronald Press), 1964.

Travers, Robert M. W., *An Introduction to Educational Research,* 2d ed. (New York: The Macmillan Co.), 1964.

Chapter 11

ADMINISTRATION

PRINCIPLE: The function of administration is to arrange the procedure of routine operations in such a way as to facilitate the duties of the departmental staff in the execution of the purposes for which the recreational service agency was established, and to preserve public trust in the agency.

The complexity of society has multiplied to such an extent that administration of any human enterprise offers problems of considerable magnitude. If the problems that confront administrators are to be resolved, in even the simplest endeavors, logical progression is required; the more intricate and larger the system, the more essential it is that a well-planned organization be produced and made effective. Organization is the arrangement of combined efforts by individuals and aggregates coordinated so that the work of the agency can be carried out with maximum efficiency, minimum waste, and optimum desirable results.

Of all the modern social agencies, few have wider dealings with the tremendous range of human interests and needs than does the community recreational service department. It can be one of the more complex undertakings which the local jurisdiction operates. Its essential purpose is to provide a comprehensive program of diverse recreational experiences to all of the people all of the time. In accomplishing this purpose the recreational agency must bring to bear the knowledge and discipline available to it from the fields of business or corporate enterprise as well as those of scientific management which are appropriate to its own administration. In addition, it must recruit highly skilled and technically competent individuals, who are professionally prepared to operate the department, together with ancillary personnel, including volunteers who can more nearly supplement and complement the recreationist. Moreover, the added precaution of economic utilization of men, materials, and money in ways that will produce efficient, systematic, and effective services of a recreational nature is required.

Only through organization can optimum service without duplication of effort and waste of material and fiscal resources be produced. No small detail should be overlooked and every individual employed or enrolled within the personnel aspect of the agency should have clearly defined duties. Departments in which every employee is always ready to think and act promptly and effectively will have the regular functions, authority, and responsibilities of each carefully assigned. Authority will be centralized, responsibility designated, coordination utilized, and relationships definitely fixed. Organization should be looked upon as the structural facet or form-giving element of the agency, whereas administration is planning, directing, and controlling the operation of the organization through coordination. Organization is a part of administration and is concerned with the arrangement of all elements pertaining to the agency in such a way that appropriate service will be engendered.

ORGANIZATIONAL CONCEPTS

Too often, recreational service agencies have no real plan of organization or, at best, a superficial one. Many agencies have simply reacted to changing times, the organization being structured about whatever personnel was available and with no thought to any logical plan. Any modifications made in these agencies have been largely ones of expediency brought about by emergency conditions. Typically, community recreational service departments start off as summer programs which, after having proved successful in attracting whatever clientele there is, become accepted by the local government as a part of an existing agency or are established as a separate member of the municipal family. Initially, the department may have been built around one person, usually the individual in charge. In time, with the accumulation of additional duties as a result of being made a full-time department, or having incurred responsibilities as a subordinate branch of a larger agency, the agency has to broaden the scope of its activities. When it is finally learned that the agency cannot carry out its functions with only the existing personnel, other individuals are hired. Unfortunately, if the agency's program has been geared to the skills of the individual worker rather than to the recreational needs of people living in the community to be served, there is bound to be a noticeable weakness in the structure of the organization. Often, the program is unbalanced, with too much emphasis on one phase and not enough on others. A constricted view of the work to be done, rather than an orientation embracing the fundamental principles of recreational service in the community determines the direction of the agency's activities. Attention is focused on petty details, while the larger problems of balance, scope, variety, and progression of activities within the program are unresolved. In this instance, concepts of coordination and cooperation are of distant concern.

Organizational Planning

When the organization is based upon logical methods, debilitating conditions cannot become entrenched. Organization takes as its rationale the idea that only through cooperation and coordination will there develop maximum output with a minimum of expense and effort. Specialization and the desire to meet the needs of total population are outgrowths of modern professional interest in the field of recreational service. Increased size adds to the problems of control through increased number of participating personnel and greater complexity of the system. Specialization concentrates expert attention on the activities specialized in and limits the possibility of error. Simultaneously, however, specialization strengthens the requirement for coordinated effort and for ways of widening the concepts of these specialists, i.e., having them look beyond their specific interests to the needs of the agency as a whole. A soundly planned organization is the structure upon which administration depends for essential cooperation, direction, control, and coordination.

Examination of the very largest recreational service departments indicates the multiplicity of functions undertaken and executed. In some instances, thousands of persons may be employed. There are specialists in a variety of recreational activities—construction and maintenance, business administration, public relations, personnel management, and an extended list of other fields. Each individual spends his vocational life in the preparation and practice in a specific area, being particularly adept to perform certain endeavors or to give expert technical guidance in his area. Through organization, functions are identified and categorized. This allows specialists to be employed to take responsibility for those functions, which should culminate in a coordinated effort that permits each specialization to function effectively while all specialities are combined to produce a common goal—recreational service. On each level of the agency hierarchy the supervisor coordinates the work of his subordinates; in turn, his work and that of others of his rank are coordinated by his superior until the executive of the agency finally coordinates all activities being carried on within the system. One of the required functions of any administrator is to effect coordination within his area of authority, whether that sphere be the department or some division of the agency. The more extensive the department, the more desirable is coordination and therefore, the greater is the need for an organization developed to facilitate the efforts of the executive and his subordinates in obtaining unity of purpose and harmony.

There is hardly an ideal organization for every recreational agency. Nonetheless, there are certain principles and standards that can be followed in the development of an organizational procedure which can be ideal for each agency. The standard should be kept constantly uppermost in the mind of the executive and should be varied from only with exceptional reason. On the other hand the structural pattern should not be maintained regardless of changing needs and other modifying pressures. The study of the standards of organization will offer reasonable choices for the development of a logical organizational plan. However, environmental as well as internal influences may necessitate deviation from what might be considered an ideal organizational plan. Political machinations, available professional personnel, financial support, community traditions, and other factors, all play an important part in any structural arrangement.

Basic Organizational Standards

As each recreational service agency has conditioning factors peculiar to itself—in terms of region, finance, authorization, legal establishment, operating and volunteer personnel available to it, public support, participant demand, pressure groups involved, financial resources available, natural and artificial resources available—a unique statement of rules and prescriptions cannot be formulated which might be applicable to the organization of all agencies. However, certain fundamental standards can be provided by which actions can be guided and from which levels of attainment may be judged. Details of application may differ as a result of unique conditions, but the following standards are valuable as underlying procedures for logical organization.

1. *Purpose.* Vital to the initiation of every recreational service agency in any sector of society, or to the transaction of any operation by the agency or its units, is a clear and definite statement relating to the purposes for which the agency is established. This explanation will result in the development of plans and emphasis upon the achievement of the aims therein set forth. The purpose for which the agency was established is the essence of that enterprise. All other activities are subordinate to the primary purpose and each must serve to substantiate and aid in the attainment of the chief purpose.

2. *Classification.* A comprehensive examination of the entire range of activities, operations, and services to be produced must be made so that each facet of the agency and its units can be identified and assigned relative responsibilities. There is little question that anyone with a good knowledge of the field of recreational service would attempt to establish a department unless all of the requirements for that department, in a specific locale, were analyzed. Recreational service agencies are organized chiefly with the aim of providing experiences of a recreational nature to all of the people in a given community, if the agency is of the municipal family, or for a particular clientele. It would therefore be decidedly foolish to establish the agency without first determining whether the public wants or is ready to accept the provision of public recreational service, whether such an agency can employ professional personnel, and whether adequate financial support will be available to permit a comprehensive and varied program at a price which the community is willing to pay. Unless the answers to these questions are positive, additional public education and dissemination of information relating to individual need for recreational experiences must be made the first order of business.

3. *Simplification.* All activities that are not essential to the production of recreational services should be eliminated, and those activities that are continued should be managed in the simplest efficient way.

4. *Functional Segregation.* The organization should be structured on the primary purpose of the agency and not around personnel. The nature of recreational service determines the chief functions of the agency, and

thus, of itself, offers the correct foundation for organization. Functions, or activities, have no limitation; people are restricted in what they can do and to what extent that may develop. Functional segregation distributes work efforts and responsibilities. Similar or complementary functions should be grouped so as to form the several major divisions of the system. For example, all requisite activities concerning business administration should be classified in one major group. All necessary activities relating to the maintenance of the physical plant of the agency should be placed in another major class, and all of the activities relating to the direct provision of recreational experiences should be put into a third category, and so on. Each of these groups will then be the foundation for a major division of the system. This provides a sound structure which prevents overlapping, duplication, and omission of functions to the detriment of the department as a whole. When a system is developed around functions, which are clearly identified and made responsible for specific outcomes, the result is one of flexibility, growth, capability, and adjustability to whatever changing conditions the environment brings. When major divisions are established to care for the respective groups of like and complementary functions, then responsibility can be fixed, valid costs of operations can be known, department budgets accurately estimated and prepared, and the necessary personnel employed.

5. *Authority and Responsibility.* Centralization of responsibility and wide delegation of authority in order to fix the former and render the latter most effective in the production of recreational services are necessary. An individual does his best work and accomplishes the greatest result when he is given a definite job to be completed in a specified time, the work being of a nature for which he is physically and emotionally suited and competently prepared to carry out. Assignments should be of a difficulty that is sufficient to demand the highest quality of effort that the person has to offer. Individual effectiveness is increased through in-service education and improved work conditions. Carefully instructed personnel know to whom and for what they are responsible; they have a better understanding of the purpose of the agency, and they are enabled to perform more efficiently, quickly, and economically those things for which they were employed to do. Similarly, improved working conditions develop morale, loyalty to the system, and dedication to the field.

Scientific formulation of work responsibilities leads to specialization of effort and develops experts in some particular activity, with resultant advantages derived from concentrated attention. Care should be exercised, however, not to narrow the scope of work to such an extent that the individual can only be confident and/or competent in one minute activity form. A certain amount of versatility is not only desirable, but vital, if the recreational service agency is to offer the most comprehensive program possible. Recreationists should be expert in two or three program categories, but should also have a wide acquaintance and knowledge of all of the program categories and resource possibilities.

An individual exercising authority should be held responsible for the execution of all activities within the limit of his authority. Conversely, no individual should be held responsible for the proper execution of operations that do not fall under his jurisdiction. Ultimately, of course, all responsibility rests with the departmental executive, e.g., the superintendent of recreational service. Although it has been stated that an executive may delegate authority, he may not delegate responsibility. To a certain extent this is true. Nevertheless, some responsibility does fall upon the individual who has been given authority to carry out a specific operation. Failure to perform adequately when proper authority to control a given operation has been received reflects unfavorably upon the delegator as well as the recipient. When authority is delegated, it should be clearly defined. There should be no overlapping of authority nor any question about with whom responsibility lies.

Standardized executive control through the delegation of authority and acceptance of responsibility requires establishment of clearly defined lines of supervision and an insistence upon chain-of-command from the executive downward. This provides a basis for discipline and coordination of all work to be produced. In addition, it stresses the probable lines for advancement within the agency hierarchy, and teaches leadership techniques and other operational knowledge to personnel who understudy their superiors.

6. *Standardization.* The substitution of standard operating procedures, in the routine of daily affairs of the agency, for policy statements concerning individual activities should be made. Particular techniques of best practice, carefully determined, should be adopted and applied throughout the agency.

Whenever feasible, certain standards of practice, expressed in terms of definite qualitative and quantitative units or patterns of behavior, should be made the model by which all performance and productivity may be evaluated. Standards of performance provide administrators with specific terms by which to measure efficiency, evaluate leadership, appraise program content, and to estimate future planning. Unless standards are introduced into the daily operations of the agency, there is no basis for comparison and no sure method for understanding whether or not the agency's efforts approximate the aims for which the agency was established. Standardization permits better control and affords a greater degree of accuracy in analyzing the system's productive capacity for the rendition of recreational service. Properly instituted standards furnish incentive to personnel to achieve a level of competency which they can clearly perceive, rather than being dependent upon some nebulous ideal about which there are no means of determination.

7. *Planning.* The satisfactory accomplishment of the agency's purpose can be attained only when there is a logical plan by which all of the system's personnel and all of its interests and functions are guided. Therefore, intelligible, sharp, and comprehensive plans are essential to effective administration.

246   Practices of Recreational Service

Planning assists achievement of aims. It defines the real interests of the system, the goals to be reached, and specifically details the priority, personnel, facilities, space, material, and money to be used in their accomplishment. The aims provide a basis for action, setting up primary objectives, and the means and techniques to be utilized in arriving at those objectives. They are not arbitrary rules or regulations, but highly practical and elastic guides which take into consideration the present environment and shifting conditions and/or needs of the community or clientele to be served. With planning the arrangement of work, the delegation of authority and the fixing of responsibility are decided upon, decisions are made as to what should be done, who will do it, how it will be performed, and when and where it should be carried out. Because recreational service is a field that deals with people, the offering is constantly changing as people's needs are continuously being modified. For these reasons, planning is of utmost significance if the agency is to satisfy demand.

Charting the System

After a department has been established it is often difficult to picture it in its entirety and see whether or not a logical plan of organization has been created. To ascertain the strengths and weaknesses in the structure and a sound basis for agency operation, an organizational chart should be drawn. The chart graphically indicates the direct relationship of functions and existence of lines of authority and responsibility as well as the interrelationships between line and staff personnel and divisions. The charting procedure is an excellent test of logic and structural soundness, inasmuch as any organization relationship that cannot be easily diagrammed is often poorly planned and unintelligible to the personnel employed within it. There are distinct advantages for the use of organization charts, particularly for the largest agencies where so many more employees are involved in agency operations. However, charting is also applicable and of benefit to smaller departments as well. The following seven (7) organizational charts (reprinted with permission of the City of Detroit, Michigan), indicate major divisions of a recreational service system, secondary or subdivisional charts, and tertiary or sectional subdivisions indicate basic activities carried on in the organization.

Chart 1
DEPARTMENT OF PARKS AND RECREATION

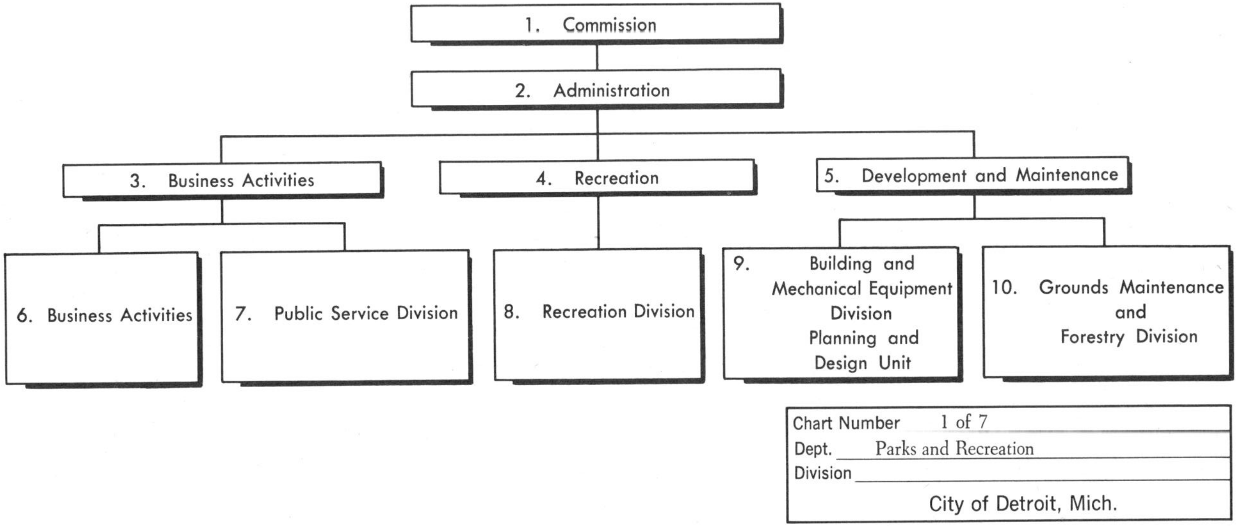

1. Commission
2. Administration

3. Business Activities
4. Recreation
5. Development and Maintenance

6. Business Activities
7. Public Service Division
8. Recreation Division
9. Building and Mechanical Equipment Division Planning and Design Unit
10. Grounds Maintenance and Forestry Division

Chart Number 1 of 7
Dept. Parks and Recreation
Division _____
City of Detroit, Mich.

CHART 1

Department of Parks and Recreation

1.   COMMISSION

Establishing policies and regulations for the management of all activities and properties assigned to the Parks and Recreation Commission by the provisions of the City Charter in accordance with directives of the Mayor and Common Council.

4   Member

2.   ADMINISTRATION

Directing all activities of the department in accordance with the policies and regulations laid down by the Commission, including a recreation program, public service activities, horticulture, grounds and building maintenance, and acquisition and development of park facilities; member, Department Report and Information Committee.

Budgeted Position: P/R 1-100

1   General Superintendent of Parks and Recreation

3.   BUSINESS ACTIVITIES

Directing, planning, coordinating, and supervising administrative, personnel, public service division, and general business management functions of the department; reviewing special reports and analyses, and evaluating adequacy of existing procedures; recommending changes in policies and appropriate actions to improve efficiency, services, and operations; reviewing and analyzing budget; examining departmental expenditures to insure conformity with budget programs.

Budgeted Position: P/R 1-100

1   Parks and Recreation Administrator (Business Activities)

4.   RECREATION

Directing, planning, coordinating, and supervising recreation functions of the department; reviewing activities reports and making field inspections to evaluate efficiency and adequacy of program and to assure full use of personnel and facilities; coordinating departmental recreational activities with recreation services of public and private agencies; coordinating recreational activities with those of the Board of Education; recommending changes in facilities and activities where analyses indicate need for change.

Budgeted Position: P/R 1-100

1   Parks and Recreation Administrator (Recreation)

5. DEVELOPMENT AND MAINTENANCE

Directing, planning, coordinating, and supervising horticultural, buildings and grounds maintenance and development functions of the department; coordinating building construction program with other departments and contractors; reviewing and analyzing activities reports and making field investigations to check work progress and to determine efficiency and adequacy of program; recommending changes in departmental policy where investigation and analyses indicate need for change; making recommendations and requests for major construction equipment purchases.

        Budgeted Position: P/R 1-100

1 Parks and Recreation Administrator (Development and Maintenance)

6. BUSINESS ACTIVITIES

Directing the personnel general office, stores and accounting, and acquisition and analysis functions of the department.
        (See chart 2 of 7)
        Budgeted Positions: 92
        Memo Position: 1

7. PUBLIC SERVICE DIVISION

Directing the activities of the Public Service Division.
        (See chart 3 of 7)
        Budgeted Positions: 14
        Memo Positions: 53
        Seasonal Positions: 23 to 224
        Contractual Position: 1

8. RECREATION DIVISION

Conducting recreation program for adults and children.
        (See chart 4 of 7)
        Budgeted Positions: 191
        Memo Positions: 2
        Seasonal Positions: 79 to 715
        Contractual Positions: 5 to 240

9. BUILDING AND MECHANICAL EQUIPMENT DIVISION PLANNING AND DESIGN UNIT

Being responsible for the buildings and mechanical equipment of the department; preparing plans, specifications, and preliminary layouts.
        (See chart 5 of 7)
        Budgeted Positions: 86
        Memo Positions: 239
        Seasonal Positions: 0 to 44

10. GROUNDS MAINTENANCE AND FORESTRY DIVISION

Planting and maintaining trees, flowers, and plants in municipal gardens; maintaining parks and playgrounds.
(See charts 6 and 7 of 7)
- Budgeted Positions: 40
- Memo Positions: 517
- Seasonal Positions: 0 to 185
- Contractual Positions: 6

Totals on Chart:
- Budgeted Positions: 4

Total Positions Utilized: 4

Totals in Department:
- Budgeted Positions: 427
  - (Vacant: 10)
- Memo Positions: 812
  - (Vacant: 1)

Total Positions Available: 1239
- (Total Vacant: 11)
Total Positions Utilized: 1228
- Seasonal Positions: 102 to 1168
- Contractual Positions: 6 to 247

Chart 2
DEPARTMENT OF PARKS AND RECREATION

Business Activities

1. Business Activities
2. General Office Unit
3. Public Service Division
4. Accounting and Stores Unit
5. Secretarial Services
6. District Offices
7. Main Office
8. Stores
9. Accounting

Chart Number 2 of 7
Dept. Parks and Recreation
Division Business Activities
City of Detroit, Mich.

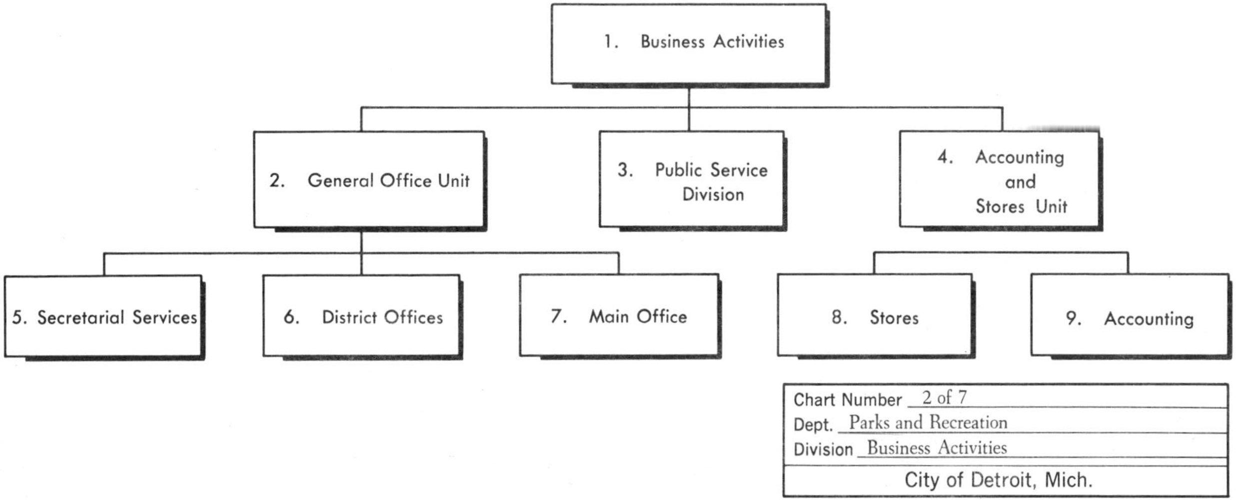

CHART 2

Department of Parks and Recreation
Business Activities

1.   BUSINESS ACTIVITIES

Directing the business management functions of the department; reviewing special reports and analyses, and evaluating adequacy of existing procedures; recommending appropriate actions or changes in policies to improve efficiency, services, and operation; reviewing and integrating the preliminary budget request and preparing a budget program; examining departmental expenditures to insure conformity with budget program.

    B   U
    1   1 - Parks and Recreation Administrator (Business Activities)

2.   GENERAL OFFICE UNIT

Supervising clerical, stenographic, mimeograph, and switchboard services for the department; preparing and processing Public Service Division contracts; reviewing and approving partial payments on construction contracts.

           B   U
           1   1 - Head Clerk
           1   1 - Principal Clerk
           —   —
           2   2

3.   PUBLIC SERVICE DIVISION

Operating, directly or by concession, the income-producing properties of the department.
         (See chart 3 of 7)
        B-Budgeted Positions: 13
        M-Memo Wage Personnel: 263
           Seasonal: 180
           Extra Labor: 58
        C-Contractual Positions: 1
        U-Positions Utilized: 277

4.   ACCOUNTING AND STORES UNIT

Supervising departmental accounting activities and the operation and maintenance of departmental storerooms and supply yards.

    B   U
    1   1 - Principal Accountant

5. SECRETARIAL SERVICES

Providing clerical and stenographic services for administration and various divisional supervisors.

B	U	
1	1	- Secretarial Stenographer
3	3	- Senior Stenographer
6	3	- Stenographer
2	5	- Typist
1	1	- Clerk
13	13	

6. DISTRICT OFFICES

Performing filing, record keeping and general clerical work in district offices.

B	U	
1	1	- Senior Typist
2	1	- Stenographer
4	5	- Typist
4	4	- Clerk
1	3	- Junior Typist
1		- Junior Clerk
13	14	

7. MAIN OFFICE

Providing typing, stenographic, and mimeograph services; operating switchboard, preparing and maintaining miscellaneous reports and records; arranging for use of school buildings for recreational purposes; receiving reservations for summer camp.

B	U	
2		- Senior Clerk
3	2	- Stenographer
	1	- Senior Typist
3	5	- Typist
2	1	- Clerk
2	2	- Telephone Operator
	1	- Junior Typist
2	1	- Junior Clerk
14	14	

8. STORES

Operating departmental storerooms and supply yards; ordering, receiving, and issuing materials and supplies; maintaining inventory; performing departmental mail pick-up and delivery.

B	U	
1	1	- Head Storekeeper
2	2	- Storekeeper

```
1    1 - Senior Clerk
3    3 - Assistant Storekeeper
2    2 - Clerk
M    1 - Public Service Attendant (Merchandising)
M    1 - Auto Deliveryman
─    ──
9    11
```

9. ACCOUNTING

Maintaining general, cost, and appropriation ledgers; processing purchase requisitions; conducting departmental audits; preparing financial statements; performing cost accounting for various departmental locations.

```
B    U
1    1 - Senior Accountant
1    1 - Semi-Senior Accountant
1    1 - Senior Bookkeeper
1    1 - Senior Typist
3    3 - Senior Clerk
1    1 - Typist
1    1 - Clerk
─    ─
9    9
```

Totals on Chart:
   B-Budgeted Positions: 62
   M-Memo Wage Personnel: 2
   U-Positions Utilized: 64

Chart 3

DEPARTMENT OF PARKS AND RECREATION

Public Service Division

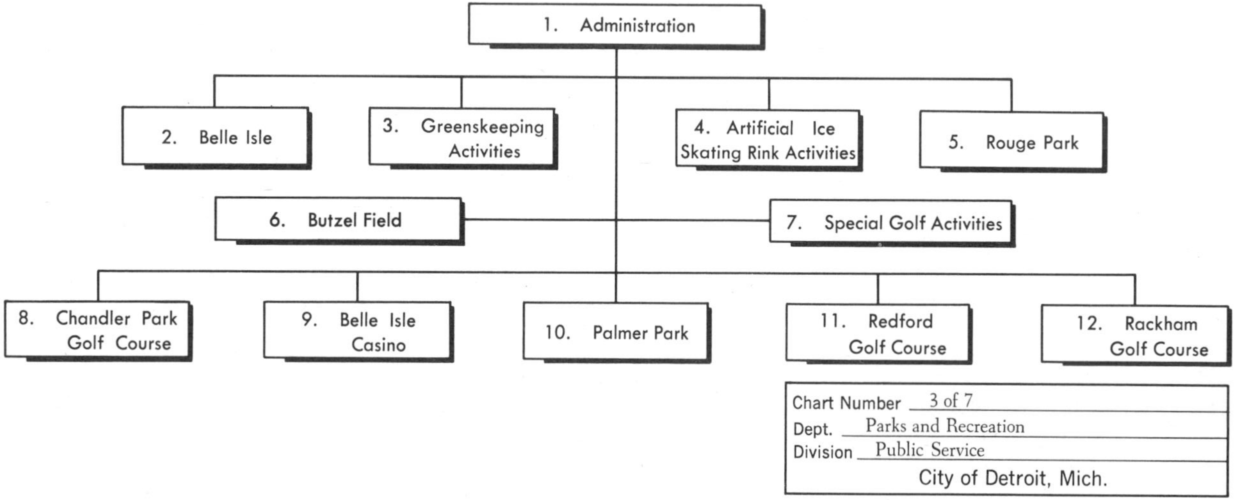

1. Administration
2. Belle Isle
3. Greenskeeping Activities
4. Artificial Ice Skating Rink Activities
5. Rouge Park
6. Butzel Field
7. Special Golf Activities
8. Chandler Park Golf Course
9. Belle Isle Casino
10. Palmer Park
11. Redford Golf Course
12. Rackham Golf Course

Chart Number 3 of 7
Dept. Parks and Recreation
Division Public Service
City of Detroit, Mich.

255

CHART 3

Department of Parks and Recreation
Public Service Division

1. ADMINISTRATION

Directing, planning, and coordinating activities relative to the operation of refectories, golf courses, Belle Isle Casino, 9 artificial skating rinks, and other revenue producing properties either directly or by concession.

```
B   U
1   1 - Superintendent of Public Service
1   1 - Assistant Superintendent of Public Service
―   ―
2   2
```

2. BELLE ISLE

Operating 6 refectories, golf course, launching ramps, canoe shelter, Memorial Park Marina, golf driving range, trackless train, and two mobile refectories; controlling 14 private concessions.

```
B   U
1   1 - Senior Public Service Supervisor
2   2 - Public Service Supervisor
M   3 - Public Service Supervisor
2   2 - Senior Public Service Attendant
        (Merchandising)
M   2 - Senior Public Service Attendant
        (Merchandising)
M   1 - Greenskeeper
```

SEASONAL

```
M   1 - Senior Public Service Attendant
        (Merchandising)
M  13 - Public Service Attendant (Merchandising)
M  50 - Assistant Public Service Attendant
M   2 - Public Service Laborer
M   2 - Truck Driver
M   1 - Truck Driver/ Park Maintenance Helper
M   4 - Laborer A
```

EXTRA LABOR

```
M   5 - Public Service Attendant
M   6 - Assistant Public Service Attendant
―   ――
5   95
```

256

3. GREENSKEEPING ACTIVITIES

Maintaining and rebuilding golf courses and bowling greens.
      B   U
      1   1 - Supervising Greenskeeper

4. ARTIFICIAL ICE SKATING RINK ACTIVITIES

Operating nine artificial ice skating rinks (one inside rink and eight outdoor rinks), including the two ice skating locations shown in other boxes on this chart (three months).

5. ROUGE PARK

Operating four refectories, golf course, and golf driving range (nine months); controlling four private concessions.
      B   U
      1   1 - Senior Public Service Supervisor
      M   1 - Senior Public Service Attendant
                (Merchandising)
      M   1 - Greenskeeper

           SEASONAL

      M   1 - Senior Public Service Attendant
                (Merchandising)
      M   5 - Public Service Attendant
      M   9 - Assistant Public Service Attendant
      M   1 - Park Maintenance Man
      M   1 - Truck Driver
      M   6 - Laborer A

          EXTRA LABOR

      M   4 - Public Service Attendant
      M   4 - Assistant Public Service Attendant
      —   —
      1   34

6. BUTZEL FIELD

Operating refectory and artificial ice skating rink.
      B   U
      M   1 - Senior Public Service Attendant
                (Merchandising)

           SEASONAL

      M   5 - Public Service Attendant (Merchandising)
      M   1 - Assistant Public Service Attendant

          EXTRA LABOR

      M   7 - Assistant Public Service Attendant
          —
          14

7. SPECIAL GOLF ACTIVITIES

Planning and organizing special golfing events and tournaments; making public appearances to demonstrate golfing techniques and to stimulate public interest in the program.

    B   U
    C   1 - Golf Professional

8. CHANDLER PARK GOLF COURSE

Operating golf course and refectory (nine months); controlling one private concession; operating artificial ice skating rink (three months); operating Connors bowling green.

    B   U
    M   1 - Public Service Supervisor
    M   1 - Senior Public Service Attendant
              (Merchandising)
    M   1 - Greenskeeper

        SEASONAL

    M   5 - Public Service Attendant
    M   1 - Park Maintenance Man
    M   1 - Truck Driver
    M   7 - Laborer A

        EXTRA LABOR

    M   5 - Assistant Public Service Attendant
    —   —
    9   22

9. BELLE ISLE CASINO

Operating Belle Isle Casino.

    B   U
    1   1 - Steward-Manager (Belle Isle Casino)
    1   - Senior Public Service Supervisor
        1 - Public Service Supervisor
    M   1 - Senior Public Service Attendant
              (Merchandising)
    M   1 - Senior Dining Room Attendant
    M   2 - First Cook

        SEASONAL

    M   1 - Second Cook
    M   1 - Public Service Attendant (Merchandising)
    M   1 - Assistant Public Service Attendant
    M   1 - Public Service Laborer

        EXTRA LABOR

    M   8 - Public Service Attendant
    M   7 - Assistant Public Service Attendant
    M   4 - Public Service Laborer
    —   —
    2   29

10. PALMER PARK

Operating golf course and two refectories (nine months); controlling two private concessions.

	B	U	
	1	1 - Senior Public Service Supervisor
	M	1 - Senior Public Service Attendant (Merchandising)
	M	1 - Greenskeeper

SEASONAL

M	1 - Senior Public Service Attendant (Merchandising)
M	6 - Public Service Attendant
M	7 - Assistant Public Service Attendant
M	1 - Park Maintenance Man
M	1 - Truck Driver
M	6 - Laborer A

EXTRA LABOR

| M | 1 - Public Service Attendant |
| M | 3 - Assistant Public Service Attendant |

  1 29

11. REDFORD GOLF COURSE

Operating golf course, club house, and refectory (nine months), and artificial ice skating rink (three months).

	B	U
	1	1 - Senior Public Service Supervisor
	M	1 - Senior Public Service Attendant (Merchandising)
	M	1 - Greenskeeper

SEASONAL

M	6 - Public Service Attendant
M	1 - Assistant Public Service Attendant
M	1 - Public Service Laborer
M	1 - Park Maintenance Man
M	1 - Truck Driver
M	7 - Laborer A

EXTRA LABOR

| M | 2 - Assistant Public Service Attendant |

  1 22

12. RACKHAM GOLF COURSE

Operating golf course and refectory (nine months).

B	U		
	M	1 -	Public Service Supervisor
	M	1 -	Senior Public Service Attendant (Merchandising)
	M	1 -	Greenskeeper

SEASONAL

	M	5 -	Public Service Attendant
	M	1 -	Park Maintenance Man
	M	1 -	Truck Driver
	M	7 -	Laborer A
	M	7 -	Laborer B

EXTRA LABOR

	M	2 -	Public Service Attendant
	M	2 -	Assistant Public Service Attendant

28

Totals on Chart:
- B-Budgeted Positions: 13
- M-Memo Wage Personnel: 263
  - Seasonal: 180
  - Extra Labor: 58
- C-Contractual: 1
- U-Positions Utilized: 277

Chart 4
DEPARTMENT OF PARKS AND RECREATION

Recreation Division

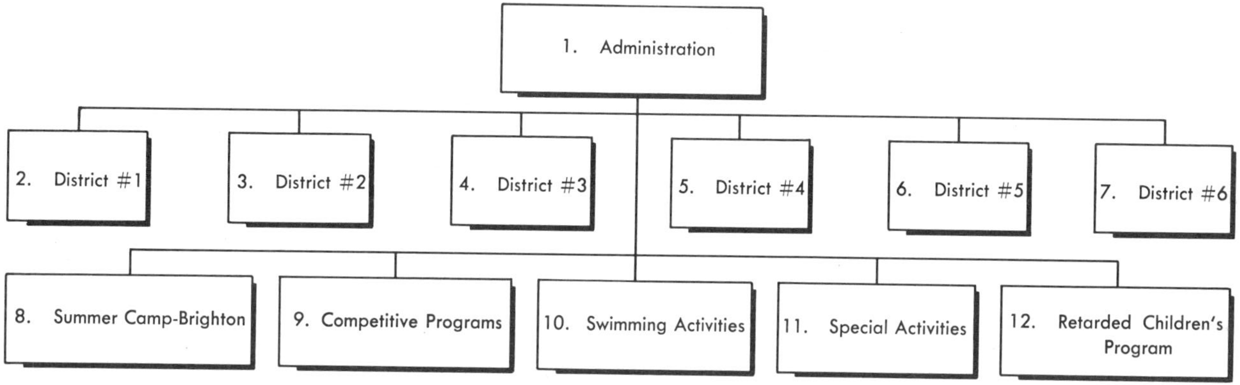

1. Administration
2. District #1
3. District #2
4. District #3
5. District #4
6. District #5
7. District #6
8. Summer Camp-Brighton
9. Competitive Programs
10. Swimming Activities
11. Special Activities
12. Retarded Children's Program

Chart Number 4 of 7
Dept. Parks and Recreation
Division Recreation
City of Detroit, Mich.

CHART 4

Department of Parks and Recreation
Recreation Division

| 1. | | ADMINISTRATION |

Coordinating, planning, and directing a municipal recreation program for children and adults, involving physical, passive, and cultural recreational activities.

```
B    U
1    1 - Superintendent of Recreation
1    1 - Assistant Superintendent of Recreation
—    —
2    2
```

| 2. | | DISTRICT #1 |

```
     B    U
     1    1 - Recreation Supervisor
              (District Activities)
     1    1 - Assistant Recreation Supervisor
     4    4 - Community House Supervisor -
              Grade II
     2    2 - Community House Supervisor -
              Grade I
    18   17 - Recreation Instructor
          1 - Recreation Leader
          3 - Recreation Leader
     6    9 - Junior Recreation Instructor
          SEASONAL

          SUMMER PROGRAM

     M   51 - Playleader
          WINTER PROGRAM

     M   21 - Playleader
    —    —
    32  110
```

| 3. | | DISTRICT #2 |

```
     B    U
     1    1 - Recreation Supervisor
              (District Activities)
     1    1 - Assistant Recreation Supervisor
     2    2 - Community House Supervisor -
              Grade II
     1    1 - Community House Supervisor -
              Grade I
     9   12 - Recreation Instructor
     M    5 - Recreation Leader
     4    1 - Junior Recreation Instructor
```

SEASONAL

SUMMER PROGRAM

M 50 - Playleader

WINTER PROGRAM

M 17 - Playleader

18 90

4. ### DISTRICT #3

B	U	
1	1 -	Recreation Supervisor (District Activities)
1	1 -	Assistant Recreation Supervisor
2	2 -	Community House Supervisor - Grade II
3	3 -	Community House Supervisor - Grade I
14	10 -	Recreation Instructor
	4 -	Recreation Leader
5	1 -	Junior Recreation Instructor

SEASONAL

SUMMER PROGRAM

M 55 - Playleader

WINTER PROGRAM

M 21 - Playleader

26 98

5. ### DISTRICT #4

B	U	
1	1 -	Recreation Supervisor (District Activities)
1	1 -	Assistant Recreation Supervisor
4	3 -	Community House Supervisor - Grade I
12	9 -	Recreation Instructor
	5 -	Recreation Leader
5	3 -	Junior Recreation Instructor

SEASONAL

SUMMER PROGRAM

M 49 - Playleader

WINTER PROGRAM

M 21 - Playleader

23 92

6. DISTRICT #5

B	U	
1	1	- Recreation Supervisor (District Activities)
1	1	- Assistant Recreation Supervisor
1	1	- Community House Supervisor - Grade II
3	3	- Community House Supervisor - Grade I
8	5	- Recreation Instructor
1	3	- Recreation Leader
4	1	- Junior Recreation Instructor

SEASONAL

SUMMER PROGRAM

| M | 59 | - Playleader |

WINTER PROGRAM

M	21	- Playleader
19	95	

7. DISTRICT #6

B	U	
1	1	- Recreation Supervisor (District Activities)
1	1	- Assistant Recreation Supervisor
3	3	- Community House Supervisor - Grade II
3	3	- Community House Supervisor - Grade I
13	13	- Recreation Instructor
	3	- Recreation Leader
6	5	- Junior Recreation Instructor

SEASONAL

SUMMER PROGRAM

| M | 50 | - Playleader |

WINTER PROGRAM

M	21	- Playleader
27	100	

8. SUMMER CAMP-BRIGHTON

Operating summer camp for nine weeks; providing a variety of recreational activities.

B	U	
M	½	- Recreation Camp Supervisor (6 months)
C	1	- Senior Physician
M	1	- General Staff Nurse
M	1	- Swimming Leader

M	1 -	Recreation Instructor
M	12 -	Camp Counselor
M	16 -	Camp Counselor in Training
M	2 -	First Cook
M*	1 -	Park Maintenance Man
M	1 -	Laborer A
M	1 -	Laborer B

37½

9. COMPETITIVE PROGRAMS

Coordinating, directing, and conducting the athletic and competitive programs.

B	U	
1	1 -	Director of Competitive Athletics (Interim)
1	1 -	Assistant Recreation Supervisor
M	½ -	Senior Recreation Instructor (Seasonal) (6 months)
1	1 -	Recreation Instructor
	1 -	Senior Typist

SEASONAL

M	1 -	Senior Baseball Instructor
M	25 -	Baseball Instructor
M	35 -	Public Service Attendant (General)
C	96 -	Baseball Umpire
C	60 -	Baseball Scorer
C	80 -	Basketball Official
C	20 -	Boxing Instructor
C	24 -	Football Official
C	36 -	Hockey Official
C	80 -	Softball Umpire

3 461½

10. SWIMMING ACTIVITIES

Operating outdoor bathhouses; planning and conducting swimming programs.

B	U	
1	1 -	Recreation Supervisor (Swimming)
1	1 -	Assistant Recreation Supervisor
19	19 -	Swimming Instructor

SEASONAL

SUMMER PROGRAM

M	2 -	Bathhouse Manager
M	4 -	Senior Swimming Instructor
M	16 -	Swimming Leader
M	16 -	Swimming Aid
M	28 -	Life Guard
M	4 -	Senior Public Service Attendant (General)

```
         M   36 - Public Service Attendant (General)
                     WINTER PROGRAM
         M   32 - Swimming Leader
                      EXTRA LABOR
         M   18 - Public Service Attendant (General)
         M   23 - Assistant Public Service Attendant
         M   12 - Lifeguard
         M    5 - Swimming Leader
         M    6 - Swimming Aid
         ──  ───
         21  223
```

11.   SPECIAL ACTIVITIES

Planning and conducting musical, choral, and summer day camp activities; coordinating pageants, dramatics, festival, and other special programs.

```
         B    U
         1    1 - Director of Specialized Recreation
                    Activities (Interim)
         1    1 - Assistant Recreation Supervisor
         7    6 - Senior Recreation Instructor (Specialties)
         2    2 - Recreation Instructor
         1      - Junior Recreation Instructor
              1 - Recreation Leader
         1    1 - Senior Seamstress
                        SEASONAL
         M   10 - Playleader
         M   12 - Piano Accompanist
         M    1 - Seamstress
         C    1 - Boys Band Director
         C    3 - Square Dance Caller
         ──  ──
         13  39
```

12.   RETARDED CHILDREN'S PROGRAM

Providing recreational program for mentally retarded children.

```
         B   U
         1   1 - Community House Supervisor - Grade II
         3   3 - Recreation Instructor
         ──  ──
         4   4
```

```
              Totals on Chart:
                 B-Budgeted Positions:        188
                 M-Memo Wage Personnel:       769
                      Seasonal:               658
                      Extra Labor:             64
                 C-Contractual Personnel:     401
                 U-Positions Utilized:       1352
```

* Year round position.

Chart 5
DEPARTMENT OF PARKS AND RECREATION

Buildings and Mechanical Equipment Division Planning and Design Unit

- 1. Buildings and Mechanical Equipment
  - 2. Heating Plants, Skating Rinks, Pools, and Laundry
  - 3. Liaison
  - 4. Building Trades and Recreation Equipment Shops
  - 5. Mechanical Equipment Repair Shop
  - 6. District Building Cleaning Maintenance and Custodial Service
    - 7. District I
    - 8. District II
- 9. Planning and Design Unit

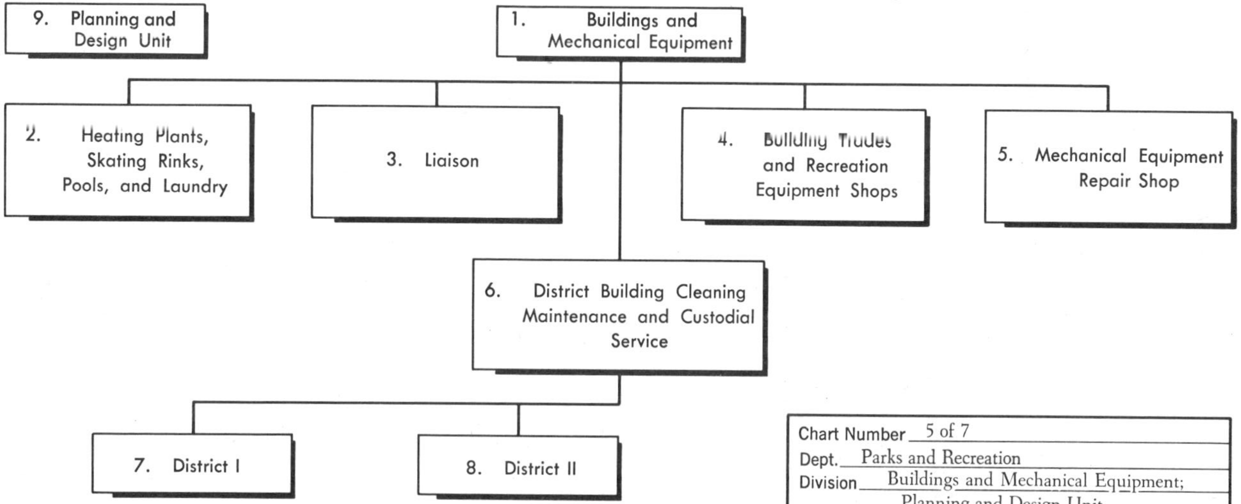

Chart Number 5 of 7
Dept. Parks and Recreation
Division Buildings and Mechanical Equipment; Planning and Design Unit
City of Detroit, Mich.

CHART 5

Department of Parks and Recreation
Buildings and Mechanical Equipment Division
Planning and Design Unit

1.   BUILDINGS AND MECHANICAL EQUIPMENT

Planning activities relative to the maintenance of buildings, the repair and maintenance of mechanical and recreational equipment, and the operation of the sign and other shops; contacting Central Building Maintenance and other city departments relative to maintenance service.

Budgeted Positions: P/R 1-500

     1   Superintendent of Building Maintenance
     1   Associate Mechanical Engineer (Maintenance)
   ─
     2

2.   HEATING PLANTS, SKATING RINKS, POOLS, AND LAUNDRY

Operating and maintaining heating plants, ice skating rinks, swimming pools, and laundry.

Budgeted Position: P/R 1-560

     1   Heating Plant Supervisor - Grade II

Budgeted Position: P/R 1-570

     1   Laundryman

Memo Positions: P/R 5-110

   1   Third Operating Engineer
   7   Boiler Operator (High Pressure)
  17   Refrigeration Equipment Operator - Third Class/Mechanical Helper (General)/Laborer A
  19   Boiler Operator (Low Pressure)
   9   Mechanical Helper (General)/Laborer A
   2   Laborer A/Mechanical Helper (General)
   1   Laborer A/Refrigeration Equipment Operator - Third Class
  ─
  58

3.   LIAISON

Serving as departmental representative on construction and maintenance work done by departmental employees and under contracts.

Memo Position:

     1   Senior Construction Inspector (Vacant)

4.   Building Trades and Recreation Equipment Shops

Fabricating and maintaining signs, recreation equipment, structures, and maintenance equipment; performing minor repairs and alternations to buildings.

    Budgeted Positions: P/R 1-510

        1   Building Maintenance Sub-Foreman

    Memo Positions: P/R 5-100

        1   Sign Painter
        1   Building Tradesman (General)
        1   Building Tradesman (Painter)
        1   General Welder
        5   Carpenter
        1   Athletic Goods Repairman
        3   Building Trades Helper

   14

5.   Mechanical Equipment Repair Shop

Repairing and maintaining construction and park maintenance equipment and tools.

    Budgeted Position: P/R 1-510

        1   Building Maintenance Sub-Foreman

    Budgeted Positions: P/R 1-520

        1   Senior Mechanical Maintenance Foreman
        1   Mechanical Maintenance Sub-Foreman

    Memo Positions: P/R 5-280

        1   Saw Filer
        9   Mechanical Tradesman (Equipment Repair)
        2   Refrigeration Equipment Operator - Third Class/Mechanical Helper (General)/Laborer A
        1   Vehicle Operator (Park Equipment)/Truck Driver
        1   Mechanical Helper (General)/Laborer A

   17

6.   District Building Cleaning Maintenance and Custodial Service

Cleaning, guarding, and maintaining departmental buildings, major comfort stations, recreation and maintenance buildings.

    Budgeted Position: P/R 1-500

        1   Supervising Building Attendant - Grade III

7.   District I

Budgeted Positions: P/R 1-530

    1   Stableman

Budgeted Position: P/R 1-530

    1   Supervising Building Attendant - Grade II
    2   Supervising Building Attendant - Grade I
    3   Senior Building Attendant

Budgeted Positions: P/R 1-540

   13   Comfort Station Attendant (one vacant)
   10   Comfort Station Matron (one vacant)

Budgeted Positions: P/R 1-550

   11   Watchman

Budgeted Positions: P/R 1-570

    8   Public Service Attendant - General (one vacant)

Memo Positions: P/R 1-540

   56   Building Attendant A
   24   Building Cleaner

Memo Positions: P/R 2-540

    1   Tree Artisan
    1   Laborer A
    8   Laborer B

Seasonal Positions:

   0 to 3   Building Attendant A
   0 to 9   Building Cleaner
   0 to 5   Public Service Attendant (General)
   0 to 5   Park Maintenance Assistant

139 to 161

8.   District II

Budgeted Positions: P/R 1-530

    2   Supervising Building Attendant - Grade II (one 4/28'd to Supervising Building Attendant - Grade I)
    1   Senior Building Attendant

Budgeted Position: P/R 1-540

    1   Comfort Station Attendant

Budgeted Positions: P/R 1-550

   12   Watchman (one vacant)

Budgeted Positions: P/R 1-570

    6 Public Service Attendant (General)
Memo Positions: P/R 2-540

   43 Building Attendant A
   19 Building Cleaner
Memo Positions: P/R 5-280

    1 Refrigeration Equipment Operator - Third Class/Mechanical Helper (General)/Laborer A
    1 Laborer A
    1 Laborer B

Seasonal Positions:

  0 to 4 Building Attendant A
  0 to 9 Building Cleaner
  0 to 4 Public Service Attendant (General)
  0 to 5 Park Maintenance Assistant

87 to 109

9.   Planning and Design Unit

Preparing plans, specifications, and preliminary layouts for construction done by departmental employees and under contract; designing landscaping for city projects.

Budgeted Positions: P/R 1-130

    1 Associate Landscape Architect
    5 Senior Assistant Landscape Architect (one 4/28'd to Assistant Landscape Architect; one vacant)

    6

Totals on Chart:
  Budgeted Positions: 86
    (Vacant: 5)
  Memo Positions: 239
    (Vacant: 1)

Total Positions Available: 325
  (Total Vacant: 6)
Total Positions Utilized: 319
Seasonal Positions: 0 to 44

Note: Seasonal and contractual payroll numbers do not, in this instance, serve as identifying information and are therefore omitted.

Chart 6
DEPARTMENT OF PARKS AND RECREATION

Grounds Maintenance and Forestry Division

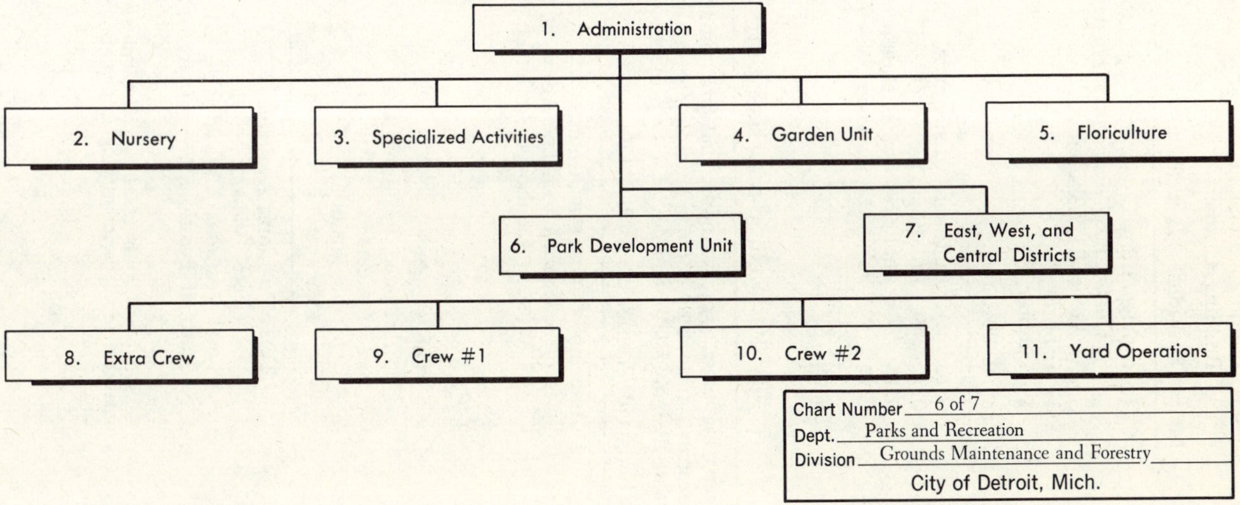

1. Administration
2. Nursery
3. Specialized Activities
4. Garden Unit
5. Floriculture
6. Park Development Unit
7. East, West, and Central Districts
8. Extra Crew
9. Crew #1
10. Crew #2
11. Yard Operations

Chart Number 6 of 7
Dept. Parks and Recreation
Division Grounds Maintenance and Forestry
City of Detroit, Mich.

CHART 6

Department of Parks and Recreation
Grounds Maintenance and Forestry Division

1. ADMINISTRATION

Planning, directing, inspecting, and devising new methods and procedures relative to forestry, landscaping, floriculture, grounds construction, park development and maintenance activities.

Budgeted Positions: P/R 1-700

- 1 Superintendent of Grounds Maintenance and Forestry
- 1 Assistant Superintendent of Grounds Maintenance and Forestry (4/28'd to Associate Forester)

Budgeted Position: P/R 1-600

- 1 Senior Park Maintenance Supervisor (4/28'd to Park Maintenance Supervisor)

—
3

2. NURSERY

Operating nursery; performing activities relative to propagation, cultivation, and maintenance of trees, vines, plants, perennials, shrubs, and evergreens; preparing such items for shipment.

Budgeted Position: P/R 1-700

- 1 Associate Forester

Memo Position: P/R 2-550

- 1 Forestry and Landscape Foreman

Memo Positions: P/R 5-180

- 1 Nurseryman
- 1 Construction Equipment Operator (General)
- 2 Tree Artisan
- 3 Vehicle Operator (Park Equipment)/Truck Driver
- 1 Park Maintenance Helper
- 5 Laborer A

—
15

3. SPECIALIZED ACTIVITIES

Trimming trees to provide clearance for public utilities; making special investigations including cause of diseases or death of trees; determining billing of utilities for tree damage; operating weed killing programs; conducting Dutch elm disease programs; making arrangements for and directing filming of divisional activities for television presentation.

Budgeted Position: P/R 1-750

   1 Senior Gardening Instructor

Memo Positions: P/R 2-550

   5 Forestry and Landscape Foreman

Memo Positions: P/R 5-200

   1 Junior Forester
  12 Tree Artisan

Seasonal Positions:

  0 to 2 Senior Tree Artisan
  0 to 4 Tree Artisan

 19 to 25

4. GARDEN UNIT

Conducting children's garden classes and clubs in schools and centers, junior forestry classes and miscellaneous gardening activies.

Budgeted Positions: P/R 1-750

   2 Gardening Instructor

Seasonal Positions:

  0 to 1 Playleader
  0 to 1 Laborer A

  2 to 4

5. FLORICULTURE

Operating 16 greenhouses and the conservatory; performing activities relative to the propagation, cultivation and maintenance of all plants, municipal flower beds, gardens, and other floral displays.

Budgeted Positions: P/R 1-700

   1 Floriculture Supervisor
   2 Floriculture Foreman

Memo Positions: P/R 2-550

   1 Senior Floriculturist
  13 Floriculturist

Memo Positions: P/R 5-190

- 1 General Gardener/Park Maintenance Man
- 1 Refrigeration Equipment Operator - Third Class/Mechanical Helper (General)/ Laborer A
- 3 Park Maintenance Man
- 1 Truck Driver
- 2 Floriculture Assistant
- 1 Park Maintenance Helper
- 8 Laborer A

Seasonal Positions:

0 to 4 Floriculture Assistant

34 to 38

6. Park Development Unit

Supervising the park development program.

Memo Positions: P/R 2-580

- 1 Park Development Coordinator
- 1 Park Development Supervisor

2

7. East, West, and Central Districts

Performing grounds maintenance and forestry activities relative to parks, parkways, and recreational areas; investigating complaints and requests for service.

(See chart 7 of 7)
Budgeted Positions: 30
Memo Positions: 388
Seasonal Positions: 0 to 173

8. Extra Crew

Working with either crew #1 or crew #2 or separately, depending on nature of project.

Memo Position: P/R 2-580

- 1 Park Maintenance Sub-Foreman

Memo Positions: P/R 5-210

- 3 Asphalt Paver/Laborer A
- 1 Park Maintenance Helper
- 3 Laborer A

Contractual Positions:

- 6 Hired Trucker

14

9.   Crew #1

Developing land owned by department for use as parks, parkways, playgrounds, and recreational areas.

Memo Position: P/R 2-580

1	Park Development Foreman

Memo Positions: P/R 5-210

1	Senior Construction Equipment Operator/ Construction Equipment Operator (General)/Vehicle Operator (Park Equipment)/Truck Driver
2	Senior Construction Equipment Operator/ Construction Equipment Operator (General)/Truck Driver
1	Asphalt Roller Operator/Construction Equipment Operator (General)/ Vehicle Operator (Park Equipment)/ Truck Driver
1	Construction Equipment Operator (General)/Vehicle Operator (Park Equipment)/Truck Driver
2	Concrete Finisher/Park Maintenance Helper
1	Vehicle Operator (Park Equipment)/ Truck Driver
1	Tree Artisan
3	Park Maintenance Man
13	Laborer A
26	

10.   Crew #2

Developing land owned by department for use as parks, parkways, playgrounds, and recreational areas.

Memo Position: P/R 2-580

1	Park Development Foreman

Memo Positions: P/R 5-210

1	Senior Construction Equipment Operator/ Construction Equipment Operator (General)/Truck Driver
1	Senior Construction Equipment Operator
1	Asphalt Roller Operator/Construction Equipment Operator (General)/Vehicle Operator (Park Equipment)/Truck Driver
1	Construction Equipment Operator (General)/Vehicle Operator (Park Equipment)/Truck Driver
1	Construction Equipment Operator (General)/Park Maintenance Man

1 Tree Artisan
  2 Park Maintenance Man
  1 Park Maintenance Helper
 15 Laborer A
 ──
 25

11.   YARD OPERATIONS

Memo Position: F/R 2-580

  1 Equipment Dispatcher

Memo Positions: P/R 5-210

  2 Vehicle Operator (Park Equipment)/Truck Driver
  2 Laborer A
 ──
  5

Totals on Chart:
  Budgeted Positions: 10
    (Vacant: 1)
  Memo Positions: 129

Total Positions Available: 139
Total Positions Utilized: 139
Seasonal Positions: 0 to   12
Contractual Positions   6

Note: Seasonal and contractual payroll numbers do not, in this instance, serve as identifying information and are therefore omitted.

Chart 7

DEPARTMENT OF PARKS AND RECREATION

Grounds Maintenance and Forestry Division   East, West, and Central Districts

1. East, West, and Central Districts
2. Ground Maintenance Activities
3. Forestry Activities

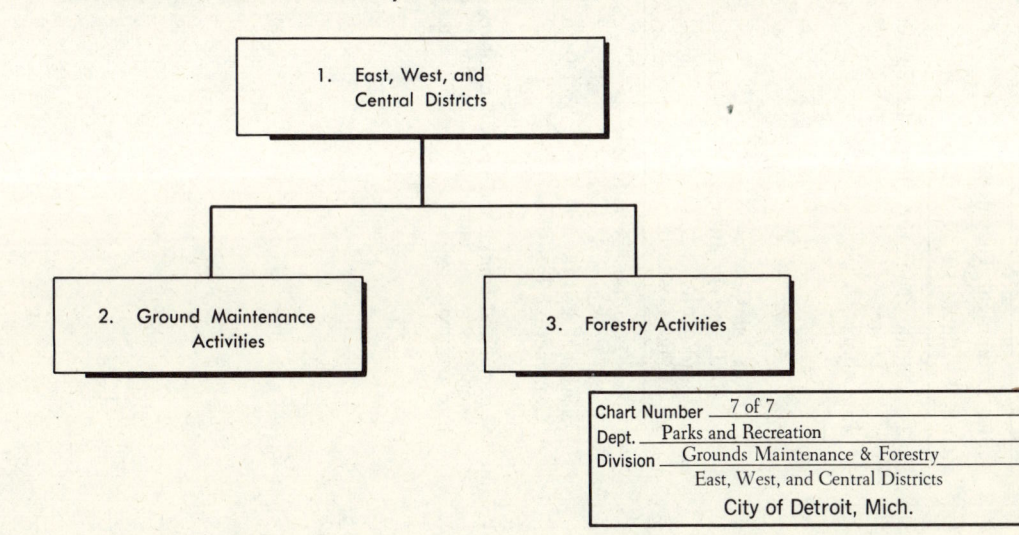

Chart Number   7 of 7
Dept.   Parks and Recreation
Division   Grounds Maintenance & Forestry
   East, West, and Central Districts
   City of Detroit, Mich.

CHART 7

Department of Parks and Recreation
Grounds Maintenance and Forestry Division
East, West, and Central Districts

1.   East, West, and Central Districts

Planning and supervising grounds maintenance and forestry activities.

    Budgeted Positions: P/R 1-700

    3   Associate Forester

2.   Ground Maintenance Activities

Performing activities relative to maintenance of parks, parkways, and recreational areas.

    Budgeted Positions: P/R 1-600

    6   Park Maintenance Supervisor
    6   Park Maintenance Foreman
    7   Park Maintenance Sub-Foreman
    1   Senior Garage Attendant

Memo Positions: P/R 5-120

   11   Park Maintenance Man
    8   Vehicle Operator (Park Equipment)/Truck Driver
   14   Park Maintenance Helper
    4   Truck Driver
   29   Laborer A

Memo Positions: P/R 5-130

   13   Park Maintenance Man
   11   Vehicle Operator (Park Equipment)/Truck Driver
    1   Auto Deliveryman
   18   Park Maintenance Helper
    1   Truck Driver/Vehicle Operator (Park Equipment)
    5   Truck Driver
   28   Laborer A
    1   Laborer B

Memo Positions: P/R 5-140

    6   Park Maintenance Man
    8   Vehicle Operator (Park Equipment)/Truck Driver
    2   Park Maintenance Helper
    2   Truck Driver/Vehicle Operator (Park Equipment)

    1 Truck Driver
  17 Laborer A

Memo Positions: P/R 5-340

    7 Park Maintenance Man
    5 Vehicle Operator (Park Equipment)/Truck Driver
    1 Truck Driver/Vehicle Operator (Park Equipment)
    2 Truck Driver
    6 Park Maintenance Helper
  17 Laborer A

Memo Position: P/R 5-350

    1 Park Maintenance Helper

Seasonal Positions:

  0 to   8 Truck Driver
  0 to   2 Public Service Laborer (Interim)
  0 to 142 Park Maintenance Assistant

TOTAL: 239 to 391

3.   Forestry Activities

Trimming, spraying, planting, and cultivating trees; investigating complaints and requests for service.

Budgeted Positions: P/R 1-700

    4 Senior Assistant Forester (one 4/28'd to Assistant Forester)
    2 Assistant Forester
    1 Junior Forester

Memo Positions: P/R 2-550

  19 Forestry and Landscape Foreman

Memo Positions: P/R 5-150

    1 Junior Forester
    4 Senior Tree Artisan
  18 Tree Artisan
    6 Vehicle Operator (Park Equipment)/Truck Driver
    2 Tree Artisan Helper

Memo Positions: P/R 5-160

    1 Forestry and Landscape Foreman
    2 Saw Filer
    3 Senior Tree Artisan
  20 Tree Artisan
    5 Vehicle Operator (Park Equipment)/Truck Driver
    6 Tree Artisan Helper
    1 Laborer A

Memo Positions: P/R 5-170

- 1 Saw Filer
- 4 Senior Tree Artisan
- 20 Tree Artisan
- 4 Vehicle Operator (Park Equipment)/Truck Driver
- 6 Tree Artisan Helper
- 1 Laborer B

Memo Positions: P/R 5-330

- 1 Junior Forester
- 4 Senior Tree Artisan
- 26 Tree Artisan
- 3 Vehicle Operator (Park Equipment)/Truck Driver
- 3 Tree Artisan Helper

Seasonal Positions:

- 0 to 17 Tree Artisan Helper
- 0 to 2 Junior Forester
- 0 to 1 Tree Artisan/Saw Filer
- 0 to 1 Laborer A

TOTAL: 176 to 197

Totals on Chart:	
Budgeted Positions:	30
Memo Positions:	388
Total Positions Available:	418
Total Positions Utilized:	418
Seasonal Positions:	0 to 173

Note: Seasonal and contractual payroll numbers do not, in this instance, serve as identifying information and are therefore omitted.

Recording the System

Providing organizational charts that clearly identify lines of authority, responsibility, and specialization is one step in making each employee cognizant of his functions and significance within the structure of the agency. In order to offer the most comprehensive and intelligible concept of the organization and its work, the recreational service agency should define the general policies of the system, detail the rules and regulations by which it operates, and attempt to standardize routine operating procedures. This vital information can be made easily available to all employees by publishing a set of directives or an administrative manual of the agency. Actually, there are several types of manuals which the recreational service department may put to good use. Among these are:

1. The administrative manual, which contains policy statements relating to the functions of the agency; operating procedures and fundamentals; personnel practices; public relations information; the organization of the system as a whole, with a detailed explanation of general duties and responsibilities; a definition of the subdivisions and their respective activities; and general information concerning the whole system.
2. The program manual, which covers all phases of a comprehensive and well-balanced series of appropriate recreational activities for the population to be served; provides rules, regulations, and instructions dealing with the teaching, guidance, and supervision of recreational experiences; suggests types of activities; and also lists a great variety of activity possibilities and resource material.
3. The divisional manual, which is applicable only to a given division and provides detailed specifications for the activities which the division carries out. The significance of such a manual is indicated from the inclusion of the following topics and items:
   a. Name of the activity for which division is responsible.
   b. Precise statement or description of the divisional activity and the range of functions covered.
   c. General duties of the division.
   d. Specific duties of personnel within the division.
   e. Coordination maintained with other divisions of the department.
   f. An organizational chart of each section of the division.
   g. Complete specifications for each section of the division.

The value to be derived from procedural manuals depends to a great extent upon the opinion of those who are most concerned with the consequences from records. The manual is a document which by its very nature undergoes periodic revisions and consistent modification. It is, therefore, subject to additions and deletions to insure that what it describes relating to the organization are valid reflections of current conditions and requirements. The worker is thus enabled to evaluate better past activities and to assist in the formulation of new recreational experiences and practices. Such records are vital if work methods and standard operating procedures are to be commonly practiced.

In very large recreational service systems the various manuals may be voluminous and in extreme detail, with a careful elaboration of the rules, regulations, policies, and procedures by which the agency is governed. Such detail is necessary if every routine phase of operation is to be adequately covered. Standard operating procedures are the result of compiled records and reports of the department over a long period of time and tend to reflect the common occurrences, behavior, functions, requirements, and control necessary for effective administration. "Going by the book" does not hinder the ingenuity and innate creativeness of the recreationist. On the contrary, it frees him from the problem of making inaccurate appraisals or using poor judgment in delicate personal contacts with the general public. The manual serves as a standard for personnel conduct of activities as well as for quick reference to establish correct practices. The manual provides a ready source of information on a wide variety of routine problems which often confront the recreationist in his dealings with the public. These published expectations of professional responsibilities for employed personnel as well as for the conduct of participants do much to offset petty annoyances and occasional personality conflicts that may arise. The manual is not the *last word* by any means, but it does offer an easy device whereby the typical problems of scheduling personnel, working attire, facility responsibility, custodial operations, plant maintenance, holidays, salary increments, routing schedules, club management, supervisory factors, liability, and the minutiae of daily on-the-job practice is reduced to an easily handled and systematized routine. By clearing away some of the clutter that usually hampers the recreationist in his practice, the manual of procedures generally permits the professional more time to experiment and develop new program ideas. Creativity is one product of standardizing operating procedures in manual form. Manuals are developed over extended periods wherein administrators and other personnel, by way of exposure to recurrent and in some cases repetitive activities, realize that much time and effort can be saved and less effort expended in handling day-to-day business of the agency.

The administrative manual usually covers the following work and personnel policies:

1. Personnel management.
    a. Any changes of address. Currently employed personnel should have their home address and telephone number on file with the central office (if a small agency) or with the facility office.
    b. Uniform dress requirements. Regulations are in effect and notice of correct attire for all staff personnel assigned to various divisions and/or activities of the department. If the department requires that a specific uniform be worn by its employees, it must provide a uniform clothing allowance and indicate where such garments and other accessories may be purchased. Otherwise it must issue a standard uniform. The dress of professional staff personnel should be appropriate to the occasion and conform to whatever detailed dress descriptions the department deems necessary. The department may also require some badge or emblem to be worn as a distinguishing insignia indicating the status of the employee.
    c. Substitutions. Employees are remunerated for work performed. All employees are hired by an authorized office and are compensated

on the system payroll as local jurisdiction demands. Under no condition can an employee absent himself from his job responsibilities and substitute another.

d. Employment schedules. Regular hours of work for all personnel of the department are fixed according to departmental requirements. Specific assignments shall normally run a full eight-hour day, not to exceed forty hours per week. Depending upon the need of the program, day and night work schedules are made up in conference with divisional and/or district superiors, depending upon the organization of the system. Because the department operates a seven-day per week program, starting in the morning and continuing on through the evening hours, a regular two or three personnel shift shall be required in order to meet the supervisory needs of the program. Such aspects of scheduling to meet day and night needs, to compensate for over-time, and to assign night duty tours on a regular basis must be taken into consideration. Any compensatory time must be taken within a specified period and may not be saved and added to the normal vacation time allowed.

e. Emergency leaves and sick time. As a standard operating procedure each employee who must be absent from his job because of illness must notify his immediate supervisor as soon as he is able on the day of illness. In the event that an employee becomes ill on the job, the immediate supervisor must be notified in order that the assignment can be covered. In the event of an emergency or radical sickness requiring an extended period off the job, sick leave allowances are in operation and time off with full or partial pay as enumerated in the work schedule will be in effect. The department will set a limit on the amount of sick leave time that can be accumulated during any one year with full compensation. Other incidents requiring time off, such as being called to jury duty will be worked out.

f. Annual leaves and vacations. The municipality will generally have some policy for vacations. Usually, employees are allowed a specified time with full pay after having successfully completed one year of service. The annual leave time is increased after continuous employment with the community. Increments in annual leave may be noted after five, ten, fifteen, or more years with appropriate increases in leave time. Specific forms for leave requests are devised by the department, and upon written application, vacations may be arranged. Vacations shall be arranged to interfere least with the program needs of the agency.

g. Remuneration. All pay rates are established in conformity with municipal policy and are subject to special provisions which reflect professional, technical, and other pay categories. The department usually has some form of pay schedule and increment plan by which continuous satisfactory employment in the department is rewarded. Step increments may be annual and at one or more steps per year depending upon worker competency and performance. It is usual to raise more highly proficient workers or those who, in the opinion of their supervisors, merit such increments. Such evaluations are made by immediate supervisors and passed upon by whatever administrative staff the department employs.

h. Staff conferences and in-service education. All employees of the department are expected to attend regularly scheduled in-service educational programs, institutes, workshops, demonstrations, or lectures. Such meetings are designed to improve employee competency and efficiency as well as for professional development. Regularly scheduled conferences for staff personnel dealing with work schedules, job assignments, program ideas, daily operations, or any other matters will be attended by all appropriate employees.

i. Program participation by departmental employees. Under no circumstance will professional personnel of the department participate in any departmental sponsored or operated recreational activities. Nonparticipation, in this instance, means as an active player or competitor. It in no way terminates the professional obligations which employees have as leaders, supervisors, or instructors.

j. Conflicts of interest. Employees may belong to whatever organizations they wish for their professional development, social enjoyment, or for other reasons. However, such affiliations should not be the cause of conflicts of interest between the employee and the department.

k. Professional education. All employees are encouraged to take advantage of any university or college professional educational courses. However, the department will stipulate the number of hours and/or courses which any employee may take while working full time in the system.

l. Functions of personnel. The job specification identifies the requirements of each position. It establishes the conditions of work which will result in an optimum contribution of the recreationist to the success of the agency as a whole. It provides the worker with a clear understanding of his duties and obligations within the system and his relationship with others. Further, it defines responsibilities of the position and the authority which it carries. The individual is therefore in the situation of best appreciating what is expected of him within these lines. Each position specification should contain the following information about a particular job:

  (1) General responsibilities.
  (2) Principal objectives.
  (3) Primary functions.
  (4) Limits of authority.
  (5) For whom responsible.

286 Practices of Recreational Service

      (6) To whom responsible.
2. Public behavior.
    a. Intoxicating or alcoholic beverages. No person shall be allowed to possess or consume alcoholic beverages in or on departmental properties. Usually, there is a municipal ordinance prohibiting the use of such beverages in public places.
    b. Profane and/or obscene language. The use of such language is considered to be offensive to public taste and as such cannot be allowed.
    c. Public health and safety. In order to maintain the health, welfare, and safety of those who utilize public recreational spaces and facilities, the following regulations may be applied. No person shall be allowed to:
        (1) Vandalize or otherwise deface or destroy public property.
        (2) Carry or discharge firearms or fireworks, slings, or other weapons.
        (3) Remove any public property from the allotted area.
        (4) Pollute or otherwise wrongfully utilize any water facility.
        (5) Kindle fires except in properly designated places.
        (6) Gamble.
        (7) Dress indecently.
        (8) Ride or drive any animal or vehicle except in places expressly for such activity.
        (9) Engage in riotous, threatening, or indecent conduct.
        (10) Conduct any business without the express permission of proper departmental officials.
        (11) Deposit any refuse of any kind except in proper receptacles as are provided.
        (12) Have animals, except cats and dogs on a leash of suitable length and strength.
        (13) Campaign politically, transmit handbills or posters, hold religious services, parade, or otherwise disrupt the normal function of the recreational facility unless such activity is officially sponsored by and part of the recreational service program.
        (14) Use narcotics or other illegal or harmful drugs or chemical substances which render rational behavior unlikely.
    d. Volunteering. All recreationists should attempt to recruit and utilize laymen as instructors, escorts, guides, and in other capacities as volunteers in order to supplement and expand the offerings of the recreational program. There are many opportunities for the provision of recreational experience that cannot be taken advantage of because of a lack of staff personnel. Volunteers make additional activities possible. The initiative of skilled, enthusiastic, and dedicated laymen should be made an integral part of every recreational service program. Volunteering can be of extreme significance in the enhancement and attractiveness of a planned program.

3. Administrative operating procedures.
    a. Accidents. Usually, only minor injuries shall be treated by departmental employees, unless a physician is a departmental employee (by contract). If an injured person requires immediate medical attention, proper authorities must be notified. First aid procedures should be instituted at once to prevent more serious injury to the individual.
    b. Accident reports. Accident report forms will be utilized whenever there is any accident involving injury to a patron or property damage suffered by any individual other than employees who are on duty at any departmental facility. Reports of injuries or property damage shall be filed in accordance with municipal regulations.
        (1) Every effort shall be made to complete all parts of the accident report, including the names, addresses, and statements of all witnesses.
        (2) In the event of very serious injuries, including the death of a participant or spectator, the supervisor of the facility shall make an immediate verbal report to his immediate superior and file a complete written report within twenty-four hours.
        (3) Departmental employees will not utilize their own vehicles to transport injured persons, unless unusual circumstances force such transportation to be used, but will request police or hospital department ambulances to render assistance.
        (4) Departmental employees will render whatever first aid is required, request medical assistance if necessary, report all facts, and in no way make commitments on behalf of the department.
        (5) In all cases of serious injury to participants, where the proximate cause appears to result from faulty equipment or a hazardous area, the departmental employee supervising the facility shall request a police photographer to photograph the area. The employee immediately concerned with the situation shall be prepared to indicate the possible cause or causes of the accident in order to guide the policeman in the subject or angle of the picture. In the event that a police photographer fails to respond, the recreational service worker should telephone his immediate supervisor and appraise him of the fact that he was unable to arrange for a photograph to be taken of the suspected area, facility, or piece of equipment.
    c. Participations. An attendance count shall be made between the hours when the facility is in operation. The attendance count shall be recorded on an official form provided for that purpose. There are several formulae utilized for taking an attendance count during the day. Any one of these may be used to determine the number of visits to the facility. The attendance count is the total number of all persons visiting the facility. Such a count shall be made each day

and recorded on the weekly report for submission to the central office.
d. Daily log. Entries in this daily journal shall record the activities conducted at the facility under immediate supervision of the local staff. Its purpose is to reflect an accurate picture of all organized activities sponsored, promoted, and supervised by the facility staff.
e. Closing hours. Usually, regular activities at any recreational facility shall cease at 10:00 p.m. However, on special occasions activities may be scheduled until a later time. The approval of superiors should be secured in advance. If the possibility of advance approval cannot be obtained, the circumstances should be reported immediately after the working day on which this deviation of schedule took place.
f. Opening hours. All personnel will arrive at their respective facilities not less than fifteen minutes prior to the officially designated time for opening. Upon arrival, employees should follow this standard procedure:
(1) Open all entrances and rest room doors.
(2) Raise the colors.
(3) Set out any special equipment.
(4) Check over all supplies.
(5) Inspect all apparatus.
(6) Designate any unsafe equipment for removal.
(7) Make entries in proper ledgers concerning any faulty equipment.
g. Inspection of facilities, equipment, and areas. It is the responsibility of the facility supervisor to make a complete daily safety check of all equipment in order to insure hazard-free utility for participants. Furthermore, each employee has the obligation of surveying all recreational areas, facilities, and equipment and report inadequacies and/or deficiencies. All hazardous situations should be reported immediately to the central office for correction. The employee must follow up by continual check until the condition is corrected.
h. Transportation. If the department has a contract for the use of buses for recreational center groups, the following procedure should be initiated. Each center is authorized a specific number of bus trips throughout the year. In addition, the department may also furnish transportation to certain city-wide and special events. In order to maximize the use of buses, recreational supervisors are requested to coordinate activities requiring transportation with nearby centers, within their district, if possible.
i. Facility improvement. A supervisor of a facility may initiate a request for improvement of the facility on a form specifically designed for that purpose. The request may concern remodeling, renovating, or

adding to the facility which would result in substantial modifications of the existing facility. The individual initiating the request for improvement shall provide full details of the proposed modifications, including estimates of the probable cost of the project, sketches, line drawings, and the reasons and need for the proposed improvement. Administrative procedures are to carry the request up through channels for consideration by the chief executive of the agency. If the request is approved, complete plans and specifications shall be drawn up and action taken upon the modifications.

j. Requisitions for supplies, materials, and equipment. It is the responsibility of the supervisor of a facility to anticipate the needs of the program and to request an adequate supply of material to carry out program operations. All requisitions shall be transmitted to the proper central storeroom at a date fixed by local need.

k. Criticisms and complaints by the public. On occasion, justifiable criticisms and complaints are received by departmental personnel. All such complaints must receive careful consideration and be reported to the proper supervisors. Where a situation appears to warrant immediate action, the proper supervisor shall be notified, by telephone, so that the matter can be attended to without delay. In reporting complaints, care should be taken to give full details concerning time, place, individuals involved, and the situations about which the complaint is made. Courtesy and intelligence may be the best way to handle many of the complaints and tend to build up good public relations.

l. Fires. Should a department facility sustain a fire from which any damage results, a telephone report must be made immediately to the proper supervisor. Such a report should be followed by a written report to the central office. The report should contain the name of the facility, the date of the fire, the hour at which the fire occurred, how it was discovered, where it took place within the facility, the extent of damage, a list of property destroyed, the cause or suspected cause of the fire, any other pertinent information which can assist in fixing responsibility, and precautions or regulations that can be taken to prevent similar occurrences.

m. Disturbances or unusual situations. Whenever any unusual condition occurs at any recreational facility, the supervisor is required to notify his immediate superior. A written report is to be made at the earliest practicable time thereafter.

n. Referral problems. Occasionally, there will come to the attention of workers problems of a nature not consistent with the work of the department. These should be referred to the proper authorities and/or other municipal agencies organized to provide assistance in the area of social welfare cases. Nevertheless, the recreationist should be knowledgeable about, and have pertinent information of, other agencies which are specifically concerned with social welfare problems.

o. Vandalism. In addition to the problem of maintaining the facility in a clean and attractive manner, all employees should be alert to detect any markings on any interior or exterior surfaces. Such offensive markings mar the facility and must be removed as soon as possible after detection.

p. Equipment utilization. All employees must be aware of the hazards which exist if equipment is utilized improperly. Employees will always insist that equipment and other apparatus be used in a manner consistent with the safety of the participant.

q. Care of equipment and supplies. Each facility will have one employee responsible for the condition and maintenance of all equipment, supplies, and material charged to the specific facility.

r. Loan of equipment. Depending upon departmental policy and philosophy, the lending of equipment, supplies, or providing material assistance to other agencies within the community, but not a part of the department, may or may not be permitted. If such lending is permitted it is usually done on a priority basis, with all departmental needs having precedence over all recipients. The policy may require the posting of a bond or payment of some fee which is held in escrow until said material is returned in the same status as when borrowed.

s. Storage and maintenance of equipment and supplies. Store all material neatly for easy accessibility under lock and key. Keep a perpetual inventory of all material in storage. Label all dangerous materials and store them in accordance with their respective instructions. Use good housekeeping procedures when dealing with combustible materials.

t. Repair and salvage operations. All damaged or worn equipment, supplies, and materials may be salvaged and repaired or renovated to the extent that they become serviceable. All such items which cannot be repaired or used at the local center should be collected and transported to the central repair shop of the agency. In order to secure correct distribution and credit, all such items will be clearly marked with the name of the center.

u. Care and use of floors. The multi-purpose use of floors makes them of great importance in the maintenance of the facility. All employees can perform an excellent service by careful supervision of participants in order to avoid abuse of wooden floors. Specific rules for the care and maintenance of all floors, whether of wood, asphalt tile, or some other material will conform to the best preventive maintenance in practice.

v. Keys to departmental facilities. Issuance of keys to all departmental facilities shall be limited to those employees requiring keys to specific facilities or centers. No unauthorized person shall have a key to a department facility. All keys are issued and accounted for by receipt.

When personnel who have custody of department keys are transferred, resign, retire, or are otherwise terminated, all keys that have been issued shall be accounted for prior to clearance. No employee shall have duplicate keys made for any facility. If an employee loses a key through negligence he shall be charged with the cost of replacement. Any loss of keys to departmental facilities must be reported immediately to the employee's supervisor.

w. Furnishings and decorations. At particular recreational facilities, live Christmas trees may be used. Only electric lights will be used for decoration purposes and these shall be installed by electricians employed by the department. Artificial Christmas trees are fireproofed by the department and almost any decoration may be used upon them. However, all decorations must conform to fire department regulations.

  (1) When installing decorations for parties or dances, care must be taken to see that such effects do not interfere with the usual program in the center. All sponsored groups using their own furnishings and decorations shall install and remove same subject to the approval of the facility supervisor.
  (2) All decorations must be installed in such ways that they will not mar the surface to which they are attached. Such decorations will conform to fire department regulations.
  (3) All flammable materials shall be fireproofed.

x. Costumes. The costume workshop is maintained to provide needed accessories for that aspect of the program concerned with dramatics and/or special events. The following procedures are used to standardize costume operations:

  (1) Ordering costumes.
      (a) The costume requisition form should be used in ordering costumes.
      (b) In ordering costumes, the supervisor should record the name of the play and characters.
      (c) In ordering costumes for song or dance groups, give the name of the dance or song.
  (2) In determining the size of costume to order, the director should refer to the following scale of measurements, to which all department costumes conform:

Girls

Size	Length	Chest	Waist	Sleeve Band
4	31	24	22	8
6	34	26	23	8½
8	38	28	24	9
10	44	30	25½	10
12	48	33	26	10½
14	50	36	26½	11

Boys

Size	Waist	Waist to Crotch Front	Back	Crotch to Cuff	Chest
4	23	8	10	14	24
6	24	9	11½	17	26
8	24½	10	12½	20	28
10	25	10½	13	23	30
12	26	11½	14	26	33
14	27	13	16	28	36

(3) Requests are filled in the order that the complete requisitions are received by the costume workshop. Partial requisitions cannot be sent for the purpose of reserving special costumes during a busy holiday season.

(4) When costumes are received at the recreational center, the director should check them immediately to be sure they are correct in size, type, and quantity.

(5) The following rules on the use and care of costumes should be observed
   (a) Children should handle costumes with care so that they are not ripped or torn.
   (b) Children should wash their hands and faces, necks and arms immediately prior to donning the costumes, even for dress rehearsal.
   (c) Children should not wear costumes at any time other than during the performance and during the dress rehearsal.
   (d) Children should not wear costumes that are too tight or too long. If costumes are too baggy, the director should either make a slight alteration or order a substitute costume.
   (e) Costumes should not be cut, nor altered on the sewing machine.
   (f) Children should be instructed to turn the costumes right side out, put them on hangers, and return them to the costume mistress or the director at the conclusion of the performance. They must be ready to be picked up by the costume truck at 8 a.m. on the day following the performance.

(6) Children are not to wear their own costumes, or costumes furnished by any other agency, when they participate in playground programs.

(7) Costumes are furnished only for playground events. It is not possible to provide costumes to any other agency no matter how worthy the work of that agency may be. The limited supply of

costumes and staff make it impossible to give service outside the department.

Much could be written about recording all manifestations of the agency program and operations, but the ramifications would be overpowering. It is enough to simply indicate the previously mentioned possible classifications of duties, functions, and responsibilities without spelling out the multiple details that constitute administrative procedure for any single agency. Large departments will, of necessity, have to submit to greater detail and variety in systematically recording standard activities undertaken on a daily basis. Nevertheless, every agency, regardless of size, should have a procedural manual to which staff members can refer. Its size and type will reflect upon the size of the department staff and all of the operating considerations which together make up the entire agency.

Significantly, administrative and other divisional manuals indicate the degree of control and influence which the department has upon public confidence and conduct, inasmuch as the largest segments of the manual are supportive of routine acts. These routine operations are a direct measure of public esteem, because where the public has continually utilized the agency's program and become accustomed to agency policy it tends to accept the department as a necessary service. Thus, routine activities require standardized procedures as a consequence of the volume of requests, suggestions, criticisms, and participations that have been received. Departmental sponsorship and organization make possible the speedy translation of recreational requests to standard operating procedures. This does not remove responsibility on the part of the department to be creative. On the contrary, it requires the agency's staff to be constantly creative in supplying new recreational concepts and activities to a public that continually demands new and broadening experiences. Routinization must not mean stagnation. Reducing many or most contingent factors to a basic routine merely saves time and effort by not having to look for answers which by the very volume of demand require standardizing. Routine quantifies particular facts, classifies them, and promotes a rapid system whereby repetitive activities may be more readily processed.

FINANCIAL SUPPORT

If recreational service on the municipal level is a distinctive governmental function, why do so many community recreational service departments experience budgetary problems? The municipal, county, state, or federal recreational service agency should be accorded the same place in the governmental hierarchy as are other long-established departments. No other department is expected to return a profit nor to underwrite its own support, yet municipal departments of recreational service are enjoined, even demanded, to return money to the general fund of the community. This is inequitable, dangerous, and indefensible.

Noted authorities in the fields of law, urban planning, public administration, sociology, and education have long and repeatedly stated that municipal recreational service must be treated as an essential governmental function and not as a retrenchable frill. Many experts spell out in detail the advisability of providing a firm tax base in support of the program and necessary facilities for the operation and maintenance of public recreational services. Why, then, do public recreational service agencies continue to depend on other than tax support for their developed activities? Should public or governmentally operated recreational service agencies be denied adequate tax support? Why do so many communities assess fees and charges for activities which are supposed to be free to the general public? How can public recreational service departments justify returning excessive amounts of money to the municipal general fund? Is there something wrong with the modern municipal concept of operating local public recreational service departments? On what basis should fees be charged, or is there ever any activity or facility which should require attached user fees? The answers to these questions constitute some of the most serious and complicated problems confronting public recreational service agencies throughout the country.

Every legitimate and legal precedent points unalterably to the fact that public recreational service is, indeed, a governmental function. If the use of the term *public* has any meaning whatsoever, it connotes accessibility by people to the services of a governmental agency without additional fees or charges. It certainly means open to the public, free of charge, and supported *in toto* by taxes. Whenever public agencies begin to assess fees and tack on charges to services that are supposed to be paid for by appropriation from the general municipal fund, then there is complete nullification of the principle of public recreational service. Such practices fly in the face of the concept of governmental function and public agency. Obviously, this is an extremely common practice. There is little possibility that any public recreational service agency exists in this country today which does not in some way supplement its tax appropriation with fees and charges. Does this mean that such practice is either good or right? Most administrators of departments defend the user fee on the basis that they require additional money to perpetuate the operation of the agency. Is this a true statement? Let us look at the facts.

Almost all of the revenue collected by municipal departments of recreational service are turned over to the general fund. Few agencies have special or ear-marked funds designed to set aside revenues for the specific purpose of extending public recreational services. The simple truth is that most municipalities use the funds that are returned to it from fees and charges, posted by recreational service departments, for other municipal functions. Such monies may be utilized to build new public buildings, augment personnel on the police and fire departments, purchase new city vehicles, maintain streets, lights, sewers, and other public works; but rarely are they employed to provide additional public recreational service. The department must still fight for its appropriation from the general fund along with all other municipal agencies.

Legitimate Sources of Recreational Funds

The impetus to place public recreational service on the same level with other local departments of the municipality has progressed despite, rather than as a result of, community sentiment. The average citizen would much rather spend his money, whatever the price, for those things from which he benefits personally than to pay a slightly higher tax rate for those services that will benefit the entire community—and himself. Human nature being what it is, selfishness and personal aggrandizement are more readily apparent and consistent than the larger view of community welfare and social betterment. The very fact that more than ten billion dollars is spent each year in the United States on personal consumption of liquor and that school, park, and recreational land and facility acquisition are so often turned down in public referenda surely bears out this view. Nevertheless, it is only on the basis of tax support that public recreational service departments can or should operate.

Donations and Grants. This by no intent means that other sources of revenue cannot be found or used. The public agency has the right to and should accept all gifts, bequests, endowments, awards, donations, and grants of real or personal property and money or other articles of value, insofar as such benefices do not involve the corporate entity in litigation or where the acceptance of such articles, items, or objects would cost more than they are worth to maintain or operate. Philanthropic organizations are more than welcome to provide financial support for experimental or continuing activities which the department can organize and administer. Subventions from the state, bond issues (which involve voluntary taxation), federal grants, rebates, and allowances are all legally constituted methods of supporting public recreational services of various types. Wherein is the rub? With all of these sources, the fundamental program of balanced activities may not be adequately supported and the cost of capital improvements are almost never carried by a general fund appropriation.

Fees and Charges. There are other possible sources of money for the public recreational service department—fees, charges, and/or concession operations. Because public recreational service is a genuine function of government and not a proprietary or profit-making effort, the idea of charging for the very services that are supposed to be free appears to negate the premise on which the public sector of the field stands. The public agency is not in *business,* nor can it afford to compete with private enterprise. It cannot sell commodities, goods, or services that are obtainable through purchase in the private sector of the community. To do so would invite massive retaliation by commercial organizations who could justifiably charge that the public agency is taking unfair advantage of its position. Yet there is a defensible position for the public agency to take in the question of assessments or user fees and concession charges.

A legitimate instance of user fee assessment would be those activities where a small group of people receive intense personal instruction in an activity which normally would not employ personnel for such a particular object. Instruction is an essential part of the recreational program. No one should have to pay for it because it is an integral part of the on-going series of activities administered by the department. However, if it were some esoteric instruction in yoga, flying instruction, or short-hand lessons, where the skills involved are not necessarily those which the typical recreationist would possess, the department could and should attach a fee for instructional services. If the activity gained such popularity that it would require the department, in the interest of extending recreational possibilities, to employ a full-time instructor to handle this activity, the fee should be withdrawn and an appropriate budgetary item substituted to support this activity. For experimental activities, where there is no background of how popular it will become or to what extent it will attract potential participants to the agency, the fee is attached. As soon as the activity proves itself and becomes a routine part of the departmental offering, all fees should be withdrawn. This, for all practical intents and purposes, is another part of the fundamental program of activities. When the activity, under such circumstances, is assumed by the department as a routine item and later loses its popularity, or interest disappears, then either it is dropped, or for those few who still want to participate, the fee is reestablished.

Maintenance of buildings, grounds, and facilities should not require user fees. Maintenance is a legitimate on-going overhead item of expense which the agency will have whether people participate in a given activity or not. The golf course will still have to be watered, mowed, cultivated, rolled, and so on, whether ten, one hundred, or one hundred-thousand people utilize it. The same thing holds true for swimming pools, beaches, community centers, parks, playgrounds, boating facilities, tennis courts, fields, courts, and other equally important areas. Fees should not be allowed for use of these places. They have been acquired, constructed, and developed as the base upon which all, or almost all, of the programmed recreational activities of the agency stand. Without them there would hardly be a program, at least not a very attractive program. Then how are these facilities to be financed? The typical answer is pay-as-you-go revenue bonds. This may in fact be a logical answer, but one vital aspect is being ignored in the rush to capitalize on the modern physical plant—a tax appropriation to cover the capital investment, or borrowing.

A few experts insist upon segregating capital from routine budget items. They maintain that any commercial enterprise would not note as an expenditure a sum disbursed to construct a storage tank, let us say, but would carry it as an asset and would establish for it a plan for depreciation and amortization. A community center, swimming pool, golf course, or park, if paid for prior to obsolescence, should be viewed as an asset. It is also true that capital expenditures in local jurisdictions do not run evenly. The financing of a swimming pool might be disastrous if it had to be paid for in one year.

The chief hazard of the separated capital budget is the concomitant inclination to rest completely on borrowed money. All bankers relish the thought of government indebtedness, but the taxpayer should demand that such practice be halted. It is no rarity for municipalities to have twenty-five per cent of their tax funds absolutely tied to the debt service, with fifty per cent of the commitment awarded to interest, and the other half for retirement of the principal sum. It has been stated that the larger and more affluent the jurisdiction, the less defense there is for debt. As Charlesworth states:

> After a society has become stabilized, however, it has no routine phases; the rounded and mixed character of its make-up gives it a constant statistical average. It is not the *nature* or the *size* of the project that determines whether bonds should be issued or assessments increased; it is the *indivisible character* of the project that is controlling. If the project is big and also indivisible, and the jurisdiction is small, borrowing must be resorted to; in all other cases the improvement should be handled in stride.[1]

There are situations where the community is so affluent that not one of its citizens would be financially hurt if fees were assessed for various services. For example, if an individual can afford a boat, he can afford the charge for mooring it at a public dock or marina. If an individual's taste runs to horseback riding, he can afford the fee for the hour he rides, particularly if this occurs in the urban center. In a community where affluence is average the individual may wish to join the public golf course association and pay a yearly fee, instead of belonging to a private country club where the dues are presumably much higher. This may be permissible. However, what of the not-so-affluent individual residing in the same community? Perhaps he too would want to play golf (the game is no longer a rich man's sport), but he cannot afford the yearly fee. He must either save his money for the fee, play only intermittently, or not at all. Is this fair? In this society an individual must learn to differentiate between what is valuable to him and what is not so valuable. If playing golf is more valuable than another activity, which may cost nothing, then the individual is obligated to save until he can afford the game of his choice. Does this void the idea of a public agency service? Does it defeat the very purpose for which the agency was established?

---

[1] James C. Charlesworth, *Governmental Administration* (New York: Harper & Row, Publishers, 1951), p. 327.

Where every individual in the community is solvent enough to have a boat and boats are an accepted recreational activity, then community marinas should be supported by tax monies. However, where the community follows the usual economic levels from wealthy to poor and boating is not considered an on-going recreational activity for all, it would be most discriminatory for the not so affluent to have to help support, by tax monies, the free use of mooring facilities. In such instances fees for such use should be fixed. Yachting, motor boating, aeroplane piloting and ownership, polo, riding to the hounds, and so on, are still not considered on-going activities of the routine recreational program. These experiences require individual wealth that is beyond most people to afford. Under these conditions, riding stables maintained by the municipality, the community airport, marina, community polo field, should all be maintained and supported by user fees. Should the time ever come when such activities are participated in by everyone, or where each individual expects to be able to participate in activities of this type, then they should be made part of the basic recreational program and supported by tax funds.

Concessions. One other possible source of revenue is available to the public recreational service department, that of profits from operating concessions. Concessions are, in fact, all of those operations dispensing goods and services not offered by the department, but farmed out on a bid and morals basis to businesses which guarantee to return money to the agency. In fact concessions have come to be looked upon, in certain quarters, as political patronage plums. Unscrupulous politicians have sometimes helped themselves to a profit at the public's expense by requiring personally owned commercial enterprises, or those with whom they have some business connection, to operate in the areas controlled or operated by the public department. If this is not the case, there are other disadvantages in having commercial operators selling commodities. The public facility, whether beach, park, center, or some other structure, has been financed from tax monies. It is illogical and not in the best interests of the citizens of the community to have private commercial enterprises operating businesses and making a profit from the taxes invested in public facilities. There is, however, a clear and purposeful step which recreational service agencies may take. Instead of backing away from the responsibility of operating refectories, and other amenity service shops and stands, the departments should actually have a complete division or bureau that does nothing else but operate such enterprises.

The goods and services that can be sold in public places or at public facilities are those items or objects that make the patron's time spent at the facility more enjoyable. This may come in terms of food, refreshments, or salable items for use at picnics, outings, for games, sports, bird-watching, or just for the use of space. The only stipulation concerning the public agency's operation is that there be no excessive profit attached to the selling. Goods and services must be provided at the lowest possible cost and should cover the expense of providing the personnel, overhead, and the cost of the commodity. Sale of space, as for the parking of cars, can be nominal to help defray the cost of constructing the parking lot, salaries of employees, with any surplus going to offset the cost of activities. The sale of locker space, checking clothing, revenues developed from vending machines can be applied to personnel wages and additional facility construction and maintenance which would not be considered a budgetary item for recreational service. Amenities items and services are justified on a proprietary basis in that they are a convenience for the patron and not a necessity for the production of satisfying experiences.

Dangers of Revenue-producing Resources. Rather than offer a detailed statement on dangers inherent in the development of fees, charges, and excessive concession profits, a listing of questionable practices and outcomes should suffice.

1. The practice of assessing fees and charges to on-going recreational activities under public agency sponsorship negates the concept of tax support and generic governmental function.
2. There is a hazard that unenlightened political or managerial authorities will use the recreational service department for the production of monies to subsidize municipal government.
3. Fees and charges attached to programmed activities defeat the purpose for which the agency was originally established.
4. One specific danger lies in the municipality's attempt to employ individuals who are not career recreationists to administer the department for business purposes rather than public services.
5. Political patronage for past favors may result in the establishment of party cronies as executives with fees and charges being used for "paying off" politically incurred debts.
6. Charging whatever the traffic will bear commercializes a public function of government, usurps the prerogatives of the private sector, restricts participation to those who can afford to pay, sets up the climate for double taxation, and places unlimited temptation upon the administrator to ignore the pre-emptive aspect of recreational service orientation in favor of simply making profits.
7. If fees and charges are permanently affixed to the municipal function of recreational service provision, it is likely that the body politic will begin to wonder why they have to continue to pay taxes to support an operation for which they have to pay an additional user fee. Enlightened taxpayers will seek to determine why an apparent public agency requires fees and charges in order to function at all. With such questioning comes a breakdown in public trust and support of the recreational service department.
8. No other municipal agency, e.g., police, fire, health, or public works, charges fees for performance of the service for which they were estab-

lished. No other municipal agency is expected to furnish a steady source of revenue which will apply to the general fund. Continued charges for services which, in theory, are supposed to be supported by taxes, will undermine the agency's governmental status and revert it to a quasi-public or proprietary function.
9. The individuals who require the public recreational service most, children, older adults, out-of-school youngsters, and others who are on the fringes of an affluent society, will be adversely affected by a pay-as-you-use agency. The very people whom the agency should be attempting to reach and satisfy are the ones who will be most discriminated against by fees and charges.
10. It may be that activities will be programmed only on the basis of profits generated. There are some activities, which because of mass appeal, can be organized with charges assessed for entrance. It would be unfortunate, indeed, if only those activities which stimulated great spectator interest would be offered as a consequence of being able to produce revenue for the municipality. There are agencies, at this time, whose policy for the selection of recreational activities is based on revenue production.

There are some general standards which apply in terms of how public recreational service shall be financed. The following concepts are thought to be of a practical and ethical approach.

1. Because society identifies recreational experience as a significant aspect of human life and has accepted responsibility for the provision of recreational services through governmental jurisdictions, in the public sector, it must furnish basic recreational activities and the financial resources needed to support such activities.
2. In order to carry out the mandate set by the body politic, governments are established to satisfy welfare needs of society. The increasing demand for public recreational facilities, spaces, and programming indicates an explicit approval of the expenditure of tax resources for such recreational service.
3. Although there is no scientifically established standard for the determination of per capita expenditures for recreational services, other municipal functions may be studied to provide some estimation of what the costs are for financing public recreational activities. It must be understood that finances are necessary not only for spaces, facilities, and personnel salaries, but for the continually expanding variety of activities which are being programmed by creative recreationists. Items are now being included in budget requests which were not in existence ten years ago.
4. Appropriated funds should be used in a discriminating manner. Although it is true that there are no special recreational neighborhoods

in communities, e.g., where a low-end socioeconomic neighborhood receives the largest center, outdoor facilities, or increased leadership personnel and higher income neighborhoods receive little, the examination of neighborhoods within the community will tend to reveal the recreational habits and consumption of recreational resources and activities by residents. Where there is a lower social and economic level prevalent in a neighborhood, the likelihood does exist that a larger percentage of appropriated tax funds should be spent there. The rationale for such a statement is the economic rule of diminishing returns. Where individuals are thoroughly capable of determining their own recreational pursuits on a private basis, they will probably seek other than public facilities for their experiences. Lower income groups, on the other hand, do not have the financial resource necessary to engage in many nonpublicly sponsored recreational activities and therefore rely upon them to a greater degree than do the more affluent. Tax money should be expended where the need is greatest and where the return for such expenditures will bring optimum fulfillment and satisfaction.

5. Wherever there are recreational user fees attached to public agency programs, there is a question of whether or not the agency is adhering to basic concepts and principles of governmental function. Essentially, all recreational activities for which there is an expected participation should be free of all costs In rare and special circumstances, i.e., experimental or special service experiences, fees may be attached. Such charges, however, should not be used to support other phases of the program. They should be at cost and be utilized specifically to offset nonbudgeted monetary needs. Such fees must be reasonable and apply only until such time as the activity is either integrated into the ongoing comprehensive program or dropped from the scheduled activities.

6. Budgeted appropriations must be scrupulously earmarked for the purpose of funding the department of recreational service. Unless tax funds are so allocated they may be used for functions other than those originally intended.

7. In general, recreational activities that are universal in appeal and which satisfy a common need must be offered free of charge.

8. Fees or charges may be justified on the basis of providing a special facility or activity to a small group when there is a lack of appeal for the activity to the general public.

9. When participation in an activity is closed to the general public and limited to a private membership exclusively, a fee for the provision of the facility, activity, or other resource services may be charged. Such exclusive activities, if provided at all, on public property should be operated at the expense of those benefiting from such services.

10. When the service is received by nonresidents who are not taxpayers in the jurisdiction where the service is rendered, a fee may be charged.

The justification for such fees comes in terms of prohibiting outsiders from utilizing such services or for making the nonresident share in bearing the cost of operation. If there were such a thing as reciprocal taxation, where municipalities prorated payments on the basis of their residents using other cities' recreational facilities and activities, there would be no justification for assessing nonresidents. However, this is not practical nor is there any precedent for it. It is equitable that those who do not bear the burden of supporting local agencies through taxation should share the cost of providing services based upon tax support.

SUMMARY

Administration is the process which attempts to coordinate and facilitate a variety of functions performed by diverse personnel in order that the most comprehensive and effective program of recreational activities will result. To this end, all phases of planning, organizing, supervising, and directing the utilization of financial support, physical plant, property, and personnel is undertaken. Proper administration is vital if organized recreational services are to be valuable to the public. Administration of recreational services has only one outcome and that is the production of high quality organized recreational experiences. The development and operation of recreational activities for people is the only reason for justifying administration. The chief purpose of all administration is the improvement, extension, and provision of high quality planned recreational opportunities in an optimum environment.

To effect a harmonious relationship between professional personnel and the normal daily requirement of public participation within the program, a detailed system of administrative procedures which often minimizes friction in handling routine matters is helpful. Such procedures, in the form of manuals, should not be interpreted as confining professional activities nor reducing professional functions to mere paper work managers. The manual is designed to alleviate purely routine reporting and will never restrict the recreationist in the performance of his professional responsibilities. All rules and regulations that are necessary and developed over a long period of time, while the department is in operation, record particular behavioral controls which assist in departmental success. These standardized procedures should never become the last word in personnel management, but are useful as guides in meeting the countless questions and problems that may have arisen over a period of years. It is important to emphasize that all recreationists employed by the department should be concerned with and participate in the development of operating manuals.

The administrative process is necessarily elastic because it deals with people and changing conditions or situations. Adroit administration strikes a nice balance between the individual needs and interests of recreationists and the smooth operation of the department. Professionalization will more than compensate for the latitude given to the recreationist in his conduct of recreational affairs. Rigidity of structure and circumscribing policies and regulations will do more to hinder the very competent worker than almost any other procedure, except, perhaps, poor supervision. Very large departments with numerous personnel are forced to enact systematized methods for working with personnel. In some instances this proves beneficial to all concerned. However, the best administration is that which allows the highly competent and professional worker to do his job and carry out his responsibilities with a minimum of direct regulation and a maximum respect for his integrity and desire to do the best job possible. Administration exists to facilitate worker needs in performing the only justifiable reason for his employment, the product on of a comprehensive, worthwhile, and satisfying recreational program.

SELECTED REFERENCES

ALLEN, L. A., *Management and Organization.* (New York: McGraw-Hill), 1958.

BAKER, BENJAMIN, *Urban Government.* (New York: D. Van Nostrand Company, Inc.), 1957.

BOWMAN, D. M., ed., *Management: Organization and Planning.* (New York: McGraw-Hill), 1963.

BLUM, H. L. and A. R. LEONARD *Public Administration.* (New York: The Macmillan Co.), 1963.

BUCHANAN, J. M., *Public Principles of Public Debt.* (Homewood, Ill.: Richard D. Irwin, Inc.), 1958.

GROSS, B., *Managing of Organizations.* (New York: The Free Press), 1964.

HJELTE, GEORGE and JAY S. SHIVERS, *Public Administration of Park and Recreational Services.* (New York: The Macmillan Co.), 1963.

ISARD, WALTER and ROBERT COUGHLIN, *Municipal Costs and Revenues.* (West Trenton, N.J.: Chandler-Davis Publishing Company), 1957.

LANHAM, E., *Administration of Wages and Salaries.* (New York: Harper and Row), 1963.

MILLETT, JOHN D., *Government and Public Administration.* (New York: McGraw-Hill), 1959.

MUSOLF, LLOYD D., *Public Ownership and Accountability: The Canadian Experience.* (Cambridge, Mass.: Harvard University Press), 1959.

NIGRO, FELIX A., *Public Personnel Administration.* (New York: Holt, Rinehart & Winston), 1959.

PFIFFNER, JOHN M. and FRANK P. SHERWOOD, *Administrative Organization.* (Englewood Cliffs, N. J.: Prentice-Hall, Inc.), 1960.

RAMANADHAM, V. V., *Finances of Public Enterprise.* (New York: Taplinger Publishing Co., Inc.), 1965.

THAYER, LEE O., *Administrative Communication.* (Homewood, Ill.: Irwin), 1961.

Chapter 12

COORDINATION

> PRINCIPLE: Diversity of interests, needs, philosophy, and program within any community requires that a common course be determined in order that total recreational service can be offered. The process of community cooperation in the interests of all can only be effected when coordination among all agencies concerned with the provision of recreational services becomes reality.

Man is a social and political animal. For this reason he relies upon interdependence in order to survive and creates government to ensure social stability and security.

Even primitive man found it necessary to organize to stay alive. The solitary hunter of prehistory met death far more often than did those who banded together in family, clan, or tribal units. Mutual protection offered survival. As human society achieved a high degree of complexity, the reliance upon others increased proportionately. The basic factor that produces this interdependence in modern society is the complicated specialization of labor. This intricate division necessitates an involved and ramified social organization so that coordination of a variety of functions on which society depends can be attained. A cursory inspection of the diverse agents and agencies upon which our survival, educational, recreational, and occupational instrumentalities exist immediately proves our mutual need and the organization required to place these devices at the disposal of the individual.

Indeed, it is the very complexity of modern existence that necessitates the type of governmental enterprise now applied. For society to cope most effectively with its health, educational, recreational, economic, social, and ideological problems, an understanding of human development, social interactions, and the role that government plays in these factors merits intensive study and serious attention.

HUMAN NATURE AND SOCIAL ORGANIZATION

Individual development is determined not only by face-to-face contacts in family encounters and direct personal friendships, but it is also influenced to a great extent by membership and participation in classes, aggregates, and other groups. These inclusive social clusters, in direct opposition to the more personal relationships, are in the nature of public concern. Thus, the public sector of life involves the individual as a member of a public rather than as a contributor by virtue of particular qualities of personality. The person is accorded consideration with regard to societal functions within the social organization. A most immediate concern is for society as a whole, in which the individual must seek his position.

Although direct interpersonal contacts have a continuing influence on the development of human nature, the "other-directed" relationships inaugurated within the total milieu of society also define the scope and consequence of the cultural environment in which the individual is nurtured. Restrictions, conditioned by custom and code, are imposed upon the person and some mediation must be attempted in order for the individual to fully realize the many avenues available to him for personal growth and development.

The whole concept of social organization is possible because of the nature of man. His aspirations are not merely concerned with interpersonal relationships, but transcend these patterns in terms of highly developed and complex social structures. The arrangements and conglomerate associations which man creates as he seeks social organization are as diverse as unique judgments can make them.

The idea of social organization developed originally from the necessity for having a division of labor. Assigned responsibilities for protecting the community gave rise to a princely class. A reliance upon some individuals to explain nature's caprice and man's future led to the formation of a priestly class. The function of supplying food, clothing, and shelter devolved upon a worker class. From these simplified divisions have sprung countless specialities, intricate organization, and manifold controls all coordinated to some extent by the interdependent need of the community. To this must be listed the aspect of control by law, common or written, first to preserve the privileges of the well-born, but more recently in order to obtain a measure of equity and justice for all. With law, the initiation of a social order is systematized. If there are also added a large and increasing population, sectionalism, ideological differences, pressure groups, and technological programs of rapid industrialization and urbanization, then the need for social organization based upon intense specialization and complete dependence by each individual upon the skills and services of productive workers is absolute.

But the social fabric is not based upon survival expediency alone. The purposes of association satisfy man's hunger to establish a lasting patrimony. Man the creator endows his environment with the change that he brings about. He is unique in the universe by virtue of his capacity to create, shape, and modify his environment. It is this last realization, the need to arrange a variety of social forms in order to advance his status, that has caused man to build in community. Thus, where speciality is required to sustain life, the effectiveness of many far exceeds the most efficient single member of the project. The structure developed by these associations is the rarest and most dynamic of all art forms—human personality.

Personality and Society

The undoubted connection between social organization and human personality clearly indicates the necessity for having some institution assume responsibility for the logical development of people. Because people embody the ideals and principles of the state in which they live, the concepts of ethics, rational values, and intelligent choices cannot be left to hopeful assimilation, but must be stringently promulgated by a social agency to whom is assigned the task of ideological education. Whatever the state is, the individual will mirror its forms on a lesser scale. For this reason, the association between personality development and social structure may be more clearly perceived in terms of value judgments.

That the relationship between the individual's development and the society in which he lives reflects the actual order of life cannot be denied. Each person must make his way in terms of the specific environment from which he comes and through the various classifications of which he is a part. All of these groups shape his personality relating to attitudes, opinions, biases, and basic beliefs. It is as a participant, observer, center of pressure, and conformer to codes, mores, and laws, or as an independent thinker and doer that the human personality grows in the complex cultural intricacy of the social world.

If the individual is of such character that the social milieu into which he is placed overwhelms him, then he is rejected or is restricted from participation. Success in the matrix of institutional arrangements means satisfaction and productivity for the individual and society. The remarkable affiliation effected between personality development and society is indicative of the instructional influence of the social order. The form of cultural agencies is an essential appliance for the directed learning of those who will have citizenship responsibilities. The models which growth should emulate are the realities of daily living as synthesized and practiced in the structure of social institutions. Many institutions shape the development of the young. Among these are the all-pervasive laws, and the occupational, ideological, educational, religious, fraternal, voluntary, and recreational agencies, performance in which assures a hearing so that one's opinions and actions are felt in guiding society. The interactions thus produced have as much effect upon individual growth and personality development as the individual may have in gaining a place in and thereby influencing the social system.

Although each person leaves some indication of having lived in a specific culture, there will be a tremendous degree of difference in terms of the influence that any one person has on society. The contributions that each makes differ radically. However, individuals come and go despite the significance of their passing, but institutional patterns vary slightly, if at all, and society remains. Therefore, institutions, because of their stability, become the constant by which individual development can be directed and measured. Thus, the individual is evaluated by what he accomplishes in the way of citizenship, his deference for law, respect for government, and recognition of the application of authority through social organization.

Social Education. The social order has two distinct, though related, functions in perpetuating itself. It utilizes the young to carry on the traditions and recognized mores in order to maintain stability and to transmit the vital information required to keep the social order operating. At the same time as it propagates the heritage of past generations, it also embodies instructional aspects that are innovational. This latter educational factor is almost culturally opposed to the former because it is concerned with modification of the social system rather than its preservation. These two seeming dichotomies are closely connected in that both are on the educational continuum. Both are necessary if society is to exist for the satisfaction and betterment of man.

The system of social conservation supposes that because a particular way of performance has served over a period of time that that method is the only method. Because it is hoary with age it is good. Complacency about how and why things are done develops and what is customary becomes the code for conduct. Nevertheless, society is dynamic and changing because people change. Thus, it seems clear that there must be room for more than mere transmission of historic fact. This opens the way for the second aspect of social education—the limitless perfectability of humanity and its institutions.

The structure of society necessitates reorganization on occasion. Sometimes this arises with revolution. Usually, however, the peaceful transition from what was, to what is, to what will be, carries with it a more powerful impact on the institutions of society than war could. Nothing short of the reconstruction of society is contemplated in social engineering and the doctrine of seeking after human perfectability. Yet, for all of this, the moderate course appears best. That is why social education is a continuum, starting from the past and going through to the future, with an effective mixture of that which has proved valuable and that which dictates change. Change of and for itself is questionable, for through modification or reconstruction an established valuable pattern may be destroyed or demeaned for something that is cheap and tawdry at best. The individual in society may be served most through the combined utilization of recreation and the preservation of significant and worthwhile traditions that are his patrimony.

Any consideration of public recreational service requires a knowledge of the jurisdictional framework into which the field fits. For this reason, a basic understanding of government and the constitutional provisions which guide its functions are offered.

THE GUARANTEES OF GOVERNMENT

In the complexities of a modern industrialized society government is an omnipotent force. From birth to death, necessarily transcribed and officially recorded, the significance of government as an all-pervasive influence in the regulation of people's lives can scarcely be misinterpreted. It is an intrinsic part of man's environment because man has planned it that way. Government guards our lives, defends our property, protects our children, and provides for our health, education, and welfare, controls and regulates our vocations, business transactions, marriages, liquor consumption, gambling, moral obligations, institutions, and makes sure that these functions are subscribed for by taxing individuals and corporate incomes. But this is only a recent phenomenon. It was not always so.

In a less complex time, perhaps as late as 1925, the government stood for restrictive activities. The maintenance of the *status quo* and adherence to the rigidities of a patriarchal culture characterized government. In simple cultures, the family is the agency of life, a microorganism of the social world, self-contained and conditioned to informally regulate fundamental behaviors on a traditional basis. Through various factors, such as discovery, development, and exploitation of natural resources, a plentiful supply of cheap labor, and the commercial genius to implement technological processes for an expanding market of goods and services, some change in the culture appears. As a culture matures in depth, intricacy, and particularization, the family begins to lose its centrality as a social institution, and becomes less important as a comprehensive agency of control. Other societal organs must then take up the reins and exert pressure for social organization. These institutions may take the form of health, welfare, educational, political, religious, recreational, or economic complexes. In many instances these forms may be governmentally operated. Government has therefore developed into a powerful force, pushed by technocracy and gaining ascendancy by filling the void left by the ineffective family unit. But what is government? Why is it organized? Is it really necessary?

Government

The state is the institution of authority and responsibility in modern society. It has become a supra-embodiment of power in order that the complexity of our social system is not thrown out of balance. Government is nothing more or less than a concept of order that has been put into practice. It is, in fact, the institutional synthesis of the principle of authority by which social organization is stabilized and maintained. Society depends upon government to regulate behavior and guaranty freedom while imposing certain obligations on individuals so that the rule of law is not shattered. In this manner, order in life is preserved.

Government has been created out of man's felt need for the organization of his own and other resources as well as for security reasons. Governments are established to safeguard man's natural rights through powers granted by those subject to such authority. The powers thus derived are utilized to provide equal dispensation of justice, defense against all subversive forces, guaranteed liberty, but not license, for all, and the promotion of the health, safety, and happiness of citizens. Explicitly engendered as a result of the formation of government is the production of public service to satisfy people's needs and to achieve cultural maturity and identity. When private enterprise fails to fulfill its obligations, then government, in all of its ramifications, moves in to provide the required services; and once in cannot be dislodged easily.

Governmental Functions. The functions of government may be viewed from three aspects concerning human activities. These are seen as promotional, restrictive, and amalgamative. Insofar as the promotional function is regarded, government is seen as an enabling body providing subsidies and generally rendering assistance in the completion of plans and operations beyond the means of private citizens to so perform. The government is looked upon as a useful tool for supporting and adding to social effectiveness; an instrument for increasing, through a pooling of tax resources, the development of individual productivity. Without such aid and service, valuable projects either could not or would not be executed by private enterprise. It is well known, for example, that the Tennessee Valley Authority was created because private power interests did not appreciate the need to provide cheap power to the relatively underdeveloped hinterlands—to the great sorrow of the private power concerns. As a result of the vacuum created by the abdication of private power corporations, the government supplied this needed service. Other illustrations might also serve to clarify this concept. Social security, civil rights laws, and a national system of super highways are facets of this promotional function. Wherever there is a lapse in service by the private sector of society, then government steps in to provide that service.

The inverse view of government sees it as a restrictive force. The prime requisite of the state is to perform police duties. But government itself is corruptible, because men govern, and it is therefore a possible source of contamination. For this reason a system of checks and balances must be established to prevent government from assuming a totalitarian form. As Jefferson said, "That government is best which governs least." His declaration stems from the view that at best government is a necessary evil and must be carefully hedged to prevent its misuse and degeneration, by unscrupulous demagogues, into despotism.

The ameliorative or amalgamated view is eclectic, taking the best features from each position and tempering them so as to achieve the worthwhile and efficacious social contributions of government together with the judicious and equitable utilization of police power guided by due process of law. Because human society is completely unpredictable and ambient—

expressing at times or in some individuals altruistic leanings and at other times or in other persons actions of bigotry, apathy, ignorance, and hate—government must function promotionally and restrictively. It is a reflection of the ambivalence of human behavior.

Promotional Government. Perhaps the most startling and significant development of the past fifty years pertaining to government endeavor is the manifestation and ramification of public welfare activities. Welfare, in the most valid meaning of the term, is the betterment of citizen life in all aspects, not merely indigent care. This proliferation of public services, an increase that is a distinct feature of all current jurisdictions, occurs on every level. To a certain extent it is an outgrowth of technological progress, a realization that scientific advancement requires some social control of the forces now placed at man's disposal. In some part it is a consequence of individual enlightenment and of an increasing knowledge that enables man to satisfy his urgent as well as luxury demands. Another factor influencing this trend is the modification of the ideas concerning the place of government in the social order. No chief cause can be given to fully explain the multiplication of governmental services or the proper sphere of governmental enterprise, it is the indisputable result of contemporary society.

COMMUNITY ORGANIZATION AND COORDINATION

The pattern of community organization stems directly from the larger complex of society of which it is an intrinsic part. The community is analogous to the family as the single building block of the greater whole. Within its structure and diverse functions may be observed the entire social order—class and caste, division of labor, and the whole social, political, religious, and economic structure. Enlarge the community and it is all of civilization.

Community organization concerns the collection and coordination of all the natural, physical, and personal resources of the community in order to satisfy felt needs. It is related to the discovery of human desires as well as to their satisfaction through the production and application of services. Community organization is both product and procedure. However, in terms of its use here it is viewed as a process, or series of coordinated efforts, resulting in the achievement of a sufficient degree of service in some area to which it is applied. The nature of this process requires group activity. The many organizations are coordinated so that their resources, personnel, specialities, and combined services can produce an effort designed to meet community needs. Community organization is a dynamic approach through continual group organization and action scrupulously applied to achieve maximum service to all citizens of the community.

Community organization may be short lived or perpetual. In the framework of providing some necessary function, e.g., recreational service, a stable program integrating all aspects of the community and affording a meaningful instrument by which individuals may lead more effective lives is required. The continuing expression of coordinated effort promotes significant contributions to citizen welfare and makes the community a better place in which to live.

Community organization attempts to contribute to positive local progress in its examination and assessment of existing community needs. By determining the segments of the community which have primary or some interest in meeting a set need, a plan of action can be formulated. Out of this analysis coordinated procedures can be attained to satisfy or help alleviate the need. In so doing, all necessary resources will be called into play. An evaluation concerning the priority of the need in relation to other community needs can be determined, and the production of effective activities can be instigated to perform whatever services are required.

The basic aims of community organization are measured in terms of cooperative agency and individual involvement for a better community and the perpetuation of effective services coordinately engendered. These ends are reached when the general public is educated to the conditions of community life, when agencies can augment their services by combining with other organizations and utilizing pertinent community resources at their disposal, and when areas of inadequate services or lapses in service can be competently filled. Community problems can be capably resolved if a useful pattern of affiliations among interested individuals, agencies, and groups is established. Generally, the following elements are effected as a consequence of community organization:

1. Parochial views by single agencies are diminished as community needs assume a more important place than do agency projects.
2. Each citizen is enabled to participate directly in solving community service deficits.
3. A process is set up to overcome gaps in service which threaten to cause social disintegration if they are allowed to persist.
4. Personal and physical resources of the community are more appropriately utilized.
5. Community cohesiveness and its conceivable correlated actions are demonstrated.
6. An awareness of the necessity for enlightening the entire community becomes manifest as agencies and individuals secure a better understanding of their place in the spectrum of community organization.
7. Friction among people is lessened or eliminated as ignorance is reduced while they work together for the common good on a prevailing problem.

The local community comes closest to the living concept of republican democracy, for the essence of democratic life resides in the functions of each community. The validity of the magnificent phrases penned by the "founding fathers" is tested at the local level. If the community is constant in its appreciation of those things which are self-evident, then democracy works and every individual is accorded his place and allowed to progress within the limits of his capacity and up to the maximum of his potential without artificial barriers to hinder him. The local community must embody living democracy if its citizens are to attain what this ideal claims is possible to achieve. The significant point of consideration then is that community spirit and cohesiveness attend the labors of every agency and institution attempting to furnish to its membership and services, the value of which underscores democratic obligations. More important, however, is the actual effect of community solidarity proven by free willingness to coordinate efforts in cooperative endeavors so that commonly held goals can be accomplished.

The community is appraised on its production of citizens who are able to function competently and effectively in a competitive society. The caliber of citizen effectiveness is almost totally dependent upon the services, of a tangible and intangible nature, which the community establishes for its self-preservation.

In this era of mass leisure, sufficient opportunity for recreational experiences promoted to enhance the life of the individual is basic to the fabric of social relationships in a worthwhile community. Legislative considerations to the contrary, local prerogatives for the rendering of these developmental opportunities must be afforded through state affirmation and dispensation if the community is to satisfy the fundamental premise that it is the locus of liberty in a nation of free men.

COORDINATING COUNCILS

Recreational service is assumed to be a local responsibility, a function, partially, of government. In nearly every community of any size there exist different organizations, outside of the public sector, which also provide many opportunities for the attainment of recreational skills and the practice of leisure arts and interests. The provisions which such groups make are augmented and made more comprehensive in depth and scope when the community has accepted its responsibility of establishing a public recreational service department supported by taxes. As do other governmental functions, a tax-supported recreational program has qualities that can strengthen and enlarge upon the offerings of other agencies. However, tax-supported services are not the only sources of organized recreational programs. All agencies play a necessary role in satisfactorily meeting the expressed needs and interest of the public.

One method of coordinating all sectors of the community is provided by some type of central council representing all of the agencies within the community who have any interest in the provision of recreational services. Such a council is the chief medium for coordinating the multiplicity of recreational sources that are available in the community. Because the council is open to all, it offers a forum for interested professionals and laymen alike to participate in community planning in the area of recreational services. It allows open discussion and debate on the best procedures in meeting community needs. It can, of course, serve as an informational clearing house for the exchange of ideas as well as receiving data on current problems, crises, and conditions, the exigency of which demands immediate attention.

The purpose of the coordinating council is to promote community betterment through the medium of recreational services and to offer a means for the exchange of ideas, experiences, problems, possible solutions, and cooperation through representatives of those agencies who make up the council. The coordinating council for recreational service may be defined as a primary policy-making body whose main efforts are designed to promote civic betterment through planned community examination and positive action. Such a body is brought into being by local ordinance, being established as a legal arm of government, by voluntary association on the part of social agencies interested in cooperative effort, as a result of citizen demand, or any combination of these. The consequences of initiating such a council will probably take the form of a study of community conditions and needs as they relate to recreational opportunities, the encouragement of close cooperation and coordination of activities by member groups of the council, and the determination of a plan or plans to secure competent action in meeting and improving services of a recreational nature that will meet community needs.

Recreational service coordinating councils have developed from the work of an individual or a small group who realized the need for the establishment of a public recreational service system or the improvement of an existing department. In some instances the council has arisen because public officials want to institute a department or have already done so. In no few cases councils have received impetus from the voluntary cooperative endeavors of public and private agency officials. In other circumstances they have been established as one branch of a parent body whose interests cover all phases of community life and functions.

Representation

Broad representation and inclusiveness must be the basic tenet upon which a council is organized. A listing of all civic, service, social, commercial, religious, business, professional, fraternal, educational, and labor groups within the community should be made and each of these organizations should be invited to supply a representative to the coordinating council. It may be that a hierarchy of councils within a large community, from the neighborhood, district, and regional councils, up to the local jurisdictional council covering the entire community, will send representatives for coordinating purposes. There is a place for every voice, for the total community should be represented. Almost every frame of reference should be permitted to receive admittance to the equitable solution of recreational needs and problems confronting the community.

Relationships

The many agencies dealing with community recreational service make logical planning on the municipal level almost impossible. Each agency attempts to arrogate to itself a series of functions which it may or may not be able to undertake. Each agency seeks autonomy, an additional slice of financial support, and a public image that will do much to enhance its prestige within the community. The complexity of community recreational service and the many agencies seeking to operate or currently operating in this field necessitate the establishment of some coordinating body that can efficiently and equitably settle questions of relationship among community agencies. Effective relationships are desperately needed. The initiation and continual production of total community recreational services requires the resources of every agency, in the community, which has a commitment to offer recreational activities. To the extent that these resources are organized to provide soundly administered services that have meaning for the development of individuals, a centralized coordinating council may be the only answer in the achievement of good order and elimination of waste within the community.

To reach the goal of beneficial cooperation among all community agencies for the betterment of public welfare in terms of recreational opportunities requires valid leadership from recreationists and the professional objectivity essential in recognizing how each sector can be integrated and thereby contribute its significant program to the entity of community recreational service. Cooperative relations among community agencies for recreational operations are exercised in many ways. At the basic level of stimulating activity for cooperative ventures is, or should be, the public recreational service department. It is the only agency that has been given primary responsibility for the provision of recreational service to the entire community. It has no specific clientele nor is its program limited by any exclusive mandate. It has been created to offer the broadest possible program to all of the people. For this reason, the public department is the logical agency to assume leadership in the development of a coordinating council.

The public recreational service department acts with the authority of government, supported by tax monies. It has the power to acquire the proper physical plant and properties and to develop these areas for maximum use by the public. It has the financial means to offer a more stable organization and inasmuch as it is brought into being by local ordinance and state enabling legislation, its permanency is relatively assured. Its control ultimately rests with the people of the community, not with any group of individuals. It answers to all of the people because it is by their will that it is established. Because government is the instrumentality by which people accomplish certain results which they require, but which they cannot do for themselves, the agency of government, in this case the recreational service department, acts for the people in supporting their needs and meeting conditions that arise in the community. The objective of community recreational service will never be completely realized unless a coordinating body, truly representative of all sectors of the community is established. Provision for this service cannot be left up to voluntary participation and accidental cooperation. The initiative must come from an agency that is chiefly concerned with organizing the entire community for recreational services.

To the end that optimum community recreational service will be the outcome, the public recreational system must coordinate its efforts with those of all other agencies which purport to offer recreational activities. It may be shown that certain innovations cannot be offered by public agencies but will fruitfully develop through private agency auspices. Particular emphasis may be placed upon specific recreational experiences by sectarian, commercial, or voluntary agencies that may be better equipped than the public recreational service department to operate a particular activity. Instead of attempting to offer the same activity and run the risk of an inferior performance and experience, as well as a duplication of what is already being done more effectively, the public department must take the view that it will best serve community needs by encouraging, cooperating with, and stimulating special interest organizations to even greater efforts. It is unwise and unnecessary to compete with another community agency in that agency's special field. There are so many other recreational activities to be offered that any duplication can only engender bitter feelings, unwelcome comparisons, a waste of time, a drain of financial resources, a misuse of personnel efforts, and needlessly restricted programming.

To assist in the development of cooperation and coordinated action by community agencies, particular policies should be widely disseminated in the community in order to alert all other recreational agencies and educate their operating officers to the idea of a centralized coordinating body. The council is established as a primary means of gaining cooperation of all community agencies. It attempts to encourage an environment of mutual trust and provide a common meeting ground wherein reciprocal commitments among and between agencies offering recreational opportunities can be fostered. The council must stimulate agency representatives to look beyond parochial limitations and adopt an attitude of community concern. One function of the council is the continual examination and evaluation of recreational opportunities, problems, and methods by which inadequate or underdeveloped recreational services can be eliminated. Community-wide projects require the resources of all agencies committed to recreational provision. Major concern today is the location and utilization of specialized physical resources such as recreational centers, golf courses, aquatic facilities, camps, and other extensive developments. Such consideration is significant to private agencies catering almost exclusively to youth as differentiated from public or private groups which may serve older adults, and other agencies which act as catalytic forces for the stimulation of recreational programs instead of actually operating programs.

Council Organization

The public recreational service department should initiate a council by inviting all community agencies, with direct or implied interest in the provision of recreational services, to send a representative to a meeting sponsored by and under the aegis of the department. The public department should organize and steer the council because it is the primary agency concerned with total recreational efforts in the community. However, some groundwork must be prepared by the public recreational agency prior to the convening of a coordinating body. Preparation must be made through a sound educational campaign calling for and explaining the need of a council.

The council must be wanted by the community and its agencies. This means that all prospective participants should feel that a council is necessary to accomplish total community recreational service. To inaugurate a council unhurried methods, preceded by carefully determined support, are required. The chief purpose of the council is to speed action and eliminate gaps in recreational services. For this reason, the organization of the council should be suitable for the given community and of uncomplicated arrangement. The functions and responsibilities of the council must be precise, easily identified, and comprehensible to all. The lack of a clear and well-specified definition of functions and responsibilities has negative consequences of misunderstanding and poor relationships between members of the council and in minor council activities. The duties and efforts of the council should be developed in precouncil conferences with future participants.

Within the council organization there may be a smaller steering committee, necessary if the council membership is of such number so as to prove unwieldy in the determination and effect of business, and several permanent committees. These permanent committees are required to perform much of the groundwork of the council. Committees of this kind are responsible for long-term functions that tend to constitute some of the most important problems confronting the community. Among these standing committees of the council are public relations, physical plants and resources, financial, programming, personnel, and legal. It is customary for the chairman of the council to appoint committee members.

Good councils do not operate in a vacuum. Instead they seek to enlist the services of technical and professional persons to serve as resources from many fields of endeavor. Intelligent and competent professional assistance is required by and is essential to the smooth and efficient performance of the council. To ensure the proper functioning of a council, adequate time must be allocated for council work. The amount of time will vary in direct proportion to the extent of activities carried on and the individual and agency commitment made to the council. Attendance at council meetings is a prime requisite for council membership. At least one council meeting each week is prescribed for any transaction of effective business in the coordination of community activities.

Determination of an agenda for council meetings will usually be the responsibility of whatever executive officer the council decides upon. In the event that a steering committee is made the executive organ, responsibility will rest with it. However, exigencies and conditions will have a great deal to do with what the council discusses and resolves. Standing committees of the council will have no small role to play in the selection and evaluation of items that require the attention of the council. The calendar of business for the year and the agenda for each council session requires careful study and planning. The agenda for each of the regular council sessions should be planned at least one week prior to the business meeting and then distributed to all representative agencies for additional comments, suggestions, and additions. Such advance notice will ensure consideration of agenda items and allow all interested agencies and individuals to discuss intelligently the various actions to be taken.

If the council is established by virtue of municipal executive order, offices, supplies, and secretarial assistance may be provided by the city. If the council is initiated by the public recreational service department, the department must furnish the necessary space, facilities, and staff personnel. Because the council is advisory and is inaugurated as a clearing house and coordinating body, it needs no budget *per se*. Agency representatives are expected to be on salary and council participation becomes a regular part of their assigned functions. The specific functions for which the council is established is written out and serves as the constitution and by-laws of the body. When the council is activated by executive order, the order is codified and becomes the basis for all council action. Where the recreational service system implements the council as a coordinating mechanism in the community, specific duties and functions are developed by the membership sitting in session.

Neighborhood Advisory Councils

The recreational councils established within each neighborhood are usually organized by the public recreational service department. In some cases, interested neighborhood residents have generated enough enthusiasm to form their own councils which support the public program. In brief, the functions of the neighborhood recreational council can be defined as follows:

1. Representing neighborhood interests within the greater scope of city- and community-wide planning for recreational services.
2. Coordinating existing activities and determining the need for additional facilities and services.
3. Establishing and consolidating social relationships within the local

neighborhood. Putting people into contact with one another where such contact did not previously exist.
4. Making an inventory of neighborhood resources in terms of physical properties owned by city, school, quasi-public and private agencies. Compiling a list of the various recreational facilities which might be useful in contributing to the total neighborhood program.
5. Providing information about the public recreational agency to all people in the neighborhood in order to engender popular support for budgetary needs in making more adequate and better recreational services available to the neighborhood. Educating the public to understand the need for professional personnel and higher standards of competency.
6. Assisting the public department in planning recreational activities as well as requesting certain facilities or equipment for specific placement within the neighborhood.
7. Supporting referendum campaigns which are designed to develop capital building, land acquisition, and special equipment for the particular neighborhood.
8. Securing volunteers to supplement professional practitioners.
9. Advising the public department on the neighborhood customs, opinions, and population characteristics.
10. Sponsoring special events of an ethnic variety which can be included in city-wide recreational planning.
11. Sending a representative to sit on a district coordinating council in order to effect community or municipal decisions affecting the neighborhood or in order to influence community attitudes towards neighborhood needs.
12. Supplementing public funds with private donations for activities, equipment, or facilities to be utilized in the neighborhood.

Neighborhood advisory councils are one method by which social growth and development is planned for and facilitated. It is a sure procedure for the involvement of people in efforts that will enhance their own enjoyment and provide them with a feeling of being part of a significant undertaking. It offers a chance to participate in shaping the course of recreational activities within a neighborhood. It enlists the interest and support of citizens at the grassroots level and assists in their own education as to the value of public recreational services. The ultimate purposes of the neighborhood council are to promote community progress through neighborhood planning and cooperation; to serve as the medium by which local residents can articulate their recreational needs, interests and problems; and to provide the focal points from which coordination will emerge among any and all agencies having responsibility for recreational services.[1]

[1] Hjelte, George and Jay S. Shivers, *Public Administration of Park and Recreational Services* (New York: The Macmillan Company, 1963), p. 95.

The Neighborhood Recreational Council

Neighborhood recreational councils, especially in large metropolitan areas, are the recipients of much attention as a community coordination possibility. Such groups are particularly fit to assume responsibility for this approach. The typical activities of study, planning, enlistment of assistance, support, and awareness are right for this form of organization. This form of council is concerned with attempting to satisfy felt needs close to the lives of local residents. In the largest urban centers such councils are not only desirable, but absolutely required to facilitate total community planning of recreational services. There is no question that neighborhood councils will, should, or can ever replace centralized coordinating bodies, but it most assuredly renders such bodies more effective.

COORDINATION THROUGH OTHER EFFORTS

The range of agencies in the modern community having community-wide interests is so varied that duplication of work, waste of time, and uneconomic utilization of financial resources usually occur. All of these organizations are autonomous and tend to act independently of one another. For this reason a great deal of overlapping, parallelism, and omissions exist in offering community recreational service. Agencies that have similar interests and concerns do not necessarily have to be in conflict with one another. The avoidance of seeming infringement upon agency prerogatives and interference in functions can be increasingly achieved by coordinated effort and cooperative planning. Coordinated effort can be realized if agencies can agree on community objectives. Some of the effective procedures which are currently used in coordinating community agency activities are described in the following paragraphs.

Policy

A basic policy can be established which emphatically states that the agency has a fundamental responsibility for coordinated action with other socially oriented organizations within the community. Policy cannot merely be annunciated by an executive and left for enactment by subordinates. The policy of coordination must be made a part of every worker's position analysis. Each employee of the agency requires preservice orientation concerning pertinent philosophy and the guides to implement such philosophy. If the new worker is enjoined to act coordinately with other community agencies in order to achieve specific community-wide goals, the likelihood exists that coordination will become part of each worker's responsibility. Executive decision does not ensure that policies will be carried out. The executive's decision to effect coordinated effort with other agencies is only a starting point. From the time that the decision is made the concept of cooperative action must permeate the entire organization.

Every employee must be imbued with the idea that cooperation and mutual planning is vital to agency success. Coordination can be realized when employees at the functional level regard it as a primary obligation in carrying out the functions of the system. Until and unless employees at the lowest level of agency hierarchy comprehend the necessity for coordinated and cooperative effort, policy statements by executives mean little.

Informal Meetings

Widespread publicity concerning recreational planning in the community is very helpful in arranging meetings. Notices should be sent to every interested agency and private citizen. A request for attendance at a specified time, place, and date should accompany the notification. The location of the meeting should be as central as is possible. The luncheon becomes the simplest device for providing and exchanging information about recreational services within the community. It is a ready means by which coordinated plans may be drawn up and disseminated. By offering a program dedicated to cooperative action in an informal and highly social setting the possibility of success is enhanced.

Meetings are arranged through the staff of all agencies who wish to be represented as well as for those agencies who are confronted by problems of mutual concern. In order to facilitate such meetings it is wise to hold them on a routinely established basis, much like the luncheon meetings of social, civic, or fraternal associations. Instead of having a guest speaker or lecturer as the featured program, the coordinating meeting will always discuss recreational plans, schedules of activities, mutual problems, conflicts that arise, and any other situations that appear to be hindering coordinated effort. The meeting form of coordinated activity does not in itself secure coordination. As usual, whenever there are close relationships needed for the production of any service, personality factors play a significant part. Without the vital equation of interpersonal good will, most coordinating efforts will not be successful. Mutual feelings of cooperation and good official relations tend to grow out of informal social occasions, personal friendship, and continual joint planning. Any plan of cooperative enterprise that assists in bringing together the representatives of agencies on various levels for the careful study of responsibilities of mutual concern can be useful if it strengthens the bonds of good will between the representatives and provides for an exchange of factual information about what each representative is doing and can do in achieving the common goal.

Institutes, Workshops, and Conferences

A more formalized procedure for the institution of coordinated action is the periodically scheduled institute, workshop, or conference which may take place within a period of one to fourteen days. Depending upon the size of the community involved and the number of separate agencies concerned with recreational problems, the duration of any confrontation will be decided. These devices to effect coordination of recreational service agencies have been employed with very beneficial consequences. The easiest method is the frequent exchange of information through conference. Conferences may be organized among interested representatives of concerned agencies. The conference may be of one to three days in duration, although it is suggested that a shorter time period alloted may be of even more value if the conferences are arranged at closer intervals. The conference may even become a routine device wherein agencies host a meeting once each month. Institute and workshops, by their very nature, are scheduled less frequently, although they may also become a regular and routinely attended function. Institutes are intensive sessions in which a great many problems and possible solutions are discussed and analyzed over a stipulated period of time—usually not less than three days nor more than two weeks. Because of the length of the institute and the concepts to be scrutinized, a much more complicated and detailed preparation is necessary to ensure the success of the mission. In most instances, specialists are brought in, either from the community or from outside sources, and special lectures, publications, program resources, and pertinent data, which have been painstakingly collected, are offered for the enlightenment of the participants. From these sessions new involvement and a rededication to the precepts of coordinated effort are intended. The success or failure of an institute is reflected, not only in representative attendance, but in the outcomes which affect community coordination.

Workshops are intensive practical sessions lasting not more than three days, in which a series of planned demonstrations, specialists, and outstanding practitioners are called upon to dramatically show how things can be accomplished. In planning the workshop, the managers should select the areas and instructional methods that will effect the greatest contribution to the development of community-wide coordination. The topics offered and the techniques utilized in handling them should be designed to stimulate the largest number of participants toward wanting to do the best possible job in fulfilling their responsibilities as professional persons. The likelihood of laymen in the audience necessitates the provision of having subjects and techniques related to the level of experience and skill most apt to produce positive responses to calls for cooperative activities.

Contract

By mutual agreement or contractual obligation, two or more agencies may seek a solution of common problems. Good administrative practice requires validated normal methods for purposes of efficiency and effectiveness. Among the routine measures that can be initiated are those of a mutually agreed upon contract specifically detailing the exact nature of areas for coordinated action. Sometimes this results in a more restrictive type of enterprise, wherein only those activities stipulated will be acted upon and individuals who are poorly motivated may seek ways of restricting joint projects by adhering to the letter of the contract. However, the contractual form of coordinated undertaking is one avenue that may be employed to establish a working relationship with another agency. Such a contract can lead, eventually, to closer agreements and ultimately produce a permissive climate wherein harmonious working relationships are standardized. Wherever possible and by whatever proper method available and feasible, the end product of coordination is justified.

Employed Coordinator

Two or more agencies may jointly employ an individual to work at the supervisory level and perform only those duties that concerned coordination. The coordinator would be free of all managerial functions and be directly responsible to the executives of the jointly employing agencies. As an employee of several agencies, each paying a proportion of his salary, he would have access to all personnel records, employees, reports, facilities, equipment, program plans, and other operational factors to which most outsiders are denied. In this position the coordinator would in effect be an assistant executive for each agency and his authority would be granted in relationship to each situation. It would be his duty to keep several coordinate units under separate auspices in constant connection and in concurrence with each other. More particularly his immediate functions would comprise:

1. Interpretation of the role of each difference in the overall plan of community recreational service.
2. Interpretation of the philosophical orientation of each agency to all other agencies in terms of community recreational service.
3. Investigation of community recreational needs and problems that could be solved by coordinated action on the parts of several agencies.
4. Recommendation of cooperative endeavors by which each agency would complement another agency's efforts.
5. Arrangement of conferences, meetings, institutes, and workshops by which mutual problems, conflicts, and unfamiliarity can be ameliorated or otherwise alleviated.
6. Development of joint projects that would demand cooperative activity to ensure success.
7. Development of joint policies, rules, regulations, and procedures that would result in the presentation of a coordinated and comprehensive program of recreational services for the community.

The idea of employing a coordinator who would be free of executive functions recognizes that coordination deals with every facet of agency operation and is not limited to policy making. This form generally commends itself to large urban centers where complex and constant relations with a variety of agencies requires a person of high intelligence, tact, and ingenuity.

The Shared Executive

Two or more agencies may employ an administrator who serves, let us say, as a director or assistant executive of some phase of a school system, as the superintendent of recreational service in a municipal recreational department, and as director of the park department. In each agency the executive receives a one-third salary. He reports to the superintendent of schools in the school system, and to the mayor or other managing authority in the municipal system. This plan may commend itself in small communities or in sparsely populated rural regions where the employment of a high salaried executive might be beyond the economic means of a small community. However, when several agencies combine to hire one executive, each agency provides but a small proportion of an overall salary which is commensurate with the level of position and the responsibilities incumbent upon the employee.

Serious negative aspects are apparent when an executive is employed by two or more autonomous agencies. The complex and sensitive relationships accompanying the position are almost overwhelming in magnitude and it is unlikely that one person will be able to assume responsibility for two or more full-time jobs and give only half or one third of his time to each. It is expecting too much of one individual to be so expert and well rounded as a specialist that he will be able to administer two or three separate agencies, each calling for a specialist in the position, when he may be competent in one, or at best, two areas. The administrator might become so entangled in the intricacies of management and direction of more than one public system, that he could not fulfill his obligations to any. Not having the time to familiarize himself with all facets concerning the administration of any one agency he could not be prepared to handle the intimate details of operating procedures to effect coordination except in stating policy lines. As has been previously indicated [2] coordination by major policy commitments does not ensure actual cooperative and coordinated practice.[3]

Nevertheless, in communities where the shared administrator is employed by two different systems, e.g., school and recreational service, the employee is able to more closely integrate curriculum with the teaching of leisure arts and skills and the municipal department's offerings with educational subject matter. In effect, each aspect reinforces the other. With the two systems employing a shared executive, the same positive results might accrue in small communities through this form of coordination as could develop from the employment of a nonexecutive coordinator within a large metropolitan center. It is still *possible* that the coordinator *might* be able to perform effectively even though the responsibility may be doubled and therefore much more difficult of doing effectively.

[2] *Supra*, see page 319.
[3] Hjelte, George and Jay S. Shivers, *Public Administration of Park and Recreational Services* (New York: The Macmillan Company, 1963), p. 96.

Interlocking Board Membership

Where policy or advisory boards or councils are established for a variety of agencies having the recreational service function, an excellent means of overhead coordination can be had through the initiation of joint or interlocking memberships. In this plan, one or more individuals, adroitly selected on a basis of broad points of view and genuine interest, are asked to serve on several separate though related boards, e.g., the recreational service board, the park board, the school board, and the library board. Presuming that such an individual would have both the necessary time and the inclination, he would be in the best situation to observe and comment upon the needs of the various agencies in question, supply information about each agency, and be sympathetic to the problems and needs of each. In his capacity as board member, with voting rights, he would thus be in a strategic position to call attention to duplication of services, glaring examples of noncoordination, and poor or faulty relationships between personnel, as well as focus public scrutiny and professional study upon such conditions in an attempt to correct them.

Exchange of Board Members

Like the interlocking membership plan of coordination, the exchange plan attempts to understand agency difficulties through the method of inviting members of one board to be voting members of other boards, when such agencies governed or advised by these boards have a direct concern with the provision of recreational service in the community. Except in instances where board members are publicly elected to serve, any board by invitation and appointment may request that an individual already serving as a member of one agency's board participate in the functions of another agency's board. When membership is by public election, the invitee may still serve in an *ex officio* capacity. A member of the school board may be asked to serve on the recreational service advisory board, whereas a member of the recreational service board can be requested to serve on the school board. In each case, these board members would bring to the respective boards an understanding of the functions of the systems with which they are familiar and in turn would learn about the departments with which they have had less experience. In broadening the knowledge of such individuals it is expected that they would more clearly recognize problem areas that confront the agencies and seek to establish an atmosphere conducive to harmonious relationships and cooperative activities.

Coordination can exist only where there is a voluntary desire to cooperate. To be particularly effective, efforts to organize the community and its various agencies of recreational service must culminate in the building and maintenance of good will with all of the operating agencies and associations. Whatever means are utilized to cultivate coordination, it must be recognized that it is relatively easy to criticize, analyze, and recommend solutions. However, each agency, as an autonomous organization, must act in a manner consistent with its frame of reference and is ultimately responsible for its own posture. Working solutions may be derived through mediation, consolidation, and education, but in the final analysis, the decision of the agency to systematically effect coordination with other community-based groups is its own and must be respected.

SUMMARY

Recreational service is so broadly constituted that it can never be the sole province of only one agency operating within the community. The provision of recreational services is not exclusive to the public sector, but properly includes many institutions, systems, and programs representing every facet of community life. Essentially, recreational endeavors are freely chosen, not only by the individual participant, but by any agency which desires to offer recreational opportunities. This overriding democratic guide permits uncounted recreational operations by public, quasi-public, and private agencies to coexist and develop, each to the betterment of all the others. Free cooperation and coordination of all efforts to promote services of a recreational nature are more significant to the welfare of the community than are jurisdictional disputes concerning which agency shall have the exclusive right to perform. The closing of gaps and the displacement of voids in the provision of recreational service are more important, meaningful, and necessary than refraining from duplicating activities. Coordination is the best means of achieving a degree of community cooperation whereby harmonious relationships will occur. From this, well-organized efforts will accommodate diverse orientations so that recreational service may receive the latitude necessary to expand and flourish in an atmosphere of mutual trust and accord. Being the broadly promotional aspect of life that it is, recreational experience must be allowed to spread across all organizations and be available and accessible to all of the people from as many agencies as wish to offer possible avenues of service.

SELECTED REFERENCES

Bruyn, Severyn Ten H., Jr., *Communities in Action.* (New Haven, Conn.: College and University Press), 1964.

Buell, B., *Community Planning for Human Services.* (New York: Columbia University Press), 1952.

Coleman, James S., *Community Conflict.* (New York: The Free Press), 1965.

Davies, J. C., III, *Neighborhood Groups and Urban Renewal.* (New York: Columbia University Press), 1965.

Dunham, Arthur, *Community Welfare Organization.* (New York: The Macmillan Co.), 1958.

Harper, Ernest B., ed., *Community Organization in Action.* (New York: Association Press), 1959.

HUNTER, F., *et al.*, *Community Organization.* (Chapel Hill, N.C.: University of North Carolina Press), 1956.
MATTHEWS, MARK S., *Guide to Community Action.* (New York: Harper & Brothers), 1954.
MERKENS, GUIDO, *Organized for Action.* (St. Louis, Mo.: Concordia Publishing House), 1959.
MCMILLEN, WAYNE, *Community Organization for Social Welfare.* (Chicago: University of Chicago Press), 1945.
National Council of Social Service, *A Handbook on Administration for Community Associations.* (London: National Federation of Community Associations), 1959.
PUNKE, HAROLD H., *Community Uses of Public School Facilities.* (New York: King's Crown Press), 1951.
RUSSETT, B. M., *Community and Contention.* (Cambridge, Mass.: Massachusetts Institute of Technology Press), 1963.
SWIFT, HENRY and ELIZABETH SWIFT, *Community Groups and You.* (New York: John Day Co.), 1964.

Chapter 13

SUPERVISION

> PRINCIPLE: The process of supervision is one of reciprocity between those receiving supervision and those providing it. It permeates all levels of the agency hierarchy and must be concerned with the development of professional and personal competencies as well as with the interpretation of policy through expert technical guidance.

Supervision is concerned with effecting the optimum recreational service possible through the enhancement of recreationist competence, primarily by reinforcing professional development, and by promoting scientific methods of analyzing functions for improved working procedures. Supervision in any field of endeavor is an attempt to improve worker competencies so that ultimately the most effective good or service will be provided. In the field of recreational service this is no less true. The final result of supervision should be the production of all of those conditions that make the rendering of recreational services most effective. Many of the problems which affect human behavior and environmental situations, and which interfere with a high rate of capacity for the accomplishment of all recreational services involve supervision.

FOUNDATIONS FOR SUPERVISION

Chiefly, three facets or governing controls must be established in an effort to make supervision the rewarding and productive process it can be in human relations. Effective supervision should be guided by a democratically oriented viewpoint, scientifically produced facts, and the logical procedures of philosophy.

Democratic Theory

The hallmark of democracy rests in equality or respect for individuality while reserving consideration for majority rule. Diverse opinion is not merely tolerated but welcomed, for in the rule of many, each person has the right and privilege to present his views and may justifiably expect them to receive some attention and, perhaps, use. It is a fundamental objective of democracy to provide optimum freedom to the individual in order that he may capitalize upon whatever potential he has, insofar as such development does not infringe upon the rights of others. Democracy holds as basic a factually educated public, honestly informed, and able to distinguish between ethical practices and immoral or criminal behavior.

Democracy means more than specific political forms; basically it is the enjoyment of liberty without license. The ideal of democracy carries with it equal rights for self-development with limitations imposed by self-discipline. Thus, individual responsibility is balanced by individual expression and by a concern for the humanity of each person. As Franseth states:

> Democracy involves not only a respect for others but also active participation with others in striving to make the world a better place for everyone. The democratic ideal can be realized only by the translation of democratic attitudes and beliefs into action. This requires intelligence and responsibility, faith and persistence.[1]

Democracy, wherever it is practiced, is participation in the dynamic interchange of groups in society by free men having maximum scope for action.

Democracy versus Anarchy. Democracy by no means implies a lack of authority or no restraint upon individuals in society. Democracy is, in fact, the antithesis of anarchy or lawless rule where everybody is free to do as he pleases regardless of the outcomes and in spite of any infringements upon others. There is, indeed, a residual authority that is to be found in expertness, fact, and equal dispensation of justice under the law. Democratic principles exist where power is derived from those who are to be governed as opposed to external authority which imposes obedience without regard for those who will be governed. A basic factor of democracy is equality. Explicit in this statement is the concept of guaranteed rights for equal opportunity. No person should receive any more consideration than any other in questions of political determination. One man, one vote, is the democratic ideal. However, in a democracy, authority is contained in moral principles generally composed and codified into what are called laws. The law applies to all, and each individual is given the same consideration. Thus, authority comes from the law rather than from personal power. It should not be imagined that there is anything supernatural about the source of law. Social idealism usually stems from social agreement through traditional practice. Over a long period of human history, certain social contracts have been found to be equitable and these have come to be the foundations and guiding rules of social conduct. The law is the embodiment of these principles and is derived from these concepts. When the supervisory process is ideally constituted, it is democratic. But this cannot mean a lack of disagreement, diversity, or discussion.

---

[1] Jane Franseth, *Supervision As Leadership* (New York: Harper & Row, Peterson and Company, 1961), p. 11.

Democracy and Leadership. Democracy is not equated with conformity. Although democracy is based upon majority rule, it still takes into account minority opinion. When the majority tyrannizes the minority, the minority has the right to seek redress and equity. There is guaranteed the equal right to be different, not so extreme that anarchy prevails and infringement of personal security is brought about, but to the extent that individuality is encouraged and the right to hold a different opinion is sustained. If the minority opinion is logical, ethical, and presented properly, it may become the majority opinion. Each person shares in the political consideration of social determination and all views are welcome; although all views are not necessarily put into practice.

Democratic application of supervision does not abrogate the authority of the legally empowered individual. When the supervisor creates a climate wherein democratic principles have conditioned the recipients of supervision, then the probability of leadership attempts on the part of group members is much more likely. Leadership contributions require complete identification with whatever matters are presented to the group (agency) for solution. In such an environment, the exercise of leadership, instead of the imposition of authority by virtue of position, augurs well for the full involvement and cooperation of the staff. Staff members will then attack problems with the same cooperative attitude and without the prodding that accompanies the typical use of supervisory authority. Barr and others state:

> A group so led thoroughly understands the demands of the situation and the action to be taken. All have been heard, all have had opportunity to present views, all have entered their objections, if any. Discussion has been free; minorities have been heard; conflicting views have been heard; and differences have been ironed out. The decision then reached by majority vote represents unity, freely achieved. It is the best thought of the group up to that moment. Discussion can be reopened by anyone as obstacles are met or new data appear. The policy and its implementation have been determined in such a way that every participant had a chance to help form them.[2]

Supervision performed as an exercise in leadership will do more to further the aims of recreational service than any dependence upon control through headship. Nevertheless, it is well to realize that there are those within some departments who are incapable of responding to democratic procedures. Such inability raises the greatest question as to the validity of the democratic process in supervision. In order to gain the cooperation that is so vital to the successful fulfillment of recreational service objectives, every consideration must be given to those individuals who display obtuseness in the face of democratically applied supervision. Just as guidance and

---

[2] A. S. Barr, William H. Burton, and Leo J. Brueckner, *Supervision*, 2nd ed. (New York: Appleton-Century-Crofts, Inc., 1947), p. 53.

counseling are extended to those who participate responsively, they must also be provided to the inert as well. When opportunities for professional growth and development have been fairly given and those who are sluggish, resistant to better methods, or who actively attempt to subvert the program are clearly recognized and labeled, then the only recourse left is the imposition of legal authority for the dismissal of these persons. Because this procedure is directed toward personnel who are supposed to be professional, it is unlikely and only in extreme instances when authoritarian measures will have to be imposed in place of leadership. To the degree that personnel are professionals, the exercise of leadership will rest with the supervisor; however, the responsibility for sharing in the decision-making function and the dynamics of leadership will be a part of every staff member's obligation.

> Group decision-making has the added asset of allowing the members of the group to identify themselves more completely with the leader and the plan because each is able to feel that he has had an important part in developing and contributing to the over-all program. Membership loyalty to the leader is intensified because every person will get his chance to have his say in the advance of group welfare and direction.[3]

Democracy and Specialization. Democratic supervision does not consist of endless group discussion offering opinions which may or may not be supported by fact. Just as democratic procedures should not be confused with anarchy, neither can they be misinterpreted to preclude expertness and specialization. In a democratic setting each person has the right to be heard, but he does not have the right to impose prejudicial hearsay or other non-supported opinion upon the group in total disregard for available tested evidence. The right to question whatever evidence is presented, to investigate the ways and directions by which the facts were ascertained, to recommend additional testing and evaluation, is inalienable in a democracy. To fly in the face of reality so that preconceived attitudes can be promulgated is a waste of time and is a manifestation of immaturity. The person who has been granted the prerogative for offering his ideas to the group, also has the mandatory responsibility for recognizing competent information, for understanding the rules of intelligible acuity, and for acting coordinately within these limits.

Democratic discourse in which every member may take part has a role for the specialist. This is particularly true regarding esoteric or highly technical phases of recreational service. Utilization of experts within democratic environments is not contradictory. Authority in the form of expertise is implied, but is not necessarily imposed upon the group. The specialist participates within group discussion with the same rights and privileges

---

[3] Jay S. Shivers, *Leadership in Recreational Service* (New York: The Macmillan Company, 1963), p. 81.

as any other participant. He is not treated as a revered entity nor given any specific distinction that would place him on a superior level to his colleagues. Any suggestion or recommendation that the specialist makes is not accepted as *the* final word until it is critically evaluated by the group. The expert's participation comes in the form of clarifying technical considerations so that abstruseness is reduced and general enlightenment follows. Conclusions reached by the expert on experimental grounds should be carefully explained so that all can appreciate the factors which tend to sustain them. Any contribution which the specialist makes to the group is not imposed by legal authority, but will be studied by the group through logical discussion and applied f additional experimental conditions support the recommended procedures.

Leadership is not unique to certain individuals, but occurs in many people at different times evoked by particular conditions. Because leadership is discerned at every level in the organization and because the staff is essentially composed of professional personnel, democratically contrived supervision seems to be the most valid and valuable process.

Science and Supervision

Science is factual knowledge accumulated by empirical methods and proved reliable through objective testing. The aim of science is to substitute fiction and fancy with unqualified truth. But science is more than a mere collection of immutable fact. Each verifiable observation and authenticated fact of science is related by theoretical concepts or general principles. Isolated truths are the specific items of general principles, and an understanding of basic laws explains a great many specifics. The goal of science is to replace the lack of relational entries and the plurality of things with correlation and oneness. Therefore, scientific knowledge consists not only of accumulated fact, but also ". . . in becoming familiar with the interpretive schemes and conceptual systems through which perceptual experience may be meaningfully organized." [4]

Beyond and with the ideas of fact and connected particulars goes the third significant feature of a scientific nature, i.e., the scientific method. Science as a method supplies a precise tabulation of existing phenomena and of what may result when working with computable and regulated cases. The usual scientific methods are controlled experimentation, laboratory examination, a variety of survey practices, analysis and authentication of archives, as well as statistical techniques. The scientific approach to supervision offers greater accuracy, less bias, more control over variable factors, greater adequacy of data, reliability, stability, validity, and a more methodical arrangement of procedures.

Ideally, scientific supervision means obtaining a precise and comprehensive understanding of current practices in recreational service. Then

[4] Philip H. Phenix, *Philosophy of Education* (New York: Holt, Rinehart and Winston, 1958), p. 326.

all scientific knowledge concerning human relations and behavior patterns is applied to improve conditions. Science focuses attention on the locus of the search for truth. Supervision, using scientific methods, is better able to set goals, determine current needs, analyze resources, and do away with uncontrolled and prejudicial attitudes. Scientific supervision means deference for whatever facts are present and correct application of the facts. It means ability to accept new facts after their derivation and validity have been authenticated. It explicitly rejects confused and unsystematic opinion and relies upon logical, stable, and skilled research.

Philosophy and Supervision

The philosophic process as applied to supervision is chiefly concerned with values and the justification for actions taken. This method is a way of appraising knowledge which is already at hand. It relates to the arrangement, rationale, explanation, and estimation of that which has been observed, experienced, and known. The factor that characterizes philosophy from all other realms of knowledge is not its specialized subject matter but the procedure and objectives which it seeks. Philosophical inquiry has as its aim the fundamental meaning and basic assumptions on which knowledge rests.

The philosophic method of extending and improving problem-solving processes proceeds quite differently from the scientific method. The objectives of the philosophic method are not limited to a single set of items and variables which are inherent in any behavioral problem and which can be readily controlled for experimental purposes, but instead include all factors and every conceivable variable which is either directly pertinent or in some tenuous way connected to the problem. The complete incidence of circumstances considered to have bearing upon any problem under philosophical study is not merely quantitative. Therefore, the philosophical method is truly characterized by an effort to integrate or compile this information in accordance with some classification of unity or agreement. As Barr and others have stated, "The method involves reflective thought upon quantitative data in their qualitative aspect (the meaning of facts), and upon qualitative data, the ideals and aspirations, the values and ends thought to make up the good life." [5]

Supervision should concern itself with the substance, the insular objectives, the appreciations of the great social structure within which recreational service operates. The community, as well as society as a whole, its means and properties, its conflicts and challenges, its goals, its social conditions, will be examined as the milieu of current recreational problems and line of conduct. Consequences will be compared in relation to what is valuable both to the immediate community and to the larger society within which all communities exist.

[5] Barr, *et al., op. cit.,* pp. 57–58.

Supervision and Creativity

Supervision is increasingly dependent upon and utilizes the concepts of democratic ideology, scientific application and methodology, and secures its logical form from the discipline of philosophic procedures. It is an inseparable combination of all three views and, as such, is as good as the contribution of these intellectual sources can make it. Supervision that is oriented to the democratic view focuses attention upon individual worth, dignity, and provides a sane basis for control through democratic processes. Science provides accuracy, impartiality, and a method for defining facts. Philosophy offers a world view of ideas and particularly the net worth or value system that underlies concepts and goals. Taken together, the three methods can produce a climate of intellectual perception and sensitivity which emphasizes logic, precision, problem-solving, individuality, and social outcomes.

There is little question then that within such a climate new ideas for attacking problems that beset society will flourish. This is creativity at its best. Any environment that permits free discussion and participation without fear of reprimand or retaliation, that considers all contributions with equal deference regardless of simplicity or expression, will necessarily call forth creative demonstrations from nearly all of the participants, perhaps from each person functioning as part of the group. Supervision is directly concerned with stimulating an atmosphere most conducive to creative expression and additionally will search out whatever hidden talent or skill reposes in the individual by offering ample opportunity for individual participation in a climate of mutual trust and confidence. However, creative representations are produced hesitantly. Real leadership must be apparent and consistently a part of the relations between supervisor and supervised. The calculated exercise of the situation to provide opportunities for contributions of a creative nature is possible only when intelligence and ingenuity are combined. Leadership and the creativity that it can elicit are absolutely necessary for the achievement of democratic principles and creative group life.

SUPERVISION IS LEADERSHIP

Broadly constituted leadership is influence with other people so that certain common ends, of value to those who participate in the dynamics of group life, are achieved. Leadership, to be effective, must have as its base the wide support of group members. Such support is established most completely where all members of the group take part in the decision-making process concerning the group.

Supervision is generally seen as a specialized body of knowledge utilizing leadership techniques which supports a persistent inclusion of all recreational service personnel in a cooperative endeavor to produce the most effective recreational service program. Creative supervision permits the infusion of new ideas and new concepts for the benefit of those who will potentially participate within the program. It mitigates hackneyed activities and allows the development of experiences that are highly imaginative, compelling, and attractive. Good supervision is not a process of telling workers what to do and then investigating in order to determine whether or not they have completed assignments. Ordering individuals to perform in certain ways and demanding strict obedience to mechanical rules and regulations discourages latent talents and encourages passivity, conformity, and mediocrity. A slavish devotion to rules and bureaucratic machinery usually produces ludicrous and sometimes rather inane results. It does not permit recreationists and other personnel to use their intelligence toward creative action but is content with routine behavior. Apropos of this form of "thinking-by-the-regulations" is the following newspaper account of the consequences of a park department employee in New York City who did some independent and valuable activity.

PRAISE BRINGS REPRIMAND *

NEW YORK (AP)—A citizen's letter of praise has been the undoing of a city parks employe who grew corn, carrots and flowers in a playground to teach children how things grow.

Plow it under, said the Parks Department, regretting that no one got permission first for the tiny garden.

The bureaucratic wheels began to turn when Mortimer Todel, who lives across from a playground in the Bronx, wrote to the Parks department: "I want to commend one of your attendants for the initiative he has shown in planting vegetables and flowers in a small portion of the park, because of the reaction of my daughter and other children, which has been excellent."

The attendant is Paul Goluboff, 47, a gardener for the Parks Department for eight years. His playground on Hudson Manor Terrace won a citation for its appearance two years ago.

Samuel M. White, the department's director of maintenance and operations, answered Todel's letter, saying he would pass the comments on to Goluboff.

He sent copies of this letter to Goluboff and Goluboff's foreman. At the end of all three copies there was this note to the foreman: "The motivation, while well intentioned, is contrary to department policy. Remove the garden prior to 8-18-64."

Goluboff and his foreman, Joseph F. Forshay, 60, have been ordered to a hearing and face possible disciplinary action for violating regulations.

Forshay said Goluboff had been authorized to grow ivy, but it wouldn't grow, so he planted vegetables and flowers. But Forshay failed to notify the head office.

"This," he said, "was a mistake."

* *The Hartford Times,* Vol. **CXXIV**, No. 223; Friday, September 18, 1964, p. 1.

PARK GARDEN GETS REPRIEVE *

    Paul Goluboff's corn, carrot and flower garden can stay—at least until the crops are in—the Parks Department decided today.
    Goluboff, a department gardener, cultivated his small plot in a city park at Hudson Manor Terrace in the Bronx to teach children how things grow.
    Goluboff's boss, Joseph F. Forshay, general foreman of District 3, thought it was a fine idea but failed to get permission from higher up.
    But the higher-ups found out about it when a parent wrote to Parks Commissioner Newbold Morris praising Goluboff and describing the garden's benefits to neighborhood children.
    Samuel M. White, Parks Department director of maintenance and operation, replied to the letter in Morris' absence and at the same time ordered the garden plowed under because it was in violation of "departmental policy."
    Public reaction to a published report of White's order was immediate.
    "The telephone calls we got! Some people called from as far as Boston," White said. "So we'll let him keep it (the garden) until the end of the growing period."

This incident was widely reported on wire service releases throughout the United States and was picked up on television and radio. It was not until the mass media played up the situation and held the department of parks up to ridicule for its nonsensical decision, that the department relented. It must be obvious to all, that better supervision and a more flexible concept of the nature of parks as a recreational facility would have precluded any such display of heavy-handed supervisory-employee dealings.

Greater recognition of the significance of the human element in administration has emphasized the need for leadership in aiding the efforts and coordinating the functions of staff personnel. With leadership as the criterion of supervision, all personnel involved in the production of recreational services will be encouraged to perform willingly and inventively, have a sense of satisfaction from it, and feel confident of having accomplished something valuable from this participation. Trust, enthusiasm, and a spirit of cooperation are achieved through leadership. Individual differences are noted and utilized, group effort is enhanced, and the development of individual staff members is promoted. The most fitting means to utilize will vary with specific conditions, but, in general, effective supervisory techniques include educating all staff personnel by keeping them well informed about all aspects of the department, supplying factual answers to all questions that arise during the course of operations, offering technical advice where needed and requested, and providing a climate of mutual confidence so that employees will seek out supervisory assistance for resolving problems or overcoming areas of weakness. Where supervisory

* New York *World-Telegram and Sun,* Friday, September 18, 1964.

emphasis is geared to the needs of staff personnel rather than to the program as such, most of the supervisor's efforts are turned to the practice of effective leadership.

Balance for Effective Performance

There is a distinctive pattern of supervisory leadership in departmental organizations which applies universally. It involves a variety of behaviors that include basic administrative method on the one hand and knowledgeable dealings with the dynamics of human needs on the other. Unfortunately, archaic thinking has produced supervisory personnel who when skilled in orthodox managerial practices were completely at a loss in handling or even recognizing the human element. Therefore, that form of supervisory leadership in which agencies should be patterned must include equilibrium between technical processes and human factors.

Supervision must embrace people and things for this is the nature of the work. It is sometimes assumed that these two factors may be treated separately, but this is not valid. There is a pressing need for people who have both technical competence and an understanding of the needs of individuals and the eccentricities of human behavior. It is desirable, from the outset, to reject the idea that all conflicts between employees and employers can be dispelled by a sentimental approach, that all a supervisor need do is display a smile, exude the milk of human kindness, and overlook technical shortcomings. Supervisory problems can never be processed in such a manner. Supervisory leadership, which relies upon objectivity as well as cooperative understanding when dealing with the human factor, is required.

The democratic approach to supervision necessitates an "other-directed," view of performance. It is employee-centered and humanistically oriented. By this is meant that supervision strives to enhance ego involvement among the workers and provides them with a working environment that brings satisfaction through achievement. Democratic leadership constantly works for a pattern of human relations which tends to elevate the worker while it de-emphasizes the traditional concepts of supervision. The old edict of "I-am-the-boss" as a *sine qua non* of supervision is slowly being replaced with a leadership system at the program level which embraces group communication, free contribution, discussion, participation, worker consultation, and ego satisfaction for all rather than a select few.

Good supervisors recognize that the supervisory process will succeed and be most forceful when it is not coercive. When leadership is dispersed as widely as is possible within the group, then unity of purpose and attainment of program objectives will be forthcoming. The extent to which all departmental members share in the decision-making process and leadership responsibilities usually determines the rate of progress that can be made toward any stated objective. Supervision based upon worker needs in any particular situation becomes supportive through technical proficiency and derives authority from the skillful handling of the situation. Any reliance upon position to effect conformity can only bring about mediocrity, passivity, and resentment. "The authority of the supervisor's position has not decreased, but it is used in another way. It is used to promote growth through responsibility and creativity rather than through dependency and conformity." [6]

Good supervision concentrates upon and utilizes individual differences to strengthen the program. Personal skills must be incorporated for best application to benefit the operation of the entire program. The differences of opinion developed as a result of background, experience, or education should provide a setting for a more comprehensive range of services to people. In making the most effective use of personal talent, intelligence, and skill, the best expression for each unique personality will find outlet. Initiative, responsibility, and self-confidence will be stimulated through the provision of full opportunity to explore a wide variety of program activities and to contribute by cooperative endeavors in the formulation of plans and policies for the continued success of the agency. Supervision must be based upon the supposition that recreationists are professional people and are therefore capable of consistent growth on the job. Acceptance of people as they are, objectively and without prejudice, is a fundamental characteristic of supervision. All traits of human personality, whether antagonistic or cooperative, are treated with the same concern for consequences to the program. Antagonistic traits require additional effort in order to align them with productive activities which will be reflected in a better series of services to agency constituents, whereas cooperative traits are the sinews of credit by which the smooth functioning of the agency is enabled to be facilitated. In either case, supervision will replace headship with leadership. Through leadership, any necessary authority will be derived from current events and the facts of evidence which the situation brings to light. Personal authority is appreciated and developed as an outcome of expertness. The scope of technical knowledge and the weight of wide experience will lend credence, respect, and support to the supervisor and promote his authority among his professional peers.

Ultimately, supervision is employed to effect a continuing schedule of appealing and enjoyable recreational activities by which the lives of participants may be enhanced. This essential purpose of supervision is contingent upon the formulation of a voluntary fusion of all staff personnel within the agency who are dedicated to the premise of service to people through planned recreational experiences. The process by which this aim will be reached is through the provision of leadership in a democratic climate, thus securing logical sequence and reliability in fitting the program

---

[6] Kimball Wiles, *Supervision for Better Schools: The Role of the Official Leader in Program Development,* 2d ed. (Englewood Cliffs, N.J.: Prentice-Hall, Inc., 1955), p. 9.

to the changing needs of people in a dynamic society. Of immediate importance is the development of a favorable climate for professional growth and increased skill among staff personnel so that agency operation can offer more varied and comprehensive activities, more expertly organized, and cooperatively planned which will be sufficient to satisfy new and constant demands of an enlightened public.

Leadership involves discovery. When supervisors want to encourage leadership they must create a setting designed to facilitate freedom to work out solutions to unfamiliar problems while establishing security in the friendly environment of the familiar. Mistakes which will occur as a consequence of attempted creative effort should not be scorned. Such errors of procedure and participation are indicative of a change in relations between the program practitioners and supervisory personnel. Permissiveness and the willingness to assume the risk of error as a form of learning may, in the long run, turn up new methods, new applications, and a greater sense of achievement and security with concomitant program successes.

Organizational Factors. Although it has been stated that supervision is a function of all personnel throughout the agency, a distinction between supervisors and other personnel who exercise supervision must be drawn. The term *supervisor* explicitly means an individual whose chief and major responsibility lies in the provision of leadership in supervisory functions. Other supervisory personnel may be any staff person whose major responsibility falls within an administrative or special service category, but who may devote a minor portion of their time to leadership activities of a supervisory nature. Typically, the program director is a supervisor as is the coordinator of activities or special events. Usually, recreational service departments reserve the title of supervisor to general, district, facility, or special activities personnel. Thus, the general supervisor has responsibility for supervising all line personnel; the district supervisor has responsibility for supervising all line personnel within a specific district of a local legal subdivision; the facility supervisor is responsible for all personnel operating certain types of facilities, i.e., centers, playgrounds, swimming pools, and so on, within an agency; and the supervisor of special activities may be responsible for coordinating special events, activities, and specialist personnel on an agency-wide basis.

The supervisor can be characterized by the following factors concerning his responsibilities and personnel relationships:

1. The supervisor is not made responsible for the operation of single units of the agency, e.g., a recreational center or a playground.
2. The supervisor is responsible for a group, class, or all units and their operational personnel throughout the entire agency.
3. The supervisor has primary responsibility within one or more assigned areas having general impact upon personnel competencies and limited or subordinated responsibility in other agency functions.

Although nearly every recreationist within the agency has some supervisory functions, only those personnel whose major responsibility is devoted to supervision of personnel, *per se,* can be characterized as supervisors. Supervision which occupies large and protracted segments of time and effort cannot be delegated to any person who has responsibilities for functions in other than supervisory areas. Those who are charged with general administration simply do not have the time to spend on prolonged leadership activities that demand large allotments of time and energy. They must rely, instead, upon those specialists who have undertaken the supervisory function as a major assignment.

SUPERVISORY FUNCTIONS

Agency supervision can be distinguished by the following responsibilities that are geared to the continuing development of agency personnel and the outcomes which technical proficiency can bring to the program.

1. Staff selection. Recruiting, selection, and assignment of personnel to suitable activities in the organization. Included within this function are screening, testing, orientation, and the maintenance of personnel records.
2. In-service education. Performing all of those necessary activities designed to promote the professional development of line personnel to make them more efficient and effective.
3. Program development. Planning, specifying, and assisting in the design of appropriate activities and events which are to be provided by personnel of the department. Helping to establish program standards and personnel expectations in the achievement of program objectives. Assisting in the development of policies that can best facilitate face-to-face program leadership. Organizing schedules in order to equalize worker load and plan for the continual flow of work, materials, facilities, and spaces required for optimum service to client participants.

Special competencies are necessary if the supervisor is to perform his functions expertly. All supervisory personnel need particular competencies if they are to contribute anything of value to the supervisory process. Competence is nothing more than the ability to apply knowledge and skill in order to effect a specific outcome. Definite factors of supervision will necessitate distinctive skills. For example, working with individual recreationists who require assistance with ambivalent feelings as they influence client participation needs a supervisor especially competent in using clinical procedures and practices.

The personal problems of employees, as well as overt job maladjustments, fall under the immediate purview of line supervisors. Resolution of such discord is the direct responsibility of the line supervisor. The supervisor may serve as a supportive person who can give guidance where and when needed so that the worker will be able to recognize weaknesses or obstacles and modify his behavior to overcome them. The supervisor can best perform his counseling function when his subordinates feel that he is readily accessible and sincerely interested in them as individuals. The supervisor should be sensitive enough to his subordinates' feelings so that he can develop a situation which will enable them to discuss their problems without their feeling that someone is prying into their personal affairs. The supervisor should be capable of giving all such problems, whether trivial or complicated, the careful consideration, sympathetic understanding, and attention necessary to alleviate the condition.

If the statement that all people constitute some problem for somebody with whom they work is considered as a starting point, the concept of therapeutic supervisory activities will be better understood. This discussion is not concerned with psychotic individuals, but the typical behaviors manifested by a few, some, or many workers at different times in a variety of work situations. It can factually be stated that many persons doing outstanding and even consummate work, not excluding supervisory personnel, may be the most irritating persons and may be doing the most damage to subordinates and colleagues alike. Almost 79 per cent of position losses, as a result of discharge, are on personality-conflict rather than competency bases. This is not only unfortunate to the individual who loses the job, but to the agency that loses a highly competent, though hard-to-get-along-with personality. In either case it is a consequent loss to society.

Problem workers with a variety of personality weaknesses can be found in nearly every agency. Hopefully, the following catalogue of behavioral patterns will diminish in proportion to the degree of professionalization the worker has attained: Those who have a chip on their shoulder, individuals constantly on the lookout for something at which to express anger; those who declare that they are being "used" or misused if called upon to take responsibility for an assignment that is not absolutely specified in the authorized position analysis; those who "move checkers" [7] instead of attending to the responsibilities of their position; those who are so insecure that they must spend inordinate amounts of time winning friends or making themselves inconspicuous so that no fault will ever be found with them, instead of doing what can reasonably be expected in terms of job functions; those who are misanthropic, pessimistic, or cynical; those who are too thin-skinned for any pressure generated on the job; those who exaggerate fact and distort the truth; and those who are simply unreliable.

> Many will recall having worked with or supervised those of belligerent disposition who resist any kind of supervision. . . . One also finds among those who work a random sampling of prima donnas, practical jokers, alcoholics, misguided do-gooders and joiners, and wearers of halos.[8]

---

[7] Jay S. Shivers, *Leadership in Recreational Service* (New York: The Macmillan Company, 1963), pp. 303–304.

[8] John M. Pfiffner, *The Supervision of Personnel Human Relations in the Management of Men* (Englewood Cliffs, N.J.: Prentice-Hall, Inc., 1951), pp. 315–316.

Supervisory leadership manifests itself in the following terms: (1) the supervisor as a director of personnel performing a management function particular to his level within the agency hierarchy; and (2) the supervisor being well versed in human relations. In the first instance he understands when to delegate authority while retaining responsibility. He can do this because of his knowledge of the competencies required to effect good program control as well as the quality of performance necessary to further the aims of the recreational service agency. He knows what should be produced by each worker. He has certain expectations for all positions for which he is responsible and this knowledge makes him completely aware of what is being done without the constant need of having to intervene in the details of work assigned to those whom he supervises. He maintains a consistent work load and arranges for any requisite materials. He is program-conscious and economy-minded without being compulsive to the point where it defeats his purposes. He is capable of coordinating his work with those of the technical staff, if the department is large enough to employ such personnel, as well as encouraging maximum participation among line personnel.

Secondly supervisory leadership revolves around the seemingly paradoxical concepts of subjectivity and objectivity in handling people. On one hand, the supervisor must be sympathetic to the divergent patterns of individual behavior, technique, and personality and still maintain an objective and decisive view of personnel. Human nature being what it is, there will always be those who attempt to take advantage of any situation (even professional practitioners) and do as little as possible for their pay. The supervisor will encounter professional persons who indulge in such hypocritical activities as lying, cheating, stealing, malingering, or subverting and circumventing agency policies and practices. The supervisor must do everything within his power to assist and guide individuals who fall into negative categories to become rehabilitated to their job obligations and opportunities or, unable to react and help them, he must have the firmness and finesse to terminate their association with the agency with the least possible distress to morale or abrasiveness to the harmony between the agency and the working force.

If personal ambitions of individuals are antagonistic to the agency's desired goals, the successful supervisor will adroitly take the necessary action to alleviate the situation. To the casual observer, the personnel action may seem abrupt or even harsh; but the supervisor views it as an unbiased decision which will facilitate organizational accomplishment of stated aims. The supervisor may have to take certain personnel actions which may prove personally distasteful to him, but he must have integrity of purpose and the requisite firmness to recommend dismissal, reprimand, or other suitable disciplinary measures when he is certain that the welfare of the people whom the agency serves demands it. Thus, management patterns present an enigma of sorts. One aspect adheres to agency needs and the coordination of many people in achieving specific goals. The other view is that of human relations wherein individual worker satisfaction orients personnel policy. Obviously, the successful supervisor must be able to steer a median course between the extremes of absolute conformity to rules and regulations and a maudlin approach to worker needs which almost always promotes some kind of corruption among those who are willing to use oversentimentality as a weapon for their own purposes.

SUPERVISORY TECHNIQUES

The precise methods that any supervisor uses as he assumes the obligations of his position will depend, to a great extent, upon how he perceives supervision. How he performs will be determined by the past experiences, knowledge, and special skills which he brings to the job. Particular techniques will be effected by his view of other people, his understanding of human nature, his basic ideas about human behavior, and his comprehension relating to the function of the recreational service agency in the contemporary world.

Disseminating Information

The effective supervisor transmits factual information throughout the agency in an effort to provide needed knowledge to all personnel, thus facilitating problem solving. When requested, he may provide information by lecture, discussion, demonstration, or workshops. He may further supply informational needs through conversation, library resources, audio-visual aides, pamphlets, posters, bulletin boards, resource persons, exhibits, individual and group conferences. Communication is vital to the efficiency of agency operation. Problems in human relations and in subsequent actions as a result of faulty communications can almost always be laid to hindrances in the process of information dissemination.

All employees want information about their orgnization, and the continued flow of factual information will promote a sense of loyalty to the agency as well as developing morale, cohesion, and security. Nothing reduces stress or anxiety so much as does true information.[9] Complete knowledge concerning the function of the agency and the contribution which each person, in every section of the agency, can make to the overall effective operation of the departmental program cannot but help to produce a climate wherein cooperation and intelligent planning will flourish.

Individual Conference

An individual conference may initiate with a supervisory request or suggestion, or it may come from any program worker. In any instance, such a meeting will be most effective when both of the conferees decide on the time, place, and agenda. The probability exists that all professional per-

---

[9] Alexander R. Heron, *Sharing Information with Employees* (Stanford University, Calif.: Stanford University Press, 1942), pp. 30–36.

sonnel want to perform their functions with the greatest skill they can command. For this reason they will appreciate supervisory conferences which will offer assistance in achieving technical proficiency.

Any individual confrontation between supervisor and subordinate may have a threatening aspect to the worker. To offset any latent hostility or deterioration of worker self-confidence, the conference must be calculated to produce an encouraging and helpful atmosphere. Simple criticism is not helpful. A careful marshalling of facts complimenting any suggestions or opinions which the supervisor may have will be more readily accepted and utilized. Mere command will not persuade the recreationist to alter his methods. As one professional to another, the supervisor must present sound evidence to support any position he takes in appraising employee techniques. Regardless of the topic under discussion, the individual conference will prove successful only to the degree which the worker accepts or rejects positive advice. In the final analysis, modification of techniques and/or behavior on the job will be accomplished if the worker sincerely feels that he *should* change. Individual interviews initiated by either the supervisor or the program worker are important for discussion of problems and handling exigency situations as they arise. Person-to-person interviews occur as the need for them exists. There are times when the program worker must speak to the supervisor immediately and cannot wait to see the latter in the field. From the supervisor's point of view, the individual conference always has a distinct purpose. He requests interviews because there is a definite plan of action that he wishes to get across or wants the worker to begin thinking about. Interviews are scheduled for one of two purposes, i.e., to explore possibilities and establish facts by which to proceed, or having determined the facts, to reach a solution to a problem. The methods of conducting interviews vary with individuals, but generally rapport must be established so that something positive will result. The interview should never deteriorate into a sham or time-wasting device.

Group Conferences

The cohesion of individuals into a high-morale group does not occur overnight. It is promoted through varied experiences in which individual staff members realize that cooperative effort is not only desirable, but necessary if satisfying objectives are to be attained. Group conferences are useful only to the extent that they meet program worker needs. If they are called to impose official regulations they are a waste of time because there are handier methods for disseminating notices and rules. Group conferences must focus on those problems which the staff, not the administration, deems important. A basic agenda which has been cooperatively planned by both supervisor and staff subordinates must be developed with the idea that it can be changed when and where necessary. Each member of the conference should have an equal opportunity to present whatever problems he has for resolution. An agenda which is discussed at reasonable length, so that each staff person knows what will be presented and therefore be prepared to offer sound suggestions and ideas, will be more effective in gaining staff support than something which is handed down from on high without any prior notice.

Perhaps the best technique for avoiding wasted time and energy is to initiate a staff conference planning committee. Responsibility for planning group conferences can best reside with this committee. It is made up of staff workers selected by the staff. It functions as a central clearing house for staff ideas that need to be heard and is evidence to the staff that they have more than lip-service control over such meetings. The committee, aside from determining the agenda, can have additional responsibility for assuring the success of the conference, i.e., arrangement of time, place, and setting for the meeting, provision for whatever refreshments might seem necessary, and the securing of the services of consultants.

Conference time should not be taken from the leisure of the participant but should be taken from time on the job. Scheduling of conferences should be worked out from the viewpoint that staff planning and administrative policy making are a part of the work assignment. Thus, the staff will be offered an opportunity to reach decisions as to the specific time for such conferences.

In order to make group conferences most effective, some thought must be given to how such meetings are operated. The success of any group conference depends, in large measure, on the skill exhibited by the individual who acts as chairman. If staff workers are unable to contribute in a democratic climate, it might be well to have one who is highly skilled in elements of group leadership. Until staff workers are competent in working together democratically, the supervisor must be prepared to chair the session. The primary function of the leader in group conferences is to create a favorable environment out of which creative contributions can be evoked. An easy and friendly atmosphere in which all participants are treated as equals does much to dispel any doubts or fears which members may have.

Group conferences can too easily be dominated by one or a few highly aggressive or outspoken individuals. The chairman must be adroit in preventing domination of the group by a select few. Conference topics must conform to the agenda and the meeting itself should be conducted in a most business-like way. Although time must be taken and given for discussion of many viewpoints and alternate solutions, speakers must not be allowed to wander so far from the topic that the conference degenerates into separate conversations without any meaning. The steady flow of ideas and the recognition of additional participants with questions or new approaches must be integrated into the total discussion. Appropriate shifts to selected topics on the agenda as well as the clarification of questions or problems that are posed will do much to facilitate the evenness of the conference. As Wiles and others have written:

... the discussion leader secures group agreement on the agenda, maintains an atmosphere that encourages full participation, is impartial toward ideas, helps the group establish its own rules of procedure, keeps discussion on the problem, summarizes as necessary, brings out issues and agreements, utilizes special abilities of group members, works toward agreement, and makes or provides for final summary.[10]

Supervisory Visitation and Observation

The chief reason for visitation by the supervisor is to provide ample opportunity, under actual working conditions, for him to study recreationist techniques, stimulate any needed worker improvement, for instructional purposes to present the most up-to-date information concerning specific activities, and to be in the best position to accurately appraise worker performance. Field visitation can be initiated by the supervisor or it may be requested by the program worker. It may vary in length, but usually a visit of not less than one-half hour is required in order to understand properly the working situation and determine needs. Regardless of expression of like, dislike, nervousness, or apprehension on the part of workers concerning supervisory visitation, even when requested, these visits are significant to the supervisory process.

Visitation should be a pleasant experience, both for worker and supervisor. Nearly all professionals are anxious to learn and seek additional opportunities for professional development. The supervisory visitation is one approach where such development and knowledge can be encouraged. When visitation is carried on in a creative and skillful way, program recreationists will advocate and look forward to them. The initial visits should be quasi-social, never brusque or demanding. As in every instance of leadership when the designated leader makes his first contact with potential followers, every manifestation of his behavior will cause some reaction. Highly inconsequential comportment can be misinterpreted or unduly stressed by those workers who are either insecure or inexperienced.

Field visitation should be a periodic and routine procedure made with the full knowledge and cooperation of the program recreationist. When the functional worker becomes accustomed to supervisory visitations, he will usually forget the presence of the supervisor and perform his functions with the same effort and competence he would exhibit during any working situation in which the supervisor was not present. When a supervisor announces his visitation in advance, the recreationist may do a more efficient planning job concerning the day's activities than he might typically do. The supervisor will then be a witness to what the functional worker honestly believes is his best effort. Prior notice of visitation has the distinct advantage of almost forcing a more complete preparation which might not be entered into and thus contributes to professional development.

[10] Kimball Wiles, Carmille Brown, Rosalind Cassidy, *Supervision in Physical Education* (Englewood Cliffs, N.J.: Prentice-Hall, Inc., 1956), p. 105.

Observation, unlike visitation, is a routine, nonperiodic, unannounced method for determining specific worker techniques and competencies in an atmosphere not made artificial by the supervisor's presence. One great drawback to supervisory observation is directly related to hostile feelings engendered on the part of those who come under observation. Many functional workers feel that observation is "snoopervision" or, more bluntly, spying. Special effort by the supervisor is absolutely necessary to dispel this unfortunate negative reaction to this most simple tool. The supervisor must establish rapport with his subordinates and create a mutual feeling of confidence. In any event, observation should be made so that the information obtained is an accurate sample of the situation in which the recipient finds himself.

It must be reiterated that observation is not spying upon a worker. The supervisor must never hide from the worker and watch him from some remote or secret place. Surprise, instead of announcement, is perfectly moral and practical. However, observation is only one specific phase of the supervisory process and must ordinarily be supplemented by other methods if a complete and factual representation of the program worker's abilities under a variety of conditions is to be made.

Informal Meetings

Random meetings between functional workers and supervisors, either on the job or after working hours, provide many chances for supervision. The supervisor must recognize that his responsibilities never cease. He is eternally on the job, for supervision is a process that occurs wherever and whenever supervisors and subordinates meet. Perhaps casual meetings are the best possible opportunities for supervision because away from the daily pressure of work assignments and responsibility, the worker's reaction to a question raised by the supervisor may shed some light upon a viewpoint that might have remained guarded or latent. Social gatherings offer excellent occasions for such explorations, because the program worker is going to be less inhibited by and less slanted toward what would ordinarily be taken for the supervisor's likes, dislikes, or opinion. Each contact a supervisor has with a subordinate may affect him so that improved work habits and higher competence can result. If the supervisor, preoccupied with his own thoughts, unintentionally passes a worker on his way to the center or other facility without a greeting, he could conceivably cause such distress to the subordinate's ego and security that his work for the day might suffer. Conversely, a cheery and spontaneous salutation can stimulate the subordinate to program efforts that no calculated situation could evoke.

Supervision is essentially a scrupulously planned process. However, the supervisor who wants to learn about the agency and its personnel will lose a great many opportunities for examination and evaluation if he relies solely upon formal procedures. It is improbable to foresee the hazards that are likely to occur in the operation of a recreational service program at any time. To a considerable extent, the supervisor's contribution to agency achievement will result from his skill in anticipating problem areas and inherent dangers to personnel as well as participants. He does this to a greater degree through his informal meetings with his workers than he does through his more formalized contacts.

IN-SERVICE EDUCATION AND DEVELOPMENT

Inherent within the supervisory process is that which deals with the professional growth of personnel. All development will be concerned with conditioning factors that affect direct relationships between recreationists and agency clientele. Among these are (1) situational factors, specifically those that influence the recreationist's typical way of life and professional growth; (2) personality factors specifically those traits of character that are developed from inherited as well as environmental effects; (3) intellectual factors, specifically those talents, enthusiasms, concepts, knowledges, and appreciations that are learned and that result in typical behaviors; (4) morale factors, specifically those conditions that promote interests and loyalty toward certain ideals; (5) ability to learn, specifically those factors that determine readiness and intent; and (6) leadership factors, specifically those that are concerned with leadership techniques.

In-service education particularly seeks to improve and encourage professional growth by constant study of the factors indicated above. In-service education begins with problems arising from environmental conditions in the agency and attempts to determine what actually produces the problem. The process fosters experimentation and analysis of facts in order to develop possible ways of solving problems as well as program practices. The program should engender development of goals consistent with participant needs in the light of the requirements of contemporary society. It must encourage recreationists to develop a sound working philosophy of recreational service based upon applied social scientific knowledge and democratic views.

In-Service Educational Activities

There are distinctive experiences which the supervisor can offer to induce professional development as in-service education. These activities are specifically designed to produce a climate which is conducive to permissiveness and which can facilitate contributions that may stimulate personal growth and technical accomplishment. Among these supervisory devised proceedings are brainstorming, discussion groups, panels, demonstrations, exhibits, field observation, library research, workshops, laboratory, and lectures.

Brainstorming. Brainstorming is generally structured, has some focal point, and is most useful in groups of not more than fifteen. Essentially, it is a verbalizing situation in which a great many ideas are expounded in a brief time period. No attempt is made to critically examine the ideas which are produced, and quantity rather than refinement of thoughts is significant here. In such a permissive atmosphere nearly all participants are encouraged to offer statements and all adverse comments are forbidden. Each person has an opportunity to contribute and no statement is considered too far-fetched.

Discussion Groups. The discussion group is somewhat informal in atmosphere, although it is oriented toward a specific problem or assignment to be carried out. Basically, the discussion group allows members to freely participate in whatever objectives are at issue and to gain a better understanding of the material under consideration.

Panels. The panel discussion constitutes a formally organized verbal presentation by two or more speakers where a single topic is focused upon. The panel form itself may become one of interaction wherein the panelists react to the presentations made, or the panel may be of a symposium type, wherein short papers are read to the group. Although there is limited participation from the receiving group, the audience may be requested to ask questions about the presentations or ask for additional information concerning the topic. Invariably, the panel presentation is restricted by time, and whatever stimulation is received can be lost if there is no follow-up by written or graphic material distribution. Where the presentations are so exciting as to induce argument or additional discussion groups, a greater learning impact may be developed.

Demonstrations. The demonstration is designed to improve specific skills or to develop techniques in relation to objectives that are sought. The experience is one that involves a planned series of activities with stress upon specific facets of performance so that the observers can plainly see sequence of action, technical movement, and necessary corrections. Demonstrations are enacted to meet the needs of observers as well as to provide concepts, methods, means, and instrumentations that can best be examined.

Exhibits. A self-explained activity, an exhibit provides large or small groups with materials, equipment, and facilities arranged in such a manner as to present some idea or to carry through some theme. Exhibits may include, posters, books, other printed materials, films, bulletin boards, flats, scale models, drawings, or other rigid or plastic materials which depict some aspect of agency operation.

Field Observation. Field observation is epitomized by the visitation of workers to an actual program operation whereby functional personnel have an opportunity to observe a highly competent recreationist perform in an environment void of artificiality. It allows staff personnel to see proficient workers conducting activities that are directly related to their respective jobs.

Library Research. Library research is universally recognized as one of the most important and probably most neglected of all in-service educational procedures. All too often a professional library is unknown within the recreational service agency. If this is not true, then getting program workers to read the material is a difficult task. There should be a continuing program of required reading by the functional worker to keep abreast of current activities and new forms of programming. Pertinent materials relating to on-going operations should be clipped out of research journals and passed around for the benefit of all personnel. Abstracting relevant material, attractively presented and stimulating in advancing ideas, must be a constant aim of supervision.

Workshops. The workshop consists of a small group of workers, generally between fifteen and twenty, whose purpose it is to develop program and resource materials for immediate and practical use. It is a planned group situation in which program workers work together to prepare materials that can be utilized in their recreational activities.

Lectures. The most highly formalized of all teaching activities, the lecture is simply the transmission of information from an expert to a group of listeners.

Laboratory. The laboratory provides a method whereby development of some skill is directed without pushing the worker into an actual encounter with participants. The laboratory serves as a protected practice session in which the worker's skills are augmented in an artificially contrived atmosphere in order that maximum guidance and directed learning can be accomplished.

Internal Communication. Employing the technique of internal communication, commonly known as the house or agency organ, is important for maintaining high morale among personnel and educating them so that they may provide accurate information about recreational services in their contacts with the public. The internal system of communication serves this purpose very adequately. It is a publication printed for distribution to the agency's own staff and is one of the most valuable methods of obtaining and retaining the support and interest of personnel. The house organ may be published monthly, or more often as need dictates, and should contain personal items, outstanding articles on new developments in programming as well as authoritative articles on departmental operations, and some form of "letter-to-the-editor" column. This latter feature is an effective means of encouraging interest. Ideas and criticisms of all kinds should be stimulated, particularly if they are constructive, although adverse criticism should also be included. Every employee of the agency should be permitted to contribute to this "open forum" column. Through imaginative suggestions it is always possible to improve the administration of the agency as well as to make the entire operation more efficient. In addition, the house organ inculcates in personnel a positive attitude toward the agency and its responsibilities, one consequence of which is a more highly competent and meaningful service to the public.

THE EFFECTS OF SUPERVISION

The outcomes of scientific supervision can readily be observed in terms of program participation, worker effectiveness, and an enthusiasm for performing in the most optimum way possible, thus assuring the agency of dedicated, high-morale employees. Organizational efficiency is deliberately enhanced by pride of professionalism and group coordination. The instillation of harmonious practice and the absence of dissension as a result of on the job communication are other products. Supervisory effects are noticed in relation to lessened worker illness requiring sickleave, a willingness to undertake additional responsibilities and to do a better job, less concern with who is responsible to whom, and a better understanding of agency functions and the personnel practices within it.

The most effective supervisors are accessible; they have an empathy for people which allows them to establish rapport. The worker, in turn, recognizes that the supervisor understands whatever problems, weaknesses, or strengths he has and is his partisan. The relationship which the supervisor has carefully nurtured is evoked through an analysis of facts, listening, and by nondirective counseling techniques. Additionally, worker productivity increases in direct relation to the supervisor's willingness to take the time to assist the program worker on the job.

Supervisory reliability is established because the relationship developed between the supervisor and his subordinates is stable. There are no great deviations from personality norms, nor are there defections from doing what is necessary when the situation requires some action. The supervisor takes disciplinary measures, is constant in his dealings with workers and their problems, but more significantly, he provides information concerning job requirements, and lines of communication are always open. Employees can rely on the premise that merit, rather than seniority, will be rewarded and that each person will be given the opportunity to contribute to the overall success of the program and earn increments and promotions.

One immediate effect of competent supervision is the lack of conflict that accrues from vague descriptions of job responsibilities and duties. Where formalized work procedures are implemented and written, confused work orders are avoided and well-established duties of workers with clear lines of authority are established. Work flow, agency rules, regulations, and policies are made readily available to all employees. Subordinate workers come to realize that the competent supervisor is consistent in his attitude towards them, that he can be relied upon to do what he says he will do, and that when he has to, he can and does make decisions. As Harris writes:

> An important aspect of good supervisory behavior is decision-making. The effective supervisors are decisive, making decisions more easily than

do poor supervisors. In the eyes of the subordinates, these decisions show good judgment. The effective supervisor is consistent in his decisions, administering equal justice to all.[11]

The following consequences will occur as a result of positively applied supervision: (1) cooperation—joint effort in the common cause of providing a varied and comprehensive recreational service. This is accomplished through the recognition of the specific contributions of each worker to the advancement of the program, and (2) creativity—constructive plans for improvement of the program and the operational activities of the agency through the efforts of self-expression and self-determination are possible because supervision seeks out the latent talents and skills and creates an environment in which ingenuity and experimentation are encouraged. As Barr and others have stated:

> . . . every normal individual is capable of creative expression in some degree. Growth and development of the total personnel including community members is definitely stimulated through creative expression. Supervision in addition to providing opportunities for creative contribution will deliberately seek latent talent, will deliberately manipulate the environment to provide settings for creative expression.[12]

Good supervision provides an atmosphere in which the thinking individual is allowed to contribute in spite of established traditions. Innovations, experimentations, and the possibility of questioning established methods are permitted. Through continual acts of exploration and invention the worker becomes more confident of his own abilities and secure in the knowledge that he will receive support and encouragement in determining answers to questions that have not been resolved satisfactorily. As the worker realizes himself through creative performance he achieves a certain sense of mastery, satisfaction, and perseverance. There is concomitantly a buildup of loyalty toward the agency which permits this activity as well as expressions of dedication, enthusiasm, and intellectual stimulation.

The competent supervisor has the functions of carrying out administrative decisions, explaining agency policy, orientation, procedures, and practices to subordinate workers, in assignments, and performing a mediating service between the program and administrative levels of the organization.

The supervisor allies himself neither with the administrator nor with the functional workers, but serves as the counselor to both. Just as he interprets decisions downward through the chain of command, he also explains

---

[11] Ben M. Harris, *Supervisory Behavior in Education* (Englewood Cliffs, N.J.: Prentice-Hall, Inc., 1963), p. 432.
[12] A. S. Barr, W. H. Burton, and L. J. Brueckner, *Supervision* (New York: Appleton-Century-Crofts, 1947), p. 62.

the needs and objectives of workers upward. It is the function of the supervisor to offer such expert and technical assistance both to the administrator and the functional workers that success in various spheres of work assigned to them is more likely to be reached.[13]

Supervisors create the guiding philosophy of the agency and are therefore obliged to assume responsibility for whatever achievement is attained within the recreational program.

SUMMARY

The supervisor must lead and seek out worker leaders, guide worker productivity, and discover better ways by which to supervise. Coordinated effort for maximum output in which the most valuable activities of a recreational nature are provided for participants is effected by scientifically applied, democratically oriented, logically controlled, and creatively endowed supervisory leadership.

The primary function of supervision is the continual improvement of the factors that effect practitioner development. These factors are immediately concerned with the establishment of a common philosophy or rational frame of reference whereby the recreationist may be guided toward common goals. Chiefly, an educational process must be established in order for continual staff development to occur. The essential function of supervision is leadership with the concomitant development of leadership within the staff as well as from participants within the program. The supervisor is not the only individual capable of leadership activities, but this is the primary responsibility that he has.

Supervision is a necessary function within any recreational service system. It provides expertness from a resource orientation in dealing with the multiform and complex problems usually confronting "line" recreationists as they deal with people. A demand for technical assistance in order to achieve continuity of purpose and maximum coordination of effort toward desired goals, i.e., optimum recreational opportunities through the program, increases the need for successful supervision. Supervision enhances in-service staff development toward professional growth. Supervision aids in the discovery of latent leadership ability and encourages creativity by arranging opportunities for discussion of new ideas, recommendation by staff for improving supervisory techniques, and sound staff morale based upon job security. The democratic process and supervision are part of the same package. Supervision will be successful only to the extent that fear or coercive pressure is eliminated.

[13] Jay S. Shivers, *Leadership in Recreational Service* (New York: The Macmillan Company, 1963), p. 284.

SELECTED REFERENCES

BEACH, DALE S., *Personnel: The Management of People At Work.* (New York: The Macmillan Co.), 1965

BURTON, WILLIAM H. and LEO J. BRUECKNER, *Supervision: A Social Process,* 3d ed. (New York: Appleton-Century-Crofts), 1955.

CROSBY, MURIEL, *Supervision As a Cooperative Action.* (New York: Appleton-Century-Crofts), 1957.

FAMULARO, J. J., *Supervision in Action.* (New York: McGraw-Hill), 1961.

FRANSETH, JANE, *Supervision as Leadership.* (New York: Harper and Row), 1961.

HALSEY, GEORGE D., *Supervising People,* rev. ed. (New York: Harper and Row), 1953.

International City Manager's Association, *Supervising Methods in Municipal Administration.* (Chicago: International City Manager's Association), 1958.

MAIER, N. R. F., et al., *Supervision and Executive Development.* (New York: John Wiley and Sons, Inc.), 1964.

PFIFFNER, JOHN M., *Supervision of Personnel: Human Relations in the Management of Men,* 3rd ed. (Englewood Cliffs, N.J.: Prentice-Hall, Inc.), 1962.

SARTAIN, AARON Q. and A. W BAKER, *Supervisor and His Job.* (New York: McGraw-Hill), 1965.

STRAUSS, GEORGE and LEONARD SAYLES, *Personnel: The Human Problems of Management.* (Englewood Cliffs, N.J.: Prentice-Hall, Inc.), 1960.

THOMPSON, C. E., *Personnel Management for Supervisors.* (Englewood Cliffs, N.J.: Prentice-Hall, Inc.) 1948.

WILLIAMSON, MARGARET, *Supervision: New Patterns and Processes.* (New York: The Association Press), 1961.

Chapter 14

PROGRAMMING

PRINCIPLE: The organization and mobilization of all the community's resources, both physical and personal, in order to produce a balanced, comprehensive, and varied continual recreational program are necessary if programming is to be performed logically.

The essence of all recreational service is the program. It is the only justification for a recreational service department. Programming consists of planning, scheduling, and implementing an organized series of sponsored recreational experiences through the utilization of all community resources in such a way as to offer routine, special, passive, active, varied, and graded activities. Community programming requires an inclusive plan of action under the auspices of a central agency, e.g., a public recreational service department. All of the activities sponsored, administered, and supervised by the system combine to form the program. Everything that the department does, whether employing personnel, constructing facilities, recruiting volunteers, or paperwork management, finds outlet in one culminating goal—the program. To this end, all of the energies, intelligence, talent, and skill of qualified personnel are organized to provide the most comprehensive program possible in order to meet the diverse needs of the people living in the community. The basis for programming lies in the concept that each individual in the community must be given the *opportunity* to participate in at least one departmentally sponsored recreational activity. There should be something for everybody in the way of recreational experiences. Because the department is charged with the responsibility for providing total community recreational service, it must offer planned experiences which may be undertaken by all of the residents of the community. Fundamentally, all of the people must be served during their leisure.

THE IDENTIFICATION AND CLASSIFICATION OF RECREATIONAL ACTIVITIES

The balanced recreational program is composed of twelve equal categories within which are to be defined many varieties of activities. These categories are coequal insofar as they contribute satisfaction, enjoyment, and other recreational values to individual participants. These twelve categories cover almost every possible recreational activity which can be planned, programmed, or scheduled and offer a diverseness which is as broad in scope as the human mind is able to determine. With few, if any, exceptions, nearly every recreational experience may be included in this classification system. Among these twelve categories are art, crafts, dance, dramatics, education, hobbies, motor performance, music, outdoor education, service activities, social activities, and special projects.

Art

Art may be defined as any personalized expression of a graphic or plastic nature representative of or symbolizing some concept. It is part of the process of communication. Essentially, it is a method of self-expression through visual factors arranged to satisfy the needs of the person who forms and creates them. It may be that only the artist can explain his work, but the explanation is neither important nor required. More importantly, art in any of its many forms provides a means of conveying ideas, moods, or personal feelings in a visual presentation. The art category may be divided into several easily distinguished parts which readily lend themselves to incorporation in a recreational program. Among these parts are the following:

Graphic Art	Plastic Art
oil painting	stone sculpture
water colors	metal sculpture
wash drawing	clay sculpture
pen and ink drawing	glass etching
finger painting	ivory carving
charcoal sketching	wood carving
pastel drawing	precious metal smithing
photography	lapidary work
dry point etching	tapestry making
silk screen printing	mosaic tile making
crayon drawing	glass blowing
	mobiles

Ramifications. All age groups may participate in art activities. Whether the child draws in crayon or the skilled artist creates in oil, each person is enabled to find expression. Art may be programmed on an instructional basis, i.e., graded classes can be organized to develop skill, technique, and ability to perform. There will always be those who are beginners. Primarily the youngest age groups will generally fall in this class. However, many older children, youth, and adults are also beginners. They need the stimulation and confidence building to be found among a group of people who come together to learn a new skill. As with all skills, other people will have had some prior experience and may be classified as intermediates.

They are not highly skilled, but have basic knowledge of materials, media, and some technique. The third class is made up of highly skilled individuals who wish to continue in an instructional session, perhaps studying under a well known artist. All of these skill levels must be considered in developing the category of art.

The noninstructional phase of art is for those persons who have the skill, talent, or knowledge to create, but lack a place in which to perform. The agency, through its schedule, can offer an art room in which people may perform without instruction. One other facet of art comes in terms of appreciation. There are those individuals who cannot or will not want to draw, paint, or sculpt. However, they may have a desire to learn about art. Art appreciation classes organized to develop aesthetic interests and an understanding of what art is may assuredly be incorporated in the art activity.

Art classes are scheduled according to ability and capacity of the individual so engaged. For young children short instructional sessions are programmed. For adults, longer sessions. Experience and exploration of community interests, needs, and requests will best assist in the establishment of the number of art classes, lessons required, equipment, spaces, and instructional leadership necessary.

Crafts

The fabrication of any material for ornamental, utilitarian, or manipulative purposes from animal, vegetable, and mineral substances may be termed a *craft*. It is a creative process of intrinsic value to those who seek satisfaction through the shaping, molding, and modification of materials. Although the line of demarcation between art and craft is thin, it is distinguishable and the two should not be confused or placed in the same classification. Although they are, or can be intimately related they are two separate categories and should be treated as such for programming purposes. Craft activities may be differentiated in the following manner: Substance—i.e., animal, vegetable, and mineral, and Functional—i.e., industrial, nature, and marine, as delineated in the Table on page 357.

Ramifications. Craft activities invade nearly every part of the recreational program and tend to enhance other categories. Crafts, of and by themselves, are extremely satisfying to the individual whether it is the small child playing with miniature hammer, nails, and saw or the highly skilled craftsman tooling an electric motor. Within these two extremes lies a multitude of experiences pleasing and expressive of individual wants, needs, and capacities. Crafts can be done in a solitary manner, but usually the craft activity organized at a recreational center is a social experience carried on in a group setting. Crafts is such an individualized medium that almost anyone can find outlet through this experience. Like art it may be organized in graded classes where instruction and supervision are maintained. Noninstructional crafts may be organized where skilled persons congregate to tinker, shape, carve, mold, hammer, or effect other changes

Craft Activities

Substance:	ANIMAL	VEGETABLE	MINERAL
	leather craft	weaving	metal craft
	shell craft	sewing	clay modeling
	bone carving	crocheting	glass making
	horn carving	needlepoint	bead craft
	taxidermy	embroidery	ceramics
		basketry	plastic lacing
		block printing	plaster of paris
		knitting	jewelry making
		paper sculpture	pottery making
		raffia work	sand sculpture
		appliquéing	stone craft
		cardboard sculpture	soap carving
		wood carving	chemical crafts
		crepe paper craft	snow sculpture
		papier mâché craft	ice sculpture
		dyeing	coral craft
		wood work	
		candle making	
		whittling	
		hooking	
		braiding	

Functional:	INDUSTRIAL CRAFTS	AUTOMOTIVE CRAFTS	NATURE CRAFTS
	electrical shop	building automobiles	fly tying
	masonry	repairing	lashing
	smithing	motor tuning	canoe repairing
	mechanical arts	boat designing	shelter building
	plumbing	plane constructing	fire making
	cabinet making	bicycle making	implement making
	tool and die making	model making	net making
	furniture refinishing	gilder building	cooking
	fur coat remodeling	motorcycle repairs	specimen mounting
	hat designing		driftwood craft
	dress designing	MARINE CRAFTS	stenciling
	gift wrapping		spatter painting
	tinkering	knot tying	vegetable printing
	bookbinding	rope making	potato puppetry
	woodworking	sail making	Indian craft
	clock making	boat repairing	
	glass grinding	surf board shaping	
	printing/book making		

in wood, metal, or leather materials. Many people, particularly adults, find a hobby interest which lasts them a lifetime as a result of attendance in a crafts activity.

Instructional leadership is of primary importance in programming crafts. Unless there is a competent worker who understands the use of media, tools, and space requirements the activity is likely to meet with little success. Leadership, either professional or volunteer, plus essential tools, work spaces, and materials are vital to crafts. Certainly, there are simple craft activities which do not need extensive tools, equipment, or expensive materials. However, such activities are more likely to appeal to younger children than to the majority of adults who wish to participate. The ingenuity of professional leadership is apparent from the production of many craft activities without expensively procured supplies and materials. Salvaged materials sometimes afford the greatest satisfaction. There is a good deal of pleasure in designing and fabricating something useful, ornamental, or manipulative from a piece of junk or scrap. With competent leadership almost any craft project is possible.

Dance

Any rhythmic movement, gross or fine, which is sustained by a regular tempo, beat, or music, may be termed *dance*. Dance has been conceived as a method of nonverbal communication, as kinetic movement to relieve tension, and as a means of social and individual self-expression. The dance category may, for ease in programming, be classified as follows:

Folk Dance	Social Dance	Choreographed Dance	Rhythmics
square	waltz	ballet	free exercise
round	*rumba*	modern	games
ethnic	tango	concert	tap
	fox trot	interpretive	clog
	fad (Twist, Watusi, Monkey, Swim, etc.)		

Ramifications. Dance like all skills must be learned. One of the most popular recreational activities, it has found almost universal expression in every culture. A dance may reflect traditions or a general contemporary feeling. Many dances are an outgrowth of religious rites or of an ethnic variety depicting the celebrations and mores of different cultural patterns. Dancing is a graceful rhythmic motor skill whose performance can be enjoyed by spectators and participants alike. Dancing as an outlet of self-expression may be of a solo type, dual, or performed in groups. Dancing fosters socialization and allows people to satisfy a basic urge to respond to a pleasing tempo.

Although social dancing still attracts the greatest number of people, square and folk dance has come to be extremely popular and interest in this form of the activity is growing. The criteria for selecting specific types of dance forms are influenced by the age, sex, prior experience, degree of skill, and the size of the group involved. Instructional phases of dance may be divided into the familiar beginner, intermediate, and advanced classifications.

Of primary importance is the presence of qualified leadership to conduct instructional activities and provide competent guidance for the inclusion of all who seek enjoyment through this medium. The various forms of dance enable almost everybody to achieve a sense of satisfaction and release of tension. The techniques involved and the objectives to which people aspire vary greatly, thus offering opportunity for individuals to experience emotional outlets. Through instructional classes for the development of needed skills, in sharing the vicarious stimulation of watching the dance as a spectator, this activity proves of immense value as a socializing mechanism and contributes to the cohesion of any group so involved.

Dramatics

Communication through aural and visual means whereby an individual can emote and express himself or reproduce the expression of others via interpretation, mimicry, symbolism, or spontaneous activity may be defined as *dramatics*. The element of performance, whether in front of an audience or not, is incorporated. The scope of dramatics is extremely broad and includes many activities among which are:

Manipulative Performance	Creative Drama	Forensic Performance	Theater
	pantomime		blackout plays
marionettes	improvisation	monologues	demonstrations
puppetry	games	dialogues	dramatizations
shadow plays	charades	debate	opera
juggling	psychodrama	public speaking	operetta
prestidigitation	sociodrama	story reading	tableaux
(sleight-of-hand)		storytelling	skits
		impersonation	stunts
		choral speech	
		radio plays	

Ramifications. The constructive utlization of a story, in either play form, pantomime, role-playing, or spontaneous re-creation, allows participants to express themselves in terms of needs and interests. Dramatics and its various forms, using a medium of reality, fantasy, and wish-fulfillment, makes the individual aware of himself and causes him to empathize with others. Every age group enjoys some aspect of dramatics. Children love to tell stories and to hear stories, to play dramatic games, to act out fairy tales. Adults enjoy a good story as does the teller.

Dramatics also includes games, improvisation, plays, and other forms which convey ideas by means of speech, action, or both. Essentially the dramatic performance is the most highly personalized of all the categories. It is the individual on whom all attention is focused and it is the individual who must interpret the idea or character about which the story is written. In creative dramatics there is no story line and the role-taker must act out his ideas spontaneously, as the mood or action dictates. Where there is a formal play, the actor has his lines to memorize and must reproduce the character prescribed by the author.

As in all planned recreational activity, a prime requisite is qualified leadership to serve in a directorial capacity, to act as a resource, or to supervise the entire presentation. Dramatics classes, appreciation of drama in its different forms, and actual performance upon the stage all require expert guidance. Dramatic presentation may be of the workshop variety where the participants learn by doing. On the other hand, when the play is performance oriented, many weeks must be taken for rehearsal, sets must be designed, lighting and other equipment accumulated, and all of the details of presentation must be planned. In many instances performers gain confidence through this participation and are able to overcome any emotional barriers that prevent them from taking part. Drama is valuable to the individual as a medium for self-expression through representations of characters and roles which may be the creation of another person.

Education

Any instructional activity wherein the primary reason for participation is the enhancement of knowledge or the learning of a new skill, idea, or subject may be termed *education*. Formal or classroom instruction of subject matter as well as informal learning experiences which are programmed specifically to teach a skill are part of this category. Although almost all recreational activity may be defined as educational, it is not the place of the recreational service department to teach subjects which might better be left to the school system. Certain educational outcomes may be carried out and noted in an organized program, but the atmosphere and the emphasis are quite different from those of the school classroom. The activities which typically form the educational category are:

Adult Education	Literary Activities	Linguistic Activities
citizenship	book clubs	foreign language groups
civics	book review groups	debating
first aid	short story writing	public speaking
curriculum subjects	library cataloguing	choral recitations
grammar	play writing	conversation
mathematics	technical writing	discussion groups
history	poetry reading	forums
geography	poetry writing	quizzes
science	Bible reading	storytelling
current events	letter writing	story reading
industrial arts		lectures
etiquette		liturgical groups
floral designs		panel presentations
horticultural arrangements		seminars
home gardening		symposia
maternity and child care		
accounting		
bookkeeping		
typing		
stenography		

Ramifications. Nothing enhances enjoyment as much as having knowledge about a given subject and being able to bring that knowledge to bear when a situation demands that it be used. Knowledge opens many doors to quiet satisfaction. It extends the promise of awareness, recognition, and appreciation to any subject. The category of education lends itself most particularly to the recreational setting because learning is enjoyable, especially when the information gained is learned during one's leisure. Formal curricula subject matter as taught by the school places emphasis upon progress toward a specific goal, with so many units learned and examinations taken. The recreational orientation of education stresses satisfaction on the part of the learner without examinations and the pressure to achieve a specific grade. Classes in recreational education are designed to improve knowledge, to increase skill, to share in social occasions, and to develop physically, emotionally, and intellectually. Generally, all programmed instruction lays emphasis on the activity or subject to be learned. The individual's interest dictates the speed and progress he will make.

Education during leisure in curriculum subjects has tended toward a variety of skill learning, such as, typing, first aid, driver safety, letter writing, short story writing, and civics. However, any subject may be offered. When literary, linguistic, or commercial courses are offered in the program they are there because a demand has been created and interested people desire them. Formal subject presentation is offered in the hope that exposure to the information will prompt additional study and provide incentive for improvement.

Competent leadership is required for the presentation of most educational subjects. Volunteers may be utilized for such skills as fur coat remodeling, furniture refinishing, or the like, but in general qualified instructors must be employed. The educational category offers opportunities for personal exposure to information about which some confusion exists. Political debate, local government in action, open forums, current events, book clubs, and other sources that stimulate the individual's thinking are valuable contributions effected in these activities.

Other forms of education are quizzes, puzzles, and mental games. These activities have received scant notice from practitioners, even though they are quite enjoyable to participants. It must be remembered that the education category rests entirely upon the mental capacity, willingness to learn, and basic interest of potential participants. It has been found that nearly everyone can learn if the material presented is stimulating, beneficial, or if the individual is motivated to acquire the information available. On these bases, education may afford the best hope in the provision of recreational experiences.

Hobbies

Hobbies are highly personalized interests having to do with the acquisition, knowledge, appreciation, manipulation, fabrication, or designing of some thing, subject, or concept. So diverse and peculiar are hobbies that any listing, no matter how extensive, would only begin to indicate the variety of human interests that can be classified as hobbies. It is probably easier to indicate the activities which are not hobbies. All activities requiring performance, such as, dramatics, sports and game participation, music, and so on, may be thought by some to be hobbies, but they are not. An interest ceases to be a hobby when the aspect of performance becomes a part of the experience. For example, music appreciation, collecting music, knowledge of music, or writing music may be considered as hobbies. However, when the individual performs music, i.e., sings or reproduces music on an instrument, the activity cannot be considered a hobby. If a hobby can be any activity, and it includes all activities, then anything and everything may be identified as a hobby. There is no basis for a definition. Definitions differentiate and set apart. If everything is accounted for under one topic, there is no difference in activities. Performance is clearly different from collecting, knowledge, or manipulation. It is a unique factor which permits classification within other categories.

Ramifications. There are some people to whom all activities of the balanced program mean little or nothing. By temperament, emotional capacity, or for other personal reasons, they do not want to participate. They do not want any part of the program. For these people, there is always one outlet which the recreational agency can offer. The highly personalized and individual hobby enables each person to select at least one area of interest to himself. He needs no others for participation. The hobby category is organized quite differently from all of the other eleven classifications. There are no classes of instruction by which a person may learn a hobby. There is no extrinsic motivation which the recreationist can bring to bear which might stimulate participation in a hobby. The recreationist may, however, organize interest groups or clubs when a hobbyist requests it.

The function of the recreationist in attempting to engage an individual's attention for hobby purposes may well come in terms of exposure. Some individuals are compelled to attempt one form of hobby or another as a result of personal observation, casual conversation, attendance at a hobby show where various displays and exhibits were demonstrated, or simply by chance encounter. However people are initiated into the mysteries of the hobby, this activity becomes an absorbing and long-time pursuit. All hobbyists are fanatics concerning their particular hobby. Nothing is more pleasing to the hobbyist than to be called upon to demonstrate or explain his interest. This is one way by which hobbies are spread. The enthusiasm which the hobbyist exhibits is contagious and usually infects an entire audience of spectators or listeners.

The recreationist has a chance to assist in the spread of hobby interests by locating hobbyists of various types and scheduling clubs that promote the exchange of information, displays, lectures, and other media for the transmission of knowledge. If hobby clubs are already in existence, then the recreationist can encourage hobbyists to utilize recreational facilities throughout the community for meetings as well as for the scheduling of hobby shows. Continual exposure of people to hobbyists and to the interests from which hobbies are developed may be the best method which the recreationist has at his disposal. Providing space and facilities for hobbyists can be fruitful in widely disseminating hobby possibilities. In the long run, most stress is placed upon the individual's capacity to interest himself in a worthwhile pursuit and to develop personal skills in undertaking total responsibility for maintaining the activity.

Motor Performance

All of those activities requiring gross and/or fine muscle control which may be devised for physiological development, extension of capacity to endure, or for competitive purposes are called motor performance. Sports, games, and conditioning experiences are one means of classifying and identifying motor performance. Sports are all of those recreational pursuits that are not restricted by time, rules, or to a distinct or specifically delimited area universally known. Games, on the other hand, have special rules and codes to which all players must adhere. Games are conducted in carefully defined and distinguishable spaces, segregated from all other activities, and are usually relegated to a selected portion of time or by units in which the game must be completed. Sports, when so regulated, may be modified to become games. Games can never be sports. Motor performance can be identified in several ways and contain the following activities:

INDIVIDUAL	DUAL	TEAM	GROUP
swimming	fencing	baseball	calisthenics
gymnastics	wrestling	basketball	weight training
tumbling	handball	cricket	circuit training
track	squash	field hockey	drills
field events	tennis	football	tug-o-war
rifle-shooting	table tennis	ice hockey	relays
pistoling	badminton	lacrosse	tag games
archery	aerial darts	rugby	ball games
equitation	horseshoe pitching	soccer	dodge-ball
rowing	shuffleboard	volleyball	pass ball
bowling	synchronized swimming	water polo	circle games
fishing	two-man sculling	polo	beater goes
surfing	billiards	softball	round
diving	paddleball	crew	slap jack
golf		curling	apparatus play
sledding			hiding games
skiing			*boccie*
ice-skating			croquet
roller skating			goal-hi
skeet shooting			stunts
walking			self-testing
sailing			
fly-casting			
weightlifting			
bicycling			

Ramifications. It is unfortunate that too many recreational programs are so heavily larded with motor performance activities and little else. Sports and games are rather easily scheduled within any program and have almost universal acceptance. Motor performance is no more important in the balanced recreational program than are any of the other categories. Nevertheless, sports and games have received an inordinate amount of emphasis. Motor performance can be very appealing to all age groups and to both sexes, and the other cultural factors may not affect its popularity. Motor performance is a part of living from the time the child expresses himself in random kinetic movement until the mature individual takes his last evening constitutional. Every waking moment has some facet of motor performance within it.

Traditionally, young males are attracted to and participate in a variety of motor skills. Young females also appreciate elementary games and rhythmical movement. As the individual matures, however, the female's interest in sports and physical games decreases. This is also true of active participation in team sports by adult males, although they may become the more fanatic of the passive spectators who follow team sports. With the popularization of sports and game competition, a result in great part of the recent world-wide coverage of the last three Olympic Games by the mass media and, in part, of the increasing attention given to the physical fitness level of all Americans, participation dramatically increased. Public relations selling by commercial establishments, such as bowling centers, have changed the image of the game and more women are bowling now than ever before. The same holds true for golf, swimming, gymnastics, and dance. Television popularization of any sport or game has been matched by an upsurge in participation. Where before females might have considered sports and game participation unfeminine, they now realize that the women participants in swimming, skiing, ice-skating, ballet, modern dance, tennis, golf, gymnastics, horseback riding, water skiing, and track not only possess beautiful figures, but are extremely feminine as well. No longer does the woman look with distaste upon motor performance. Another basic reason lies with the public school system which promotes physical education activities from the elementary level through the college level. Physical education, as an academic requirement, has done much to foster carry-over value for recreational participation long after the individual has left school.

The recreationist therefore has the responsibility of programming all forms of motor performance throughout the year. He plans to meet the needs, skills, and experiences of all of the people in the community. The standard for selection of motor activities into the program are not how many will be spectators, but rather, how many will take an active part. The schedule of physical recreational experiences should include both highly organized and formal activities and self-directed, informal, and free play activities. Within this format there should be some motor performance that has an appeal for each individual according to his own skills, proficiency, experience, and prior exposure. There must be instruction on each level of ability through clinics, workshops, and both individual and group practice. Competition is valuable in the motor performance, but emphasis upon extrinsic awards and winning at any price must be avoided. The justification for participation should be the enjoyment and satisfaction derived from playing the game and taking part in the sport.

Whenever there is serious thought given to competition, a place should be established for all those who wish to participate. The highly skilled performer certainly has a place in the recreational games program, but so does the individual with little ability and no experience. The intramural program, with its intention of allowing every interested person to play the game, may be the best method available in meeting the needs of people. Intramurals should not be confused with the specialist team. They are designed to offer equal opportunity, where participation will be against those of average skill. The intramural program consists of competition among those persons who frequent one recreational facility. It may consist of double or single elimination tournaments, ladder or pyramid contests, or round robin tournaments. It may or may not be co-recreational, although the latter might promote greater interest at one age and deter interest at another. In any case, the recreationist will be in the best position to organize such an activity.

Intermurals are those competitive activities organized between two or three neighborhood recreational facilities, e.g., centers or playgrounds, and conducted on the same basis as intramurals. The difference here is that an off-facility event can be scheduled and additional interest may be secured. Extramurals are those highly competitive events scheduled on an interdistrict and city-wide basis with great emphasis upon skills. They serve to focus attention upon the individual or single team and are useful in meeting the needs of those who have great ability, skill, and experience.

In whatever way the various forms of motor performance are programmed, they have a natural appeal. There are motor skills for the physically fit and unfit, for the strong, the weak, those who have endurance and those who have little stamina. There are activities which demand poise, balance, flexibility, agility, speed, and grace. There are other activities which require hand-eye coordination. Sports have many values, not the least of which is to offer the opportunity of belonging to a team, receiving personal satisfaction in attaining some objective, or simply enjoying the exhilarating effects of whatever game is being played.

Music

Any activity which produces vocal or instrumental tonal or atonal sounds having some form of syncopation or tempo is music. Music may be thought of as being either vocally or instrumentally produced, a combination of these forms, the act of creating music, and an appreciation of performance.

Music is a means of expression and can motivate action, evoke personal response, and elicit mood changes by appealing to and stimulating emotional reactions. Music may be classified into several component parts, among these are:

Vocal	Instrumental	Appreciation
community singing	solos quintets	concerts
barbershop quartets	duets septets	recordings
solos	trios octets	radio
glee club	quartets motets	musicology
a cappella choirs	band	
chorus	rhythm band	**Combination**
ensembles	orchestra	opera
madrigal singing	symphony band	operetta
round singing		musicals
singing games		variety and talent shows
choraling		parades
		pageants
		festivals
		circus

Ramifications. Music has an appeal for all ages, both sexes, and in some of its various forms may be performed, listened to, or appreciated by receptive people. Singing by oneself, in groups, formally, or spontaneously, participating in ensembles for instruments, composing, song writing, learning to appreciate the technique of a virtuoso, or just listening to any recorded music has a significant place within most recreational programs. The ability to enjoy music is easily acquired, for there is a particular type of music for every taste. Musical activities may come in terms of graded instruction for individuals or groups, appreciation classes, programmed background music to coincide with other activities, musical shows, talent shows, choral presentations during religious ceremonies or holidays, and community sings.

Some musical activities may be arranged in contests whereby performers attempt to create the most perfect type of their form. This is not to be confused with talent shows or other contests of that kind. Illustrative of talent contests are the barbershop quartet, marching band, fife and drum corps, and other musical groups which, although practicing for their own pleasure and satisfaction, are brought together once each year to perform en masse or as contestants.

Recreationists may be able to stimulate interest in the establishment of small ensembles whose members may never want to perform in public, but who utilize the recreational facility as a place for practice sessions. The development of brass choirs, string quartets, vocal groups, rhythm bands, jazz combinations, and string bands can arise from such organization.

The recreational service agency should act as a musical clearing house for the community by maintaining an adequate library from which records, tapes, and books on music could be borrowed. At every opportunity the department should sponsor community concerts, music under the stars, band exhibitions, glee clubs, *a cappella* choirs, and other music groups which may interest people and allow them to find a satisfying and creative outlet through music.

Outdoor Education

All nature-oriented activities based upon the physical, biological, and natural sciences expressed by the living in, collecting of, acquiring knowledge about, and finding appreciation in the outdoor environment may be considered as outdoor education. Outdoor education may be represented by the following:

Biological Science	Physical Science	Natural History
agriculture	chemistry	anthropology
agronomy	physics	ecology
biology	astronomy	paleontology
bacteriology	geology	archaeology
botany	mineralogy	mythology
floraculture	oceanography	nature lore
horticulture	geography	Indian lore
icthyology	topography	folk lore
ornithology	speleology	conservation
entomology	spectroscopy	
silviculture	meteorology	Outdoor Living
pomology	lapidary	
genetics		camping cave trips
zoology		hiking excursions
		climbing tours
		hunting

Ramifications. Broadly stated, outdoor education embraces all of the learning activities that deal directly with the wise utilization and appreciation of the natural environment. It consists of learning by actual performance in the natural laboratory of all outdoors.

The degree to which the aims of outdoor education is achieved will nearly always be the effect of the leadership provided. The leadership necessities of outdoor education, inclusive of all activities carried on under this category, require more than skill or technique in nature study, conservation, camping, or other specialities. Important as highly developed teaching skills are, they do not compensate for high quality leadership. Soundly planned and administered, the category of outdoor education provides the best features of schooling, camping, recreational experiences, and skill development of the individual. Within the natural setting the individual has the opportunity of being himself. This necessarily suggests, without temporizing, an optimum situation in terms of environment, facilities, program, and leadership. High quality outdoor educational experiences must operate under maximized criteria in order to promote good health habits, physical vigor, and human welfare.

Outdoor education, particularly that phase of it known as camping, offers excellent modalities and experiences for the development of participants who might otherwise be stifled in a less permissive atmosphere. Here the individual is, for a little while, taken away from the normal routine of school, home, or business, and placed in a dynamic situation under the guidance of professionally prepared personnel. This type of organized activity may eventuate in the individual's own appreciation for and indulgence in outdoor educational activities on his own at a later time.

In an outdoor environment the individual is able to express himself most freely. There are no distractions, noisome cities, densely populated neighborhoods, or the loneliness of isolation from one's peers, unless isolation is what the individual seeks. Here the needs of the individual are satisfied. The child or adult has an opportunity to live in proximity to nature. Whatever value there is in looking upward to the sky on a spectacularly starry night, seeing a clear moonrise, watching ribbons of light stream across the face of earth at dawn, catching the first drops of a summer shower, standing in appreciation of a magnificent autumnal coloring, or gazing at the panoramic view to be found after a long climb is fully realized. Living close to nature teaches each person something of how best to appreciate the resources of the land. The therapeutic value of outdoor education comes from simply being in the outdoors, living at an unhurried and unharried pace, learning whatever new skills one is capable of performing, and experiencing an entirely new series of activities or re-learning valuable skills which have been forgotten through disuse.

The recreationist has an ethical obligation to help preserve and conserve natural resources. At every season of the year there is some aspect of outdoor education which can be incorporated into the program. Through this instillation of awareness on the part of participants, a highly vocal and mobilized effort can be made and sustained for the preservation of open spaces, wilderness areas, and other natural phenomena necessary for such activity to occur. While teaching people to appreciate the value and beauty of the outdoors, converts may be won. Those who are most vociferous for the maintenance of natural places in the face of entrenched opposition have had some chance to camp, climb, hike, or bird watch. The organization of nature interest clubs, gardening clubs, astronomy clubs, nature craft activities, wilderness tours, and other stimulating experiences of this kind is an essential aspect of the comprehensive and balanced recreational program. The department should take advantage of any open space, stream, waterway, forest, game refuge, or park in which to inculcate and dramatically present to active and potential participants the inherent values of recreational activities in the outdoor setting.

Service Activities

All of those activities voluntarily engaged in by people who wish to assist others in learning, appreciation, skill development, or in making the community a better place in which to live as a result of their interest, talent, and sense of responsibility may be termed *service activities*. It is the selfless giving of time, energy, and sometimes money, purely for the satisfaction derived from helping another person or an entire community. Perhaps more than any other activity, service to others may be considered as the most rewarding. It is just as enjoyable as any of the other activity categories, requires the same sense of personal expression, and may result in an even greater or intense emotional response of well-being and warmth as the recipient of the service succeeds in the undertaking where assistance was given. Watching an individual develop skill, knowledge, emotional maturity, or an appreciation of a variety of subjects as a direct consequence of one's own instruction, guidance, or support provides the donor with a feeling of achievement and a sense of self-esteem for being able to help when another individual depended upon it. Service to others may be attained even when the volunteer does not work directly with other people. By offering time, skill, or technical knowledge, a more valuable recreational experience can be provided. Service activity is as broad as the entire field of recreational service. However, for simplification, services may be organized around these classes:

COMMITTEE WORK	DIRECT ACTIVITY LEADERSHIP	NONLEADERSHIP WORK
membership on:	art hobbies	stage lighting
boards	crafts music	clerical work
councils	dance outdoor	registering contestants
interest groups	drama education	receptionist
resource groups	education motor performance	decorators
committees	service activities	fund raisers
	social activities	transportation
	special activities	ushers

Ramifications. Every community has the potential personal resource of special skills and an infinite variety of talents waiting to be discovered. It is the responsibility of the recreationist to ensure a balanced program by investigating the possibility of incorporating the service phase of recreational experience into the program. To whatever extent an individual possess some talent or ability, it may be useful to others and therefore a viable contribution to the community at large.

Lifelong skills acquired as a result of occupation, hobbies, education, or living within one community may be the basis on which one can effect voluntary services to others. There is no phase of the program that may not be made more valuable to participants as the result of some volunteer's experiences and donation of time or effort.

Of necessity, volunteers must be recruited. This is best done by a survey performed in the community by staff members of the recreational service department. Some volunteers simply walk into the agency and ask to be allowed to help in any way. However, for the most part volunteers must be sought. The department should maintain a list of possible volunteer positions needed in the conduct of the program, the operation of the agency, or in assistance of enlisting support for the department. With these slots in mind, people may be recruited. Many people would like to help, but feel that they do not have special talent or do not realize that they do not have to be skilled in program in order to be useful and make a valuable contribution. Unfortunately, too, some administrators do not recruit nor do they want volunteers assisting in the program because they feel that volunteers require more time than is worthwhile to give them. Such an attitude on the administrator's part is not only one bred of ignorance, but is completely out of keeping with the idea that volunteer service is an integral part of the recreational program.

Recruitment of volunteers may be facilitated if relevant sources are determined before any drive is carried on. Retired individuals, high school-aged youngsters, hobbyists, fraternal organization members, and others are prime targets as recruits. The same fervor utilized for developing good public relations with the public should also merit consideration in developing a corps of volunteers for the department. Once individuals have been recruited, a screening process must be instituted so that those who can be placed within the various voluntary classifications may be indicated. Individuals with a high degree of program skills should be placed in a related sector, those who have administrative or clerical experience in the appropriate sector, and those who may perform significant work for the department in other areas should also be so indicated. An experienced interviewer for the department should be employed in the screening process, and written statements of potential volunteers should tend to clarify their aims and primary sense of purpose in offering their time.

After the initial action of recruitment and screening has occurred, there should be a basic orientation to the agency in terms of philosophy, functions, and goals. In this way the would-be volunteer can be made to recognize what the agency is attempting to do, why it performs in the way that it does, and the contribution that it makes to community welfare. After the orientation, there should be a period of in-service education to prepare the volunteers for service in any facet of agency operation. For those who will work with recreationists at a variety of facilities, scheduled observations and tours should be made as well as a brush-up of skills and methods of instructing and supervision. For those who will be participating as administrative assistants, office management techniques should be thoroughly explained and demonstrated. There is room in the daily operation of program to include all who want to lend their time and energy.

There are certain drawbacks to the utilization of volunteers, but their positive benefits to the program far outweigh any undesirable characteristics. It is true that volunteers may not be as reliable as paid employees and that they will not owe first allegiance to the agency. However, the agency should do everything in its power to stimulate loyalty and dedication in the volunteer just as it does for the employed individual. Moreover, the dependable volunteer frees the professional worker to do a more extensive and inclusive job of programming than might be allowable without additional help.

For all the negative reasons listed as to why volunteers should not be assigned or utilized, there is one over-riding fact for their incorporation—service is a recreational activity and it must be considered if the recreational program is to be balanced with something for each person's taste and satisfaction. Recreationists have the mandatory obligation to serve people and they can do this in one respect by offering opportunities for providing service to others through volunteer efforts. The benefit which volunteers contribute is so great that no program may be considered successful without them. The value received from a dedicated and skilled volunteer is incalculable to the agency. No program should be without as many as can be recruited.

Social Activities

All experiences of a recreational nature wherein two or more people come into close contact and where there is some direct relationship so that communication exists are social. With the exception of solitary recreational activities, all situations of a recreational nature are intensely social. Communication, in this sense, does not have to be verbal. It is enough if people can satisfy their need to belong to a group by merely being present at an activity in which the group is involved. Communication can be verbal or nonverbal. Close proximity, coincidental participation in the activity, and common interests often open avenues of receptivity and acceptance which are essential to sociability. Because social activities are generic to every category of the recreational program, only a sampling of these experiences is listed. Social activities may be grouped as follows:

Formal Activities	Informal Activities
parties	games
banquets	active
ceremonials	mental
programmed dances	musical
concerts	party
dinners	table
balls	community singing
teas	social dancing
festivals	conversation
holiday celebrations	coffee klatches
commencements	drop-ins
	pot-luck suppers

Special Projects

Activities which are out of the ordinary, conducted at intermittent intervals, require extra effort, and add variety and spice to the otherwise routine daily experiences of the program come under the heading of special projects. Such activities may involve participants who might not be attracted to the standard recreational activities. Special projects may be conducted throughout the year, but each special project is unique and is programmed only once in any given year. These feature presentations are complex and take strenuous effort at all stages, whether planning or actual operation, if they are to be successful. They must be colorful and exciting if they are to draw active participants and spectators. Almost any idea or theme will serve as the vehicle for a special project. However, most projects are classified in the following manner:

Exhibitions	Festivals	Musicals
art show	fairs	band day contests
craft show	circus	parade
animal show	field day	opera
hobby show	carnival	operetta
gymnastic exhibition	block party	pageant
horticultural show	community picnic	symphony concert
tableaux	holiday celebrations	talent show
nature exhibit	yacht regatta	

Ramifications. Special projects spotlight, correlate, and include many if not all of the other program categories. The special event may be looked upon as a culminating activity for a season, a month, or for a unique occasion. The special must be coordinated with other phases of the program and maintain the balance between routine and the change of pace which such an activity provides. Special projects are those events calculated to stimulate the individual who participates in the daily activities offered by the department as well as the stay-away. It affords the once in a while excitement necessary to attract new participants, and sustain those who do the daily work provided.

Key events which trigger the special project should be built around midyear and year-end periods. The summer festival, Christmas carnival, or winter frolic requires, perhaps, six months to one year of planning and preparation for success. For this reason, the special project cannot be programmed on a routine basis. It would surely sap the energies and creative expression of those required to do the work. Special projects that take place too frequently lose their speciality and become commonplace. The recreationist must know when to inject the special into his program. There is a natural progression of events which lead directly to a culminating activity inclusive of all the other recreational experiences that have gone before. In the normal course of events, every three month segment of a program may terminate with a modified special event, every six month segment with a major special project. Within these time periods other special events may be programmed, but they cannot be of the magnitude of the semiannual projects. Holidays make excellent themes around which a special event can take shape. But there is no single month within the year that does not contain a holiday or commemorative date of some note. Therefore recreationists in charge of programming special projects would do well to limit the occasions for such activities. The less they are performed in any given year, the greater the anticipation and satisfaction at the occurrence.

PLANNING FACTORS IN PROGRAMMING

The recreational program is not a series of individual activities strung together without any compensating factors. It is a carefully integrated and planned combination of many activities selected on the basis of individual and group interests, related ideas, and themes which are organized to achieve particular aims. Among these aims are the realization of personal fulfillment, satisfaction, enjoyment, physical and mental health, and the development of positive social relationships. Essentially, programming is the balanced correlation of leadership personnel, required space, facility, or equipment, a specified activity, and a participant at a time and place, both convenient and attractive, for some performance to occur. Presumably, the performance of an activity of a recreational nature, either as a passive spectator or as an active participant, will result in certain values necessary to the recipient.

Participant Planning

One of the basic concepts of programming is to involve as many potential participants as possible during the planning stage. Programming cannot be carried on without the support of those who will ultimately benefit from activities and voluntary association with organized recreational experiences. The recreationists may not simply dictate to the community at large the content of the program and expect instant acceptance and large attendance. There will always be some people who need to be told what to do, when to do it, with each phase carefully scheduled and arranged for their convenience. However, there is no guarantee that even those who require such assistance will participate. More likely, the recreationist must work with representatives of neighborhoods or with specific groups as a whole. His function is to enable them to operate and develop a program which is consistent with their interests and needs. When individual workers are assigned to small groups, each group may have a recreational program of its own, based upon the skills, knowledge, interest, and needs of the membership. When, however, the recreationist functions at the community level, as is most often the case, he must work with a small sample of the citizens in the community. If the department organizes neighborhood advisory councils and utilizes them in planning the program the recreationist acts as a transmitter and catalytic agent. He serves as a guide, advisor, and resource person, or taking a more active part in formulation, offers selected choices which are practical, stimulating, and capable of meeting the needs of the recipients.

Whether planning the program for one center, one playground, or other neighborhood facility, the recreationist should constantly seek out individuals who appear to be leaders or those who indicate a desire to assist in the production of a program. In order to involve as many different people as possible in any given neighborhood, there should be committees set up for each facet of the program. Additional committees may be organized for administrative and nonleadership purposes. These local committees can meet weekly, provide ideas for activities for the following week, and serve as part of the public relations medium in disseminating information about the program. One member of each committee may be elected to participate in an overall steering or coordinating council for the neighborhood. In this manner potential participants can be attracted to the program in the valid assumption that they have had a significant part in developing it. Participation is almost completely assured and support will invariably be generated when people feel that they have contributed their own energy and talent in planning activities. Ego involvement with some phase of the program will induce those very persons to ensure the success of the presentation. Participant planning plays another important role in the programming: it is in itself part of the recreational program and can be a most enjoyable and satisfying experience because it is one aspect of the service category. Participation in behind-the-scenes negotiations, devising activities for others to encounter, and generally performing a useful and necessary task in planning sessions is just as recreational as are the activities normally thought of in that respect.

Individual Need

The planning of an activity as well as the experience itself must be kept within the bounds of practicality and reality insofar as the potential participant is concerned. Successful accomplishment within any given recreational act, even the desire to perform in such an activity, is predicated upon the individual's capacity, ability, and limitations. The mental equipment possessed by the individual will enable him to accept certain responsibilities and facilitate his performance. With individuals of limited mental ability, there is a definite requirement on the part of the recreationist to protect them from situations where failure and resulting frustration and unhappiness are inevitable. However, the professional has the obligation of stimulating participation in those areas where they are capable. Individuals without any physical, mental, or emotional handicap are limited only by lack of knowledge, experience, and practice. There may also be a limitation imposed as a result of a lack of interest, but the competent leader will attempt to overcome this lack by exposure of the individual to stimulating and attractive situations. In any event, nonhandicapped people may achieve to whatever extent their capacity will allow. For those potential participants with some handicap, the recreationist must develop modified activities in which success may be attained.

As in all planning, individual welfare and satisfaction is uppermost. Although recreationists usually work with large numbers of people, the individual, rather than an aggregate, is the ultimate determinant of success or failure in programming. The recreationist can never forget that all activities must contribute something of value to the individual. Programming mass or spectator events can be justified solely in relationship to the values derived by the participating individuals. This does not militate against programming mass activities, but emphasis should not be laid on how many attended a given activity. This is a false system of appraisal in measuring the success of the activity. What the participation has done for the individual, what he has achieved, whether or not he has learned anything, developed socially, emotionally, physically, or mentally are the criteria upon which any recreational experience should be evaluated. It is to individual need and interest that programming must be oriented.

Time

Time is the basis on which the recreational program operates. Leisure is the free time which people have to participate in recreational experiences. The work of the recreational service department finds its rationale for establishment in the leisure which people have to spend. At almost any time during each day of any week there will be those in the community who have free time. One of the elemental procedures necessary, if the public agency is to serve its constituents well, is to determine who has leisure and when. On this foundation the program structure will be built.

Program content will be made more interesting if it is related to current events, incidents, occurrences, or historical and traditional situations. The timeliness of activities assists in arousing and maintaining interest and participation in planned activities. Time is significant in planning the program because it involves all persons residing in the community. Of necessity surveys must be made to find out what age and sex groups are free to participate. Planning the playground or center program will rely upon these two factors. While the adult age group will remain stable, except in communities having a high population of "shift" workers in local industry, the children and adolescent age group free time components change. If the program includes preschool age children, activities must be planned for them when they can attend. Consideration must be made for parents if their presence is required. School age children will not be available to the program during school hours throughout the academic year. Working adults will usually participate only during evening hours and on the week ends. These time elements are therefore of extreme importance in the development of the program.

Obvious as it may seem, time can be segmented into the following components for utilization in programming: hour, daily, weekly, monthly, seasonally, and annually. The entire program hinges on time and the proper scheduling of leadership, facilities, equipment, and activities.

Hourly segment. Dividing the recreational day into hourly segments is of assistance in programming for children whose attention span is short and who may be expected to be restless if activities are prolonged. Typically, each hour is indicated in terms of the commencement of particular activities as well as by half-hour segments for the younger age groups.

Daily Schedule. A daily listing of all activities to be offered by the recreational facility on an hourly basis is very desirable. The daily program is designed to meet the needs of the facility and the neighborhood it is intended to serve. Unless each neighborhood has the same population composition and the facility is duplicated along with staff positions, each daily program will be different. The difference will be determined by the population to be served, the leadership employed, the facility and space available, and other administrative factors. Among the considerations which influence the daily program will be the age, occupational status, and sex of people living within the neighborhood. In designing the daily program to meet the needs of the population, the recreationist should be aware of when activities at the facility will be practical. For example, preschool age children will probably make use of the recreational facility during the morning hours from 9:00 a.m. until 11:00 a.m. The department should also be prepared for some activity for the mothers of these children.

Some time before noon, older retired adults may make use of the facility and an appropriate series of activities must be planned. Out-of-school youth tend to frequent the facility in the early afternoon as do the preschoolers. After three o'clock in the afternoon, children of elementary school age begin to utilize the facility. Although some of the children under eleven years will probably leave for supper and not return those children who are between the ages of twelve and fourteen may come back to the facility until 8:00 p.m. The senior high school age group begins drifting into the facility sometime after 7:00 p.m. and will generally stay until closing. Older adults rarely remain after 10:00 p.m. Young adults may be expected to arrive after 8:00 p.m. and remain until closing. If the facility is open during the week end, as it should be, there will be a noticeable shift in usage by children. The elementary school age child will arrive earlier and remain later. This is not true for the adolescent or older adult. Their arrivals and departures tend to be constant.

Weekly Schedule. A weekly program assists the recreationist in planning for recurrent and instructional activities. It provides a feeling of continuity and allows participants a chance for selecting specific activities in advance and makes them aware of the times at which they begin. The weekly schedule enables the recreationist to enhance the program by adopting his activities and materials to appropriate themes. Themes add color to the routine activities and provide a carry-over from one day's activities to the next with a culminating event at the end of each week. The variety of interests and the diversity of activity offerings prohibit the scheduling of all such experiences during any one day. Weekly scheduling facilitates the incorporation of diversity and variety for recurrent, intermittent, and unique recreational activities to be programmed.

Monthly Schedule. Of chief consideration in planning a monthly program is the inclusion of sequential and graduated activities which culminate in a special project, usually based on some theme, that demonstrates many of the activities carried on at the recreational facility. Such an event presents the opportunity of correlating activities in order to enhance each one. By combining the different categories into one monthly special event, many more participants can perform. City-wide tournaments, various leagues, and those activities which require not less than two or three weeks of preparation before they can be introduced should be included in the monthly plan. Among the activities for which additional time is needed are formal plays, double elimination tournaments, some craft projects, certain art objects, and innumerable exhibits, displays, and shows. The month-to-month schedule of activities may be quite applicable in neighborhoods where the recreational program has been newly established. Because the recreationist responsible for the neighborhood facility must have time to acquaint himself with the special character of the neighborhood, it is unlikely that programs will be scheduled for longer periods than one month in advance. Only after prolonged contact has been made with the neighborhood, and those variable factors which can influence the program have been determined to some extent, will there be an attempt to program for time periods longer than one month.

Seasonal Schedule. The changing seasons offer countless opportunities for the construction of an interesting and comprehensive recreational program. Seasonal programming tends to follow the traditional activities which have been utilized by many locales throughout the country. Except in regions where there are extremes, the four seasons provide a natural setting for the development of various and highly diversified experiences. With seasonal shifts, different themes and culminating special events may be brought into the program. Seasonal programming offers the chance for planning three months in advance. It is reasonably assumed that where the recreational service department is well established, long-range planning of recreational activities on a neighborhood, district, and community-wide basis follows. The content of the seasonal program is not merely the proliferation of daily, weekly, and monthly programs. It operates on the basis of special projects which may be profitably introduced only once, at a specific time of the year, and for that reason requires scrupulous attention to many planning details. The nature of the event is such that it may take many weeks and even months for plans to materialize and for the prior preparation necessary to ensure success. Invitational contests, tournaments, and meets usually require at least three months of intensive preparation. A holiday celebration with parades, exhibits, demonstrations, and other planned events may occupy a six-month planning session before it is ready for production.

Seasonal planning considers the nature of the activity to be offered, the community factors operating to influence participation, the time such an activity requires for successful presentation, local traditions and expectations, and the adequacy of the departmental staff to stimulate interest and attract attention. Typically, the themes under which the seasonal program operates are essentially related to the conditions that prevail during any given three-month period. For example, the summer season of June, July, and August will allow a larger number of children to participate in outdoor activities than at any other time of year. The winter season of December, January, and February offers opportunities for a special winter carnival or festival that can occur at no other time.

Annual Schedules. The recreational program for the entire year is developed from all of the preceding time segments. However, there are some facets of the yearly program that should be emphasized. There is no period during the year when the public recreational service should not be operating at maximum capacity. It is unrealistic for any recreationist to assume that people have no interest in recreational activities at certain times of the year. Such an assumption is pure nonsense. As Hutchinson states:

> The interests people have for leisure activity do not wane as the days become shorter during the year. An examination of the shift in emphasis of the commercial amusement attractions during the winter shows very little differences in the desires people have for activity. The differences lie in *where* the activities take place rather than *when* they take place.[1]

Public recreational service agencies are established to serve people during their leisure. Leisure is increasing. Particularly is this true among various occupational groups whose work hours have remarkably decreased in the past five years. Older adults, after retirement, have almost unlimited leisure. Better working conditions, increased fringe benefits, vacation periods, longer week ends, and holidays are the times around which public recreational service agencies should concentrate their programming function. These are the times in which people are free to participate. The recreational service day should begin at 9:00 a.m. and continue to 11:00 p.m. during the week. On week ends the length of the day may be even longer. Inasmuch as there are always people in the community who have

---

[1] John L. Hutchinson, *Principles of Recreation* (New York: A. S. Barnes and Company, 1949), p. 187.

free time at all hours of the day and evening, the public program must consider scheduling activities all of the time. Public agencies cannot afford to exist on a part-time basis. They have been established as full-time operations and have the responsibility for offering services whenever people have the leisure to utilize them. Leisure has become almost universal, in this country. For these reasons public recreational agencies must remain open and operating each and every day of the year, subject only to staffing requirements. There is no such idea that recreational services are a sometimes thing. People seek recreational activities all the time. The public department is obliged, therefore, to operate all of the time.

Themes

One of the ways in which activities can be made more attractive and stimulating to the potential participant is the organization of recreational experiences around some central idea. In this way, every activity that is planned and organized by the department focuses attention on a single concept and contributes to its presentation. Themes are topical ideas that lend a common element to every activity which can be scheduled within the program. They provide a basic aim that lends color and effect to the most routine activities. Essentially, themes offer natural opportunities for the integration of various categories of activities into a combined presentation. Such combination actually increases the satisfaction of participation as the different parts are joined together in one symmetrical event. An example of the utilization of a theme which integrates many activities might be a winter carnival or summer festival. Depending upon the overall activity, let us say a musical in this instance, many features of the program could be exhibited. The categories of art, crafts, dance, drama, music, motor skills, service, social activity, and special event, could be combined. Artists could be called upon to paint appropriate sets and scenes; crafts would be brought into play for the construction and design of sets, stage, lighting, and properties; music and dramatics are part of such activity; all dramatics is intensely social. The service category would enlist the assistance of volunteers to act as ushers, curtain raisers, lighting technicians, coaches, make-up designers, grips, sound technicians, publicity agents, and so on. Motor performance might be included if the musical featured any aspect of gymnastic, fencing, or other physical skill. There is little question but that the entire performance would be a special event. The theme of festival or carnival would be the point of departure for the entire program.

To a lesser extent, themes can play an important part in making program activities more enjoyable during every week of the year. Each week can be devoted to one theme. Each month and season may also be appropriately concerned with themes. The progressive nature of instructional activities invites thematic concepts. As the individual develops greater skill in whatever activity interests him, a variety of themes can serve as incentives for additional practice and ultimate presentation or exhibition. Themes may be organized around the following:

holidays (national)	seasonal
traditions (local, regional)	religious
ethnic and cultural	commemorative
patriotic	miscellaneous

Gradation

Every category, except hobbies, service, and special projects, will offer opportunities for instruction to be given. A program that is free from the taint of stagnation must be progressive in scope. Progress is best maintained as individuals are enabled to develop proficiency in the activities that interest them. Gradation of activities requires a tripling of program activities. By this is meant that each skill taught at the recreational facility may be offered at the beginning level, intermediate level, or advanced level. Beyond this requirement is the differentiation of age groups into which classes are divided. In crafts, for example, there are projects designed to familiarize the individual with tools, material, equipment, and the finished product. At each age, there will be crafts appropriate to the needs of the group. With maturity and responsibility, more complicated and intricate crafts may be introduced. At the youngest age level simplified and easily understood projects are included. But even at the youngest ages there will be those who show precocity or unusual advancement. Such individuals should not be held back and deprived of more advanced techniques. They will tend to drop out of the program if their interest cannot be maintained. Graded instructional courses prevents, in most instances, the withdrawal of participants because of boredom, possession of a high degree of skill, or association with individuals who are not capable of handling tools and materials. It is possible through this instructional sequence to maintain contact with program participants from earliest childhood through old age. The graded aspect of programming facilitates modification of activities to meet mental, physical, or maturation limitations. Gradation is necessary in the program because it allows people to acquire skills and interests that will have carry-over value for them.

Balance

The recreational program must serve all interests, needs, personalities, and levels of skill. For these reasons it must contain a variety of activities in which all people may seek satisfaction. Balanced programming has to do with the inclusion of many activities within all categories in order to attract participation. There should be something for everyone in a public recreational service program. Each individual should be able to find something of interest if the program is correctly balanced. There will be a compelling program which can stimulate interest and desire to learn among all citizens in the community. Balance is particularly important in providing equal opportunity for participation. Because the categories must cover all, or nearly all, recreational experiences in which people show interest, there should be enough variety to offset emphasis on any single category.

Balance indicates diversity. It means consideration for skill levels attained by individuals as well as organizational forms by which the activity is programmed. There must be opportunity for both active participation and passive appreciation, for solitary as well as group experiences, for performance as well as looking-on, for motor skills as well as mental skills, for giving service as well as receiving service. Progressive aspects of the activity are also considered in terms of individual development and proficiency achieved. In the balanced program there is a place for the beginner, the individual who has some knowledge or skill, and the advanced or highly skilled and resourceful person. There is, in short, equilibrium among the various component parts of the program.

Flexibility

The ability to meet any contingency or condition as a result of changing interests, weather, population, or for circumstances beyond the control of the recreationist is termed *flexibility*. Alternate courses of action planned in the event of unexpected conditions damaging or destroying primary plans must be handled with the same judgment and concern as are scheduled activities. A sudden rain storm, snowfall, illness, damage to a vital facility, or other emergency situation should be arranged for with a reserve plan. Modification of the site, adaptability of the activity to meet the needs of potential participants is always part of the sound program plan. The alternate activity includes professional personnel, facility determination, any transportation requirements, planned activities, and method of ready communication to publicize whatever changes have to be effected.

Foreseeability, that is, the recognition that there always exists a possibility of disruption or curtailment, places the burden of detailed secondary planning in the hands of the recreationist. The alternative activity may be a duplicate of the scheduled activity with the exception of location and/or facility. A primary example of alternative planning and flexibility is illustrated by the understudy role in any play. Featured players always have back-up actors in the event that some emergency renders them unable to go on with a performance. An open-air concert, art exhibit, or hobby show should not be cancelled because of rain. Plans should be made to move the performance indoors. Even rain or snow days contribute to flexibility. If all those concerned, either as performers, exhibitors, or spectators know that an alternate date has been made in the event of inclement weather, then cancellation of an activity on a given day will not ruin the effort which has gone into its production. At worst, only a few potential participants may be lost. Wherever possible, however, the activity should be held at the same time on the same day, but at an indoor facility. In this way, those who are prepared to attend will not be disappointed and none will be lost to the activity.

Leadership

In programming recreational activities, an essential element that influences the success or failure of the activity to meet its stated objective is leadership. In developing plans for the inclusion of all recreational categories, serious consideration must be given to the adequacy of staff requirements necessary to achieve proper instruction, supervision, and guidance. The one ingredient without which public recreational service loses much, if not all, impact is the quality of professional leadership available. Every one of the categories is predicated upon sufficient professional personnel available to conduct activities and offer leadership resources. Community-wide programming necessitates full-time employed personnel to give continuity, comprehensive planning, and daily attention to the operational functions of the agency. Volunteers or part-time employees may assist in the development of program and broaden opportunities, but they cannot replace professional leadership. The program is only as valuable as an adequate personnel force can make it.

Spaces, Structures, and Facilities

The development of an adequate program of recreational service depends upon the design, construction, and maintenance of indoor and outdoor areas appropriate to the conduct of program. Requirements range from quiet corners in a playground or park to immense spaces in which camping, hunting, fishing, mountain climbing, or other outdoor activities may be programmed. Many recreational activities simply cannot be organized with any expectation of success unless specific facilities are available and accessible to participants. The public recreational service department is required to acquire, design, sometimes to construct, and always to maintain physical plants and properties of a size and type sufficient to carry all phases of the program. However, acting in coordination and conjunction with other sectors of the community, including churches, youth serving agencies, other municipal buildings, and schools, such properties may also be considered as potential recreational resources.

The modification, renovation, or reconstruction of existing buildings may result in additional useful space which can make the facility a better place in which to conduct the program. The wise utilization of all possible available areas as well as modern design for the multiple use of formerly restricted spaces allows for the inclusion of additional activities. Successful programming is concerned with availability and accessibility of recreational facilities for public use. Space requirements for activities to be included necessitate the development of a well-balanced series of structures and outdoor places which are suitable in terms of size, situation, and attractiveness. Suitability also means placement of rooms within a building, ease of supervision by personnel, traffic flow, building design, color scheme, cleanliness, comfort, and interior decor. Many activities also require special equipment, materials, and instruments if they are to be programmed.

SUMMARY

The recreational program is the single most important function with which the recreational service agency concerns itself. Every conceivable means and effort must be taken to ensure the well-balanced, comprehensive, and varied program. Programming represents all of the directed energy which the agency has at its disposal to effect the most valuable, satisfying, and attractive program possible. (Programming is influenced by many far reaching factors, including community fabric and milieu; individual need, interest, and capacity; social, economic, and educational levels; previous experiences; occupation; and many tangible and intangible aspects of the culture of which it is a part.)

All recreational programs are justifiable under the principle of providing something for each person in the community at all times. Success in recreational programming depends upon logical planning, standards of activity selection and development, and techniques for their implementation. Programming is a complicated process requiring professional leadership and support. Ultimately, programming is effected by an arrangement of competent leadership, interesting activities, and recreational places at which performance occurs. Detailed planning based upon certain knowledge of the community and its people, resources, and potential are of inestimable value in establishing a sound program in which all people may attain satisfaction, enjoyment, and a feeling of personal well-being.

SELECTED REFERENCES

BAIRD, FORREST J., *Music Skills for Recreation Leaders.* (Dubuque, Iowa: Wm. C. Brown), 1963.

BUTLER, GEORGE D., *Playgrounds: Their Administration and Operation,* 3d ed. (New York: The Ronald Press), 1960.

DONNELLY, R. J., W. G. HELMS, and E. D. MITCHELL, *Active Games and Contests,* 2d ed. (New York: The Ronald Press), 1958.

FREEBERG, WILLIAM H. and LOREN E. TAYLOR, *Programs in Outdoor Education.* (Minneapolis, Minn.: Burgess Publishing Company), 1963.

HAUGEN, ARNOLD O. and HARLAN G. METCALF, *Field Archery and Bowhunting.* (New York: The Ronald Press), 1963.

KAPLAN, MAX, *Music in Recreation: Social Foundations and Practices.* (Urbana, Ill.: Stipes Publishing Company), 1955.

KLEINDIENST, VIOLA K. and ARTHUR WESTON, *Intramural and Recreation Programs for Schools and Colleges.* (New York: Appleton-Century-Crofts), 1964.

KRAUS, RICHARD, *Recreation Today: Program Planning and Leadership.* (New York: Appleton-Century-Crofts), 1966.

LIEBERS, ARTHUR, *The Complete Book of Water Sports.* (New York: Coward-McCann, Inc.), 1962.

MONTGOMERIE, NORAH, ed., *To Read And To Tell.* (New York: Arco Publishing Co., Inc.), 1964.

NICKELSBURG, JANET, *The Nature Program at Camp.* (Minneapolis, Minn.: Burgess Publishing Company), 1964.

THE ATHLETIC INSTITUTE, *The Recreation Program,* 2d ed. (Chicago: The Institute), 1964.

VAN DER SMISSEN, BETTY and OSWALD H. GOERING, *A Leader's Guide To Nature-Oriented Activities.* (Ames, Iowa: Iowa University Press), 1964.

VOSS, GUNTHER, *Reinhold Craft and Hobby Book.* (New York: Reinhold Publishing Corp.), 1963.

Chapter 15

PLANNING

PRINCIPLE: Proper planning is the only logical method to forestall chaotic measures and appalling expenditures resulting from the growth of population, attrition of natural resources, expansion of urban metropolises, and modification of conditions arising from technology and scientific advances.

Planning is a continuous process that attempts to preserve the best features of the community while forecasting future needs. Planning for recreational service is the study of human needs and the scientific examination of contemporary resources, demographic growth, and urban expansion. It analyzes the related problems of land usage and the management of such use by correctional and developmental applications. It is concerned and related to the orderly control of the physical development of the community, although it cannot be separated from program planning. In nearly every respect, physical planning is the obverse of program planning. Programming invariably influences the direction which physical planning takes.

The chief function of planning is to collect and make available the technical data and expertise necessary to ensure that more adequate, harmonious, and accessible recreational spaces and facilities are developed according to need and on a sound priority basis. Planning is really an attempt to prevent waste while resolving a host of problems concerning area beautification, traffic congestion, and the redistribution of population. Planning is also concerned with the proper distribution of recreational spaces and the proposals for construction of the required varied facilities to provide the indoor and outdoor activities which make up the balanced program. One purpose of planning is to promote, extend, and to make available the necessary areas and physical plants for a more perfect administration of public recreational service.

PLANNING PROCEDURES

The most important part of any planning program is the preparation of a comprehensive plan dealing with a particular problem, in this case that of recreational service. Because planning objectives are based upon logical decisions and alternatives in order to meet current and future needs, the plan is essentially a compilation of physical, demographic, political, and economic resources in the development of the community. All planning procedures are usually predicated upon the completion of surveys to gather information about the community, the collation of such information as well as the development of a master plan and the implementation of that plan.

Collection of Data

Initially, a survey must be undertaken to assess the community. At this stage all physical qualities of the community are noted and listed. Included in this study would be data on existing open spaces, forest and water resources, topographic features, residential areas, commercial areas, industrial areas, transportation methods, streets and other traffic carriers, all public buildings and structures, private agency buildings and structures, sewage lines, dams, reservoirs, and parks or reservations located adjacent to or nearby the community. The second phase of the survey would be to indicate the community potential. Any suggestion for renewal, renovation, or correction should be indicated in proposals for the continued development of the community along recreational lines.

All community estimates and appraisals are made in terms of historical background information and research concerning the community and its growth. Of extreme significance would be the demographic aspects of the community: the growth, distribution, density, composition, and movements of population in the community as well as such social manifestations as schools, churches, health facilities, all recreational agencies, protective agencies, and financial and economic trends observable in the community. As the purpose of obtaining factual information is to aid in the preparation of a master plan, attention must be focused on assembling only that data which is of significance to the development of the plan.

Master Planning

Fundamentally, the plan is a guide for the long-time development of the community. In preparing the master plan, the first objective is to indicate the outstanding community features in correct relation. For purposes of recreational planning, the location and form of land uses, the features and sites of proposed open spaces, the transportation systems and traffic patterns, the location of public buildings, and the distribution and types of public utilities together with specific proposals for their development and extenuation are necessary. Other projects which will affect the plan, although not particularly related to these factors, are concerned with urban renewal, greater efficiency of transit systems, alleviation of traffic congestion, and other long-term public improvements. The recreational service master plan attempts to forecast the development of the community in terms of twenty-five-year periods. For this reason, a detailed and accurate diagnosis of current activities and reliable information pertaining to projected growth is basic to any decision making predicated on the plan.

A contemporary trend in residential planning has been to identify areas in terms of neighborhood units. In many communities, neighborhood patterns have spontaneously developed around suburban or newly constructed outlying shopping centers. However, there are some well-planned neighborhoods. The local or neighborhood unit concept is a recent innovation promoted by urban planners which has, as a main object, the development of easily defined intrinsic neighborhoods arranged around a local recreational center or complex having at least one school within the area. Generally, these publicly planned neighborhood units are delimited by natural barriers, e.g., major traffic arteries, railroads, waterways, cultivated green spaces, or wooded areas which serve as buffer zones.

Typically, the neighborhood is planned to provide residential housing for the population, an elementary school to serve that population, and recreational facilities suitably designed and adequate to meet the requirements of local residents. Amenities agencies are frequently mapped out for development on the rim of the unit, specifically at traffic junctions, and contiguous to districts of a similar nature in adjacent neighborhoods. The street system and traffic load capabilities must be given significant consideration. The vehicular arteries and pedestrian streets must be designed to facilitate traffic movement, but prevent use by through traffic. In order for the neighborhood unit to function most effectively, vehicular traffic cannot be allowed to discourage the cross movement of people. Major traffic carriers can act as well as any natural physical feature as a distinct barrier to pedestrian use in an area. Attention must also be focused upon the protective services of the community and the structures needed for the maintenance of effective police, fire, and health departments.

PUBLIC LAND USE FOR RECREATIONAL SERVICES

In almost every community, but particularly the large urban center, there are sections of land reserved for public and quasi-public utilization. These uses are chiefly concerned with the provision of services to the entire community or some part of it. Contained in this classification are lands reserved for streets, public utilities, buildings, buffer zones, schools, and all types of recreational facilities. The policies under which these various land uses operate cannot be segregated from the agency responsibilities to which they relate. Therefore, it is necessary to omit additional mention of these services of government and concentrate on the one function of primary interest—recreational service.

Land and spaces categorized as recreational cover a wide variety of uses including playgrounds, parks, reservations, playfields, community centers, beaches, camp grounds, swimming pools, outdoor theatres, golf courses, riding trails, bicycle paths, tennis courts, auditoriums, gymnasiums, band shells, arboretums, zoological and botanical gardens, museums, scenic vistas, historical sites, water ways, forests, and other open spaces of different types. Recreational areas and spaces include quasi-public and privately owned lands and facilities which are available for public utilization.

The amount of space segregated for recreational purposes in any given community varies greatly with the local conception of providing for public recreational service. If the community feels that recreational experience is a vital governmental function designed to meet the changing needs of people, the likelihood exists that a greater proportion of the available land will be devoted to recreational uses. Where a community does not accord value to recreational experience, the amount of land made available for recreational purposes decreases. Recreational spaces differ significantly from community to community and within different neighborhoods of a single community. The space necessary for recreational uses depends a great deal upon the physical situation of the community as well as upon the interests, age groups, occupational factors, and educational, social, and economic level that are characteristic of its people. At this time there are only educated estimates as to the space requirements for recreational use in the community. Such rules of thumb may run anywhere from five to ten per cent of all the community land available to one acre per every hundred persons residing in the community. The basic error of such figures is that they do not consider population mobility, density, or need.

Site location and variety of utilization are probably of greater importance than the total allotment of space set aside for recreational uses. Recreational facilities and areas must consider all of the people residing in the community as well as transient populations. The chief factor concerning amount of space devoted to recreational objectives is its accessibility to the population which most requires it. Facilities designed to meet the recreational needs of the local neighborhood have to be located within one quarter mile of almost every resident. The facilities must be easily accessible without hazard from vehicular traffic nor barred by any natural or man-made physical objects. On the other hand, regional parks and camping and picnic facilities need not be closely situated to the local population. They may be located on the outskirts of the community, or in distinct but accessible sections of the community without regard to distance. The utilization of such outlying or peripheral facilities is intended for a mobile population which will travel some distance to reach the site.

Recreational site planning requires scrupulous attention to the acquisition of open space for future population needs. Careful consideration must also be given to present residential districts, population composition, population trends and movement, population distribution and density, future population composition, distribution, and density as well as other governmental services essential to the health, education, welfare, and safety of the population. Other factors which affect long term recreational site planning will be concerned with street plans, present and future school sites, and other public building construction.

In the selection of sites for recreational purposes, every effort must be taken to make basic use of areas which for all other practical intents and purposes would prove to be uneconomical, unfeasible, or otherwise undesirable. Such areas are prime spots for scenic viewing, hiking trails, and nature paths, and have program value. Thus, steep hillsides may be converted to winter sleigh riding, skiing, or tobogganing areas. In the summer, the hillside might serve as an observatory, beginner's hill for novice mountain climbers, as part of a cross country or steeple chase run, and so on. Deep gorges, ravines, rocky promontories, so-called submarginal lands, swamps, bogs, and other equally unsuitable land for commercial or industrial development may very well be excellent for recreational purposes. These various areas may be easily incorporated into the program by making use of them as passive or active recreational spaces. Bird watching, hunting, geological explorations, collecting minerals, studying the ecological process of a given environment are all potentially worthwhile recreational experiences. However, these lands should not be bought, leased, or accepted for recreational use unless they are situated in suitable locations. A deep ravine, for example, does not have to be accessible to the general public if it can be reached by an interested climber. In fact, accessibility may not be the only standard for selection. Availability for the purposes to which such areas are intended for use may make them desirable recreationally, if for no other reason. When the space is to be utilized for tot-lots or neighborhood playgrounds, it must be of adequate size and situated within the neighborhood where it will be convenient to those whom it will serve.

Standardized Recreational Facilities and Their Placement

Every community should have a variety of basic recreational facilities in which all of its people may find a balanced series of recreational experiences. Ideally, a small playground or tot-lot, with minimum equipment, should be situated at the center of every one hundred children under six years of age. This area can be ten thousand square feet or less in size and located in such a site that children could have access to it without crossing any street. The play lot can be fenced in, contain a large sand pile and a few pieces of ceramic tile or concrete forms, gaily planted, and have benches set in on all sides. Parents would thus be the means of supervision and the sandbox and blocks play of early childhood could be satisfied.

The neighborhood playground should be exactly what its designation implies. Every neighborhood within the community should have a playground.[1] The playground is essentially designed, although not exclusively, for children between the ages of six to fifteen. The neighborhood playground may have from three to ten acres, contain multipurpose areas, a

[1] Charles L. Mee Jr., "Putting the Play in Playgrounds," *The New York Times Magazine,* November 6, 1966, Section 6, pp. 112, 117, 119–120.

shelter, toilet facilities, quiet games area, court games area, and sufficient space to conduct a comprehensive and balanced program for the individuals who attend. In many instances the playground can be night-lighted and thereby serve an older age group. It is not uncommon to find tennis courts, volley ball courts, handball courts, *boccie,* and basketball layouts, as well as the aforementioned facilities on playgrounds. The neighborhood playground should be adjacent to or in close proximity to the local elementary school, thereby taking full advantage of any availability of the school for recreational purposes. The neighborhood served by the local playground will have a radius of not less than one quarter of a mile. The park-school concept, which incorporates this plan, has been implemented in Minneapolis, Chicago, Skokie, Providence and other cities. This is the construction of school buildings either on or adjacent to park sites so that the combined facility can be used for both educational and recreational purposes.

The district recreational center is an indoor facility containing the space and equipment necessary for the on-going year-round production of a highly effective and diversified program of recreational activities. It will serve all age groups and be open from morning until late at night to meet its primary obligations. It will be adjacent to an intown park of not less than twenty-five, nor more than forty acres, containing a variety of passive and active areas, including at least one fully equipped and staffed playground, walking paths, a variety of playing fields, courts, appropriate plantings, and picnic spots. The district center should be able to serve the needs of people from an area within a radius of between one half to three quarters of a mile.

The regional recreational complex is a tract of land not less than one hundred acres and ranging up to two thousand acres. It contains a highly diversified series of terrain features, has facilities of many types, and may also be planned to house the community's zoological and/or botanical exhibit. It may be located near a museum of natural history, art museum, or other educational center. There is every likelihood that the complex may have a field house constructed upon it for a variety of sports and games activities, at least one outdoor theater and band shell, a relatively large lake, boating facilities in summer and ice-skating facilities during the appropriate winter months. It may have an outdoor stadium as well as golf courses and one or two swimming pools or other aquatic areas. If the regional complex is located close to a major waterway, i.e., river, sound, bay, ocean, gulf, or great inland lake, it will probably have marina and beach facilities. Generally, there will be well-designed spaces for almost every recreational taste. Walks for strolling, bridle paths, bicycle paths, an observatory, bird sanctuary, scenic vistas, fountain displays, reflecting pools, and picnic and camping areas may well be part of such a regional center. This may be considered to be the chief recreational plant of the community, and, depending upon the density of population, may very well be able to care for all of the people. Except in the largest urban centers, one such regional center is all that is necessary. As many as ten to twenty of this type of complex may be required to administer to the citizens of the great metropolitan cities. It is a necessary correlate that only with easy accessibility by major transit systems or by a series of high speed traffic arteries will these regional complexes serve the purpose for which they were created. The ability to attract patronage to these centers depends, to a significant extent, upon the mobility of the population and the available transportation systems, both public and private.

No community can be considered fully prepared to promote the most comprehensive coverage of recreational services unless it has within a short distance from its border a noncity-owned recreational reservation. Such a facility is usually operated by the county, state, or federal government and can be within two hours' drive, by express highway, from the city limits. The reservation may be part of the county park system, a state park or forest, or a national park, forest, or monument. Any of these facilities will have special features of a natural phenomenon type or man-made attractions which draw attendance. Panoramic views from promontories, spectacular waterfalls, mountains, gorges, fall coloring, trees, ocean views, geologic remains, scientific curiosities, quiet glades, and an abundance of natural and artificially created areas on which a wide diversity of recreational activities may occur will be expected of the reservation. This last facility may not be within the power of the community to provide, because it must rely upon other governmental levels to furnish it. However, with increasing federal and state awareness of the need for open space acquisition and the development of these areas for recreational purposes, there is every reason to believe that the community can request such governments to plan for the acquisition and development of such facilities. Because the city itself will have no jurisdiction, it must join with other communities and request planning and development assistance from county or state government with funds from the federal government to supplement and underwrite the costs. If communities work together for these additions, they may find higher jurisdictions more receptive to such needs. There has long been a movement to develop parks every one hundred miles in some states.[2] With the present availability of federal funds this movement may become reality. Although far-sighted men realized the need for the acquisition and preservation of scenic areas and the development of permanently established recreational parks which would help to conserve our natural resources, it is only now with an emergency of our own making, in terms of destroyed resources, that after forty years of warning something of positive value is being done.[3]

---

[2] Barrington Moore, *A State Park Every Hundred Miles,* Bulletin, National Conference on State Parks (Washington, D.C., 1921), 4–7.
[3] Raymond H. Torrey, *State Parks and Recreational Uses of State Forests in the United States,* National Conference on State Parks (Washington, D.C., 1926), 259 pp.

Without really opening a Pandora's box of confusing statements, reiteration of a chief consideration cannot be made too often. The community should be able to rely upon the city school system for utilization of every school building within the public domain. Each school, with its central location and abundant rooms and facilities may serve admirably as a local neighborhood recreational center if of the elementary type, as a district center if of the junior high school type, and as a regional center if of the senior high school type. The tremendous expenditures of tax funds for the design, construction, and maintenance of these school buildings makes it mandatory that they be used to a maximum extent. No city can afford to allow these schools to stand vacant when there are so many people to be served. The school buildings are a valuable primary recreational facility and should be so employed. The other alternative is, of course, the major construction of purely recreational buildings and centers. The cost of these additional facilities when schools are so well suited for this role indicates a complete abdication of responsible political behavior on the part of those who have jurisdiction over the school system. Every effort must be made to incorporate the school building and its entire surrounding physical plant into the municipal recreational service system. That this idea has not received greater impetus and effect is due to a lack of knowledge on the part of governing politicians and the resultant crises which may be perpetuated if there were a strong municipal movement to take over the operation of the city school system.

The traditional employment of boards of education is fast being outmoded. While it is not the intent of this book to deal in prophecy, it may happen that in the future there may very well be a decided move against local school districts and the school boards which operate them in favor of districts which are congruent with the municipal limit and a municipal agency to operate the school system. There certainly appears to be no trend toward municipal government taking over operation of the school system, but we may yet see that day. School systems no longer need the protective benefit of nonpolitical school boards (if such were ever of value) and the day is fast approaching when municipal governments will operate school systems just as they operate other protective and promotional agencies. When this happens, as it most surely will, school buildings will become an organic part of the community recreational system and their utilization for recreational purposes will enable them to be employed at a greater economical rate in proportion to their original cost of construction. Whether or not school systems remain under the operational jurisdictions to which they are now attached has little to do with the case. School buildings and the abutting grounds must be made available for public recreational purposes. The sooner school authorities permit such use on a daily basis throughout the year, particularly on week-ends, during holiday periods, and over the summer months, the better the community will be insofar as its recreational capacity to serve its constituents is increased.

The Recreational Planning Survey

In order for the municipality or other local subdivision to prepare a priority schedule for the selection of sites, acquire lands, develop properties, and institute a program, there must first be undertaken a careful survey of the community to gauge the present and future need. In outline form, the following subjects are included in any recreational survey performed in the community:

1. *Historical Factors*
    a. Establishment of the community.
    b. Neighborhood development.
    c. Traditions.
2. *Physiographic and Other Features*
    a. Land and water area involved.
    b. Topography.
    c. Elevation above sea level.
    d. Streams, rivers, lakes, and other waterways.
    e. Average monthly temperatures and precipitation.
    f. Scenic, scientific, historical, or other cultural features.
    g. Geopolitical boundaries.
3. *Legislation*
    a. State enabling acts and statutes.
    b. Municipal ordinances and codes.
    c. Zoning laws or restrictions.
    d. Building codes.
4. *Population Data*
    a. Estimated or actual present population.
    b. Population distribution, density, and composition.
    c. Ethnic groupings.
    d. Racial groupings.
    e. Population migration (trends and movements).
    f. Occupational distribution.
    g. Age groups.
5. *Housing Data*
    a. Rental values by neighborhoods.
    b. Existing housing projects and their populations.
    c. Proposed housing or subdivisional developments.
    d. Character of homes by neighborhoods.
6. *Community Organization*
    a. Governmental organization.
    b. Protective agencies (police, fire, civil defense).
    c. Preventive agencies (health and sanitation departments).
    d. Promotional agencies (school system, libraries, conservation).
    e. Welfare agencies.

f. Private organizations
      Churches
      Youth serving agencies
      Social, civic, and fraternal groups
      Business and professional groups
      Philanthropic agencies
   g. Coordinating agencies or councils.
   h. Special interest groups.
7. *Recent Municipal Studies and Surveys*
   a. U.S. census.
   b. Master plan or city plan studies.
   c. Urban renewal projects (if any).
   d. Land use maps.
   e. Streets and traffic pattern surveys.
   f. Neighborhood layouts and patterns.
   g. Drainage and sewer systems.
   h. Priority schedules for municipal construction (if any).

SOCIAL EXAMINATION

The analysis of cultural factors which directly influence the provision of recreational service is necessary if social pressures are to be understood and balanced by essential recreational opportunities. Recreational experiences are universally desired as having personal value and also because they contribute to the common good. Any activity recognized as encompassing such values will, of necessity, be of significant concern to almost every type of social institution. Agencies that attempt to teach about the constructive use of leisure are confronted by numerous and sometimes conflicting community standards. The organization of human leisure and the operating practices for the development of soundly planned and conducted recreational activities face an increasing number of friction producing pressures as social values become modified and human institutions undergo startling metamorphoses.

Contemporary society is in the midst of a social revolution, one that is rapidly dissociating itself from a passive and controlled philosophical discussion to a highly verbal and aggressively active movement. As with all revolutions some violence to people, institutions, and ideas is bound to occur. The impact of the social revolution has focused attention upon inequalities in many areas of human contact. In the wake of abdication by state and local governments to fairly administer and see that justice is done, the Federal Government has had to take some drastic measures. New legislation aimed at the immorality of social injustice, discriminatory practices, disenfranchisement of a large block of legally constituted voters, and an upsurge in what might be termed social disintegration has caused new problems and requires new methods on the part of recreationists attempting to meet their professional obligations.

Greater mobility, automation, cybernetics, massive leisure, problems arising from the possession of leisure without the skills to utilize it correctly, greater per capita wealth, larger numbers of people possessing a higher level of education, less illiteracy, greater distribution of more information through the mass media, and other related factors that have a tendency to sweep away former standards of behavior have left a residue of guilt, fear, hostility, frustration, and anarchical situations thinly veiled by a veneer of obedience to legal authority. In this social milieu, every aspect of the community must be examined because so many impingements upon the wise use of leisure are apparent. The community must be carefully analyzed in terms of its people, its natural resources, its existing facilities, the probability of acquiring additional spaces and facilities, problems which result from encroachment, pollution, waste, inefficiency, and inadequate personnel.

With an expanding economy, a larger proportion of our people being educated at the college level, a larger work force, the desertion of certain moral and ethical behaviors in the face of an uneasy world situation, all have produced a restless and searching type of behavior. Into this charged atmosphere the recreational service agency must come to do the work for which society initially established it. Social status, sex, age, vocation, education, migration, and the continued destruction of great natural resources all combine to bring about a serious threat against the programming of recreational activities that can meet the divergent needs of people. Nevertheless, the recreationist must bend all of his effort to produce a balanced series of activities which can attract the individual and enable him to take advantage of opportunities that are presented. To this end, community examination is undertaken. By considering all of the possible factors which might influence the planned recreational program, the recreationist assumes the most efficacious position possible in formulating the type, and scope of the different activities necessary in developing the comprehensive program.

FACTORS INFLUENCING THE PROGRAM

Among the general and specific factors influencing the programming of recreational services in any community will be the following: region, demography, agency structure, departmental jurisdiction, and the community viewpoint.

The Region

The term *region* is used in its typical sense to convey the idea of a homogeneous geographic area. In a broader sense region may be defined as any contiguous areas which have common characteristics, geographically, are joined as the result of extensive interdependent factors, e.g., economic activity, population, and geographic segregation, or have common problems as a result of shared resources, e.g., water pollution, mass transportation difficulties, labor market, trade centers, and industrial facilities. Regions may be of an intrastate or interstate variety. A single state may be apportioned into distinct segments called regions. These regions are based upon the same characteristics as would qualify regions of an interstate type. They are distinguished by geographic proximity or contiguity, share common problems, or are related as a result of economic development. The grouping of regions for purposes of programming recreational experiences may best be made on an intrastate basis. However, there are several groupings of regions which might be applied to continental United States in terms of regional government or even federal governmental programs of recreational service. In each instance, the designated region has been employed in order to reveal more thoroughly those factors which might influence programming. Among the most common regional groups are:

1. The triad: the Northeast, the Southeast, and the West.
2. Nine multi-state regions: New England, Middle Atlantic, Great Lakes, Old Confederate, Plains, Southwest, Rocky Mountain, Pacific Northwest, and Western.
3. Modified multi-state regions: Atlantic Coast, Gulf Coast, Ohio Valley, Tennessee Valley, Northern Plains, and so on.
4. The individual states.
5. Intrastate Categories.
6. Metropolitan regions.

Climatic Factors. Each region, except those of the intrastate categories, will have climatic variations that have a direct and significant influence on programming recreational services—seasonal changes, mean temperature, and the rain cycle. Moderate and severe weather conditions will invariably affect the type and kind of recreational activities which can be produced successfully within a given region. For example, in certain sections of the country, outdoor recreational facilities and activities can be offered eleven months of the year; in other regions less than four months may be profitably spent outdoors. These climate extremes will find reflection in the type of facilities that have to be constructed and maintained and in the form of activities which predominate programs. The amount and intensity of rainfall, the length of days, and the duration of twilight or evenings will have a marked influence on whether recreational experiences are building or open space oriented.

Topographical Factors. Topography refers to terrain features of a region and includes such things as land elevation, flatness, ruggedness, hills, mountains, and gorges, valleys, canyons, sloping land, coastlines, contours, and other prominences which can be useful or a hindrance to certain aspects of any recreational program. Where geologic features abound they can be used directly in the program. Mountain climbing, spelunking, collecting, viewing, conservation are all suitable for a planned program of recreational activities of an outdoor type. Flat uninteresting vistas, little or no contour lines, or sparse vegetation may not provide resources for the already named activities, but they can lend themselves to other experiences equally enjoyable, i.e., fields for sports and games, quarter horse racing, drag strip racing, cultivation, soil erosion abatement, and other forms of recreational activity. Each region of the country, even on the plains, offers some recreational opportunity insofar as topographic features are concerned. However, where the lack of rugged or interesting terrain provides little in the way of nature-oriented activities, man-made construction may be one solution to recompense for the natural deficiency.

Natural and Man-made Resources. Among the natural resources that could be employed for recreational purposes in any community program would be those contained in regions where large tracts of wilderness and open space still exist in spite of creeping urbanization. Forests, caverns, and water resources of all kinds, e.g., coastlines, estuaries, gulfs, bays, oceans, lakes, rivers, streams, swamps, marshlands, tidal reaches, geologic formations, fish, game, and wild fowl refuges and preserves constitute the regional resources of a natural type which can be programmed for a planned series or organized recreational experiences by departments whose jurisdiction encompasses such an environment. On the other hand, metropolitan areas, which are characteristic of other regions, offer the variety of the urban center. Such facilities as zoological and botanical parks and gardens, museums of art, science, and natural history, concert halls, tall buildings, world famous historical sites, churches, tombs, bridges, harbours, and port facilities are but a few of the fascinating resources which can be incorporated in a series of planned recreational activities. Urban-based departments have at their command the vast city as a facility which can be used for guided tours of many types, entertainment, education, and achievement in all phases of recreational experiences. It readily lends itself to every aspect of the balanced program. Whereas it is valid to state that man can construct nothing to equal nature's infinite variety of color, beauty, and design, it is also reasonable to know that man is capable of compensating for the lack of natural abundance by creating artificial projects which offer enjoyment and opportunity of a different sort. Although the city does not afford the vistas of a mountain, desert, or forest region, it does provide a fascinating setting of its own. Man has gathered together a complex of resources and facilities to satisfy every sense and need within the confines of an urban region. The goods and services available within the city and the city, taken *in toto,* can be a remarkable recreational resource.

Traditions. Specific regions of the country have, and are noted for traditional activities. The tidewater region of Virginia is noted for fox hunting, the lake region of Minnesota is known for fishing, the Rocky Mountain region in Colorado is noted for skiing as are the Green and White Mountains of Vermont and New Hampshire. Sailing and boating are particularly fancied along the Atlantic and Pacific coasts, but nowhere is there more enthusiasm for this traditional activity than in the New England region. The South has had a tradition of cotillion dances, and raccoon and opossum hunts, while the Southwest is noted for the rodeo. Basketball has been a Midwestern activity and horseracing is well known in Kentucky. Regions within the states of Ohio and Pennsylvania support Amish, Mennonite, and Dunker communities whose traditions are still quite puritanical. The blue laws of New England and in some parts of the South also affect forms of recreational and leisure activity. The Plains region has had the tradition of state fairs, community festivals, and agriculturally based recreational experiences. Those regions which are heavily forested and have been employed in the lumbering industry gave rise to the traditional activities associated with logging camps, e.g., woodchopping contests, tree climbing, log rolling, timber-topping, and so on. Regional differences in climate, history, settlement, economy, natural resources, and such situations as trade, industries, transportation media, or communication centers have helped to shape the form of recreational activity that is generally considered to be characteristic of particular regions. These traditions are so ingrained and expected that they must be integrated into all planning conditions for community-based recreational service programs. To ignore traditional activities is to weaken the total effectiveness of the balanced program. Many potential participants can be lost if a well-known or customary recreational experience is omitted. In any program setting it is better to work from the familiar to less well-known activities in order to fulfill the instructional responsibility of making additional opportunities available to people.

Demography

The study of population is one of the most crucial factors that can influence considerations of programming recreational services in any community. The number of persons in the population of a specific geographical area and the density, or dispersion, with reference to the unit area and resources are the chief components of demography. Knowledge of the size and distribution of population for any area is most rewarding to the recreationist researcher who attempts to objectively identify and classify population statistics. These two aspects are the easiest to obtain and are subject to quite accurate and reliable measurement. Size and distribution of population are, however, only two of several conditions affecting the type and variety of recreational services needed in a given area. Other factors modifying and having direct consequences on programming include social, economic, and vocational status, educational level, previous recreational experience, residence, migration, ethnic groupings, religious affiliation, sex, race, age, and political association. The direction and intensity of the effect on programming of any alteration of these factors as well as in the size of population are apparent. The variety, magnitude, and gradation of activities actually realized by people stem from the correlation of all of these features.

Residence. In determining the composition of the population of a given community it is first necessary to classify the nature of the area in which people live. Any region may be divided into rural and urban categories. In recent years the phenomenon of a growing suburban population has also been classified. The residence of the population is the most significant criterion of present basic variances in the environmental pressures, both natural and artificial, that human beings encounter which tend to mold personal development. Within the restrictions controlled by genetic inheritance, residence is one of the most important existing forces shaping particular personality traits which any individual will acquire.

Rural society offers a distinct contrast to urban society. Agriculture is still the predominant occupation of the rural dweller. Sparsity of population, a high degree of ethnic and cultural homogeneity, and a considerable vocational, social, and territorial permanency characterize the rural resident. Nature rather than nurture is the outstanding feature in the life of the rural population. Restricted social and political contact within a limited geographical region produces a more conservative outlook. In almost every way the urban dweller is dissimilar from his rural counterpart. Even with mass media of communications providing greater informational dissemination, news reporting, and diversity of opinion, the influences on the country man and the city person are profoundly different. There is, however, a third residential basis on which to classify population—suburban. This is the current phenomena of population migration from the urban to a more rural setting without the accompanying characteristic of an agrarian economy. The suburban resident is an urban worker who generally resides in a community which depends for its economic base upon providing amenities. It is, in fact, a satellite of the urban center located anywhere from ten to fifty miles from the central core of the city, but attached umbilically to the central city by means of one or more express highways. Suburbia represents a new classification of residency for population analysis. Neither rural nor urban, it has a few characteristics of both. It is a completely gray area that defies general categorization. There are many divergent natural and man-made environments that impinge upon the individual living in suburbia with the result that specific traits which distinguish rural and urban populations are difficult to type. Depending on many variables, the suburbanite is a composite of rural and urban traditions, mores, and economics. The homogeneous factors that can be discerned within rural populations may also be seen in suburban residents. The heterogeneous facets that mark the urban population are also to be found in the suburban population.

What continually confounds the whole idea of urban-suburban-rural categories are the criteria to be utilized in any classification system. If the basis for classification is strictly number then the size of the community may segregate rural from urban. If, however, it is a question of incorporation, economics occupations, or density, then rigid classification becomes more difficult to apprehend. This latter concept is utilized in order to more accurately reflect the various degrees through which one passes as mobility from the most rural to the most urban situations occur. The effect of population density on recreational programming is considerable. Urban centers rely much more upon man-made facilities and structures and there is a greater need for such structures to accommodate a larger population. A greater variety of structures exist and a more diverse and comprehensive program is available to the urbanite than to the rural dweller. There is more probability that the city will have a large and efficient department of recreational service offering many specialists and other ancillary personnel who are prepared to program a comprehensive and continuing series of recreational experiences. In rural areas where sparsity of population is usual, together with the fact that more than one million farm families are leaving rural areas for urban centers each year, the likelihood is that no agency program exists or if there is one it depends upon natural resources for a greater proportion of recreational activities. There are exceptions to this generalization. In the main, however, rural programs of recreational activity are characterized by poor facilities, small departments in terms of the number of personnel employed, and reliance upon routine and time-honored activities.

Ethnic Groups. Only population density and the rural-urban dichotomy take precedence over the classification of ethnic or land of national origin. The extreme importance that ethnic background has for programming recreational activities may be better understood from the significant differences between the cultural backgrounds and economic status of native and foreign born. Ethnic patterns and the heritage and traditions brought to this country from other cultures have tremendous impact upon programming. Each ethnic group, whether foreign born, first or fifth generation, looks with a certain amount of pride upon its nativity. Even after a high degree of assimilation has occurred, there is still a feeling of affiliation to the traditions and cultural displays that have been developed over centuries of social intercourse. For these very pertinent reasons, recreational service departments must determine the size and variety of ethnic groups residing within the given community and attempt to involve these citizens through the production of activities that are representative of national origin. Typical of ethnic group heritage and tradition are those activities which have gained national flavor and support. St. Patrick's Day parades, Columbus Day ceremonies, and observances honoring such national heroes as Baron von Steuben, Count Casimir Pulaski, Kosciusko, Garibaldi, Lafayette, and others, comprise certain activities of an ethnic origin. The Mardi Gras of New Orleans, the Chinese New Years of New York's and San Francisco's Chinatowns, and Pilgrims Progress in Plymouth, Massachusetts, are all examples of ethnic activities which have become part of the folkways of America.

The force that ethnic factors exert upon recreational programming is so clear that its exclusion from the organized program makes reasonable a suspicion that a less than professional job is being performed. Ancestral heritage colors and offers many opportunities for a variety of wholesome and interesting experiences to be included in the program. Ethnic dances such as the Hora, Kazatski, Schottische, flamenco, tarantella, and so on, can be of significant interest for their respective programming. Foods of foreign lands may be emphasized during a fair, festival, or through a cooking class. Cooking *aficionados,* as well as those who would be attracted to a cooking class sponsored by the public recreational department, would delight in learning to make shish-kabab, lasagna, goulash, sukiyaki or any of the countless food varieties available. Cooking and baking contests, cook-outs, celebrations, and special events can always be made more enjoyable when food with an ethnic flavor is introduced.

Ethnic sports and games have had a great influence upon typically American leisure activities. The Italian game of boccie, the American Indian game of lacrosse, the Scandinavian gymnastic or Turnverein societies, the Middle European game of soccer, the English sport of punting or rowing, the Scandinavian sport of skiing, the Dutch sport of ice-skating, the Swiss sport of mountain climbing, the French sport of bicycle racing, the central European sport of distance running, and many other recreational activities including archery, wrestling, fencing, judo, kendo, bowling, handball, golf, tennis, animal breeding and showing, volleyball, polo, as well as mah-jongg, whist, chess, pinochle, and cribbage are all of ethnic import. Thematic materials for hundreds of activities utilizing ethnic backgrounds can do much to involve people in traditional or new and exciting recreational experiences.

Race. Racial characteristics condition the acceptance and involvement of some recreational activities, but for the most part racial factors have a social, political, and regional connotation. All races have the same needs. However it is in the social sphere that problems occur. Legislation has been introduced to prevent discrimination on the basis of race or minority status, but recreational activities are performed at a level on which no amount of punitive or restrictive legislation will have any effect. Social intercourse, association, affiliation, and membership are all social matters and as such are psychologically or emotionally motivated. Although the public recreational service department has an obligation to offer a program for all people residing in a given community, there is little likelihood that any great degree of racial integration on a social basis will be attained until racial prejudice is eliminated.

Mass spectator and a few individual activities may be programmed without regard to race. This will also be valid for instructional classes, and most of the program categories. However, those activities which are intensely social, e.g., dance, parties, club associations, and perhaps dramatics, will tend toward segregation as a result of racial factors. Nevertheless, the public department must organize activities wherever residents live regardless of race. The department must provide opportunities for all forms of recreational experience in spite of racial imbalance and ignorance. Because there is *de facto* segregation of races in terms of residency, the problem of integration becomes less important concerning neighborhood activities. Where, however, neighborhoods are changing as a result of Negroes moving in and Caucasians moving out, the problem reaches severe proportions. In a few enlightened communities, racial factors do not play an essential role in influencing the type and kinds of recreational activities that can be programmed. Most communities find that only certain forms of recreational activities can be scheduled because of race problems.

Integration and involvement in recreational activities will always be an individual affair. Participation in planned recreational activities that are racially integrated will invariably be subject to ambivalent emotions. Real or fancied slights can provide fuel to an already explosive situation. Nevertheless, recreational opportunities should be made available to all who may want to participate. Such participation being a highly individualistic prerogative must be as attractive and enjoyable as possible to counter bigotry and ignorance.

Age Composition. One of the more important facts pertaining to population is the age structure of the people in a given community. It is not an overstatement to say that data concerning the age and sex of the population are among the most valuable to the recreationist. The professional practitioner requires information concerning the number and sex of the population of particular ages and their proportion to the population of the total community. Data concerning age and sex distribution is invaluable in planning for facilities and specific activities of the recreational program. The recreationist realizes that there are age group characteristics which will have a marked effect on the kind and gradation of organized recreational experiences which can be offered by the public department. In order to plan the recreational program logically, the recreationist must be well acquainted with age group characteristics and make every effort to satisfy those that are generalized as well as those that are displayed by individuals.

Sex Composition. Until the age of seven years, young children play with their own or the opposite sex without apparent preferment. Soon after entering the first grade, however, both sexes generally show some signs of hostility toward one another. By the time the child is eight selection of companions is decidedly marked on the basis of sex, and within two years almost complete segregation of sexes becomes extant. The typical consequence of any contact among boys and girls between the ages of ten and twelve is usually antagonistic. Withdrawal by either sex begins with distance, followed by scorn, and finally by overt hostility. With the onset of adolescence hostility converts to shyness. During middle childhood the sexes want to be separate and prefer being with their own group in most activities. This period of sex differentiation, when the two groups initiate standards of behavior for themselves, is of extreme importance to social development. The barriers of this age are of particular significance to the recreationist in terms of guidance and leadership of probable recreational activities to be planned for either group.

Individual differences in rate of development are quite pronounced after the age of six and sex variances are great. Fine muscle coordination begins to manifest itself, with the female acquiring this ability earlier than the male. By twelve years of age, girls are physiologically advanced almost two years ahead of boys. At age seventeen, growth rate is nearly equal for both sexes; and by twenty there is little or no distinction in the rate of development. The growth and development of males and females engender conflict as metabolic and other physical changes bring disturbing patterns with them. That these adjustments are natural mean little to the individual undergoing them. Obviously, there are also going to be psychological pressures and some anxiety that may show through conflicting social relationships.

It is during this emotionally stressful period that both sexes need understanding and support from their immediate families, but even more so from professional personnel who work with them. The anxieties that are produced at this stage of development may not be well understood by the child undergoing them. The importance of good peer relations is, therefore, essential. One sure method for assisting at this crucial time is for the organization of heterosexual groups which, through recreational activities, can provide satisfactory outlets for physical, psychological, and social needs. A variety of interest and skill groups should be initiated to include such experiences as art, crafts, sports, and service programs. As Wilson and Ryland also have indicated:

> Dancing is the outstanding medium through which teen-agers experiment in heterosexual relationships. Mass activities which include all forms of the dance and group games should have prominent places in programs for these young people. Adolescents need the anonymity of large mass activity; but they need also the individualization which the small intimate group provides. On the one hand, they need the opportunity, afforded by the mass activity, to escape for a time from the conflict within them; on the other, they need the help of the small group in facing reality. Program content should recognize no limitations of media through which the adolescent finds help in working on such problems as emancipation from his family, vocational choice, relationships with the opposite sex, and realization of himself in relation to society and to his religious beliefs.[4]

The awkwardness which is generally associated with adolescence is commonly a thing of the past by the time late adolescence begins. The older individual has learned to control his rapidly maturing body and has the coordination and strength to utilize it successfully. Characteristically, phys-

[4] Gertrude Wilson and Gladys Ryland, *Social Group Work Practice—The Creative Use of the Social Process* (Boston: Houghton Mifflin Company, 1949), p. 108.

ical strength becomes an important factor in selecting activities for both sexes. Males are eager to acquire highly complicated physical skills and participate in competitive sports and games, almost to the exclusion of all other activities. Females, on the other hand, withdraw from activities where muscular ability is a determining asset. This probably accounts for the popularity of competitive athletics among males at this stage and the relative disinclination of most females to participate either as passive spectators or active participants. To a great extent, physical strength, stamina, and skills carry a pronounced social prestige among boys of this age.[5] Girls, however, are not particularly concerned with strength and therefore concentrate on developing skills which require finesse, grace, and poise. They would rather participate in such motor skills as dancing, diving, archery, fencing, and gymnastics, where muscular coordination is of greater consequence than strength.

As the individual matures and enters the realm of adulthood, the factors of individual difference become more noticeable. The incompatibilities of adolescence give way to heterosexual adjustments as each person attempts to reconcile himself to the responsibilities and privileges of adulthood. Recreational interests for both sexes tend toward stabilization and are of a sedentary character. Males who have participated in physical activities may continue participation when their organization is involved in planning and scheduling such experiences for them. There is a continuation of activities such as swimming, golf, bowling, fishing, hunting, and for the more enthusiastic male, handball, tennis, squash, and other physical fitness exercises. Recreational activities for the adult male in general, however, are more diversional, passive, and entertaining than strenuous. There is a reliance upon social groupings and men join more clubs or interest groups. The female adult, except for an elite few, has resisted participation in athletic competition and this noninterest is carried over into adult life. Women generally find their recreational outlets in social groups, the arts, music, service activities, religious association, and activities which appear to be more in keeping with feminine tastes and interests. These sex differences and inclinations must be part of the recreationist's plan when attempting to develop a program of possible recreational activities.

Social Status. As in all other cultures and societies, there is a social class system in the United States. This system of social status is closely connected to economic level, residence, family background, education, and other factors. Some individuals have been so indoctrinated with the idea of social class that they can identify only with whoever else is also clearly affiliated with or an integral member of the same class. It is not uncommon for such individuals to consider attending a specific school and no other, entering a specific occupation and no other, or attending a specific function or functions at a particular place or places and no others. All

---

[5] H. E. Jones, "Physical Ability as a Factor in Social Adjustment in Adolescence," *Journal of Educational Research,* Vol. **40** (1946), 287–301.

people are influenced by the standards and values of their environment. Social situations are sufficiently strong to shape attitudes, and opinions, and select companions.

Social status is the degree of influence possessed by an individual in any communuity based upon recognized criteria that are sharply defined. Among these criteria are family affiliation, economic worth, occupation, religion, race, residence, and the residue of all these interrelated components that form the power structure of the community. Each person brings to any group a complex of values, opinions, behaviors, skills, and experience which in turn affect, in various ways, the objectives, size, cohesiveness, variety of activities, and affiliations. Each person is molded by environmental and social forces that originate in the customs and codes of the social class from which the individual comes.[6] As a result of previous and concomitant social experiences, one person may be highly skilled in group living, whereas another may be unable to identify himself with any particular group. Not everybody is fortunate enough to become a part of a group. Even with association, not all individuals are capable of seizing the opportunities of relating and performing well the functions assigned to a group situation. The significance of social experience makes obvious the need for considering the placement of individuals within the program. Individuals who have experienced satisfaction in social living are better able to function in involved group situations and can achieve their objectives. The social background of individuals prepares them for the assumption of different roles in a variety of groups. Those who are not well prepared either need more intense professional assistance or they fail in their specific goals and gain little satisfaction.

Social status has another effect on potential participants within any recreational program. Some people feel that they cannot participate if the "wrong" people are also in attendance. There are those who look down upon what they call "the lower class." Such bias prohibits joining any group, regardless of the interest they have for it, when those whom they consider socially inferior are also participating. With upward mobility and greater opportunities for the attainment of more education and better occupations increasingly prevalent in this society, this aspect of social life is slowly dying. Nevertheless, it is still a factor that requires attention on the part of recreationists who program.

Educational Level. Although the educational level is relatively unimportant to participants in children's recreational activities, it begins to take on greater significance as the individual matures. With older children, and particularly young adults, varying educational levels and intellectual experiences create a diversity of interests, ability, and skill which can be a divisive force. Educational differences may be so pronounced that individuals, who might have come from the same social environment, find that

---

[6] Jay S. Shivers, *Leadership in Recreational Service* (New York: The Macmillan Company, 1963), pp. 148–152.

they have little in common; or if they have one thing that brings them together, they find that they have no idiom for mutual understanding and contact. Almost all recreational service departments bring many people together to form groups of varying interests. It is in the artificially contrived groupings, prevalent and necessary for recreational agencies, that educational levels are so far ranging. Where such groups are brought into being as a consequence of some over-riding civic problem, a recreational activity of common interest, or some other shared experience, the inherent conflicts originating from differences in educational background can be transcended for a short time. Only with the assistance of a skilled recreationist, to surmount the wide variance of knowledge and maintain the group in spite of differences of this sort, will there be any value to participants. The programmer must carefully analyze educational background and intellectual attainment of potential participants when planning recreational activities.

Occupational Range. There is little question but that vocational position merits serious thought in programming for public recreational agencies. Occupational identity frequently serves as a major basis for establishing groups in organizing recreational activities. Employment in a particular occupation does not necessarily mean that the individual associates only with those who are similarly employed. However, social involvement with others who are employed in the same capacity, on the same level economically, or especially within the same firm is continually observed and seems to be a natural outcome of employment. Except in urban based employment, where workers have to commute to their place of business, the likelihood of social relationships developing beyond those with whom one shares a working environment is quite slim. Even today, there are distinct lines drawn between those who are employed in the trades, in factories, or in the professions. Lawyers, bankers, physicians, scientists, and engineers are more probably in the same economic bracket, receive about the same social approbation or community recognition, and usually maintain the same area of residence. For these reasons they are more nearly likely to belong to the same social, political, civic, or religious associations. They will typically move in the circle of relationships closed to others. In like manner, people who are employed in the same factory, or horizontally, in the same industry, will tend to find their social acquaintances and outlets at this level. There are some tradesmen who, by virtue of tremendously increased wages, have been able to afford greatly improved residential circumstances and for this reason may be accorded a social status previously denied them. A materialistic culture still places extreme importance on the economic worth of the individual and money derived from employment assists in the upward climb.

Whether or not vocational position is a basis for the formation of recreational groups, and this is questionable because so many other factors are involved, the recreationist should realize the significance of occupational identity in programming. It is simply one more conditioning facet which represents population composition.

Religious Affiliation. In a country of complete religious heterogeneity, religious affiliation can never mean church domination of the cultural life of the people as it does in countries where an established church is supported with state funds. However, church and sectarian associations still influence many social customs and contribute a great deal in the colorful ceremonies, rituals, taboos, and moral values of those who participate. To a very considerable extent, religious denomination plays a large role in establishing specific recreational experiences that are associated with sectarian affiliation. Many nationally recognized holidays, and more particularly regional observances, are of an essentially religious nature. Christmas, Easter, Yom Kippur, Rosh Hashonah, Purim, Hanukkah, St. Patrick's Day, St. Valentine's Day, Thanksgiving Day, saints' feast days, Halloween, Mardi Gras, and many other events celebrated during the year are basically religious occasions which, through many generations, have been modified to meet the social and cultural demands of modern society. Nevertheless, to orthodox, conservative, and even reformed individuals of many faiths, these holidays still carry predominant religious overtones. Perhaps the Sabbath has the deepest religious meaning for most sectarian practitioners and colors the recreational program in terms of what and when activities can be scheduled.

In some instances, it is helpful to know the religious affiliation of potential participants when planning a program of activities. There are sectarian groups in the United States which discriminate against a variety of recreational activities and in some instances against anything that may be termed recreational. The South, for example, is well known as a "Baptist Belt." Although the Southern Baptist Convention, based in Nashville, Tennessee, has long been an initiator of church recreational programs, there are other Baptist congregations which strictly frown upon dancing, card playing, and other recreational activities. Depending upon the region, and which sectarian form has the plurality, the recreationist will be wise to heed local religious customs and make the most of religious holidays, festivals, and other ritualistic events by utilizing them as program themes or structuring an entire activity or series of activities with the religious observance as its keynote.

Migration. An equally important factor for consideration in programming recreational services is the movement of people. People immigrate to a place, community, or region, or they emigrate from some place. The movement of people, whether to, from, or within a given location, is of tremendous social significance. Migration directly affects the social structure and has a powerful influence upon the personalities of individuals. Through migration the individual dissolves almost all of his social obligations and sheds the ties of group association and the positions which gave him status in them. Cut adrift from all his former primary and special interest groups, separated from his class identification, the individual must attain a role for himself in the new community, find a place for himself in new associations, and establish himself within the social structure of his residential neighborhood. The migrant severs the role of indigenous person and assumes that of foreigner. The whole process of becoming accepted and finding a position within the class structure of the new community may be slow and painful.

Whenever population movement becomes a question of radical change in the shifting of residence or state of allegiance, the dislocation that follows may be passed along for several generations. Particularly is this true where a new language must be learned and different customs assimilated. Many of the millions of migrants who came to the United States during the late nineteenth and early twentieth century never completely adjusted to the new society. The ethnic dislocation was so severe that it necessitated a ghetto-like existence for the newly immigrated. This is somewhat valid today as different racial groups migrate from southern communities to northern and far western metropolitan areas. That such radically different groupings and cultures have caused painful environmental pressures can be clearly observed in the rash of race riots which erupted across the country during the middle 1960's. The outbreak of lawless rioting in the Watts district of Los Angeles in the summer of 1965, followed by similar clashes in Natchez, Mississippi, Springfield, Massachusetts, and Chicago, Illinois, have all been linked in some way to migration.

Migrants, whether from different regions of the country or from foreign countries face a long assimilation process which is typically slow and difficult. As long as they live, in some cases, they are marked by some distinguishing physical or social characteristic of the stranger. They are never fully at ease, nor completely able to comprehend their social environment. Foreign-born migrants may continue to live in the cultural existence of their previous homeland. More often than not, there is a second generation carry-over, especially where the original language spoken at home is not the vernacular tongue. The older generation finds protection and status in the cultural patterns of the Old World. The children try to break away, obliterate all traces of their foreign heritage, and seek acceptance and total assimilation with the new customs of contemporary society. These situations can lead to family conflict and tend to color the view which the migrant has of the community.

There are three types of migration which typically affect the recreationist's concept of programming. For analytical purposes migration may be identified as population movement out of a community, into a community, and internal movement. This facet of migration has a great deal to do with the density and distribution of the population. Forecasting population movement, e.g., noting internal trends, is important for the development and construction of recreational spaces and facilities. Land acquisition, prior to the build-up of the size of the population in one section of a community, is a valuable consequence of such forecasts. The analysis of population by region of origin, and occupational, educational, economic, and social level will mean much in terms of programming. Recreationists must not only account for permanent residents, but must also plan for transient populations upon which the community may depend. The tourist trade has become a most lucrative economic base for more than one city. But urban growth and a spreading population in one or more directions remain the biggest problems for prognosticating internal migration by recreationists. Planning the program to accommodate present and future area residents will influence the kind and type of activities and necessary facilities to be employed.

Previous Recreational Experience. Although all people have the right to participate in public recreational activities and share equally in the services which are offered, all do not have the same capacity to receive value from such opportunities. The factor of previous recreational experience and the concomitant skills developed by such experiences must be recognized by the recreationist and taken into consideration as he attempts to program recreational activities. There is no standard description of how prior experience in a recreational situation will affect the skill and practice of any individual. It is well known that certain individuals never become skilled in specific activities regardless of how long they practice. This is readily observed in many motor skill activities. However, these individuals feel comfortable and knowledgeable in the activity of their choice even when they do not achieve great skill. Much the same can be indicated for a variety of other recreational categories.

Age, intellect, and natural ability play important roles as to whether or not an individual will be able to engage, with a high degree of skill, in recreational activities. Very young children, without any previous knowledge or experience in activities, require a good deal of direct supervision and guidance in learning activity skills. This is also valid for those individuals who, for medical or social reasons need constant direct supervision if they are to benefit from a therapeutic, educational, or rehabilitational program, are not in sufficient contact with reality, or whose pathological behavior prevents them from abiding by socially accepted norms. As individuals become more familiar with activities through practice, they are better able to use their personal resources to greater advantage and find increasing success in what they do.

With a history of previous recreational experiences and the related development of skills, people require less direct supervisory assistance and can effectively achieve satisfaction independently. Initially, people may need total assistance in terms of instruction, planning, organizing, and operation. With continued performance, however, this need diminishes until the recreationist may be employed minimally as a resource, for some technical problem which skill alone cannot solve, or in an advisory capacity. Programming then comes under the influence of previous experience as it concerns the degree of skill which the individual has developed and his ability to take complete advantage of opportunities afforded by agency operation. The more familiar and confident people are within the setting of recreational activities, the more likely is it that they will require a broader spectrum of activities from which to choose. Familiarity, in this instance, requires a comprehensive and dynamic program.

THE AGENCY STRUCTURE

The essential aspect of agency structure comes in terms of a sufficient number of recreationists able to offer a well-balanced program. The department should have one division that is totally concerned with programming. The root of agency structure is determined by an adequate number of personnel equipped to perform in a competent manner. Division of labor into specialities and a complete description of duties and responsibilities for these line personnel are basic if comprehensive recreational services are to be provided. All activities of the program are performed at a variety of facilities and these areas and structures should be manned to a degree sufficient to carry out the primary function of the agency.

The most desirable facility arrangement will closely correspond to the number of neighborhoods situated within the community. In very small communities—under 5,000 population—there may be only one recreational center with an attached playground. This may be supplemented by school department facilities. In the largest urban centers, however, there will be not less than one playground in each neighborhood and these will be augmented by many other various spaces and specialized structures on a district, community, and metropolitan basis. In any event, the personnel requirement will change with the size of the facility and the participant needs at the facility. There may be very small playgrounds, relatively isolated, in some large urban areas which because of size will not admit an attendance that necessitates more than one worker during each eight-hour segment of operation. However, the usual personnel commitment for a neighborhood playground is two recreationists per session during the morning, afternoon, and evening. If attendance warrants, more workers should be deployed at these recreational facilities.

Recreational centers are usually structures containing club rooms, auditorium, sometimes a gymnasium, multi-purpose room, art and craft room, lounge area, office and supply rooms, and other specialized areas for the continuous programming of many recreational experiences. The larger and more complex the center, the more it will be necessary to secure an adequate staff for its operation. The typical center usually employs one full-time director and an assistant director, complemented by one or more full-time program workers, and as many specialists as are needed to offer a diversified program of instruction, game, social, and other self-directed activities. The utilization and employment of part-time workers as well as volunteers to complement career employees is also a valuable and integral part of the program.[7]

Employment Practices

The large urban department of recreational service employs a permanent corps of career recreationists to perform the program operational responsibilities of the department. The employees function as directors, assistant directors, functional or program workers, and specialists (program skills). These are line personnel specifically qualified and held directly responsible for the production and effectiveness of the program. They are subordinate to a district supervisor in charge of a geographic area or of specified facilities who in turn coordinates program events, e.g., city-wide sports, special events, dramatics, and so on, with the assistance of supervisors in these specialities. There may be four or more of these district supervisors, depending upon the size of the city and the districts into which it can be divided for most efficient operation. Typically two, but less than five, neighborhoods constitute a district. In a major metropolitan area, the department may divide the city into three basic categories and have line supervisory personnel in charge of all recreational programming for their respective areas. Thus, the common denominator of the city will be the neighborhood; this gives way to the district, which in turn converts to a community. Two or more communities equal a city. The district supervisor is responsible to a community supervisor who reports to a general supervisor or other administrative designee. In charting such an organizational plan, the largest agency is taken as an example in order to illustrate more clearly the major employment categories and the typical lines of authority and responsibility. The ramified structure of a large department more nearly indicates the responsibilities of various workers, whereas it is difficult to illustrate employment practices with smaller agencies. Smaller departments simply reduce all overhead personnel, have fewer program workers, and capitalize on part-time and seasonal employees. In small communities there are almost never any full-time specialists employed. Rather, the specialist is hired on a *per diem* basis, for a specific activity session, or is employed at a particular time of the year.

Every department organizes its program staff in a way that will prove most effective to meet the conditions and needs of the local situation. Although there is no one best plan, there are organizational procedures that appear to be more valuable in fixing authority for functions and delegating responsibility for operations. **Figure 16-1** is such a plan.

This chart can best be understood in terms of the large metropolitan recreational service department. There are two community supervisors, each responsible for four district supervisors. The district supervisors are

[7] *Supra,* pp. 369–371.

412 Practices of Recreational Service

FIGURE 16-1. Hypothetical Organization of Recreational Program Division.

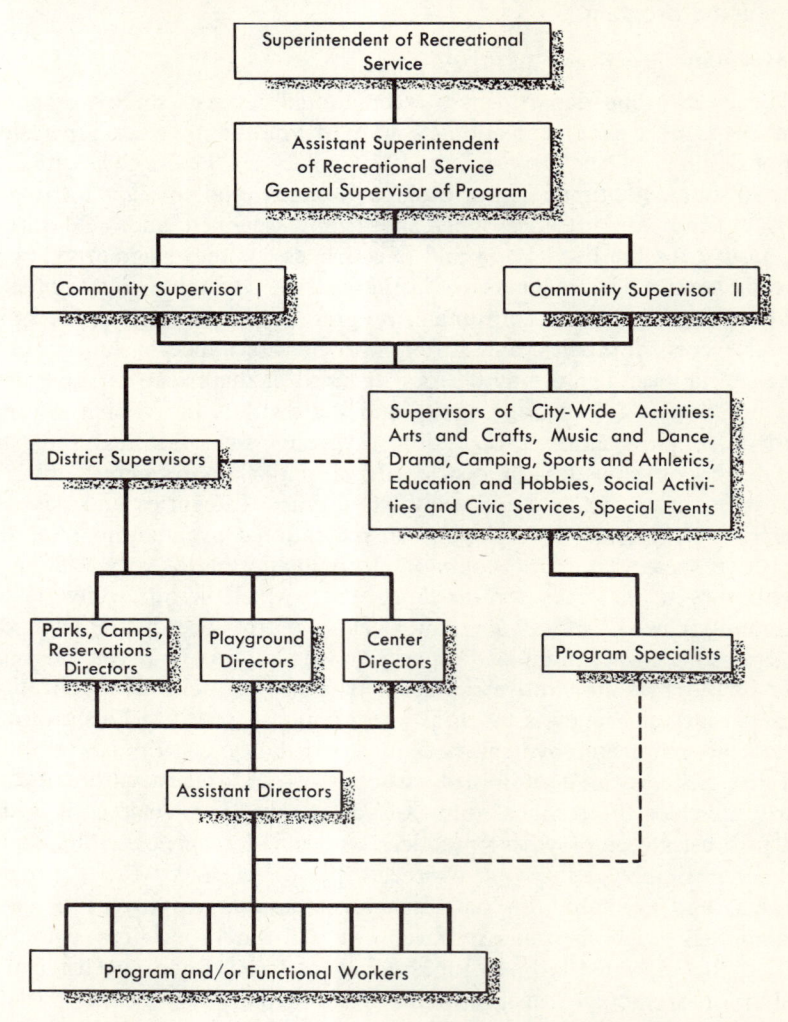

```
                    ┌─────────────────────────────┐
                    │ Superintendent of Recreational │
                    │           Service            │
                    └──────────────┬──────────────┘
                                   │
                    ┌──────────────┴──────────────┐
                    │   Assistant Superintendent  │
                    │    of Recreational Service  │
                    │  General Supervisor of Program │
                    └──────────────┬──────────────┘
              ┌────────────────────┴────────────────────┐
    ┌─────────┴─────────┐                    ┌──────────┴────────┐
    │ Community Supervisor I │              │ Community Supervisor II │
    └─────────┬─────────┘                    └──────────┬────────┘
              │                                         │
              │                         ┌───────────────┴──────────────┐
  ┌───────────┴───────┐                 │ Supervisors of City-Wide     │
  │ District Supervisors │ ─ ─ ─ ─ ─ ─ ─│ Activities: Arts and Crafts, │
  └───────────┬───────┘                 │ Music and Dance, Drama,      │
              │                         │ Camping, Sports and Athletics,│
              │                         │ Education and Hobbies, Social │
              │                         │ Activities and Civic Services,│
              │                         │ Special Events               │
              │                         └───────────────┬──────────────┘
   ┌──────────┼──────────┐                              │
   │          │          │                   ┌──────────┴──────────┐
┌──┴───┐ ┌────┴───┐ ┌────┴──┐                │ Program Specialists │
│Parks,│ │Playground│ │Center │               └──────────┬──────────┘
│Camps,│ │Directors │ │Directors│                         │
│Reservations│       │        │                          │
│Directors│                                              │
└──┬───┘ └────┬───┘ └────┬──┘                           │
   └──────────┼──────────┘                              │
              │                                         │
     ┌────────┴────────┐                                │
     │ Assistant Directors │                            │
     └────────┬────────┘                                │
              │           ─ ─ ─ ─ ─ ─ ─ ─ ─ ─ ─ ─ ─ ─ ─
   ┌──────────┴──────────┐
   │ Program and/or Functional Workers │
   └─────────────────────┘
```

responsible for all of the recreational facilities within their respective districts, of which there are eight. Each district is composed of four neighborhoods and each neighborhood contains one large playground and one recreational center. Every neighborhood recreational center has a swimming pool. All programming is performed through the general supervisor. City-wide events are coordinated at the community supervisory level. City-wide supervisors maintain close liaison with district supervisors and may be considered "staff" personnel as are specialists. Supervisors of city-wide activities schedule classes conducted by program specialists at the various recreational facilities, i.e., centers, playgrounds, parks, and so on, by arrangement with district supervisors who clear program calendars with directors of facilities. City-wide events are scheduled and cleared in the same manner.

FIGURE 16-2. Hypothetical Organization of Recreational Program Division.

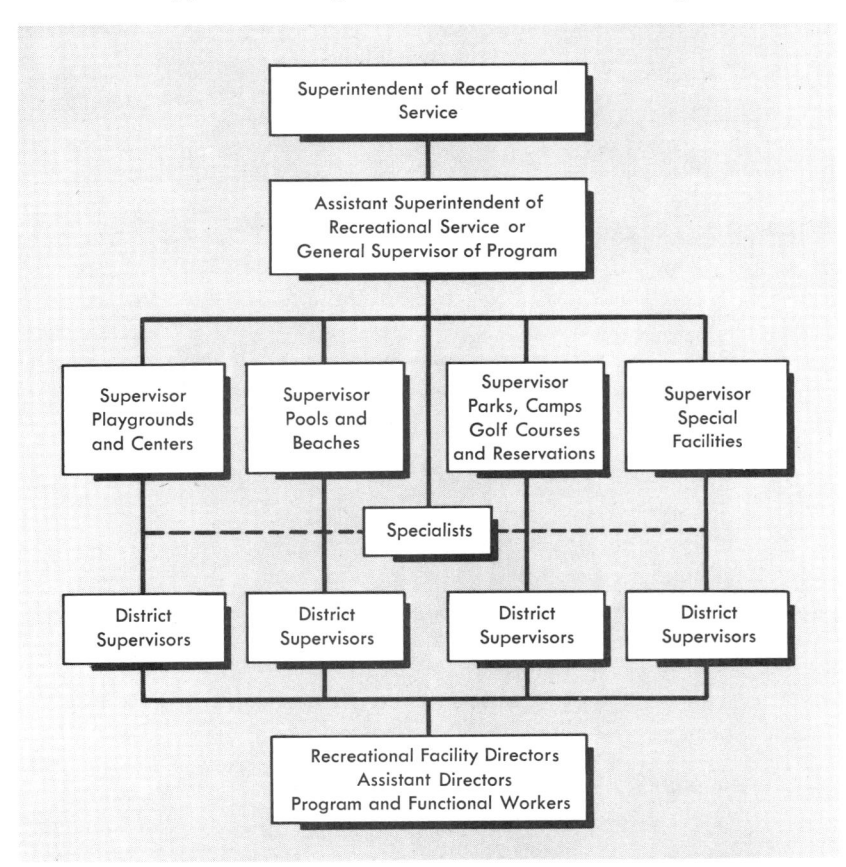

```
                    ┌─────────────────────────┐
                    │ Superintendent of       │
                    │ Recreational Service    │
                    └───────────┬─────────────┘
                                │
                    ┌───────────┴─────────────┐
                    │ Assistant Superintendent│
                    │ of Recreational Service │
                    │ or General Supervisor   │
                    │ of Program              │
                    └───────────┬─────────────┘
        ┌───────────────┬───────┴───────┬───────────────┐
   ┌────┴─────┐   ┌─────┴────┐    ┌─────┴────┐    ┌─────┴────┐
   │Supervisor│   │Supervisor│    │Supervisor│    │Supervisor│
   │Playgrounds│  │Pools and │    │Parks,    │    │Special   │
   │and Centers│  │Beaches   │    │Camps,Golf│    │Facilities│
   │          │   │          │    │Courses & │    │          │
   │          │   │          │    │Reserv.   │    │          │
   └────┬─────┘   └─────┬────┘    └─────┬────┘    └─────┬────┘
        │               │   ┌───────────┴┐              │
        │ - - - - - - - - - │ Specialists│- - - - - - - │
        │               │   └────────────┘              │
   ┌────┴─────┐   ┌─────┴────┐    ┌──────┴───┐    ┌─────┴────┐
   │ District │   │ District │    │ District │    │ District │
   │Supervisors│  │Supervisors│   │Supervisors│   │Supervisors│
   └────┬─────┘   └─────┬────┘    └──────┬───┘    └─────┬────┘
        └───────────────┴────────┬───────┴──────────────┘
                    ┌────────────┴──────────────┐
                    │ Recreational Facility     │
                    │ Directors                 │
                    │ Assistant Directors       │
                    │ Program and Functional    │
                    │ Workers                   │
                    └───────────────────────────┘
```

This chart represents a proliferation of district supervisory positions in the largest metropolitan recreational service systems and superimposes a functional supervisory level of community-wide services above the district level. The executive in charge of recreational programming for the system has direct responsibility for utilizing specialists and maintains close direction of such personnel. The line of authority in the employment of staff specialists enables the program executive to channel staff personnel into the "line" at a point which is convenient for coordinating city-wide events, providing instructional sessions, and for arranging schedules.

Figure 16-2, while introducing functional supervisory aspects of community-wide services does away with line personnel control of specialists and places coordinating functions with the executive in charge of the program division. This may appear to be an effective method for ensuring proper coordination and program planning, but it also places a crushing burden on the program supervisor because he is the administrator responsible for the total recreational service program for the city. By inverting the functional and district supervisory positions, additional personnel must be employed when there are a sufficient number of distinguishable facilities to warrant a supervisor. In medium size departments these city-wide functional supervisors may report directly to the superintendent. When, however, the department is large enough, there will be another executive interposed. Although these supervisors are responsible for the performance of two or more definable functions, e.g., program and maintenance, they will remain responsible to the executive in charge of the program division. All other divisions of the system, i.e., business administration and engineering, are considered to be staff functions and are coordinated at the divisional level.

Again, these charts illustrate the organization of a large metropolitan recreational service system. In smaller agencies the same aspects of departmental structure and organization apply, but the duties and functions of personnel are telescoped considerably and either consolidated or eliminated. In small departments there will be no intermediate supervisory level and the probability is that directors of facilities will report directly to the chief executive of the organization. Such consolidation may make for ease in personnel management, but it leaves a great deal to be desired in terms of providing effective recreational services for the total community.

Financial Considerations. Perhaps the fundamental necessity influencing all programming within the agency structure is the factor of money. The chief ingredient for the production of the program may be personnel, but unless financial support is available there cannot be the paid professional leadership so vital to programming. Programming can still be provided and a well-balanced series of recreational experiences can be offered if recreationists are employed. The highly qualified professional can, by ingenious methods, perform prodigious feats by turning junk into salvageable crafts material, converting vacant lots into playgrounds, and old loft buildings into teen-age club rooms. By utilizing existing public structures and facilities, competent leadership can provide opportunities for a stimulating, comprehensive, and balanced recreational program. However, the time spent in searching for these properties, volunteers, and materials may more profitably be expended in bettering the program, giving expert technical assistance and instruction to participants, and organizing the community for recreational services. This latter function can be fruitfully attained when there is sufficient monetary support to supply the diverse structural, space, and equipment needs of a well-rounded recreational program.

There are certain facilities which the most highly competent recreationist cannot provide. One cannot teach swimming if there is no aquatic facility available. There are art, craft, sport, and music activities which cannot be included within the recreational opportunities afforded by a community simply because they do not exist. The financial factor is one that exercises indomitable influence on what can be programmed, where the activity takes place, who provides the guidance, instruction, supervision, or leadership for the experience, and whether or not it will be open to all community residents or only a paying few. Recognition of financial need governs, to a large extent, the size of the agency, the ability of the department to meet the diverse needs of people, the inclusion of staff specialists, and even the mundane responsibilities of having the necessary filing cabinets to maintain the reports and paperwork detail of the program.

Administrative Procedures. There are certain standard administrative practices which have direct influence on the program. Unless these operating procedures are utilized, the possibility of having an ineffective, and therefore, a dissatisfying program offering is distinctly probable. These administrative techniques are concerned with the maintenance of good public relations,[8] the development of sound personnel policies and practices,[9] the efficient recording of daily occurrences throughout the system,[10] and continual appraisal and evaluation of departmental performance.[11] Even more important and having greater impetus upon the recreational opportunities programmed by the agency will be the commitment of administration toward the system. By this is meant the professional career administrator's view of his obligation to his department, his community, and his field.

Administrative techniques must make logical use of current research and any new applicable methods for more valuable presentations. There must be constant emphasis upon the employment and development of professional personnel and all of the environmental factors that encourage career workers to improve their own techniques. The community must be continually surveyed so that population analysis and trends can be made and recognized. The administrator must feel the need to call attention of the proper authorities to any deficiencies that can affect the provision of maximum and balanced recreational service to the community. This may be in terms of water pollution and waste, land encroachment upon recreational spaces for other governmental functions, inequitable salary standards, interference with departmental operations by other municipal agencies, unfair reporting or misleading statements reported in mass media, and other political or social pressures which can wreak havoc and cause dissension and dissatisfaction among the staff of the department.

First and last, the administrator must be a professional with total per-

---

[8] *Infra,* Chapter 16.
[9] George Hjelte and Jay S. Shivers, *Public Administration of Park and Recreational Service* (New York: The Macmillan Company, 1963), pp. 194–223.
[10] *Ibid.,* pp. 253–287.
[11] *Infra,* Chapter 17.

sonal commitment to the field of recreational service. He must insist that all other positions calling for professionals are filled with recreationists and specialists competent to carry out those functions assigned to them. All of the administrative procedures should have but one end and justification— the production of a program of recreational experiences designed to satisfy all of the people in the community. This is the ideal situation for which administrative techniques are geared. The probability of attaining this goal may never be realized, but it is the standard by which all facets of the program and, in a larger sense, the department are compared.

DEPARTMENTAL JURISDICTION

The department which has cognizance over the recreational service provision for any community has a great deal to do with how that service will be programmed. Where there is a separate and autonomous agency primarily responsible for the direct provision of community recreational services, all efforts will be focused upon that chief goal. There will be no stinting of monetary resources, personnel, facilities, or equipment for the fulfillment of that function. When, however, other overhead agencies become the administrative unit for undertaking the recreational service function, along with whatever primary function the agency was established to perform, then recreational service in the community suffers from being a subordinate objective.

When the municipality has seen fit to consolidate two separate, but related agencies, such as the park department and the recreational department, the recreational service function will deteriorate unless the executive in charge of the consolidated department is a recreationist. Too often, in consolidation moves, the municipal government places the former superintendent of parks in the position of departmental chief executive. In most instances the former park executive is schooled in forestry, horticulture, engineering, or landscape architecture and does not appreciate nor understand the nature of programming recreational activities. Hence, the budgetary allotment for programming and leadership becomes progressively smaller while funds for grounds maintenance, landscaping, facility construction, and other park-oriented objectives take precedence.

The recreationist, in the same position, considers the park to be part of the total recreational spaces and facilities to be utilized under the unified department. There is an allocation for the maintenance of areas and facilities, with emphasis on planning, design, and construction of needed new projects. However, the essential nature of the department is given its proper due, i.e., the provision of a balanced, comprehensive, and competently supervised recreational program.

In other situations when the overhead agency has a primary function of education, welfare, health, public works, conservation, police, or fire fighting, recreational programming usually deteriorates. When the recreational service function becomes secondary to the main job for which the agency was created, that secondary function is relegated to the orphan class and is systematically downgraded. Most administrators, who have not been professionally prepared as career recreationists, simply do not have the understanding or necessary background and skill to focus attention on this vital community service. They are content to administer their first calling, and delegate sinecures, supernumeraries, or other questionable personnel to the job of programming.

When the primary function of the agency bears little relation to that of recreational service, but recreational activity is considered a necessary facet, or it contributes in some way to the welfare of agency constituents, then recreational activity is oriented toward some end other than that usually associated with public recreational service departments. Military service organizations, for example, program recreational activities for service personnel in an effort to promote morale, keep their personnel on the base, and enhance community relationships. School institutions program recreational activities which are basically educational in content, closely tied to the formal curriculum. Church agencies offer recreational activities to their members as a direct outgrowth of moral teaching and in an attempt to cultivate spiritual values. Youth serving and social agencies often provide recreational services in order to develop good character in youth and community-oriented behavior among the groups which they serve. Treatment centers, and penal institutions administer recreational activities as having direct value in maintaining patient or inmate morale, in teaching new skills, in the process of social or physical rehabilitation, and in the production of new ideas, habits, and attitudes which will assist the individual to live a better and more wholesome life after leaving the institution. Every agency has a primary mission to perform. In the course of effecting its chief aim, it may introduce recreational activities to stimulate interest or attract additional support. In any event, the programming of recreational activities on an organized basis is performed for some motive aside from individual enjoyment and satisfaction. Recreational activities are used as means to achieve a different end. They are utilized to promote the orientation of the agency.

COMMUNITY VIEWPOINT

One other important factor which influences programming outcomes is the support the agency receives from the government of the community in which it is situated. There are many departments, which are autonomous, unable to do the most effective job of programming because the local government, while giving lip-service support, does not really feel the need for monetary expenditures which could increase staff positions and offer a more comprehensive program. Even if the citizens in a community want the service, they may face a recalcitrant board of finance, mayor, city manager, or other local governing body which overrides their petitions. This latter action is done at the elected officials' own risk, although voters seldom remember either campaign promises or the vagaries of the incumbent.

If the community is unwilling to support a public recreational service department, if it is not ready to assume the financial burden of taxation necessary for the operation of the agency, then it may always turn to quasi-public or private agencies. In these circumstances, programming becomes a tentative thing. The quasi-public agency requires a great deal of private contribution for its support, although it does have a small appropriation from tax funds. Generally, quasi-public agencies that perform the recreational function are attached to some municipal department, e.g., the police athletic or fire athletic league. United Givers or Community Chest funds invariably support one or more agencies which provide recreational services. Unfortunately, such agencies do not operate on a full-time basis. When they do operate full time, they usually restrict their services to a select clientele. When private agencies are the only means for providing recreational services to the community, the entire population can never be served. Private agencies always restrict their clientele to those individuals who are members of the organization, thus, effectively screening out all others who are not members.

SUMMARY

Essentially, planning is concerned with the selecting of possible ways of providing recreational service. It is a procedure that involves a careful examination of the community in terms of population, natural resources, traditions, economic capability to sustain and support the agency and its program, and a supply of competent staff personnel to carry out plans once they have been settled. No aspect of community life can be overlooked in planning for recreational activities. Every possible source of disaffection must be considered and all resources, whether personal or physical, should be included. The community is a complexity made up of complexities. Communities are people and people contribute the greatest difficulties in resolving problems dealing with recreational service. It is a fundamental rule, therefore, that the problems of people, their uniqueness as individuals, and the additional conflicts engendered as a result of social intercourse require carefully planned and systematically analyzed ideas. Planning is the method by which research procedures are applied in an attempt to offer better recreational services immediately as well as at some future point in time.

SELECTED REFERENCES

BARTHOLOMEW, H. and J. WOOD, *Land Uses in American Cities*. (Boston, Mass.: Harvard University Press), 1955.

CHAPIN, F. STUART, *Urban Land Use Planning*, 2nd ed. (Urbana, Ill.: University of Illinois Press), 1964.

CLAWSON, MARION, *Land and Water for Recreation.* (Chicago, Ill.: Rand McNally and Company), 1963.
DELAMATER, JAMES B., *Design of Outdoor Physical Education Facilities for Schools and Colleges.* (New York: Teachers College Press), 1963.
ECKBO, GARRETT, *Urban Landscape Design.* (New York: McGraw-Hill), 1964.
FRIEDMANN, JOHN and WILLIAM ALONSO, eds., *Regional Development and Planning.* (Boston: Massachusetts Institute of Technology Press), 1958.
LEWIS, H. M., *Planning the Modern City,* Vol. I. (New York: John H. Wiley), 1949.
PERLOFF, HARVEY S., ed., *Planning and the Urban Community.* (Pittsburgh: The University of Pittsburgh Press), 1961.
HAAR, CHARLES M., *Land Planning Law in a Free Society.* (Boston, Mass.: Harvard University Press), 1951.
———, *Land-Use Planning.* (Boston, Mass.: Little, Brown and Co.), 1959.
RATCLIFF, RICHARD U., *Urban Land Economics.* (New York: McGraw-Hill), 1949.
SITTE, C., *City Planning.* (New York: Random House), 1965.
THE ATHLETIC INSTITUTE, *Planning Areas and Facilities for Health, Physical Education, and Recreation,* rev. ed. (Chicago: The Athletic Institute), 1965.
WEBSTER, DONALD H., *Urban Planning and Municipal Public Policy.* (New York: Harper and Row), 1958.
WILLHEIM, SIDNEY, *Urban Zoning and Land Use Theory.* (New York: The Macmillan Co.), 1962.
WINGO, LOWDON, *Cities and Space.* (Baltimore, Md.: Johns Hopkins University Press), 1963.

Chapter 16

EDUCATION

PRINCIPLE: It is a professional mandate that the public be made to recognize the variety and diversity of recreational opportunity available through planned and organized recreational activities. All people must be educated to understand the facts and nature of recreational service.

Public education relevant to the field of recreational service may be defined as a basic instructional plan of cooperatively utilizing every available ethical means of informing all citizens of the values to be derived from its public recreational systems, in order that understanding and appreciation may be engendered and fostered. In this way, awareness of opportunities and attitudes of receptivity can be developed so that better personal relations between the agency and the public will be encouraged. The necessity for public goodwill is indispensable if the people for whom recreational services are organized and administered are to receive benefits and take advantage of the satisfying experiences offered to them. Essentially, however, goodwill is an outgrowth of recognition, and recognition is dependent upon comprehension.

PUBLIC EDUCATION AS NECESSITY

People have too long been ignorant of the truth concerning public recreational service. To some extent, this has been the fault of recreationists themselves. Too few recreational agencies have undertaken the arduous task of enlightening the public about the real story of the field or of the functions and role which the particular agency plays in community life. The public simply does not realize that the public recreational service department is the best single agency for securing satisfying, enjoyable, safe, and planned experiences specifically designed for the happiness of the participating individual. As a public service organization the recreational service system is under a mandate to provide facts applied to the operation, administration, and the results generated therefrom. People who have little or no knowledge of the field of public recreational service, or of the departments operating in the field, cannot be reasonably expected to appreciate the offerings. In fact, it would be surprising if without knowing of the availability or understanding the nature of recreational opportunities, any persons were to take full advantage of the services provided.

Recreationists have tended to find fault with the public for its apparent apathy and nonsupport of public departments. The fault does not lie with the public, but is in large measure a problem caused by the systems themselves. Recreationists have taken small pains to clear up misunderstandings, smooth conflicts, or provide explanations of the department's functions, responsibilities, and services to the public. Whatever misconception has arisen comes from a basic lack of effort on the part of recreationists to extend the agency's usefulness through the development of good public relations. It is quite comprehensible, therefore, to accept the reasons why the humanitarian feature of recreational service has not received its fair share of appreciation and why the public has allowed the recreationist to work in relative obscurity. As education enhances knowledge, awareness of the field, and status for recreationists, there will be a concomitant development of goodwill toward public recreational agencies which is essential for them to accomplish most effectively the fundamental promise of providing recreational opportunities for all of the people all of the time.

Chiefly, there are two considerations that make it necessary for the public to know about the field of recreational service and the public agencies which carry on the work: (1) that the entire community may profitably avail itself of the services offered; and (2) the recreational systems may properly be empowered to extend their utility. In rendering services recreational departments must perform several functions: programming recreational activities; employment and professional development of competent staff; planning, design, construction, and maintenance of physical plants and facilities; and administration. It is apparent that public education is focused on the best interests of the community, but there is reciprocity in that the department enjoys considerable benefit as well. Until recreational agencies can attract greater support through participation, they will not be enabled to offer a comprehensive series of activities, make more adequate recreational places and facilities, employ the best prepared and competent leadership, nor effectively administer the complex facets of agency operation. Public education through the provision of greater identification and discovery of significant value to the community is of specific benefit to the recreational service department. Offering authoritative, timely, and interesting information will attract favorable attention and advance the interests of the field as a whole and the agency in particular.

Outcomes of Public Education

The objectives of public education must be clearly understood, worthwhile, in good taste, and reachable. The objectives should be easily definable and basic to the nature of the agency. There is a need for identification of the public to which the campaign of education is directed. Every public relations program must be appropriate for what it is attempting to accomplish. The fundamental idea that is being promoted must be socially sound and have general appeal and value for the public. A public relations program must have desirable goals and should support only that which is in good taste. The whole concept of ethical practice revolves around this point. Consideration must be given to current public opinion. This is particularly important where the agency is attempting to educate persons of all positions and status and specifically if the idea to be disseminated is new, different, or likely to encounter objections. Unless it can be related to accepted beliefs it is likely to be dismissed without much thought. The larger goal of public education must be attainable. This can be realized through careful planning. It is true that coincidental situations, facts, or conditions may be highly publicized and gain attention and success. However, the procedure of public education should not rest upon the startling news event nor fortuitous circumstances. There must be a definite, intelligent, and carefully devised plan with scrupulous attention given to all details.

A careful well-organized plan of public education should:

1. Develop public appreciation of recreational service.
2. Expose people to a wider variety of possible recreational experiences.
3. Disseminate information about the recreational system and develop knowledge and understanding of department functions.
4. Encourage genuine good public relations between the citizens and their department.
5. Modify negative attitudes and opinions which adversely affect the department.
6. Suggest a more precise survey and analysis of the community in order to determine needs and resources wherein the recreational agency can assume a more vital and rightful role.
7. Cooperate and coordinate activities with all other recreational organizations within the community to provide total community service.
8. Foster a definite desire on the part of employed personnel to understand the work of the department and effect better relations and closer contact with the public.
9. Clearly define the economic support necessary if the public system is to be enabled to carry out its ethical mandate.
10. Justify the necessity for the construction and maintenance of additional recreational facilities and areas in order to meet community needs.
11. Stimulate participation among citizens in utilizing existing facilities and areas and taking part in planned recreational activities.
12. Remove political patronage from the public department.
13. Clarify and explain professional personnel standards in terms of more effective recreational offerings promoted in the safest manner.
14. Publicly explain the position of the recreational service system as the chief source of skilled and continuous provision of recreational experi-

ences so that it may be widely understood that this service is available to the community.
15. Encourage volunteers to offer their time, talents, and skill in broadening recreational opportunities.
16. Avoid competition for the same participants among all agencies offering recreational opportunities in the community.
17. Promote voluntary contribution, endowments, gifts, and bequests.
18. Discover and list every segment of the public which may be of significance in shaping opinion favorable to the agency.
19. Encourage private citizens to consult the agency for information and program resources in seeking personal nonprogrammed recreational experiences.
20. Improve the relations of agency and mass media for a more valid and sympathetic presentation of departmental practices and policies.

All of these outcomes are developed through a sound, carefully organized plan of public education; but in order that these benefits may be effected, a complete analysis and study of the appeals and content of the program is essential. There must be a detailed and systematic plan for initiating and sustaining a successful program of public education.

Planning Public Education

Before the public recreational service department can undertake the necessary action of educating its community, it must develop a plan that will systematically utilize every possible means of ethical practice in order to organize a comprehensive and unified campaign. There are countless opportunities throughout the year which lend themselves to effective and colorful use in educating the public. These situations and occasions should be coordinated into the campaign and every advantage must be taken of them. However, the public education program cannot be an intermittent affair of hit and miss, trial and error. There must be a sound and logical procedure by which each facet of the campaign is fitted into a complete and intelligible picture. The campaign, like the recreational program itself, is on a distinct schedule of predetermined events. A successful public education program is the culmination of a regularly released series of items which have continuity and thereby build interest. Scheduled events released to all mass media in a prearranged sequence must be made on a periodic and routine basis at times previously set in order to awaken public anticipation which may eventuate in support. Every item released at definitely spaced intervals is concentrated on increasing the education of the public.

A successful effort will be made only with a clear understanding of the recreational service department which is to be the reciprocal beneficiary of the educational campaign. Every facet of the department should be carefully researched to make certain that all the facts are known before the campaign is initiated. Questions that must be answered concern a knowledge of the history of the department, how, when, and why it was established, and information about its development, functions, policies, and personnel. It is particularly desirable in the case of policies to know why they came into existence. How does the department benefit the community? Who has guided the development and operation of the agency? What is its position in the municipal government? In the life of the community? Has it been progressive in meeting changing conditions as well as in planning for future situations? What are the advantages that will accrue if the department is given community support? What are the opportunities and resources available which will have a positive effect upon the community and its citizens? These questions answered with the truth will do much in affecting public education and engendering public commitment and support for the recreational system.

Analysis of the Public

The chief fact to be provided concerns the public to which the appeal is to be made. What does the public already know about and how do they react toward the public recreational service department? Reasonably accurate answers to many questions may be found through the use of the well-established statistical sampling method. A carefully selected sample of a fractional part of the public may be surveyed to determine answers for the entire aggregate. Sampling surveys may be conducted by personal interview, by mail, by telephone, or through a panel of permanent or periodically selected individuals. After the questions have been asked of the persons making up the sample, the responses must be analyzed, evaluated, and verified if they are to be utilized as guides for a public educational program.

STAFF REQUIREMENTS

Employed personnel of the recreational service department are all the staff that a public education program usually requires or has. However, some larger departments may be fortunate to be able to employ one or more public relations specialists who will be responsible for the technical dissemination of material that serves to educate the public. The number of staff personnel needed to operate a continuous public education program will depend, in large measure, upon (1) the quantity of material to be collected and studied; (2) the amount of writing to be performed; (3) the media to be utilized; (4) the coordination necessary for centralized and decentralized phases of the program; and (5) the mechanical and routine work which can be done by nontechnical personnel. The smaller and one-man departments will have to rely upon the recreationist to get the job done or will need to recruit volunteers who can offer assistance. The larger and more efficient metropolitan departments will undoubtedly have a specialist who has the function of public relations only. Many successful education staffs consist of a supervisor, sometimes a writer or editor, secretarial assistance, and clerical help.

The permanent staff of the largest urban systems may consist of a director or supervisor-in-charge, an assistant, several interviewers, at least one analyst, one or more writers, an editor, a photographer, clerks, typists, and secretaries. The effectiveness of the public education program will be contingent upon the competency of the director and his assistants. It is also dependent upon the degree of centralization of authority, and upon a clear line of demarcation of duties and functions. The director of public relations should have an important voice in the formulation of policies concerned with the management of public education. This means that his technical counsel should be observed in order for him to carry out his assignment and details of the program in the way that will best serve the interests and needs of the department and the community.

The employment of a public relations director, on either a full or part-time basis, realistically assists the realization of a workable procedure of public education. The public relations director must be a specialist in the field of mass communications and should be thoroughly familiar with recreational service. Such a person will know how best to gain attention and sustain public interest. He must have enthusiasm and a good imagination. Such characteristics are indispensable to one who must stimulate support with new ideas and initiate action. The director is the best qualified person to advise on the methods for public education.

STANDARDS OF PRACTICE

Unlike commercial operations and other business ventures, the public recreational service department must conduct its public relations in strict accordance with a professional code of ethics. The public agency cannot be ruled by the competitive element, but must function in a way that is most beneficial for the community and its citizens. A program of public education must utilize every possible ethical means of providing the truth about the agency and its operation to all of the people. Furthermore, there is the necessary concomitant of offering information about the entire field of recreational service and its attendant parts. Publicity is not the answer. A soundly developed plan of factual content interestingly presented and disseminated in the best manner for attractiveness and impact requires attention to the smallest detail. Exaggeration, personal aggrandizement, and statements that distort the real objective of the agency must be shunned.

PRODUCING THE EDUCATIONAL PROGRAM

Prior to the initiation of any educational program of public relations, research is necessary to disclose points of conflict and other areas of misapprehension between the public and the recreational service system.

Whenever there are any discoveries of public apathy, nonsupport, or unfavorable opinions as a consequence of certain policies which the agency follows, a planned series of explanations and procedures to remedy unfriendly attitudes must be undertaken. More specifically, some citizens may have developed erroneous ideas concerning the fees and charges which the department sets or budgeted expenditures because of inability or unwillingness to analyze the public record. Much progress has been made in recent years in making annual reports containing financial earnings and expenditures which are intelligible to laymen. The presentation of interesting, attractive, and simple reports, which are widely disseminated, may be one of the more significant features of departmental public relations. Other citizens may have developed a dislike for the department because of a poor first impression gathered when meeting with an employee who was discourteous, indifferent, or ignorant. Misrepresentations in scheduling activities, errors in the program which occur frequently, a parochial or competitive view of other agencies in the community may inspire public irritation and ultimate rejection of the agency. Such attitudes are dangerous if existent and continued. One disenchanted individual may be the beginning of a movement to abolish the department as an unneccessary frill and a waste of the taxpayer's money. Whatever the cause of ill will, it must be corrected and the facts of correction appropriately publicized.

A program of public education needs to employ every form of media which can be effective in widely publicizing the true nature of the department and its functions. Five specific avenues are available to recreational service systems for the attainment of this objective: oral presentations, literary presentations, graphic presentations, a combination of these means, and the organization itself.

Oral Presentations

Education may be greatly promoted by word of mouth. However, such education may be positive or negative depending upon the information obtained. True statements concerning the public recreational service department can be beneficial, but slanderous statements, dishonest or biased statements can do much to hurt the system. Surprisingly, but unfortunately, some departmental personnel either become disaffected, disloyal, or through ignorance speak of the agency in terms that can best be described as detrimental. Upon the superintendent, therefore, lays the responsibility of providing such personnel with the correct information and taking steps to dissuade those staff persons from their negative opinions. All personnel of the department have an important role to play in public education. Professionals, most particularly, should be so well informed about the responsibilities, functions, and operation of the agency that they are ready, willing, and able to discuss the department intelligently and explain its workings to all who wish or need to know.

Participants. Probably the most effective means of educating the public with respect to the recreational institution is through the program participant who has achieved satisfaction or enjoyment in a given activity. Unless the department can offer a program that is geared to meet the recreational needs of all of the people in the community, it should not undertake a plan of public education; in fact, it has not lived up to the reason for its establishment and should be abolished. Unless the public recreational service department is prepared to offer a comprehensive program of great variety and diversity under the guidance and direction of competent recreationists, it is not representative of the ethical practice which makes recreational service a great humanitarian field of endeavor. By providing the type of program which will generally meet the needs of people, a public department of recreational service will best publicize itself ethically. The participant who is satisfied, who has enjoyed an activity, and who feels he has achieved in some way can do more to educate and gain public support for the agency than can any other medium. This is the essential reason for the existence of the agency—to satisfy participants. A satisfied participant will do more than any other method to counteract adverse opinion because he is a member of the public and he has had direct experience with the system.

Staff Personnel. Employed personnel are especially influential in gaining satisfied participants, and their words as well as performance are a vital asset in public education. Staff personnel, whether professional, technical, or ancillary, are in constant contact with members of the public. The first contact that an individual may have with the department will probably be with an employee. If the employee takes an interest in the person, attempts to answer whatever questions are asked, knows about the program offerings, facilities, and schedules, and displays courtesy, the likelihood is that the department will reap great benefits. Conversely, ignorance, rudeness, curtness, and affectation can do much to ruin any image which the agency must maintain.

Personnel employed by recreational agencies invariably talk about their work. They relate incidents that occur daily. It is of the utmost importance that all personnel be encouraged to give a true picture of the department and what it stands for. Personnel management procedures afford excellent opportunities to carefully recruit, screen, and induct intelligent and competent individuals. The scientific management of personnel offers many techniques to prevent employee discontent and promote loyalty. In order to preclude disaffection, the recreational service department must treat its personnel with consideration. Every staff member must be made to understand the intrinsic role he plays in contributing to the overall effectiveness of the agency. Each employee must be made to believe that upon him rests the image of the system. In a sense this is the truth, for all employed personnel contribute to the operating efficiency, the adequacy of program opportunities, and the maintenance of the agency. Regardless of the position of the employee, he should be indoctrinated with the idea that whatever he does contributes in no small way to the production of recreational services for the entire community. If the employee really feels that his work is important and he receives recognition for doing a good job, he will usually react with sincere interest, dedicated loyalty, and satisfaction in his work, which in consequence will produce favorable public education. Devotion to duty, however, is not enough. All employees must be taught the basic facts about the agency, the respective policies, and this must be reinforced periodically through in-service education. It is apparent that public recreational service departments will be handsomely repaid by treating their employees in such a manner.

Speakers Bureau. The recreational service department should recruit staff members to represent it at a variety of meetings whenever speakers are in demand. A roster of speakers should be developed so that every phase of agency operation or specialization can be explained. A well-selected speaker with a prepared talk presented to any community club, association, or organization does much to encourage interest and fosters learning about the agency. Staff employees, who are selected for the bureau, should be good public speakers, be able to deliver an interesting statement, and must be well acquainted with the agency and its operations. He must be capable of fielding questions on agency policy as well as be able to answer any questions concerning programming, facilities, or other general facts of operation. Questions dealing with specific administrative detail should be referred to the proper authorities. The function of educating the public can be promoted by seizing every opportunity to reach as many organizations as is possible with appropriate talks.

Advisory Councils and Committees. Every public recreational service agency should establish a lay advisory council or committee to assist in planning the program as well as offering an indication of public interest. Such associations should be formed on a neighborhood basis, for individual playgrounds, centers, and for specific age groups, e.g., youth, older adult, and parent, as well as for the community as a whole. These groups of elected or selected representatives become the cadre from which word-of-mouth information spreads. Usually, these groups have numerous contacts, or they occupy strategic social positions in their respective neighborhoods. Each member of a committee or council is thereby able to speak with many other people concerning those aspects of the public recreational service department about which they are familiar.

In order to afford impetus to the work of public education it is absolutely essential to educate committee and council members themselves. All of these individuals will be willing to give of their time and energy for the benefit of the department. Significantly, this is considered to be a very satisfying recreational experience for those who participate, and they are participating on a voluntary basis in any case. To begin with, they have assumed a certain responsibility by becoming members of committees and councils. However, their energies must be channeled correctly so that what they have to say will be factual and contributory to the good of the agency and the community. Periodically, members of these groups should be given an indoctrinating talk regarding the department. To improve their knowledge of the agency and stimulate their enthusiasm, a visit to all centers of operation can be arranged.

Radio. Radio is a natural channel for public education. In contacting a mass audience, perhaps one of the largest will be reached by radio. Broadcasters are generally willing to utilize ideas and material which have news value or human interest and popular appeal. One of the finest avenues available for the formation of positive public opinion and, incidentally for the education of the public, is through radio commentators, who usually have quite an audience following. Spot announcements, as well as news or special features, can be made. However, arrangements with broadcasting stations must be made well in advance, script or other materials must be submitted for clearance, and the program itself must be carefully prepared so that its presentation will be as perfect as possible.

Telephone. The telephone can be a striking means for quickly informing the public about specific activities, changes in plans, or answering inquiries. Most important is the way in which the telephone is used. The person answering a telephone for the agency should maintain a pleasant tone of voice and be able to respond efficiently and in a courteous manner. One of the ways in which telephone communications can be established is the chain phone call. If departmental volunteers can form a telephone link, information about any number of departmental problems, activities, facilities, or necessary support can be swiftly dispatched. The chain call simply asks that the first person telephone two friends who in turn each call two friends, and so on. It may be that particular groups will have a telephone corps wherein each member has a selected list of members to phone. In this way, all of the members are quickly contacted and informed about any modifications of schedule or provided with whatever data is necessary. Chain telephone calls have proved extremely effective in political campaigns and there is no reason to suspect that they cannot be just as significant, if correctly used, by local recreational service departments.

Sectarian Agencies. Much factual information can be disseminated to the public via the pulpit. By obtaining the cooperation of the local council of churches or the ministerial association, it is possible to gain the undivided attention of those who might not, in the ordinary course of events be swayed or contacted by other means. One Sabbath day each should be set aside by ministers for a discussion on the public recreational service department. A tie-in can be offered between such an address and almost any of the biblical passages concerning work, leisure, the Sabbath itself and the meanings that this has for each individual. The minister may give the address himself, or it may be delivered by a selected speaker. If the minister decides to speak, he should be provided with informative material concerning the agency so that he may be sufficiently prepared to offer enlightening concepts to his congregation.

Schools. Schools constitute one of the most important fields for the dissemination of public recreational service information. It is at once a captured audience and a fertile area for the implantation of facts that will serve the community immediately and in the future. Scheduled arrangements can be made with school superintendents and the principals of each school for providing regular appearances of qualified speakers for talks on the field of recreational service and the specific department of the community. Not only can interesting information about the department and its program be offered, speakers who appear at career guidance assemblies, which most high schools arrange, can do much to assist in the recruitment of volunteer, part-time, and potential full-time employees. Many extracurricular groups are recreationally oriented. These activities, sponsored by the school, can become an excellent avenue whereby a qualified representative of the department can appear as part of the club or organizational program for one or more meetings. A definite message can therefore be communicated to young and developing minds.

Clubs, Societies, Associations. A staff representative who can deliver a stimulating and informative talk dealing with departmental plans, programs, or operational practices will be in demand at the various social, civic, business, professional, and other interest groups of the community. Hard-pressed program chairmen of these organizations are always seeking appropriate topics with which to enhance membership participation. The well-selected speaker with a prepared talk can do much to further the work of educating the public through the instrument of the spoken word.

Literary Presentations

The written word, coming from an intelligent recreationist capable of stating an idea, can shape public opinion. Recreational service departments have utilized the printed statement for a long time, but, unhappily, the type of writing they generally produced was formal, dogmatic, dull, full of statistics, and contained information not designed to be highly readable by the public. The public recreational service department must publish reports and keep records because it is accountable to the people for what it does. Furthermore, citizens want to read and understand what is reported to them. Legal discourses, financial statements, and long, dry, uninteresting literature cannot accomplish an educational purpose because the reader's attention and interest will be lost after the first insipid page. If the public recreational service agency really desires to educate the public by literary means, they must supply information that is interesting as well as informative. In smaller departments the responsibility for compiling this material rests with the executive, with another staff person, or rarely, with a volunteer. By far, the employment of a specialist on a full- or part-time basis to write and edit such material is vastly superior. The literary output of the agency can find its way to the public in many ways. Every form of written information can be utilized and fitted into the planned program of education.

Published Periodicals. Daily newspapers and weekly or monthly magazines are effective methods of placing the achievements and goals of the public department before the general public. The necessity for current events and timely news is obvious. News must be interesting and, when possible, entertaining. It must attract attention, sustain reader interest, create favorable attitudes, and gain support. Literary efforts should be as dramatically presented as possible, for dramatic presentation is often more convincing than straight copy. It makes the underlying reason for the copy not only interesting, but easy to remember. Human interest features, a novel combination of familiar subjects, a question asked in dramatic form, or an offer of service may become dramatic and stimulating methods for presenting material. Every news item should be clearly pointed. Care must be taken to create the impression desired. No written effort should ever be issued if it cannot be fully substantiated by the facts.

Good reporting is based upon the news of the department. The person in charge of developing educational material can well begin by compiling sources that can be used in news releases. Among these are

SIGNIFICANT EVENTS
    Appointment of advisory council members
    Meetings of the council, neighborhood councils, committees
    Anniversary of the department establishment
    State or national occasions which can be tied into the agency's activities
    Annual banquets, dinners, celebrations
    Annual national conference
    Annual state conference
    Annual district or regional conference
    Local pageants, commemorations, or traditional events
    Tournaments and program contests
    Awards of merit to employees
    Opening of an exhibition
    Construction of a new or improved facility or area
    Program demonstrations
    National holidays, festivals, patriotic occasions
    Special weeks, days, or months, e.g., Recreation Month
REPORTS ON SPECIAL STUDIES
    Reports on community recreational conditions
    Reports on community surveys and master plans
    Reports on construction
    Reports on land acquisition
    Reports on federal grants
    Reports on institutes, workshops, and staff development program
PERSONALITIES
    Visits by dignitaries
    Personal accomplishments of participants
    Visits by interested community groups
    Winners of leagues, tournaments, games, contests

Employee advancement within the department
Interviews by departmental employees
Contributions to the community made by employees outside of the agency
Recognition and awards to individuals for voluntary service
Endorsements of the department by local officials and prominent citizens

DEPARTMENTAL POLICIES
New rules and regulations governing certain events or facilities
New employment policies
Public conduct policies
Policies regarding hours of facility operation

Newspapers are the chief published medium of both news and educational information. Indeed they have come to be known as the great national university. It is here that the true story of the public recreational service department may be told. Because the extent to which news, feature, and human interest items are used is subject to the attitudes of the newspapers, it is necessary to know something about the way in which they are organized. The individuals who make up the editorial board, the various departments and specializations of the newspaper should be well known to the recreational service employee who is directly concerned with placing information with the newspapers. Because each editor generally supervises and determines the nature of all material to be used as news which will appear in the paper, it is desirable to cultivate that person assiduously. The maintenance of friendly relations with city, managing, and departmental editors is extremely important. Among the general rules that can be followed when working with editors are:

1. Trivialities should be omitted.
2. The educational program should be planned before presentation.
3. Personal calls should be brief and never just before a deadline.
4. Try to accommodate an editor at every opportunity.
5. Do not conceal any facts.
6. Make the releases interesting and timely.
7. If doubtful about the benefit of any story to the department, trust the editor's judgment.

In many communities, the public recreational service department may become a good source of news for newspapers. If the department can generate enough news it may become important for newspapers to assign a reporter to cover the agency and bring in departmental stories. There is no sound reason why the public department should not accord special privileges to newspapers. The situation is one of mutual appreciation. If the department expects to have its stories printed in the newspaper, reporters must have free access to the department. The resulting newspaper publicity is of several specific types: straight news stories, feature articles, editorials, departmental column, society columns, news pictures.

Standard Practice for Typed News Releases. Educational information intended for newspapers and magazines should generally be prepared so as to conform to commonly recognized standards of practice. For example:

1. Copy should be on white paper, standard size (8½ inches by 11 inches).
2. Releases should be typed clearly, double- or triple-spaced and on one side of the paper only.
3. The release date should appear in the upper right hand corner of the first page.
4. There should be an indication of whether it is for morning or afternoon release.
5. The source of the release should appear in the upper left hand corner of the first page.
6. Copy should begin not less than one third down the first page and have ample margins of not less than one inch on either side.
7. No headings should appear on the story.
8. All pages must be numbered consecutively.
9. Copy should conform to the style of the prospective user.
10. Each paragraph should be self-contained and not carried over from one page to another.
11. The word *more* should appear at the bottom of the page if additional copy appears on the next page.
12. The release should be folded so that the copy shows on the outside.
13. Duplicate copies should not be sent to competing media.
14. Editorializing should be avoided.
15. Finish should be indicated by an end mark, e.g., "30" or #.

These standards relating to copy in the preparation of news releases are the result of experiences with many magazine and newspaper offices. Other media have special rules in addition to these and they, also, must be respected if the educational program is to go forward. In the preparation of a feature story, special care must be given to the lead or topic sentence. This is a brief introductory statement. It should tell, within thirty words the answers to who, what, when, where, why, and sometimes how. The lead must be so written that if it is the only sentence that the reader actually digests he will have the essential elements of the story. He may not have all the details but he will at least have the basic facts. The story itself should be so constructed that it may be cut at any point and still be coherent and informative. If at all possible the story should be limited to one page.

Contests and School Papers. The department of recreational service may well sponsor elementary through college essay contests, especially at a time which is traditionally oriented to recreational activities. Many subjects dealing with public recreational services may be utilized in such compositions. English teachers are usually willing to cooperate in learning endeavors such as this inasmuch as these stimulate the regular classroom work.

The school or college paper may be an effective medium to publicize the department effectively. If the department organizes activities which include the student body, in part or whole, there is greater likelihood that the paper will carry features, facts, perhaps a regular column, and an editorial concerning departmental offerings, the need for public support, or other helpful statements which win friends for the department. The utilization of clip sheets, which are printed to look like a miniature newspaper page or galley proofs, may be useful to the department in regularly keeping school periodicals informed of programmed activities and other information.

Magazines and Sunday Supplements. Magazines offer a channel for certain kinds of public education. However, it is generally not possible to obtain space in the same way or on the same subjects as in the newspapers. Nevertheless, it is possible to get magazines to run excellently prepared stories of great detail and length which may add to the educational program. It is difficult, but not impossible, for a writer to reach the editors of magazines because of the nature and requirements of the publications. Material submitted to them must conform to their required patterns. Several publications in the recreational service field are rendering invaluable assistance. However, these serve mainly to educate those who are already employed within the field, rather than the lay public. Among the general magazines which carry articles dealing with the field are *Reader's Digest, Life, Look, Saturday Evening Post, Good Housekeeping,* and *Family Circle.* The class magazine group includes such periodicals as *House and Garden, Better Homes and Gardens,* and *House Beautiful.* The news magazines such as *Time* and *Newsweek* have special sections devoted to leisure and recreational activity. The business magazines such as *Fortune,* and the trade, technical, or professional magazines provide a fertile and relatively easy access for gaining acceptance. All of these magazines should be sought by recreational service departments as a means of educating the public. There are many possibilities—factual articles, descriptive essays, and pictures with news value.

Departmental Bulletins. Mimeographed or printed bulletins should be distributed by every recreational service agency. They may contain a feature story, specific facts about the agency, e.g., number of employed personnel, activities offered, facilities, up-coming events, or they can be devoted to the publication of current policies and contain actual pictures of sponsored recreational activities. Bulletins may be useful in mailings and may also be placed in the lounges of recreational centers and other public buildings for general distribution.

Pamphlets and Directories. A small, comprehensive booklet about the public department can be of inestimable help in educating the public as to the organization, administration, and operation of the agency. The purpose of the departmental pamphlet is to help explain the services of the department in language that is interesting and understandable. The use of a pamphlet of this type is very effective, particularly when complemented by other media. Directories are indexes of services, facilities, activities, special or current events offered, and names of supervisors and other employees, and may also list supplies, materials, and equipment as well as literary resources. An alphabetical listing of all recreational agencies within the community supplemented by commercial agencies of various types completes the directory.

Departmental or House Organ. Mention has been previously made of the necessity for maintaining goodwill among employees and educating them so that they can speak with factual authority of the many services and facets of the department in their respective contacts with the public. The departmental or house organ is an internal magazine written and edited for, and sometimes by, employees rather than administrative staff. It is published by the agency for distribution and free circulation solely among the members of the operating staff of the department. It may also be distributed to volunteers and their auxiliary personnel who contribute time and effort toward departmental success. It is a publication which can be issued once each month and constitutes one of the most effective means for securing the interest of all workers. Needless to say, the departmental organ can be produced only in the largest agencies having numerous employees.

The departmental magazine may run from a single sheet of mimeograph or letterpress periodical to the more nearly complete journal containing from four to 35 pages. House organs generally cover the following subjects:

AGENCY INFORMATION—such items as pay schedules, work schedules, appointments of new supervisors, construction of new facilities, advancements, availability of higher positions, expansion of the program, contests, line and staff arrangements, personnel policies, and official announcements.
EMPLOYEE INFORMATION—awards for special service, recognition for superior job performance, commendations received, promotions, new employees, retirements, obituaries, staff meetings, conference participation, employee interviews, and service anniversaries.
EFFORTS TO INCREASE EFFECTIVENESS—reduction in waste, staff development programs, safety, health, suggestions and criticisms of all sorts, technical articles, resources available, editorials, and letters to the editor.
GENERAL INTEREST ITEMS—articles by members of the staff, book reviews, current events, classified ads, personal improvement articles, recipes, fashion notes, interior decoration, hobbies, quotations, family news, and personals.

To be effective the departmental organ must be highly readable. It must have a pleasing format, neat printing, and attractive illustrations or pictures. Such a periodical should be geared to meet the needs of its readers. It should, as a matter of course, represent the mutual interest of the department and the staff. Although a great deal of the information printed in the journal may be informative, it needs to reflect the reciprocal feeling of respect which the administration has for the staff. The internal journal assists in orienting employee attitude. It serves as one medium by which the agency can build mutual trust and confidence between itself and its operating personnel. It offers an outstanding opportunity for the department to win the interest and influence the actions of those who should know the agency best—the employed staff. Public education, like charity, begins at home.

Annual Reports. Annual reports may become an effective instrument for informing the public about the organization and administration of the public recreational service department. Chief among the reasons for publishing an annual report are (1) to conform with legal requirements of public accountability; (2) to establish a permanent record of the accomplishments, operations, and financial disbursements of the agency; (3) to familiarize people with the program of activities, facilities available, and professional personnel who conduct and supervise activities; (4) to recognize all those who have contributed to the rendering of public recreational service within the community; and (5) to stimulate interest, provoke attention, and encourage participation in the program. The annual report must be something more than a statistical accounting of how many people participated or how much money was spent for the maintenance of buildings, grounds, tools, and equipment. It must be readable, thought provoking, attractive, and informative. This means that bone dry profit and loss statements, meaningless numbers, and percentages that offer calculated misrepresentations must be omitted. There are ways to present financial statements, participation statistics, and factual information that are interesting, bright, and attention getting.

Pictures constitute an important part of any annual report. Photographs of special events, of the standard operating activities, and of highlights during the year should be selected to give a sound understanding of the opportunities provided by the departmental program. Graphic artwork, carefully inserted, can do much to alleviate the tedium of going through a set of figures. Comprehensive summaries of fiscal facts can be profitably included along with a statement of budget needs and projected plans. The annual report may be an excellent selling device in gaining additional support for anticipated needs. If it is well prepared it serves as a significant educational medium.

Letter Writing. All letters should be personal and informal, unless they are required to be formalized by the nature of an inquiry or in requesting information from a specific resource. Many agencies make the mistake of not replying immediately to questions or criticisms. All replys should be mailed within three days of receipt of incoming mail. Nothing infuriates an individual so much as not having a mailed inquiry answered or having to wait weeks or months for an answer. All letters should be written with the following concepts in mind:

1. What is the basic objective of the letter?
2. What facts, opinions, or impressions are to be conveyed?
3. Does the opening sentence capture the idea to be transmitted?
4. Does the tone of the letter approach the subject from the recipient's orientation?
5. Does the letter contain a worthwhile idea?
6. Is it positive?
7. Is it integrated around one primary idea?
8. Does it include any inconsequential material that detracts from the ruling idea?
9. Does it omit any essential points?
10. Are all facts and ideas in logical sequence and intelligible?
11. Is it cordial?
12. Does it express confidence?
13. Does it fully answer any questions which the correspondent asked?
14. Is it neatly typed?

Many recreational departments have found it good practice to send a brief, informal letter to any new residents. If the community is small enough so that all new arrivals are known by some central agency, e.g., a realtor's clearing house, new residents can be easily contacted. During the start of a new playground operation, the opening of a new center, or other recreational facility, a list of participants can be made and letters can be sent to them encouraging suggestions for improvement of the activities or offerings. Letters such as these can be extremely effective in promoting goodwill and, incidently, call attention to new activities, facilities, or other innovations which the department sponsors.

Graphic Presentations

Visual presentations are a valuable method for public education. Stimuli received through the visual sense are normally lasting and impressive. People appear to understand a great deal more if they are shown something, rather than told about it. Graphic presentations seem to promote greater comprehension and longer-lasting remembrances of any given subject.

Exhibits. Every recreational service department should direct that each permanent recreational facility must have an exhibit in a particular place for inspection at all times. An outstanding idea is for the various facilities to set up exhibits depicting the series of operations and recreational activities chiefly performed at the facility. For example, a swimming pool might display a collection of action photographs of water shows and/or competitive events; a playground might offer a permanent exhibit of art, crafts, hobby, or nature oriented activities; a recreational center might set up an exhibit of a model of a proposed new center or feature a bound scrapbook indicating the highlights of the variety of activities carried on there; the golf course might display a schematic diagram of the links with the various flora that are utilized and the watering system to maintain the greens and fairways; the neighborhood or community park could have a scale model of the park with all of the trails, playing areas, picnic spots, activity places, and aesthetic views or outstanding natural phenomena specifically marked; the central office of the department might carry an instructive permanent exhibit of model records and reports. In every division, unit exhibits of this nature might be available for the edification of visitors touring the agency. Permanent exhibits can usually be kept up to date by replacing, whenever necessary, obsolete items with those of more immediate interest.

Posters and Bulletin Boards. The strategic placement of striking posters and bulletin boards is valuable in the promotion of neighborhood and city-wide recreational services. Posters should be artistically contrived, and be able to tell a story with a well-designed format. Posters may be large or small, irregularly or regularly shaped, and placed almost anywhere. They should be used where people congregate, e.g., in bank and food store windows or on counters, in the lobby of the local motion picture theatre, at entrances to recreational facilities, or on supporting columns or posts. Attractively created and colorful posters can serve as one exciting medium for the enlightenment of the public.

The utilization of bulletin boards can do much in publicizing the department's schedule of activities. Bulletin boards are always regular in shape, although they may be of any size suitable for the purpose to which they have been erected. They must be installed at points where they can be seen immediately, or situated where the traffic volume is heaviest. Pictures and notices placed on the board should be kept current. The board itself should never appear too cluttered, but should be kept neat and so designed as to produce the most pleasing effect. Bulletin boards may be open or have glass coverings. In either instance they can be enhanced by artfully concealed lighting, direct or indirect, which can do much to draw the attention to a specific spot on the board.

Combined Presentations

There are many opportunities to educate the public through a combination of media. Some of these are the following.

Motion Pictures. Many progressive departments have filmed and produced motion pictures describing the work and the activities of the department which are available free for use by selected agency employees in assisting in public education. Most recreational service departments usually cannot afford to produce motion pictures for public distribution. However, there are several excellent films available for showing by recreational agencies. This means of education is particularly valuable inasmuch as the public is educated and entertained simultaneously. Many phases of recreational service may be shown to the public through the medium of motion pictures. There is little question that the field of recreational service can be vividly portrayed by this means. The public has always accorded much interest in films and this can be advantageously exploited by departments with imaginative administrators.

Television. Television is an exciting medium that has received less attention than it should because it attracts viewers in every locale. The simple fact that there are now in the United States more than 67 million receivers is an indication of the vast potential which this means has to offer. Perhaps television has superseded almost all other media in its ability to instantaneously transmit significant news in a visual manner. Then too, well-known commentators have developed an extremely large following and do much to shape public opinion as well as to report information. Telecasting costs are so phenomenal that paid advertisements are calculated in the thousands of dollars for announcements that take seconds to deliver. It is unlikely that recreational service departments could ever budget enough money to sponsor a telecast. However, through the good graces of television stations, time is often given for a variety of local current events features. The station continually seeks out sources which either make news or are concerned with human interest stories. For this reason, departments can make arrangements to televise a series of regularly scheduled telecasts dealing with the operation of the agency in its manifold categories. To be fully effective, telecasts must occur at stated periodic intervals so that they may be scheduled for viewing release at a time when the public is prepared to see them. The telecast should become an established routine and not an intermittent, hit or miss, program. If arrangements can be made wherein the telecasts occur once each week, each program will be part of a series developing one central theme. Whatever the presentation is, it should be concerned with recreational services in the community, with the public department in particular, should never be longer than 15 minutes, should be free from technical jargon, precise, very interesting, and should always emphasize the relationship between individual achievement, satisfaction, and the recreational opportunities available through the departmental operation. It is sound judgment to reinforce the telecast with a printed pamphlet for distribution to interested parties or for general distribution at recreational centers.

The television program, or, if time does not permit, the message, must be carefully prepared so that its presentation will be as compelling as possible. To any spoken message there might also be photographs or videotapes of activities currently offered by the department. In addition, there might well be some entertainment offered, if it is of good quality, from the participants in the music, dance, art, or drama activities of the program. One public recreational service department has, for years, been able to select different groups from various centers and playgrounds throughout its community and do "live" presentations in the studio. Such performances have earned the department an outstanding reputation. The following description of a typical television announcement may be helpful in procuring time from local stations.

Television Continuity from X Recreational Service Department

Time: 25 seconds
Words: 54

VIDEO	AUDIO
Slide #_____ (Photograph of activity group)	Public recreational service needs you. It is your local avenue to personal enjoyment, satisfaction, and fun. Your participation in any of these offered activities will give you a sense of achievement—art, crafts, music, drama, sports, hobbies, or outdoor education.
Slide #_____ (Pamphlet offer with X department name and address)	Learn more about your recreational service department. Write today for this free pamphlet.

Tours. A most useful way of gaining goodwill for the department is by conducting guided tours through the agency. Visitors may see the department and its various operations by one of three types of tour.

Individuals may be guided through the department almost every day. Persons of local influence who indicate a desire to see the agency at work should be taken on an intelligently guided tour throughout the system. It is important to remember that each department must be shown in actual operation. Only in this way can the individual making the visit best gain an understanding of what competent recreational service really means. At the conclusion of the tour the individual may be presented with one of several brochures, pamphlets, or even a copy of the annual report which will help to reinforce what has been observed.

Groups may be taken throughout the recreational system. Arrangements should be made to accommodate as many local community organizations as is possible. However, specific days should be set aside on a routine basis and standard invitations to tour the department should be given to civic bodies. School groups of all grades may be effectively indoctrinated by the group tour method. Close alliance must be maintained with the local school system for this reason. Among the groups whose influence upon community life will be significant if they are favorably impressed by the tour will be parent-teacher associations, business and professional women's association, service clubs, church groups, the taxpayer's alliance, and other civic-minded organizations.

The public should be invited to a general open house at the department at least twice during the year. National Recreation Month and December present excellent opportunities for the public to visit and observe the system. The itinerary for such tours must be well planned and conducted. Features of unusual interest can be called to the attention of the visitors and items of special significance can be selected for demonstration so that a better appreciation may be acquired pertaining to the services available from the department. It is necessary that insofar as possible the normal course of activities can be presented for observation by visitors touring the system. Each division of the system can then be exhibited in its routine functions, i.e., performing those activities and providing the facilities, personnel, and recreational experiences which have come to be expected in the usual skilled manner.

Special Media. All of those items which can be used to remind the public about the field of recreational service and the local department can be included in this phase of public relations. Such items as decals, stickers, inserts, tickets, postage meter messages, lapel buttons, hats, and other novelties can be utilized to carry a particular statement. Such messages may be a few words, e.g., "Conserve Parks," "Public Recreational Service," "Volunteers for Service," and so on, to one page statements for insert under car window wipers, in telephone directories, or into shopping bags at local food markets. Each of these items, alone or in a combination, can do much to publicize the recreational services offered by the local system. The real effectiveness of such media comes in terms of perpetually reminding the public that the department exists to serve and that the facts of availability are equally accessible.

Slides and Illustrated Lectures. Photographic slides, line drawings, and other illustrations can be used in furthering the education of the public. They are well employed in augmenting talks and lectures given on the public department of recreational service and for stressing the numerous activities offered by the system. Although slides can be made without color, those in color are very striking. A series of slides or film strips showing all phases of producing a pageant, parade, drama, circus, or field event—from inception to completion—may prove stimulating to the public. Added enjoyment and comprehension of the scope of recreational experiences available to the total community can be furnished by a series of pertinent scenes taken at various sites throughout the agency. Good photography and coloring will do much to heighten such scenes. Simultaneous records, tape recordings, or a speaker may provide additional emphases where necessary.

THE ORGANIZATION OF THE DEPARTMENT

If the recreational service department wishes to gain the goodwill of its community, it must enter into the life of the community. Departmental personnel should participate in all projects which have to do with the encouragement of education, the improvement of health and welfare, and the furtherance of economic prosperity. This participation can be made when staff personnel, acting as good citizens, become involved with and take an active part in such civic bodies as the League of Women Voters and the school board, and join whatever social or political association they so desire. Through such interest and contact the public department has ample opportunity to present its own cause and, specifically, to stress the contributory part it plays in the life of the community.

Organization

The departmental structure will play an important part in assisting in public education. How the department is arranged for the promotion and operation of recreational services will do much to influence public opinion for or against the department. If the departmental structure is limited or ineffectual, particularly is this true of one-man departments, the reception afforded it by the community will therein be reflected. It should be quite apparent that the basic organization of the public department is an accurate indicator of its impact upon the community.[1] If the community has little regard for the agency it will block steady development in terms of additional personnel, facilities, financial support, and other indices of status. Where, however, the department is provided with an internal structure designed to meet the multitudinous recreational needs of the community, there is a positive indication that the agency is highly regarded or that over a period of time it has been allowed to develop and receives public support. All large agencies were not established at current size. They have had to justify their existence through many valuable services to the community over many years. When recreational service is thought to be a frill, an unnecessary device for padding the city payroll, or a function which can be cut at the first sign of economic retrenchment, then it may validly be stated that the public department has not enlightened the citizens of the community concerning its significance.

Another facet of organization comes in terms of professional practitioners or recreationists employed by the department. If the department is heavily loaded with technicians, maintenance personnel, custodians, and groundskeepers, there is every reason to believe that the public will not be well educated in understanding agency functions. The chief idea of such personnel is to maintain facilities and wait for orders from the agency hierarchy. They do not plan, neither do they program. This is not

[1] As indicated in Chapters 11, 15, pp. 293, 415.

surprising for they are not equipped to deal with the problems of organizing and administering a complex program of varied and extensive activities of a recreational nature. They are not educationally prepared to handle the human problems and situations that continually confront the recreationist. Professional education, if not extensive field experience, is the major difference which sets the professional apart from the technician. It is this difference that allows the recreationist to understand the reason why, as well as how, recreational activities are initiated and carried on. There is an entire philosophical orientation provided to the professional person which is wholly absent from the less educated. It is for these reasons that a department heavily staffed with technical and maintenance personnel may not be able to clearly communicate with and educate the public. Technicians may be able to competently instruct an activity, under supervision, but they are not as capable nor as likely to function as planners. Not being able to completely visualize the need for public education they are more nearly to forget it. The recreationist, on the other hand, is constantly under obligation to educate the public to understand its own recreational needs, both personally and collectively, as an outgrowth of professionalistic principles. The recreationist has learned that careful attention to public needs and desires is as much a part of programming as skill and knowledge of activities. The employment of recreationists, therefore, will generally produce a public relations and education program.

Facilities

Universally, the first impression to be received by the potential recreational participant, casual visitor, or critical observer is the state of the recreational facility. An effective means of forming a good opinion of the agency is through a well maintained and attractive facility. The center, park, swimming pool, or playground does not have to be expensively appointed, nor does it have to be of the most modern design or very large. If the facility in question is maintained in such a manner as to present a neat and clean exterior, painted where paint needs to be applied, metalwork polished, woodwork and masonry in a good state of repair, walks swept, grounds without litter, plantings pruned or in a physical state of obvious upkeep, then a good impression is made. The facility should be appropriate for the site on which it is situated. It should be of size adequate to meet the participant and spectator demands of the neighborhood, it should be attractive and inviting. There should never be a stale odor pervading its atmosphere. It should be well lighted, well ventilated, and colorful and carefully decorated to make the visitor want to examine it and perhaps find a place for himself in some activity being offered there.

A dingy looking facility, painted battleship gray or olive drab, has a demoralizing effect upon those who might want to utilize it. Unfortunately, many aquatic facilities utilize these colors and also fail to keep the locker areas free from excess moisture and noxious smells, and are poorly ventilated and/or lighted. Poor maintenance practices reduce the effective utilization of the facility by people who do not care for such a fetid environment. Recreational centers should always be bright and cheerful. Recessed lighting, well-placed bulletin boards and posters, a comfortable lounge area, and all of the equipment and areas necessary for the provision of a comprehensive indoor recreational program should be available and scrupulously inspected each day for signs of wear. Crafts rooms should be separated from other recreational activities because of noise, odors due to chemical reagents used, or because of the type of materials employed. All facilities should be regularly checked for safety factors, fire fighting equipment, and control of noise, dirt, or any negative features. Not only will such a care and maintenance program do much to earn respect for the agency, such practices will also lengthen the life of the facility and the equipment utilized within. Preventive maintenance coupled with well-designed and competently supervised facilities can be a most effective method for the development of good public attitudes about the agency and a positive first impression so vital to the encouragement of public support of the system.

Program

The primary reason for the establishment of any recreational service department is the operation of a comprehensive and varied program of recreational activities. This above all is the chief educational device for developing public appreciation of and respect for the department. A soundly administered program which provides opportunities for participation in activities from which people gain enjoyment and satisfaction is a public relations medium of incomparable value. The program itself can provide all of the elements which will cause word of mouth dissemination of positive opinions about agency performance. As was indicated earlier in this chapter,[2] a participant or spectator who enjoys himself is already sold on the importance of the department and will probably support recommendations calling for additional financial support for facilities, leadership, and program. Conversely, all of the readily available means for disseminating information for public education come to nothing if the final proof for the existence of the department is a mediocre program at best. Unless the department can produce a program which can, in some way, reach almost every individual living in the community with at least one recreational experience in which that person will find self-realization, skill, confidence, achievement, satisfaction, creativity, or just plain fun, it is not functioning in the manner for which it was organized. A balanced program offers the last best hope of any recreational service department to influence the community on its behalf. It is an educational device that can expose potential participants to experiences of a recreational nature to which they may have never given thought. The program can assist in the development

[2] *Supra*, pp. 426–427.

of new skills and the continued use of acquired skills, and raise the aspirations of those who have never considered themselves to have any skills at all. A well-planned, competently supervised and led activity can search out latent talents, inspire reticent individuals to attempt to learn something about which they may have thought but never dared try, and assist in the growth and recreational development of every person it contacts. In such an idealized setting, the positive nature of the experience must inevitably lead to the recognition and appreciation of the department's role in community affairs.

An Example of Events in a One-year Program of Public Education

January

1   Release of annual report.
7   Radio broadcast. Local station 11:00 a.m. "Your Recreational Service Department."
14   Newspaper release. Feature story, "Public Recreational Service and the Community."
21   Talk before the Junior League Club. Luncheon meeting, "The Need for Recreational Service."
28   Group tour of public recreational system for Junior League. Afternoon.

February

1   Open forum at X recreational center. 8–9:30 p.m. "Volunteering as a Recreational Activity."
8   Radio broadcast. Local station 11:00 a.m. "Recreational Service and the Conservation of Natural Resources."
15   Newspaper release. Feature story, "Encroachment on Our Parks."
22   Talk before the Civitan. Luncheon meeting, "The Function of the Public Recreational Service Department."
28   Group tour of public recreational service system for Civitan. Afternoon.

March

1   Newspaper release. Announcement of district conference on professional preparation.
7   Talk before Junior Chamber of Commerce. Luncheon meeting, "The Financial Value of a Community Recreational Service Agency."
14   Group tour of a public recreational service system for Junior Chamber of Commerce. Afternoon.
21   District conference on professional preparation.
28   Radio broadcast. Local station 11:00 a.m. "The Need for Professional Practitioners."

April

1   Newspaper release. Announcement of essay contest dealing with relation of recreational service department to community.
2   Junior high school talk. Assembly period. "Junior Leaders of Playgrounds." High school talk. Assembly period. "Your Future in the Field of Recreational Service."
9   Radio broadcast. Local station 11:00 a.m. "The Recreational Service Master Plan."

16	Group tour of public recreational system by high school students. Afternoon.
18	Newspaper release. Announcement of playground leaders institute.
23	Dissemination of pamphlets throughout community concerning, "Fees and Charges—How They Can Be Eliminated."
30	Telecast. Local station 12:00 a.m. "Humanitarianism and Public Recreational Service."
30	Group tour of public recreational system by junior high school students.

MAY

1	Newspaper release. Announcement of winner of essay contest.
8	Radio broadcast. Local station 11:00 a.m. "The Role of the Department of Recreational Service in Human Achievement."
15	Talk before League of Women Voters. Luncheon meeting. "Pollution of Our Waterways—Steps to Abatement."
22	Telecast. Local station 12:00 a.m. "Therapeutic Recreational Service and the Homebound Handicapped."
25	Talk before Business and Professional Women's group. Luncheon meeting. "Coordination for Total Recreational Service."
31	Newspaper release. Feature story, "Regional Recreational Complex Development."
31	Group tour of public recreational system by League of Women Voters. Afternoon.
31	Newspaper release. Announcement of program for Playground Leaders Institute.

JUNE

1	Newspaper release. Announcement of National Recreational Service Month.
7	Radio broadcast. Local station 11:00 a.m. "Leisure Arts and Skills."
14	Open house at all recreational facilities throughout system. 2–5 p.m.
21	Talk before Lions Club. Luncheon meeting at X recreational center. Talk: "The Public Recreational Service Department Operation," followed by group tour of center.
23	Newspaper release. Feature story. "Needed—A Federal Recreational Service."
25	Career Guidance Day at high school. Assembly period. "Recreational Service—Field of the Future."
30	Magazine article, "Public Access to Public Facilities."
30	Newspaper release. Announcement of Summer Festival. July 4th celebration.

JULY

1	Talk before Grange group. Dinner meeting. Talk: "Rural Recreational Opportunities."
2	Newspaper release. Summer festival schedule of activities culminating in pyrotechnical display on Fourth of July.
7	Talk before city manager's group. Luncheon meeting. Talk: "Public Recreational Service as a Governmental Function." Tour of system for group.
14	Radio broadcast. Local station 11:00 a.m. "Guides to Camping Out."
21	Newspaper release. Feature story. "Federal Funds for Local Recreational Development."
28	Talk before Associated Women's Clubs. Luncheon meeting. Talk: "The Need for Neighborhood Recreational Advisory Councils."

30 Talk before Exchange Club. Dinner meeting. Talk: "Coordinating Councils in the Community."
31 Telecast. Local station 12:00 a.m. "Departmental Policies in the Operation of Parks and Playgrounds."

August

1 Newspaper release. Announcement of Carnival.
8 Talk before local Bar Association. Luncheon meeting. Talk: "Liability and Public Recreational Service."
15 Radio broadcast. Local station 11:00 a.m. "Teenage Councils."
22 Newspaper release. Feature story. "Teenage Leaders in Volunteer Assignments."
29 Talk before local labor organization. Dinner meeting. Talk: "The Problem of Supervision."
31 Newspaper release. Announcement of Carnival schedule of events.

September

1 Newspaper release. Announcement of National Recreational Congress and departmental participants.
3 Talk before Veteran's group. Luncheon meeting. Talk: "Special Services in the Community," followed by tour of agency.
8 Talk before Parent-Teacher's Association. Dinner meeting. Talk: "Recreational Services and the Schools."
15 Talk before the Daughters of the American Revolution. Luncheon meeting. Talk: "The Constitutionality of Public Recreational Service," followed by tour of agency.
22 High school talk. Assembly period. "Horizons Unlimited."
23 Radio broadcast. Local station 11:00 a.m. "Hobbies and Their Value."
30 Newspaper release. Feature story. "It's Your Program."

October

1 Talk before sectarian group. Dinner meeting. Talk: "The Church and Public Recreational Service."
8 Newspaper release. Announcement of Halloween party and program.
15 Radio broadcast. Local station 11:00 a.m. "Music Appreciation."
18 Newspaper release. Feature story. "The Establishment of Community Theater."
23 Talk before junior high school. Assembly period. "So You Want to Volunteer."
30 Telecast. Local station 12:00 a.m. "Swimming, a Year Round Sport."
31 Newspaper release. Announcement of aquatics classes in swimming, boating, and lifesaving.

November

1 Newspaper release. Announcement of Thanksgiving Day ceremonial observance.
10 Newspaper release. Announcement of Veterans Day program.
14 Radio broadcast. Local station 11:00 a.m. "Each One Teach One."
21 Newspaper release. Feature story. "Physical Fitness and Recreational Activities."
24 Newspaper release. Announcement of Pilgrims Progress as special event.
30 Talk before Chamber of Commerce. Luncheon meeting. Talk: "Land Values and Good Park Planning."

December

1   Newspaper release. Announcement of Christmas pageant and open house at all facilities throughout the system.
5   Talk before local realtors' association. Luncheon meeting. Talk: "Land Dedication in Real Estate Subdivisions."
10   Radio broadcast. Local station 11:00 a.m. "Something for Everyone—the Principle of Recreational Service."
15   Newspaper release. Feature story. "Christmas and Recreational Service."
21   Telecast. Local station 12:00 a.m. "Christmas Music by the Recreational Service Department Concert Band."
24   Public hearing on land acquisition and new facility construction.

It stands to reason that the foregoing schedule of appearances and messages disseminated through a variety of media are not the only things that can be done. These are merely some suggestions of what can be utilized. It is very apparent that each day throughout the year can be heavily invested with public relations devices to assist in the education of people living in the community which the public recreational department serves. The ideas previously listed barely touch the wellspring of information and facts that can be so readily offered for the development of goodwill and favorable opinion. For example the well-planned program of public education also has daily information schedules of activities. Advantage should be taken of every facet that can be exploited for instructional purposes.

SUMMARY

Public education and all of the devices utilized in maintaining good public relations are necessary to provide mutual understanding between the department and the general public. It is the employment of all legal and ethical devices so that the department can interpret its function to the public. Because the department of recreational service is a public agency, it has an obligation of accountability and a duty for providing public education to all citizens. It must therefore develop an awareness on the part of the public of the significance and social value which the department has in the community. The edification of the public has a two-fold purpose: (1) it raises the status of the department within the community, thereby enabling the department to continue to grow and develop; and (2) the department is enabled to provide greater recreational services to the community and make such experiences more widely known and available to more people. In these ways will the department provide its greatest contribution to community life.

SELECTED REFERENCES

Baus, Herbert M., *Publicity in Action*. (New York: Harper and Row), 1954.
Canfield, B. R., *Public Relations: Principles, Cases and Problems*, 4th ed. (Homewood, Ill.: Richard D. Irwin), 1964.

DAPPER, GLORIA, *Public Relations for Educators.* (New York: The Macmillan Co.), 1964.
GILBERT, D. L., *Public Relations in Natural Resources Management.* (Minneapolis: Burgess), 1964.
GRAY, GILES W., and WALDO W. BRADEN, *Public Speaking,* 2nd ed. (New York: Harper and Row), 1963.
HAMLIN, HERBERT M., *Public and its Education.* (Danville, Ill.: Interstate Printers and Publishers), 1955.
LESLY, PHILIP, ed., *Public Relations Handbook,* 2d ed. (Englewood Cliffs, N.J.: Prentice-Hall, Inc.), 1962.
LOIZEAUX, MARIE D., *Publicity Primer,* 4th ed. (Bronx, N.Y.: H. W. Wilson Co.), 1959.
PIMLOTT, J. A. R., *Public Relations and American Democracy.* (Princeton, N.J.: Princeton University Press), 1951.
SCHOENFELD, CLARENCE A., *Publicity Media and Methods: Their Role in Modern Public Relations.* (New York: The Macmillan Co.), 1964.

Chapter 17

EVALUATION

PRINCIPLE: Continual procedures designed to determine the value of the recreational service agency in the community are essential if the public department is to realize its objectives in the provision of a comprehensive and balanced program of activities to meet the recreational needs of people.

The idea of evaluating recreational agencies in any of the three sectors of society, e.g., public, quasi-public, and private, is not new. Everyone who has ever been to a recreational agency intuitively knows the good points and bad aspects of the service received. Almost every layman fancies himself an expert on the subject of recreational service. After all, "Isn't recreational activity a subjective and personal matter?" Because evaluation continues uninterruptedly, it is absolutely necessary that its standards, devices, and techniques be understood. Methods must be developed for gathering facts as to how closely the recreational agency approximates its goals, and the sources of these facts need to be identified. Evaluation must be based upon reliable measurement. Therefore, instruments or measuring devices that are accurate, consistently applicable to the areas undergoing evaluation, and easily administered by competent professionals are required.

MEASUREMENT, EVALUATION, AND APPRAISAL

Measurement, evaluation, and appraisal are sometimes used synonymously. Unfortunately, for misusers, the words do not mean the same thing. Measurement is the procedure used to determine the quantity of a given item or subject. It indicates how much of a thing, item, or phenomenon is actually present. Evaluation, on the other hand, is concerned with the qualitative aspects of phenonmena. It is a process which attempts to assign pertinent values or characterize a given subject in terms of what it is worth. Essentially, evaluation asks how close a specific behavior, activity, or service comes to a presumed goal. Appraisal may be a means of assigning value to an item or subjects, but the assignment of value is performed concomitantly with the activity to be appraised. It may be likened to concurrent auditing wherein the objective is to compare what is being done, when it is being performed against a known standard. Thus, appraisal is concerned with how adequately a particular thing compares with a known value.

EVALUATION AND APPRAISAL FOR RECREATIONAL SERVICE

Evaluation is a process wherein measuring devices are utilized in order to determine whether or not a recreational service agency within the community is meeting the objectives for which the agency was created. Goals have been defined and every attempt must be made to reach them. Evaluation is the method by which inadequacies, once discovered, are corrected. It is a post-operative effort that is utilized to determine whether the services provided by the agency have actually been those which were originally formulated for the agency. Evaluation is never a finite activity. It is concerned with an on-going recreational program, not with one that has ceased to function.

Planning for evaluation must be carefully arranged so that each facet of agency operation comes under close scrutiny. A system of standards must be set up so that outcomes may be measured against them. In evaluating any recreational service department, the community in which the agency is situated must also be appraised. No department, however well staffed and administratively productive, can overcome the deficits of an apathetic population, poor natural resources, or a governmental organization which is unsympathetic to the aims of the agency. For this reason community attitudes, organization, and resources must be examined if a true evaluation of services is to be recorded. The evaluation of recreational service departments will manifest interest in the production of efforts designed to meet the recreational needs of the community's populace as well as in all of those educational factors involved in stimulating public participation. Each phase of evaluative planning focuses attention on what was produced and achieved in terms of what should have been attained.

Appraisal is a procedure whereby current activities are observed and measured for sufficiency, competency, and effectiveness. The primary concerns of appraisal are methods utilized and adequacy of items brought under investigation. It is a pre-operative and concurrent operational procedure designed to determine how activities are carried out during the actual performance of the activity. It serves as the basis on which evaluation is made. Appraisals conducted prior to action will be chiefly interested in spaces, facilities, property, and equipment. Appraisals that are concurrent are devoted to personnel and activity procedures. The methods used for appraising any aspect of the department are by observation, examination, and inspection.

Criteria for Evaluation

Establishing a program of evaluation requires the development of well-defined goals. Initially, consideration must be given to the items in which evaluation of the agency may be made. Additionally, objectives should be indicated which establish what the agency is attempting to accomplish and what all personnel should achieve. Agency objectives will best be understood and accepted when there is a cooperative effort on the part of all professional personnel at every level of the agency hierarchy. Neither the executive alone, nor supervisors alone, should set objectives to be reached. Objectives should be broadly stated. However, the wide latitude of objectives must be susceptible to singular means for enactment. Other objectives will inevitably grow out of an appraisal of participant performance. Evaluation can never be looked upon as something apart from the performance of professional services to people. It is an integral factor of what the recreationist does to make his function more effective. Evaluation of performance is as significant as performance itself.

In establishing criteria, a distinct set of areas is readily apparent. These areas can be grouped in general as organization, legality or jurisdiction, finance, administration, personnel, planning, programming, spaces, structures, facilities, education, and coordination. Thus, twelve separate areas emerge as having need for evaluation. These may be stated as:

1. The implementation of recreational service having to do with the organization of the agency.
2. Legal aspects, including the authority to organize and operate the agency.
3. Adequate financial support, from tax and other sources.
4. Operational aspects for the administration of the agency.
5. Personnel standards and professional development.
6. Planning for recreational services.
7. Programming recreational activities.
8. Adequacy of recreational spaces.
9. The development of recreational structures or physical plant.
10. The diversity and variety of recreational facilities to meet needs.
11. Education and the development of public relations.
12. Coordinated agencies and procedures for comprehensive service.

WHY EVALUATION IS NECESSARY

One of the most important purposes of evaluation is to accommodate the recreational service offerings to meet the differing needs of individuals within the community. The program is not some concrete form into which people are pushed. It is an adaptation of many activities and experiences which fulfill and satisfy the recreational desires of people. People are not expected to conform to some rigid program structure. The program is adjusted to fit people. Evaluation assists in identifying the specific needs which people have. It reveals the strengths and weaknesses of the recreational agency and its program. It provides the bases upon which to compare one department's program with another's. It makes feasible a study of the progress of a program between different dates, the development of standards, and the need for possible improvement. Generally, the evaluative process is continued for the following reasons:

1. To ensure that the recreational program meets the stated needs and desires of the people in the community it intends to serve. Of major concern is the validity of the program. Does the program actually perform the functions which it purports to perform?
2. To promote professional growth and education among the staff members of the recreational service system. An evaluation of personnel practices in terms of efforts made and effects produced in the way of professional competency during time on the job should be undertaken.
3. To ascertain the flexibility of policies within the system. Have rigid specifications been adopted which preclude modification in the face of changing times and conditions? Are the aims of the public agency consistent with the public expectation in the community? There must be a definite concern for new ideas, concepts, methods, and activities as well as the opportunity for professional growth and expression. There should not be the maintenance of *status quo* insofar as personnel relationships are involved. The day of regimented thinking has long since passed and evaluative procedures may more nearly democratize most administrative activities. Whether or not people verbally express themselves in terms of personal needs being met by the activities of the program, their thoughts, advice, suggestions, and intellectual participation in the formulation of agency policies should be taken into consideration.
4. To appraise personnel quality and qualifications in relation to specific functions within the system.
5. To develop firmer foundations of agency philosophy so that a logical frame of reference is developed. The philosophy of the agency involves principles of practice, ethical and moral conduct, and the orientation from which all departmental operations stem. There is also a concern for an understanding of the historical function of the agency and the reasons for its establishment. Where necessary, current practices must be up-dated inasmuch as the achievement of ideal ends require practical techniques.
6. To effectively gauge public sentiment, attitude, and awareness of the public recreational service system. To judge whether or not an effective public relations presentation and interpretation of fact is being made for the system to the community.
7. To increase knowledge gained through practice and to additionally test current practice as to applicability in the public recreational setting. Comparisons must be made between what is being done on a standard basis as opposed to what the department is doing. There is a necessity to ascertain the strengths and weaknesses of all departmental prac-

tices by contrasting them to what is conceived as a national norm for communities of the same size and type. To compare what other similar agencies are producing, the techniques being utilized, and the product which is being developed in relationship to the system.
8. To appraise existing facilities, physical property, and plant as to their adequacy, accessibility, safety features, attractiveness, appropriateness, availability, and utilization.
9. To seek out and eliminate any detrimental features within the program or the agency.
10. To add any feasible and constructive devices, methods, and experiences to the system in order to provide the most efficient and effective service to the people of the community.
11. To promote recognition of the agency and the field of recreational service as a whole on the part of the citizens of the community.
12. To replace outmoded concepts and invalid ideas which the public may have concerning the recreational agency.
13. To promote, insofar as is possible, the professionalization of the agency personnel and the services provided.
14. To avoid unnecessary expenditures of public monies because of inadequate coordination of community agencies in the provision of recreational services.
15. To ensure the agency and its personnel against political upheaval and partisan politics.
16. To ensure that adequate provision of spaces, areas, and facilities will be safeguarded against any encroachment by establishing protection in perpetuity through dedication of all physical property for public recreational purposes only.

Major Areas to be Evaluated

1. Space, physical plant, and equipment.
    a. Adequacy.
    b. Safety.
    c. Availability.
    d. Attractiveness.
    e. Appropriateness.
    f. Multiple use.
    g. Accessibility.
2. Programming.
    a. Program content:
        Is the program comprehensive, balanced, and flexible?
        Are community resources utilized maximally?
        Does the program reflect the purpose and policies of the agency?
        Is every effort made to involve lay participation in the organization of activities?

Are all segments of the population considered?
Does the program meet the recreational needs of people living in the community?
  b. Program meaning:
Is there carry-over value for individuals in activities of the program?
Does the individual obtain a sense of achievement, self-expression, satisfaction, and enjoyment from participation?
Does the individual attain a sense of belonging to some group, does he identify with a group as a result of participation in programmed activities?
Are individual differences in skill, maturity, intellect, prior experience, age, and sex taken into consideration?
Is there opportunity for creativity?
Is there opportunity for socialization?
Does the activity promote good will?
3. Staff.
  a. Qualifications:
Educational preparation.
Prior experiences in a professional setting.
Personality factors.
Leadership ability.
Intelligence.
  b. Technique:
Are the skills and knowledge adequate to fulfill professional duties and responsibilities?
  c. Sufficiency:
Is there adequate professional personnel for staffing program and agency needs?
Is there effective supervisory leadership?
Is there an effective in-service educational program?
Are there opportunities for professional advancement?
Are material aids and devices utilized to encourage continuous professional development on the job, i.e., professional books, journals, audio-visual aids, pamphlets?
4. Administration.
Are administrative processes handled in the most efficient and economical way?
Is work processed as rapidly as possible?
Is there effective coordination between the public agency and all other agencies?
Are records and reports maintained so that past performances can be analyzed?

METHODS OF EVALUATION

Of vital consideration, if evaluation is to proceed, is the selection of suitable methods and the construction of easily understood and appropriate instruments of evaluation. Those methods and instruments that are most compatible and economical in providing valid information for the particular purposes established will be utilized. Selecting or constructing instruments of evaluation is essentially a two-part procedure: (1) identification of what is to be measured, and (2) acquiring an instrument that will do the most accurate and valid testing.

All phases of recreational experience simply cannot be evaluated. The public will probably not allow itself to be tested, either individually or en masse, because they will undoubtedly feel that such a program is time consuming and unnecessary. There are no rating scales to measure the genuine satisfactions engendered in the performance of an activity or the enjoyment generated through participation in countless experiences of a recreational nature. Attitudes, interests, and personality aspects can be validly tested, but only in terms of a small random sample of the total public. In all likelihood, evaluation of public attitude and understanding of public recreational service will have to be learned through public relation and educational devices rather than tests. There are, however, certain obvious participations which can be easily measured, if this is an objective which the agency desires. Quantitative measurements are rather easily contrived. These represent the "how much or how many" variety and are useful in identifying the use to which various facilities and activities are put. With such quantitative factors an accurate measurement of how popular a given activity within the program is, and the intensity of use a particular facility, center, or area gets. Such information may prove useful when planning for additional areas, facilities, and activities. There are many standards and norms set for measuring physical activities, e.g., how fast, how far, how high. There are few applicable instruments which can provide a qualitative measurement in terms of satisfaction received, pleasure attained, aesthetic interest stimulated, or attitude modified. Assuredly, there are tests that will indicate this information, but they are expensive to run, require a great deal of time, and an inordinate amount of cooperation from testees. The question arises, are they readily applicable? Only where there is an extreme desire on the part of the layman to subordinate his personal interests to the rather dubious satisfaction of assisting a public agency in the performance of one of its functions can these measurements be made. Does this mean that no evaluation can be made? The only reasonable answer is no. Evaluation can and must be made, but its basis should be oriented to those topics and subjects that are more easily valued. The facilitation of the process is in no small way a very significant factor in determining whether any evaluation can be profitably made.

The following topics, standards, and recommendations are offered as an illustration of selected areas for examination, relative to items of information which the public agency might want to evaluate.

TOPIC 1.

Organization and Structure for Initiation of Recreational Service

Requirement

There should be a distribution of personnel for achieving a satisfactory recreational program through the division of duties, responsibilities and authority.

Recommendation

A department of public recreational service will be organized as a functional agency of the local, civil subdivision so as to enable it to perform the functions for which it was created.

In effect, this will mean the allocation of financial support to competently staff the organization, provide operating expenses, capital expenditures, and long-range planning for maximum efficiency.

Detailed Development of the Recommendation

1. Initiation of the agency.
    a. Approach the managing authority or legal governmental body of the community with factual information relevant to the need for setting up a service agency within the municipal family responsible for the provision of activities and experiences of a recreational nature.
    b. Supplement this effort with planned visitations of local, civic, professional, business, fraternal, social, school, religious and other service agencies in order to indicate the value that the organization of a public department would have for the community.
    c. Utilize the mass media of communication for presentation of ideas to the general public concerning the initiation of a public agency and its values to them.
    d. Obtain a written statement guaranteeing the institution of the agency against political machinations and indicating the specific responsibilities that the agency will have.
    e. Attempt to establish the recreational agency as a municipal department.
2. Functions of the agency.
    a. Here we are concerned with the reasons for which the agency was created. Thus there must be listed the specifics relating to the operations to be conducted by the agency. There will be included a statement giving unshared and primary responsibilities to the agency for the provision of recreational service in the community.

b. The agency should have the legal power to utilize any and all public structures, to house activities of a recreational nature, sponsored by the agency if such and where such activities do not interfere, hinder, or conflict with the principal purpose for which those structures were created.
c. The agency should employ only professionally prepared individuals in full-time positions; employ only competent individuals, preferably professionally prepared, in the special activities necessary for the performance of the program.
d. The agency should be the authority on the selection and placement and acquisition of such spaces, structures and facilities for the maximum utilization and effectiveness in terms of recreational service for the community.

TOPIC 2.

Legal Responsibility for Recreational Service Within the Community or the Agency

Aspects

1. Responsible to the executive.
2. Responsible to the legal board or commission.
3. Responsible to the lay advisory committee.
4. The agency functions as another department of the city, with an executive.

Requirement

An autonomous agency functioning within the civil subdivisional management having a separate legal auspice called a board or commission which operates the agency and has full authority to make policy, appoint positions, or otherwise maintain and administer the agency.

Recommendation

A policy-making body must be called into existence under legal authorization, empowering said body to operate the agency, employ necessary personnel, and delegate such functions, responsibilities, and authorities to an executive manager which will effectively permit the organization to successfully fulfill its manifold obligations and services.

Detailed Development of the Recommendation

1. Formation of the board or commission.
   a. The policy-making body should be formed by municipal authority when they have a legal instrument, such as an ordinance which brings into existence a legal board either for a specified period of time or for perpetuity.

b. Such a code is binding upon all parties unless rescinded or revoked by another act in accordance with legal and constitutional procedure.
2. Functions of the board or commission.
   a. Generally the board or commission should administer the maintenance operation and management of the recreational agency, including full responsibility for hiring and firing personnel, entering into contractual obligations with other public and private organizations, complete control of the finances, authority to make and interpret policies governing the agency, and other such functions which are proper to the most effective administration of the public recreational service agency.
   b. The board or commission should be empowered to sue and be sued in terms of legal liability, to purchase, acquire and develop property, develop and construct facilities, and purchase and maintain equipment and other physical properties.
3. Organization of the board or commission, including offices, duties, term of office and method of selecting membership.
   a. The board will consist of a specific number of members not to exceed seven and always an odd number.
   b. Appointment to the board shall either be by direct authority from the office of the governing authority of the local legal subdivision or by direct and popular election by the citizens of the community. Board members may either elect or select their own officers. However, in some instances the chairman may be appointed by the local governing authority of the community.
   c. If election is the prescribed method for board membership then all members shall have the same tenure in office for a prescribed number of years not exceeding two. Board members may succeed themselves for as many times as they are elected.
   d. Officers of the board should be provided—Chairman, Vice-Chairman, Secretary (done by the administrator plus being the executive officer of the board and ex-officio member), may also delegate responsibility in particular areas to specific members of the board.

TOPIC 3.

Financial Support

Requirement

An appropriation equal to the amount needed for the full operation and administration of all recreational service should be made.

A national standard of $8.00 per capita has been suggested as an ideal figure; but depending upon the interest of the community, the economic status of the community, and present or anticipated recreational resources, areas, or facilities of a personal or physical nature, the fiscal amount appropriated would be whatever is available.

Recommendation

An annual appropriation made from the general subdivisional fund will be earmarked for recreational service operations. This sum could be anywhere from $2–$8 per capita, depending upon the willingness and need of the citizens to pay for and receive recreational services.

Detailed Development of the Recommendation

1. General fund appropriation.

That money supplied from general taxes received from the community and apportioned out to the various municipal agencies for their current fiscal operations.

This appears to be the most uncomplicated and direct means for providing financial support to the recreational agency if the sum appropriated falls within the national standard set and if it actually allows effective operation of the recreational service department.

Where the local legal authorities do not provide sufficient funds for the effective maintenance and administration of their service agency, it will be necessary to support whatever funds are made available so that services can be offered.

2. The recreational mill levy.

An amount of tax money stipulated by state law which may be collected from the citizens of a community in order to operate a recreational service agency.

It is necessary for a popular referendum to take place in order to pass a mill levy which generally does not exceed three mills.

Upon the completion of the referendum and if the motion for a millage levy is passed, such monies as are collected will be utilized exclusively for the operation of the recreational agency.

The mill levy may be for a stipulated number of years or longer and may also be rescinded by popular vote.

The mill levy may be considered a vote of confidence, but it may also engender certain fractional rivalries within the municipal family because other municipal agencies may look with disfavor upon the recreational department which appears to be receiving an inordinant share of comfort and security. Thus the levy must be used discriminately.

3. The bond issue.

A legal instrument indebting the community for a specified sum within a specific period of time.

It is utilized in the construction and development of large capital outlays for land acquisition, construction of buildings and purchase of expensive equipment.

Only passed by popular referendum.

4. Special assessments.

Those levies laid upon specific individuals for improvements within a particular area when such improvements affect only the residents of that area rather than the community at large.

5. Fees and charges.

Utilized to supplement any financial support appropriated to the agency.

Such fees and charges must never be utilized for profit making, nor should they be excessive, exorbitant or of such nature to prohibit individuals from entering into or participating in recreational activities sponsored by the recreational agency.

The fee and the charge must be used sparingly and may be justified only in terms of providing extraordinary services, or activities not possible under the appropriated funds for the operation of the agency.

Corollary—better to allow an individual to participate in a recreational activity than to omit him from that activity because he has not the monetary means for entrance.

For items over and above the appropriated amounts in the budget, but just for service, not for profit.

TOPIC 4.

Administration of the Recreational Agency (processes applicable to the management, direction and coordination of money, materials, and men in the achievement of stated goals)

Requirement

The management and control of all personnel and operations having as their objective the achievement of policy in accordance with a logical philosophy as decided upon by legal authority in serving the recreational needs of the people within the local subdivisions.

Recommendation

The administrative processes for fulfillment or enforcement of public policy will be implemented for the facilitation and effective operation of the recreational agency's service functions.

Detailed Development of the Recommendation

1. Record keeping.

The organization and maintenance of documents relating to the daily operational activities of the agency. Such documentation will be rendered most effective by the standardization of format, duplication of materials to be transmitted to the various concerned sections of the agency for action, the utilization of such forms as required, and the storage of these materials in repositories for current and future reference.

Records will concern all aspects of the agency's operations, including financial, personnel, maintenance, program, supplies, architectural and engineering drawings and plans, policy statements, correspondence, insurance, tax, various and sundry reports, and other legal papers which must be filed for reference.

The maintenance of records and the operation of a filing system are necessary if the agency is to profit by its successes as well as its failures. The records of the agency serve as primary resources in the development of better activities, consistency of policy aims, and avoidance of duplication, and assists in the implementation of better services provided to the people.

Records will help the professional development of personnel, assist in the in-service educational procedure, and indicate the progress or regression of individuals or groups being served by the agency.

2. Standard operating procedures.

Those methods which have been found to be successful and appropriate in carrying out the varied functions for which the agency was created.

Includes such routine devices as the daily inspection of materials, supplies, equipment and facilities of the agency, the routine aspects of personnel practice including vacations, leaves, transfers, employment and discharge, chain of command authorizations, staff meetings, the scheduling of activities, the priority policies, and other features of agency operation which become standardized for efficiency and economy.

Standard operating procedures will never be applied to program activities. The program shall always be highly flexible and unique in every way that may be conceived to retain its uniqueness.

3. Office management.

Concerned with the assignment of duties and responsibilities within the central office of the agency in order to more efficiently carry out the routine accumulation of paper work and to more speedily process the requests of the operational workers of the agency.

Office management is basically concerned with the maintenance of records and the flow of work procedure from the time a request for supplies or information is brought into the office to the time the request is satisfactorily answered or fulfilled.

It is further concerned with the acquisition and maintenance of specific office machines which may be used in the process of creating or formulating various reports, records of a personnel or financial nature, answering or writing correspondence, duplicating or printing, directing information outward to mass media of communication, to individuals, to the staff and for the clerical work necessary in fulfilling the aforementioned tasks.

4. Work flow efficiency.

The processing of all material from a raw state to a finished state without duplication and in the most direct way possible.

It is concerned with correct placement of lighting, the optimum degree of heat and ventilation, the careful use of color, the sanitary effect of cleanliness, the correct placement of machinery, the identification of efficient personnel, their placement so that maximum productive potential may be achieved, and the speedy dispatch of paper work from start to finish without undue time loss or hesitancy in the transmission of such material.

5. Maintenance.

Basically concerned with the upkeep of physical properties owned, operated or utilized by the recreational agency.

It is divided into two aspects:

a. Interior housekeeping which includes cleanliness, attractiveness and supply inventories within the buildings themselves, i.e., window washing, illumination maintenance, proper heat, power and ventilation, floor cleanliness (sweeping, mopping and waxing where applicable), interior painting, furniture, sanitary facilities, and other services related to the preservation of the structure.

b. Exterior maintenance including grounds keeping, horticulture arrangements, i.e., lawns, shrubs, trees, and plants, road ways, walk ways, paved, asphalt or composition surface areas, equipment utilized in the recreational program, i.e., playground, sports, fencing, exterior illumination, shelters, sanitary facilities, drinking fountains, and exteriors of buildings.

Maintenance may also be concerned with the repair, replacement, or construction of program aids, including certain pieces of equipment, signs, posters, markers, benches, litter baskets, and any other physical property or equipment utilized in the preservation of property.

Maintenance is generally concerned with the custodianship of buildings and the conservation of physical property.

TOPIC 5.

Planning for Recreational Services

Requirement

A broad framework guiding future substantive actions and operations in the recreational agency. These principles are concerned with the development and accumulation of pertinent information, the analysis of that information for categorizing into classes for easy comprehension, the projection of alternate courses of action, and the appraisal of the consequences of such diversified courses.

Recommendation

The initiation of planning procedures to guide the development of the recreational agency and to enhance the functions of that agency, in order to avoid the waste of duplication, inefficiency, and deficient concepts, will be undertaken.

Detailed Development of the Recommendation

1. Analysis and research.

Is concerned with the collection of basic material and information relating to current concepts of recreational programming, design, construction, and maintenance of structures and facilities, investigation of comparative agencies, study of professional literature pertinent to the field of recreational service for philosophy, principles, ethics and practices, the examination of the collected data in order to determine whether or not the agency is keeping abreast of current professional concepts in each of the aforementioned areas, i.e., physical plant, philosophy, program and practices.

Research may be carried on by statistical representation, survey, i.e., questionnaire, public opinion polls, group meetings, or open forums. Observation of activities in which people participate, inspection for supervisory purposes of such activities will be involved in this analysis.

Research will attempt to determine whether or not the recreational services provided for by the agency are adequate and effective in meeting the needs of the agency's clientele and the population of the wider community.

2. The master plan.

Is a detailed construct concerning the socioeconomic, political, geographic, topographic, and educational investigation of the community in order to determine the most effective placement of physical recreational resources and the employment of competent, professionally prepared individuals to operate the activities afforded by such physical resources to meet the potential population trends and recreational needs of present and future residents of the community. Such a plan must be coordinated with other physical structures of the community including the school system, other municipal agency services, i.e., police, fire, health, public works, streets, parks, parkways and lighting developments.

The master plan is usually undertaken as a 25-year directive.

Factors to consider:

a. The economic feasibility of such a master plan.
b. Whether or not the community is interested.
c. Demand upon the citizenry.
d. Increased and more interesting activities.
e. Is the community in on the planning procedures?
f. Political institutions of the city.
g. Under what agency does the city recreational department operate?
h. The population—its ethnic and constitutional makeup, the type of people, and the classes within the population.

3. The priority schedule.

A time table for the implementation of physical recreational facilities in accordance with the master plan.

The master plan is a layout, but the priority schedule is a time table for the construction of the facilities already laid out.

Takes into consideration what is most important, what is needed immediately for the greatest number of people, and what can be done for the amount of money available.

Then lay out the land acquired, first priority, in terms of what is needed. The acquirement of suitable land for recreational purposes has first priority. When the land has been obtained it must be planned appropriately (laid out) in terms of open spaces, various facility emplacements, structures, access areas, and so on, so that community recreational needs may be met.

4. The five-year plan.

Consists of an immediate appraisal of the community which includes immediate past studies concerning traffic placements, water mains, sewer and lighting systems within recent periods of time. Concerns the relationship of immediate population movement, takes into consideration the necessity of developing facilities in accordance with a population increase within the next five years. Only concerned with that five-year period. It is, therefore, one of considerable limitation and limited physical developments.

This plan is generally concerned with specific neighborhood developments rather than community developments. The content of the plan will therefore be oriented to several neighborhoods within the community which appear to be gaining in population and with the provision of facilities to accommodate that increase. The development of facilities will necessarily be curtailed to building structures, individual playgrounds, individual parks or other facilities rather than with complex installations.

5. The three-year short-term plan.

This plan will be initiated in terms of population increase for one neighborhood within the community. This plan, rather than concerning many aspects of the community, will be related to meeting the needs of the fastest growing neighborhood of the community and the provision of recreational services and facilities in that neighborhood. Such a facility will usually be the neighborhood playground or the renovation of an existing building for increased use.

This plan makes necessary a comprehensive look at the community in terms of individual neighborhoods so as to determine the growth potential in terms of population, economic resource, and recreational need in that area.

6. The emergency plan.

Concerned with the provision of recreational services and development or renovation of facilities in densely populated sections of the community. Concerned with meeting recreational deficits within heavily populated regions of the community rather than with the acquisition of land or development of new facilities in outlying regions.

The emergency plan, as its name implies, is concerned with meeting the urgent and immediate recreational needs caused by underdeveloped property or lack of adequate space and facilities.

Must be undertaken because of lack of foresight on the part of the administrators of governmental authorities to see the necessity of recreational planning in relation to the growth of the community.

Will never keep up with population growth, is inadequate to say the least, and is instigated as an expediency measure to affect demand.

Indicates that no master plan is available.

7. Spot surveys.

Are appraisals of the community taken at random which indicate whether or not the provision of recreational service is adequate and therefore meeting the needs of the citizens of the community. The spot survey may be made in terms of the questionnaire, personal interviews, or observation.

Its most useful function is to indicate whether or not the program and the facilities are adequate, well attended and well operated.

TOPIC 6.

Personnel Standards

Requirement

Incumbents in recreational positions must have an educational and experiential preparation that will enable them to perform the essential work of serving the public's recreational needs.

Such personnel will be on a professional level combining qualities of competence, dedication, knowledge, and personal integrity to effectively function and carry on the duties and responsibilities of office.

Recommendation

Only such personnel will be employed on a full-time professional basis as can demonstrate their theoretical and practical knowledge and professional efficiency.

Minimum standards for entrance into the field of recreational service include graduation from an accredited college or university with major work in recreational learning and additional experience and educational preparation at the position level with attendant salary, duties, and responsibilities becoming higher, more difficult and complex. Appointment to professional recreational service positions requires minimum standards of education and experience. Such positions carry certain job specifications, duties, and functions. With progressively more responsibility, authority, and higher salary as tenure on the job lengthens, job pressures also mount. As the incumbent obtains more experience and is, consequently, given more authority and responsibility the complexities at this level of the organizational hierarchy become more intense.

Detailed Development of the Recommendation

1. Job analysis, specifications, and minimal qualifications.
2. Personnel salaries and step increments.
3. Professional experience, affiliation, and preparation.
4. In-service education.
5. Appointment, advancement, transfer, disciplinary actions, seniority, merit, work schedules, leaves, retirement, and other work practices.
6. Line and staff division of functions.

TOPIC 7.

Program Standards

Requirement

The program of any recreational service agency consists of all those activities provided by the agency which meet the recreational needs of the constituent public. The program contains a balance of activities which is produced on a full-time, year-round basis in which all age, sex, racial, religious, economic, or social status groups and the individuals which make up these groups may participate according to their several respective abilities and experiences.

Recommendation

The program will contain a balance of activities featuring recreational living experiences that provide social, cultural, emotional, physical, and moral values for participating individuals.

The program will consist of the following activities which may be further subdivided:

1. Physical and athletic experiences.
    a. Individual, dual, group and team, competitive and noncompetitive activities.
    b. Games.
    c. Aquatics.
    d. Sports.
2. Dance and rhythmic experiences.
3. Art.
4. Outdoor education and camping.
5. Dramatics.

6. Musical.
7. Educational.
8. Social.
9. Special project.
10. Civic service.
11. Hobby.
12. Crafts.

Detailed Development of the Recommendation
1. Possible activities and the criteria for their selection.

   It is ridiculous to select activities on any basis other than considering the objectives of the activity as being measurable.

   Some concepts are already inherent within the activity. They are not valid as criteria. The recreationist has to develop other forms of criteria for the activity.

   Criteria in terms of activities that can be measured:
   a. Social acceptability (Does it abide by the law?).
   b. Enjoyment (by attitudinal survey).

   It is up to the recreationist to find out if the person does enjoy the activity he's in. If he does not, the recreationist has to find out why and do something about it. The recreationist serves a leadership function and is not there just to provide. Some people go into an activity for reasons other than enjoyment, and the recreationist has to determine what those reasons are, the return factor and duration factor included.

   c. Safety precautions

   With precautions no activity is dangerous. Human uniqueness is the X factor, not the inherent danger of an activity.

   d. Skill (by rate of return to the activity, perseverance in the activity, and achievement).

   Is measurable and indicates whether or not the recreationist is performing the instruction obligations.

   e. Participation (by number who participate and the quality of it).

   Evaluation by number simply involves "how many" in terms of a number.

   The worker's evaluation of the activity in terms of the intensity or extent of the individual's participation.

   Selection of activities to be determined by geography, region, topography, climate.
2. Evaluation.
3. A balance of the full range of activities offered.

   In terms of the twelve activities of the well-balanced and well-rounded program. There must be adequate presentation of all these activities.
4. Equal opportunity in terms of age, sex, race, social, economic status.

TOPIC 8.

Recreational Spaces

Requirement

Any land, water, or physical structure, space, or area, i.e., physical property, which may be utilized for recreational purposes or which has historic, aesthetic, scientific or scenic value should be acquired as part of the public's legacy in conserving the natural open, wooded, and water spaces for present and future utilization.

Recommendation

That all land which has historic, aesthetic, scientific, or scenic value which may be feasible to acquire and hold for public benefit will be so acquired and held; that all current space holdings will be carefully investigated in order to discover present and potential recreational use in terms of population movement, subdivisional development, arterial construction, or other land diminishing encroachments on the public domain.

Detailed Development of the Recommendation

1. Land acquisition.

    Interested in acquiring sites for recreational purposes. These sites must be located in areas such that they are accessible for utilization and acquirable for the amount of money that the community has to spend. The land itself must not need too much development before it can be utilized.

    Land acquisition is necessary if recreational services in the community are to keep pace with the growth of the community. It is not necessary if the community shows no growth over a period of time.

    As people realize the possibilities in recreational activities, and recreationists have educated along these lines, the need arises for the acquiring of various spaces; the public wants to get these areas for their use. Much of this land must be inside the community, as well as all of the areas outside of the community, to take care of the newly educated public.

    Utilized to conserve potential recreational space in the face of encroachment of all kinds and by anyone. Acquire the land and dedicate it in perpetuity before all of the many commercial and private organizations have moved in.

2. Nomenclature, size, site, and characteristics.

    What the land is called—park, playground, reservation, refuge, conservation site, wilderness area, and so on.

    Size should range from 5000 square feet to several hundred acres within the community for any one area. Should have one acre of land for every 100 people, according to experts' estimates.

Site should be well located, dry or able to be quickly drained, not needing to be cut or filled extensively, easily accessible, not dangerous, placed so it can be utilized by people who have necessity to use it.

Characteristics refer to topographic and terrain features, the characteristics of the land.

3. Land use patterns.

Examine zoning laws of the community to determine land use patterns. Where will transportation, industry, and schools be placed, so that one can tell where it will be more feasible and important to place recreational facilities, structures, areas.

Get the land dedicated by the public in perpetuity for the provision of recreational services. To fight encroachment—an aroused public is the best bet.

TOPIC 9.

Recreational Structures

Requirement

Any physical structure designed and constructed in such a way as to serve primarily and directly as a center for recreational activity or which may have a secondary recreational potential (indirect value for recreational experience although the principal purpose is oriented towards some other endeavor).

Recommendation

Physical structures will be designed and constructed to primarily serve as functional recreational centers where feasible. When existing physical structures have been designed with some purpose other than recreational service as their main function, they should be utilized as supporting centers until such time as pertinent structures may be erected.

Detailed Development of the Recommendation

1. Primary structures.

Buildings constructed for functional recreational activities and experiences, e.g., pools, parks, zoos, centers, botanical gardens, and so on. These items may have secondary purposes also, but they are primarily designed for and used for recreational purposes.

2. Supportive structures.

Structures utilized primarily for purposes other than recreational purposes, e.g., schools (activities for learning experiences), hospitals (structures for medical and health services), churches (structures for religious purposes). These structures should be used for recreational service providing such use does not interfere with the purpose for which the structures were originally intended.

TOPIC 10.

Recreational Facilities and Traffic Patterns

Requirement

All facilities which may be utilized for some recreational purpose should be considered in an inverse priority order (highest to lowest), in terms of their primary purpose. Facilities and equipment may only be appraised in view of population size, density and actual usage involved, particularly expendable equipment.

Recommendation

Such facilities as are necessary to accommodate public usage within or around a specific community shall be built, maintained, and operated in accordance with enumerated supervisory processes, design details, and relationship of population to any single facility, i.e., density, and construction types in conformity with local zoning and inspection codes.

TOPIC 11.

Public Relations and Recreational Service

Requirement

This is a procedure that serves as an information gatherer and distributor, i.e., reception and transmission of data. Its functions are those of the sounding board and analytic machine in defining the public's interests and desires and where the policies, plans, and services of the recreational agency may be interpreted.

This procedure utilizes many media—oral, visual, and physical in reaching the public eye, ear, and taste. By the same token, there are many instruments for gathering and analyzing public demands and interests.

Recommendation

The inauguration of a specific section within the recreational agency (if the organization is large enough) or the delegation of the public relations function to one employee of the organization, i.e., a public relations specialist, for the gathering, dissemination, and interpretation of information concerning agency policy and service to the public and the collection, analysis, and assessment of the recreational needs of the public.

Detailed Development of the Recommendation

1. Transmission.
    a. Program.

b. Evaluation of the program.
c. Utilizing the mass means of communication.
d. Listing of material via flyers, leaflets, brochures.
e. Advertising gimmicks.
f. Meetings, forums, discussion.
2. Reception.
a. Suggestion boxes.
b. Interviews.
c. Conferences.
d. Inventories.
e. Check lists.
f. Check sheets.

TOPIC 12.

Coordinated Agencies for Service

Requirement

The public recreational service agency is uniquely equipped to serve as a clearing house and coordinating body which can effectively schedule, channel, and direct activities of a recreational nature by other social institutions of all types within the community.

Recommendation

The public recreational service department will initiate such action as required to effectively coordinate recreational activities of various kinds, presented and promoted by the several social institutions within the community. To this end the public recreational agency will organize a community agency council or other such designated committee, council, board, or conference which will plan, schedule, and coordinate recreational experiences and services within the community so as to avoid economic and material waste through duplication and competition for the same public by many different agencies.

Detailed Development of the Recommendation

1. Technical assistance.
   Provided by any one agency whose personnel have the skill, knowledge or ability to perform or teach activities of a recreational nature which are necessary for the provision of recreational services within the community. Such technical knowledge may also be of a nature not primarily recreational, but which when applied will enhance recreational service, i.e., legal advice, accounting procedures, mechanical or other material.
2. Speakers bureau.
   The coordinating agency will have a roster of names of personnel employed by the various agencies who have speaking ability and tech-

nical or special knowledge of one or more special areas and who may be utilized to communicate necessary information to various groups within the community relating to their specialization.
3. Scheduling.
   The main function of the interagency body will be to coordinate activities and services in such a manner that each segment of the public shall be served, that each agency shall provide an optimum presentation depending upon the resources at its command, and that local traditions, mores, and laws shall be adhered to concerning such provision without duplication of such services.
4. Committee organization.
   Shall concern the membership, make-up, in terms of the number of individuals who shall sit upon the council. It may be necessary to have a large council made up of several members of each agency which wishes to contribute preparations for the resolution of recreational problems and conflicts within the community.
   The council may elect from its number a smaller group which may serve as an executive board with rotating membership so that each agency will have representation.
   Said board to meet weekly as opposed to the monthly meetings of the council; set policy and make decisions regarding daily presentation of recreational activities within the community.
   In the event that this set-up is not feasible, it may be that an interorganization council, having as its membership the executives of contributing agencies within the community, shall meet periodically, not more than once a month and decide recreational policies, programs and presentations in and for the community.
5. Agendas.
   Will consist of all pertinent problems relating to the provision of recreational services within the community. Proper subject for discussion at the council is any problem of a recreational nature, whether it be personnel, program, or physical property for resolution by that body.
   The exercise of the veto shall be avoided and majority vote shall carry any measure and be binding on any representatives on the council.
6. Material analysis.
   The council shall serve as a clearing house for the dissemination of information, new publications, and other professional materials relating to the most current techniques in the provision of recreational service to the community. Each member shall be obliged to share his knowledge and technical skills with other council members for maximum services of an optimum nature, thereby benefiting all citizens of said community.
7. Representation.
   Representation shall be derived through any voluntary request from any public, quasi-public, or private agency within the community having any concern with recreational activity.

Based upon the standards and objectives identified and defined by the agency, a simplified score sheet may be drawn up to facilitate the comparison of the public department to the suggested criteria. The score form can contain a listing of all pertinent items that should be evaluated; a standardized score may be devised pertaining to the significance of the item insofar as provision of recreational service is concerned, and then the department's operation may be carefully analyzed and scored. Where the department attains maximum scores, it may generally be stated that the item is being successfully fulfilled. Where any deficiencies are noted, either no score will be given, or a lesser score will be appropriate. It will then be necessary to make recommendations for future substantive action if the evaluation process is to serve any worthwhile purpose. Thus, inadequacies will eventually be alleviated. The score sheet which follows is the type of standardized form that may be utilized in the evaluation process.

DETERMINING ATTITUDES AND RELATED CONCEPTS

The attitudes, interests, values, motives, and appreciations of the individual who is a potential participant within the recreational program are important to recreationists in several ways. Chiefly, they affect those things of which he is aware and recognizes, and second, modification in them often is a particular objective of public relations devices. The terms indicated above apparently refer to feelings stimulated by the social milieu in which the person finds himself.

Attitudes may be defined as positive, negative, or neutral learned responses relating to a given subject or thing which can affect behavior. They are usually based upon emotional or psychological feelings rather than logic and systematic reasoning about the given object. Interests, on the other hand, are those subjects or things to which an individual is positively attracted. There is a definite pleasantness related to interests. Values refer to those things which are considered by the individual to be most significant or worthy. Essentially, values denote the individual's basic choices as to ends and means. Appreciation may be resolved into an emotional response toward an appealing object or thing. It connotes awareness, recognition, and an aesthetic fulfillment or satisfaction from seeing, hearing, or having contact with a given subject. Motives reflect an immediate need for fulfillment. They are drives to action. Motives indicate an unsatisfied condition or tension within the organism. When tension is diminished as a result of specific action taken, then the organism has regained balance and satisfaction results. Satisfaction and equilibrium within the organism is a consequence of successful tension reduction by virtue of some behavioral manifestation.

EVALUATIVE INSTRUMENT

Organization and Structure (30) (Options)	Maximum Point Score	Departmental Score	Modifications Needed and Any Comment
1. Written policy to establish a department.	10		
2. Unshared responsibility for providing a service.	10		
3. The establishment as an independent municipal department.	10		
4. Established as a subordinate agency.	5		
5. Combination of tax-supported agencies.	5		
6. Established as a combination of nontax-supported agencies.	4		
7. Provided by a church, YMCA, or other denominational agency.	3		
8. Provided as a quasi-public department.	3		
9. Provided only by commercial enterprise.	1		
10. Provided only by private organizations.	0		

Legal Board or Commission (50)	Maximum Point Score	Departmental Score	Modifications Needed and Any Comment
1. Establishment of a general body to operate the recreational agency.	14		
2. Legal body composition.	4		
3. Terms of office.	10		
4. Number of members.	5		
5. Chief executive as secretary of legal body.	10		
6. Meetings of the board.	5		
7. Officers.	2		
8. Establishment of a lay advisory body.	1		
9. An indirect legal board.	1		
10. No board-head reports to some municipal official.	0		

Financial Support (100) (Options)	Maximum Point Score	Departmental Score	Modifications Needed and Any Comment
1. From the general tax support appropriation.	25		
2. Funds earmarked.	20		
3. Bond issues for capital improvement.	15		
4. Fees and charges appropriate to the situation.	5		
5. Minimum operational budget $2.00 per capita. Debit one point for each 25¢ under. Credit two points for each $1.00 over.	10		
6. Personnel appropriation—82%. Credit ½ point for every 1% over. Debit 1 point for every 5% under.	15		
7. Facilities maintenance—15%. Debit 1 point for every 5% over.	5		
8. Expendable program items—3%.	5		
9. Millage levy appropriation.	10		
10. Special taxes.	5		
11. Operational expenditures—75%. Debit 1 point for every 5% under.	5		
12. Capital expenditures—25% (equipment). Debit 1 point for every 5% over.	2		

Administration (80)	Maximum Point Score	Departmental Score	Modifications Needed and Any Comment
1. Written policy.	10		
2. Budget-making procedure.	10		
3. Day-to-day reports.	10		
4. Basic operating records.	6		
5. Overall scheduling of activities.	4		

ADMINISTRATION (80)	MAXIMUM POINT SCORE	DEPARTMENTAL SCORE	MODIFICATIONS NEEDED AND ANY COMMENT
6. Standard operating procedure for purchasing.	4		
7. Official board records.	5		
8. Records and receipts.	8		
9. File for unfilled requisitions.	2		
10. Classified expenditures record (all except capital equipment).	5		
11. Capital outlay record.	1		
12. Perpetual inventory.	5		
13. Nonappropriated funds record.	5		
14. Comprehensive filing system.	5		

PERSONNEL STANDARDS (250)	MAXIMUM POINT SCORE	DEPARTMENTAL SCORE	MODIFICATIONS NEEDED AND ANY COMMENT
1. Minimal educational qualifications.	25		
2. Position classification under either civil service or merit system.	25		
3. Listed personnel salary ranges and step increments.	25		
4. Written job analysis for each position.	20		
5. Experiential requirements depending on job analysis.	15		
6. Written job description.	10		
7. Personnel practices.	25		
8. Recruitment programs.	10		
9. On-the-job educational practices.	10		
10. In-service educational program.	15		
11. Orientation of personnel.	5		
12. Retirement plans.	5		
13. Fringe benefits.	5		
14. Part-time functional workers as required.	5		

Personnel Standards (250)	Maximum Point Score	Departmental Score	Modifications Needed and Any Comment
15. Line and staff organization	60		
a. Requirement for executive officer full time.	15		
b. General supervisory positions on full-time basis depending upon size of population, 1 per 50,000 or less.	10		
c. Facilities director full-time at year-round facility.	10		
d. Full-time program leader for 10,000 population or less. Also serve as director of playground or assistant director of facilities.	10		
e. Part-time functional worker as required.	5		
f. Specialists or instructors for specific activities 1 per 50,000 population.	10		

Planning (50) (Options)	Maximum Point Score	Departmental Score	Modifications Needed and Any Comment
1. Comprehensive study of the community	20		
a. Physiographic factors.	3		
b. Economic factors.	3		
c. Community features and characteristics.	2		
d. Recreational resources of a personal nature.	2		
e. Recreational resources of a physical nature.	2		
f. Current recreational services provided.	3		
g. Population factors.	1		
h. Population trends.	1		
i. Metropolitan movement.	1		
j. Housing data and subdivision growth.	1		
k. Recent municipal studies.	1		

Planning (50)	Maximum Point Score	Departmental Score	Modifications Needed and Any Comment
2. 3–5 Year recreational projection	10		
a. History and location of community.	1		
b. Local governmental structure.	1		
c. Economic factors.	1		
d. Current recreational services.	1		
e. Physical recreational resources.	1		
f. Recreational personnel duties and number.	1		
g. Activities making up the recreational program.	1		
h. Land acquisition.	1		
i. Commercialized recreational services.	1		
j. Community agencies performing any recreational services.	1		
3. Property schedule	10		
a. Land aquisition.	2		
b. Construction of facilities.	2		
c. Construction of permanent structures.	2		
d. Construction of special areas.	2		
e. Construction for present emergency needs.	2		
4. Recreational surveys	10		
a. Factual data on outdoor physical resources.	1		
b. Factual data on indoor physical resources.	1		
c. Factual data on current recreational services.	1		
d. Factual data on operating recreational personnel.	1		
e. Density of population to be served.	1		
f. Characteristics of the population.	1		
g. Geopolitical boundaries.	1		
h. Agency which administers recreational program.	1		
i. Probable resources which are available.	1		
j. Structures of a nonrecreational nature that can be utilized for recreational activities.	1		

Program (150)	Maximum Point Score	Departmental Score	Modifications Needed and Any Comment
1. Criteria for selection of activities	50		
a. Social acceptability.			
b. Safety precautions necessary.			
c. Skill required.			
d. Participation required.			
e. Self-expressive.			
2. Balanced program	60		
a. Art.			
b. Crafts.			
c. Dance.			
d. Dramatics.			
e. Education.			
f. Hobbies.			
g. Music.			
h. Nature-oriented activities.			
i. Motor skills.			
j. Service activities.			
k. Social activities.			
l. Special events.			
3. Equalized opportunity	40		
a. Sex differences.			
b. Age differences.			
c. Economic level.			
d. Racial characteristics.			
e. Religious affiliation.			
f. Social status.			
g. Active participation.			
h. Passive participation.			

Recreational Spaces (80)	Maximum Point Score	Departmental Score	Modifications Needed and Any Comment
1. Land acquisition.	25		
2. Nomenclature land use patterns.	20		
3. Location of land in relation to population density.	20		
4. Size of the land parcel.	10		
5. Topographical characteristics.	5		

Recreational Structures (60)	Maximum Point Score		Departmental Score	Modifications Needed and Any Comment
		1 for each:		
1. Municipal camp.	3	50,000 pop. or less		
2. Band shell.	1	80,000 pop. or less		
3. Shelter houses.	2	3,200 pop. or less		
4. Recreational piers.	1	2,500 pop. or less		
5. Stadium of 1,500 seats or more.	1	50,000 pop. or less		
6. Gymnasium.	5	10,000 pop. or less		
7. Auditorium.	3	13,000 pop. or less		
8. Recreational centers (neighborhood).	8	10,000 pop. or less		
9. Natatorium.	1	3% of pop. or less		
10. Outdoor theater.	1	78,000 pop. or less		
11. Club rooms.	3	30,000 pop. or less		
12. Multi-purpose rooms (should hold 40 persons).	3	3,000 pop. or less		
13. Special activity rooms.	1	8,000 pop. or less		
14. Library.	1	100,000 pop. or less		
15. Field houses.	1	130,000 pop. or less		

Recreational Structures (60)	Maximum Point Score		Departmental Score	Modifications Needed and Any Comment
16. Game room.	5	8,000 pop. or less		
17. Lounge.	2	8,000 pop. or less		
18. Bleachers.	3	2,500 pop. or less		
19. Pavilions.	2	2,300 pop. or less		
20. Maintenance and custodial operations.	5			

Geographical and topographical factors will affect evaluation of this section.

Recreational Facilities (60)	Maximum Point Score		Departmental Score	Modifications Needed and Any Comment
1. Playgrounds.	3	1 acre per 150 pop. or less		
2. Playfields.	3	1 acre per 150 pop. or less		
3. Parks.	3	1 acre per 100 pop. or less		
4. Arboretum.	1	1 for 180,000 pop. or less		
5. Zoo.	1	1 per 2,500,000 pop. or less		
6. Bathing beach.	1	1 per 3% pop. or less or 50,000 pop. or less where feasible		
7. Baseball diamond (lighted or unlighted).	2	1 per 8,000 pop. or less		
8. Softball diamond.	2	1 per 2,500 pop. or less		
9. Tennis courts (indoor-outdoor).	2	1 per 2,000 pop. or less		
10. Basketball courts (indoor and outdoor).	2	1 per 10,000 pop. or less		

Recreational Facilities (60)	Maximum Point Score	Departmental Score	Modifications Needed and Any Comment
11. Football field.	1	1 per 35,000 pop. or less	
12. Wading pools.	1	1 per 1% pop. or less	
13. Volley ball and badminton courts (indoor and outdoor).	1	1 court per 2,000 pop. or less	
14. Handball courts (outdoor and indoor).	1	1 court per 75,000 pop. or less	
15. Archery range (indoor and outdoor).	1	1 per 25,000 pop. or less	
16. Rifle range (indoor and outdoor).	1	1 per 100,000 pop. or less	
17. Locker rooms, showers, toilet facilities.	2	1 per each gymnasium	
18. Trailways.	1	1 per 100,000 pop. or less	
19. Kitchen facility.	1	1 per every large recreational center (community center)	
20. *Boccie* courts.	½	1 per 250,000 pop. or less	
21. Bowling greens.	½	1 per 250,000 pop. or less	
22. Soccer and field hockey field.	½	1 per 150,000 pop. or less	
23. Golf course.	2	1 hole per 3,000 pop. or less	
24. Track field.	1	1 per 150,000 pop. or less	
25. Marina (where feasible).	1	1 per 150,000 pop. or less	
26. Bicycle trails (where feasible).	1	1 per 10,000 pop. or less	
27. Picnic area.	2	1 per 2,000 pop or less	
28. Botanical gardens.	1	1 per 150,000 pop. or less	
29. Nature trails (where feasible).	1	1 per 10,000 pop. or less	
30. Skating rink (indoor and outdoor).	½	1 per 50,000 pop. or less	
31. Apparatus, equipment and supplies (as required).	5	For facilities as required	

RECREATIONAL FACILITIES (60)	MAXIMUM POINT SCORE	DEPARTMENTAL SCORE	MODIFICATIONS NEEDED AND ANY COMMENT
32. Design. Indicates layout, functional use of space, safety features, supervisory features, availability of facility, accessibility of facility, architectural features of the layout.	5		
33. Construction. Types of materials to be used, economical materials, materials that will blend in with a surrounding design all best suited for the purpose.	5		
34. Maintenance and custodial operation. Number of personnel necessary to maintain the facility, service inside and outside, and materials for this.	5		

PUBLIC RELATIONS (40)	MAXIMUM POINT SCORE	DEPARTMENTAL SCORE	MODIFICATIONS NEEDED AND ANY COMMENT

1. Policy
  a. Community service attitude by staff personnel.
  b. Definite community relations program in effect.
  c. Periodic review of public relations.
  d. Community relations committee.
  e. One person responsible for public relations.
  f. Coping with possible areas of friction.
  g. Directing points of public conduct for good will.
  h. Staff members taking active part in community affairs.
	10		

Public Relations (40)	Maximum Point Score	Departmental Score	Modifications Needed and Any Comment
2. Facilities	10		
a. Open house held recently.			
b. Acceptable appearance of facility.			
c. Established plan for taking care of visitors who just drop in.			
d. Printed material to be handed to all people.			
e. Encouragement of community members to visit the recreational agency and program.			
3. Mass media for communications	5		
a. Do local community people know where to go for information?			
b. Know where to get accurate information.			
c. Avoidance of trivial news releases.			
d. News releases made without discrimination.			
e. Adherence to deadlines.			
f. Means of communication notified concerning events of interest to them.			
4. Speakers bureau	5		
a. Procedure for handling requests for speaker.			
b. Visual aid assistance when needed for speaker.			
c. Available roster of staff members who can speak well on their specialization.			
d. Manuscript cleared through administration channels.			
5. Technical assistance	5		
a. Agency acts as central coordinating agency for service.			
b. Agency furnishes technical assistance to other agencies or private individuals when requested.			
c. Specialists available to answer questions relative to their area.			
d. Facilities placed on priority basis for public and private uses.			

Public Relations (40)	Maximum Point Score	Departmental Score	Modifications Needed and Any Comment
6. Community awareness	5		
a. Conducting of periodic public opinion polls.			
b. Citizen awareness of staff affiliation to the agency whenever they perform in the community.			

Coordinated Agencies (10) (Options)	Maximum Point Score	Departmental Score	Modifications Needed and Any Comment
1. Board or committee of community service agencies.	5		
2. Recreational agency serves as coordinating body for community service agencies.	4		
3. Recreational agency serves as clearing house for scheduling recreational activities in the community.	2		
4. Recreational agency sets aside space so that community agencies may meet.	1		
5. Recreational agency provides technical and clerical assistance so that service agencies may operate and function effectively.	2		
6. Neighborhood committees or councils in operation sponsored by the recreational agency.	3		
7. Definite policy of cooperation between the recreational agency and other tax-supported agencies.	2		
8. The cooperating agencies act on the basis of long-range planning.	2		
9. Definite plan of cooperation between the recreational agency and all the nontax supported recreational agencies.	1		
10. There is no coordination for recreational service in the community.	0		

Dimensions of Personality

Attitudes have various dimensions. All the dimensions, or degrees of intensity, are matters of inference. They can be measured to determine how any individual reacts to particular stimuli, in this instance the recreational service agency and the activities which are produced by the agency.

Protaganism. Protagonism is the dimension usually considered and measured. It is the degree to which an individual shows favoritism for a specific attitude object.

Pitch. Pitch is the degree of feeling the individual has toward a given attitude object.

Readiness. Readiness is the rapidity with which an attitude can be stimulated in an individual's mind. It is concerned with the primary thoughts that immediately come to the person upon direct confrontation with any provocative stimulus.

Constancy. Constancy is reflected in the variety of attitude objects toward which an individual maintains the same attitude. Thus, a person may be spoken of as being "radical," "liberal," "reactionary," or "conservative," because he has a single constant attitude toward a broad range of objects.

Measuring Attitudes and Related Concepts

Techniques for evaluating and measuring attitudes are numerous and vary widely. Although attitudes can be inferred from observable behavior (attendance at activities, efforts to provide voluntary service by instruction, monetary donations, or technical assistance), a great deal of the methodology concerning attitudes has been instrumented by verbal indexes.

Self-testing. These measuring devices are guided response items used to determine attitudes and interests through self-report efforts. By randomly selecting a public which will cooperate in responding to such tests the department may ascertain attitudes towards phases of agency program, activities, and facilities.

Scales. A variety of scaling instruments can be utilized to determine attitudes towards a given object. A scale is constructed by arranging statements relating to a particular subject under investigation. The testee simply checks the statement within a given range—from highly favorable to decidedly unfavorable or hostile to—so that the attitude object is indicated.[1]

Interest Inventories. Interest inventories are measured by standardized instruments that require an individual to select subjects in which he manifests interests from a large number of activities. Generally, interest inventories are based on knowledge that (1) successful achievers in vocational fields have similar interests, and (2) the interests of those persons in one field differ significantly from those in another occupation.[2]

---

[1] A. L. Edwards, *Techniques of Attitude Scale Construction* (New York: Appleton-Century-Crofts, 1957).

[2] G. Frederick Kuder, *Kuder Preference Records* (Chicago: Science Research Associates, Inc., 1948).

488   Practices of Recreational Service

Sociometric Tests. The sociometric test procedure requires each member of a group, such as a typical recreational group, to choose one or more members for a given purpose. Sociometric data may be useful in improving a person's social adjustment and indicate the individual's degree of social acceptability by his peers.[3]

Projective Testing. Projective techniques have been developed by presenting the subject with an ambiguous stimulus which calls for a response that can be interpreted so as to gain insight into the personality of the subject.[4]

It must be emphasized that all such attitudinal, interest inventory, and projective techniques may well be applied to professional personnel of the departmental staff in order to evaluate their suitability and compatibility for the responsibilities which recreationists undertake. As in all evaluation programs, measuring the effectiveness of staff personnel is essential if professional development and worker efficiency and effectiveness are to be encouraged, and even more important, improved.

SUMMARY

The traditional utilization of measurement and evaluation has been to gauge dimensions of attitude, interests, motives, and values as well as to determine the variables of personality structure. There has also been a direct concern for the quantitative rather than qualitative aspects of recreational service because such items were relatively easy to program and measure. Recreationists have normally been directly concerned with how many individuals participated in a given event at a specific facility rather than with the intensity of satisfaction received by each individual who thereby participated or looked-on. The difficulties of obtaining information revealing the quality of participation are not insurmountable, and, with better measuring devices and more easily administered tests, satisfaction as well as attitudes, motives, and values will become known.

For attitudes, interests, values, and motives, the most accurate and reliable measuring instruments are observations, self-reporting devices, rating scales, and inventories based upon successful achievers. Peer evaluation may also be helpful in determining the social acceptability of the individual within a group to which he belongs.

Evaluation is the process whereby the quality or worth of anything is discovered. Generally, this involves a comparison of the status of the item or subject in question with a standard suitable to a determination of its worth. Before recreational service outcomes may be measured, they must be understood so as to be disposed to measurement. Thus, nonpersonality

---

[3] Helen H. Jennings, *Sociometry in Group Relations,* rev. ed. (Washington, D.C.: American Council on Education, 1959), pp. 15–16.
[4] H. H. Anderson and G. L. Anderson, *An Introduction to Projective Techniques* (New York: Prentice-Hall and Company, 1951).

phenomena can be measured solely in relation to their dimensions, properties, or attributes. Dimensions must be chosen for measurement in terms of the nature of the phenomenon, the object of the measurement, the accuracy required, and the standard to be used in evaluation. The general dimensions usual to most phenomena of recreational interest are identity, number, and organization of segments, time, rate, place, intensity, and activity.

SELECTED REFERENCES

FEAR, R. A., *Evaluation Interview.* (New York: McGraw-Hill), 1956.
HEYEL, CARL, *Appraising Executive Performance.* (New York: American Management Association), 1959.
LARSON, LEONARD A. and RACHEL D. YOCUM, *Measurement and Evaluation in Physical, Health, and Recreation Education.* (St. Louis, Mo.: The C. V. Mosby Company), 1951.
LATCHAW, M. and C. BROWN, *Evaluation Process in Health Education, Physical Education and Recreation.* (Englewood Cliffs, N.J.: Prentice-Hall, Inc.), 1962.
MARTINDELL, JACKSON, *Appraisal of Management,* rev. ed. (New York: Harper and Row), 1965.
MICHAEL, STEPHEN R., *Appraising Management Practices and Performance.* (Englewood Cliffs, N.J.: Prentice-Hall, Inc.), 1963.
SUPER, D. E. and J. O. CRITES, *Appraising Vocational Fitness,* rev. ed. (New York: Harper and Row), 1962.

APPENDIX

APPENDIX

Pictured is a graphic representation of a public recreational agency as it supports the community welfare.

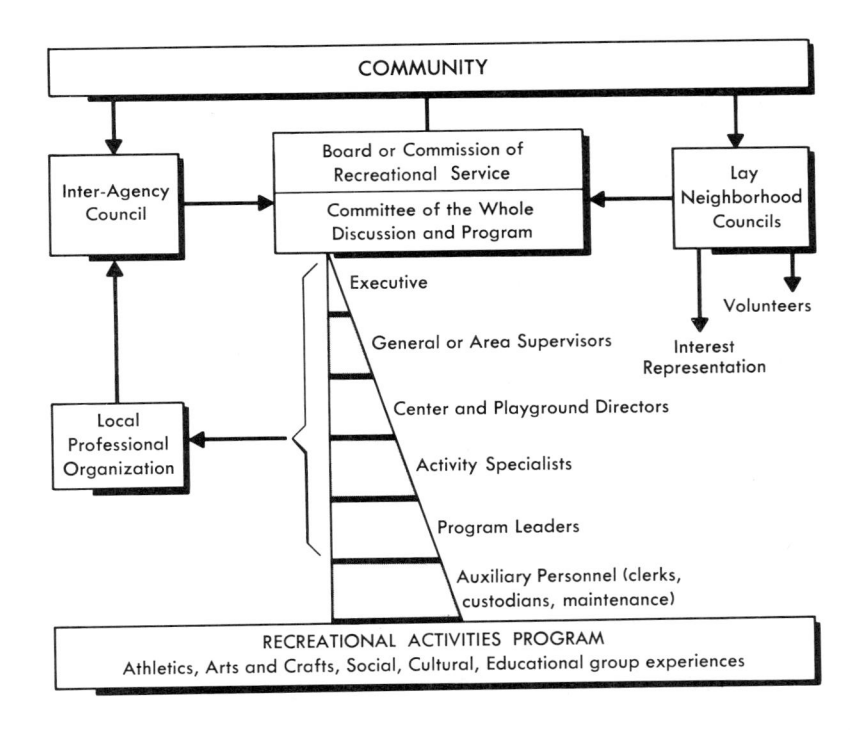

```
                              COMMUNITY
                                  |
        +-------------------------+-------------------------+
        |                         |                         |
   Inter-Agency      Board or Commission of             Lay
     Council         Recreational Service          Neighborhood
                   Committee of the Whole             Councils
                   Discussion and Program
                                                      Volunteers
                         Executive
                                                       Interest
                   General or Area Supervisors      Representation

    Local          Center and Playground Directors
  Professional
  Organization     Activity Specialists

                   Program Leaders

                   Auxiliary Personnel (clerks,
                   custodians, maintenance)

              RECREATIONAL ACTIVITIES PROGRAM
     Athletics, Arts and Crafts, Social, Cultural, Educational group experiences
```

SAMPLE ORDINANCE FOR THE CREATION OF A BOARD, COMMISSION, OR COUNCIL OF RECREATIONAL SERVICE

Whereas, the Recreational Enabling Legislation enacted by the State of ———, provides that

a. Each city, town or village which is incorporated shall be governed by the provisions of this charter, and shall be a municipal corporation.

First. To sue and be sued.

Second. To purchase and hold real estate and personal property for the purpose of establishing and maintaining indoor and outdoor recreational facilities and spaces.

Third. To sell and convey real and personal estate owned by it, and to make such order respecting the same as may be conducive to the interest of the municipality, and to exercise jurisdiction over same.

Fourth. To make all contracts and do all other acts in relation to the property and concerns of the municipality necessary to the exercise of its corporate or administrative powers.

Fifth. To exercise such other or further powers as are herein conferred.

b. Each city, town, village or other such civil subdivision may provide for the operation, equipping, and maintaining of public recreational facilities, areas, and spaces through any existing body or through a recreational service board, commission or council.

c. Each municipality may levy taxes in an amount not exceeding three (3) mills on the dollar of assessed valuation of all taxable property within such municipality for general revenue purposes and for general improvements. Provided, however, the governing authorities of any municipality may make additional levies for special purposes as authorized by law, provided the aggregate of all such special levies does not exceed the limitation prescribed therefor by law.

Whereas, it is the considered judgment of the (legal governing body of the civil subdivision involved) _____ _____ that adequate public recreational service of the (civil subdivision) of _____ can best be promoted by placing the recreational system or agency under the supervision and direction of a legally constituted board, commission, or council as authorized by the State Code of _____; therefore, be it

Resolved, By the (civil subdivision in question) _____ _____.

Article 1. That there is hereby created a recreational board, commission, or council which shall be known as the "_____ _____ of (the local civil subdivision)."

Article 2. That the board, commission or council shall be composed of five members, to be appointed by the (appropriate legal body or officer of the civil subdivision) with the power to provide, operate, and maintain public recreational areas, spaces, and all physical facilities subject to all responsibilities of the Enabling Legislation indicated in the State Codes of _____. The membership shall serve for periods of five years, and up until the time that successors shall be appointed, except that the members appointed first shall be so appointed that the office of one member shall expire annually thereafter. Vacancies will be filled in the same manner as original appointments and for any unexpired terms. All members will serve without compensation.

Article 3. That the recreational board, commission, or council (hereinafter known as the board), shall appoint from its membership a president and any other officers it feels necessary for the orderly procedure of its primary business, and may adopt by-laws, rules, regulations, and policies covering its procedures not inconsistent with the provisions of the State Codes. The Board of Public Recreational Service shall, on occasion, make such rules governing the operation of the recreational facilities and spaces operated by the board. The board shall hold periodic and regular meetings at designated times and places at its discretion.

Article 4. That the board of recreational service shall operate, maintain, and direct all of the recreational facilities, spaces, and structures, both indoor and outdoor, owned or controlled by the (civil subdivision in question).

Article 5. That the board of recreational service may receive, accept, and otherwise obtain, at its discretion, any grant, gift, bequest or services, real estate, money, equipment, or donations from any individual or group, to be utilized as specified by the giver, or by the terms of acceptance. The board shall have no authority to enter into any contract or incur any obligations or contracts binding upon the (local civil subdivision), other than current indebtedness as contracted to be fully completed during the then current fiscal year, and all within the legal fiscal instrument of appropriations made by the governing authorities of (local civil subdivision).

Article 6. That the board of public recreational service shall have the power to hire an executive officer, hereinafter known as the Superintendent of Recreational Service and/or Parks, who possesses the required professional preparation and experience and who, by actual field practice, has demonstrated his capabilities in organizing, supervising, managing and otherwise controlling a community recreational service agency or system, administer a recreational program, and direct the professional activities of such other personnel as may be deemed necessary for the effective operation of the recreational program.

Article 7. That the legal authority of the (local civil subdivision) appropriate sufficient funds, budgeted to the board of recreational service, to be disbursed by the fiscal accounting authority of the (local civil subdivision), upon specified forms (usually vouchers) issued by the board and within the budget appropriations made. Monies receipted by the board from sources other than budget appropriations shall be accounted for and deposited by the (local civil subdivision), to the credit and utilization of the board, and paid out as the budget appropriation funds are disbursed. However, funds received by gift, bequest, donation, or otherwise shall be paid out in terms of the award, or in accordance with the acceptance thereof.

Article 8. That the recreational service board shall make complete and comprehensive records of its operations in order to report to the governing body at such times as may be designated by the legal authority.

Article 9. That such powers as are now or may hereafter be provided by statute, code, ordinance, or law of the State of ———— or by ordinances of the (local civil subdivision) relating to the growth, development, and management of recreational agencies, physical facilities, and other spaces devoted to recreational activities, are now vested in the board of public recreational services, to be exercised by it subject to any and all restrictions contained in such powers and ordinances.

Article 10. That all resolutions and ordinances of (local civil subdivision) in conflict herewith are hereby repealed.

Article 11. That this resolution will be in effect and carry full force 30 days after its passage.

Adopted this _____ day of _____ 19____

Index

A

Abraham, 21
Absorption, *see* Consumption
Accreditation, 203
Achaeans, 27
Action, 79; *see also* Recreation
Activities, *see* Recreational Activities
Addams, Jane, 97
Adjustment, 134
    process of, 57
Administration, 119–120, 240–302, 455, 461–463
Administrative manual, 282–293
Administrative procedures, 287–293, 415–416
Adolescence, 135–136, 403–404
Aeneas, 27
Affluence, 133
Age, 133–134
Agency purpose, 243
Agency structure, 410–416
    employment and, 411
Akkad, 18
Alaska Purchase, 151
America, 34
American Association of Group Workers, 74
American Association for Health, Physical Education, and Recreation, 73, 74
American Recreation Society, 73
American Revolution, 35
Annual reports, 436
Antiquities Act, 152
Applications of research, 236
Appraisal, 450–451
Arcadia, 24
Aretê, 24, 25
Aristocracy, 16, 19, 24, 30, 32, 36–38
Aristotelian philosophy, 85, 86
Arizona, 152, 154
Art, 16, 355–356
Assateague Island National Seashore, 96
Assyria, 20–21
Athenians, 26
Attica, 24
Attitude modification, 34, 35, 39–44
Attitudes, 474

Attitudinal measurement, 487–488
Atypical, 141–143
Augustus, 30, 31
Authority, 244–245

B

Babylon, 19–20
Barr, A. S., 329, 332, 351
Behavior, 60–62
Bernard, L. L., 53
Boston, Mass., 101, 102, 111, 113, 164
Brainstorming, 347–348
Brockman, C. Frank, 165
Brown, J. S., 57
Brubacher, John S., 214
Bucher, Charles A., 70
Bulletin boards, 438
Bureau of Outdoor Recreation, 105, 106, 115, 153
Businessmen, 70
Butler, George D., 139

C

Caesar, Gaius Julius, 30
California, 98, 152, 154, 159, 160, 166
Calvin, John, 33, 34
Calvinism, 34, 35, 44
Campgrounds, 165
Carr-Saunders, A. M., 193
Carthage, 28, 29
Catharsis, 50, 56, 81, 82
Central Park, New York City, 163
Chalcolithic age, 27
Chaldea, 20, 21
Chapman, John Crosby, 71
Charges, *see* Fees
Charlesworth, James C., 297
Charting, 246 ff.
Chicago, Ill., 101, 113, 390, 408
Christian Church, 32
Church, 43–44

499

Class, 24, 28–31
Class distinction, 16, 38, 39
Classification, 243
Colorado, 96, 164, 397
Combs, Arthur W., 61, 62
Community organization, 310–325
Community viewpoint, 417–418
Comparative-causal survey, 229
Competition, 70
Complacency, 77; *see also* Homeostasis
Concessions, 298–299
Connecticut, 99, 156
Connecticut River, 156
Conservation, 121–122, 149 ff.
  compatibility of recreational use and, 174–175
  incompatibility of recreational use and, 168–172
  preservation versus, 149–150
Constitution, 92 ff.
Consummatory act, 46, 52, 59, 61
Consummatory experience, 75, 76, 77, 78, 80, 86–88, 90
Coordinating councils, 312 ff.
  neighborhood advisory, 317–318
  neighborhood recreational council and, 319
  organization of, 316–317
  relationships and, 314–316
  representation on, 313
Coordination, 120–121, 319 ff., 472–473
  board membership exchange and, 324–325
  contracts and, 321–322
  coordinator and, 322
  informal meetings and, 320
  institutes and, 320–321
  interlocking boards and, 324
  policy and, 319
  shared executive and, 323
Correlation, 232
Cotton, Joseph, 34
Counts, George S., 71
Crafts, 356–358
Creativity, 333
Crete, 23, 24
Criminal act, 77
Cro-Magnards, 13
Cro-Magnon, 13
Cuber, J. F., 143
Cultural achievement, 128–129
Cutten, George B., 67
Cyrus, 20, 22

D

Dance, 358–359
Dancing, 17
Danford, Howard G., 213
Darwinism, 36, 37
Decision making, *see* Leadership
Delaware Water Gap National Recreation Area, 96
Democracy, 327 ff.
  anarchy versus, 328
  defined, 327–328
  leadership and, 329–330
  specialization and, 330–331
Democratic ideals, 130
Demography, 398–410
  age groups and, 402
  educational level and, 405–406
  ethnic groups and, 400–401
  migration and, 407–409
  occupational range and, 406–407
  race and, 401–402
  religious affiliation and, 407
  residence and, 399–400
  sex composition and, 402–404
  social status and, 404–405
Departmental jurisdiction, 416–417
Departmental organization, 442–445
  facilities and, 443–444
  program and, 444–445
  structures and, 442–443
Detroit, Mich., 246
Diocletian, 31
Disciplinary powers, 206–208
District center, 390
District of Columbia, 96
Donations and grants, 295; *see also* Finances
Dordogne, France, 13
Dorian, 24, 27
Dramatics, 359–360

E

Economics, 41–42
Economic limitations, 145
Education, 36, 37, 120, 129, 139–141, 360–361, 420 ff., 443
  necessity of, 420–421
  outcomes of, 421–423
  planning for, 423–424
  staff requirements for, 424–425

Educational programs, 425 ff.
  combined presentations in the, 438–441
  graphic presentations in the, 437–438
  literary presentations in the, 430–437
  oral presentations in the, 426–430
Egypt, 15, 17
Empathy, 81, 82, 185, 186
Enabling legislation, 127
Encroachment, 144, 161–164
Energetics, 60
Enlightenment, 34
Entropy, 89
Epicureanism, 54
Equality, 131 ff., 132–133
Escape, 81, 82
Ethics, 129
  code of, 205 ff.
Etruscans, 28
Eudaemonism, 54
Europe, 12, 14
Evaluation, 122–123, 450 ff.
  appraisal and, 450–451
  criteria for, 451–452
  defined, 450
  major areas of, 454–455
  measurement and, 450
  methods of, 456–474
  necessity of, 452–454
Exclusiveness, 201
Exhibits, 437–438
Exploitation, 156–161
Extramurals, 365

F

Facilities, 443–444
Family functions, 112
Federal Bureau of Recreational Services, 105, 106
Federal Power Commission, 157–159
Fees, 295–298
  user assessment for, 296
Finances, 460–461
Financial considerations, 414–415
Financial support, 293–302, 459–461
Fitzgerald, Gerald B., 102
Florida, 96, 99
Food and Agriculture Act, 153
Franseth, Jane, 328
Freud, Sigmund, 54, 56, 89
Frobenius, Leo, 53, 54, 86, 87

G

Gadsden Purchase, 151
Genesis, 21, 23
Gerontological factors, *see* Age
Gilgamesh, 19
Government, 308–310
  defined, 308
  functions of, 113, 309
  promotional, 310
Grand Canyon, 168, 171–173
Grand Coulee Dam, 96
Greece, 64
Greeks, 24–27, 64
Green, A. W., 170
Groos, Karl, 49–51
Group conference, 343–345
Gulick, Luther H., 51, 97
Gutsmuths, Johan, 49

H

Hall, G. Stanley, 52
Hamilton, Edith, 27
Hammurabi, 19
Harlow, Harry F., 57
Harris, Ben M., 350
Hartford, Conn., 163
Health, 126
Hebrews, 21–23
Hedonism, 20, 29–31, 49, 54–58; *see also* Motivation
Hellenic age, 24–27
History, *see* Leisure
Hjelte, George, 116
Hobbies, 361–363
Home rule, 99, 100, 101
  defined, 101
Homeostasis, 57–62; *see also* Motivation
  complacency as, 59
  defined, 59
  equilibrium as, 59
  recreation as, 61
Homo neanderthalensis, 12, 13
Homo sapiens, 13
Horace, 30
House organ, 535–536; *see also* Public Relations
Hudson River, 157
Huizinga, Johan, 32, 76
Hull House, 113
Humanism, 92

502 Index

Humanitarianism, 196 ff.
Hutchinson, John L., 138, 378

I

Idaho, 152, 154
Ill and handicapped, 141–143
Illinois, 99
In-service education, 347–349
Incompetence, 146, 201, 204, 205, 208
Indiana, 96, 98, 99
Indiana Dunes National Lakeshore, 96
Individual conference, 342–343
Individual differences, 132
Information disseminiation, 342
Instinct, 46, 88, 89; see also Motivation
  recreation theories of, 49–54
Interest patterns, 78, 79
Interests, 474
Intermurals, 365
Internal communication, 348–349, 435–436; see also House organ
Intramurals, 365
Italy, 27, 28

J

Jacks, L. P., 65
Jacob, 21, 23
Jefferson, Thomas, 309
Johnson, George E., 53
Judaism, 22

K

Kentucky, 98, 398
Key Largo Coral Reef, 96
Kitto, H. D. F., 25, 26
Knossos, 23, 24
Korea, 103

L

Lake Meade, 96
Land and Water Conservation Fund Act, 153
Law, 328
Leadership, 146–147, 177–189, 329 ff.
  characteristics of, 188–189

Leadership (*Cont.*):
  counseling as, 185
  decision making and, 177 ff.
  democracy and, 177 ff.
  human needs and, 178 ff.
  inadequacies of, 146–147
  individual differences and, 181 ff., 185, 186
  instruction as, 183, 184
  learning and, 180 ff.
  motivation and, 179 ff.
  social behavior and, 187
Lee, Joseph, 51–52, 97
Legality, 92–109, 458
Legislation, 95 ff.
  enabling, 99 ff.
  federal, 104–106
  local, 101 ff.
  recreational services and, 95
  state, 97–100, 106–108
Leisure, 5, 7, 12–14, *et passim*
  acceptance of, 43–44
  activities in, 35
  civilization and, 15–40
  education for, 130
  human development and, 12–15
  man and, 13–15
  recreational service and, 39–44
Leisure class, 16, 19, 25, 26, 29, 33, 36–39
  sports and the, 39
Leisure and security, 12 ff.
Licensing, 202 ff., 212
Lies, Eugene T., 67, 68
Livy, 30
Logic, 224
Los Angeles, Calif., 101, 408
Louisiana, 99
Louisiana Purchase, 151

M

Maintenance, 463
Masochism, 56
Master planning, 386–387, 464–465; see also Planning
Materials Disposing Act, 153
Mather, Cotton, 34
Measurement, 450–451
Measures of central tendency, 231 ff.
Megalopolis, 104, 154–156
Menes, 15; see also Egypt
Mesopotamia, 15–23

Michigan, 99
Middle Ages, 33
Migration, 407–409
Milwaukee, Wisc., 102
Minneapolis, Minn., 101, 390
Minnesota, 154, 397
Mission 66, 115
Missouri, 99
Missouri Act, 99
Montana, 154
Morrill Act, 151
Motion pictures, 438–439
Motor performance, 363–365
Mt. Rushmore Memorial, 115
Muir Woods National Monument, 159
Music, 365–367
Mycenae, 24

N

Nash, Jay B., 79, 80, 81
Nashville, Tenn., 407
Natchez, Miss., 408
National Capital Parks, 96
National Education Association, 73
National forests, 168
National monuments, 167–168
National Park Service, 96, 160, 171
National parks, 115, 167
National Recreation Association, 115
National Recreation and Park Association, 210
National Recreation Resources Review Commission, 104
National Wilderness Preservation System, 153, 161
Natural phenomena, 144 ff.
Natural resources, exploitation of, 156–161
Neighborhood
 advisory councils, 317–318
 recreational councils in, 319
Neighborhood Guild, 113
Neighborhood playgrounds, 389–390
Neolithic, 14, 27
Neumeyer, Esther S., 66, 67, 111
Neumeyer, Martin H., 66, 67, 111
Nevada, 96, 152, 154
Newark, N. J., 101, 113
New England, 34, 111, 398
New Hampshire, 98, 166, 397
New Mexico, 152, 154
New York, 98, 99, 157, 158, 159, 166

New York City, 101, 113, 158, 162, 163, 334
New York Times, 158, 172
Nineveh, 20
Non-predictability, 197–199; *see also* Professionalism
Normative-survey, *see* Research
North Carolina, 98, 154

O

Oakland, Calif., 101
Objective time, 68
Objectivity, 205 ff., 336, 341; *see also* Professionalism
Office management, 462
Ohio, 398
Operation Outdoors, 115
Opportunity, 131 ff.
Oregon, 152, 154
Organization, 119, 240 ff., 442–443, 457, 458
 defined, 240
 planning for, 241–242
 standard of, 243–246
Outdoor education, 367–368
Outdoor recreational areas, 164–168
Outdoor Recreation Resources Review Commission, 115
Overstreet, H. Allen, 65

P

Pack, Arthur N., 66
Paleolithic, 12–14
Pangburn, Weaver W., 67, 68
Park movement, 114 ff.
Parkways, 165–166
Participation, 69
Patrick, G. T. W., 49
Pennsylvania, 99, 166, 398
Personal interests, 128–129
Personality, 306–307
Personality dimensions, 487
Personnel management, 283 ff.
 policies for, 283–286
Personnel standards, 466–467
Phenix, Philip H., 140, 195, 206
Phenomenal self theory, 61–62
Philadelphia, Penn., 114
Philosophy, 224, 332–333
Physical fitness, 125–126

Physiological need, 58–60
Picnic areas, 166
Planning, 122, 245–246, 385–418, 463–466
  data collection for, 386
  definition of, 385
  facility placement and, 389–392
  land use and, 387–389
  master, 386–387
  surveys for, 393–394
Play, 46–56, 83–85
  catharsis and, 50–51, 56, 81
  consummation and, 52
  education as, 51
  instinct and, 47–52
  practice theory of, 50–51
  psychoanalytic theory of, 56
  recreation as, 85
Police power, 92, 94, 113, 309
Political expediency, 144–146
Posters, 438
Principle, 3–10
Privileged communication, 202
Problems in recreational service, 237–238
Profession
  characteristics of, 193 ff.
  defined, 194
  education for, 194 ff.
  recreational service as, 192 ff.
Professional association, 201–208
Professional practice, 212–215
  ethics and, 214–215
  public welfare and, 213
  search for truth and, 213–214
Professionalism, 132, 192–216
Professionalization process, 208–212
Programming, 124–125, 354 ff., 444–445, 454–455
  art and, 355–356
  craft and, 356–358
  dance and, 358–359
  defined, 354
  dramatics and, 360–361
  education and, 360–361
  hobbies and, 361–362
  motor performance and, 363–365
  music and, 365–367
  outdoor education and, 367–368
  planning factors, 373–383
    balance, 380–381
    flexibility, 381–382
    gradation, 380

Programming, planning factors (*Cont.*):
    individual need, 374–375
    leadership, 382
    participant planning, 373–374
    space, structures, and facilities, 382–383
    themes, 379–380
    time, 375–379
  service activities and, 369–371
  social activities and, 371
  special projects and, 372–373
Program influences, 395–418
Program standards, 467–468
Promotional government, 114
Proprietary functions, 295
Protestant ethic, *see* Calvinism
Protestantism, 33
Providence, R. I., 390
Public behavior, 286
Public debt, 297
Public domain, 151 ff.
Public laws, 153
Public recreational service, 118–148
  financial support of, 293–301
  legitimate sources of funds for, 295–299
Public relations, 420–448, 471–472
Public School Athletic League, 101
Public service, 294, 309

R

Rainwater, Clarence E., 111, 116
Raup, R. Bruce, 59–60
Recapitulation theory, 52–53
Reclamation Act, 152
Record keeping, *see* Recording
Recording, 281–293, 461–462
Recreation, 24, 25, 39, 46–90, 127, *et passim*
  activity concept of, 79–83
  antisocial acts and, 74, 75
  behavioral manifestation as, 68
  defined, 46
  freedom concept of, 75
  leisure as, 63–68
  play as, 85
  prime motive concept of, 69
  religion and, 72
  traditional concepts of, 63
  unity concept of, 85–88
  virtue concept of, 73–75

Recreational activities, 16, 17, 20, 23, 33, 35, 36, 40, *et passim*
  classification of, 354–383
Recreational programming
  balance in, 380–381
  facilities needed for, 382–383
  flexibility of, 381–382
  graduation in, 380
  individual need and, 374–375
  leadership for, 382
  participant planning for, 373–374
  themes for, 379–380
  time factors and, 375–379
Recreational service
  administration of, 119–120, 240 ff.
  conservation and, 121–122
  coordination of, 304 ff.
  education for, 420 ff.
  equality of, 131 ff.
  evaluation of, 122–125, 450 ff.
  functions of, 118 ff.
  organization of, 119
  planning for, 122, 385 ff.
  practices of, 219 ff.
  programming of, 124–125, 354 ff.
  provision of, 96–99
  public, 118
  research in, 219 ff.
  social limitations on, 132 ff.
  supervision of, 123–124, 327 ff.
  values of, 125 ff.
Recreational service movement, 113–116
Recreational values, 125 ff.
  cultural achievement as, 128–129
  democratic ideals and, 130
  ethical practices and, 129–130
  health and, 126
  physical fitness and, 125–126
  safety, 127–128
  satisfaction as, 126–127
  social intercourse and, 128
Recreationist, 5, *et passim*
  defined, 212
Redwood trees, 159–160
Reformation, 33, 34
Region, 395–398
  climate of, 396
  defined, 395
  resources of, 397
  topography of, 396–397
  traditions of, 397–398
Regional complex, 390–391
Regional deficiencies, 144–146

Registration, 201 ff.
Religion, 16–17, 71–72
Renaissance, 33
Research, 219–238, 464
  methods of, 221 ff.
  clinical, 233
  descriptive, 228–229
  experimental, 229–233
  historical, 227–228
  outcomes of, 233–235
Research literature, 235–237
Reserved timbered areas, 166
Responsibility, 244–245
Restrictive legislation, 114
Revenue sources, 299–300
Riggs, A. F., 71
Rignano, E., 59
Riis, Jacob, 97, 113
Roadside rests, 165
Rochester, N. Y., 101
Rome, 27–32
Romney, G. Ott, 65, 79
Roosevelt, Theodore, 159
Rugg, Harold, 81
Ryland, Gladys, 403

S

Sabbath, 22, 23, 114
Safety, 127–128
St. Augustine, 32
St. Augustine, Fla., 114
St. Louis, Mo., 101
Sand gardens, 101, 111
Sargon, 18
Satisfaction, 126–127
Save-the-Redwoods-League, 160
Scenic Hudson Preservation Conference, 157, 158, 159
Schedules, 376–379
Scheduling, 473
Schiller, J. C. F. von, 50
Science, 331–332
Scientific inquiry, 224–225
Scientific method, 225–226
Schola, 26
School utilization, 392
Schwartz, Bernard, 94
Self-expression, 40–41
Senescence, 133–134
Seriousness, 83, 84; *see also* Play
Service activities, 369–371
Services, 118, 131

Sex, 136–137
Shadow Mountain, 96
Skokie, Ill., 390
Slavery, 25, 28, 29–31, 64
Snygg, Donald, 61, 62
Social activities, 371
Social class, 16
Social education, 307
Social examination, 394–395
Social intercourse, 128
Social limitations, 132 ff.
 age and, 133–134
 economic status and, 136–139
 education and, 139–141
 illness and, 141–143
 leadership inadequacies and, 146–147
 regional deficiencies and, 144–146
 sex and, 136–137
 social status and, 137–139
 youth and, 135–136
Social movement, 111 ff., 137–138
Social organization, 304–306
Soil Conservation Act, 152
Southern Baptist Convention, 407
Sovereignty, 92 ff.
Space, 469–470
Special projects, 372–373
Spectatoritis, 79, 80, 81
Spencer, Herbert, 49, 50
Springfield, Mass., 408
Staff, 455
Standard deviation, 231; *see also* Research
Standard error, 231; *see also* Research
Standard operating procedures, 282 ff.
Standardization, 245, 462
Standards, 8
State parks, 167
State recreational services, 107–108
Statistical factors, 230 ff.
Statistical significance, 231–232
Status quo, 143
Structures, 470–471
Subjective time, 68
Sumer, 15, 18
Sumeria, 16, 18–19
Supervision, 123–124, 327–352
 democracy and, 327–352
 leadership as, 333–339
 philosophy and, 332
 science and, 331–332
Supervisory effects, 350–352
Supervisory functions, 124, 339–342

Supervisory observation, 346
Supervisory techniques, 342 ff.
Supervisory visitation, 345–347
Supremacy, 92 ff.
Surplus energy theory, 50; *see also* Recreation

T

Technique, 199–200
Techniques, 9–10
Technology, 36, 37
 leisure and, 40, 41
Television, 439–440
Tennessee Valley Authority, 152, 309
Terramara people, 27
Testing, 201
Texas Purchase, 151
Theodore Roosevelt National Memorial Park, 115
Therapeutic recreational service, 75
Thorndike, E. L., 54, 55
Tiglath Pileser, 20
Towle, Charlotte, 197
Troland, L. T., 54, 58

U

United States, 92, 93
 Army Corps of Engineers, 153
 Bureau of Reclamation, 172
 Constitution of, 132
 Department of Agriculture, 115
 Department of Health, Education, and Welfare, 96, 105
 Department of the Interior, 96, 105, 115, 153, 173
 Department of Urban Affairs and Housing, 105
 Forest Service, 154, 161, 164
 Supreme Court, 32, 132, 159
Ur, 15, 19, 21
Urban congestion, 145
Urban encroachment, 155
Urbanization, 42–43, 112, 114, 138, 154 ff.
Utah, 152

V

Values, 474
Van Sickle, C. E., 29, 31

Index

Variability, 199
Veblen, Thorstein, 37–39
Vermont, 98, 397
Virgil, 30
Virginia, 397
Vocationalism, 69
Volunteering, 286, 369–371
  negative aspects of, 371
  positive aspects of, 370
Von Eckardt, Wolf, 155

W

War, 76, 77
  play and, 76
  sport and, 77
Washington, 96, 99, 152, 154
Water Pollution Control Law, 153
Weeks Law, 152
Welfare, 310
Wells, H. G., 129
Wetlands Acquisition Program, 153
White House Conference on Aging, 115
Wilderness areas, 154

Wilderness lands, 166–167
Wildlife Restoration Act, 152
Wiles, Kimball, 344
Wilson, Gertrude, 403
Wilson, P. A., 193
Wisconsin, 99
Withers, William, 81
Work, 40–41
Work flow, 462–463
World War II, 42, 102, 152
Wyoming, 152, 154

Y

Yellowstone National Park, 151
Yosemite National Park, 96
Young Men's Christian Association, 113, 137
Young Women's Christian Association, 113, 137

Z

Zakrewska, Maria, 113